D0203651

FROM POLIZIANO TO MACHIAVELLI

FROM POLIZIANO TO MACHIAVELLI

FLORENTINE HUMANISM IN THE HIGH RENAISSANCE

Peter Godman

PRINCETON UNIVERSITY PRESS

PRINCETON, NEW JERSEY

PUBLISHED BY PRINCETON UNIVERSITY PRESS, 41 WILLIAM STREET,
PRINCETON, NEW JERSEY 08540
IN THE UNITED KINGDOM: PRINCETON UNIVERSITY PRESS,
CHICHESTER, WEST SUSSEX

LIBRARY OF CONGRESS CATALOGING-IN-PUBLICATION DATA

GODMAN, PETER.
FROM POLIZIANO TO MACHIAVELLI : FLORENTINE HUMANISM IN
THE HIGH RENAISSANCE / PETER GODMAN.
P. CM.
INCLUDES BIBLIOGRAPHICAL REFERENCES AND INDEX.
ISBN 0-691-01746-8 (CLOTH : ALK. PAPER)
1. HUMANISM—ITALY—FLORENCE—HISTORY. 2. FLORENCE (ITALY)—
HISTORY—1421–1737. 3. RENAISSANCE—ITALY—FLORENCE.
4. ITALIAN LITERATURE—ITALY—FLORENCE—HISTORY AND
CRITICISM. 5. ITALIAN LITERATURE—15TH CENTURY—
HISTORY AND CRITICISM. I. TITLE.

DG737.55.G63 1998 945′.51—DC21 97-44320

THIS BOOK HAS BEEN COMPOSED IN BEMBO

PRINCETON UNIVERSITY PRESS BOOKS ARE PRINTED
ON ACID-FREE PAPER AND MEET THE GUIDELINES FOR
PERMANENCE AND DURABILITY OF THE COMMITTEE ON
PRODUCTION GUIDELINES FOR BOOK LONGEVITY
OF THE COUNCIL ON LIBRARY RESOURCES

HTTP: //PUP.PRINCETON.EDU

PRINTED IN THE UNITED STATES OF AMERICA

1 3 5 7 9 10 8 6 4 2

SEBASTIANO FLORENTINO

AMICISQUE TUBINGENSIBUS

Perché non essendo dalla natura conceduto alle mondane cose il fermarsi, come le arrivano alla loro ultima perfezione, non avendo più da salire, conviene che scendino; e similmente, scese che le sono, e per li disordini ad ultima bassezza pervenute, di necessità, non potendo più scendere, conviene che salghino.

(Machiavelli *Istorie fiorentine* 5.1)

CONTENTS

PREFACE

IN 1494 Angelo Poliziano, the most revered (and reviled) scholar-poet of the Italian Quattrocento, followed his patron, Lorenzo de' Medici, to the grave. Four years later Niccolò Machiavelli became Second Chancellor of the Florentine Republic. Dismissed from that post in 1512, imprisoned and tortured, he then set about writing the works that have made him famous. Between Poliziano's death and Machiavelli's maturity, Florentine humanism changed. How and why are the questions asked in this book.

It has no hero. Which may raise eyebrows, given the celebrities who frame its title. Their juxtaposition is intended to pose a problem. Of Poliziano, his works and their character, there are many excellent studies. Of Machiavelli and his "moment," there are more. Yet seldom the twain do meet and, between the distinct perspectives of these competing specialisms, issues common to them both are lost from sight. One such issue is the response of Machiavelli's generation to the intellectual legacy of Poliziano and his peers.

If that response has seldom been considered, it is because studies of this period, concentrated on two individuals, pay less attention to the culture that they shared. Poliziano and Machiavelli are viewed as the instigators of a method, a movement, an ideology; the focus is trained rather on their influence than on the milieux in which they moved; and the vista is still seen through an optic formed by the hagiography of scholarship and the praise of great men.

Many are the accounts of the rise of "critical philology" in Poliziano's *Miscellanea.* Nowhere is it noted that, in the city of their origin, the approach that they had developed was disowned as soon as their author had passed away. Amid scandal and obloquy, Poliziano was laid to rest at San Marco, clad in the habit of a Dominican *frate,* on Savonarola's command. That imperative yet enlightened champion of scholastic thought is often miscast as a fanatic, a retrograde enemy of the humanism with which Machiavelli has been linked. What kind of humanism? No adequate definition has been offered—nor can it be, until we understand more about the humanists with whom, for a lengthy and formative part of his career, Machiavelli worked. So it is that he, like Poliziano, appears more isolated than he in fact was. The lesser luminaries that surrounded them have been eclipsed by these stars in the Florentine firmament.

Its configuration, during the late Quattro- and early Cinquecento, altered rapidly. The internal politics of the Republic and the external stimulus provided by other Italian centers of learning transformed intellectual life at this original but receptive capital of Renaissance culture. From Ferrara and Venice, from Rome and Milan came new impulses to which Florentine thinkers reacted. Some of them, less known but more representative than their eminent contemporaries, perceived change as a crisis that they sought to resolve from positions that Poliziano, dependent on the Medici, and Machiavelli, reliant for his limited influence on Pier Soderini, never achieved. By one of them, in particular, no account of Florentine humanism in the High Renaissance can afford to pass: Marcello di Messer Virgilio di Andrea di Berto Adriani.

Not, in the present state of scholarship, a name with which to conjure. The history of classical philology leaps from the Poliziano of the 1490s to Pier Vettori in the second quarter of the sixteenth century, leaving a lacuna in which Marcello Virgilio languishes. Political history assigns him a marginal role on the stage where Machiavelli takes the limelight. And Marcello Virgilio scarcely exists for the history of humanism, because it has its own teleology, which, in the case of Florence, culminates with the year 1494—and comes to a dead end. So dead, that posterity conflates this forgotten figure with his homonymous grandson.

Yet Marcello Virgilio has a claim to attention. He was Poliziano's successor in his Chair at the Studio and the First Chancellor of Florence when Machiavelli was the Second. Unlike his predecessor, who died at the tender age of forty, and his colleague, who lost his office upon the restoration of the Medici, Marcello Virgilio possessed a talent for survival. Throughout Savonarola's ascendancy and fall, during the "popular" Republic, after the return of Lorenzo's dynasty, Marcello Virgilio lived on, retaining his dual function, publishing little, and founding a family of professors.

A man for all seasons? An assiduous opportunist? A "mediocrity, embellished by survival and seniority, [which] gains respect among colleagues, if not always in the wider world," as a historian of Oxford (R. Syme, *Some Arval Brethren* [Oxford, 1980], p. 115) shrewdly observes? Perhaps. Or perhaps not, if we are willing to renounce the comforting simplifications offered by models of greatness and decline. For at "the heart of the city"—to use a phrase recorded by Marcello Virgilio in his protocol of one of the earliest meetings of Florence's ruling elite that he attended—he stood, observing and commenting on the course of events with the authority of a spokesman. His voice—now engaged and direct, now studiously ambiguous—has not been heard, because most of his works are unpublished.

A sample, analyzed in this book, is set in the context of Florentine intellectual history during his lifetime. The accent is placed rather on the period—its thought, culture, and politics—than on the individual. An edition with commentary of Marcello Virgilio's *inedita* is to follow in a sequel. It will deal more fully with biographical and paleographical problems, with his work at the Chancery, and with further details of his official—not "civic"—and philological humanism. The material is many-sided, instructive, and (it seems to me) entertaining. It invites, and enables, us to look afresh at a culture that admitted few saints and no heroes.

ACKNOWLEDGMENTS

IN 1752 Angelo Maria Bandini published, at Arezzo, his *Collectio veterum aliquot monimentorum ad historiam praecipue litterariam pertinentium,* which was promptly denounced to the Inquisition. Hilarity was not remarked in the Holy Office, although the *Collectio* is an amusing book. Taken together with his *De florentina Iuntarum typographia eiusque censoribus annales* of 1791, it both offers a panorama of Florentine culture during Machiavelli's lifetime that remains unsurpassed and presents a challenge to orthodoxy, by stationing him in the company of humanists whose names are unfamiliar and whose works are unread today. To the modern inquisitors of Machiavellian scholarship, guardians of the doctrine that he stands alone, the *Collectio* might still exude an odor of heresy.

The world knows the depth and originality of Bandini's scholarship; it is perhaps less aware that he had a sense of humor. Often, when I thought that I had discovered a document in the Florentine libraries and archives, it was to find that he had printed it, in whole or in extract, two-and-a-half centuries before me; and as I pondered his selection of sources, it became apparent that he was alive to the multiple ironies of this subject. Bandini has been my guide and companion, and I have tried to write a book that might have made him smile.

What kind of smile, may be left to the readers' better judgment. They should be in no doubt about my debt to Paul Oskar Kristeller's *Iter Italicum.* If what I owe to that monumental work is emphasized in this place, it is because borrowings from Kristeller are more common than acknowledgments of him; and I do not wish to participate in what seems to me to have become a conspiracy of silent plunder.

A book of this kind, which draws on unpublished and rare sources, would have been impossible to write without periods of research in Italy, assisted by travel subventions from the Deutsche Forschungsgemeinschaft and the Volkswagen Stiftung, to which I record my gratitude. I thank, with warmth, the librarians in Florence, several of them friends, who went out of their way to assist me—in particular Gustavo Bertoli, Rosaria D'Alfonso, Adriana Di Domenico, Gianna Rao, and Isabella Trucci. The wit and urbanity of Father Leonard Boyle made the manuscript room of the Biblioteca Apostolica Vaticana a *locus amoenus.* To the courtesy of His Eminence Joseph Cardinal Ratzinger, Monsignor Joseph Clemens, and Monsignor Alejandro Cifres Gimenez, I owe access, granted at short notice, to the archives of the Roman Inquisition and Congregation of the Index. Some of the results—provisional and preliminary to forthcoming studies—are considered in the Appendix.

The ideas that lie behind this book initially took form in German, when I had the pleasure to teach Florentine humanism to a group of gifted students at Tübingen. I am much indebted to the stimulus of Frank Bezner, Jens Brandt, John Frymire, Tobias Leuker, Uwe Neumahr, and Michael Rupp. The patient intelligence of John Frymire proved invaluable, not only in the technical organization of my work. I have profited, in many conversations, from the openness and insight of Riccardo Fubini. Other colleagues and friends have commented on parts of previous drafts, and I am grateful for the help and criticism of Robert Black, Alison Brown, Daniela Mugnai Carrara, Jill Kraye, Lilly Morgese, Vivian Nutton, Brian Richardson, and Donald Weinstein. Preparatory studies have appeared in *Arcadia, Interpres,* and *Rinascimento.* I thank the editors of these journals for permission to draw on my earlier writings. To the kindness of Alessandro Cecchi I owe the photographs, from the Galleria degli Uffizi, that appear on the cover. It is timely to draw attention to the splendid catalogue, *L'officina della maniera: Varietà e fierezza nell'arte del Cinquecento fra le due repubbliche, 1494–1530* (Venice, 1996), that illuminates Florentine art of the period studied in the pages that follow.

To Sebastiano Timpanaro, with admiration and affection, and to my friends in Tübingen, with love for Italy and its culture, the dedication of this book indicates what its author cannot express:

E quanto l'arte intra sé non comprende
la mente, imaginando, chiaro intende.

(*Stanze* 119.7–8)

ILLUSTRATIONS

SIGLA AND ABBREVIATIONS

SIGLA

G	Garin, *Prosatori,* pp. 886–901.
L	BMLF, Pluteo 90, sup. 39.
N	BNCF, II.V.78.
n^1, n^2	Variants/corrections in *N*.
P	BMLF, Pluteo 90, sup. 37.
P^1	Bibliothèque Nationale (Paris), Ital. 1543.
R	BRF, 811.
S	BMLF, Strozzi 106.

ABBREVIATIONS

ACDF	Archivio della Congregazione per la Dottrina della Fede (Vatican City).
ASF	Archivio di Stato (Florence).
ASI	*Archivio Storico Italiano.*
Bandini, *Annales*	A. M. Bandini, *De florentina Iuntarum typographia e eiusque censoribus annales,* 2 vols. (Lucca, 1791).
BMF	Biblioteca Marucelliana (Florence).
BMLF	Biblioteca Medicea Laurenziana (Florence).
BNCF	Biblioteca Nazionale Centrale (Florence).
BRF	Biblioteca Riccardiana (Florence).
Curtius, *ELLMA*	E. R. Curtius, *European Literature and the Latin Middle Ages,* trans. W. R. Trask, with a new afterword by P. Godman (Princeton, 1990).
DBI	*Dizionario biographico degli Italiani* (Rome, 1960–)
IMU	*Italia medioevale e umanistica.*
Machiavelli, *Opere*	Niccolò Machiavelli, *Tutte le opere,* edited by M. Martelli (Florence, 1992).
Pico, Poliziano, e l'umanesimo	P. Viti, ed., *Pico, Poliziano e l'umanesimo di fine Quattrocento* (Florence, 1994).
Politiani Opera	*Angeli Politiani Opera,* 3 vols. (Lyons, 1533).
TLL	*Thesaurus linguae Latinae* (Munich, 1900–).

FROM POLIZIANO TO MACHIAVELLI

I

AT LORENZO'S DEATHBED

FROM THE HILLS of Fiesole, in the country retreat presented to him by his patron, Angelo Poliziano on 18 May 1492 wrote to his friend at Milan, Iacopo Antiquario, about the death of Lorenzo the Magnificent. His letter, a masterpiece of Renaissance Latin prose, offers us an insight into Florentine humanism during the last years of this Medicean house-philologist and his master:[1]

> It is common practice (*vulgare*) for one who replies rather late to a friend's letter to excuse himself with the pressure of excessive business. I, however, cannot attribute my delay in writing back to you less swiftly than I should have wished so much to the things I had to do (although there was no lack of them) as to the bitter grief caused me by the death of that man thanks to whose patronage I was until recently considered, and indeed was, by far the most fortunate of all professors of literature. With the demise of him, the sole instigator of my scholarship, my passion for writing has perished too, and almost all my enthusiasm for my past studies has faded away.[2]

Vulgare: there is nothing popular or common about Poliziano's letter. He was aware that he was writing in one of the most sophisticated genres of Renaissance literature,[3] about the classical theory and practice of which he had lectured during his first year (1480–81) as professor of poetry and oratory

[1] *G* has been collated with the following manuscripts: *P* fols. 23ᵛ–31ᵛ; *S* fols. 134ᵛ–140ᵛ; and *P*¹ fols. 57ʳ–61ᵛ. For bibliography, see *Pico, Poliziano, e l'umanesimo,* pp. 105 (no. 33) and 121–23 (no. 41). All translations, here and elsewhere, are my own.

[2] "Vulgare est ut, qui serius paulo ad amicorum litteras respondeant, nimias occupationes [*G, P*¹, *S:* excusationes *P*] suas excusent. Ego vero quo minus mature ad te rescripserim, non tam culpam refero [*P*¹: confero *G, P, S*] in occupationes, quamquam ne ipsae quidem defuerint [*P:* defuerunt *G, P*¹, *S*], quam in acerbissimum potius hunc dolorem, quem mihi eius viri obitus attulit, cuius patrocinio nuper unus ex omnibus litterarum professoribus et eram fortunatissimus et habebar. Illo igitur nunc extincto, qui fuerat unicus auctor eruditi laboris, videlicet ardor etiam scribendi noster extinctus est, omnisque [*G, P, S:* omnis *P*¹] prope veterum studiorum alacritas elanguit."

[3] On Renaissance letters, see Najemy, *Between Friends,* pp. 19–57 with further bibliography; and C. H. Clough, "The Cult of Antiquity: Letters and Letter Collections," in *Cultural Aspects of the Italian Renaissance: Essays in Honor of P. O. Kristeller* (New York, 1976), pp. 33–67.

at the Florentine Studio,[4] in a course on the *Sylvae* of Statius.[5] Drawing on Cicero and, particularly, Demetrius of Phalerum, Poliziano distinguished between the types of letter, humorous or serious, and the kinds of subject appropriate to the genre.[6] More personal than an oration and less pedantic than a treatise, the *epistola* should cultivate a gay and relaxed tone, unless it deals with philosophy and politics. Distinct from the dialogue, with its extemporaneous and colloquial character, the letter is to derive its style from eclectic imitation[7] and draw its substance from all branches of learning: "No part of this republic of men of letters (as it were) should be neglected by me; determined attention must be paid to every aspect."[8]

Two concepts central to Poliziano's thought are united in this sentence: the notion that an individual mode of expression, based on multiple models that it freely adapts, can emulate in its variety and equal or surpass through its independence the example set by the classics, together with the ideal of the unity of learning, centered on the study of letters and language, known since antiquity as *enkyklios paideia.*[9] Poliziano styles himself, in the opening paragraph, a professor of literature and refers to scholarship. These terms, in the uncharacteristically modest but revealing usage of his later years, amount to a partial retreat from the lofty aim that he had set himself in the first *Centuria* of his *Miscellanea* (1489). There, combining exaltation of himself, Lorenzo de' Medici, and Giovanni Pico della Mirandola with denigration of his enemies, the ambitious philologist had cast this triumvirate as partners in the enterprise of reconstructing a comprehensive culture.[10] Now, in 1492, the alliance is diminished, and he is reduced to the level of a client, bereft of his patron. The wider world should share his grief. Lorenzo's death was of concern not only to Angelo Poliziano and Iacopo Antiquario, but also to the entire "republic of men of letters."

Antiquario, himself a man of letters, courtier, and diplomat, had been on cordial terms with Lorenzo de' Medici.[11] He had the ear of the Sforza, rulers

[4] For Poliziano's lectures, see L. Cesarini Martinelli, "Poliziano professore allo Studio fiorentino," in *La Toscana al tempo di Lorenzo il Magnifico,* 2:463–81.

[5] *Commento inedito alle Selve di Stazio* (ed. Cesarini Martinelli). See below, pp. 66ff.

[6] Ibid., pp. 15–23, with Najemy, *Between Friends,* pp. 48ff.

[7] On the theory of imitation in Poliziano and its antecedents, see M. L. McLaughlin, *Literary Imitation in the Italian Renaissance: The Theory and Practice of Literary Imitation from Dante to Bembo* (Oxford, 1995), pp. 187ff. See further below, pp. 45ff.

[8] "Nulla mihi huius veluti literatorum rei publicae neglegenda pars est, sed universis pro virili parte consulendum." *Commento inedito alle Selve di Stazio* (ed. Cesarini Martinelli), p. 20, ll. 10–12.

[9] For the concept and bibliography, see I. Hadot, *Arts libéraux et philosophie dans la pensée antique* (Paris, 1984), pp. 263–93; and G. Rechenauer in *Historisches Wörterbuch der Rhetorik,* vol. 2 (Tübingen, 1994), cols. 1160–85. See further below, pp. 81ff.

[10] See further below, pp. 85ff.

[11] See E. Bigi in *DBI* 3 (Rome, 1965), pp. 470–72. Still useful is G. B. Vermiglioni, *Memo-*

of Milan,[12] prime targets of Florentine foreign policy. And he acted, through his numerous contacts and voluminous correspondence with scholars, as an intermediary, a mediator, and an agent of these self-appointed guardians of high culture. A letter to him, in the month following Lorenzo's death, was more than a private communication. It had a public and political aim, serving to reassure Milan and other Italian centers of learning, with their humanist-servants as attentive as Poliziano or Antiquario to the interests of their masters, that power had transferred smoothly (without the murmurs of dissent or misgiving recorded by less partisan sources[13]) from Lorenzo the Magnificent to Piero, his heir.

The same purpose, which shaped the epistolary collection that Poliziano intended to dedicate to Piero de' Medici,[14] was reflected in the swift manuscript diffusion[15] and the rapid publication of this letter. Long reluctant to venture into print, Poliziano had recently made the acquaintance of that egregious entrepreneur of scholarship, Alessandro Sarti.[16] On a journey to visit Italian libraries, made in the company of Pico between 4 and 9 June 1491, he had halted at Bologna, and had been brought, by Sarti, into contact with the printer Platone Benedetti.[17] When, on 25 June 1492, this letter issued from Benedetti's press, it formed part of an undertaking to publish or reprint selected works by its author and to inform a broader readership than Iacopo Antiquario how, at Florence, the Medici wished Lorenzo to be commemorated.

Commemoration, mingling the public with the personal, is the objective that shapes Poliziano's style. The initiative for writing, as he presents it, was not taken by him, but by Antiquario, to whose request he acceded, fulfilling the duties of friendship:

> "But since you, with great affection, wish to learn about the disaster that has befallen us" and to know what part that great man played in life's final act, de-

---

rie di Iacopo Antiquario e degli studi di amena letteratura esercitati in Perugia nel secolo xv . . . (Perugia, 1813).

[12] Gilbert, *Machiavelli and Guicciardini,* p. 261; and cf. F. Catalano, "Il ducato di Milano nella politica dell'equilibrio," in *Storia di Milano,* vol. 7, *L'età sforzesca, 1450–1500* (Milan, 1956), pp. 227ff., and *Milano dell'età di Ludovico il Moro,* Atti del convegno internazionale 28 February–4 March 1983, 2 vols. (Milan, 1983).

[13] E.g., Parenti, *Storia fiorentina,* pp. 23ff.; and see further below, pp. 18ff.

[14] See M. Martelli, "Il 'Libro delle Epistole,'" in idem, *Angelo Poliziano,* pp. 205–65.

[15] See below, pp. 26ff.

[16] See J. Hill Cotton, "Alessandro Sarti e il Poliziano," *La Bibliofilia* 64 (1992): 225–46; P. de Nolhac, "Etudes aldines III: Alde Manuce et Ange Politien," *Revue des bibliothèques* 6 (1896): 311; and Branca, *Poliziano,* pp. 2–9, 234–36.

[17] P. Veneziani, "Platone Benedetti e la prima edizione degli 'Opera' del Poliziano," *Gutenberger Jahrbuch* 85 (1988): 95–107; and cf. Godman, "Poliziano's Poetics," pp. 115ff. The manuscript P^1 was Benedetti's exemplar.

spite my tears and my deep aversion from recalling and (as it were) reliving the sorrow, I will grant your request, irresistible because it is so well-meaning, for neither do I desire to fall short of the standards of friendship established between us nor am I capable of doing so. Indeed, I am also convinced that it would be both too uncivilized and too discourteous, were I to presume to deny anything at all to you or to that towering figure who wished me so well. Nonetheless, because it is in the nature of the subject about which you ask me to write that it can be grasped more readily by silent reflection and meditation than expressed by either words or letters, I now qualify my obedience to your wish with this strict condition: that I do not promise what I cannot deliver and that, if I can do anything for your sake, I on no account refuse it.[18]

The modesty, conventional in such a context, is qualified by the ambiguous language of obligation. Ambiguous because, emphasizing his deference to Antiquario and his debts to Lorenzo, Poliziano brings himself to the fore. His waning enthusiasm for *studia* contrasts with his patron's steadfast devotion to him (*mei tam studioso*). "That towering figure," in his final act on life's stage,[19] had all the composure of an ancient philosopher, looking down on the vanity of human striving, including his own. Not only Platonism but other schools of pagan thought, blended with Christianity, interested Lorenzo[20] and contributed to form his image.[21] Syncretic and dramatic, this client's letter reflects both the sacred and the profane culture of his master.

[18] "'Sed si tantus amor casus cognoscere nostros' [*Aeneid* 2.10] et qualem se ille vir in extremo quasi vitae actu gesserit audire, quamquam et fletu impedior et a recordatione ipsa quasique retractatione doloris abhorret animus ac resilit, obtemperabo tamen tuae tantae ac tam honestae voluntati, cui deesse pro instituta inter nos amicitia neque volo neque possum. Nam profecto ipsemet mihi nimium [*G, P*[1], *S:* om. *P*] et incivilis viderer [*G, P*[1], *S:* videre *P*] et inhumanus, si tibi et tali viro et mei tam studioso rem ausim prorsus ullam [*P, P*[1], *S:* nullam *G*] denegare. Ceterum quoniam de quo tibi a nobis scribi postulas, id eiusmodi est, ut facilius sensu quodam animi tacito et cogitatione comprehendatur, quam aut verbis aut litteris exprimi possit, hac lege tibi iam nunc obsequium nostrum astringimus, ut neque id polliceamur quod implere non possimus, et si quid tamen possimus [*P*[1], *S:* possimus . . . possumus *P:* et si quid tamen possimus om. *G*], tua certe causa non recusemus."

[19] For the metaphor, see Curtius, *ELLMA,* pp. 138ff.; A. Demandt, *Metaphern für Geschichte: Sprachbilder und Gleichnisse im historisch-politischen Denken* (Munich, 1978), pp. 332ff.; and L. Cesarini Martinelli, "Metafore teatrali in Leon Battista Alberti," *Rinascimento* 29 (1989): 3–52.

[20] See Hankins, "Lorenzo de' Medici as Patron of Philosophy," pp. 15–53; J. Kraye, "Lorenzo and the Philosophers," in Mallett and Mann, eds., *Lorenzo the Magnificent,* pp. 151–66; and A. Brown, "Platonism in Fifteenth-Century Florence and Its Contribution to Early Modern Political Thought," in eadem, *The Medici in Florence,* pp. 215–45.

[21] On the image of Lorenzo, cf. Rubinstein, "Lorenzo's Image in Europe," pp. 297–312, and "Formation of the Posthumous Image," pp. 94–106; E. Gusberti, "Un mito del Cinquecento: Lorenzo il Magnifico," *Bulletino dell'istituto storico italiano per il Medio Evo* 91 (1984): 187ff.; Bullard, *Lorenzo il Magnifico,* pp. 3–132; and the exhibition catalogue *Lorenzo dopo Lorenzo.*

A "mirror for princes" composed about a "non-prince,"[22] its silences and omissions are no less notable than its explicit eloquence.

His subject, declares the professor of oratory, is beyond the compass of rhetoric. With the contemplation accorded to the study of spiritual texts, he ruminates on his theme.[23] Feigning speechlessness before the ineffable, Poliziano recommends a *meditatio mortis*. Then begins the graphic narrative:

> For almost two months Lorenzo de' Medici suffered from those pains which, because they attack the cartilage of the internal organs, are aptly called hypochondriac. They are rightly considered very trying because they are most painful, although they never prove fatal in their violence. But in Lorenzo's case—I should say by the will of fate or through the ignorance and negligence of his doctors—it came to pass that, while his suffering was being treated, he contracted an extremely dangerous fever that gradually penetrated not (as is usual) into his arteries and veins but into his limbs, internal organs, muscles, bones, and marrow. Because it crept into his system subtly and secretly—as it were, with a light tread—it was hardly observed at first; then, when it had given clear signs of its ominous presence, it was treated less carefully than it should have been, and it so totally weakened and afflicted Lorenzo that not only did his physical forces disintegrate but also almost his entire body was consumed and wasted away. So it was that, on the day before he gave up the ghost, as he lay ill in his villa at Careggi, there occurred a complete breakdown that left no hope of recovery. With his customary wisdom, Lorenzo understood this. His first priority was to summon a doctor for his soul in order to confess to him the sins of his whole life according to Christian custom. Afterwards, at close quarters, I heard that confessor marveling as he related that he had never seen anything greater or more wondrous than the way in which Lorenzo, constant and prepared for death, with not the slightest sign of fear, remembered the past and provided for the present, thinking ahead to the future in the same spirit of deep faith and wisdom. And then, in the middle of the night, as he rested and meditated, it was announced that the priest had arrived with the sacrament. Lorenzo, at that moment, was truly shaken, saying: "Far be it from me to make Jesus, my creator and redeemer, come to this bedroom. I ask you to carry me immediately; carry me to meet the Lord." As he said this, he lifted himself up as far as he could and, counterbalancing his physical weakness with his strength of mind, went to the hall, leaning on the arms of members of his household, to meet the old man, before whose feet Lorenzo fell in tearful supplication. "Most gentle Jesus," he said, "will you deign to visit this most wicked servant

[22] See below, pp. 13ff.

[23] For the term and the mode of reading, cf. J. Hamesse, "Il modello della lettura nell'età della scolastica," in *Storia della lettura nel mondo occidentale,* ed. G. Cavallo and R. Chartier (Rome, 1995), pp. 92ff.

of yours? But why have I said servant? I am rather your enemy and a most ungrateful one at that. For you have heaped upon me so many favors and I have never listened to your words, so often committing high treason against you. In the name of that love with which you embrace the whole human race—which brought you down from heaven to us on earth and arrayed you in the dark vestments of our humanity; which compelled you to suffer hunger, thirst, cold, heat, travails, mockery, slander, beatings and blows and finally even death on the cross—I humbly implore you, Jesus my savior, to turn your gaze from my sins, so that when I stand before your tribunal, to which I have long felt myself plainly summoned, my transgressions and wrong-doings will not be punished but forgiven through your good deeds on the cross. Let your most precious blood intercede on my behalf—that blood which you shed in order to liberate men on the lofty altar of our redemption!" As he said these and other things, Lorenzo wept; and all those who were present wept with him. Eventually the priest ordered him to be lifted up and carried to his little bed so that the sacrament could be administered more comfortably. For a while Lorenzo refused but, not wishing to disobey a man older than himself, he allowed himself to be persuaded after expressing almost the same opinion, and received the body and blood of the Lord filled with the Holy Spirit and in awe of God's majesty.[24]

[24] "Laboraverat igitur circiter menses duos Laurentius Medices e doloribus iis [*G:* his *P,* P^1, *S*] qui, quoniam viscerum cartilagini inhaereant, ex argumento hypochondrii appellantur. Hi tametsi neminem sua quidem vi iugulant, quoniam tamen acutissimi sunt, etiam iure molestissimi perhibentur. Sed enim in Laurentio—fatone dixerim an [*G, P, S:* ac P^1] inscitia incuriaque medentium—id evenit ut, dum curatio doloribus adhibetur, febris una omnium insidiosissima contracta sit, quae sensim illapsa, non quidem in arterias aut venas, sicuti ceterae solent, sed in artus, in viscera, in nervos, in ossa quoque et medullas incubuerit. Ea vero, quod subtiliter ac latenter—quasique lenibus vestigiis—irrepserat parum primo animadversa; dein vero cum satis magnam sui significationem dedisset, non tamen pro eo ac debuit diligenter curata, sic hominem debilitaverat prorsus atque afflixerat, ut non viribus modo, sed corpore etiam paene [*G, P, S:* paene etiam P^1] omni amisso et consumpto distabesceret. Quare pridie quam naturae satisfaceret, cum quidem in villa Caregia cubaret aeger, ita repente concidit totus, nullam ut iam suae salutis spem reliquam ostenderet. Quod homo, ut semper cautissimus intelligens, nihil prius habuit quam ut animae medicum arcesseret [*P,* P^1, *S:* accerseret *G*], cui de contractis tota vita noxiis Christiano ritu confiteretur. Quem ego hominem postea mirabundum sic prope audivi narrantem [*G, P, S:* Quem . . . narrantem om. P^1] nihil sibi unquam neque maius neque incredibilius visum, quam quomodo Laurentius constans paratusque adversus mortem atque imperterritus et praeteritorum meminisset et praesentia dispensasset et de futuris item religiosissime prudentissimeque cavisset. Nocte dein media quiescenti meditantique sacerdos adesse cum sacramento nunciatur; ibi vero excussus sibi [*P:* om. *G,* P^1, *S*]: 'Procul,' inquit, 'a me hoc absit, patiar ut Iesum meum, qui me finxit, qui me redemit, ad usque cubiculum hoc venire. Tollite hinc obsecro me quam primum, tollite ut Domino occurram!' Et cum dicto sublevans ipse se [*G, P, S:* sese P^1] quantum poterat atque animo corporis imbecillitatem sustentans, inter familiarium manus obviam seniori ad aulam usque procedit, cuius ad genua prorepens supplexque ac lacrymans: 'Tune,' inquit, 'mitissime Iesu, tu nequissimum hunc servum tuum dignaris invisere? At quid [*G, P:* quod P^1: quondam *S*] dixi servum? Immo

Lorenzo's illness[25] is the only medical phenomenon observed and recorded by Poliziano. About fever, he had created in his youth a poetic myth no less allusive, refined, and distant from reality than his other literary works,[26] the utility of which was now being questioned. The purple prose and elegant verse that had sufficed to make a reputation in the 1470s were gradually being supplanted, in the changing intellectual atmosphere of the late Quattrocento, by different and more serious pursuits. Doubt was being cast, at the time when Poliziano wrote, on the role of "men of letters"—nowhere more searchingly than at Ferrara, whose medical humanists decried as ornamental the erudition practiced by *grammatici* such as him, contested the self-sufficiency of philological research, and sought to apply classical scholarship to issues of life and death.[27] Did Poliziano understand the disease that he recounted with such urbanity? Was he capable, on the basis of the Greek physicians whom he studied, of prescribing a cure? Or was this stylish writing a mere exercise in rhetoric—as polished, elementary, and superficial as the Latin composition practiced in the schools?

An echo of that controversy, which struck at the very foundations of the edifice of *enkyklios paideia* that Poliziano wished to construct, is audible in his polemic against "the ignorance and negligence of . . . doctors." More actual and personal than a cliché of the bereaved and the sick, it voiced resentment at a profession that was gaining, within humanist circles, a lucrative prestige denied to the traditional *grammaticus*. Placed on a lower rung in the academic hierarchy, and recently worsted by a leading medical human-

---

vero [*G, P*^{1}, *S:* om. *P*] hostem potius, et quidem ingratissimum, qui tantis abs te cumulatus [*G, P*^{1}, *S:* cumulatis *P*] beneficiis nec tibi dicto unquam audiens fuerim et tuam totiens maiestatem laeserim. Quod ego te per illam, qua genus omne hominum complecteris, charitatem, quaeque te caelitus ad nos in terram deduxit, nostraeque humanitatis induit involucris, quae famem, quae sitim, quae frigus, aestus [*P*^{1}: aestum *G, P, S*], labores, irrisus, contumelias, flagella et verbera, quae postremo etiam mortem crucemque subire te compulit; per hanc ego [*P, P*^{1}, *S:* om. *G*] te, salutifer Iesu, quaeso obtestorque avertas faciem a peccatis meis, ut cum ante tribunal tuum constitero, quo me iam dudum citari plane [*P, P*^{1}, *S:* plene *G*] sentio, non mea fraus, non culpa plectatur, sed tuae crucis meritis condonetur. Valeat, valeat in causa mea sanguis ille tuus, Iesu, preciosissimus, quem pro asserendis [*P, P*^{1}, *S:* afferendis *G*] in libertatem hominibus in ara illa sublimi nostrae redemptionis effudisti!' Haec atque alia cum diceret lacrymans ipse lacrymantibusque, qui aderant, universis. Iubet eum tandem sacerdos attolli atque in lectulum [*G, P*^{1}, *S:* lectum *P*] suum, quo sacramentum commodius administraretur, referri. Quod ille cum aliquandiu facturum negasset, tamen ne seniori suo minus foret [*P:* foret minus *G, P*^{1}, *S*] obsequens, exorari se passus, iteratis eiusdem ferme sententiae verbis, corpus ac sanguinem dominicum plenus iam sanctitatis et divina quadam maiestate verendus accepit."

[25] See A. Costa and G. Weber, "Le alterazioni morbose del sistema scheletrico in Cosimo dei Medici il Vecchio, in Piero il Gottoso, in Lorenzo il Magnifico, in Giuliano Duca di Nemours," *Archivio de Vecchi* 33 (1955): 55ff., to which little is added by E. Panconesi and L. Marri Malacrida, *Lorenzo il Magnifico in salute e in malattia* (Florence, 1992), pp. 39ff.

[26] *Angeli Politiani, Sylva in scabiem* (ed. Perosa). See Perosa, "*Febris:* A Poetic Myth," pp. 74–95.

[27] See further below, pp. 96ff.

ist, this professor of literature took his revenge by slights on the competence of physicians. Here as elsewhere, Poliziano's abuse sustained an old-fashioned tone, recalling the low invective of Petrarch, another "man of letters" with upward aspirations.[28]

Ineffectual physicians of the body are temporarily replaced, by the prescient Lorenzo, with "a doctor for the soul." The distinction, ultimately derived from Aristotle (*Nicomachean Ethics* 1102*a*), was to become fundamental in Florentine culture of the late Quattro- and early Cinquecento.[29] Again like an antique sage, "that great man" foresees the end, and provides for the present, past, and future. These are not only the attributes of a philosopher but also the qualities of a prophet—the role claimed by Girolamo Savonarola (soon to arrive on the scene), and by his antitype of the next generation, Niccolò Machiavelli.[30] The division between the secular and spiritual realms, obscured by Savonarola's political influence and reasserted by Florentine humanism after 1494,[31] is here bridged by the conduct of Lorenzo, who displays all the humility, piety, and humanity of a Christian prince formed by the preaching of the friars.[32]

Pietas toward God and his servants is matched by Lorenzo's concern for his heir and for the state. The private virtues of the ruler complement his sense of public responsibility:

> Next he began to console his son when the others were absent, urging him to bear the hardships that had to be with equanimity, admonishing him that heaven's protection, which had never failed him among so many changes of fortune and circumstance, would not abandon Piero; that he should pursue the path of virtue in a good frame of mind, for what has been well pondered is conducive to favorable results. After this Lorenzo remained absorbed in meditation for a time and then, after sending the others away, he called the same son to himself, admonishing, instructing, and teaching him many, many things that had never been known publicly but that were, as we have heard, all full of sin-

[28] See K. Bergdolt, *Arzt, Krankheit, und Therapie bei Petrarca*. Cf. B. Martinelli, "Il Petrarca e la medicina," in Petrarca, *Invective contra medicum* (ed. Ricci), pp. 205–49.

[29] Cf. Ficino's commentary on Plato's *Symposium* 1.2: "Verum episcopus et medicus, alter ad animorum, alter ad corporum curam abire coacti," in Ficino, *Opera omnia* 2.2:1321. See further below, pp. 292ff.

[30] See below, pp. 269ff.

[31] See Chapters IV and V.

[32] See D. d'Avray, *Death and the Prince: Memorial Preaching before 1350* (Oxford, 1994), pp. 117ff. The prayers and contrition of Lorenzo reflect the prescriptions of the *Arte del bene morire,* which circulated widely in Florence and was attributed to Domenico Capranica, cardinal of Fermo (on whom see A. Stenad in *DBI* 19 [Rome, 1976], pp. 147–53). Cf. *Arte del bene morire* (Florence, 1472) [= BRF, B.R. 175], b*iiii*ff., d*ii*ff.; on the ascription, see R. Rudolf, "Der Verfasser des 'Speculum artis bene moriendi,'" *Anzeiger der phil.-hist. Klasse der österreichischen Akademie der Wissenschaften* 88 (1951): 387–98.

gular sanctity and wisdom. One of these precepts, however, that I was privileged to learn, I shall record. "The citizens," said Lorenzo, "will undoubtedly recognize you as my successor. I have no fear that you will command the same authority in this Republic that we [Medici] have possessed up to this day. But since every city is, as they say, a body with many heads and it is impossible to satisfy each individual, remember in crises of this kind to follow that counsel which you understand to be the most honorable and pay more attention to the common good than to particular interests." And Lorenzo commanded that his funeral, following the example set by his grandfather Cosimo, should be conducted within the limits suitable for a private citizen.

Then there arrived from Pavia your friend Lazzaro, a doctor of great expertise—as it seemed—who, however, was summoned too late in the day. Not wishing to leave anything untried, he attempted to concoct a very costly medicine out of gems of all kinds and pearls crushed together. To this Lorenzo reacted by asking the members of his household (a few of us had by now been admitted) what that doctor was doing, what on earth he was up to. When I replied that he was preparing a poultice to warm the vitals, Lorenzo, recognizing my voice at once and gazing at me with his usual look of good humor, said: "Look, Angelo, look!" Barely able to raise his arms, which were drained of energy, he clasped both my hands very tightly. Sighs and sobs took hold of me and I tried to hide them by hanging my head, but he remained serene, never ceasing to hold fast my hands. When Lorenzo realized that I was still prevented by my sorrow from attending to him, he released them from his grasp little by little, as if feigning not to do so. I threw myself to the ground again and again in the antechamber of his bedroom, weeping and giving rein (so to speak) to my tearful grief. Presently, however, I returned, having dried my eyes, as far as I could.

When Lorenzo saw me—and he saw me immediately—he called me to him again and asked very gently what his friend Pico della Mirandola was doing. I replied that he was staying in the city because he feared that he would be a nuisance to Lorenzo if he came. "But were I not afraid," he replied, "that the journey here would be a nuisance to Pico, I should avidly wish to see and speak to him for the last time before I pass away." "Do you want him to be summoned?" I asked. "Indeed I do," said Lorenzo, "as soon as possible." So it was that I followed his wish. Pico came, sat down, and I kept watch at Lorenzo's knees, in order to hear my patron more easily as he spoke in a faint voice that was beginning to fail. Good God, with what courtesy and kindness—I would almost say with what charm—he received Pico! Lorenzo asked him first to forgive him for having caused him this bother, attributing it to his love and goodwill toward him, and saying that he would more willingly give up his soul if he had first feasted his eyes, as he died, on the sight of a man whom he loved dearly. Then he turned to conversation that was, as usual, urbane and intimate. Furthermore, he joked with us a good deal, and then, gazing at Pico and me, said:

"I only wish that I could put off the time of my death to the day when I should have completed your library."[33]

The advice that Lorenzo gives to his son had recently been imparted to Piero by a Chancery official, Filippo Redditi. His *Exhortatio ad Petrum Medicem* of

[33] "Tum consolari Petrum filium—nam reliqui aberant—exorsus, ferret aequo animo vim [*G, P, S:* cum P^1] necessitatis admonebat, non defuturum caelitus patrocinium, quod ne sibi quidem unquam in tantis rerum fortunaeque varietatibus defuisset, virtutem modo et bonam mentem coleret, bene consulta bonos [*G,* P^1, *S:* bonus *P*] eventus paritura. Post illa contemplabundus aliquandiu quievit; exclusis dein [*G,* P^1, *S:* deinde *P*] ceteris, eundem ad se natum vocat, multa monet, multa praecipit, multa edocet [*G, P, S:* docet P^1], quae nondum foras emanarunt, plena omnia tamen, sicuti audivimus [*G, P:* audimus P^1, *S*], et sapientiae singularis et [*G,* P^1, *S:* et singularis et *P*] sanctimoniae: quorum tamen unum, quod scire nobis [*P,* P^1, *S:* nobis scire *G*] quidem licuerit [*G,* P^1, *S:* licuit *P*], adscribam. 'Cives,' inquit, 'mi Petre, successorem te meum haud dubie agnoscent. Nec autem vereor, ne [*G, P, S:* nec P^1] non eadem futurus auctoritate in hac republica sis, qua nos ipsi ad hanc diem fuerimus. Sed quoniam civitas omnis corpus est, quod aiunt, multorum capitum, neque mos geri singulis potest, memento in eiusmodi varietatibus id consilium sequi semper, quod esse quam honestissimum intelliges [*G, P,* P^1: intelligis *S*], magisque universitatis quam seorsum cuiusque rationem habeto.' Mandavit et de funere, ut scilicet avi Cosmi exemplo iusta [*G,* P^1: iuxta *P,* corr., *S*] sibi fierent intra modum videlicet eum, qui privato conveniat.

"Venit dein [*G,* P^1, *S:* deinde *P*] Ticino Lazarus vester medicus—ut quidem visum est—experientissimus, qui tamen sero advocatus, ne quid inexpertum relinqueret, pretiosissima quaedam gemmis omne genus margaritisque conterendis medicamenta temptabat [*G, P,* P^1: tentabat *G*]. Quaerit ibi tum ex familiaribus Laurentius (iam enim admissi aliquot fueramus) quid ille agitaret medicus, quid moliretur. Cui cum ego respondissem epithema [*G,* P^1, *S:* epichema *P*] eum concinnare, quo praecordia foverentur, agnita ille statim voce ac me hilare intuens, ut semper solitus: 'Heus,' inquit, 'heus, Angele!'; simul brachia iam exhausta viribus aegre attollens [*G, P, S:* attollens aegre P^1], manus ambas arctissime prehendit. Me vero singultus lacrymaeque cum occupavissent, quas celare [*G,* P^1, *S:* clare *P*] tamen reiecta cervice conabar, nihilo ille [*G,* P^1, *S:* illo *P*] commotior, etiam atque etiam [*G,* P^1, *S:* etiamque etiam *P*] manus retentabat. Ubi autem persensit fletu adhuc praepediri me, quominus ei operam darem, sensim scilicet eas quasique dissimulanter omisit. Ego me autem continuo in penetrale thalami conicio flentem atque habenas, ut ita dicam, dolori et lacrymis laxo. Mox tamen revertor eodem siccatis, quantum licebat, oculis.

"Ille ubi me vidit—vidit autem statim [*G,* P^1, *S:* om. *P*]—vocat ad se rursum, quaeritque perblande quid Picus Mirandula suus ageret. Respondeo manere eum in urbe, quod vereatur, ne illo, si veniat, molestiae [*S:* molestior *G, P,* P^1] sit. 'At ego,' inquit vicissim, 'ni verear, ne molestum sit ei hoc iter, videre atque alloqui extremum exoptem [*G, P, S:* exopto P^1], priusquam plane a vobis emigro.' 'Vin tu,' inquam [*G, P, S:* igitur P^1], 'arcessatur [*P, S:* accersatur *G:* accessatur P^1]?' 'Ego vero,' ait ille, 'quam primum.' Ita sane facio; venerat iam, assederat, atque ego quoque iuxta genibus incubueram, quo loquentem patronum facilius utpote defecta iam vocula exaudirem. Bone Deus! qua ille hunc hominem comitate, qua humanitate, quibus etiam quasi blanditiis excepit [*G,* P^1, *S:* excipit *P*]! Rogavit primo [*P,* P^1, *S:* primum *G*] ignosceret quod ei laborem hunc iniunxisset, amori hoc tamen et benivolentiae in illum suae adscriberet, libentius [*G,* P^1, *S:* liberius *P*] sese animam editurum [*P, S:* editurus *G,* P^1], si prius amicissimi hominis aspectu morientes oculos satiasset. Tum sermones iniecit urbanos, ut solebat, et familiares. Nonnihil etiam tunc quoque iocatus nobiscum, quin utrosque intuens nos: 'Vellem,' ait, 'distulisset me saltem mors haec ad eum diem, quo vestram plane bibliothecam absolvissem.'"

1489 is an indirect panegyric on *il Magnifico,* continuing a tradition of praising the father while addressing the son begun by partisans of the Medici shortly after Cosimo's death in 1464.[34] Poliziano, extolled as Piero's tutor in Redditi's work,[35] had been shown it with anxiety: "I tremble in fear at the thought of submitting my little book to Poliziano's critical judgment, just as if I were to hold out a stick to an elephant in a Roman amphitheater."[36] Both the analogies and the trepidation were well founded. Critic and scourge of others' productions, Poliziano counted among his own an unpublished chapter on elephants.[37] Expert in the art of literary emulation, he took Redditi's oblique panegyric on Lorenzo to a direct conclusion, and attributed to the father words of wisdom that his predecessor as encomiast had offered to the son.

Redditi surpassed, and his work consigned to the shelf (where it remained for 250 years),[38] Poliziano concentrated on two related topics that affected him intimately: his own position and that of the dynasty. During this deathbed dialogue, from which others had been excluded, confidential advice had been given to Piero by Lorenzo;[39] and if Poliziano proposed to initiate his readers into one of its secrets, it followed that his source could only have been father or son. Privileged access to the great suggested flattering complicity with those less favored, but what was revealed to them amounted to no secret at all: the necessity for a first citizen, without the title and status of prince, to consider the common good rather than particular interests, and to consult with "the most honorable"—meaning other members of the optimate oligarchy at Florence. This, an adaption of precepts by Cicero (drawing on Plato), was a commonplace of Medicean encomium, on which Redditi had already played the changes.[40] In the same spirit, Lorenzo himself had warned Piero, before his departure for Rome on 26 November 1484 with the sons of the Florentine ambassadors, that "although you are my son, you are no more than a citizen of Florence, like them."[41] Not a lord but a *civis*

[34] See Benivieni, *Ἐγκώμιον Cosmi ad Laurentium Medicem.* See further below.

[35] Ed. Viti, pp. 23, 508–11.

[36] Ibid., pp. 92, 23–25: "Ad acrem tamen Politiani censuram meum pervenire libellum non aliter pertimesco, quam si in Romano theatro stipem elephanto essem porrecturus."

[37] See pp. 106ff. (criticism); 111ff. (elephants).

[38] The *editio princeps,* by Giovanni Lami, was published in 1742.

[39] A Medicean genre: writing to Lorenzo and Giuliano de' Medici about their deceased grandfather Cosimo, Bartolomeo Scala (on whom see below, pp. 126ff.) recorded the advice that the dying patriarch had given to his son Piero. See BNCF, Magl. VIII, 1439, fols. 74^{v}ff.

[40] Cicero *De officiis* 1.85; Plato *Republic* 342*e* and 420*b;* Redditi, *Exhortatio* (ed. Viti), pp. 8, ll. 90ff.; 9, ll. 110ff.; 12, ll. 207ff.; 24, ll. 10ff. On Lorenzo's constitutional position, fundamental are Rubinstein, *Government of Florence,* esp. pp. 228ff.; Kent, "*Lorenzo . . . Amico,*" pp. 43–60; and Brown, "Lorenzo and Public Opinion," pp. 61–85.

[41] "Poiché per esser mio figliuolo, non sei però altro che cittadino di Firenze, come sono ancor loro." L. de Medici, *Scritti scelti* (ed. E. Bigi), p. 637. Often quoted, the advice is best analyzed by Kent, "*Lorenzo . . . Amico,*" p. 50.

with the personal authority to which, in a echo of one of his own letters, the Lorenzo of Poliziano's alludes,[42] *il Magnifico* wished his heir to understand that the primacy of the Medici depended on the support of their allies and partisans. That lesson was meant as a reassurance to the adherents (and opponents) of the house. By Lorenzo's successor, less receptive to his father's example than to the divisive conduct of his tutor,[43] it was promptly ignored. The price was paid two-and-a-half years after Poliziano's letter, when the Medici were exiled from Florence.[44]

The title *pater patriae* bestowed on Cosimo was not conferred on Lorenzo. Urged by his father's encomiasts to follow his example,[45] that son, shrewder than Piero, emulated it not only in the simplicity of his "private citizen's" funeral, but also in his collection of books and patronage of scholars.[46] They—or rather, the select group of two headed by Poliziano—are contrasted with the doctor Lazzaro, at whose dubious fame and expensive remedies Lorenzo pokes fun. Humor gives way to pathos when, in the midst of his suffering, the dying man requests Pico's attendance. The count sits by his side, the client-scholar at his knees. Not with the peremptoriness of a prince but with the courtesy of a friend, Lorenzo exemplifies the paradox of his apparent equality and innate superiority. His power is intrinsic, requiring neither submission nor show; his urbanity is apparent, even on the brink of death; and the Socratic wit of this philosopher-ruler, as lively as Cosimo's,[47] is directed at his famous but unfinished library.

Its construction, as reported by Poliziano, had been undertaken for himself and Pico. Redditi had made a similar point, when he extolled Lorenzo as "the unique hope and refuge of men of learning"[48] and praised, more generally and conventionally, his subvention of scholarship. Poliziano was more

[42] "Io non sono signore di Firenze, ma cittadino con qualche auctorità, la quale mi bisogna usare con temperanza et iustificazione." L. de' Medici, *Lettere* 6 (1481–82), ed. M. Mallet (Florence, 1990), p. 100 [= 525], quoted by Kent, "*Lorenzo . . . Amico,*" p. 52.

[43] See below, pp. 125ff.

[44] See N. Rubinstein, "Machiavelli and Florentine Republican Experience," in Bock, Skinner, and Viroli, *Machiavelli and Republicanism*, p. 15.

[45] A. Brown, "The Humanist Portrait of Cosimo de' Medici, *Pater Patriae,*" in eadem, *The Medici in Florence,* pp. 3–52; and cf. Bartolomeo Scala's letter to Bartolomeo Platina of 1474, edited and discussed by Brown, "Scala, Platina and Lorenzo de' Medici in 1474," in *Supplementum Festivum: Studies in Honor of P. O. Kristeller,* ed. J. Hankins et al. (Binghamton, N.Y., 1987), pp. 137–44. On Platina's *De optimo cive* (ed. F. Battaglia [Bologna, 1944]), Cosimo, and Lorenzo, see Rubinstein, "Cosimo *optimus civis,*" p. 55 (with further bibliography).

[46] See J. Hankins, "Cosimo de' Medici as a Patron of Humanistic Literature," in Ames-Lewis, *Cosimo "il Vecchio,"* pp. 69–94; and A. de la Mare, "Cosimo and His Books," in ibid., pp. 115–56. On Lorenzo's funeral, see S.T.S. Strocchia, *Death and Ritual in Renaissance Florence* (Baltimore, 1992), pp. 215ff.

[47] A. Brown, "Cosimo de' Medici's Wit and Wisdom," in Ames-Lewis, *Cosimo "il Vecchio,"* pp. 95–114 (= eadem, *The Medici in Florence,* pp. 53–72).

[48] Ed. Viti, pp. 20–21, ll. 440–468, and cf. pp. 25–26.

personal. He referred not to the Medicean books available to "the public" at San Marco but to the private collection in Lorenzo's palace in the Via Larga—to a heritage of which he and Pico are represented, by their benefactor's last words, as heirs.[49] No rivals were admitted, not even those men of learning once closest to Cosimo. A process of exclusion is detectable in this letter, qualified by a later and partial attempt at reconciliation.[50] Conspicuous by his absence from the scene is Ficino, whose several accounts of Lorenzo's father on his deathbed are motivated by a desire to emphasize his own proximity as favorite. "Come and bring with you your translation of Plato *On the Highest Good,*" Ficino was requested by the expiring Cosimo, having been commanded to render into Latin Xenocrates' *On Death.*[51] That parallel was in Poliziano's mind when he stressed his own and Pico's intimacy with Lorenzo, while relegating Ficino to the wings of his drama.

A new character is introduced, more forceful than the absent Ficino and less affectionate than the departing Pico:

> To be brief: Pico had barely left when Girolamo Savonarola of Ferrara, a man distinguished for his learning and saintliness and an excellent preacher of heaven's teaching, entered the bedroom and urged him not to waver in his faith. Lorenzo said that it was unshaken; Savonarola told him to live in the future with absolute purity, and Lorenzo replied that he firmly intended to do so. Savonarola admonished him to bear his death, if need be, in a calm state of mind. "There is nothing more agreeable," Lorenzo declared, "if God has so decreed." Savonarola was making to leave when Lorenzo said to him, "Father! Wait! Give me your blessing before you go." Hanging his head, with a humble expression and an aspect of unqualified piety, he promptly repeated Savonarola's words and prayers duly and correctly, not moved in the slightest by the grief of his loved ones, so evident that it could no longer be concealed. You would have said that everyone stood on the verge of death, except Lorenzo.[52]

[49] See Piccolomini, *Intorno alle condizione;* E. B. Fryde, *Greek Manuscripts in the Private Library of the Medici,* 2 vols. (Aberystwyth, 1996); idem, "The Library of Lorenzo de' Medici, in idem, *Studies in Humanism and Renaissance Historiography* (London, 1983), pp. 159ff.; Branca, *Poliziano,* pp. 108–56; S. Gentile, "Lorenzo e Giano Lascaris: Il fondo greco della Biblioteca Medicea Privata," in Garfagnini, *Lorenzo il Magnifico,* pp. 177–94. See further below.

[50] See below, pp. 22ff.

[51] See Hankins, *Plato in the Italian Renaissance,* 1:267ff.

[52] "Ne multis: abierat vixdum Picus, cum Ferrariensis Hieronymus, insignis et doctrina et sanctimonia vir, caelestisque doctrinae praedicator egregius cubiculum ingreditur, hortatur ut fidem teneat; ille vero tenere se ait inconcussam; ut quam emendatissime posthac vivere destinet: scilicet facturum obnixe respondit; ut mortem denique, si necesse sit, aequo animo toleret [*G, P*[1]: tolleret *P, S*]. 'Nihil vero,' inquit ille, 'iucundius, si quidem ita Deo decretum sit.' Recedebat homo iam, cum Laurentius: 'Heus!' inquit, 'benedictionem, pater, priusquam a nobis proficisceris.' Simul demisso capite vultuque et in omnem piae religionis imaginem formatus, subinde ad verba illius et preces rite ac memoriter responsitabat, ne tantillum quidem familiarium luctu aperto iam neque se ulterius dissimulante commotus. Diceres [*G, P*[1], *S:* diceris *P*] indictam ceteris, uno excepto Laurentio, mortem."

This visit was the homage due, by the prior of San Marco, to the patron who had secured his election to an office that was in the gift of the Medici.[53] If Savonarola, not yet the prophet of redemption he was to become,[54] says nothing directly, his reported words contain no hint of censure. Absolution, already granted by the priest who preceded him, had not been requested; and the focus is trained on Lorenzo's wish for benediction.[55] The blessing of Savonarola, sought as a tribute to his growing influence, underlines his harmonious relations with the Medici. The thought is less that of a tyrant admonished than that of the lowly exalted (Luke 1:52). Through his meekness, *il Magnifico* reveals his grandeur. In his abasement, he displays his authority—submitting to the "excellent preacher of heaven's teaching." The inversions that establish his singularity are completed in the delicate understatement of the final sentence: "You would have said that everyone stood on the verge of death, except Lorenzo."

Indifferent to grief and superior to suffering, this model of Aristotelian virtue combines temperance (*Nicomachean Ethics* 1118*a*–*b*) and greatness of spirit (ibid., 1123*b*ff.) with the wit of a gentleman (ibid., 1128*a*). All the more cogent, therefore, is the support that Lorenzo lends to Poliziano's polemic against doctors:

> He alone among the throng showed no sign of pain, agitation, or sorrow, until his last breath maintaining his usual firmness of mind, steadiness, even temper, and greatness of spirit. Nonetheless, the doctors continued to press their attentions upon him, not wishing to seem to do nothing, tormenting him with their busy officiousness; but he did not refuse or oppose anything that they thrust on him—not because he had the faintest hope of holding on to sweet life but in order to avoid giving the slightest offense to anyone while dying. He endured all with such strength, up to the very last moment, that he made several jokes about his own death. Thus, when someone offered him food and asked how it pleased him, Lorenzo replied: "As much as is usual for a man passing away." After that he gently embraced each individual and humbly sought forgiveness if, on account of his various illnesses, he had been too severe or trying. Then Lorenzo concentrated all his attention on the extreme unction and commendation of his departing soul. There followed the recitation of the Gospels, in which the crucifixion inflicted on Christ is described. Lorenzo indicated his almost complete understanding of the words and the sense at times by moving his lips in silence, at times by raising his weary eyes, occasionally by

[53] For Savonarola's position in 1492, see Martelli, "La politica culturale del ultimo Lorenzo," drawing on Weinstein, *Savonarola and Florence*. Cf. G. C. Garfagnini, "Firenze tra Lorenzo il Magnifico e Savonarola," *Critica storica* 18 (1991): 9–30.

[54] Cf. G. C. Garfagnini, "Pico e Savonarola," in *Pico, Poliziano, e l'umanesimo,* pp. 149–57; and cf. below, pp. 134ff.

[55] For the controversy over the interpretation of this scene, see Ridolfi, *Studi savonaroliani,* pp. 115ff. and 265ff., and idem, *Vita di Savonarola,* pp. 75ff.

a movement of the fingers. And finally, with his gaze continually fixed on a small crucifix made of silver and magnificently adorned with pearls and jewels, which he repeatedly kissed, Lorenzo de' Medici passed away.[56]

With the intrusive bustle of the physicians is contrasted the calm equanimity of the sage. Once again, Lorenzo does not make the others the butt of his wit; the joke is at his own expense. Preserving the courtesy that distinguished his summons to Pico and the obedience that marked his conduct with Savonarola, he submits to their pointless ministrations and begs pardon from his entourage. Passing from this world in serene splendor, he is qualified for equal eminence in the next. Heady with incense, the image of Lorenzo de' Medici held up for veneration by this canon of Florence's cathedral[57] is nothing less than the icon of a secular saint.

The sacred and the profane, the ancient and contemporary elements in Poliziano's portrait, are blended in the summary that follows:

He was a man born to every form of greatness, who against the alternating, repeated buffets of fortune continually trimmed his sails, so that you would not have been able to tell whether he was more constant in favorable circumstances or more calm and temperate in adverse conditions. His intelligence was so great, so versatile, and so perceptive that, where others consider it of tremendous moment to excel in a specialized field, he was of equal distinction in them all. Indeed, I think that there is no one who is unaware that in this manner probity, justice, faith, and holiness found in the heart and mind of Lorenzo de' Medici their favorite abode and altar-piece. How compelling his graciousness, kindness, and affability were, is demonstrated by the goodwill toward him of the whole people and absolutely every order of society. Yet among all his gifts, liberality and magnificence were the most splendid, raising him in almost im-

[56] "Sic scilicet unus ex omnibus ipse nullam doloris, nullam perturbationis, nullam tristitiae significationem dabat; consuetumque animi rigorem, constantiam, aequabilitatem [*G, P:* aequalitatem *P*[1], *S*], magnitudinem ad extremum usque spiritum producebat. Instabant medici adhuc tamen, et ne [*G, P*[1], *S:* om. *P*] nihil agere viderentur, officiosissime hominem vexabant, nihil ipse [*P:* ille *G, P*[1], *S*] tamen aspernari, nihil aversari, quod illi modo obtulissent [*G, P, S:* attulissent *P*[1]], non quidem quoniam spe [*G, P*[1], *S:* spem *P*] vitae blandientis illiceretur [*G, P, P*[1]: alliceretur *S*], sed ne quem forte moriens vel levissime perstringeret. Adeoque fortis ad extremum perstitit, ut de sua quoque ipsius [*G, P*[1], *S:* om. *P*] morte nonnihil cavillaretur; sicuti cum porrigenti cuidam cibum rogantique mox quam placuisset respondit: 'Quam solet morienti.' Post id blande singulos amplexatus petitaque suppliciter venia, si cui gravior forte, si molestior morbi vitio fuisset, totum se post illa perunctioni summae demigrantisque animae commendationi dedidit. Recitari dein evangelica historia coepta est, qua scilicet irrogati Christo cruciatus explicantur, cuius ille agnoscere se verba et [*G, P, S:* verbaque *P*[1]] sententias prope omnis [*P, P*[1]: omnes *G, S*], modo labra tacitus movens, modo languentis [*P, P*[1], *S:* languentes *G*] oculos erigens, interdum etiam digitorum gestu significabat. Postremo sigillum crucifixi argenteum margaritis gemmisque magnifice adornatum defixis usquequaque oculis intuens identidemque deosculans expiravit."

[57] See *Pico, Poliziano, e l'umanesimo,* pp. 346–47 (no. 146).

> mortal glory to the ranks of the gods, for he did nothing simply in the interests of fame and renown but everything for love of virtue. His concern for men of letters; the vast respect—even reverence—that he showed each of them; the huge expenditure of effort and application that he devoted to seeking out all over the world, and buying, volumes in Greek and Latin; the enormous sums that he spent on this enterprise will make not only the present age or century but even posterity itself understand that, at the death of Lorenzo, it suffered an immense loss![58]

Constancy in the face of Fortune's changes was not only an Aristotelian virtue (*Nicomachean Ethics* 1100*b*) that characterized the wise man of several philosophical schools, notably the Stoics; it had also been a key theme of encomia on Cosimo de' Medici.[59] Lapo da Castiglionchio, in the preface to his translation of Plutarch's *Life of Themistocles,* had employed the metaphors used by Poliziano,[60] and Vespasiano da Bisticci, among others, had referred to the all-round excellence of Lorenzo's father.[61] Poliziano, bent on making his patron an embodiment of the ideal of *enkyklios paideia,* continues the process with an admiration not shared by all Lorenzo's contemporaries. They noted, and resented, his hunger for glory, even in petty matters—his jealousy, rages, and *prepotenza.*[62] With the probity and justice, the affability and graciousness that the panegyrist extols, they contrasted the sharp financial practices, the

[58] "Vir ad omnia summa natus, et qui flantem reflantemque totiens fortunam usque adeo sit alterna velificatione moderatus, ut nescias utrum secundis rebus constantior an adversis aequior ac temperantior apparuerit. Ingenio vero tanto ac tam facili et perspicaci, ut quibus in singulis excellere [*P, P*[1], *S:* excedere *G*] alii magnum putant, ille in [*P, P*[1], *S:* om. *G*] universis pariter emineret. Nam probitatem, iustitiam, fidem, sanctitatem [*P:* om. *G, P*[1], *S*] nemo, arbitror, nescit, ita sibi Laurentii Medicis pectus atque animum quasi gratissimum aliquod domicilium templumque delegisse. Iam comitas, humanitas, affabilitas quanta fuerit, eximia quaedam in eum totius populi atque omnium plane ordinum benivolentia declaratur. Sed enim inter haec omnia liberalitas [*G, P, P*[1]: libertas *S*] tamen et magnificentia explendescebat, quae illum paene immortali quadam gloria ad deos usque provexerat; cum interim nihil ille famae dumtaxat causa et nominis, omnia vero virtutis amore persequebatur. Quanto autem litteratos [amore *P erased:* om. *G, P*[1], *S*] homines studio complectebatur, quantum honoris, quantum etiam reverentiae [*G, P, S:* reverentia *P*[1]] omnibus exhibebat, quantum denique operae industriaeque suae conquirendis toto orbe terrarum coëmendisque linguae utriusque voluminibus posuit, quantosque in ea re quam immanes sumptus fecit, ut non aetas modo haec aut hoc saeculum, sed posteritas etiam ipsa maximam in huius hominis interitu iacturam fecerit!"

[59] See Brown, "Humanist Portrait," pp. 7ff. (cited in note 45).

[60] *Vitae* (Rome, 1470), fol. 81^{v}. The common source is Cicero *De officiis* 2.19 (cf. 1.90). For its use in the language of diplomacy, cf. the Milanese ambassador, Sacromoro: "Troppo alza le vele per bonanza," "Molto alza le sue vele quando gli pare havere vento prospero," cited by Brown, *Bartolomeo Scala,* p. 61n; and cf. Bullard, *Lorenzo,* p. 24.

[61] *Vitae,* vol. 2, ed. A. Greco (Florence, 1976), pp. 168 and 193. For Lorenzo's "ingegno universale" in the post-restoration panegyrics of Francesco Guicciardini and Niccolò Valori, cf. Rubinstein, "Formation of the Posthumous Image," pp. 99 and 100.

[62] See Kent, "The Young Lorenzo, 1449–69," in Mallett and Mann, eds., *Lorenzo the Magnificent,* pp. 4ff.; and Brown, "Lorenzo and Public Opinion," pp. 67ff.

manipulated elections, and—after the Pazzi conspiracy of 1478—the authoritarian style of a party boss accompanied in the streets by a band of armed thugs.[63] And although Poliziano was not alone in attributing divine qualities to his secular saint,[64] Lorenzo's mercifulness to the people and munificence to the church could also be construed as the political and economic tactics of a would-be *signore.*

Liberality and magnificence, the Aristotelian attributes of the great-minded that Cosimo had possessed,[65] are presented as manifestations of the selfless *virtus* that Vasari, in his famous portrait, was to highlight.[66] Aristotle's ethical categories had long influenced memorial preaching on the prince;[67] and Savonarola, in his *Arte del ben morire* of 1496, was to celebrate disinterested *virtù.*[68] The altruism of Lorenzo, as depicted by Poliziano, found expression in support for "men of letters," upon whom and whose libraries he lavished "enormous sums." The benefits were reciprocal. Grateful admiration of the learned guaranteed the ruler's immortality. Praising Lorenzo's merits, natural and inherited, Poliziano stresses continuity—in particular, a continuity of patronage reaching from grandfather to father and, by implication, to the son and heir. Now Piero, by a logical progression of self-interest, enters the scene:

> Yet we are now consoled in our profoundest sorrow by his children, most worthy of so distinguished a father. The eldest of whom, Piero, barely twenty-one years old, bears with great responsibility, prudence, and authority the heavy burden of the entire Republic, so that it is thought that his father Lorenzo has forthwith returned to life in him. The other son is the eighteen-year-old Giovanni, both a splendid cardinal at an age in which no one has ever attained such a rank, and a legate appointed by the supreme pontiff with jurisdiction not only over the patrimony of the Church but also over his fatherland. He proves himself to be of such character and stature in his conduct of, and excellence in, complex affairs that he will attract the attention of everyone and arouse unbe-

[63] Kent, "*Lorenzo . . . Amico,*" pp. 59ff.

[64] Ibid., pp. 46 and 57. Cf. Scala (BNCF, Magl. VIII, 1439, fol. 76^r): "Civitates, quarum rectores et principes . . . vicarii putantur in terris deorum."

[65] *Nicomachean Ethics* 1122*b*. Cf. A. B. Fraser Jenkins, "Cosimo de' Medici's Patronage of Architecture and the Theory of Magnificence," *Journal of the Warburg and Courtauld Institutes* 33 (1970): 162–70.

[66] See P. Rubin, "Vasari, Lorenzo, and the Myth of Magnificence," in Garfagnini, ed., *Lorenzo il Magnifico,* pp. 427ff. with fig. 1. Cf. Rubinstein, "Formation of the Posthumous Image," p. 104.

[67] D'Avray, *Death and the Prince,* pp. 136ff.

[68] (Florence, 1496), reprinted with an introduction by E. v. Rath (Berlin, 1926). See D. Weinstein, "*The Art of Dying Well* and Popular Piety in the Preaching and Teaching of Girolamo Savonarola," in *Life and Death in Fifteenth-Century Florence,* ed. M. Tefel, R. G. Witt, and R. Gotten (Durham, N.C., 1989), pp. 88–104. Cf. A. Tenenti, *Il senso della morte e l'amore della vita nel Rinascimento (Francia e Italia)* (Turin, 1957), pp. 112–14, 329–31.

lievably high expectations, which he will satisfy to the full. The third son then is Giuliano, a stripling with sensitivity and good looks, whose marvelous sweet temperament, combined with uprightness and intelligence, has entranced the entire city. Even though I shall say nothing about the others for the moment, on the subject of Piero I cannot restrain myself from noting a testimony from his father that is of recent date.

About two months before his death, sitting in his study, Lorenzo (as was his wont) mused with us about philosophy and literature. He said that he intended to spend the rest of his life in these studies with me, Ficino, and Pico della Mirandola, far from the bustle of the city. I said that the citizens would never allow this, for they appeared to need his authoritative guidance more and more every day. Smiling, Lorenzo replied: "But presently I shall give up my role to your pupil and place on his shoulders this heavy burden." When I asked whether he detected in Piero, who is still a young man, such strength that we could rely on him with good faith, Lorenzo said: "I see such a great and solid foundation that I expect with full confidence that he will be able to bear anything I wish to build upon it. Do not think, Angelo, that any Medici before Piero has had such character as he displays. In consequence I hopefully predict that—unless a number of tests of his intelligence which I have made deceive me—he will yield to none of his ancestors."

Indeed, Piero promptly gave ample and clear signs of the validity of his father's wise prediction by being constantly at his side when he was ill and attending himself to almost everything, even the lowliest of tasks, showing great patience at sleepless nights and missed meals, never stirring from Lorenzo's bedside except for urgent affairs of state. Although a wondrous sense of filial duty was apparent on his features, nonetheless, he avoided increasing Lorenzo's suffering during the illness by revealing his own grief, swallowing (as it were) all his groans and tears with incredible steadfastness. So it was that, in this saddest of moments, we witnessed a most entrancing spectacle (so to speak), for Piero's father, in his turn, improvised to avoid making his son gloomier by his own sorrow, pretending to be in a different mood, and held back his tears for Piero's sake, never seeming either disturbed or broken in spirit as long as he was present. In this way both of them struggled with their feelings and sought to conceal their delicate sentiments with considerate delicacy.

When Lorenzo passed away, the courtesy and dignity with which our Piero received all his citizens who thronged to his house can scarcely be described; nor can the appropriateness, variety, and gentleness of his responses to their grief, consolations of the hour, and promises of support. Scarcely expressible, too, is the immense skill that Piero showed in organizing the family's affairs, in making good all the damage done by this grievous blow to its vital interests; receiving, encouraging, and giving heart to even the most insignificant retainer of the Medici who was downcast and depressed at the adverse circumstances; never faltering in his service to the Republic at any time or place, never failing any individual or falling short in any duty, down to the last detail. That is how Piero seems to have clearly established his course and to have begun, at full speed, a journey that will lead him soon to follow (so it is thought) in his father's footsteps.[69]

[69] "Ceterum consolantur nos maximo in luctu liberi eius, tanto patre dignissimi. Quorum qui maximus natu Petrus vixdum primum et vigesimum ingressus annum tanta iam et gravitate et prudentia et auctoritate molem totius reipublicae sustentat, ut in eo statim revixisse genitor Laurentius existimetur. Alter annorum duodeviginti Ioannes et cardinalis amplissimus, quod nunquam cuiquam id aetatis contigerit, et idem pontifici maximo non in [*G, P^1, S:* om. *P*] ecclesiae patrimonio dumtaxat, sed in patriae quoque suae dictione [*P:* ditione *G:* dicione *P^1, S*] legatus, talem tantumque se iam tam arduis negotiis gerit et praestat, ut omnium in se mortalium oculos converterit atque incredibilem quandam, cuique [*P:* cui *G, P^1, S*] responsurus planissime est, expectationem concitaverit. Tertius porro Iulianus impubes adhuc, pudore tamen ac venustate neque non probitatis et ingenii mirifica quadam suavissimaque indole, totius sibi iam civitatis animos [*P^1, S:* totius iam sibi animos civitatis *G:* totius sibi animos civitatis *P*] devinxit. Verum ut de aliis in praesenti taceam, de Petro certe ipso cohibere me non possum, quin recenti re testimonium hoc loco paternum adscribam.

"Duobus circiter ante obitum mensibus, cum in suo cubiculo sedens, ut solebat, Laurentius de philosophia et litteris nobiscum fabularetur, ac se destinasse diceret reliquam aetatem in his [*P:* hiis *P^1, S:* iis *G*] studiis mecum et cum Ficino Picoque ipso Mirandula consumere, procul scilicet ab urbe et strepitu, negabam equidem hoc ei per suos cives licere, qui quidem in dies viderentur magis magisque ipsius et consilium et auctoritatem desideraturi. Tum subridens ille: 'Atqui iam,' inquit, 'vices nostras alumno tuo delegabimus, atque in eum sarcinam hanc et onus omne reclinabimus.' Cumque ego rogassem, an adhuc in adolescente tantum virium deprehendisset, ut ei [*P, S:* eis *G, P^1*] bona fide incumbere iam possemus: 'Ego vero [*G, P, S:* om. *P^1*],' ait ille, 'quanta eius et quam solida video esse fundamenta, laturum spero haud dubie [*G, P^1, S:* om. *P*] quidquid inaedificavero. Cave autem [*P, P^1, S:* igitur *G*] putes, Angele, quemquam adhuc ex nostris indole [*G, P^1, S:* indolis *P*] fuisse tanta, quantam iam Petrus ostendit, ut sperem fore atque adeo augurer, nisi me ipsius ingenii aliquot iam experimenta fefellerint, ne cui sit maiorum suorum concessurus.'

"Atque huius quidem iudicii praesagiique paterni magnum profecto et clarum specimen hoc nuper dedit, quod aegrotanti praesto fuit semper, omniaque per se paene etiam sordida ministeria obivit, vigiliarum patientissimus et inediae; nunquamque [*P, P^1, S:* numquam *G*] a lectulo ipso patris, nisi cum maxime respublica urgeret, avelli passus. Et cum mirifica pietas extaret in vultu, tamen ne morbum aut sollicitudinem paternam moerore suo adaugeret gemitus omnis [*P, S:* omnes *G, P^1*] et lacrymas incredibili virtute quasi devorabat. Porro autem quod unum tristissima in re pulcherrimum ceu spectaculum videbamus, invicem pater quoque ipse, ne tristiorem filium tristitia sua redderet, frontem sibi ex tempore velut aliam fingebat ac fluentes oculos in illius gratiam continebat, nunquam aut consternatus animo aut fractus, donec ante ora natus obversaretur [*P, P^1, S:* observaretur *G*]. Ita uterque certatim vim facere affectibus suis ac dissimulare pietatem pietatis studio nitebatur.

"Ut autem Laurentius e vita [*G, P^1, S:* e vita Laurentius *P*] decessit, dici vix potest quanta et humanitate et gravitate cives omnes suos Petrus noster ad se domum confluentes exceperit, quam et apposite et varie et blande etiam dolentibus, consolantibusque pro tempore suamque operam pollicentibus responderit; quantam deinde et quam solertem rei constituendae familiari [*G, P:* familiarum *P^1:* consuetudine familiar(i)um *S*] curam impenderit, ut necessitudines suas omnes gravissimo casu perculsas sublevarit, ut vel minutissimum quemque ex familiaribus deiectum [*G, P, P^1:* deiectumque *S*] diffidentemque sibi adversis rebus collegerit, erexerit, animaverit, ut in obeunda quoque republica nulli unquam aut loco, aut tempori [*G, P, P^1:* tempore *S*], aut muneri, aut homini defuerit, nulla denique in parte cessaverit. Sic ut eam plane

If this family portrait of a traditional consolation[70] includes members of the Medicean entourage such as Poliziano, Lorenzo's dealings with other rulers are not depicted. Foreign policy painted out of the frame, domestic difficulties are smoothed away.[71] No sign, naturally, of the disaffected nephews, Lorenzo and Giovanni, sons of Pierfrancesco;[72] nor does any other Florentine optimate figure in the picture. And since none of "the many heads" of the city whom his heir had been urged to consult appears at Lorenzo's deathbed, the unacknowledged tension between the appearance of power-sharing and the reality of hegemony is simply resolved in a partisan view of Cardinal Giovanni, occupied in the hunt for benefices;[73] of Giuliano, insignificant enough to be praised on account of his good looks; and—above all—of Piero de' Medici and his omnipresent tutor.

With Poliziano, Pico, and Ficino, it is reported, Lorenzo had planned to spend his remaining years in the study of philosophy and literature. The name of the third of these scholars makes an impression here. After his fall from grace in the 1470s,[74] Ficino, in the late 1480s, began to return to Lorenzo's favor.[75] Never the leader of a "Platonic Academy,"[76] his philosophical influence over the ruler-sage was second to Pico's, with whom he had more than once crossed swords.[77] Allied with Pico was Poliziano, equivocally deferential to the older man, on whose admonitions to Lorenzo that he should imitate Cosimo and prefer virtue to wealth, power, or honor[78] this letter draws. *Il Magnifico*'s "conversion" to philosophy, announced by Redditi in correspondence with the Bolognese humanist Filippo Beroaldo,[79] had been celebrated by Pico in the dedication to his *De ente et uno* of the previous year, without mentioning Ficino. If he drew closer to Lorenzo between 1491 and

institisse iam viam atque ita pleno gradu iter ingressus videatur, brevi, ut putetur, parentem quoque ipsum vestigiis consecuturus."

[70] For the tradition, see P. von Moos, *Consolatio: Studien zur mittellateinischen Trostliteratur über den Tod und zum Problem der christlichen Trauer,* vol. 1 (Munich, 1971), pp. 298ff.

[71] Cf. F. W. Kent, review of Lorenzo de' Medici, *Lettere,* vols. 5 (1480–81) and 6 (1481–82), ed. M. Mallett, *Renaissance Quarterly* 49 (1996): 131.

[72] See Brown, "Lorenzo and Public Opinion," pp. 71ff.; and eadem, *The Medici in Florence,* pp. 73–102.

[73] G. B. Picotti, *La Giovinezza di Leone X* (Milan, 1927), pp. 67–159; and Bullard, *Lorenzo il Magnifico,* pp. 148ff.

[74] See Fubini, "Ficino e i Medici," pp. 3–52, and "Ancora su Ficino e i Medici," pp. 275–91.

[75] See M. M. Bullard, "Marsilio Ficino and the Medici: The Inner Dimensions of Patronage," in Verdon and Henderson, eds., *Christianity and the Renaissance,* pp. 467–92; and Hankins, "Lorenzo de' Medici," pp. 34–35.

[76] Hankins, "Myth of the Platonic Academy," pp. 429–75.

[77] See M.J.B. Allen, "The Second Ficino-Pico Controversy: Parmenidean Poetry, Eristic, and the One," in *Marsilio Ficino e il ritorno di Platone: Studi e documenti,* vol. 2, ed. G. C. Garfagnini (Florence, 1986), pp. 417–58 with further bibliography.

[78] Bullard, "Marsilio Ficino," pp. 478ff.

[79] Ed. Viti, p. 110. On Beroaldo, see below, pp. 92ff.

1492,[80] the distance between him and his rivals was scarcely bridged by this gesture of half-hearted reconciliation. Poliziano and Pico continue to occupy the foreground. Ficino, paid the ambiguous compliment of an honorable mention, remains absent.

Absent, too, is Landino, another of Lorenzo's former teachers.[81] The thesis in defense of the active life that he had attributed to his pupil in the *Disputationes camaldulenses* of 1473[82] had later been rejected, Poliziano implies. Rhetoric, rather than philosophy, was what *il Magnifico* in his youth had learned from Landino;[83] and that, in the altered atmosphere of Lorenzo's last years, was no longer enough. The eloquent poet of love and pastoral idyll depicted in Poliziano's *Nutricia* of 1486[84] had become a graver statesman during his maturity. The desire to relinquish the world of politics that runs throughout Lorenzo's verse, from the *Altercazione* to the *Rappresentazione di San Giovanni e Paolo,*[85] finds its last and least convincing expression here, in his yearning for contemplation.

The alleged wish to withdraw from the world had a political purpose: to indicate that Piero's succession had been prepared. The unqualified joy at the passing of power to him, like the general grief of the citizens at the loss of his beloved father that Poliziano describes, is intended to stifle the mumblings of discontent and suppress the exultation at the death of a detested "tyrant" recorded in their diaries by other Florentines opposed to the ruling house.[86] The flawless conduct of its new head in public is matched by his filial devotion to Lorenzo at his bedside. No speech is attributed to Piero. He is to be judged by his actions—as restrained and attentive as those of the ideal courtier, whose art is expressed by its concealment in Castiglione's work of that title.[87] Hiding his sorrow, Piero conducts with Lorenzo a wordless dialogue, tribute to their unspoken understanding. When the father breaks his

[80] See V. Branca, "Lorenzo e il Poliziano della *Miscellaneorum Centuria Secunda,*" in Garfagnini, ed., *Lorenzo il Magnifico,* p. 202.

[81] See R. Cardini, "Landino e Lorenzo," in *La Toscana al tempo di Lorenzo il Magnifico,* 2:449–61. See further below, pp. 81ff.

[82] Ed. P. Lohe, pp. 26–35. See further below, pp. 185ff.

[83] "Haec igitur habui, quae declamatorie et, ut apud Landinum me exercere soleo, magis quam philosophice mihi pro vita civili dicenda viderentur." Landino (ed. P. Lohe), p. 35, ll. 18–20.

[84] See below, pp. 62ff.

[85] On the *Altercazione,* see Rubinstein, "Lorenzo's Image in Europe," p. 312 and n. 97; on the *Rappresentazione,* M. Martelli, "Politica e religione nella Sacra Rappresentazione di Lorenzo de' Medici," in *Mito e realtà del potere nel teatro: Dall'antichità classica al Rinascimento* (Viterbo, 1988), pp. 189–216; and cf. N. Newbigin, "Piety and Politics in the *Feste* of Lorenzo's Florence," in Garfagnini, ed., *Lorenzo il Magnifico,* pp. 39ff.

[86] Cf. A. Rinuccini, in *Ricordi storici* (ed. G. Aiazzi), p. cxlvi: "Perniziosissimo e crudelissimo tiranno alla città nostra."

[87] See P. Burke, *The Fortunes of the Courtier: The European Reception of Castiglione's "Cortegiano"* (Oxford, 1995), pp. 29ff.

silence to voice trust in the son, he speaks—to Poliziano—not of "my heir" but of "your pupil." Unlike his heroes, the sometime tutor with an eye to the future is seldom reticent about himself.

To this prodigy of ambition, those of nature take second place. The *portenta* that preceded Lorenzo's death are described after it, in a manner that betrays Poliziano's purpose:

> About the funeral I've nothing to say. It was celebrated according to the example set by his grandfather's in the way that (as I have mentioned) Lorenzo had prescribed as he lay dying. There was a great throng of people of every kind, so great that we have never seen its like. Moreover, these wonders immediately preceded the death, roughly three in number, although others are also bandied about. On the fifth of April, at about the third hour, three days before Lorenzo passed away, during a sermon from the pulpit in the church of Santa Maria Novella, a woman suddenly rose up, struck with terrible fear, among the packed crowds and ran out in a frenzy, screaming hideously: "Look, citizens, look! Do you not see the raging bull who with his flaming horns has leveled this huge church to the ground?"
>
> Then, at the first hour of the watch, when the sky was unexpectedly covered with foul clouds, the highest point of the great basilica [Santa Maria del Fiore], which with wondrous artistry tops a roof that has no match in the entire world, was repeatedly struck by lightning, with the effect that huge parts of the building were torn down, especially in that part adjacent to the Medici palace; while enormous pieces of marble were ripped out by a terrifyingly violent force. There had been a clear premonition of this, for a gilded ball, like others that can be seen on the same high level, was blasted by a bolt, as a further sign portending a particular loss to that family. And it is also worth mentioning that, no sooner had the thunder rumbled, than the sky cleared.
>
> During the night on which Lorenzo died, a star that was brighter and larger than usual loomed over the villa where he was passing away, and was observed to fall and disappear at the very moment when it was known that he had given up the ghost. For three nights without interruption torches are said to have run from the hills of Fiesole above the church where the remains of the Medici dynasty are buried, shining brightly and then, after a brief interval, vanishing. Furthermore, a very fine pair of lions, in the pit where they were publicly held captive, battled so fiercely that one of them was seriously injured and the other killed. At Arezzo, on the very top of the fortress, twin flames are reported to have burned like St. Elmo's fire for a very long time; and beneath the walls of the city a she-wolf repeatedly let out blood-curdling howls. Some people—for such is their cast of mind—even interpret as a monstrous event the fact that a doctor among our contemporaries held to be a great expert committed suicide because his professional skill and diagnosis proved mistaken. Deciding to throw

himself down a well, this medic made, by his destruction, an offering of expiation to the head of the Medicean house.

But I now see that, although I have been silent about many weighty matters in order to avoid lapsing into a form of flattery, I have gone on at greater length than I intended initially. That I have done so is to be partly ascribed to my desire obediently to follow your wish, my most excellent, learned, wisest, and dearest of friends, for what you wanted could not be satisfied by hurried brevity. Yet there was also another motive: that a certain bittersweetness, like a tickle, drew me to recall and cherish the memory of Lorenzo de' Medici. If his equal or like, once or twice, chances to be produced by our age, we will be able boldly to compete with antiquity for the splendor and glory of its fame.[88]

[88] "De funere autem nihil est quod dicam. Tantum ad avi exemplum ex praescripto celebratum est quemadmodum ipse, ut dixi, moriens mandaverat. Tam magno autem [*G, P, S:* autem magno *P*[1]] omnis generis mortalium concursu quam magnum nunquam antea [*P, P*[1], *S:* ante *G*] meminerimus. Prodigia vero mortem ferme haec antecesserunt, quamquam alia quoque vulgo feruntur: Nonis Aprilibus, hora ferme diei tertia, triduo ante quam animam edidit Laurentius, mulier nescio quae, dum in aede sacra Mariae Novellae [*G, P*[1], *S:* om. *P*], quae dicitur, declamitanti e pulpito dat operam, repente inter confertam populi multitudinem expavefacta consternataque consurgit, limphatoque cursu et terrificis clamoribus: 'Heus, heus!' inquit, 'cives, an hunc non cernitis ferocientem taurum, qui templum hoc ingens flammatis cornibus ad terram deiicit [*P*[1], *S:* deicit *G, P*]?'

"Prima porro vigilia, cum caelum nubibus de improviso foedaretur, continuo basilicae ipsius maximae fastigium, quod opere miro singularem toto terrarum orbe testudinem supereminet, tactum de caelo est, ita ut vastae quaepiam deiicerentur [*P*[1], *S:* deicerentur *G, P*] moles, atque in eam potissimum partem, qua Medicae convisuntur aedes, vi quadam horrenda et impetu marmora immania torquerentur. In quo illud etiam praescito non caruit, quod inaurata una pila, quales aliaeque in eodem fastigio conspiciuntur, excussa fulmine est, ne non ex ipso quoque insigni proprium [*G, S:* proprie *P:* prodigium *P*[1]] eius familiae detrimentum portenderetur [*G, P*[1], *S:* protenderetur *P*]. Sed et illud memorabile, quod, ut primum detonuit, statim quoque serenitas reddita.

"Qua autem nocte obiit Laurentius, stella solito clarior ac grandior suburbano imminens, in quo is animam agebat, illo ipso temporis articulo decidere extinguique visa, quo compertum deinde est eum vita demigrasse. Quin excurrisse etiam faces trinoctio perpetuo de Faesulanis montibus supraque id templum, quo reliquiae conduntur Medicae gentis, scintillasse nonnihil moxque evanuisse feruntur. Qui [*P*[1], *S:* quid *G, P*] quod et leonum quoque nobilissimum par, in ipsa qua publice continentur cavea, sic in pugnam ferociter concurrit, ut alter pessime acceptus, alter etiam leto sit datus. Arreti quoque supra arcem ipsam geminae perdiu arsisse flammae, quasi Castores, feruntur, ac lupa identidem sub moenibus ululatus terrificos edidisse. Quidam illud etiam (ut sunt ingenia) pro monstro interpretatur, quod excellentissimus—ita enim habebatur—huius aetatis medicus, quando ars eum praescitaque fefellerant, animum desponderit, puteoque se sponte [*G, P*[1], *S:* se de sponte *P*] demerserit, ac principi ipsi Medicae, si vocabulum spectes, familiae sua nece parentaverit.

"Sed video me cum quidem multa et magna reticuerim, ne forte in speciem adulationis inciderem, longius tamen provectum quam a principio institueram. Quod ut facerem, partim cupiditas ipsa obsequendi obtemperandique tibi optimo, doctissimo prudentissimoque homini mihique etiam [*P:* om. *G, P*[1], *S*] amicissimo, cuius quidem studio satisfacere brevitas ipsa in [*G, P*[1], *S:* inquam *P*] transcursu non poterat, partim etiam amara quaedam dulcedo quasique

Among the "wonders" listed here and later interpreted by Machiavelli as premonitions of "Italy's ruin" (*Istorie fiorentine* 8.36), it is the lightning that struck Santa Maria del Fiore that contemporary sources emphasize.[89] With echoes of the signs accompanying Christ's passion (Matthew 27:45ff.) and allusions to those recounted by Cicero and Lucan,[90] Poliziano's *portenta* raise Lorenzo's death to the level of a metahistorical tragedy.

Tragic were its consequences in the cause célèbre of Pier Leone, the physician who, according to some, took his own life in remorse and, in the opinion of others, was killed by the Medici as revenge for his failure correctly to diagnose Lorenzo's illness.[91] Insidiously ("for such is people's cast of mind"), the suicide or murder is presented by Poliziano as an act of expiation. In a pun on the Latin *medicus* ("physician") and *Medica . . . familia* ("the Medici"), the refinement of the writing jars with the brutality of the thought, as the doctor's reputation is sacrificed on the altar of the philologist's vendetta with his profession. Concluding his address to Antiquario and, through him, to the world of learning, the gratified mannerist feels no incongruity in recording a "tickle of bittersweetness." Conscious of having created a masterpiece, he preens himself on his art. Its style and idiom are less those of a citizen of the republic of letters than those of a prince—as aristocratic, superior, and insufferable in Poliziano's chosen sphere as Lorenzo, to many, appeared in his. How insufferable, may be measured by the reactions of other intellectuals to this letter.

. . . . .

Five weeks later, on 26 June 1492, Marsilio Ficino corresponded with Filippo Valori, ambassador and intermediary between the Hungarian court and the Florentine elite.[92] Marginalized in Poliziano's account of their patron's last hours, Ficino had other reasons for disgruntlement at being overtaken by the times. His Latin translation of Plotinus, published at Lorenzo's expense,

---

titillatio impulit recolendae frequentandaeque eius viri memoriae. Cui si parem similemque nostra aetas unum forte atque alterum tulit, potest audacter iam de splendore nominis et gloria cum vetustate [*G, P, P*[1]: venustate *S*] quoque ipsa contendere."

[89] The claim of M. Martelli ("Schede sulla cultura di Machiavelli," p. 291), "In tutti gli altri e sopratutto gli cronisti, di nessun altro prodigio si fa parola, se non del fulmine," is misleading. Cf. Bullard, *Lorenzo il Magnifico,* pp. 39ff.

[90] Cf. Cicero *In Catilinam* 3.18 and *De consolatu suo* 2.15ff.; Lucan *Bellum civile* 1.526ff.

[91] See L. Frati, "La morte di Lorenzo de' Medici e il suicidio di Pier Leoni," *ASI* 5 (1889): 255–60.

[92] For the letter, see *Supplementum Ficinianum* (ed. P. O. Kristeller), pp. 63–64. On Filippo Valori and Ficino, Kristeller, "Domenico Sforazzini (1686–1760) e la sua biografia di Marsilio Ficino," *Interpres* 6 (1986): 132–33, 146–47, 154. For context, cf. Branca, *Poliziano,* pp. 125ff.; and L. Elekes, "La politica estera di re Mattia e gli stati italiani nella seconda metà del secolo xv," in *Rapporti veneto-ungheresi all'epoca del Rinascimento* (Budapest, 1975), pp. 251ff.

had appeared in May—just days after its dedicatee's death.[93] "I write, in my usual manner, as a philosopher," declared the senior scholar, reclaiming the territory on which his junior had begun to trespass. Although Poliziano's letter was "full and elegant" (*latius elegantiusque*), it had missed an essential point. Lorenzo's soul had transmigrated to Piero, in "Pythagorean" terms, or—in the words of the Gospels (John 14:9 and Matthew 11:27)—"He that hath seen me, hath seen the Father," "All things are delivered unto me of my Father." Poliziano's analogy between Piero and Lorenzo becomes Ficino's identification; the spiritual undertones of the earlier letter are brought to the fore; and as the younger Medicean client is trumped in the art of courtly flattery, so it is insinuated that his elder is the true philosopher, in contrast to the full but empty elegance of the "professor of literature." Poliziano's implied offer of reconciliation is implicitly declined.

His pupils shared this skepticism. In mid-April 1492, Marcello Virgilio, a disaffected student of the humanist, corresponded about the passing of *il Magnifico* with another of his teachers, Demetrius Chalcondyles.[94] Resenting Poliziano's competition in the teaching of Greek language and philosophy, and loathing his enemy's polemic against Byzantine émigrés such as himself, Chalcondyles had moved, as recently as September 1491, from his chair at Florence to one at Milan. There Marcello Virgilio's letter reached him, mentioning the lightning that had struck Santa Maria del Fiore but none of the other prodigies described by Poliziano. Volubility on this topic contrasted with silence on others. Savonarola figured at Lorenzo's bedside in his client's encomium, but not the prophecy of God's wrath delivered during the sermon of a "sophist," as Marcello Virgilio characterized the *frate,* who had struck fear into many.[95] Pier Leone's tragic fate, described with a sympathy lacking in Poliziano's account, moved Chalcondyles to horror. It marred, he wrote back on 4 May, the end of a great man whom he remembered with gratitude.[96] It was in this atmosphere of grief, shock, and suspicion that the commemorative epistle that, with a "tickle" of self-regard, Poliziano had sent to Milan fell (or was thrust) into the hands of a sometime colleague not inclined to share its author's satisfaction.

The "Lord of the Flies" (Ψυλλάνθρωπος), as Poliziano was called by Marcello Virgilio and others,[97] paraded himself in Florence as the authority on

[93] Cf. P. Trovato, "Il libro toscano nell'età di Lorenzo: Schede e ipotesi," in *La Toscana al tempo di Lorenzo il Magnifico,* 2:542ff.; and A. M. Wolters, "The First Draft of Ficino's Translation of Plotinus," in Garfagnini, ed., *Marsilio Ficino e il ritorno di Platone,* 2:305–330 (cited in note 77).

[94] On Chalcondyles, see below, pp. 147ff.; on Marcello Virgilio, see below, pp. 144ff. et passim. The letter is edited by Vermiglioni, *Memorie di Iacopo Antiquario,* pp. 266–68 (cited in note 11).

[95] Ridolfi, *Vita di Savonarola,* pp. 73–74.

[96] "Mortem Laurentii maculavit et notam haud parvam atque infamiam et familiae et civitati inussit." Ed. Bandini, *Collectio,* pp. 23–24.

enkyklios paideia, wrote the incensed Chacondyles on 23 June 1492.[98] "Poetry and oratory, dialectic and philosophy: he promised 'great and unheard-of things.'" That this was indeed how Poliziano was perceived by his admirers since 1490, a correspondence between Michele Acciari and his fellow student, Michele Alessi, confirms.[99] To Chalcondyles, such pretentions seemed absurd, for he recognized their origins—"He began from my basics"—and the sneer became satire with feigned astonishment at the polymath's descent from high politics to the "profession of letters."

The allusion was to the beginning of Poliziano's letter; the jibe directed at the false humility affected by that literary politician. His style was Ciceronian, Chalcondyles archly suggested, aware that Poliziano, a year earlier, had poured scorn on the purism of one of Cicero's epistolary imitators.[100] If Poliziano "boasted" that he had sent his letter to Antiquario, the word was calculated to strike a chord, for boasting was a trait noted even by the writer's fans.[101] Combining open mistrust with veiled praise, Chalcondyles observed that the account given of Lorenzo's death ought to be assessed in Florence, for it was evident that, at the beginning and end of his work, Poliziano had "inserted many other things, lending wondrous expression to his learned intelligence." Less a tribute to the erudition and ability of this virtuoso than an invitation to check his narrative against the facts, Chalcondyles' words pre-

[97] See below, pp. 122ff.

[98] The text has been edited twice—in full by E. Legrand, *Cent-dix lettres grecques à François Filèfe,* pp. 349–50; and in part by S. Gentile in *Pico, Poliziano, e l'umanesimo,* pp. 100–101 (no. 32). Gentile mistakenly takes the following extract to refer to Pico: "Ψυλλάνθρωπος autem (nam recte tali nomine eum notatis), preter ea volumina tam Greca quam Latina, que hoc anno scribis eum percurrisse in facultate poetica, oratoria, dialectica, et philosophie(!) cepisse etiam nuper ab elementis nostris (ut ais) 'magnaque et inaudita' polliceri. Per hec ominari sibi nescio quid mihi videtur, qui ex tam alto gradu ac spe multo maiora administrandi, que πρὸς σύστασιν τῆς πολιτει ΄ας οὐχ ἥχιστα τείνει, ad licterariam professionem descenderit. Epistolam vero eius Ciceronianam, quam iactitat huc ad Iacobum Antiquarium misisse, nos etiam vidimus: sed eam vos melius istic cuius sit integritatis iudicare poteritis. Ceterum principium ipsius et circa finem multaque alia, que hinc inde interserit, mirifice eius ingenium exprimunt et doctrinam." The "free" use of the Greek genitive—*philosophie*—in the first sentence betrays Chalcondyles' origins. Cf. E. Schwyzer, *Griechische Grammatik,* vol. 2 (Munich, 1950), p. 133, 3; and R. Kühner, *Ausführliche Grammatik der griechischen Sprache* 2, 1 (Hanover, 1898), p. 363 n. 11. Not strictly parallel to Chalcondyles' hyperbaton are the passages cited by R. Kühner and C. Stegmann, *Ausführliche Grammatik der lateinischen Sprache,* 4th ed., 2, 1 (Darmstadt, 1962), pp. 473ff. with 443ff.

[99] "Tranquillum [Suetonium] prosequitur . . . lecturus . . . *Nutricia* sua . . . interpretatur Aristotelis *Ethica,* in quibus non tam oratorum atque poetarum interpres quam prestantissimus phylosophus apparet." Edited by D. Delcorno Branca, "Un discepolo del Poliziano: Michele Acciari," *Lettere italiane* 28 (1976): 479. For the courses, see Cesarini Martinelli, "Poliziano professore," pp. 476ff. (cited in note 4).

[100] See below, pp. 46ff.

[101] Cf. the letter of another pupil, Girolamo da Panzano, on 11 July 1486: "Politianus tuus nunc maxime, ut inquit ille, sua '*se iactat in aula*' [*Aeneid* 1.140]." Ed. Branca, *Poliziano,* p. 75.

supposed an animus shared by pupils of the "Lord of the Flies." Just as he was constructing, on building blocks taken from his former colleague, a vainglorious monument of *enkyklios paideia,* so he might be exposed as Cicero's plagiarist.

Such was the bitterness, behind the scenes, that Poliziano's masterpiece aroused among some of the intellectuals who knew him all too well. Their number included Marcello Virgilio, who, two years later, was to become his successor in his chair. At Florence, when he wrote, the position of this Medicean client was less secure than he pretended. Asserting its strength, Poliziano exposed its precariousness. The hauteur of his manner, so closely identified with the cultural ideology of the ruling house, proved near-fatal to his scholarly approach when the Medici fell from power.[102] And Chalcondyles, in a negative sense, was right when he characterized this letter as Ciceronian. Its stylistic practice is eclectic, but its portrayal of the intimacy of an ideal statesman with scholars and *viri boni* is colored by Cicero's image of the "Scipionic" circle.[103] That circle, as its Florentine imitator described it, was closed and exclusive. After Lorenzo's death, Poliziano was to become increasingly isolated.[104] Even in the claustrophobic "republic of men of letters," it was difficult to maintain his illusion of a self-sufficient elite; and it is salutary to glance, by contrast, at the same events as perceived by artisans in the street. One of them was that engaging coppersmith, Bartolomeo Masi.

In April 1492, Masi noted in his diary that Lorenzo had passed away and that he had been a great man. On what grounds was this opinion formed? On account of the magnanimity, generosity, or patronage of scholarship celebrated by Poliziano? Not a bit of it. To the rhetoric of humanism, Masi was impervious. He had different and concrete criteria. He knew that Lorenzo had been important, because the "Sultan of Babylon" had sent him a giraffe.[105] And what a giraffe it was! Graceful and hornless, with long legs and an arching neck, it had a tail like a calf's, an insatiable appetite, and the sprightliness of a lamb.[106] The marvelous beast had entertained the likes of Masi until, bumping its head on a window ledge, it came to a premature end. To Lorenzo's passing, after this ardent encomium, Masi half-heartedly returned, assigning to the achievements celebrated by Poliziano less space and less enthusiasm than he devoted to the giraffe, which the philologist does not mention. The primacy of the Medici, the feuds of scholars, and the cult of

[102] See below, pp. 151ff.

[103] Cf. *De officiis* 1.55 and *Pro Archia poeta* 16, with H. Strasburger, "Der 'Skipionenkreis,'" *Hermes* 95 (1966): 66ff. Observe, too, Cicero's use of *titillatio* at *Cato* 47 and *De natura deorum* 1.113.

[104] See below, pp. 130ff.

[105] On Lorenzo's giraffe and its donor, see F. Babinger, "Lorenzo de' Medici e la corte ottomana," *ASI* 121 (1963): 336 n. 91, 350–51. See further below, pp. 106ff.

[106] Masi, *Ricordanze di Bartolomeo Masi* (ed. S. O. Corazzini), pp. 18ff.

antiquity were not the only subjects that attracted attention at Florence in the late Quattrocento. Nor was the coppersmith's indifference to the "Quarrel of the Ancients and the Moderns" evoked by the man of letters, in the final sentence of his letter, a sign of general apathy. Poliziano's brand of humanism, no longer impregnable, was being challenged within the city. Whispers of criticism had been anticipated by ringing dissent. A voice, passionate and prophetic, had begun to call for change.

II

THE PRISON OF ANTIQUITY

"MUCH has changed," wrote that severe yet scintillating theorist of poetry, Girolamo Savonarola, in his *Apologeticus de ratione poeticae artis* of 1491. "We too, like the ancients, can add words or subtract them . . . for who today employs the archaic forms that were current in their times? Yet there are some who have so fettered themselves, who have enslaved their own intellects in the prison of antiquity so completely that they are even reluctant to diverge from its usage and wish to say nothing that the ancients have not said."[1]

This vivid metaphor, like much else in Savonarola's poetics, was calculated to disturb the complacency of the humanists to, and against, whom it was directed. The self-proclaimed rediscoverers of ancient literature, from Poggio to Poliziano, had vaunted their enterprise as an act of liberation from the captivity of barbarism, the servitude of neglect.[2] Now, in 1491, at what is conventionally regarded as a high point of the Florentine Renaissance, Savonarola was deflating their pretensions, representing them as prisoners, as bondsmen, as slaves.

Or so a startled humanist might have misconstrued the polemical tones of the *Apologeticus*. Its point, in context, was more precise. Savonarola was not indiscriminately hostile to the study of antiquity and the pursuit of humane letters, nor was he an enemy of poetry. An apologist for the scholastic organization of learning, proceeding from Aristotelian and Thomistic premises, Savonarola reasserted the dependence of poetry upon logic within a quadripartite division of philosophy.[3] For the liberal arts extolled by the humanists he had little regard. *Humanitatis studia,* he declared in his preface, had not oc-

[1] *Scritti filosofici* (ed. G. C. Garfagnini and E. Garin), 1:250, ll. 19ff.: "Possumus ergo et addere et minuere sicut illi potuerunt, nam et multa iam mutata sunt. Quis enim hodie dicit 'vostras' et 'volt' et 'intellegere' et alia multa, quae apud antiquos erant usitata? Quidem enim adeo perstrinxerunt se et carceri antiquorum intellectum proprium adeo manciparunt, ut nedum contra eorum consuetudinem aliquid proferre nolint, sed ne velint quidem dicere quid illi non dixerunt."

[2] See Poggio's letter about the discovery of the integral *Institutio oratoria* at St. Gall in 1416: "[Quintilianum] . . . foeditatem illius carceris, squalorem loci, custodum saevitiam diutius perpeti non potuisse." Ed. Garin, *Prosatori,* p. 244. See further below, p. 44.

[3] See E. N. Girardi, "L' 'Apologetico' del Savonarola e il problema di una poesia cristiana," *Rivista di filosofia* 44 (1952): 412–31; O. B. Hardison, *The Enduring Monument: A Study of the Idea of Praise in Renaissance Literary Theory and Practice* (Chapel Hill, N.C., 1962), pp. 13–16; and C. C. Greenfield, *Humanist and Scholastic Poetics, 1250–1500* (London, 1981), pp. 246–56.

cupied his attention for twenty-two years.[4] Instead he had been concerned with "the more serious disciplines"—with theology and philosophy—which dealt with incorruptible and eternal truths. Their basis was Scripture. The humanists' attempt, through a misuse of allegory and a perversion of metaphor, to liken the particular, mutable, and transient perceptions of secular literature to the universal verities of Biblical revelation Savonarola dismissed out of hand. It was absurd to glorify classical poetry as a source of encyclopedic knowledge; in the hands of frivolous aesthetes, it had dwindled into mere decoration and frills. Neither verbal artifice nor meter nor rhythm is constitutive of poetry but Aristotle's "imaginative syllogism." Ruled by reason, this minor medium should voice, in subdued style, arguments that are to be assessed in terms of their truth-claims; and Plato, on Judgment Day, would rise up and prove him right.[5] So it is that Girolamo Savonarola, advocate of content's primacy over form, can conceive of poetry *sine versu*.[6]

That arresting idea is linked to his critique of those who had chosen to abnegate their intellectual freedom. Savonarola's target was less humanism in general than a specific type of humanist: the purists, the "Ciceronians," who never deviated from a syllable laid down in the master's canon.[7] Their ideology of imitation, denying all possibility of development and precluding any change (except for the worse), entailed subjection to an inflexible classicism. Upon these pusillanimous pedants Savonarola, the scholastic modernist, poured scorn.

Hence a paradox for those who have wished to cast him as a reactionary opponent of progress. In the fifteenth-century "Quarrel of the Ancients and the Moderns,"[8] Savonarola took the side of the avant-garde. From different criteria, he came to the same conclusions as Valla, Poliziano, and (later) Erasmus,[9] rejecting ideals of absolute excellence, confined to one period of classical literature, which entailed condemning all that came later as decline. Acknowledging the fact that language, like culture, alters, and welcoming the process of its renewal, Savonarola argued against purism with a rigor lacking in the poetics of his humanist predecessors and contemporaries.[10]

[4] In *Scritti filosofici* (ed. Garfagnini and Garin), p. 210.

[5] Ibid., pp. 265–66.

[6] Ibid., pp. 248–49.

[7] Still fundamental is R. Sabbadini, *Storia del ciceronianismo*. See further below, pp. 48ff.

[8] See H. Baron, "The Querelle of the Ancients and the Moderns as a Problem for Renaissance Scholarship," in idem, *In Search of Florentine Civic Humanism,* 2:72–100; and S. S. Gravelle, "Humanist Attitudes to Convention and Innovation in the Fifteenth Century," *Journal of Medieval and Renaissance Studies* 11 (1982): 193–209.

[9] See G. W. Pigman III, "Imitation and the Renaissance Sense of the Past: The Reception of Erasmus' Ciceronianus," *Journal of Medieval and Renaissance Studies* 9 (1979): 155–77. On Valla and Poliziano, see below, pp. 39–40.

[10] From the large bibliography, the following surveys may be singled out: G. Barbieri Squarotti, "Le poetiche del Trecento in Italia," in *Momenti e problemi di storia dell'estetica,* vol. 1

That is why, in this central field of their endeavor, he was more than a match for the champions of *studia humanitatis*. Savonarola had a system. In the scholastic hierarchy of the disciplines re-erected in his *Apologeticus,* poetry was taught to know its proper—inferior—place. Beneficiary of Lorenzo de' Medici's patronage; mentor of Giovanni Pico della Mirandola; prior of San Marco, where Poliziano was to be admitted, in the last weeks of his life, as a *frate* and, like Pico, laid to rest, Savonarola wrote from a position of growing authority—a position strengthened, and complicated, for the humanists by his sympathy with a form of modernism that enlightened circles at Florence claimed as their own. Small wonder that, outflanked on the battlefield of poetics, they retired from the fray or returned to it later, cowed and trembling.[11]

Savonarola was impressive and intimidating. His censure, in the *Apologeticus,* touched on other subjects from which those who professed them derived income and prestige: grammar, in his opinion not a *scientia* save in the loosest sense;[12] the study of letters divorced from philosophy;[13] the separation of language from the substance of reality.[14] "Not in ignorance but out of zeal for God," wrote this reformer of contemporary culture, ". . . I bite the poets sharp and strong."[15] The metaphor is exact. In the *Apologeticus,* a brief but brilliant tract written in the persona of a repentant poet[16] and renegade from the *studia humanitatis,* Savonarola had exposed their points of intellectual vulnerability, and sunk his teeth into their flabby flesh.

. . . . .

These views, in Poliziano's immediate circle, were not unprecedented. If the trenchancy with which Savonarola criticized the weaknesses of literary hu-

---

(Milan, 1959), pp. 255–324; A. Buck, *Italienische Dichtungslehren vom Mittelalter bis zum Ausgang der Renaissance* (Tübingen, 1952); Curtius, *ELLMA,* pp. 221–34; F. d'Episcopo, "L'estetica del poeta-teologo e l'enciclopedismo di Niccolò Perrotti," *Res publica litterarum* 4 (1980): 43–66; Greenfield, *Humanist and Scholastic Poetics;* C. Mésionat, *Poetica theologia: La "Lucula Noctis" di Giovanni Domenici e le dispute letterarie tra '300 e '400* (Rome, 1984); Robey, "Humanist Views," pp. 7–25, and "Virgil's Statue at Mantua and the Defence of Poetry: An Unpublished Letter of 1379," *Rinascimento,* 2d ser., 9 (1969): 183–203; G. Ronconi, *Le origini delle dispute umanistiche sulla poesia (Mussato e Petrarca)* (Rome, 1976); F. Tateo, "Poesia e favola nella poetica del Boccaccio," *Filologia Romanza* 5 (1958): 267–342; C. Trinkaus, *In Our Image and Likeness,* vol. 2 (Chicago, 1970), pp. 679–704; R. Stillers, "Dichtungstheorie in der italienischen Renaissance: Ein Bericht über ihre Erforschung seit 1960," *Romanisches Jahrbuch* 32 (1981): 48–68; R. G. Witt, *Hercules at the Crossroads,* pp. 209–26, and "Coluccio Salutati and the Conception of the Poeta Theologus in the Fourteenth Century," *Renaissance Quarterly* 30 (1977): 538–46.

[11] See below, pp. 151ff.

[12] *Apologeticus* (ed. Garfagnini and Garin), p. 222.

[13] Ibid., pp. 249, 263.

[14] Ibid., p. 250.

[15] Ibid., p. 245.

[16] Ibid., p. 216.

manism and asserted the vitality of medieval traditions of thought was distinctive, his views had been anticipated six years earlier by "that marvelous youth," Pico, in a letter that he had addressed to the Venetian scholar Ermolao Barbaro, who, on 5 April 1485, had written to congratulate him on his achievements in Latin and Greek literature and to urge him not to waste his time with the "barbarians" of medieval philosophy.[17] At Florence, on 3 June 1485, a Pico affecting to be divided between the pursuit of humane letters and the study of scholasticism composed his reply.[18]

Ermolao's letter, he declared, had given him and Poliziano sensual pleasure. "Reading it, Venus upon Venus seemed to blossom in such fertile abundance that, applauding without interruption, we have scarcely a moment to draw breath."[19] A tone of jocular intimacy established, Pico pretended to regret the time he had spent on Thomas Aquinas, Duns Scotus, Albert the Great, and Averroes. Such "barbarians" are "dirty, vulgar, uncivilized," yet to one of them is attributed a fictive speech, "as unbarbaric as possible," in defense of his "barbarism."

What follows this ironical introduction is an oration that luxuriates in refinements of rhetoric. Proclaiming his ignorance, the "barbarian" philosopher displays a sovereign command of classical literature. His theme is Cicero's distinction between *eloquentia* and *sapientia,* which had played an important role in previous humanist debate;[20] his intention—like Savonarola's in the *Apologeticus*—is to assert the superiority of content over form and style. The search for choice diction is a pleasing pastime, but undesirable in a serious thinker. Persuasion is a useful weapon in political life, where lies and deception reign. From the public domain of the orator, the philosopher maintains his distance. He is no whoremonger. To sexy virgins he prefers the frumpish matron.

All this in purple prose. No reader of the speech that Pico attributes to his "barbarian" has failed to observe that he possesses every attribute of the verbal elegance that he claims to reject. Few seem to have noted that he parodies the explicitness that is such a salient feature of humanist eloquence and, shifting his ground from the scholastic Aristotelians repudiated by Pico, embarks on a defense of the medieval Platonic ideal of the implicit, with its attendant qualities of secrecy and indirectness. They were praised by Aristotle's Greek interpreter, Themistius,[21] whom Barbaro had translated into Latin

[17] *Epistolae, orationes, et carmina* (ed. V. Branca), vol. 1, *ep.* 68, pp. 84–87. A translation of Barbaro's and Pico's correspondence, with brief discussion, is offered by Q. Breen, "Giovanni Pico della Mirandola on the Conflict of Philosophy and Rhetoric," *Journal of the History of Ideas* 13 (1952): 284–412.

[18] Ed. Garin, *Prosatori,* pp. 804–23.

[19] "Novae fertiliter inter legendum efflorescunt Veneres, ut perpetua quadam acclamatione interspirandi locum non habemus." Ibid., p. 806.

[20] Cicero *De inventione* 1.1, with J. E. Seigel, *Rhetoric and Philosophy.*

[21] See J. Pépin, *La tradition de l'allégorie de Philon d'Alexandrie à Dante* (Paris, 1987), p. 207.

in 1481. Pico echoes the terminology of that translation,[22] but in a manner that hints at its limits, for what he discerns beyond them is the theory, current and influential since the twelfth century, of *integumentum*.[23]

Integumentum means "covering" and "shrouding": the outward form as opposed to the inner core. Arrayed in apparent ugliness, this shroud contains a mysterious beauty of hidden truth. That is why the philosopher proclaims his preference for frumpish matrons over sexy virgins—for a mode of expression that is "disheveled, bloated, clumsy" rather than one "prettily tricked out with the character or suspicion of shamelessness." "Otherwise my words would not display Athene's cloak but be driven away, in their profanity, from the holy rituals."[24]

This is the language of initiation, employed in the Platonism of the High and Late Middle Ages. Warding off the common herd, Pico's philosopher speaks in the same hieratic terms as Bernardus Silvestris, Alan of Lille—or Poliziano himself in the preface to his incomplete translation of the *Charmides*.[25] The argument in favor of implicitness does not flinch from paradox, lauding naked expression in a style clothed in splendid *colores*.[26] Obliqueness combined with profundity is the aim of this subtle "barbarian," a *concordia oppositorum* unattainable in the shallow lucidity of the purists. Their linguistic narrow-mindedness imports philosophical incoherence, he argues,

[22] On Barbaro and Themistius, see J. Kraye, "Philologists and Philosophers," in *Cambridge Companion to Renaissance Humanism,* pp. 144ff. On Pico and Barbaro, see F. Bausi, "Il 'dissidio' del Giovane Pico tra umanesimo e filosofia (1484–87)," in *Pico, Politiano e l'umanesimo,* p. 39, and cf. idem, "Per Giovanni Pico della Mirandola: Tre schedi filologico-linguistiche," *Interpres* 14 (1994): 272–78, reprinted in his *Nec rhetor neque philosophus.*

[23] See, best, E. Jeauneau, "L'usage de la notion d'*integumentum* à travers les gloses de Guillaume de Conches," in idem, "*Lectio Philosophorum,*" *Recherches sur l'École de Chartres* (Amsterdam, 1973), pp. 125–92. Cf. P. Dronke, *Fabula: Explorations into the Uses of Myth in Medieval Platonism* (Leiden, 1985), pp. 47–67.

[24] "Comatam orationem semper cinaedam. Quare nos nostram malumus capillis hirtam, globosam, inexpeditam, quam cum impuritatis vel nota vel suspicione belle comatam. Alioquin Palladis peplum non revelaret, sed a sacris uti profana repelleretur." Ed. Garin, *Prosatori,* p. 810.

[25] Cf. "Vulgo non scripsimus. . . . Nec aliter quam prisci suis aenigmatis et fabularum involucris arcebant idiotas homines a mysteriis, et nos consuevimus absterrere illos a nostris dapibus, quas non polluere non possent, amariori paulum cortice verborum." Ibid., p. 812, with Alan of Lille, *Anticlaudianus,* prologue, ed. R. Bossuat (Paris, 1955), pp. 55–56, for the same use of *aenigmata* and *involucra* and "ne porcorum pedibus conculcata margarita depereat, ne derogetur secretis, sed eorum magestas divulgetur indignis." See Poliziano, Preface to Plato, *Charmides* (ed. J. Hankins), 2:625–26, ll. 115–22: "Prisci illi theologi Homerus, Orpheus, Hesiodus, Pythagoras item et hic ipse, de quo agimus, Plato aliique quam plurimi Musarum veraeque sapientiae antistites multiplicem illam totius philosophiae cognitionem *per quaedam fabularum atque aenigmatum involucra integmentaque* tradiderint et quasi septibus quibusdam cancellisque obstruxerint, *ne religiosa quodammodo Eleusinarum dearum mysteria profanarentur* . . . et quasi suibus . . . margaritae obiicerentur." Dated by Hankins (ibid., pp. 450–53) to c. 1479.

[26] Ed. Garin, *Prosatori,* p. 816.

for if names are arbitrarily imposed on things, then there is no reason to condemn an Arab's or an Egyptian's word for the same object, no justification for choosing a Latin rather than a French, English, Spanish, or—medieval—Parisian term.[27] Solecism is relative; language is dispensable but not the heart; "one cannot be humane without polite literature, yet one is not human without philosophy."[28] And if Pico, after his philosopher's speech, closes with a likeness of himself to Plato's Glaucon in the *Republic* (358*b–e*), seeking to provoke his interlocutor Barbaro into praise of the subject he has appeared to attack, he and the multivocal "barbarian" speak with one voice when they assail grammarians: "These elementary schoolmasters (*grammatistae*) turn my stomach! Possessed of a couple of etymologies, they vaunt and promote themselves with such boastfulness that they think that philosophers are nothing compared to them."[29]

A grammarian rose to the challenge. In 1494—when Savonarola was advancing toward an ascendancy that, during the lifetime of Lorenzo de' Medici, he had not yet reached and *il Magnifico*'s son stood in dire need of support—Poliziano wrote to his pupil, Bernardo Ricci, secretary to the Florentine orator at Milan, where malicious gossip about Pico's alleged stylistic incapacity was circulating. Attaching his friend's letter, Poliziano observed: "You should not be displeased that he destroys eloquence, for so eloquently does he destroy it that, in the act of destruction, he builds it up again."[30]

This observation is true. It is also beside the point. Pico's objective was not simply to prove himself a master of ambiguous eloquence. The ambiguity was functional, inherent in his medium, and employed to insist, against the empty artifice of humanist rhetoric, on the truth-claims of veiled form and indirect exposition. When Pico's "barbarian" likens his mode of writing to that of the *prisci,*[31] he means both the ancient and the medieval advocates of a platonizing polysemy. They, distinguishing between the oratorical brilliance that moves the crowd and the opaqueness suited to the initiate, had asserted a freedom, both conceptual and stylistic, that classicizing grammar, with its rigid rules, mythological ornamentation, and trivial etymologies, did not

[27] Ibid., p. 818.

[28] "Non est humanus, qui sit insolens politioris litteraturae; non est homo, qui sit expers philosophiae." Ibid., p. 820.

[29] "Movent mihi stomachum grammatistae quidem, qui cum duas tenuerint vocabulorum origines, ita se ostentant, ita venditant, ita circumferunt iactabundi, ut prae seipsis pro nihilo habendos philosophos arbitrentur." Ibid., p. 822. Cf. p. 806: "Vivimus celebres, o Ermolae; et posthac vivemus, non in scholis grammaticorum et paedagogiis, sed in philosophorum coronis, in conventibus sapientum, ubi non de matre Andromaches, non de Niobes filiis atque id genus levibus nugis, sed de humanarum divinarumque rerum rationibus agitur et disputatur."

[30] "Quae displicere non debet, propterea quod eloquentiam destruit. Destruit enim sic eloquenter, ut adstruat hoc ipso quod destruit." *Politiani Opera,* 1:264. For context, see Martelli, *Angelo Poliziano,* pp. 237ff.

[31] See note 25.

permit. For Pico, as for Savonarola, classicism was a prison. Restrictive and superficial, it hardly scratched the surface of the relationship between *verba* and *res*.

The integumental Platonist of 1485 and the Aristotelian scholastic of 1491 were in agreement. From different but related standpoints, Pico and Savonarola cast doubt on the humanist enterprise of imitating antiquity. Both were in sympathy with pluralism against purism, arguing for the priority of content over form. Both considered the study of poetry and eloquence, without the tutelage of philosophy, to be misdirected. Against this background of debate, conducted by two of Florence's leading intellectuals (the one to become his intimate ally, the other his spiritual guide), about subjects that he taught at the Studio, Angelo Poliziano pursued his career as professor of poetry and eloquence.

. . . . .

That career began in 1480, after reconciliation with Lorenzo,[32] to whose patronage he owed his appointment to a chair. As professor and as Piero de' Medici's former tutor, Poliziano remained a client of Florence's leading family. Independence was possible only in the intellectual sphere; and even there, the triumph of literary humanism, like the rise of "critical philology" and "historical method," so often celebrated as his achievements, are less notable than the opposition roused by his character and approach. Rigorous, polemical, and self-advertising, Poliziano cultivated a virtuosity that had solid, if limited, foundations and a noble but overstated aim. Through hard labor in the margins of incunabula or manuscripts and meticulous investigation of textual problems, he attempted to ground an ideal of *enkyklios paideia* in philological erudition, where his supremacy would be unchallengeable. Yet between his theory of unified learning and his specialized practice, a tension is detectable; and if he was both more and less than a historical critic, he never lost sight of the need for a system.

Systematic research found paradoxical expression in an "Alexandrian" aesthetic.[33] Linked by hindsight to the method of Karl Lachmann,[34] Poliziano, in his own context, more often resembled Callimachus.[35] Classification and

[32] On the troubles of the years 1478/79, still fundamental is Picotti, "Tra il poeta e il lauro," pp. 3–86.

[33] The term "Alexandrian" is employed below in the metaphorical sense in which it was used by A. Warburg (*Gesammelte Schriften*, vol. 2 [Leipzig, 1932], p. 534, with E. Gombrich, *Aby Warburg: An Intellectual Biography* [London, 1974], pp. 214–15), to refer not to the origins of antiquarian scholarship and poetry at Ptolemaic Alexandria but to their later Greek and Latin traditions. See below, pp. 56ff.

[34] Classic is Timpanaro, *La genesi del metodo del Lachmann*, 2:4ff. Cf. Kenney, *The Classical Text*, pp. 5ff., and Grafton, *Joseph Scaliger*, 1:35ff.

[35] For the analogy, see below, pp. 59, 91.

analysis provided the basis from which this poet-philologist cultivated an appearance of improvisation. Stylish variation, witty charm, and light incompleteness are opposed, in his writings, to ponderous perfectionism and tedious elaboration.[36] Poliziano's art lay in its concealment. What he concealed at the level of form, but never failed to realize at that of content, was the urge to exactitude that motivated his literary and scholarly works.

They form a unity. Their complementary development, between the year of his appointment as professor and that of his death, reveals a thinker who continued, with distinctive emphases and original departures, a line of debate that others had initiated. Bold and original, Poliziano was not alone. He pondered, no less deeply than Pico and Savonarola, the same issues of modernism and classicism that exercised his contemporaries; and he began publicly to reflect on these subjects in his inaugural lecture of 1480, when he spoke about Quintilian and Statius.

The choice of these authors was significant. Unlike Cristoforo Landino, on whose "hour" of instruction Poliziano's contract forbade him to encroach, "lest it be said, tacitly or expressly, that he was competing" with his former teacher,[37] the new professor did not adhere to the orthodox classics, Virgil and Cicero.[38] Selecting Statius, whose *Sylvae* had been rediscovered in the Quattrocento, Poliziano disassociated himself from the canon and methods of interpretation established at Florence[39] and entered into competition with a Roman philological approach developed by, among others, Domizio Calderini, upon whose methods and memory he commenced (as he would continue) to pour venom and bile.[40] It is Quintilian, however, to whom the greater part of Poliziano's inaugural lecture is devoted—an author who had engaged his attention from his earliest years. As he annotated the Milanese edition of the *Institutio oratoria* (1476), Poliziano had in his mind Cicero's rhetorical theory.[41] An intertextual reading of Quintilian's work led him to compare it further with the *Dialogus de oratoribus* by Tacitus.[42] And that comparison between the three masters of Latin rhetoric was suggested

[36] See Maier, *Ange Politien,* pp. 99ff., 203ff.; Bigi, *La cultura del Poliziano,* pp. 90ff.; and A. Bettinzoli, "Le 'Sylvae': Questioni di poetica," in idem, *Daedaleum iter,* pp. 67ff.

[37] Verde, *Studio,* 2:26–27. Cf. the clause of 21 November 1482: "Alia hora quam dns. Christophorus Landinus, ita ut nec tacite nec expresse dici posset ipsum esse concurrentem dicti dni. Christophori." See further below, pp. 81ff.

[38] On Landino's orthodox classicism, see Cardini, *La Critica del Landino.*

[39] See Cesarini Martinelli, "In margine al commento," pp. 96–145.

[40] See J. Dunston, "Studies in Domizio Calderini," *IMU* 11 (1986): 71–152; C. Dionisotti, "Calderini, Poliziano e altri," *IMU* 11 (1986): 153–85; and S. Timpanaro, "*Atlas cum compare gibbo* (Marziale VI.77)," in his *Contributi di filologia,* pp. 337–43. See further below, pp. 81, 94ff.

[41] See Godman, "Poliziano's Poetics," pp. 131ff. On the 1476 edition (BNCF, B.R. 379), see Perosa, *Mostra,* p. 19 (no. 4); and Cesarini Martinelli, "In margine al commento," p. 119.

[42] See below, pp. 44ff.

by the writings of another Roman philologist, greater than Calderini—Poliziano's unacknowledged master, Lorenzo Valla.[43]

Valla was, in the final quarter of the Quattrocento, the *magnum nomen* of Italian and European philology.[44] Unlike Calderini, he could not be abruptly dismissed. At Florence, in the highest quarters, Valla's thought had provoked heated debate. Poggio Bracciolini, accomplished humanist and controversial chancellor, had composed inflammatory polemics against Valla's *Comparison of Cicero and Quintilian.*[45] Smoke without fire, its indignant author retorted: he had never argued for Quintilian's superiority.[46] Cicero was "by far the greatest of Latin authors, comparable or preferable to Demosthenes," as he had written in the margin of his codex of *Institutio oratoria* (10.1.105);[47] and Cicero remained Valla's prime linguistic model in the influential *Elegantiae.*[48] What he had sought to demonstrate, there and in the *Comparison,* was the interdependence of the oratorical works of Quintilian and Cicero.[49] This position was resisted by the purists, who could neither grasp nor accept his unflattering distinction between the master and his followers.[50] Ciceronianism had been challenged by Valla's insistence on the importance of the integral *Institutio oratoria;*[51] and Poliziano, a regular user of the *Elegantiae,*[52] entered knowingly, at the beginning of his professorial career, into a controversy. At stake was less Quintilian's superiority over Cicero than the question, posed but not settled by Valla, of the relationship between their theories of eloquence.[53]

As a continuator (however tacit) of Valla's attempt to place Quintilian, after

[43] Analogies between Valla and Poliziano are signaled by Camporeale, *Lorenzo Valla,* p. 97; and Wesseling, "Poliziano and Ancient Rhetoric," pp. 192–93.

[44] For a different view of Valla's standing and influence, see Grafton, *Joseph Scaliger,* 1:12–14.

[45] Cf. L. Cesarini Martinelli, "Note sulla polemica Poggio-Valla e sulla fortuna delle *Elegantiae," Interpres* 3 (1986): 45 et passim; and S. Camporeale, "Poggio Bracciolini contro Lorenzo Valla: Le Orationes in L. Vallam," in *Poggio Bracciolini, 1380–1980* (Florence, 1982), pp. 137–61.

[46] Cf. his sarcastic letter to Giovanni Tortelli of 5 August 1441, *Laurentii Valle epistolae* (ed. Besomi and Regoliosi), pp. 29–31.

[47] "Cicero Latinorum maximus et multo maximus Demosthenique vel comparandus vel anteponendus." Paris, Bibliothèque Nationale, lat. 7723, fol. 120^r.

[48] See Cesarini Martinelli, "Note sulla polemica," and V. de Caprio, "Elegantiae di Lorenzo Valla," in *Letteratura italiana le opera,* vol. 1, ed. A. Asor Rosa (Turin, 1992), pp. 668ff.

[49] "Neminem posse neque Quintilianum intelligere, nisi Ciceronem optime teneat, nec Ciceronem probe sequi, nisi Quintiliano pareat." *Antidotum primum* (ed. Wesseling), p. 108.

[50] Cf. L. Cesarini Martinelli, in *Lorenzo Valla e l'umanesimo italiano,* p. 35.

[51] *Antidotum primum* (ed. Wesseling), p. 108.

[52] Cf. Munich, Bayerische Staatsbibliothek, clm. 745, fols. 169^r–217^r (Poliziano's course of 1483–83 on Virgil's *Eclogues*); Angelo Poliziano, *Commento inedito all'epistola ovidiana di Saffo a Faone* (ed. Lazzeri), p. 108 (*ad indicem*); and idem, *La commedia antica et l' 'Andria' di Terenzio* (ed. Lattanzi Roselli), p. 73 (*ad indicem*).

[53] Cf. Leeman, *Orationis Ratio,* 1:290ff.; and M. Winterbottom, "Cicero and the Silver Age," in *Éloquence et rhétorique chez Cicéron,* Entretiens sur l'antiquité classique 28, ed. W. Ludwig (Geneva, 1981), pp. 237–66, esp. pp. 254ff.

Cicero, at the center of the study of Latin prose, Poliziano was less unique than his inaugural lecture intended to suggest.[54] Local factors also played a role in his choice of subject. Anxious, after quarrels with Lorenzo's wife Clarice,[55] to justify his tutorial practice to his patron, he had appealed to Quintilian's example.[56] Turning from the dubious diligence of Piero de' Medici to the studious youth of the Florentine Studio, the new professor advanced his case with careful ambiguity: "I have undertaken to interpret the *Institutio oratoria* . . . which, even if it seems most meticulous and learned, is not to be preferred to Cicero's writings in the same genre."[57] The circumlocution is characteristic of the style and argument of Poliziano's inaugural lecture: a preference intimated by denial, a solemn subscription to conventional categories with an ironical hint that they are being undermined. His theme is the hierarchies of a canon: who comes before whom? That issue, in the wake of the Valla-Poggio polemic, still glowed with controversy.

Following this initial hint of ambiguity comes the topos: "Let us enter new paths, virtually untrodden before, leaving behind those old and well-worn."[58] The topos consists in a reference to Quintilian with a distinctively Ciceronian flavor;[59] and from this allusion, Poliziano begins to develop his own view of Roman literary history, raising the issue of whether Statius was second-rate. The *Sylvae* were unfinished and Virgil stood, in relation to their author, as Cicero had stood to Quintilian. But are matters so clear-cut, even regarding the status of the "princes of Latin eloquence"? Poliziano begins to relativize:

> What prevents us from not immediately offering to the young the highest of authors but those (so to speak) of lower and, as it were, second rank whom they should learn, with the intention of making it easier for them to imitate the greatest writers?[60]

54 For precedents and context, see J. O. Ward, "Renaissance Commentators on Ciceronian Rhetoric," in *Renaissance Eloquence: Studies in the Theory and Practice of Renaissance Rhetoric,* ed. J. J. Murphy (London, 1983), pp. 158ff.

55 Cf. Picotti, "Tra il poeta e il lauro," pp. 39ff.; M. Martelli, "Nota a Poliziano, *Epigrammaton Latinorum* XXIX," *Interpres* 3 (1980): 270–81; and Angelo Poliziano, *Sylva in Scabiem* (ed. P. Orvieto), pp. 8ff.

56 Picotti, "Tra il poeta e il lauro," p. 77: "Summi magistrorum Quintiliani praecepta."

57 "*Oratorias institutiones* enarrandas susceperim . . . etsi maxime accuratae eruditissimaeque videri possunt, Ciceronis tamen eodem in genere *non* fuisse *anteferendas*." Ed. Garin, *Prosatori,* p. 870.

58 "Novas tamen quasique intactas vias ingrediamur, veteres tritasque relinquamus." Ibid. Cf. Valla's inaugural lecture of 1455: "Mihi tamen aliam quandam ingrediam viam, ne detrita et pervagata et iam quasi fastidium moventia vobis inculcare videor." *Laurentii Valla opuscula tria* (ed. Vahlen), p. 93. See further below, p. 44.

59 *Institutio oratoria* 1, pr. 3 and 10.2.10. Cf. Cicero *Orator* 3.12.44–47.

60 "Quid enim prohibet vel ideo adolescentibus non statim summos illos, sed hos (si ita placet) inferioris quasique secundae notae auctores discendos praebere, ut imitari illos facilius possint?" Ed. Garin, *Prosatori,* p. 870.

Imitation, a central problem in humanist culture that determined its stance toward antiquity,[61] was also a practical matter. How were the young to be taught to write Latin, prerequisite for a career in the church and in many of the professions? At the level of didactic theory, Poliziano proposes a model of graduated difficulty. At another level—that of style—he modifies his own proposal by conflating Cicero, a "highest author," with Quintilian, a "writer of lower rank,"[62] and affirming the value of the apparent inferior. Both, in the passages on which the professor draws, discuss change and progress, to which rivalry provides a spur.[63] In rivalry with them, he transforms the metaphors with which they had depicted imitation[64] from prunings of restraint into props of support.[65] To scale the heights requires encouragement, but also demands divergence. Divergence, exemplified in Poliziano's own imitative strategies, is a principle of pluralism.

Pluralism now becomes the guiding theme of his inaugural lecture, which employs intertextuality to argue a historical case:

> My view of Statius, with whom we are dealing, is so very different from those [negative] opinions that have been reported that, just as I would affirm that nothing can be found in all the immense store of Latin literature that easily surpasses these books [of his *Sylvae*] in weighty themes, solid content, or sustained style, so it seems to me virtually an established fact that these works are of such stature that, in terms of heroic grandeur or multiplicity of subjects, or varied artifice of expression, or knowledge of geography, mythology, history, and customs or of their recherché learning and recondite style, there is nothing in the entire range of Latin poetry that you should prefer to them.[66]

The double negatives so insistent in this sentence, its circumlocutions and pleonasms, drive home a more profound point. The key word is "store"—

[61] See below, pp. 45ff.

[62] *Institutio oratoria* 12.2.26–27 and *Orator* 1.4–5.

[63] E. H. Gombrich, "The Debate on Primitivism in Ancient Rhetoric," *Journal of the Warburg and Courtauld Institutes* 39 (1966): 34; and E. Fantham, "Imitation and Evolution: The Discussion of Rhetorical Imitation in Cicero, *De oratore* 2, 87–97 and Some Related Problems of Ciceronian Theory," *Classical Philology* 73 (1978): 1–16.

[64] *Institutio oratoria* 10.7.28 and *De oratore* 2.21.88.

[65] "Nam quemadmodum novellis vitibus humiliora primum adminicula atque pedamenta agricolae adiungunt, quibus se gradatim claviculis illis suis quasique manibus attollentes in summa tandem iuga evadant, ita nec statim ad ipsos sicuti primi ordinis scriptores vocandi adolescentes, sed humilioribus iis, qui tamen haud abiecti humi iacentesque sint quasi paulatim invitandi sublevandique videntur." Ed. Garin, *Prosatori,* p. 870.

[66] "In hoc quidem, de quo agimus Statio, longe mihi ab iis, quae dicta sunt, aliena mens fuerit, ut enim non ierim inficias posse aliquid in tanta Latinorum supellectile inveniri, quod his libellis vel argumenti pondere vel mole ipsa rerum vel orationis perpetuitate facile antecellat, ita illud meo quasi iure posse videor obtinere eiusmodi esse hos libellos, quibus vel granditate heroica vel argumentorum multiplicitate vel dicendi vario artificio vel locorum, fabularum, historiarum consuetudinumque notitia vel doctrina adeo quadam remota litterisque abstrusioribus nihil ex omni Latinorum poetarum copia antetuleris." Ibid., p. 872.

suppellex, which occurs, in a comparable context, at *Institutio oratoria* 8 pr. 28.[67] There the subject is the comprehensiveness of the learning to be acquired by the rhetor's pupil. Quintilian's argument is verbal; Poliziano's, more ambitious. Proceeding from theme and style to substance, he arrives at the concept of an integrated culture. And that is the focus of Scaevola's remarks in Cicero's *De oratore* 1.35.165, the terms of which are here borrowed and adapted. The strategy reflects the same movement of thought detected in the paragraphs above: Quintilian's position is associated with Cicero's, and, after a concession to the traditional arguments for the superiority of other Latin poets, Statius's claims are advanced by an ambiguous negation.

The mannerism is employed with irony. If Statius himself is not in fact, but is merely considered, second rate, what are the grounds for received opinion? The answer, still couched in Quintilian's theory of emulative imitation, is a burlesque of conventional hierarchies:

> And so, just as Statius laid claim, virtually in his own right, to the second rank among the epic poets in his *Thebaid* and *Achilleid,* so in the verse of the *Sylvae,* in which his success was without rival, he—in my judgment—surpassed himself to the same extent as Virgil excelled him in the higher genre.[68]

Following the vertiginous movement of this sentence, which member of Poliziano's audience could have readily grasped who stood above, before, or behind whom? These pyrotechnics of qualification are not meant in earnest. Enlarging the classical canon, they poke fun at the purists who restricted it with such solemnity.

That canon, as taught in the schools, traditionally began at the top of the hierarchy, with Homer's *Iliad* and Virgil's *Aeneid:*

> We read the *Aeneid* first and contrast it with Greek literature, in particular with Homer; and then Statius's *Sylvae*—an excellent work, unique in its genre—which we consider not only a subject for public lectures but worthy to be thoroughly studied, imitated, and reproduced by orators and poets.[69]

The terms in which Poliziano's argument is couched are taken from a passage of Quintilian that he had annotated attentively,[70] only to depart from it. After epic, the *Institutio oratoria* stations tragedy, which Poliziano substi-

[67] Cf. below, p. 277.

[68] "Itaque ut in *Thebaide* atque *Achilleide* secundum sibi inter eius ordinis poetas suo quasi iure locum vindicarit, ita in his *Sylvarum* poematis, in quibus citra aemulum floruerit, tam sese ipse—ut meum est iudicium—post se reliquit, quam eundem Virgilius Maro in superioribus antecesserat." Ed. Garin, *Prosatori,* pp. 872–74.

[69] "Nos tamen et *Aeneidem* in primis legimus et Graecis illam praecipue Homeroque opponimus; et Statii *Sylvas*—egregium atque in eo genere unicum opus, quodque auctori suo felicissime omnium sucesserit—non solum publice enarrandas sed ediscendas *etiam et oratoribus aeque poetisque* imitandas exprimendasque censemus." Ibid., p. 876.

[70] *Institutio oratoria* 1.8.5 with BNCF, B.R. 397, fol. 16^{r}.

tutes with the *Sylvae,* applying to their author a positive version of the negative judgment on Lucan[71] by Quintilian, which had stimulated a long and intense controversy.[72] The leaden Lucan, replaced by the "silver" Statius, rubs shoulders with "golden" authors in Poliziano's enlarged canon.

To the purists, a provocation; to Quintilian, a direct response. He had advocated emulative imitation—a freedom, motivated by rivalry, to alter—now applied to the *Institutio oratoria* itself. And as that work is refashioned through a series of allusions to Cicero, the closed system of its Roman classification is opened to the flexible criteria of an "Alexandrian" aesthetic. Poliziano's style, expressive of his different and more dynamic concept of literary history, illustrates how canons can be altered, authorities displaced, new and less-established members such as Statius admitted into what was viewed by the Ciceronians as an exclusive club.

If "minor" authors might be revalued, what did it mean to speak of "the great" or "the best"? How was a classic to be defined, and such a definition applied to Quintilian? Understanding of his work, Poliziano had demonstrated, depended on comprehension of Cicero's. Yet preference for the *Institutio oratoria* should on no account be construed as an assertion of canonical priority. Quintilian's rhetorical theory, he argues, is simply fuller, richer, more complete and consistent than Cicero's, who changed his views from the unpolished *De oratore* to the one-sided *Brutus*. That book deals with the training of the rhetor, not with the entire art of oratory; and it concentrates on the "best kind of speech."[73] This evokes a criterion that is central both to Cicero's writings[74] and to Poliziano's argument. The full range of the "types of style" (actually related, in the *Brutus,* to "the importance of individual idiom"[75]) is needed to fathom the tradition that reaches from Cicero to Quintilian. The inference is clear: the "best" is not enough. Where, then, did Poliziano himself stand? As a revelator of novelty? Or as a relativizer of these positions?

The second stance is the one that he initially assumes—first by recalling, only to deny its relevance in this context, the image of untrodden paths at beginning of his inaugural lecture; then by evoking the topos of "the fault of age" employed by Valla at the opening of his *Elegantiae;* and finally by bor-

[71] *Institutio oratoria* 10.1.90: "Magis oratoribus quam poetis imitandus."

[72] See G. Martelotti, "La difesa della poesia nel Boccaccio e un giudizio su Lucano," *Studi sul Boccacio* 4 (1967): 265–79; K. Borinski, *Die Antike in Poetik und Kunsttheorie,* vol. 1 (reprint Darmstadt, 1965), p. 131; P. von Moos, "Poeta und Historicus im Mittelalter: Zum Mimesis-Problem am Beispiel einiger Urteile über Lucan," *Beiträge zur Geschichte der deutschen Sprache und Literatur* 98 (1976): 93–130.

[73] *Institutio oratoria* 9.2ff. A passage emphasized by Poliziano in his annotation ad loc., BNCF, B.R. 397, fol. 168^{v}.

[74] Cf. E. Fantham, "On the Use of Genus-Terminology in Cicero's Rhetorical Works," *Hermes* 107 (1979): 441–58.

[75] Ibid., p. 458.

rowing the metaphors of prison and liberation with which Poggio had vaunted his discovery of the integral *Institutio oratoria*.[76] Setting himself in the line of these pioneers, Poliziano proceeds to usurp their place:

> Why should it be considered a fault of mine that [Statius and Quintilian] have acquired in me their very first interpreter? Why should it not be a reason for universal gratitude that I have not hesitated to repay a public debt from (as it were) my own pocket?[77]

This is less repayment than theft. The metaphor of coinage, employed by Quintilian to describe linguistic usage, had been adopted in Valla's philosophy of language[78] before being filched from him by Poliziano.

Not, it might seem, the strongest of positions from which to assert one's originality. Yet the claim is swiftly made good. Quintilian had commented unfavorably on the "decadence" of Seneca at *Institutio oratoria* 10.1.125, and the Ciceronians applied his criticism indiscriminately to all writers of the postclassical age. This is the position that Poliziano stands on its head by drawing, for the first time in such a context, on Tacitus's *Dialogus de oratoribus*:[79]

> And finally I set no great store by the objection that the eloquence of these writers was corrupted by the age in which they lived, for if we examine the issue more justly, we shall understand that it was not so much corrupt and that eloquence was depraved, as the style of speech had altered. Nor should we too hastily conclude that what is different is worse.[80]

[76] "Sed neque inusitatas vias indagamus, cum veterum libros auctorum in manus sumpserimus, qui tamen si minus in usum consuetudinemque hominum aliquot iam ante saeculis non venerunt, non tam ipsorum culpa quam fortunae ac temporum iniuria effectum est. Quid enim nunc attinet superiorum calamitatem temporum memoria repetere? Quod sine summo dolore facere vix pie possimus, quibus insignes illi atque immortalitate dignissimi scriptores partim a barbaris caesi foedeque laniati sunt, partim ab his ipsis ad nostrorum usque parentum memoriam velut in carcerem coniecti atque in compedibus habiti, vix tandem aliquando, sicut erant semilaceri atque trunci multumque a seipsis immutati suam hanc patriam revertunt." Ed. Garin, *Prosatori,* pp. 876–78. Cf. p. 31 above, and *Elegantiae* 1, pref. ("Non nostra sed temporum culpa"). For Poggio, see above, note 2. On Poliziano's use of Poggio's exemplars of Quintilian and Statius, cf. V. Fera, in *Lo spazio letteraria di Roma antica,* vol. 3, ed. G. Cavallo et al. (Rome, 1990), pp. 523–24. See further, pp. 51ff. below.

[77] "Quod quidem si me nunc primum auctore adipiscentur, cur mihi tandem id vitio vertatur, aut cur non summa potius gratia ab omnibus habeatur, quod quasi mea privata pecunia publicum omnium aes alienum dissolvere non dubitarim?" Ed. Garin, *Prosatori,* p. 878.

[78] See S. Camporeale, "*Institutio oratoria* I, 6, 3 e le variazioni sul tema di Lorenzo Valla: *Sermo e interpretatio,*" *Memorie Domenicane,* n.s. 25 (1994): 233–44.

[79] Cf. P. Smiraglia, "Il problema del *Dialogus de Oratoribus* in età umanistica: qualche nota in margine," in *Miscellanea A. Campana* (Padua, 1981), 2:729–41 (who does not discuss this passage). The debt to Tacitus, but not the relationship to Quintilian, is registered by J. von Stackelberg, *Tacitus in der Romania: Studien zur literarischen Rezeption des Tacitus in Italien und Frankreich* (Tübingen, 1960), p. 61.

[80] "Postremo ne illud quidem magni fecerim, quod horum scriptorum saeculo corrupta iam fuisse eloquentia obiciatur, nam si rectius inspexerimus, non *tam corruptam atque depravatam*

Linking the words of Aper, champion of progress and exponent of innovation in Tacitus's *Dialogus,*[81] with Quintilian's aspersions on Seneca, Poliziano reveals a historical understanding of the relationship between the two works. Quintilian had offered an aetiology that Aper, at *Dialogus* 18.3, refuted on the grounds that there had been no decline.[82] The relevance of that argument to the Quattrocento debate about purism and allied issues is direct and patent: against the Ciceronians, who professed to believe that, after the master, all was decadence; against the models of regression propounded, in other historiographical contexts, by Flavio Biondo and Leonardo Bruni;[83] against the authority of the very Quintilian whom he claims to praise, Poliziano adopts from Tacitus a modernist's relativism.

"The style of speech had altered": just as Cicero's presence in Quintilian is highlighted to demonstrate their interdependence, so the views of Tacitus's Aper are manipulated to illustrate the process by which the restrictive standards of purism can be overcome. In Poliziano's historical theory, exemplified in his eclectic practice,[84] every author, at any stage of the Latin tradition, has a validity that must be assessed both in his own terms and in relation to his precursors and followers. The emphasis is rather on diversity within continuity than on the hierarchical model of rise and fall; on achievement within specific genres instead of the primacy of the "best mode of speech." Chronology abrogated, conventional canons are then dissolved into particular genres. Intertextuality was nothing new in the Italian Quattrocento, but in this dynamic form—with this exact understanding of the agreement and dissent between the three chief theorists of Roman rhetoric—it was unprecedented. When he proclaimed his originality in his inaugural lecture, Poliziano was both exaggerating and telling the truth.

. . . . .

To an audience in search of models for its own Latin writings, this oration offered a new approach to the traditional subject of *confronti* or comparisons.[85] Its basis was Roman rhetoric; its product, the "transposition of a his-

---

illam, quam dicendi mutatum genus intelligemus. Neque autem statim deterius dixerimus quod diversum sit." Ed. Garin, *Prosatori,* p. 878.

[81] See R. Syme, *Tacitus,* vol. 1 (Oxford, 1958), pp. 105 and 116.

[82] See C. O. Brink, "Quintilian's *De causis corruptae eloquentiae* and Tacitus' *Dialogus de Oratoribus,*" *Classical Quarterly* 39 (1989): 472ff., esp. pp. 496–97. Cf. K. Heldmann, *Antike Theorien über Entwicklung und Verfall der Redekunst* (Munich, 1982), pp. 255ff.

[83] See A. Mazzocco, "Decline and Rebirth in Bruni and Biondo," in *Umanesimo a Roma nel Quattrocento* (Rome, 1982), pp. 249–66; and N. Rubinstein, "Il Medio Evo nella storiografia italiana nel Rinascimento," in *Concetto, storia e immagini del Medio Evo,* ed. V. Branca (Florence, 1973), pp. 429–33.

[84] On Poliziano's stylistic eclecticism, see Rizzo, "Il latino nell'umanesimo," pp. 386 and 408.

[85] On the humanistic genre of "confronti," see Sabbadini, *Il metodo degli umanisti,* pp. 48ff.

torical sequence" into one of "expressive possibilities,"[86] fully realized eleven years later in a letter that Poliziano directed to the Roman purist, Paolo Cortesi, who had sent him a collection of epistles that aped Cicero's style. Declining Cortesi's gift, Poliziano now expanded the relativism of his inaugural lecture into a full-blooded pluralism:

> I am sending back the letters that you have diligently collected, and (to speak freely) I am ashamed of having misspent valuable time reading them. For, apart from a very few, they do not deserve study by any scholar or collection by you. I shall not explain which I approve of, which I condemn. I wish no one, on my authority, to feel complacent or dissatisfied with himself. Yet there is a point of style in which I differ from you considerably. You are not accustomed to giving your approval, so I gather, unless a writer composes a pen-portrait of Cicero. But the appearance of a bear or a lion seems to me much more honorable than that of an ape, even if it is more like a man. Nor, as Seneca affirmed, is it true that the leading figures in [Roman] eloquence resembled another. Scorn was poured by Quintilian on those who thought themselves Cicero's twin brothers because they were capable of ending a periodic sentence with the words: "it would seem to be." Horace decries those who are imitators, and nothing more than imitators. To me it seems that those who only compose by imitating are like the parrot or the magpie, spouting forth what they do not understand. What they write lacks vigor and vitality; it wants movement, feeling, and character; it is supine, sleepy, snoring. Nothing in it is true, solid, effective. "You do not express," someone will object, "Cicero." So what? I am not Cicero; but (it seems to me) I express myself.
>
> Moreover there are some, my dear Paolo, who search for their style like beggars plead for crumbs of bread; they do not live for the day but eke out a living from day to day; and then, unless they have at hand the book from which they pick out what they can, they are incapable of putting three words together, and these they debase with unlearned juxtapositions or unseemly barbarisms. For that reason their style of speech is always shaky, unsteady, feeble, unkempt, and undernourished; and them I cannot stand, for they also have the nerve to sit in judgment over men of learning: that is to say, over those whose style has long been matured by recherché learning, many-sided reading, and lengthy practice.
>
> But to come back to you, Paolo—whom I dearly love, to whom I owe much, to whose abilities I pay full tribute—I ask you not to shackle yourself with that superstitious belief which prevents you from taking pleasure in anything that is fully your own and from ever averting your gaze from Cicero. For when you have read, thoroughly and long, Cicero and many other authors of quality—

On the influence of the medieval *accessus ad auctores,* R. Rizzo, "Una prolusione del Poliziano," p. 762 and n. 5.

[86] Gombrich, "Debate on Primitivism," p. 35 (cited in note 63).

when you have absorbed them, learned them off by heart, and thoroughly digested them—filling your mind with their multifarious knowledge, and make ready to compose something yourself—then and only then should I like you "to swim without support" (as they say) and occasionally make up your own mind—casting off that neurotic obsession with copying Cicero, and Cicero alone—to try at long last your full potential. For those whose bewildered gaze is fixed solely on such absurd "outlines," as they are called, are not even capable of portraying them adequately—believe you me! They inhibit the drive of their own intelligence, like placing an obstacle before a runner, or (to use an expression of Plautus) create a hindrance. For just as no one can be a good runner if his only objective is to follow in others' footsteps, so nobody can write well if he does not venture to diverge from the rules. And, finally, I should like you to know that it is the mark of a misguided lack of intelligence to produce nothing by oneself, but always to imitate. Farewell.[87]

[87] "Remitto epistolas diligentia tua collectas, in quibus legendis (ut libere dicam) pudet bonas horas male collocasse. Nam praeter omnino paucas, minime dignae sunt, quae vel a docto aliquo lectae vel a te collectae dicantur. Quas probem, quas rursus improbem, non explico. Nolo sibi quisquam vel placeat in his, auctore me, vel displiceat. Est in quo tamen a te dissentiam de stylo nonnihil. Non enim probare soles, ut accepi, nisi qui lineamenta Ciceronis effingat. Mihi vero longe honestior tauri facies aut item leonis quam simiae videtur, quae tamen homini similior est. Nec ii, qui principatum tenuisse creduntur eloquentiae, similes inter se, quod Seneca prodidit. Ridentur a Quintiliano qui se germanos Ciceronis putabant esse, quod his verbis periodum clauderent: *esse videatur.* Inclamat Horatius imitatores, ac nihil aliud quam imitatores. Mihi certe quicumque tantum componunt ex imitatione similes esse vel psittaco vel picae videntur proferentibus quae nec intelligunt. Carent enim quae scribunt isti viribus et vita; carent actu, carent affectu, carent indole; iacent, dormiunt, stertunt. Nihil ibi verum, nihil solidum, nihil efficax. 'Non exprimis,' inquit aliquis, 'Ciceronem.' Quid tum? Non enim sum Cicero. Me tamen, ut opinor, exprimo.

"Sunt quidam praeterea, mi Paule, qui stylum quasi panem frustillatim mendicant, nec ex die solum vivunt sed et in diem; tum nisi liber ille praesto sit, ex quo quid excerpant, colligere tria verba non possunt, sed haec ipsa quoque vel indocta iunctura vel barbaria inhonesta contaminant. Horum semper igitur oratio tremula, vacillans, infirma, videlicet male curata, male pasta. Quos ferre profecto non possum iudicare quoque de doctis impudenter audentes, hoc est de illis, quorum stylum recondita eruditio, multiplex lectio, longissimus usus diu quasi fermentavit.

"Sed ut ad te redeam, Paule—quem penitus amo, cui multum debeo, cuius ingenio plurimum tribuo—quaeso,ne superstitione ista te alliges, ut nihil delectet quod tuum plane sit et ut oculos a Cicerone nunquam deicias. Sed cum Ciceronem, cum bonos alios multum diuque legeris, contriveris, edidiceris, concoxeris et rerum multarum cognitione pectus impleveris ac iam componere aliquid ipse parabis, tum demum velim, quod dicitur, 'sine cortice nates' atque ipse tibi sis aliquando in consilio, sollicitudinemque illam morosam nimis et anxiam deponas effingendi tantummodo Ciceronem tuasque denique vires universas pericliteris. Nam qui tantum ridicula ista, quae vocatis 'lineamenta,' contemplantur attoniti, nec illa ipsa—mihi crede!—satis repraesentant et impetum quodammodo retardant ingenii sui currentique velut obstant et, ut utar Plautino verbo, 'remoram' faciunt. Sed ut bene currere non potest, qui pedem ponere studet in alienis tantum vestigiis, ita nec bene scribere, qui tamquam de praescripto non audet egredi. Postremo scias infelicis esse ingenii nihil a se promere, semper imitari. Vale." Ed. Garin, *Prosatori,* pp. 902–4.

Consider the metaphors with which this vivacious style abounds: the bull and the lion as opposed to the ape, the parrot, and the magpie; supine slumber in contrast to swimming and running; begging for crumbs rather than digestion and absorption. All are attested in classical Latin literature,[88] but what is significant here is their combination. Just as Poliziano parades the multiple authorities of Seneca and Quintilian, Horace and Plautus (while alluding to others), so he lays out a mosaic of metaphors, the pattern of which derives from "contamination," contrast, and antithesis.

Antithesis is fundamental to Poliziano's style. So, too, are implication and innuendo, underlined by repetition. The hapless Cortesi, damned with faint praise, is ironized not only by a virtuoso display of the learning that he lacks but also by a superior command of the author whom he adulates. Take the word "outlines" (*lineamenta*), twice attributed to Cortesi. The term is weaker than "image" (*imago*);[89] and in Cicero's usage it occurs—to cite only texts known to Poliziano—either in negative contexts[90] or in antithesis to solidity of construction[91] (which lies behind the comparison, in the first paragraph, between "a pen-portrait of Cicero" and "nothing . . . solid"). The Ciceronian *superstitio* reproduces only the outlines: Cortesi is implied, by the ill-chosen vocabulary imputed to him, to be no connoisseur of The Master's style.

A point that is driven home. The images of the bull, the lion, and the man are also Ciceronian. At *De oratore* 2.16.69, Antonius defends, with these examples, his decision to omit rules. "When the category is grasped, the subspecies follows. No art requires professional instruction in its every aspect; the fundamentals enable the student, unaided and without difficulty, to master the details."[92] For an exponent of prescriptive purism like Cortesi, whose every word was supposed to derive from the hallowed canon of Cicero's works, Poliziano's advocacy of creative freedom in terms derived from The Master was intended to be gall and wormwood.

The allusion, elegant and malicious, is capped by a barb at the aberrant standards of Ciceronianism. An "ape" may be "more like a man"—the first category of example cited by Cicero at *De oratore* 2.16.69—but the "apes of Cicero" are bloodless, brainless, boring. The reversal of convention is strik-

[88] See D. Coppini, "Gli umanisti e i classici: imitazione coatta e rifiuto dell imitazione," *Annali della Scuola Normale di Pisa,* Classe di lettere e filosofia 3, 19 (1989): 276ff.; and T. H. Greene, *The Light in Troy: Imitation and Discovery in Renaissance Poetry* (New Haven, Conn., 1982), pp. 54ff.

[89] See R. Daut, *Untersuchungen zum Bildbegriff der Römer* (Heidelberg, 1975), pp. 32–54.

[90] *Verrines* 2.4.98 and *Orator* 56.186, with J. G. Sandys, *Marcus Tullius Cicero: Ad Marcum Brutum Orator: A Revised Text with Introductory Essays and Critical and Explanatory Notes* (reprint Hildesheim, 1973), pp. 204–5 ad loc.

[91] Cf. *De natura deorum* 1.123.

[92] See A. D. Leeman, H. Pinkster, and H.L.W. Nelson, *Marcus Tullius Orator Libri,* vol. 3 (Heidelberg, 1985), p. 277. See, too, Daut, *Untersuchungen,* p. 40.

ing. *Scimia di Cicerone* had, in living memory, possessed a positive resonance at Florence. For Filippo Villani, it had been a term with which to praise Coluccio Salutati.[93] In Poliziano's hands, it becomes a term of ridicule. That imitation of nature and imitation of antiquity were identical was a Renaissance commonplace,[94] but not one that licenses a contrast between "mimesis" and "fantasy."[95] For imitation, understood as Poliziano practices it, entails an imaginative liberty paradoxically faithful to Cicero's example. By the Ciceronians, however, this paradox is scarcely perceived. Only the outlines of the image, where nature and antiquity intermingle, are dimly discernible to the ape. Yet in the freer sphere of true mimesis, the bull bellows and the lion roars.

Sometimes their sounds are muted, in complex associations of style and thought that eschew the simple correspondence between model and imitation expounded by Cortesi. So with the sentences that run from "Scorn was poured by Quintilian . . ." to the end of the first paragraph. Quintilian's ridicule of the Ciceronian mannerism "it would seem to be"[96] had already been exploited, for polemical purposes, by Valla in his writings against Poggio.[97] To none of his precursors did Poliziano stand closer than to Valla, as his inaugural lecture had shown;[98] from Valla, therefore, he distances himself—less by the anaphora of succeeding sentences than by the repeated personal pronouns culminating, after an ironical aside, in the verb "I express."

"Myself" is its object, to which the *Institutio oratoria* gives rise. Its force is defined by a contrast, dependent on the same verb and a similar argument. At *Dialogus* 23.1, Aper (tacitly alluding to Quintilian) makes fun of those who end their period with the same cadence. "It would seem to be," sniffs Aper, and continues: "For I have retained this unwillingly and omitted many things that are only approved and expressed by those who call themselves ancient orators." Quintilian's critique of affected archaism stimulates Aper's satire of Ciceronianism. Both are applied to Cortesi, while the avant-garde standpoint of the *Dialogus* is espoused by Poliziano. "I express . . . myself" does not simply imply "self-expression."[99] It also evokes the modernist's derivation of individual style from plural models.

Flaunting Plautine diction, Poliziano combines it with his variant on an

[93] Sabbadini, *Storia del ciceronianismo,* p. 11.

[94] See R. W. Lee, "Ut Pictura Poesis: The Humanistic Theory of Painting," *Art Bulletin* 22 (1940): 204.

[95] *Pace* M. Kemp, "From 'Mimesis' to 'Fantasia': The Quattrocento Vocabulary of Creation, Inspiration and Genius in the Visual Arts," *Viator* 8 (1977): 347–98. See, too, M. Baxandall, *Giotto and the Orators: Humanist Observers of Painting in Italy and the Discovery of Pictorial Composition, 1350–1450* (Oxford, 1971), esp. pp. 44ff.

[96] *Institutio oratoria* 10.2.18.

[97] Sabbadini, *Storia del ciceronianismo,* p. 21.

[98] See above, pp. 39ff.

[99] Cf. Greene, *Light in Troy,* p. 150 (the same point, differently argued).

originally Ciceronian proverb. It is the Plautus of *Curculio* who gives rise to the metaphor of begging[100] and, in case his correspondent has not grasped the innuendo, Poliziano underscores it with a second example: "(To use a Plautine expression) a hindrance."[101] The thought underlying these allusions is similar to that expressed in Poliziano's prologue to the same writer's *Menaechmi:*[102] against the "supercilious, arch-necked herd,"[103] which looks down on Plautus, this lover of archaic Latin[104] asserts the dramatist's claim to stand beside Cicero.

The empire of Latinity is wide. Ignorance is the province of Ciceronians, whose pretensions to superior culture are belied by their limitations. Contaminating the proverbial expression "incapable of putting three words together"[105] with loftier diction, Poliziano throws an anticipated charge of "contamination" back on his critics. His ideal of erudition ("recherché learning, many-sided reading, lengthy practice") has affinities with the views expressed at *Dialogus* 30.2–3 and with the opinions of Cicero and Quintilian that lie behind it, but it would be mistaken to ignore an echo of Daniel 12:4 or the predominantly Biblical and Late Latin flavor of the verb "matured."[106] A further provocation, calculated to discomfort Cortesi. For how was this "jeune ambitieux," with his eye on a career at the Roman Curia, to object to the faint (and spurious) odor of sanctity in Poliziano's prose?

In the mixture of metaphors that follows, the polemic is completed. Seneca's images of digestion (*Ep.* 84.6), Quintilian's "time and trouble" (*mora et sollicitudo: Institutio oratoria* 10.3.9—a positive recommendation for beginners, applied here negatively), and his criticism of remaining "in others' footsteps" (ibid. 1, pr. 3) lead to a stinging conclusion. At the end, as at the beginning, of the letter, the implied situation is that of a master who has transcended the prescriptions of his art, speaking down to a freshman shackled by rules, the sense of which he imperfectly grasps. Understatement and association contribute as much to the message as blunt and direct argument: Cortesi's inability to "swim" unaided (cf. Horace *Sermones* 1.4.120; Ovid *Tristia* 3.4.11) evokes, by contrast, the "buoyant facility with words" (*innatans illa*

[100] "Non solum de die, sed etiam in diem vivere." A. Otto, *Die Sprichwörter der Römer* (reprint Hildesheim, 1971), p. 114, s.v. p. 8. For *frustillatim,* cf. Plautus *Curculio* 576.

[101] For *remora,* cf. Plautus *Poenulus* 928.

[102] See G. Bombieri, "Osservazioni sul prologo ai *Menaechmi* di Angelo Poliziano," in Cardini et al., eds., *Tradizione classica e letteratura umanistica,* 2:489–506; and Martelli, *Angelo Poliziano,* pp. 62–71.

[103] "Superciliosum, incurvicervicum pecus." *Prologus* 42.

[104] See H. D. Jocelyn, "Gli studi del Poliziano sulla poesia latina arcaica," in *Validità perenne dell'umanesimo: Angelo Cini de' Ambrogini e l'universalità del suo umanesimo,* ed. G. Tarugi (Florence, 1986), pp. 133–39.

[105] "Colligere tria verba non possunt." See Otto, *Sprichwörter,* s.v. p. 1.

[106] On *fermentare,* see *TLL* 6.1:526.

verborum facilitas: Institutio oratoria 10.7.28) acquired, and absorbed, by Poliziano from the whole of Latin literary history.

Convinced of the need to revise the Ciceronian dogma from the ground up, Poliziano had implemented a scorched-earth policy. Its scars were still visible more than two decades later, when Cortesi wrote his *De cardinalatu.* Looking back on this letter, he criticized his opponent for changing his language like an article of clothing with the weather, for employing unusual vocabulary in order to gratify modern taste.[107] That, Poliziano might have answered, was precisely his point.

Cortesi's other major work is motivated by an attempt to respond to this challenge. Yet the effort, in *De hominibus doctis dialogus,* to trace a schema of scholarly progress in an idiom derived from Ciceronian rhetoric entailed notable difficulties of critical expression;[108] and even when Cortesi seems to be acknowledging the justice of Poliziano's case, as in his criticism of Andrea Contrario,[109] his reluctance to give ground is more salient than has been thought.[110] It is not just that the unrepentant Ciceronian describes Contrario, with Poliziano's word, as an "ape." It is also striking that Cortesi continues to think in terms of the "best kind [of speech]"—the very Ciceronian term criticized in Poliziano's inaugural lecture and demolished in his letter on imitation. Its imitative practice had demonstrated, triumphantly, the limitations of a single "expressive possibility" and indicated a way out of the labyrinth in which Cortesi chose to remain trapped. The claims of modernity demanded a pluralism that opened up a new perspective, without limits or barriers, on Latin literature. Imitation was not the end of that perspective but the means by which it gained focus.

. . . . .

How, then, did the claims of pluralism stand in relation to the merits of individuality? Poliziano's taste for republican writers, his preference for late

[107] "Ex quo iure a litteratissimo homine Angelo Politiano de verborum Latinorum utendorum ratione saepe dissensi puer, propterea quod homo ingenii luce et doctrinae confidentia magnus, non modo de industria verborum insolentiam exquirere, sed etiam *orationis tanquam vestis usum probare velle videretur, qui temporum conditione mutetur, quique quo inusitatior et recentior commentitia concinnitate sit, eo gratior esse novitati soleat.*" Cortesi, *De cardinalatu,* fol. M.6. For context, see R. Cardini, "'Antichi e Moderni' in Paolo Cortesi," *La rassegna della letteratura italiana,* ser. 8, 3 (1991): 20–28.

[108] See G. Ferraù, ed. (Palermo, 1979), pp. 13–15.

[109] Ibid., pp. 172, ll. 11–14: "Sed Andream Contrarium placuisse quibusdam scio, quod illa lumina Ciceronis ingeniose admodum consectari videretur. Sed aliquanto tamen abest *ab optimo genere imitandi* et, ut scite amicus noster ait, non ille quidem ut alumnus, sed ut *simia effingit.*"

[110] T. M. Graziosi, ed., *De hominibus doctis* (Rome, 1973), pp. 62–64 and n. 125.

Latin authors, amounted to more than a desire to deviate from the well-trodden path of the acknowledged classics. It also reflected a determination to widen the scope of historical understanding. How he believed that history should be conceived and executed is formulated in the *Praefatio in Suetonium,* composed as an introduction to his course of 1490–91.[111]

Poliziano studied and annotated Suetonius in the Milanese edition of 1475,[112] which, among other later writers such as Eutropius and Paulus Diaconus, contained the *Historia Augusta.* That compilation left its mark both at the beginning and at the end of his *Praefatio in Suetonium.* Near its opening, Poliziano cites the examples of Severus Alexander and Zenobia;[113] at its conclusion he draws up a list of historians in which the *Scriptores historiae augustae* figure prominently.[114] The list amounts to a programmatic alternative to Quintilian's canon at *Institutio oratoria* 10.1.101ff.: no Thucydides or Herodotus, no Livy or Sallust. Instead Dio, Herodian, Plutarch, Procopius and Suetonius, Tacitus, Orosius, Eutropius, Paulus (Diaconus), "Aelius Spartianus," and the rest. A parade of imperial historians, in short, headed by the bogus biographers of the *Historia Augusta.*

Their roll call is drawn from the speech of "Vopiscus" at *Probus* 2.7—a revealing choice, because that chapter deals with one of the central themes developed in the *Praefatio in Suetonium:* the relationship between history and biography. If, in the late fourth century, the biographical cast of Latin historiography needed to be affirmed only in response to the challenge of Ammianus Marcellinus,[115] in the late fifteenth, the issues were less clear-cut. Setting out from Suetonius and the *Historia Augusta,* Poliziano's *Praefatio* finds, among many conventional features,[116] a point of original reflection on the methods of universal and individual history.

Poliziano was writing this *Praefatio* while preparing to lecture on the *Nutricia,* 790 Latin hexameters dealing with the Graeco-Roman poetic tradition that he regarded as a masterpiece.[117] That work opens with one of the most exalted celebrations of poetics in Quattrocento literature. All the more striking, therefore, is the invidious comparison (adapted from Lucian *De historia conscribenda* 8), in the prolusion on Suetonius, between poetics and history:

> Now if you consider its claims to fame, you will not compare poetics in any respect with history. For truthfulness is either wholly denied to poetry or, if as-

[111] *Politiani Opera,* 3:117–34; and see G. Brugnoli, "La *Praefatio in Suetonium* del Poliziano," in idem, *Studi suetoniani* (Lecce, 1968), pp. 185–203.

[112] BNCF, B.R. 91. See Perosa, *Mostra,* pp. 20–21 (no. 6).

[113] *Politiani Opera,* 3:118.

[114] Ibid., p. 134.

[115] See R. Syme, *Ammianus and the Historia Augusta* (Oxford, 1968), pp. 94ff.; and A. Cameron, "Literary Allusions in the Historia Augusta," *Hermes* 92 (1964): 375–76.

[116] Cf. R. Black, "The New Laws of History," *Renaissance Studies* 1 (1987): 134–35.

[117] On the *Nutricia,* their character and background, see below, pp. 70ff. Cf. F. Bausi, "Sui *Nutricia* di Angelo Poliziano: Questioni esegetiche e testuali," *Interpres* 14 (1994): 163–97.

> cribed to it in the final analysis, only in the measure in which it most closely conforms to, and resembles, history. And he is to be considered the greatest of poets who most readily inspires trust in his listeners.[118]

The primacy of history over poetry is matched by its ascendancy over philosophy:

> I declare that philosophy will never be able to keep on course without the guidance of history . . . for just as there is general agreement that teaching by examples is more effective and efficient than instruction by precepts, so the human race could more readily renounce philosophy than history.[119]

The terms of this comparison evoke Aristotle's *Poetics* 1451*b* and recall, more particularly, the preface to Valla's *Gesta Ferdinandi regis Aragonum* (8ff.),[120] where Poliziano's precursor set out to vindicate, against Aristotle, the superior cognitive status of history.[121]

Departing from a position similar to Valla's in the long-standing debate about history's relationship to poetry and philosophy, Poliziano alters its terms. His subject is less *universalia* than universal as opposed to individual history:

> But since I have spoken enough for the moment (as it seems to me) about universal history, I should like to add a little on the subject of the biographers of famous men who, in my view, surpass those who served up an indigest mass of different people, places, and periods in the same measure as individual details can be more accurately rendered and more easily imitated and copied than a general picture.[122]

The governing thought here is not so much the classical distinction between history and biography[123] as the ancient subsumption of that genre (the sep-

[118] "Iam nec poeticen quidem, si ad gloriam spectes, ulla ex parte cum historia contuleris, quippe cui aut omnino fides abrogetur aut tum denique habeatur, cum sese maxime ad historiae imitationem conformet et is haberi summus poetarum debet, qui quam facillime quorum velit auditoribus faciat fidem." *Politiani Opera,* 3:122.

[119] "Ne ipsa quidem philosophia, inquam, sine historiae adminiculo suum cursum tenebit unquam . . . utqui valentius, efficaciusque docendi genus per exempla quam per praecepta esse nemo non fateatur, ita prolixius humanum genus historia quam philosophia demeretur." Ibid., p. 125.

[120] Ed. O. Besomi (Padua, 1973), pp. 5ff.

[121] See Regoliosi, "Lorenzo Valla," pp. 549–71.

[122] "Sed quoniam de ea universa satis (ni fallor) pro tempore locuti sumus, pauca etiam de illustrium vitarum scriptoribus persequamur, qui mihi quidem tanto eos antecellere videntur, qui multifariam illam hominum, locorum, temporumque diversorum quasi *sylvam* in medium exponunt, quanto et diligentius singula quaeque exprimere et facilius imitari atque effingere quam universa quis possit." *Politiani Opera,* 3:126. (*Sylva* is translated as the Latin equivalent of ὕλη for reasons considered below.)

[123] See A. Momigliano, *The Development of Greek Biography* (Cambridge, Mass., 1993), esp.

arate existence of which Quintilian does not acknowledge) under history.[124] Pursued by Petrarch, Matteo Palmieri, and many others,[125] this view of biography as the preeminent form of individual history provided a foundation for Poliziano's own ideas.

The particular that for Valla, in his reaction to *Poetics* 1451*b,* was history's vulnerable point, requiring defense, is, in Poliziano's opinion, its chief strength. His *Praefatio in Suetonium* justifies individual history not by its proximity to Aristotelian *universalia* but by its ability to distinguish details. *Singula,* that is, as opposed to the *sylva* or indigest mass of generalities. It is a philologist who writes, bent on the particular. His contrast is stark, his tone polemical. Against whom is the polemic directed?

None of the Latin historians or orators whose works were used in Quattrocento discussions of history offered such an antithesis, nor did the Greek writers—Herodotus and Thucydides, Appian, Lucian, and Herodian—whose works had begun to be translated in the fifteenth century.[126] Poliziano's reference is to an author hitherto attested only as a philological source in the second *Centuria* of the *Miscellanea:* the most vocal champion of universal history in the Graeco-Roman world, Polybius.[127]

Polybius reenters historiographical debate in Poliziano's *Praefatio in Suetonium,* only to be roundly rejected. To universal history, the genre of Polybius's choice, is applied, with a fresh technical exactitude, the unflattering word *sylva.* Used of oratory by Cicero at *De oratore* 3.24.93, the term now recovers its original historiographical connotations for the first time since antiquity. The "unmethodical mass" of Tauriscus—known to Poliziano through pseudo-Plutarch's *Life* of Homer and Sextus Empiricus[128]—is contrasted with the systematic clarity of individual analysis. The type of history advo-

---

pp. 105ff., with B. Gentili and G. Cerri, *History and Biography in Ancient Thought* (Amsterdam, 1988), pp. 61ff. Cf. R. Syme, "Biographers of the Caesars," in idem, *Roman Papers,* vol. 3, ed. R. Birley (Oxford, 1984), p. 1270.

[124] Cf. Cicero *De oratore* 2.163, with R. Syme, *The Historia Augusta: A Call for Clarity* (Bonn, 1971), pp. 25ff.

[125] See M. Miglio, "Biografia e raccolte biografiche nel Quattrocento italiano," *Atti della Accademia delle scienze dell'istituto di Bologna,* Classe di scienze morali 63 (1974–75): 166–99.

[126] See E. B. Fryde, "Some Fifteenth-Century Latin Translations of Ancient Greek Historians," in idem, *Humanism and Renaissance Historiography* (London, 1983), pp. 83–114.

[127] Cf. 1.4.1–8, with F. Walbank, *A Historical Commentary on Polybius* (Oxford, 1957), 1:9, 44–46 and 12:24, with P. Pédech, *Polybe: Histoires Livre,* vol. 12 (Paris, 1961), pp. 117–18. On the philological use of Polybius in the second *Centuria* of the *Miscellanea,* see A. Momigliano, "Polybius' Reappearance in Western Europe," in idem, *Sesto contributo alla storia degli studi classici e del mondo antico,* vol. 1 (Rome, 1980), p. 115. On Polybius's polemic on this subject, cf. idem, *Classical Foundations,* pp. 59ff., and below, p. 271.

[128] See G. Cerri, "Crasso, Taurisco e la 'selva senza metodo,'" *La parola del passato* 27 (1972): 312–20. For Poliziano's knowledge of Sextus Empiricus, see Cesarini Martinelli, "Sesto Empirico," pp. 327–58.

cated by Polybius is thereby dismissed as unmethodical and jumbled—in terms of the theory that he had implicitly repudiated.[129]

Poliziano's alternative is plainly stated: "And so I will never concede that Plutarch and Suetonius have done less for mankind than Herodotus or Sallust."[130] Here, characteristically expressed in a double negative, lies the core of his historiographical position. Poliziano's sympathies were with a tradition that embraced writers as diverse as Petrarch and Boccaccio—or, at Florence, Filippo Villani and Vespasiano da Bisticci.[131] Reinforced by the enthusiasm for Suetonius, the interest in Nepos, and the craze for Plutarch, this strong biographical current in the mainstream of Quattrocento historiography was one of the approaches to the past that Poliziano, in the *Praefatio ad Suetonium,* set out to affirm. The philological controversies that surrounded the text of Suetonius in the early 1490s[132] were thus accompanied by a different but related debate, in which the traditional view of exemplary history was employed to justify the biographical genre that he practiced.

If Suetonius, like Plutarch, provided one instance of Poliziano's antithesis between individual and universal history, it remained for him to distinguish, in terms of method, between the wood and the trees: "While it is difficult for everyone to imitate diverse examples that have been heaped together, it is easy to do so on the basis of material that has been separated, sorted, and classified."[133] Plutarch, with his nearness to political historiography, was not needed to argue this point. Suetonius—or rather, the systematization and classification that Poliziano associated with his name—now became the focal point on which hung his defense of the "antiquarian approach."[134]

For the Suetonius with whom Poliziano displays the closest affinities is less the author of *De vita Caesarum* than the compiler of *De poetis* and *De grammaticis*—known through fragments preserved in Jerome's translation of Eusebius's *Chronicle,* Isidore, Aulus Gellius, Servius, and other sources. Origin or filter of much biographical information about the Latin poets,[135] Sueto-

[129] See S. Mazzarino, *Il pensiero storico classico,* vol. 1 (Rome, 1990), p. 490; cf. ibid., pp. 485ff.

[130] "Itaque numquam ego aut Plutarchum minus hominibus quam Herodotum aut Suetonium quam Sallustium fateor contulisse." *Politiani Opera,* 3:126–27.

[131] Cf. E. Cochrane, *Historians and Historiography in the Italian Renaissance* (Chicago, 1981).

[132] See V. Fera, "Polemiche filologiche intorno allo Suetonio del Beroaldo," in *The Uses of Greek and Latin: Historical Essays,* ed. A. C. Dionisotti, A. Grafton, and J. Kraye (London, 1988), pp. 71–88.

[133] "Ita imitari congesta in unum varia exempla difficile sit omnibus, separata autem atque digesta facile cuivis liceat." *Politiani Opera,* 3:127.

[134] Momigliano, *Classical Foundations,* pp. 54ff., esp. p. 66, and his "Problems of Ancient Biography," *Quarto contributo alla storia degli studi classici e del mondo antico* (Rome, 1969), p. 86.

[135] R. Caster, *Suetonius "De grammaticis"* (Oxford, 1995), pp. xxiiiff.; and R. Blum, *Die Literaturverzeichnung im Altertum und Mittelalter* (Frankfurt am Main, 1983), pp. 64ff. Cf. below, pp. 60ff.

nius contributed to establish a model of linking work to life that Poliziano was to follow. But because *De poetis* and *De grammaticis* offered no guide to Greek literature, he parted company with his Latin sources and looked elsewhere: to the legacy of "Alexandrian" antiquarianism and to Hellenistic poetry, which had exercised a formative influence on him early in his career.

. . . . .

In 1472–73, Poliziano began to make excerpts from the *Anthologia Planudea*[136] that anticipate his later research. His interest in that collection centered on epigrams dealing with the lives and work of Greek poets; and he included a number of verse aphorisms by Diogenes Laertius that are transmitted by Planudes but omitted in Ambrogio Traversari's Latin translation of the *Lives of the Greek Philosophers*. Aesthetics had little to do with Poliziano's study of Hellenistic poetry: his focus was strictly biobibliographical; and his concern with the indirect tradition of Diogenes Laertius—read in the original, avoiding the byway of Walter Burley and eschewing the omissions of Traversari—points forward to the studies conducted seven years later, at the beginning of his professorship.[137]

In 1479–80, as one of a series of attempts to assemble a proto-encyclopedia of the arts and the sciences,[138] Poliziano gathered materials on the history and theory of poetry. He circumscribed that subject more narrowly than Landino, who, in the *Comento sopra la Commedia di Dante,* published in 1481,[139] linked the course of classical poetry to the development of vernacular verse. Christian literature is also excluded by Poliziano. Poetic history, its chronology based on Jerome's Eusebius, began, for him, with Zoroaster and Prometheus, Orpheus, and Linus, halting at Claudian. Its limits were determined by a classicism more generous than that of the purists but less expansive than that of his teacher, from whom he differed fundamentally in the attention paid to Greek.

The Greek sources studied and copied by Poliziano in 1479–80 reveal much about his approach. They were not apologists of *belles-lettres,* but writers for whom literature was often marginal; by whom theological and ethical questions were neglected; and who analyzed poetic personality and production in verse in biographical form with bibliographical methods. An example of the interests reflected in Poliziano's notes is provided by the *Lives*

[136] See E. Mioni, "L'*Antologia Planudea* di Angelo Poliziano," in *Medioevo e Rinascimento veneto con altri studi in honore di L. Lazzarini,* vol. 1 (Padova, 1979), pp. 541–55 with bibliography.

[137] See L. Cesarini Martinelli, "'De poesi et poetis,'" pp. 455–87.

[138] Cf. eadem, "Un ritrovamento polizianesco: Il fascicolo perduto del commento alle 'Selve' di Stazio," *Rinascimento* 22 (1982): 183–212.

[139] Landino, *Scritti critici* 1:100ff., esp. pp. 130ff.

of Eminent Philosophers. Their sphere of inquiry, Diogenes Laertius taught him, was superior to that of the poets. Hence Poliziano excerpted the reports (3.5) that Plato consigned his verse to the flames and (9.110) that Timon regarded poetry as a leisure activity, signaling Solon's prohibition of Thespis from performing tragedies (1.59–60) and Pythagoras's descent to Hades, where Hesiod and Homer were being punished (8.21). Method rather than content was the professor's first concern. Diogenes Laertius's efforts to distinguish between the genuine and spurious works of the philosophers, his fascination with the multiple identities of namesakes and consequent lists of homonyms, are enthusiastically recorded in Poliziano's extracts. From the lengthy treatment of Aristotle in Book 5 of the *Lives of Eminent Philosophers,* for instance, are singled out only the details of his career (5–11) and the catalogue of his writings (22–27). From the fourth book of Diogenes Laertius, the future author of a celebrated passage on the interpretation of poetry at *Miscellanea* 1.4 recorded not the image of Cleanthes' lantern that he was later to employ so effectively,[140] but the less exhilarating information that there had been a "frigid elegiac poet" with the same name. Facts curtly registered by Diogenes Laertius about minor versifiers whose works have been lost engaged Poliziano's attention no less than legends that had accrued to major figures. The derivative, compilatory, bibliographical character of the *Lives of Eminent Philosophers,* which, to their most celebrated student, was to appear their weakest point,[141] seemed their main strength to Poliziano as he explored the world of "Alexandrian" erudition that Diogenes Laertius opened to him.

That approach did not render obsolete the questions traditionally asked about poetic theory. Boccaccio rubs shoulders with Laertius in Poliziano's excerpts. From the summary and expansion of previous positions offered in Book 14 of *Genealogiae deorum,* he inherited a context for the fresh material that he was unearthing; and the chief problem that his research now posed was whether this traditional Latinate framework could accommodate the different, more comprehensive picture beginning to emerge from his Greek sources.

As excerpted and arranged by Poliziano, they reflected lines of inquiry that set him apart from other Florentine scholars. Allegory is seldom emphasized, at least not in the Neoplatonizing forms favored by Ficino and Landino; instead he concentrates on the concept of poetry as *fabula,* the fictitious exterior that contains philosophical truth. Thus a certain coherence between the views recorded in some of the extracts from Boccaccio and others from Laer-

140 See below, pp. 85ff.

141 "Ein Schriftsteller, der . . . so viel und mit solchem Unverstande abschreibt." F. Nietzsche, "Beiträge zur Quellenkunde und Kritik des Laertius Diogenes," in *Gratulationsschrift des Paedagogiums zu Basel* (Basel, 1870), p. 1. Cf. idem, "De Laertii Diogenis fontibus," *Rheinisches Museum* 24 (1869): 201.

tius. Posidonius's definition of poetic style (singled out from *Lives of Eminent Philosophers* 7.60), for example, contained a theory of significant expression compatible with Boccaccios's in a passage that Poliziano culled from *Genealogiae deorum* 14.7. Similar criteria guided him to Plutarch's *Moralia*.

These criteria were threefold. First, a rationalistic conception of art and literature that was distinctively (but not exclusively) Plutarchan.[142] Second, attention to the "fabulous" in poetry, which sets it apart from philosophy and likens it to theology—without, however, going so far as to assert, in the quasi-mystical manner of Florentine Neoplatonists, their identity as "poetical theology." And third, the nonaesthetic criteria by which poetry can be judged: its instinctiveness, its comprehensiveness, its truth.

From this followed an interest in Plutarch's attitude to Homer. A single passage of the *De primo frigido* (950*e–f*) arrested Poliziano's curiosity because it portrayed the father of poetry as a natural philosopher. By contrast, almost the entire pseudo-Plutarchan *Vita Homeri* is paraphrased, for it described its subject as the source of universal learning and depicted his works as an encyclopedia of knowledge.[143] To these central preoccupations, the allegorical features of the Life (more marginal than some have allowed[144]) take second place: attention is focused on the all-encompassing verities that Homer expresses in "enigmatic and mythical language."

So it was that Poliziano reconstructed the ancient "Greek belief that all men had *learned* from Homer since the beginning"[145]—a belief that he supplemented with Strabo's defense (1.2.3–10) of the didactic value of poetry against Eratosthenes' view of it as mere entertainment. Here, as in Eustathius's commentary on the *Iliad,* Poliziano found material that served to answer the questions posed by his previous extracts: affirmations of the cognitive status of poetry, centered on the figure of Homer, and assertions of the utility of its mythical elements, which Strabo (1.2.7–9) represented as indispensable in the growth of understanding. The link, philosophical and didactic, between medium and message underlies his concern, aroused by Boccaccio, with *fabula,* which runs through the excerpts from Plutarch (*De Iside et Osiride* 354*c*), Strabo, and Eustathius, combining these sources in a syncretism that is not without piquancy. For the arguments that Plutarch directed against the Stoics' criticisms of poetry are developed by Poliziano on the basis of Strabo's Stoic defense.

[142] See A. M. Tagliasacci, "Le teorie estetiche e la critica letteraria in Plutarco," *Acme* 14 (1961): 71–117.

[143] Cf. R. Lamberton, *Homer the Theologian: Neoplatonist Allegorical Reading and the Growth of the Epic Tradition* (Berkeley, 1986), pp. 40–41.

[144] See A. Ludwich, "Plutarch über Homer," *Rheinisches Museum für Philologie* 72 (1917–18): 559ff.; and M. Wehrli, "Zur Geschichte der allegorischen Deutung Homers im Altertum," diss. phil., Basel, 1928, p. 26.

[145] R. Pfeiffer, *History of Classical Scholarship: From the Beginnings to the End of the Hellenistic Age,* 2 vols. (Oxford, 1968), 1:167.

An implicit dialectic about poetry is thus present in the organization of the excerpts that the newly appointed professor made from Greek writers in 1479–80. It went hand in hand with classification by category: again biographical, in the brief notes taken from the Suda or the longer transcription and paraphrase of the *Vitae* of Pindar; inscriptional, oracular, and anecdotal in the extensive passages copied from Pausanias; and literary-historical in the short selections from the *Anthologia Planudea* that supplement Poliziano's earlier compilation. "Alexandrian" learning and literature, together with Byzantine scholarship from the tenth century to the Paleologan revival, provided the context from which his understanding of the Greek canon grew: an understanding rooted in the particular; concentrated on personalities; mistrustful of broader periods, general trends, or wider movements; largely and deliberately exclusive of the evidence provided by Latin.

This was the context of the historiographical position assumed in the *Praefatio in Suetonium*. Against the critics of antiquarian research, in defense of "the authors of local history, chronography, genealogy, erudite dissertations" attacked by Polybius,[146] Poliziano affirmed the value of the minute methods applied in his own work. The biobibliographical attention to literary—especially poetic—texts; the concern with chronology, inscriptions, monuments; the entire apparatus of "Alexandrian" erudition reconstructed in the studies that were fundamental to his teaching of poetry and its history lie behind the *Praefatio in Suetonium*. They provide one motive for our comparison between Poliziano and Callimachus. Another is offered by the reserve that both expressed toward Aristotle.[147] History, in the *Praefatio*, is set above philosophy; poetry below them both. The criterion of *universalia* is jettisoned as summarily as the form and pretensions of universal history. The wood is relegated to the background; at center stage stand the trees—the individual and the detail, meticulously observed.

All of which was argued by a scholar to whom, by common accord, the discovery of Aristotle's *Poetics* amounted to a revelation, alienating him from the doctrine of "poetic frenzy" propagated in the milieu of Ficino and Landino, and leading him to adhere to what has been called a "naturalistic" aesthetic, with lasting consequences for his adult thought.[148] Such are the received opinions about Poliziano's relationship to Aristotle's poetics and literary history. They crumble under scrutiny.

. . . . .

[146] Momigliano, *Classical Foundations,* p. 59.

[147] On Callimachus, see Pfeiffer, *History of Classical Scholarship,* 1:137ff.; and K. O. Brink, "Callimachus and Aristotle: An Inquiry into Callimachus' ΠΡΟΣ ΠΡΑΞΙΦΑΝΗΝ," *Classical Quarterly* 40 (1946): 11ff. esp. pp. 16–19.

[148] See Branca, *Poliziano,* pp. 12ff., esp. p. 15; and R. Cardini, review article in *La rassegna della letteratura italiana* 81 (1977): 465–71. More cautious are S. N. Tigerstedt, "Observations on

The Greek text of the *Poetics* had begun to circulate in Italy before the third quarter of the fifteenth century.[149] Aristotle's work played an important role in the debate about the status of history, poetry, and philosophy, to which Valla gave impetus and to which Poliziano made a contribution. The *Poetics* also figure in his course of 1484–85 on Terence's *Andria,* which opens with a Latin version of the theory of mimesis and the origins of comedy and tragedy outlined at 1447*b*–49*a* of Aristotle's work;[150] they are used in Poliziano's lectures on the *Odyssey* of 1489;[151] and they made some impact on other aspects of his teaching.[152] In the large but incomplete corpus of his extant writings, which abounds with references to classical authors of every kind, neither the quantity nor the quality of these allusions is imposing—not because Poliziano neglected the *Poetics,* but because he viewed them through an "Alexandrian" optic, significant indications of which are provided by the marginalia preserved in his own manuscript of Aristotle's work.[153]

Poliziano annotated the *Poetics* in ways similar to those in which he excerpted the writings of Diogenes Laertius, Plutarch, and Pausanias. His interest in *fabula*[154] intersected with a concern for the relationship between poetry, history, and philosophy[155] that is reflected in the *Praefatio in Suetonium.* These themes, however, were not exclusively Aristotelian, and many of Poliziano's notes on commonplace topics, such as poetry as "a speaking picture,"[156] merely repeat what he had already observed in 1479–80. He aligned Aristotle's work with his reading in later Greek authors, and in doing so shunned many aspects of the *Poetics* that are distinctively Aristotelian. Less poetry, viewed in the abstract, than poets engage Poliziano's attention; not tragedy but the names of tragedians and tragic characters. Hence the lists—closely comparable to his extracts from, and marginalia to, the Suda or other sources—of *dramatis personae,* of historical allusions, of antiquarian details.

the Reception of Aristotle's Poetics in the Latin West," *Studies in the Renaissance* 15 (1968): 11; and E. Garin, "La diffusione della Poetica di Aristotele dal sec. XV in poi," *Rivista critica di storia e filosofia* 28 (1973): 449.

[149] See N. G. Wilson, *From Byzantium to Italy: Greek Studies in the Italian Renaissance* (London, 1992), p. 39.

[150] Ed. Lattanzi Roselli, pp. 3–4, and cf. pp. 14, 10–15, 26.

[151] Bibliothèque Nationale ms. grec 3069, 52^r–119^v, partly printed by L. Dorez, "L'hellénisme d'Ange Politien," *Mélanges d'archéologie et d'histoire* 15 (1885): 25–28. See, too, Wilson, *From Byzantium to Italy,* p. 104.

[152] Cf. Poliziano's lectures on Statius, *Commento inedito alle Selve di Stazio* (ed. Cesarini Martinelli), pp. 55, l. 21; 59, l. 15; and on the *Epistola Sapphus, Commento inedito all'epistola ovidiana di Saffo a Faone* (ed. Lazzeri), pp. 58, l. 3; 90, l. 2; on his course on the *Fasti,* see below. Cf. Tigerstedt, "Observations," p. 11.

[153] The following paragraphs are based on a study of BMLF Plut. 60, 14, Poliziano's copy of the *Poetics.*

[154] "Simplex et composita." BMLF, Plut. 60, 14, fol. 8^v.

[155] Ibid., fol. 7^v.

[156] Ibid., fol. 29^r.

No hint of the hierarchy of literary forms present in Aristotle's views on epic and tragedy; no trace of the theory of generic evolution developed in the *Poetics*. Action and personality; unity and decorum; *peripeteia, anagnorisis,* and *katharsis:* Poliziano scarcely registers Aristotle's opinions on these subjects or passes over them in silence.

That silence is eloquent. The concepts of *mimesis* and *technē,* so prominent in the *Poetics,* are not faithfully represented at the beginning of Poliziano's lectures on the *Andria.* All that interested him there was an account of the origins of tragedy and (especially) comedy. An explanation provided in broadly Aristotelian terms, the *Poetics* seldom figure in the remainder of the course. And their limited use, in this instance, serves to highlight why the numerous annotations that he made on his manuscript of the *Poetics* display such a marked reserve toward Aristotle's central ideas. A concept of *technē,* encompassing all mimetic art and assimilating the poet to an abstract, impersonal tradition,[157] was the polar opposite of Poliziano's "Alexandrian" insistence on the importance of individual writers. The historical pluralism espoused in his inaugural lecture and exemplified in his letter to Cortesi precluded any notion of ordered evolution, natural perfectibility, or biological decline. The inference is plain: Aristotelian concepts of literary history ran counter to Poliziano's assumptions and practice. In the margins of his manuscript, as in the courses that he delivered at the Studio, he selected those details from the *Poetics* that suited his purposes, while rejecting their author's principal theories.

Confronted with complex ideas, such as *mimesis* and *technē,* Poliziano skimmed the surface, while avoiding the uncongenial implications of the depths. What he sought from Aristotle was information on subjects that already engaged his interest, which remained focused on a Greek tradition of scholarship and literature not uniformly hospitable to the philosopher; Poliziano therefore sought common denominators between the Aristotelian *Poetics* and later writers on literary history, some of which had become commonplaces in Hellenic and Roman tradition. An instance is the topos of poetry's pedagogical and civilizing role, which has been ascribed to his enthusiasic reception of Aristotle,[158] ignoring its widespread attestation in Horace, Suetonius (*De poetis* = Isidore 8.7.1–2), and Cicero—to say nothing of Bruni, Landino, or other Quattrocento precedents. Fresh antiquarian details aside, Poliziano chiefly found, in Aristotle's text, evidence of what he knew or wished to have confirmed.

That the *Poetics,* to him, were no revelation is further suggested by early evidence. Had he "converted" to an Aristotelian "naturalism"—breaking with, or establishing his distance from, the Platonism of Ficino and

[157] See S. Halliwell, *Aristotle's Poetics* (London, 1986), pp. 60ff. and 109ff.

[158] Branca, *Poliziano,* p. 15. On the topos in ancient literature, see C. O. Brink, *Horace on Poetry,* vol. 2 (Cambridge, 1971), pp. 384–85; for a wider context, Curtius, *ELLMA,* pp. 210ff.

Landino[159]—why is it that his lectures on Ovid of 1481–82 display a debt to both the older scholars? Commenting on *Fasti* 6.5–6 ("There is a god in us . . ."),[160] Poliziano cited, among other parallels, Plato's *Phaedrus* and *Ion*—and Aristotle's *Poetics* 1455*a*. The link between Ovid's text and the doctrine of *poeticus furor* was not a difficult one to see, nor was Poliziano the first to recognize it. The point had already been established by Ficino, citing many of the same authorities, in the subsection "On Poets" of *Theologia platonica* 12.2.[161] All that Poliziano added to Ficino's argument was the reference to Aristotle's work.

The *Poetics* as a witness to the Platonic doctrine of poetic frenzy—this passage sits uneasily with their alleged separation. Did the divorce occur later in Poliziano's career? The answer is negative because, in this central sphere of his literary theory, he continued to subscribe to Ficino's and Landino's positions. Consider three examples, taken from the opening of the *Nutricia*—published in 1491, but already completed on 8 October 1486[162]—where Poliziano offered his final and most considered views on one of the two subjects that he was employed to profess:

> (1) . . . Now is the moment for the action: where the burning frenzy drives me, let me follow to the goal set by my intellect, duty, and hopes!
>
> (2) Come now, let me expound this divine madness
> which rouses men's hearts with mighty frenzy,
> that intelligence, high heaven's kin, so fertile
> of progeny who boldly wreathed their learned brows
> with Apollo's laurels and made their distinguished names
> immortal throughout the aeons of time! . . .
>
> (3) . . . For just as the reflection of a star shines
> into a mirror; like a spring, with its clear, elemental force,
> as if preserved in flawless glass, glows at the sun's ray,
> so the melodies of resounding heaven mold
> and inflame poets with resplendent purity.[163]

[159] Cardini, *La Critica del Landino,* pp. 171–73, following E. Garin, "L'ambiente del Poliziano," in *Il Poliziano e il suo tempo,* pp. 22–24 and 26–28.

[160] Angelo Poliziano, *Commento inedito ai "Fasti" di Ovidio* (ed. F. Lo Monaco), p. 448.

[161] *Marsile Ficin: Théologie platonicienne* (ed. R. Marcel), pp. 203–4.

[162] See below, pp. 77–79.

[163] **(1)**"En agedum: qua se furor incitat ardens, / Qua mens, qua pietas, qua ducunt vota, sequamur!" (vv. 32–33). **(2)**"Nunc age, qui tanto sacer hic furor incitet oestro / Corda virum, quam multiplices ferat enthea partus / Mens alto cognata polo, qui praemia doctae / Frontis Apollineas ausi sibi nectere lauros / Inclyta perpetuis mandarunt nomina saeclis, / Expediam!" (vv. 139–44). **(3)**"Nam ceu tralucet imago / Sideris in speculum; ceu puro condita vitro / Solis inardescit radio vis limpida fontis; / Sic nitidos vatum defecatosque sonori / Informant flammantque animos modulamina coeli" (vv. 158–62 and cf. 189ff.).

More than a decade after he had first read and studied the *Poetics;* nine years after his attempt, in his course on the *Fasti,* to marry Aristotle's work with the theories espoused by Ficino; in a poem interpreted publicly with jealous pride, on which hung this ambitious scholar's hopes for advancement, the doctrine of *poeticus furor* still found in Poliziano a keen exponent.

Behind these passages lies not only Plato but also the adaptations of his *Ion* and *Phaedrus,* under the influence of Ficino, in Landino's proemium to his *Comento dantesco* of 1481.[164] Its sequence of thought, proceeding from the ancient and divine origins of poetry to "poetic frenzy" and the antique tradition of poets, foreshadows the structure of the *Nutricia.* And from Ficino, in whose writings the Platonic image of the mirror is recurrent,[165] Poliziano derived a further stimulus:

> . . . The creator in highest heaven, growing weary
> of our sluggish spirits and hearts languishing
> in long sleep, bestowed on us the divine art of poetry
> to guide our will, like a charioteer.
> You bend our resistance to your control,
> you spur us on when we are slow,
> civilizing our uncouthness, for you were the first
> who made bold to strike from our hard hearts
> their hidden spark, the first to cherish Prometheus's flame,
> kindled in heaven.[166]

Unprecedented in Latin poetics was this identification of poetry with the charioteer of Plato's *Phaedrus* (246*b*). Yet in Ficino's translation of that work, and the exegesis that accompanied it,[167] the equation of the charioteer first with the intellect and later with its rational powers anticipates Poliziano's stress, in the *Nutricia* (vv. 40, 66, 84), on the link between reason and poetry's civilizing force. The thought, wholly un-Aristotelian, was an ancient commonplace into which fresh life had been breathed by Poliziano's adaptation of Ficino's Platonism.

Modification and extension of his views and those of Landino were possible in this context, but of a break with the doctrine of *poetic furor* and a conversion to Aristotelian "naturalism" neither the *Nutricia* nor any other work by Poliziano displays the slightest trace. The turning point, in respect of Aris-

[164] Cristoforo Landino, *Scritti critici e teorici,* 1:140ff.; and cf. Cardini, in ibid., 2:206.

[165] See M.J.R. Allen, *Icastes: Marsilio Ficino's Interpretation of Plato's Sophist: Five Studies and Critical Edition with Translation* (Berkeley, 1981), pp. 184ff.

[166] "Ab aetherio genitor pertaesus Olympo / Socordes animos, longo marcentia somno / Pectora, te nostrae, divina Poetica, menti / Aurigam dominamque dedit. Tu flectere habenis / Colla reluctantum, tu lentis addere calcar, / Tu formare rudes, tu prima extundere duro / Abstrusam cordi scintillam, prima fovere / Ausa Prometheae coelestia semina flammae" (*Nutricia* 67–74).

[167] *Marsilio Ficino and the Phaedran Charioteer* (ed. M.J.R. Allen), pp. 53, 61, 99, 185–86.

totle, occurred in the last three years of his life, under the influence of Pico, who directed him to the logical and metaphysical works of a philosopher whom Poliziano had hitherto been inclined to ignore, to subordinate to later sources, or to "harmonize" with Plato and his Quattrocento interpreters.

No fundamental revaluation of Poliziano's ideas or methods occurred with his limited reception of the *Poetics*. He continued to work as before, his gaze fixed on the world of "Alexandrian" erudition that he had discovered for himself, eschewing the techniques of Neoplatonic allegory but accepting, while varying, the doctrine of *poeticus furor* that Ficino and Landino had bequeathed him. In the mental world of the Florentine Callimachus, the *Poetics* appeared with not a bang but a whimper.

. . . . .

Poliziano's reserve toward Aristotle can be understood in terms of the intellectual choices that he had made before 1491: for pluralism against purism; in favor of an open concept of literary tradition as opposed to a closed and exclusive canon; the consequent dissolution of conventional hierarchies into individual genres; together with an overriding emphasis on change and eclecticism, on the individual rather than the universal, on history in preference to poetry. During that same year he published (not once, but twice) the *Nutricia,* on which he had already lectured and to which he often referred in the first and second *Centuriae* of his *Miscellanea.*[168] From this poem, in which he had invested his arcane learning, Poliziano expected rich yields of patronage. Conscious of having created a new kind of work, he enigmatically described it as a *poetarum historia.*

The enigma is posed by Poliziano's thought on both these subjects. If history, in his view, was superior to poetry, what then should be the status and purpose of a "history of the poets"? If truth was located in the particular, and priority attributed to the concrete, what was the cognitive value of the highly general, frequently abstract, notions of poetics so intensely debated before and during his lifetime? Landino's solution to these problems was a "suffocating reduction of all history" to a single unvarying principle.[169] That principle was *poeticus furor.* Relativized in the *Nutricia,* it provides a mythopoeic account of causality, circumventing earlier contrasts between a "poetry of art" and a "poetry of inspiration." Both coexist harmoniously in Poliziano's revised perspective, which, proceeding from "poetical frenzy" and its manifestations, goes on to the legendary seers of Greek mythology and the Hebrew prophets, before continuing with their Graeco-Roman successors.

[168] See below, pp. 91–92, and Godman, "Poliziano's Poetics," pp. 113–24.

[169] Cardini, *La Critica del Landino,* p. 94.

Yet poetics, in the *Nutricia,* do not stand alone. They are bound in close nexus with reason, which depends on an alliance between poetry and eloquence that was embodied in the title of this professor's chair:

For as soon as wisdom, sole ruler of the universe,
supported by lovely eloquence, put forth its sweet tune,
at the moment when the sound impinged on the unresponsive ears
of the barbarous crowds, they rushed together,
astounded at the voice's measured melody, at poetry's mysterious laws.
Rubbing shoulders and alert, motionless and intent,
the masses began to learn the difference
between habit and right conduct, the source and limits of rectitude,
how faith should be kept, justice made equitable,
tradition maintained; the standards of propriety and reason,
the social bonds and agreements which reconcile men.[170]

So Poliziano recurs to the Ciceronian praise of eloquence as civic wisdom, classic in Italian culture,[171] combining two disciplines that enabled him to formulate specific answers to the general questions raised by his earlier work. Less transcendental eloquence than technical rhetoric shaped his approach to the issue of the "history of the poets." The detail of systematic analysis, not clouds of theory, lies behind half (vv. 339–719) of the *Nutricia,* where the originality of Poliziano's thought on the subjects that had concerned him during his entire career emerges with clarity.

Poetics, in the Quattrocento, were nothing new. The novelty of the *Nutricia* lay in their combination of theory with history, organized according to a system that Poliziano describes as "poetica et poetarum historia per membra decurrens." *Membra* means 'section, division, branch'; the allusion is to Pliny's *Natural History;*[172] and the method is that of a taxonomist, as formulated in the *Praefatio in Suetonium:* "Individual details . . . separated, sorted, and classified" according to a *ratio carminum* or a ruling principle of poetry. How did this system, in practice, function?

The expression first occurs in the course on the (pseudo-) Ovidian *Epistola Sapphus* that the professor gave in the spring of 1481.[173] Like Poliziano's other lectures, it is concerned with the problem of literary genres. Inter-

[170] "Nam simul ac pulchro moderatrix unica rerum / Suffulta eloquio dulcem sapientia cantum / Protulit et refugas tantum sonus attigit aures, / Concurrere ferum vulgus numerosque modosque / Vocis et arcanas mirati in carmine leges / Densi humeris, arrecti animis, immota tenebant / Ora catervatim, donec didicere quid usus / Discrepet a recto; qui fons aut limes honesti; / Quive fide cultus; quid ius aequabile; quid mos; / Quid poscat decor et ratio; quae commoda vitae / Concilient inter se homines, quae foedera rebus" (vv. 75–85).

[171] See A. La Penna, "La tradizione classica nella cultura italiana," in *Storia d'Italia,* 5, 2 (Turin, 1973), pp. 1343 and 1345.

[172] 7.16.72: "Cum membratim historia decurrent." Cf. *TLL* 8:644, 1ff.

[173] *Commento inedito all'epistola ovidiana di Saffo a Faone* (ed. Lazzeri), pp. 4, 9, and 11.

preting Statius, for example, he offered a panorama of Greek and Latin verse, organized generically;[174] in his *Praefatio in Persium,* he wrote a history of satire;[175] while Poliziano's lectures on Terence's *Andria* examine the development of tragedy and comedy,[176] drawing on an exceptional command of Greek and Latin sources. The range and diversity of his scholarship led him further than Quintilian, who, at *Institutio oratoria* 10.1, was neither attempting to be comprehensive nor seeking to compose a monograph of genre criticism. But Quintilian, Poliziano's starting point, remained his point of reference. The *Institutio oratoria* was fundamental to the program announced in his inaugural lecture and implemented in subsequent courses, the first of which was devoted to the *Sylvae.*

Their place in the history of Roman literature had been redefined, in 1480, by modifying and extending Quintilian's terms.[177] The system that lay behind them was, however, firmly in Poliziano's mind when, rejecting a classification according to chronology, epoch, or period, he went on to depict Graeco-Roman poetry as a unity and to order it both by genres and by authors. These dual features of his inherited system, different from the modern,[178] were indivisible from one another: "The selection of authors presupposes a classification of genres."[179] For Quintilian they had not been of equal weight. Authors play the leading role at *Institutio oratoria* 10.1, and rivalry between individuals, rather than impersonal evolution, is the principle according to which their relationship is defined.[180]

Such remained Poliziano's emphasis, even when he sought to outdo Quintilian in the conspectus of discrete genres that precedes his course on Statius's first *Sylva.* Greek and Roman poets are considered together, instead of being separated into different national traditions. Quintilian's definitions of lyric and epic are altered with the aid of (John) Tzetzes' commentary on Lycophron's *Alexandra;*[181] their order and hierarchy are changed—lyric directly following epic, as proposed in the inaugural lecture[182]—and new information is added, stressing the proximity of Latin poets to the Greeks,[183] highlighting subgenres, listing additional authors, enumerating different and more

[174] *Commento inedito alle Selve di Stazio* (ed. Cesarini Martinelli), pp. 52–61.

[175] See Cesarini Martinelli in Angelo Poliziano, *Commento inedito alle Satire di Persio,* ed. L. Cesarini Martinelli and R. Ricciardi (Florence, 1985), pp. xxxv–lxxvi, 3–13.

[176] See above, p. 60.

[177] On Quintilian's practice, see P. Steinmetz, "Gattungen und Epochen der griechischen Literatur in der Sicht Quintilians," *Hermes* 92 (1964): 454–64.

[178] Discussed by G. Genette, "Genres, types, modes," *Poétique* 32 (1977): 389–421.

[179] Curtius, *ELLMA,* p. 248.

[180] Cf. T. G. Rosenmeyer, "Ancient Literary Genres: A Mirage?" *Yearbook of Comparative and General Literature* 34 (1985): 82.

[181] *Praefatio in Statium,* ed. Cesarini Martinelli, p. 52, ll. 3–8–p. 53, ll. 21ff. For the attribution of this commentary to John (not Isaac) Tzetzes, see N. G. Wilson, *Scholars of Byzantium* (London, 1983), p. 190.

[182] See above, p. 42.

[183] *Praefatio in Statium,* ed. Cesarini Martinelli, p. 53, l. 8 (the Suda on Parthenius).

elaborate divisions. The detail of Poliziano's conspectus is more sophisticated and varied than Quintilian's, but the underlying suppositions remain the same. The unity of the whole tradition, like the individuality of the single genre, derives from its named exponents, among whom an instigator or inventor is, wherever possible, identified. Generic rules, when mentioned, are empirically induced from a practice that is less analyzed than evoked; and if the triad *poetica, poema, poesis* is adduced from Diomedes' *Ars grammatica,*[184] its specific purpose is to classify into a "general group" (*commune genus*) the first of Statius's *Sylvae.*[185] Consistent with the plan announced in his inaugural lecture, Poliziano opens the canon of *Institutio oratoria* 10.1 to embrace the mixed modes of later classical poetry, enlarging Quintilian's account of the "individual types of poetry"[186] and of those who composed them, without essentially altering the basis of his system.

"Individually," "individual genres," "individuals": the terms in which Poliziano characterizes his approach[187] point to the *Praefatio in Suetonium.* The "artifice" of the *Sylvae* is accordingly anatomized into rhetorical categories.[188] The first poem, for example, belongs to the epideictic genre,[189] and the *Epistola Sapphus* to the deliberative, because it is a *suasoria.*[190] From that follows an analysis of figures and tropes that, among other virtuoso feats of rhetorical classification, distinguishes no less than sixteen types of "sentiment."[191] What Poliziano understands by the "ruling principle of poetry," in his opening remarks on the *Epistola Sapphus,*[192] is the organization of a poetic work, derived from the rhetorical features of its formal structure.

From those features, he was not averse to inventing poetic biographies and constructing poetic personalities. The evidence about Sappho available to him in 1481, for example, was relatively extensive; and much of it is assembled at the beginning of his lectures on the *Epistola Sapphus.*[193] Poliziano cites multiple testimonies to the reputation and life of the poetess, discriminating between them. Was Sappho a native of Eresus or Mytilene? The ancient authorities diverge.[194] He judiciously leaves the matter open, while refusing to accept the fabrication of a "second Sappho" transmitted by the

[184] Ibid., p. 59, ll. 19ff.

[185] Ibid., p. 60, l. 13.

[186] Ibid., p. 51, l. 21.

[187] Ibid., p. 51, ll. 20, 21; p. 52, l. 1.

[188] Ibid., p. 61, ll. 10–14: "Sed ut distinctius agamus utque vos facilius singula percipiatis, talem rationem inivimus, ut sententiam primo ipsam explicemus, tum ordinem lectionis aperiamus, mox singula ipsa verba diligentissime exponamus, deinde quae ad artificium pertinerent exequamur."

[189] Ibid., p. 66, ll. 11ff. Cf. p. 192, ll. 11ff.

[190] Ed. Lazzeri, pp. 76, ll. 25ff. and 82, ll. 4ff.

[191] Ibid., p. 82, ll. 9ff.–p. 85, l. 13.

[192] Ibid., pp. 3–4, ll. 9–12.

[193] Ibid., p. 4, ll. 20ff.

[194] Cf. A.S.F. Gow and D. L. Page, *The Greek Anthology: Hellenistic Epigrams,* vol. 2 (Cambridge, 1965), p. 42.

Suda.[195] At this factual level, in his course on Statius, Poliziano displays the same thoroughness and rigor that are evinced by the *Vitae* of Pindar[196] and of Ennius.[197] But when the professor addresses, later in his lectures on the *Epistola Sapphus,* questions unanswered in his opening remarks about the personality and work of the poetess, he descends to a different plane.

Between Sappho's life and writing, Poliziano assumes a direct correlation, which he illustrates by rhetorical procedures that are poles apart from the stringency of his source criticism. Sappho, he observes, was a woman—which leads to Aristotle's unflattering characterization of her sex in the *Historia animalium.*[198] She was also a lover—which produces a list of parallels from Greek and Latin sources.[199] "She is said to have been learned, with a charming, delightful character and unaffected habits": a partial paraphrase of *Anthologia Planudea* 16.310, supplemented by scraps of information and gossip from Horace, Maximus of Tyre, and Herodotus.[200] That, however, was enough to warrant a long string of epithets matched to the *Epistola Sapphus,* serving to validate its author's reliability—and Poliziano's own.

The precision is spurious, the procedure a variant on the ancient habit of concocting an author's life on the basis of his or her works.[201] The biographical trustworthiness of the *Epistola Sapphus* is affirmed by an argument of traditional circularity, which reveals the authority of the dual system that Poliziano continued to implement. If information about the life was wanting, it had to be made up. Just as the "ruling principle of poetry" could be construed in rhetorical categories, so they could supply aspects of the poet's biography lacking in classical sources but demanded by the model that Poliziano had inherited. His invention, on such a feeble basis, of Sappho's personality is a testimony to the strength of Quintilian's authority.

That strength was reinforced by the importance that Poliziano attached to imitation and its corollary, rivalry or *aemulatio,* the relevance of which to an understanding of Graeco-Roman poetry is underscored by *Institutio oratoria* 10.2. Practiced with sophistication in his own Latin and Greek verse, the theory of emulative *imitatio* inclined Poliziano to view genres as potentialities that gained substance through competition between those who employed them. This is salient in his account of the origins and development of satire in the *Praelectio in Persium.* Poliziano makes due allowance for the transition

[195] Ed. Lazzeri, p. 5, ll. 19–23. On the "second Sappho" in the Suda, see D. A. Campbell, *Greek Lyric,* vol. 1 (London, 1982), p. 7 ad 3 (n. 1).

[196] *Commento inedito alle Selve di Stazio* (ed. Cesarini Martinelli), pp. 679ff.

[197] Ibid., p. 523, ll. 23ff.

[198] *Commento inedito all'epistola ovidiana di Saffo a Faone* (ed. Lazzeri), p. 90, ll. 10–14.

[199] Ibid., p. 90, ll. 15–26; p. 91, ll. 1–13.

[200] Ibid., p. 91, ll. 13ff.

[201] Cf. M. Lefkowitz, *The Lives of the Greek Poets* (London, 1981), pp. viiiff. and 36, with J. Fairweather, "Fiction in the Biographies of Ancient Writers," *Ancient Society* 5 (1974): 231–75.

from a rural custom of Athenian "popular culture" to a religious ritual, mimicked and altered by poets employing different forms.[202] He traces the Roman genre of "biting satire," in Fescennine verse, to the rise of a more elaborate form in which the "choruses of the satirists" parodied the solemn gestures of the establishment.[203] Distinct from this development, the Atellan farce migrated to Rome, to be stripped of its sting by law and replaced by Lucilian and Menippean satire.[204] Analyzing the various types of writing subsumed under the composite label of satire, Poliziano finds one of the key explanations for its continuity in a tradition of *imitatio,* the characteristics of which his *Praelectio* itself concludes by imitating.

So, too, with the account, initially in Aristotelian terms, of mimesis in the course on Terence's *Andria.* Comedy and tragedy—whether born together, as Aristotle asserts, or emerging (as Donatus claims) in a different order[205]—have their own instigators, continuators, conventions. Various explanations of origin are admitted, and room is made for theories of a direct relationship between literature and life;[206] but what fosters the growth of a genre such as comedy is "artifice"[207]. "Artifice" derives from the technical adeptness of the poet, whose attitude to his precursors is both mimetic and agonistic, involving progressive refinement and increasing complication.[208]

Poliziano was not a mere formalist. Recording and welcoming the process of change, he highlighted the mutable features of each genre with which he dealt. Yet his approach, both as professor in the lecture room and as researcher in the study, was always systematic. The consequent urge to classify entailed reliance on the austere instrument of rhetoric, which enabled him to compare texts within and across genres, identifying their common features without minimizing their individuality. Rhetoric was employed to probe the mechanics of poetry, not to portray its character. Criticism in that sense it is idle to seek from Poliziano's lectures.[209] His imaginative interpretations of verse were advanced in the same medium—in the series of poetic *praelusiones,* composed between 1482 and 1491 and known as *Sylvae.*[210] Intended as introductions to academic courses, which the humanists usually wrote in prose, Poliziano's attempts, in verse, to recreate the distinctive styles and themes of

[202] *Praefatio in Persium,* ed. Cesarini Martinelli and Ricciardi, p. 5, ll. 78ff.

[203] Ibid., p. 7, ll. 116ff.

[204] Ibid., p. 11, ll. 234ff.

[205] *La commedia antica et l' "Andria" di Terenzio* (ed. Lattanzi Roselli), p. 13, ll. 18ff.

[206] Ibid., p. 8, ll. 7ff.

[207] Ibid., p. 9, ll. 2ff.

[208] Ibid., p. 9, ll. 1ff.

[209] Cf. Cardini, *La Critica del Landino,* pp. 49–50.

[210] See G. Ponte, "Poetica e poesia nelle *Sylvae* del Poliziano," *La Rassegna della letteratura italiana* 63 (1959): 390–416; and E. Klecker, *Dichtung über Dichtung: Homer und Vergil in lateinischen Gedichten italienischer Humanisten des 15. und 16. Jahrhunderts.* Wiener Studien, Beiheft 20 (Vienna, 1994), pp. 12–20.

major Greek and Latin poets marked a new departure in this genre.[211] He was proud of this innovation—referring, in the *Miscellanea,* to the *Sylvae* both as a vehicle and as an object of exegesis[212] and publishing them earlier than most of his other writings.[213] But it was to the *Nutricia*—the fourth and final of the *Sylvae*—that Poliziano attributed pride of place, and it is now pertinent to ask how his theory of the "ruling principle of poetry," developed in technical and academic contexts, was applied, in practice, to the verse that sought to unite his ideas on literary history and theory.[214]

. . . . .

There, in the *Nutricia,* his taxonomical method artfully concealed under an appearance of disorder, Poliziano organized *per membra* the writers of Greek and Latin poetry. Each genre is portrayed in terms of its exponents, whose works are mingled with details of their biographies. Narrative is minimal; chronology plays no role. Graeco-Roman poetry again forms a timeless unity; and in its sempiternal present the jealous Ennius, placed after Ovid (vv. 454ff.), surveys with a shudder the appropriation of his themes by Virgil (vv. 476–77).

Ennius himself is a thief from, and a critic of, Naevius (v. 474), Ovid the successor and rival of Callimachus (vv. 434ff.). Decimus Laberius and Publilius Syrus depend on the mimographers Sophron and Philistion (vv. 699–702). Imitation and rivalry are dramatized through personal envies and public contests, the terms of which are frequently set by Quintilian. The preference for Tibullus rather than Propertius expressed at *Institutio oratoria* 10.1.93, for example, is reversed by Propertius's victory over his rival in a contest enacted at *Nutricia* 539–42. Horace, the lyric "bee from Venusia," stings Lucilius and initiates a line of acerbity continued by Persius and Juvenal (vv. 640ff.). The allusion is to *Institutio oratoria* 10.1.94, but its range is extended, while the metaphors of aggression are borrowed from the satirists themselves.

[211] There exists no systematic study of this genre. See recently F. Rico, *El sueño del humanismo* (Madrid, 1995), pp. 161–90; and M. Campanelli, "L'oratio di Lorenzo Valla per l'inaugurazione dell'anno academico," in Valla, *Orazione per l'inaugurazione dell'anno academico,* pp. 25–61. Useful collections of material in the reprint (Munich, 1970), introduced by B. Gerl, of K. Müller, *Reden und Briefe italienischer Humanisten* (Vienna, 1899); and C. Trinkaus, "A Humanist's Image of Humanism: The Inaugural Orations of Bartolomeo della Fonte," *Studies in the Renaissance* 7 (1960): 90–132.

[212] See pp. 91ff. below. Cf. the commentary on the *Ambra* of his pupil, Pomponaio Petreio, ed. A. Perosa (Rome, 1994).

[213] See A. Perosa, "Studi sulla tradizione delle poesie latine del Poliziano," in *Studi in onore di U. E. Paoli* (Florence, 1956), pp. 539–62.

[214] For background, see M. McLaughlin, "Histories of Literature in the Quattrocento," in *The Languages of Literature in Renaissance Italy,* ed. P. Hainsworth et al. (Oxford, 1988), pp. 63–80.

Competition lends life to Poliziano's dual system. Genres, subject to classification but open to variation, are depicted as no less changeable than the individuals upon whose rivalry they depend. Virgil eyes Lucan sternly (v. 509), recalling the goddess Rhamnusia at Statius *Sylva* 2.6.73, who—to make the reference plain—is adduced two lines later as the motive-force behind Nero's command that the poet commit suicide (vv. 511–13). It is envy that links the leading authors of Roman epic—not only Virgil and Lucan but also Statius, bound to the others by insidious echo.

Rivalry provides the dynamics of a tradition that Poliziano often ironizes. The portrayal of Virgil at 509–11, for example, inverts the claim at *Nutricia* 350–52 that he is immune to the emotion felt by others. Confronted with Lucan's achievement, the poet promptly falls prey to *livor.* Here as elsewhere in the poem, a pluralistic view of literary history is linked to the process and consequences of emulation. Jealousy is felt even by the acknowledged master, in Latin, of the genre traditionally regarded as supreme. In Poliziano's *poetarum historia,* no hierarchy is secure from challenge, no canon safe from competition, no author superior to his rivals.

That is why both Virgil and Homer receive brief notice in the *Nutricia.* Obscure authors rub shoulders with celebrities; "minor" genres jostle with "major" for place. Room is made for the combative Archilochus (vv. 644ff.) and the comfortable Oppian (vv. 421ff.); original research assigns generous space to Ennius (vv. 454ff.) and Pindar (vv. 558ff.); while Ovid—potentially too familiar a writer to claim much attention—is lent prominence through his debts to Callimachus (vv. 426ff.). And as long-standing positions are revised while newcomers are imposed, the stylistic device of variation embodies Poliziano's "ruling principle of poetry," with its emphasis placed on provisionality and change.

The *Nutricia* thus represent a *summa,* in compressed form, of Poliziano's reflections on literary history. They demonstrate how ancient poetry, systematically classified, can be understood as a whole without conforming to conventional hierarchies, canons, or stereotypes. The rivalry of individual authors advances a tradition that reaches from the mythical past to the present, encompassing Dante and Petrarch, Boccaccio and Cavalcanti, to culminate in Poliziano's patron and pupil (vv. 720–90). What came between is ignored. Continuity with the ancient world is restricted to modern Italian culture—chiefly, among the Italians, in a Florence presided over by that modern Maecenas, Lorenzo de' Medici (vv. 728ff.).

From Orpheus to Lorenzo, prince of poets—the *poetarum historia* of the *Nutricia* has its own teleology, a teleology produced by methods for which the *Miscellanea* alone are applauded today. In none of Poliziano's works is the inadequacy of the distinction between philology and poetry more evident than in the *Nutricia,* which their author rightly placed at the center of his oeuvre, loudly proclaiming their original contribution to the study of the ancient world and passing over, in silence, their debts to his Renaissance precursors.

. . . . .

Petrarch figures in the poem (v. 723) only as the author of the *Triumphi*. Some of those verse catalogues point in a direction that Poliziano followed. Related to the *Triumphi* is *Laurea occidens,* tenth part of Petrarch's *Bucolicum carmen,*[215] from which, in a spirit of tacit rivalry, Poliziano goes out of his way to distance his work. The *Nutricia* are not bucolic. They cultivate complexity rather than *obscuritas*.[216] Allegory plays no role in Poliziano's poem. It is fundamental to the *Bucolicum carmen,* in which Petrarch celebrates an ideal of solitude and contemplation, alien to worldly involvement.[217] The *Nutricia* ignore this antithesis, and exalt the achievements of Poliziano's patron. "Civic" humanism versus the *vita contemplativa*? The contrast is too simple. Lorenzo in the *Nutricia* is extolled for his poetic prowess; and *sylva,* exceptionally in the *Laurea occidens,* acquires a sense of "literary club."[218]

The tenth *Bucolicum carmen* was one of the allegorical poems by Petrarch that inspired a commentary, associated with Benvenuto Rambaldi da Imola,[219] that transmits Petrarch's own attempt to offer a key to the interpretation of his work by providing the names of the poets whom he describes in it with calculated obscurity. The same procedure is followed in the margins of the earliest editions of the *Nutricia*. No conclusive proof, this, of dependence on the commentary inspired by Petrarch, for many of the incunables that Poliziano annotated are also filled with authors' names; but it indicates a similarity of approach that is more than casual. Despite differences in mode, manner, and content, both the *Nutricia* and the *Laurea occidens* were written to inspire exegesis. Both challenged their readers to solve erudite problems—to spot references, recognize allusions, and divine the identities of poets.

For Petrarch, the ancient tradition of poetry embraced Christian Latin authors[220] whom Poliziano excludes from his purview. Insofar as the *Laurea oc-*

[215] References are to the edition of G. Martellotti (Rome, 1968). For affinities between the *Triumphi* and *Laurea occidens,* see Martellotti, "L'inedito Weiss," in idem, *Scritti petrarcheschi,* ed. M. Feo and S. Rizzo (Padua, 1983), pp. 165ff., and G. Ponte, "Problemi petrarcheschi: La decima egloga e la composizione dei *Trionfi,*" *Rassegna della letteratura italiana* 69 (1965): 517–29. Further bibliography in Petrarca, *Triumphi* (ed. M. Ariani), pp. 333–35.

[216] On *obscuritas* in Petrarch's bucolic, see K. Krautter, *Die Renaissance der Bukolik in der lateinischen Literatur des XIV. Jahrhunderts: Von Dante bis Petrarca* (Munich, 1983), pp. 128ff.

[217] Ibid., pp. 106ff.

[218] Ed. Martellotti, p. 41 ad 1.

[219] Ibid., 12–13, with A. Avena, ed., *Il Bucolicum carmen e i suoi commenti inediti* (Padua, 1906), pp. 227ff.

[220] *Laura occidens* 311ff.

cidens has a principle of organization, it derives from topography—from the places that Silvanus, its author's persona, visits during his imagined odyssey through the poetic past. Odysseus, however, had a sense of direction. Silvanus is often tossed on the high seas. Deprived of *Institutio oratoria* 10.1 by a lacuna in the copy of Quintilian's work that he possessed, Petrarch regarded as "great additions" the information he later supplied to his text on the basis of Ovid's *Ex Ponto* 4.16 while denying, with false modesty, any claim to completeness.[221] How falsely, the superior scholarship of the *Nutricia* amply demonstrates.

At *Laura occidens* 188ff., for example, Petrarch paraphrases *Ex Ponto* 4.16. His theme is forgetfulness, and he lists poets such as Fontanus and Montanus whose works have not survived. At 254ff., again drawing on Ovid, Petrarch names further lost authors, making much of his borrowed credentials. Poliziano will have none of this: a swift allusion to the *Ex Ponto* suffices (*Nutricia* 535–37), and the wraiths resuscitated by Petrarch are consigned to oblivion. No Largus or Lupus; no Tuscus or Tuticanus. Names that, for Petrarch, advanced an aspiration to higher learning are demoted by Poliziano to the anonymity of cross-references.

Archias, on the same principle, is not worth mentioning, although (or perhaps because) Cicero's oration in his favor had influenced Petrarch's speech on his laureation,[222] leading to the appearance of this lost poet at *Laurea occidens* 268–69. Marius and Thucydides, misinterpreted by Petrarch, are excluded from the *Nutricia;* while Pisander and Panyassis, Euphorion and Tyrtaeus—known to Poliziano through Quintilian (*Institutio oratoria* 10.1.54, 56)—figure prominently (vv. 397ff.). Silent correction of Petrarch's errors is accompanied by enlargement of his horizon, through the use of sources unknown or unavailable to Poliziano's predecessor.

Quintilian was important in this regard. So, too, was evidence drawn from Greek. Artfully combined, they outclass the *Laurea occidens*. Around Sappho, for instance, Petrarch had grouped, on the basis of allusions in Latin writers, a canon of classical love-poets, succeeded by Pindar (vv. 88–101).[223] That order is reversed by Poliziano (*Nutricia* 558ff.), with Pindar appearing first, his biography enlarged and his primacy affirmed on the authority of *Institutio oratoria* 10.1.61 and *Anthologia Planudea* 9.184 and 571. Anacreon succeeds him, perhaps because of his age (ibid., 16.306–7, 309); then come Alcaeus, Stesichorus, and Simonides—a common trio in the *Anthology*'s epigrams, which serves to modify the sequences followed by Petrarch and Quintilian. Sappho (who, like Anacreon, is not mentioned at *Institutio oratoria* 10.1) com-

[221] Cf. Martellotti, "Aspetti della filologia del Petrarca," in idem, *Scritti petrarceschi,* pp. 540–41.

[222] See G. Gensini, "Poeta et historicus: L'episodio della laurea nella carriera e nella prospettiva culturale di Francesco Petrarca," *La cultura* 18 (1980): 166–94 with further bibliography.

[223] See Martellotti, ed., pp. 50–53.

pletes the procession—as both the ninth of the Aeolian lyric poets (*Nutricia* 619–20) and the tenth of the Muses (vv. 637–39).

Combining material from the *Anthologia Palatina,* Poliziano varies its canons with a mastery to which Petrarch did not rise, establishing simultaneously his independence from Quintilian, whose account he supplements. The competitive spirit is patent; the corrections appear thick and fast. That Oppian was not Ap[p]ian, that he wrote in Greek (not Latin), that his patron was Antoninus Pius are, like the separation of the two Varros whom Petrarch had conflated, further stages in the same punctilious process. In covert rivalry with their immediate antecedent in the Renaissance, Poliziano's *Nutricia,* which extol *aemulatio,* implement it with devastating results. After his exercise in the genre pioneered by Petrarch, the *Laurea occidens* was intended to become as obsolete as the myth of Thucydides' verse.

. . . . .

Petrarch, like Dante, signified for Poliziano the boundary of a new age. That boundary is marked in the *Nutricia* by a classicism stricter than even Petrarch's.[224] Exclusion of the Christian poets of late antiquity and the Middle Ages establishes a symmetry between the beginning of the work, which depicts the rise of the arts of learning with poetry as their queen, and its conclusion, which evokes the rebirth of ancient literary culture in Renaissance Florence.

This schema had precedents. At Padua, Sicco Polenton, in his account of Latin literature completed in 1437, had traced the origins and development of the arts, especially poetry, to the history of which are devoted Books 2–4 of his *Scriptores illustres linguae latinae.* Organized biographically on the lines of Cicero's *Brutus* and Jerome's *De viris illustribus,* that history, in Sicco's eyes, was discontinuous. After Horace, sleep. After Juvenal, sleep again. Following a brief interlude of semiconsciousness in late antiquity, a long millennium of slumbering darkness, fitfully illuminated by beacons of medieval verse. Then the gradual dawning of a new day with the Paduan "prehumanists," Mussato and Lovati, until the Muses began to stretch themselves, rub their eyes, and move their limbs at the advents of Dante and Petrarch.[225]

Sicco's panorama of the classical tradition, more limited in range and less rigorous in method than that of the *Nutricia,*[226] had a focus that was to be narrowed further by Poliziano. Available to his circle in a version of 1426,[227] Books 2 to 4 of the *Scriptores illustres linguae latinae* represent poetry as the

[224] See T. E. Mommsen, "Petrarch's Conception of the 'Dark Ages,'" *Speculum* 17 (1942): 226–42.

[225] Ed. B. Ullmann, p. 129, ll. 2ff.

[226] See A. Ghisalberti, "Medieval Biographies of Ovid," *Journal of the Warburg and Cortauld Institutes* 10 (1946): pp. 25ff.

[227] On Pietro Crinito's copy—BRF 121—see Ullmann, in Polenton, *Scriptores illustres,* p. xvi and n. 3.

principal vehicle of *translatio studii*.[228] More than a history of literature, the work represents an attempt to write cultural history. Sharing his assumptions and smoothing away his discontinuities, Poliziano follows the course of such studies beyond Dante and Petrarch to the Florence of the Medici.

"Poets," declared the Florentine Filippo Villani, writing a century earlier than Poliziano, "acquired fame among mortals before all others."[229] Guardians of learning, they possessed encyclopedic knowledge.[230] From Villani's perspective a long tradition is traced, beginning with Claudian and continuing, after intervening gloom, with the splendid triumvirate of Dante, Petrarch, and Boccaccio, to whose number Poliziano adds Cavalcanti and Lorenzo. This addition was both natural in context and consistent with local conventions. For the teleology and temporal limits of the *Nutricia* were shaped by the genre of *laus Florentiae* practiced by Villani and developed by his continuators.

Chief among them, in Poliziano's milieu, was Landino. Between his proemium to the *Commento dantesco* and the second book of Villani's *De origine civitatis Florentiae et eiusdem famosis civibus* there exist analogies. Both organize their accounts of the disciplines in which Florentines had excelled to lend prominence to poetry; and at *Nutricia* 728ff., Lorenzo is singled out as the equal or superior of Dante and Petrarch. The same claim is made by Landino in the introduction to his *Vergilii interpretationes,* published in 1488 and dedicated to Piero de' Medici,[231] who is urged to emulate the literary achievements of his father. With an identical admonition, the *Nutricia* (780ff.) end. It is a matter for conjecture whether this poem (known in the Florentine Studio since 1486) was echoed by Landino, or whether Poliziano—after 1488 but before its publication in 1491—had added the encomium on Lorenzo to his work, following Landino's precedent. What matters here is less the issue of priority than the fact of affinity. As with *poeticus furor,* so with the *laus Florentiae*. Landino and Poliziano, motivated by similar aims, worked with the same conventions.

Patriotic and uncritical, those conventions naturally precluded the aspersions on Dante's "uncouthness" that Poliziano had voiced in the preface to the collection of vernacular verse known as the *Raccolta aragonese*.[232]

[228] On this concept, see below, p. 257.

[229] *De origine civitatis Florentiae et de eiusdem famosis civibus* 2 (= *Liber de civitatis Florentiae famosis civibus*), ed. G. C. Galletti (Florence, 1847), p. 20 (Roberto de Bardis, *ad initium*). On Villani, see G. Tanturli, "La Firenze laurenziana davanti alla propria storia letteraria," in Garfagnini, ed., *Lorenzo il Magnifico,* pp. 16ff.

[230] Ibid., p. 6.

[231] Landino, *Scritti critici e teorici,* p. 224, ll. 18–20. See further below, pp. 184ff. Cf., too, Pico's letter of 15 July 1484, ed. Garin, *Prosatori,* pp. 796ff., with P. Thompson, "Pico della Mirandola's Praise of Lorenzo (and Critique of Dante and Petrarch)," *Neuphilologus* 54 (1970): 123–26.

[232] See D. de Robertis, "Lorenzo aragonese," *Rinascimento* 34 (1994): 3–14, and cf. Cardini, *La Critica del Landino,* pp. 202ff., and idem, "Landino e Dante," *Rinascimento* 30 (1990): 175–90.

Landino's eloquent defense of Dante, in the proemium to his commentary, is implicitly accepted in the *Nutricia*. Preferences once expressed for the poets of the Duecento—with the exception of Cavalcanti, already assimilated by Ficino and Pico to Florentine tradition—are now dropped. An double-edged attempt at conciliation with the leading opponent of philological method can be discerned in Poliziano's work, which lends the unflattering words of one of Landino's pupils, two decades earlier, a different and less negative sense.

In 1465 Lorenzo Guidetti had inveighed against the "petty details of history" adduced by "those more interested in ferreting out minutiae than in seeking to understand larger issues."[233] This contrast, stimulated by a refusal on Landino's part to accept the subordination of poetry to history and to employ new critical techniques, is resolved in the *Nutricia* by an ingenious harmony of opposites: a Landinian poetic married with a *poetarum historia,* founded on philology and attached to a panegyric on Florentine verse. "Petty details of history" are thereby reconciled with the grand vistas and blended with the local view favored by Landino; yet the poetic diplomacy remains ambiguous. His lesson learned, his message received, Poliziano's former teacher was left by the *Nutricia* to reflect on how effectively his own criteria could be satisfied by procedures that he had professed to scorn.

. . . . .

More directly than Landino, another member of Poliziano's milieu had reason to feel threatened by the *Nutricia:* a member who had left Florence for Rome in 1483, after a polemical exchange with his sometime friend, only to return, a year later, to teach on a reduced salary; a courtier no less assiduous than Poliziano in seeking patronage, whose success in gaining the favor of Matthias Corvinus suggests why his rival, who had inscribed a manuscript of the *Nutricia* to the king of Hungary in 1486, decided against making the dedication public;[234] an antagonist whose ambitions and career ran parallel, along the axes of Florence, Buda, and Rome, to those of Poliziano: that able but conventional humanist, Bartolomeo Fonzio.

At the beginning of the academic year 1485–86, Fonzio delivered, as a *praelusio* to his course on Horace's *Odes,* an *Oratio in laudem poetices facul-*

[233] Cardini, *La Critica del Landino,* p. 268; and Grafton, *Defenders of the Text,* pp. 23ff. See further below, pp. 119ff.

[234] See Godman, "Poliziano's Poetics," pp. 113ff.; S. Caroti and S. Zamponi, *Lo scrittoio di Bartolomeo Fonzio* (Milan, 1974), p. 16; and Branca, *Poliziano,* pp. 126ff. Cf. Fonzio, *Bartolomeus Fontius, epistolarum libri III* (ed. L. Juhàsz), ep. 2.11, p. 36, ll. 9–10. The letter, dated "III. Cal. Februarii 1488," promises a dedication of his work on Valerius Flaccus. Cf. ep. 2.12 (ibid.) and the inscription of Fonzio's collected Latin poetry, *Saxettus,* to Mathias Corvinus's son in *Bartolomeus Fontius: Carmina,* ed. J. Fògel and L. Juhàsz (Leipzig, 1932), p. 1.

tatis.[235] Not by chance did Poliziano present, in the next academic year, the *Nutricia* to the same audience, transposing the same theme into verse and developing it with a virtuosity lacking in Fonzio's pedestrian prose. Indebted to Landino, Fonzio had dealt with subjects discussed in the proemium to the *Commento dantesco: poeticus furor,* the civilizing effect of poetry, its ancient traditions continued by Dante and Petrarch. Like eloquence and history—the topics of separate orations that he gave in 1481 and 1482—poetics are judged by Fonzio in terms of their moral instructiveness, their ethical utility. Pedagogical clichés, worn thin by unceasing repetition in humanist circles, form the substance of his *Oratio in laudem poetices facultatis;* and nothing is more probable than that, when Poliziano expounded the *Nutricia* to packed crowds,[236] he was intending to demonstrate, as publicly as possible, that the common subject could be treated differently.

Poetics, united with eloquence and history, were set on a new basis by that *praelusio.* No longer presented as a source of moral examples but combined with other disciplines, they embodied an encyclopedic ideal of learning to which lip service had been paid by Fonzio's rhetoric. Philological techniques that he had never thought of employing in such a context transformed the schema that both humanists derived from Landino. These differences in substance were matched by divergences in form and style. In the competitive atmosphere of the Florentine Studio, its leading expert on *aemulatio* selected the loftier medium to convey his higher message. Above the plodding Fonzio soared the poet Poliziano, his superiority proved to mutual friends and shared pupils. The challenge was unmistakable, the provocation patent. How did Fonzio respond?

Between 1489 and 1490, Fonzio composed a work, *De poetice,* which he dedicated to Lorenzo de' Medici.[237] Its model is the *Nutricia,* camouflaged by prose, and it employs many of the same sources, expanding, wherever possible, on topics that they treat briefly or implicitly. Book 1 of *De poetice*—typically—deals with little that Poliziano had not already made plain. *Poeticus furor* is linked to the dignity of the art, its antiquity and its utility. Advancing the claims of poetry against those of other disciplines, Fonzio draws on a debate that had been conducted for generations. Identifying the ancient seers and prophets as theologians, he repeats clichés that Poliziano had eschewed. And an assertion, in Book 2 (the chief source of which is Horace's *Ars poetica*), that rhetoric is inferior to poetry does not prevent Fonzio from going on, in Book 3, to classify poetic genres and their practitioners in rhetorical terms.

These terms were familiar to those who, like Fonzio, had already heard

[235] BNCF, Magl. M.7, p. 3ª.

[236] See pp. 91ff.

[237] Ed. C. Trinkaus, in "The Unknown Quattrocento Poetics of Bartolommeo della Fonte," *Studies in the Renaissance* 13 (1966): 40–122.

Poliziano lecture on Statius's first *Sylva* or who had attended his expositions of *Nutricia* 339–719. Why, is simply explained. In Book 3 of *De poetice,* Fonzio lifts his conspectus of Graeco-Roman poetic genres from the lectures of his antagonist, varying the model they provided on the basis of the ancient evidence they cite. When he differs from Poliziano, it is to introduce cosmetic changes—to transmit opinions that had been too commonplace, or adduce sources too banal for inclusion in the course on Statius and in the *Nutricia.* Furnished by them with both the motive and the material for a counterattack, this skillful tactician could afford to wage a campaign of attrition against his adversary on the subject of satire,[238] while biding his time for the main offensive.

It was not slow in coming. In 1490–91 Poliziano was planning a further set of lectures on the *Nutricia,* which he had not yet published. With the addition or expansion (perhaps in response to Landino's example) of 728–90, which praise the Medici dynasty, the poem was now eminently suitable for dedication to Lorenzo or his son. The moment had been prepared, the audience was waiting. The reactions of his Florentine pupils to the *Nutricia* had been enthusiastic. *Centuria prima* of the *Miscellanea* had advertised their scholarly importance. Combining poetry and philology, they would swell Poliziano's reputation and vaunt his intellectual independence, while affirming his political loyalty. It was at this point that Fonzio chose to strike.

Timing was his strong suit. Just as he anticipated Poliziano in winning the favor of Matthias Corvinus, so he beat him to Lorenzo de' Medici. Presenting the *De poetice* to their patron first, Fonzio thwarted the author of its unacknowledged model from doing the same. The dedication of a work, in this humanist battle of the books, was no less important than its contents, as their author had grounds to observe in 1491, when inscribing the *Nutricia* instead to Cardinal Antoniotto di Pallavicino Gentile. Outmaneuvered by Fonzio, Poliziano found it opportune to recall, in short order, a long-standing project to become papal librarian. So it was that what he called his *opus eruditissimum,* so expressive of Florentine patriotism, on which Poliziano had set such high hopes, came to be dispatched to Rome. The cardinal was not his first choice of dedicatee, nor probably his second, but his third. The alternatives, however, were limited by sources of patronage intended to advance the career of a man of letters. Better a fresh attempt at the Vatican than wasted effort in Florence. Even poetry, highest of the arts, was not above cultural politics.

Cultural politics, at Florence, were changing rapidly. A new dispensation had been announced by Savonarola in ringing tones, compelling the sympathies of those, such as Pico and Lorenzo, to whom Poliziano stood closest.

[238] Poliziano's lectures on Juvenal were delivered in 1485–86. That Fonzio's course on Juvenal took place in 1487–88 (and not in 1486–87) is established by A. F. Verde, "Un terzo soggiorno romano del Poliziano," *Rinascimento* 22 (1982): 260. Cf. Verde, *Studio,* 2:84–91.

The *Nutricia* belonged to the older order, in which literary pursuits—learned and refined, yet exclusive and elitist—needed no justification other than the approval of the patron upon whose munificence they depended. Lorenzo's interests, allegedly more philosophical and certainly more religious, were now different. Within a year he would be dead. In 1491, recognizing that poetry and eloquence were no longer sufficient in the altered atmosphere of the city that his work celebrated, the Florentine Callimachus wanted out. His thoughts turned (not for the first time) to Rome, where he sent the *Nutricia,* prefaced by a plea for intercession on his behalf with Pope Innocent VIII. On the scene that Poliziano had hoped to dominate, his supremacy was challenged. The philologist's thought on matters of literary history was being purloined or ignored; resistance was mounting to the technical scholarship on which he had based his *poetarum historia;* and few, even in his own milieu, shared his passion for spelling "Virgil" with an *e.*

III

THE ANGEL FROM HEAVEN

VIRGIL or Vergil? Was this, in 1489, a pedant's quibble or the sign of a "revolutionary transformation," a "sweeping innovation in philological method"[1] perceived for the first time as a vehicle of "historical study"[2] and heralding the rise of historicism?[3] In the first *Centuria* of Poliziano's *Miscellanea,* chapter 77, the problem is presented in different terms. With violent invective against unnamed detractors, Poliziano celebrates both his approach and himself.

The *Miscellanea* are as much concerned with their author's present as with the classical past. Linking questions of ancient orthography, textual criticism, and exegesis to partisan interests, they mirror a culture—or rather reflect, through a highly individual optic, particular strains within it. Less secure and unique than is often supposed, Poliziano was not only a philologist, nor should the technical advances made in this product of his "Alexandrian" scholarship[4] blind us to its self-imposed limitations. Consider, for example, what the Florentine Callimachus has to say about Virgil/Vergil:

> At issue when I say Vergil with an *e,* which is now beginning to gain favor among certain scholars through my influence, rather than Virgil with an *i,* which has been all too common usage, are a number of monuments of great antiquity to which I have paid close attention and which I shall gladly adduce on account of certain vile characters, filled with malignity and thoroughly deserving all hatred and contempt, who, although they remain at the level of primary-school pupils, have the nerve to rub shoulders with learned promoters of literature as if they were its censors.[5]

[1] Grafton, *Joseph Scaliger,* 1:37; idem, *Defenders of the Text,* p. 57.

[2] Kenney, *The Classical Text,* pp. 5ff.

[3] A. Scaglione, "The Humanist as Scholar and Politian's Conception of the 'Grammaticus,'" *Studies in the Renaissance* 8 (1961): 50–51; and Kelley, *Foundations of Modern Historical Scholarship,* p. 48.

[4] Cf. Timpanaro, *La genesi,* pp. 4ff. For the term "Alexandrian," see p. 37 above.

[5] "Ceterum ut ego Vergilium dicam magis per 'e,' quid iam placere quibusdam per nos etiam doctis incipit, quam Virgilium per 'i,' quod vulgo nimis obtinuit, in causa sunt veterrima aliquot monumenta, nostrae observationi patrocinantia, quae libens equidem subiiciam propter propudiosos nescio quos et aeruginis plenos, odio omni fastidioque dignissimos, qui, quamquam semper elementarii sunt, vindicare tamen inter doctos fautores audent sibi censuram litterarum." *Politiani Opera,* 1:645–46.

Should Poliziano be taken at his withering word? Why such aggressive statements of loathing and disdain? Against whom, to what end, were they directed?

Behind the triumphant tone sustained throughout the *Miscellanea* can be detected a certain defensiveness. In this passage, for instance. Rather than criticize living enemies, Poliziano preferred to flail the dead: the conveniently deceased Calderini he never spared from attack.[6] But the anonymous targets of his animus, at chapter 77, are alive and kicking. They are *elementari:* the pupils of primary schoolmasters, teachers of rudimentary subjects at a level below the *grammatistae* who turned his friend Pico's stomach.[7] In short: presumptuous pedants, with whom Poliziano himself might have been easily confused.

No, no. Such confusion is unjustified, for these intellectual pygmies are beneath our giant's notice. Or they would be, had they not pretended to the censor's authority reserved by Quintilian, at *Institutio oratoria* 1.4.3ff., for the *grammatici* who were the purveyors of *enkyklios paideia* (cf. ibid., 1.10.1–6), which Poliziano had already proclaimed as his ideal. Writing, at *Miscellanea* 1.4, that the "interpreter of the poets ought to labor in the night-watches by the light not only of Aristophanes' lantern but also by that of Cleanthes" and declaring that "not just the schools of philosophers should be taken into account but those of writers on law, medicine, dialectic, and the entire sphere of learning which we call *encyclia,*"[8] he was responding to Pico's aspersions on the lowly *grammatista* by appeal to Quintilian's lofty conception of the *grammaticus.*[9] Philosophy (mentioned three times in as many sentences) is integrated by this polymath into the study of literature and related subjects. *Semidocta sedulitas,* by contrast, merely gives itself airs. Defining what he is not at *Miscellanea* 1.77 by denouncing what his opponents are, Poliziano, the champion of *enkyklios paideia,* has in mind both the critique of Pico, *noster amor* (1.4), and the slights cast on the pursuit of "petty details" by Landino and his school.[10]

Landino is lauded in chapter 77

> as a man both eloquent and erudite, a long-standing and celebrated teacher of *belles-lettres* at Florence, to whom I owe a great debt for training in elementary subjects during my youth, and who is now (so to speak) my professional col-

[6] See above, p. 38, and pp. 94ff. below.

[7] See above, p. 36.

[8] "Qui poetarum interpretationem suscipit, eam non solum (quod dicitur) ad Aristophanis lucernam, sed etiam ad Cleanthis oportet lucubrasse. Nec prospiciendae autem philosophorum modo familiae, sed et in iureconsultorum et medicorum item et dialecticorum et quicumque doctrinae illum orbem faciunt, quae vocamus Encyclia." *Politiani Opera,* 1:517–18.

[9] Cf. below, p. 116, and see Billanovich, "Auctorista, humanista, orator," p. 159.

[10] See above, p. 76.

> league, enjoying such secure fame and continuing to support me as I struggle and strive in the intellectual race that he seems to receive and interpret any praise which I acquire as if it were bestowed on himself.[11]

The ambiguity of the final clause is obvious and has been remarked on,[12] but not the venomous equivocality of the lines that precede it. Landino, a dubious celebrity resting on faded laurels, accepts those freshly plucked by Poliziano. He advances, while his teacher—"so to speak," his colleague—remains on the shelf. And what had Landino taught Poliziano? *Rudimenta*—the elementary subjects practiced by his despised detractors. Implicitly demoted from the professorial *cathedra* to the schoolmaster's stool, the leading critic of philological method at the Florentine Studio is left with the option of taking at face value his pupil's words—or of eating his own.

Landino's criticism of "petty details" was not entirely his own, nor was Poliziano's polemic on this theme wholly new. At Florence, during the late fourteenth and the early fifteenth centuries, the problems discussed at *Miscellanea* 1.77 had given rise to bitter debate. At the center of the dispute stood the hyper-classicist Niccolò Niccoli, to whom Poliziano, in his many acerbic moments, bears an uncanny resemblance.[13] Exacting, difficult, and sharp of tongue, Niccoli provoked invective.[14] *Against That Slanderous Scoundrel* is the title of Leonardo Bruni's work of 1424, in which he inveighed against the limits of his enemy's culture. "Niccoli understands nothing about philosophy, mathematics, rhetoric, and jurisprudence," blasted Bruni, anticipating components of the ideal of unified learning that Poliziano was to invoke at *Miscellanea* 1.4. "He is interested only in puerile grammar. He fiddles about with diphthongs."[15]

Orthography had attracted passionate interest and strong antipathy among several generations of Florentine humanists. Manuel Chrysoloras, Coluccio Salutati, Poggio Bracciolini, and others were deeply concerned with the subject of spelling. It defined, and expressed, their attitude to tradition and innovation, to the concept of correctness.[16] Niccolò Niccoli was pilloried by his opponents because (as they depicted him) he carried formalism to ster-

[11] "Landinus, homo et eloquens et eruditus et Florentiae iamdiu doctor bonarum litterarum celebratissimus, cui se praeceptori adulescentiae meae rudimenta magnopere debent, et qui nunc in professione quasi dixerim collega, locata iam in tuto sua sibi fama, nobis adhuc in studio laborosissime decertantibus ita favet, ut quicquid ipsi laudis acquirimus, quasi suum sibi amplecti atque agnoscere videatur." *Politiani Opera* 1:647.

[12] Cardini, *La Critica del Landino,* p. 171.

[13] On Niccoli, see G. Zippel, *Niccolò Niccoli* (Florence, 1890), reprinted in *Storia e cultura del rinascimento italiano,* ed. G. Zippel (Padua, 1974), pp. 68–157; and P. A. Stadter, "Niccolò Niccoli: Winning Back the Knowledge of the Ancients," in *Vestigia: Studi in onore di G. Billanovich* (Rome, 1984), pp. 747–64.

[14] See Davies, "An Emperor without Clothes?" pp. 95–148.

[15] *Oratio in nebulonem maledicum,* ed. Zippel, *Storia e cultura,* p. 136, ll. 6ff.

[16] See Gombrich, "From the Revival of Letters," pp. 93–110, esp. p. 646.

ile excess. Made sensitive to the same charge by Pico, anxious to avoid any imputation of superficiality, Poliziano, at *Miscellanea* 1.77, set out to show how orthographical issues were neither elementary nor provincial but formed part of the empire of *enkyklios paideia,* over which he aspired to hold sway. Not only in his rancor did Poliziano resemble Niccoli. Here as elsewhere in the *Miscellanea,* their author's cultural enterprise amounted less to a revolution than to a continuation of previous debates.

That enterprise of "discovering and reviving antiquity" was caricatured by his critics as an outrage (*flagitium*) on moral grounds. Poliziano, they asserted, abused his *otium.* He wasted time and effort with frivolous trivia. "Had not Caesar himself descended to such subtleties (*tenuitas*)?" replied the unperturbed *grammaticus.* It is not just to blame him for engaging in higher scholarship (*altiora studia*), for if he is interested in small issues, they are of great moment. "To them I devote myself as though I were passing not from leisure to study but from study to leisure . . . without design, by chance, free from care, like taking a relaxed stroll along the beach, gathering seashells in the meantime."[17]

This engaging image points to a change effected in the *Miscellanea.* Against the Renaissance tradition inspired by Cicero's writings and example, which from Petrarch to Bruni and beyond had equated *otium* and *negotium*[18] and regarded leisure as freedom for literary pursuits,[19] Poliziano affects an aristocratic nonchalance. The higher scholar, as portrayed by him, is a gentleman, different from the withdrawn humanist and the intellectual monk. In the solitude of their cells, in the privacy of their studies, these anchorites of the mind seek refuge from the cares of the world. Care-less and untroubled, he claims *otium* by right—without apology or excuse—and gathers at random the objects of his eclectic interest. This systematic thinker can afford to assume an unsystematic air, because his model is Medicean. Writing to Piero de' Medici about the qualities that had made his grandfather Cosimo great, Poliziano singled out for special praise the fact that "despite doing countless things, he gave the impression that he had nothing to do."[20]

Doing nothing is preferable to "yawning,"[21] like his detractors, or "grunting in the mire" (*oscitationes et grunnire in coeno*). With feigned langor, the gentleman-scholar lifts a finger to prove his credentials. An ancient inscrip-

[17] "Non ut ab otio ad studium, sed ut a studio ad otium me refero, et in quae non tam feror ex professo quam casu incido, ceu si littoribus ex commodo inambulans, conchas interim colligam securus." *Politiani Opera,* 1:286.

[18] See H. Baron, "The Memory of Cicero's Roman Civic Spirit in the Medieval Centuries and in the Florentine Renaissance," in idem, *In Search of Florentine Civic Humanism,* 1:94–133.

[19] Cf. ibid., p. 141, and the collection of essays in B. Vickers, ed., *Arbeit, Muße, Meditation: Betrachtungen zur "Vita activa" und "Vita contemplativa"* (Zürich, 1985).

[20] Cited by Baron, *In Search of Florentine Civic Humanism* 1:131 and n. 62.

[21] Cf. again Bruni's polemic against Niccoli: "Ex bibliotheca plane dormitorium fecit: simul ac librum aperit, *ad paginam stertit.*" Zippel, ed., *Storia e cultura,* p. 136, ll. 2–3.

tion on a marble table at Orvieto is adduced, together with one in stone at "Sutrium." Agents had inspected them on his behalf, but oral reports were not sufficient. The eyes must supplement the ears; monuments give way to manuscripts: Poliziano looks into the orthography of the Florentine Pandects[22] and the Roman Virgil.[23] And so the hunt is on: a codex of Donatus's commentary on the poet "in the hands" of Landino offered, by its indubitable age and authority, corroborative evidence of Poliziano's theory.[24] Two manuscripts, written "in Lombard script,"[25] of Augustine's *City of God* and of Columella consulted in "the public library of the Medici family"[26] at San Marco, were compared with a "very old book" containing Seneca's *Epistles* made available to this detective by Lorenzo's secretary Niccolò Michelozzi.[27] Not to mention "many volumes of venerable antiquity" that Poliziano had showed to (among others, as need and occasion arose) his "friend and scholarly aide," Jacopo Modesti.[28] The chase ended with the prize catch of two antique epitaphs from Rome, reproduced, at *Miscellanea* 1.77, from a collection presented to Lorenzo de' Medici by Fra Giocondo of Verona.[29]

A manuscript hunt, therefore, conducted in the spirit of a sleuth. But also a catalogue of evidence and witnesses, presented in the manner of an advocate's brief. Is this the modern "habit of full and precise quotation from sources," the product of "historical method"? Certainly, in the sense that priority is assigned to the oldest testimonies. Yet the mystique of *vetustas* was not invented in 1489: such criteria had long been shared by the antiquarians, ancient and modern, in whose mold the *Miscellanea* are cast.[30] More is at stake in Poliziano's parade of testimonies. "Wondrously old," the Roman manuscript of Virgil was viewed by this investigator among "the innermost recesses of the Vatican library." Other codices are preserved or collated by colleagues, patrons, and friends: by Michelozzi, *elegantis homo ingenii;* by Fra Giocondo, "not only the most meticulous but also indubitably the most expert of all mortals in ancient inscriptions and monuments"; even by the superannuated Landino, who had in his possession a valuable Donatus. The

[22] See Branca, *Poliziano,* pp. 182ff.; Perosa, *Mostra,* pp. 54–56 (no. 47); and N. G. Wilson, *From Byzantium to Italy: Greek Studies in the Italian Renaissance* (London, 1992), pp. 109–11.

[23] Vatican lat. 3867 with Branca, *Poliziano,* pp. 91ff.

[24] BMLF, Pluteo 45.15. See Perosa, *Mostra,* p. 31 (no. 15); and Rizzo, *Il lessico filologico,* pp. 128–30.

[25] Rizzo, *Il lessico filologico,* p. 129.

[26] Ibid., p. 86.

[27] See Branca, *Poliziano,* p. 100 n. 1; on Michelozzi, ibid., pp. 40–41, 74–75, 137; and see further below, p. 238.

[28] Ibid., pp. 182ff., 245–46.

[29] See L. A. Ciapponi, "Appunti per una biografia di Giovanni Giocondo da Verona," *IMU* 4 (1961): 131–58.

[30] See Momigliano, *Classical Foundations,* p. 70. Cf. above, p. 82.

range and status of his connections, as much as the antiquity of his evidence, buttress Poliziano's position; the network of the Medicean circle, its agents and its resources, lends support to his case. Clinched by appeal to *ratio et res ipsa* and linguistic examples, it had been pleaded publicly—before Modesti and other collaborators or pupils.

High culture placed beyond their reach, the burden of contrary proof is then passed to Poliziano's unequal opponents, who must find weightier testimonies and more telling arguments. "Ancient custom," enlisted on his side against "modern ignorance," is less an object of historical research than a weapon of adversarial intimidation. Privileged access to the libraries of popes and the collections of magnates enables this gentleman-scholar casually to gather, like seashells, treasures from which the *elementarii* are excluded. While they sweat in the schoolroom, he strolls on the beach. These plebeian pedants would be well advised to spell "Virgil" with an *e.*

. . . . .

A single syllable, an individual letter can establish a world of difference. Such is the message, both technical and intellectual, of *Miscellanea* 1 from the outset. The first chapter deals with Cicero's attribution to Aristotle of the word *endelechia*—'continuous action of the mind'—at *Tusculan Disputation* 1.22, which John Argyropoulos had criticized as inauthentic, proposing instead *entelechia* or "perfection."[31] Where and when his late teacher had voiced this view, Poliziano does not specify.[32] Such inexactness, coming from the alleged pioneer of precise citation, is suspicious. There is no sign that Argyropoulos's opinion on this subject had provoked, at the Florentine Studio between 1457 and 1489, the slightest ripple of controversy.[33] Seized upon by Poliziano, it becomes the occasion (or the pretext) for a "defense of Cicero from calumny." The advocate of classicism then mounts a case for the classic advocate against his modern detractors, postponing to the fourth chapter the programmatic statements that provide the motive and justification of his work. This should give pause. *Miscellanea* 1 opens not with the nocturnal lanterns of Aristophanes and Cleanthes but with the harsh lights of a show trial. It is worth inquiring why.

The personae of the advocate, the censor, and the gentleman are linked, in the first *Centuria,* by a complex cultural strategy. Philology provides the tactics with which the dramatis personae on Poliziano's stage are divided into friends and enemies. Lorenzo and Pico are the allies who occupy the limelight; other figures are marginal or relegated to the wings. The villain of the

[31] *Politiani Opera,* 1:224–30.

[32] The expression "dictitare ausus est," like the verbs *utebatur* and *aiebat,* is frequentative in sense and indicates lectures.

[33] See E. Garin, "'Ενδελέχεια e ἐντελέχεια," pp. 177–87.

piece is Domizio Calderini, supported by a large if anonymous cast of abecedarians, charlatans, and fools. Yet there are some who play an ambiguous part in this drama of exclusion—neither rank outsiders nor members of the elite. They fall between Poliziano's categories of eulogy and condemnation, and he is never more equivocal than when he seems to praise them. These men were his teachers. Landino provides one example; Argyropoulos another.

Argyropoulos, by a calculated symmetry, appears both at the beginning and at the end of *Miscellanea* 1. In the *coronis* Poliziano discusses his own philosophical interests. During his youth, he had been taught the subject by two "most excellent men," Ficino and Argyropoulos. Taste and inclination, however, had led him to prefer Homer. Yes, he had studied both Platonic and Aristotelian philosophy, but "with sleepy eyes" later opened by the arrival at Florence of that "singular fellow—or rather that hero, so richly endowed with every gift of fortune, physique, and intelligence," Pico della Mirandola. Pico has brains and beauty, memory and eloquence; he is "an expert in every branch of philosophy; he knows various literatures and languages; he has a comprehensive grasp of all the disciplines."[34] What Poliziano saw in Pico was a living embodiment of *enkyklios paideia*.

Those who need heroes cannot dispense with demons. Argyropoulos was not polished: he had a blunt manner, a thick accent, and a beard.[35] This had not prevented Poliziano, in his youth, from addressing to his teacher a flattering Greek epigram or receiving greetings of a honeyed cordiality that, in 1489, had become bile.[36] Argyropoulos, by then, was perceived as a threat, indirectly admitted in the first sentence of *Miscellanea* (1.1):

> Argyropoulos from Byzantium, once my philosophy teacher, was considered very learned, for he was by no means uninterested both in Latin literature and in the wisdom contained in the Decretals, and in all the disciplines that Martianus [Capella] calls cyclical.[37]

The reserve is evident from the style: "once ['long ago': *olim*] my teacher," "was considered" (*est habitus,* not *erat/fuit*), *minime incuriosus*—a double negative, the emphatic force of which, in Poliziano's subtle Latinity,[38] is less positive than the superlatives (*cumulatissimus, perspicacissimus, consultissimus*) showered on Pico.[39] Yet he and Argyropoulos are measured by the same standard, for the Greek, too, had been regarded as a proponent of *enkyklios paideia*.

[34] *Politiani Opera,* 1:697.

[35] See A. Field, *The Origins of the Platonic Academy of Florence* (Princeton, 1988), p. 109 and n. 10.

[36] See Zippel, *Storia e cultura,* pp. 195–96.

[37] "Argyropoulos ille Byzantinus, olim praeceptor in philosophia noster, cum litterarum Latiniarum minime incuriosus, tum sapientiae Decretorum, disciplinarumque adeo cunctarum, quae cyclicae a Martiano dicuntur, eruditissimus est habitus." *Politiani Opera,* 1:505.

[38] See above, p. 41.

[39] *Politiani Opera,* 1:697.

Argyropoulos, unlike Poliziano, did not found his version of that ideal on the study of grammar and literature. Inferior disciplines (for him), they were propaedeutic to ethics and natural science, mathematics and metaphysics.[40] Precedence was assigned by Argyropoulos to philosophy. Newly susceptible, as he concedes in the *coronis* of *Miscellanea* 1, to the claims of that subject, but wishing to establish his theory, formulated at chapter 4, that the *grammaticus* was the supreme exponent of *enkyklios paideia,* Poliziano found himself divided from his former tutor, in the Quattrocento *disputa delle arti,*[41] by a different approach to the same concept. That is why chapter 1—and not chapter 4—opens the *Miscellanea.* The *grammaticus* sets out to show that he, with philological methods, is the qualified interpreter of philosophical texts. Attacking Argyropoulos on his own grounds, Poliziano aims to demonstrate that he understood Aristotle more intimately than the leading Aristotelian of recent memory—to prove that he knew Greek better than this presumptuous Greek.

Presumptuousness, in Poliziano's eyes, was a characteristic of schoolmasters. Argyropoulos is accordingly represented as a humble *Graecus magister,* in contrast to the noble Cicero, "father and prince of Latin eloquence." The controversy is thus elevated (or inflated) into a clash of cultures. Between the classical Romans and the ancient Greeks, with whom Poliziano and Argyropoulos are respectively identified, there exists an abiding enmity. "They are unwilling to admit us Latins to the circle of those who share in their language and learning. They think that we possess the scrapings of Hellenism, its slices and its skin: they the fruit, the whole, and the core."[42] Confronted with the perennial arrogance of Greek scholarship, Poliziano, like "any Latin professor," has a duty to defend "Cicero's glory."

That entailed both refuting Argyropoulos and discrediting the Greek commentators upon whom he drew. Citing the later Latin authorities who had held Cicero in high regard, Poliziano abandons the hyper-classicism that characterizes his poetics and literary history[43] and enlists the aid not only of Boethius, Macrobius, and Augustine but also of Thomas Aquinas and Albert the Great—representatives of a scholasticism that he would later deplore as barbaric ignorance[44] but here hailed for their enlightened learning: "Good God, what men were these!" Illustrating with historical exempla how the Latin philosophical tradition, united in its esteem for Cicero, was no less rich or continuous than the Greek, Poliziano again adopts an advocate's proce-

[40] Field, *Origins,* p. 113. Cf. J. E. Seigel, "The Teaching of Argyropoulos and the Rhetoric of the First Humanists," in *Action and Conviction in Early Modern Europe: Essays in Memory of E. B. Harbison,* ed. T. K. Rabb and J. E. Seigel (Princeton, 1969), pp. 237–60.

[41] See Garin, ed., *La disputa delle arti.*

[42] "Vix enim dici potest, quam nos aliquando, id est, Latinos homines, in participatum suae linguae doctrinaeque non libenter admittit ista natio. Nos enim quisquilias tenere litterarum, se frugem: nos praesegmina, se corpus: nos putamina, se nucleum credit." *Politiani Opera,* 1:506.

[43] See above, pp. 56ff.

[44] See below, pp. 114ff.

dure that has been dismissed as "not strictly relevant to his case."[45] This is to miss its point and piquancy. For the *auctoritatum moles* amassed to plead in favor of Cicero is modeled on the same techniques with which "the prince of eloquence" had presented his own cases for the defense.[46]

Rhetorical arguments are now turned against the Greeks and their dubious legacy. Poliziano's next contention is not that Cicero had understood Aristotle's ideas correctly—this follows an account of the history of the text. And it is constructed in such a way that Cicero is made to intervene at a crucial stage in the transmission: after the alterations ineptly made by Apellicon (a bibliophile rather than a philosopher) to the already damaged works of Aristotle, following centuries of neglect by the declining Peripatus, but before Alexander of Aphrodisias, who flourished during the reign of the emperor Severus. Poliziano's sources are Strabo (13.609) and Plutarch (*Life of Sulla* 26).[47] No word of the list of Aristotle's writings by Diogenes Laertius (5.22ff.), which he knew and had studied attentively,[48] for it might have complicated a picture consistently unfavorable to Greek scholarship. Only when Sulla conquered Athens and transferred the books to Rome could a new edition be prepared by Tyrannicon and Andronicus.[49] Naturally Cicero did not use their work, for "what was to prevent him" from resorting to the archetype—"if not uncorrupt," then merely defiled by Apellicon's scribbles? The thought here is the same as that which animates chapter 77: the earliest reconstructible state of the text is employed to assert the priority and (therefore) the superiority of Cicero. Attributing—on no evidence—manuscript research to the "prince of eloquence," Poliziano fashions him in his own image.

If this hypothesis does not satisfy his readers, he offers a second: Plato, in the *Phaedrus,* describes the soul in perpetual motion; why should Cicero, like subsequent interpreters, have not assumed that Aristotle shared his view? Is not Pico working day and night on a *Concord of Plato and Aristotle*? Another sleight of hand, for Argyropoulos's discussion of the source and its context is never fully reported by Poliziano. According to him, his teacher had merely

[45] Wilson, *From Byzantium to Italy,* p. 105.

[46] For the theory, cf. *De oratore* 1.20, 2.51, and *Orator* 120, 132, cf. for the practice (e.g.), *Pro Archia poeta* 3.4–7, *In Verrem,* 2.4. See H. Schoenberger, "Beispiele aus der Geschichte, ein rhetorisches Kunstmittel in Ciceros Reden," diss. phil. Erlangen, 1910, pp. 13ff.; H. W. Litchfield, "National Exempla Virtutis in Roman Literature," *Harvard Studies in Classical Philology* 25 (1914): 27ff.; and von Moos, *Geschichte als Topik,* p. 624 (s.v., with bibliography).

[47] See I. Düring, *Aristotle in the Ancient Biographical Tradition* (Göteborg, 1957), pp. 382, 392–95; and cf. A.-H. Chroust, "The Miraculous Disappearance and Recovery of the Corpus Aristotelicum," *Classica et mediaevalia* 23 (1962): 50–67.

[48] See above, p. 57, and P. Moraux, *Les listes anciennes des ouvrages d'Aristote* (Louvain, 1951), pp. 312–13.

[49] Düring, *Aristotle,* pp. 412–25, and idem, "Notes on the Transmission of Aristotle's Writings," *Acta Universitatis Gotoburgensis (Göteborgs Högskolas Årsskrift)* 54 (1950): 66–70.

affirmed that *entelechia* was "the more Aristotelian word"; that Cicero had been deceived by its verbal similarity to *endelechia;* and that Peripatetic usage proved him wrong.

Adducing later exegetes whom, on grounds of their lateness, he had previously disqualified, Cicero's defender refrains from spelling out the implication of his mode of reasoning: that the Roman philosopher understood Aristotle better than the Greek Aristotelian tradition, because he interpreted him Platonically. Instead, conjecture props up conjecture, punctuated by demands for negative proof ("What was to prevent him . . .?" "Why should he not . . .?"), and Cicero's authority, less established than asserted with a row of favorable epithets, is shakily supported by that of Pico's unfinished work. With these "historical methods," the "most noble lion" of Latin culture is protected from the "baying of the hounds of the lamp"—from "that nation" of Greeks which included Aristotle, whose text Poliziano reveres, and Argyropoulos, whose memory he damns.

. . . . .

The elimination of rivals and the trouncing of critics are effected, in the first *Centuria,* with the materials of a philologist and the means of an advocate. Playing, often simultaneously, the roles of counsel both for the prosecution and for the defense, Poliziano contemplated the ancient world with a litigious vision formed by Quattrocento controversies. This had the drawbacks of partisanship but also real advantages, making the *Miscellanea* actual and engaged. "It is not right," he declared in a stirring sentence from their preface, "to renew things that have practically died out, unless they have not merely continued to mature but are capable of being re-established on an entirely new basis."[50]

That basis was exclusive. The contents of the *Miscellanea,* which could be discussed with Lorenzo on horseback,[51] were not on offer to the *populus.* Reserved for the elite, for the study and lecture room, they were withheld from the marketplace and council chamber.[52] Writing to Poliziano soon after the publication of the first *Centuria,* Marco Lucido Fazzini, bishop of Segna, described him as "absolutely Latinate," "one of the very few—that is to say, the most learned—not the mass of minor *littérateurs,* assistant teachers, and the mob."[53] Music to Poliziano's ears, inspiring him to resound in a higher

[50] "Nec enim renovare sit probum, quae iam pene exolerunt, si modo haec ipsa non vetustescere adhuc, sed veterascere de integro possint." *Politiani Opera,* 1:213.

[51] Ibid.

[52] "Non se populo venditant, sed paucis modo paratur," "Nos ista certe non foro et curiae, sed cubiculo et scholae paravimus." Ibid., p. 214.

[53] "Te plane Latinum esse iudico," "Politanus paucorum—id est doctissimorum—est, non turbae literatulorum ac paedagogorum et vulgi." Ibid., p. 81.

key: "I am not one of those," he replied to Fazzini, "who will allow that the Latin language has largely come to a halt because everyone fears the ignorance of the common herd."[54]

A teleology is thus entailed by Poliziano's exclusiveness, linking him to the great authors of the past and licensing his liberty in the present. At stake is the recurrent theme of authority: both his own and that of his critics. They are represented in the preface to *Miscellanea* 1 as "intestine torturers" and "stage-show censors."[55] "That name was most odious to him," Poliziano insincerely assured Iacopo Antiquario, who had objected to the abuse leveled at Calderini in the first *Centuria*. "'Censor' is the apt term for his enemies; he eschews that invidious title, preferring to be compared with the ancient poets who slaughtered one another in gladiatorial contests of literature, while the people called for encores."[56] "The people" are those whom, in its preface, Poliziano had ruled out from the readership of his work; and the censorial authority that his letter to Antiquario demurs is what he claims in *Miscellanea* 1.

The premise for such a claim was cultural continuity. Heir of Cicero, beneficiary of the Latin heritage and interpreter of the Greek, Poliziano stationed himself on a par with the ancients, not beneath them. The teleology of the *Miscellanea* leads directly to their author from the most elevated reaches of classical scholarship and letters; and the assumption of equality is borne out in his practice, which unites exegesis with poetry. How, is illustrated by *Miscellanea* 1.80,[57] where Poliziano offers an interpretation of "a little-known story about Tiresias and Pallas, in which the meaning of Propertius [4.9.57–58] is revealed."[58] A similar tale is told by the Egyptian Abammon in a letter to the philosopher Porphyry. Proclus, however, attributes the epistle to Iamblichus. This is why Virgil writes, "Look not back" [*Eclogue* 8.102], and why Odysseus is given a similar warning by Homer's Leucothea [*Odyssey* 5.350].

All of which is, strictly speaking, nonsense. Ficino, in the preface to his translation of Iamblichus's *De mysteriis,* writes simply that the philosopher "introducit vero Porphyrio respondentem Abamonem Aegyptum sacerdotem pro Anebo discipulo suo, ad quem Porphyrium misit epistolam."[59] About Abammon and his real or attributed works, neither Poliziano nor his

[54] "Non . . . ex eorum sum numero, qui cessare linguam Latinam magna ex parte patiuntur, dum quisque illa reformidat, quae vulgo hactenus ignorata sunt." Ibid., p. 82.

[55] "Ceu tortor intestinus iugiter excruciat," "censores pulpitarii." Ibid., p. 489.

[56] Ibid., pp. 89–90.

[57] Cf. Grafton, *Joseph Scaliger,* 1:36–37; and Wilson, *From Byzantium to Italy,* pp. 107–8.

[58] *Politiani Opera,* 1:649.

[59] *Marsilii Ficini Opera Omnia,* 2.2:1878 (= p. 873). For context, see B. P. Copenhaver, "Iamblichus, Synesius and the Chaldean Oracles in Marsilio Ficino's *De vita libri tres:* Hermetic Magic or Neoplatonic Magic?" in *Supplementum Festivum: Studies in Honor of P. O. Kristeller,* ed. J. Hankins et al. (Binghamton, N.Y., 1987), pp. 448ff.

contemporaries had any further information. They knew, however, that Homer and Virgil had lived long before the Neoplatonists, and were therefore in a position to note this deliberate reversal of chronology. It occurs before Poliziano prints the Greek text of *The Bath of Pallas,* accompanied by a stylish and faithful translation, in order to demonstrate Propertius's dependence on Callimachus.[60] Ironically introduced by this spoof on source-criticism, the Greek and Latin poems are situated not in a historical context but in a timeless zone of themes and motifs, where Poliziano ranges freely from the past to the present.

In the present, center stage is assigned to his own works. An antichronological approach, which his philology here shares with his poetics and literary history,[61] enables him to cite the motif of Teiresias as it occurs in his *Ambra* and *Nutricia.* Confidently placed in a line of succession from the ancient *poetae docti,* the Quattrocento Callimachus presents his own verse as worthy to bear comparison with any specimen of classical literature. In this period of transition from a manuscript culture to one of the printed book, however, a borderland existed between the public and private domains; and it was necessary to admonish his readers to observe his authorial rights:

> You should know that this is *my* interpretation; it stemmed from me before it surfaced in anyone's commentary, as the same *Sylvae* that I have quoted—made public (*editae*) many years previously—will prove. The second of them I expounded publicly a long time ago before packed crowds, with numerous note-takers. Let, therefore, what I have created belong to me, as it should.[62]

Fear of stolen thunder motivates such sentences. The *Ambra* had been printed probably in 1485; the *Nutricia* were not to issue from the press until 1491. What, then, did Poliziano mean by describing as "tot abhinc annos edita" a poem that, on 11 July 1486, his pupil, Girolamo da Panzano, had characterized as "nondum . . . edita"?[63] Girolamo alluded to publication. His teacher referred to lectures, in which he had expounded the *Nutricia* before large audiences that had taken all-too-serviceable notes. Both therefore drew on distinct senses of the ambiguous verb *edere,*[64] and both were telling the

[60] See Wilson, *From Byzantium to Italy,* p. 108, and, on the typography, J. Irigoin, *Les débuts de la typographie grecque* (Paris, 1992), pp. 30–31.

[61] See p. 66.

[62] "Illud item scito est opus, nostrum hoc esse interpretamentum et a nobis denique fluxisse prius quam in ullius commentariis ebulliret, quod et *Sylvae* per se ipsae, quas citavimus, *tot abhinc annos editae* probabunt, quarum videlicet alteram magno sumus olim conventu publice multis excipientibus interpretati. Sit ergo nostri iuris, quod nostri fuit muneris." *Politiani Opera,* 1:652.

[63] See Branca, *Poliziano,* p. 75.

[64] For this sense of *edere,* see Rizzo, *Il lessico filologico,* pp. 312–13. Cf. Godman, "Poliziano's Poetics," p. 121 and n. 39.

truth—a truth that indicates how jealously, how defensively, Poliziano regarded the diffusion of his writings before they appeared in print.

. . . . .

That theme recurs frequently in *Miscellanea* 1, and provides a key to understanding the character and function of the work. Before sending it to press, its author had been assailed by doubts. Accused of plagiarism, Poliziano had to restrain himself from leveling the same charge against others. Suspiciously similar to *Centuria prima,* the *Annotationes centum* by Filippo Beroaldo of Bologna had come out in 1488, and the same year a rumor had spread that Poliziano had lifted, from the unpublished *Cornucopiae* of Niccolò Perotti,[65] the entire contents of his own book. Part of this problem was solved by the appearance, in 1489, of the *Cornucopiae.* Now everyone could see, Poliziano smugly reflected, that what divided him from Perotti was thicker than the wall that had separated Pyramus and Thisbe.

So the *coronis.*[66] Strikingly, it attributes the rumor of plagiarism from Perotti not to Poliziano's enemies but to his friends. He had shown a draft of *Miscellanea* 1 to *aliquot amici* and they, or those to whom they had spoken ("non satis certo auctore"), had concocted a fictive line of transmission. Poliziano, they gossiped, had got hold of a manuscript of the *Cornucopiae* via Lorenzo de' Medici, who had exercised pressure on Federico da Montefeltro, duke of Urbino. To this imaginative constructor of textual histories, malice had attached an imaginary construction in his own style, reducing his high ideal of *enkyklios paideia* to the humbler level of Perotti's encyclopedic compilation. Malevolent this tittle-tattle may have been, but it was not stupid. It caricatured Poliziano's method, pilloried his purpose, and revealed much about the atmosphere in which he believed he was operating.

Belief is not always identical with truth, yet Poliziano had grounds for his opinion. False friendship is the subject that links his open dismissal of Perotti in the *coronis* with a subdued critique of Beroaldo. "A great friend of mine," declared Poliziano, "not inexpert in these matters, a competent man of letters, who mentions my name not without goodwill and kindness." Again, double negatives voice apparent conciliation. It was needed, because Poliziano was convinced that Beroaldo had drawn on interpretations of Statius and Horace that he had advanced, years before, in his lectures. Professing a generous readiness to overlook these correspondences, in private he boiled with rage. "[Beroaldo] has lifted this from my pupils' notes!" "Patently plagiarized!" "Superfluous, as usual!" "This is my opinion, not his!" "He hasn't read Plutarch!": These are among the indignant remarks made on the *An-*

[65] On Perotti, see the contributions gathered in *Res Publica Litterarum: Studies in the Classical Tradition,* vol. 4 (1980).

[66] *Politiani Opera,* 1:695–98.

notationes centum in the seclusion of Poliziano's study.[67] Only an urbane echo of this fury filtered through to the *coronis:* "Pereant," Donatus had observed, "qui ante nos nostra dixerunt." Poliziano is willing to say the opposite, if only due credit is given and priority acknowledged, so that "not everything be shared between friends."

The insistence on honest and exact attribution, like the apparent precision with which histories of texts are traced in *Miscellanea* 1, represents more than academic principles of research applied to the literature of the ancient world. It reflects the circumstances in which Poliziano wrote his book, the state of mind in which it was brought out. In 1489 he was, on the strength of his few publications, far less well-established than Beroaldo.[68] The first *Centuria* is thick with references to the three previous *Sylvae,* because they were the only writings (apart from his account of the Pazzi conspiracy) by this no longer young man in a hurry that had hitherto passed through the press. In Poliziano's eyes, the *Nutricia*—known but not yet printed—resembled conjectures and interpretations that, against his will, had entered the public domain. They occupied a limbo that he was disposed to regard as infernal. This is why *Miscellanea* 1, traditionally regarded as a monument to the Renaissance's written culture, offers such eloquent testimony to the oral tradition of Poliziano's work-in-progress.

Chronicling the evolution of his ideas, he explains their origins in lecture courses or impromptu lessons, and adduces witnesses who will vouch for the trustworthiness of his procedure. Only once does Poliziano temper an otherwise defensive tone. At chapter 68 he states that his famous proposal of *Calybon* in Catullus 66.48 had been diffused prior to publication, because Pico had leaked it, "as he knows . . . and freely admits." Pico and Poliziano are, beside the dedicatee Lorenzo, the heroes of *Centuria prima.* If their names do not appear in the *Index auctorum,* it is because, confined to ancient sources and modeled on Pliny,[69] that manifesto of *enkyklios paideia* is organized according to languages, subjects, and categories that the duumvirate transcends. Partner in Poliziano's enterprise of reconquering the realms of integrated learning, Pico is at least the equal of the Greeks and Romans.[70] He initates his companion into "the sacred precincts" of Hebrew at chapter 14; he is a guide to the secrets of philosophy in the *coronis* and at chapter 90 (where Barbaro and Girolamo Donà momentarily enlarge the alliance); he is about to

[67] Edited and discussed by Lo Monaco, "Poliziano e Beroaldo," pp. 103–65.

[68] Ibid., p. 105.

[69] "Enimvero ne putent homines maleferiati nos ista, quaeque sunt, de faece hausisse neque grammaticorum transiluisse lineas, Pliniano statim exemplo nomina praetexuimus autorum, sed honestorum veterumque duntaxat, unde ius ista sumunt, et a quibus versuram fecimus." *Politiani Opera,* 1:488.

[70] Ibid., p. 492, with the quotation "Cedite Romani scriptores, cedite Graii" from Propertius 2.34.65.

complete his *Concord of Plato and Aristotle* and his *Heptaplus* (chapters 1 and 4). *Miscellanea* 1 announces a common and continuing project, which required a novel form.

That form—open-ended, flexible, and extensible—has been viewed as a breakthrough in the history of scholarship.[71] The first *Centuria,* it is true, amounts to more than an edition or commentary. But it also represents less. Less in terms of Poliziano's own ambitions, for, while recovering intellectual property stolen by others and pledging more to come, he was exploiting the advantages of a selectivity that enabled him to gloss over what, in 1489, he had failed to accomplish. By then he had abandoned earlier hopes of producing the edition of Catullus[72] that, in 1473, at the age of eighteen, he had planned with the ambition of youth. Convinced that, by conjecture, he had restored most of the corrupt text to soundness, he recorded the triumph in the subscription to his copy of the *editio princeps.* Twelve years later, after further efforts, adolescent confidence had given way to mature doubts. "Today I do not approve of many of my corrections. . . . A number of them . . . deserve to be erased." Still more uncertain is a letter to Alessandro and Lattanzio Cortesi of 1486. They had heard that Poliziano had written a commentary on Catullus. No, no, he demurred. "Some marginalia were quite useful . . . but not yet worth publishing."

So it was that, three years before the appearance of the first *Centuria,* by the familiar route of acquaintances and rumor, Poliziano became aware that the learned public had associated a Catullan commentary with his name. The problem had been further complicated by the publication, in 1485, of Antonio Parthenio's commented edition and by others' appropriation of conjectures and interpretations that Poliziano regarded as his own.[73] Taken together with his marginalia to incunables of Quintilian and Ovid,[74] his notes on the *editio princeps* reflect a prolonged attempt, over many years, both to improve the text and to interpret its place in Roman literary history, which circumstances and self-criticism had drawn to a close. Yet Catullus remained a sensitive part of Poliziano's intellectual biography, and writing about the poet in the first *Centuria,* he is at his most autobiographical.

In 1473, when he was making his first Catullan emendations, Domizio Calderini visited Florence. *Miscellanea* 1.19 reports that, on hearing Poliziano's explanation of poem 84, the elder scholar declared that "he had learned more from a single student on that day than from any professor in many previous years."[75] In chapter 9, before refuting Calderini's opinions on

[71] Grafton, *Joseph Scaliger,* 1:22ff.

[72] Valuable discussion by Gaisser, *Catullus and His Renaissance Readers,* pp. 42ff., on which the next paragraph draws.

[73] Ibid., pp. 43–44, 69.

[74] See Godman, "Poliziano's Poetics," pp. 130ff. with notes.

[75] *Politiani Opera,* 1:548.

a point of geographical interpretation, Poliziano had assassinated his character: "*Nimium sui . . . admirator,* a captious quibbler whenever the opportunity arose, convinced of his own superiority and contemptuous of others."[76] This thumbnail sketch amounts to an inadvertent self-portrait, inspired by resemblances between the two men that were too close for comfort. The Roman philologist had gained patronage from the Medici that their Florentine protégé coveted; Calderini had published commentaries on authors, such as Ovid and Statius, to whom Poliziano had devoted attention that had not yet been immortalized in print; and—embarrassingly—there was also the small matter of that epitaph composed by him, some nine years earlier, on his present bête noire. Still more embarrassing, had their author recognized it, is the contradiction between his chapters 9 and 19. The nineteenth demonstrates (against the ninth) that Calderini was an admirer not only of himself but also of Poliziano. By the modest and self-effacing standards of *Miscellanea* 1, the judgment of this miscreant had therefore been impeccable—at least once.

There lay the rub. Chapter 19 passes directly from events of 1473, when Calderini had praised Poliziano for work on Catullus that he had never finished, to those of 1480. Then his eulogist, dead for two years, had not been forgotten or forgiven. The chronology of this ambivalent enmity is significant, because it shapes Poliziano's autobiographical narrative at chapter 19, determining what he chooses to recount and what he prefers to omit. One rainy day in the spring of 1480, he relates, he had taken shelter in a shop at Verona, Catullus's birthplace, where he had entertained himself and a crowd of onlookers by explaining "almost the entire works" of the poet. Neither the choice of author nor the emphasis on the completeness of the exposition, at this date, was fortuitous. After visiting Verona, Poliziano went to Torri del Benaco, on Lake Garda, where he inspected Calderini's books.[77] That symbolic pilgrimage from the scene of his triumph as a Catullan interpreter to the place where his epitaph was inscribed on his rival's tomb is suppressed from chapter 19.

Laying Calderini's ghost to uneasy rest and asserting himself as the prime exegete of Catullus were linked with the issue of plagiarism in Poliziano's obsessive mind. He craved total recognition—more than that won by any competitor or filched by any imitator—and it had been provided by his audience in Verona, which had marveled at his erudition. Yet the praise, even then, was not wholly disinterested. The throng had included a descendant of Dante and—"unless I am mistaken"—Battista Guarino. Poliziano knew he was not mistaken, for Battista's son, Alessandro, attributed to his father the interpretation of the aspirates in Catullus 84 that appears at *Miscellanea*

[76] Ibid., p. 524.

[77] See R. Weiss, "In memoriam Domitii Calderini," *IMU* 3 (1960): 315–16.

1.19.[78] Baccio Ugolino, among others, had been present to witness this spectacle. He had heard Angelo applauded as "an angel sent from heaven."

The implied affidavit recalls the role of Jacopo Modesti at chapter 77 and the other friends or students to whom manuscript evidence had been shown. Chapter 44 insists that "an ancient commentary in Lombard letters" had been displayed "publicly" to Poliziano's lecture audience.[79] "Publicly," in 1480 and 1481, he had advanced interpretations of Statius's *Sylvae* and Ovid's *Fasti,* it is affirmed in chapter 58, at a point where Calderini's name recurs.[80] To a "public audience" at the Florentine Studio, the same course on Ovid, with the same date, and one on Horace's *Satires* had been offered, according to the *coronis*. There the unnamed but identifiable addressee is Beroaldo.[81] And if, at chapter 68, Pico had leaked an emendation that had become "common currency" (*pervulgatam*), he would "willingly" confirm its authorship.[82] (At whose prompting, it is superfluous to ask.) Testimonials, documents, and dates confirm the sequence of Poliziano's studies, establishing a retrospective authority that he wrests from Calderini and others. Treating himself like an archetype, damaged in transmission, he reconstructs his original readings, correcting transgressions in the past and menacing punishment for the future. The very title of his work—*Centuria prima*—contains both a promise and a threat: more might be meted out to "the crows and the vultures" that "feed from the corpses when the eagle is sated."[83] Never sated with vendetta, Poliziano perceived, eagle-eyed, a danger at every turn—from false friends and unscrupulous enemies, from plagiarists and pedants, from ex-teachers and indiscreet pupils, from The Conspiracy Of Persons Known And Unknown Who Denied The Angel Sent From Heaven.[84]

. . . . .

On earth, *Miscellanea* 1 was received with enthusiasm by some, criticism by others, and irony by one. The singular Nicolò Leoniceno, professor at Ferrara, was both a philologist of note and a medical scholar of distinction.[85] He was also perhaps the most convincing physician of the Italian Renaissance because, following a regime prescribed by himself, he lived to the age of 96. A militant exponent of Hellenism, Leoniceno led a crusade against

[78] Gaisser, *Catullus and His Renaissance Readers,* p. 69.

[79] *Politiani Opera,* 1:592.

[80] See ibid., p. 618.

[81] Ibid., p. 694.

[82] Ibid., p. 636.

[83] Ibid., p. 549.

[84] Cf. the epigram on Poliziano, with the same pun, by Giovanni Crasso in Angelo Ambrogini Poliziano, *Prose volgari inedite e poesie* (ed. Del Longo), p. 182.

[85] On Leoniceno's life, work, and connections, see Mugnai Carrara, "Profilo di Nicolò Leoniceno," pp. 169–212.

the "barbarians" of the Arabo-Latin tradition of medieval medicine.[86] On friendly terms with Pico, with whom he saw eye to eye on astrology, similarly insisting on the primacy of content over form,[87] Leoniceno was also in contact with Battista Guarino, whose humanism included the natural sciences and philosophy;[88] and Guarino had passed to him Poliziano's gift of *Miscellanea* 1. When Leoniceno wrote his letter of thanks, in February 1490,[89] it was with the familiarity of mutual acquaintances and with a related but different conception of scholarship.

Poliziano's senior by a quarter of a century, Leoniceno occupied a more prestigious chair. Professors of theoretical and practical medicine like him, who often taught philosophy, were capable of commanding higher salaries and status than their colleagues in the arts.[90] Sensitive to his humbler rank in the hierarchy of learning, Poliziano, at the time Leoniceno wrote, was seeking to improve it, by taking advantage of an opportunity provided by the change in his formal position at Florence a year before the publication of the first *Centuria*. In 1488, his contract had been altered, allowing him to teach whatever he chose.[91] He now aimed to annex the superior subjects, elevating the lowly *grammaticus* into a high priest of *enkyklios paideia*. How Leoniceno reacted to the claims advanced in his book, was not indifferent to this ambitious intellectual in the winter of 1490.

The reaction from Ferrara was urbane, its tone delicately *de haut en bas*. The first *Centuria* had given him pleasure, wrote Leoniceno, because it had enabled him to return to the *studia humanitatis* that he had relished during his youth.[92] Wryly reminding Poliziano of the propaedeutic function of the *artes* that he professed, the exponent of more elevated disciplines then reassured him that, with *Miscellanea* 1, he felt at home in a wider world: "I found things that are not only of great benefit to the study of literature, poetry, and oratory but also much that is pertinent to medicine and philosophy." This allusion to *Miscellanea* 1.4 was then capped by a reference to the *coronis*. "You learned (as you write) Platonic and Aristotelian philosophy from excellent teachers in your youth. Now you have Pico. With his guidance you will, in short order, achieve the same eminence in philosophy that you have already won in literature." So much for Poliziano's polemic against Argyropoulos.

86 Mugnai Carrara, *La biblioteca di Nicolò Leoniceno,* pp. 16ff.

87 Cf. Pico, *Disputationes* 1.1 (ed. E. Garin), pp. 61–63. Cf. pp. 34–36 above.

88 E. Garin in *Ritratti di umanisti* (Florence, 1967), p. 73. Cf. Grafton and Jardine, *From Humanism to the Humanities,* pp. 1–28.

89 *Politiani Opera,* 1:37–38.

90 See Kristeller, "Philosophy and Medicine," pp. 431–42; N. Siraisi, *Arts and Sciences at Padua: The Studium of Padua Before 1350* (Toronto, 1973); and P. Kibre, "Arts and Medicine in the Universities of the Late Middle Ages," in *Les Universités à la fin du Moyen Age,* Actes du congrès international de Louvain, ed. J. Paquet and I. IJsewijn (Louvain, 1978), pp. 213–27.

91 Verde, *Studio,* 2:26–9.

92 *Politiani Opera,* 1:37.

Leoniceno's double-edged compliment insinuated that the aspiring philosopher had fallen short of his professed goal. In an elegant echo of Poliziano's own words, it suggested that, if Argyropoulos's critic had profited little from his former tutor, he should turn to Pico, skeptic of the verbal arts. Closing his letter with compliments to Lorenzo and Piero de' Medici, this intimate of the younger man's allies at Florence could afford the luxury of understated condescension.

The angel from heaven had met his match. Leoniceno could be neither denigrated nor ignored. Regarding philology as instrumental,[93] he was not disposed to accept its claims to be the foundation of *enkyklios paideia*. What interested the professor of medicine about the first *Centuria* was its contribution to his own fields of endeavor. That, he implied, could be greater. Poliziano was compelled to take this view seriously because Leoniceno's subject, together with philosophy, was an essential component of the ideal of an integrated culture, as defined by himself. Writing back, he acknowledged his correspondent's case, admired his translation of Galen, and declared: "Your congratulations that I have dedicated myself wholly to philosophy have filled me with good hope. I shall persevere, since I have had success with the specimen that I have offered to the public."[94] Pico would help him in an undertaking that he knew to be incomplete, but that he regarded optimistically. To what extent was that optimism justified? How far did Poliziano's ideas change, during the last four years of his life, in response to the demands of medicine and philosophy?

. . . . .

Philosophy, especially the thought of Aristotle, is viewed in *Miscellanea* 1 from the perspective of the Latin tradition.[95] Greek writers on medicine appear at the margins of the first *Centuria,* incidentally cited in support of non-medical arguments.[96] Yet Poliziano had already begun to interest himself in this field and in the related one of Greek botany before 1489. From the physician Paolo dal Pozzo Toscanelli he had bought manuscripts of Galen in 1487;[97] he had annotated excerpts from Dioscorides and other authors during the same and subsequent years;[98] and he had even produced a translation

[93] See N. W. Gilbert, *Renaissance Concepts of Method* (New York, 1960), pp. 102–4; W. F. Edwards, "Niccolò Leoniceno and the Origins of Humanistic Discussion of Method," in *Philosophy and Humanism: Renaissance Essays in Honour of P. O. Kristeller,* ed. E. P. Mahoney (Leiden, 1976), pp. 283–305; and D. Mugnai Carrara, "Una polemica umanistico-scolastica," pp. 31–57.

[94] *Politiani Opera,* 1:38–39.

[95] See p. 87 above.

[96] E.g., *Miscellanea* 1.34 and 38 (Galen), 50 (Dioscorides and Paul of Aegina), 61 (Dioscorides).

[97] See A. Perosa, "Codici di Galeno," pp. 75–76. See further below, p. 205.

[98] Ibid., pp. 79ff. Cf. Hill Cotton, "Materia medica nel Poliziano,"in *Il Poliziano e il suo tempo,* pp. 237–45; and idem, "Frosino Bonini," pp. 157–75.

of Galen and Hippocrates, now lost. Pico approved of it, wrote Poliziano to Lorenzo on 5 June 1490, when the *bella cosa et utile* was almost complete. What he now needed was the opinion of an expert, and he should be grateful if Lorenzo's doctor, Pier Leone, would cast an eye over the work.[99] Among the papers found after Poliziano's death was an incomplete commentary on Galen's *Aphorisms,* and his library contained no less than fourteen medical manuscripts. What particularly concerned him, he explained in his letter to Lorenzo, was the difficult problem of Latin equivalents for technical terminology in Greek. That was one of the subjects that, with mounting intensity, he pursued between 1490 and 1494 in response to the challenge issued by Leoniceno.

If much united the two scholars, more divided them. The rhetoric of a crusade against "barbarism," for example, they shared but employed differently. When Leoniceno inveighed against the "barbarian" Averroes and medieval medicine,[100] Poliziano could express sincere agreement. When the professor at Ferrara extended his criticisms to include Pliny, a canonical and popular author among literary humanists, his colleague at Florence recoiled. Having declared himself, in *Miscellanea* 1, the advocate of Latin learning, Poliziano had sought to prove that any notion of its inferiority to Greek was unfounded. Leoniceno was doubly disquieting to him because he not only asserted the priority of Hellenistic botany and medicine but also argued that Pliny was dependent upon them. This argument in the stemmatic spirit of the first *Centuria* seemed to conclude by equating an *auctor* of classical antiquity with an Arabic "barbarian" on the strength of a specialist competence to which mere *grammatici*—like Poliziano—could not pretend. Leoniceno was a famous teacher and trainer of physicians. He insisted that Greek botanical and medical literature should not be treated as an object of philological study but applied to the cure of disease. Poliziano, who had stylized a clash of cultures in his book, was now faced with a real one. The ensuing controversy with Leoniceno over Pliny led him to restate some of his most entrenched convictions.

Their debate began in correspondence. Leoniceno had censured, in a lost letter, Pliny's confusion of the Greek *kissos* ('ivy') and *kisthos* ('rock-rose') with the Latin *hedera.* Similarity of names, he asserted, had led to errors of fact; the rich ambiguity of Greek technical terms was leveled into false homonyms by the Latin encyclopedist. Poliziano would have none of this, sensing from the first the personal implication of Leoniceno's reasoning. He appeared to regard Pliny as a kind of inept philologist, tinkering with words and ignorant of empirical research. Hence, in Poliziano's reply,[101] an echo of Petrarch's polemic against *medici*[102] ("Health is more at risk from doctors than

[99] Poliziano, *Prose volgari inedite e poesie,* p. 77. On Pier Leone, see above, p. 26.

[100] For context, see N. Siraisi, *Avicenna in Renaissance Italy,* pp. 67ff.

[101] *Politiani Opera,* 1:40–44.

[102] See above, p. 10.

from disease"), coupled with a grammarian's insistence on exact interpretation. What interested him was less the observation of nature than the punctuation of Pliny's text. Poliziano drew attention to a parallel from Ovid, discussed the relationship of the *Historia naturalis* to the work of Theophrastus, and admonished his correspondent: "I should be glad, Leoniceno, not to see a Latin author tarred with the same brush as the barbarians. Pliny's authority is to be taken very seriously. You should either abandon the attempt or assail him more powerfully."

The counsel of caution fell on deaf ears. Leoniceno took the offensive in a tract that, published in 1492 under the polemical title *De Plinii . . . erroribus,* opened a campaign that he was to continue into the next century. Recurring to the theme of his first letter of congratulation, he sharpened its sting: "I do not think that the common if heretical opinion applies to you, that a man of eloquence is incapable of judging other disciplines."[103] Having evoked the specter of professional incompetence, Leoniceno combined flattery of Poliziano with blame of the writer whom he defended: a parasite of Dioscorides, the foremost authority on the subject of medicinal herbs and simples, Pliny was responsible only for the introduction of original error and should be demoted to the same grade as the Arab Serapion. Had not Ermolao Barbaro, "a great expert in all the disciplines," been preparing a work that Leoniceno hoped would uncover Pliny's "innumerable errors," he would list them at greater length.

The factual truth of Leoniceno's attack on Pliny[104] was less material, to his opponents, than the realignment in the categories of learning advocated by his work. For *De Plinii . . . erroribus* 1 argues that not only the humanists but also contemporary doctors, who derived their knowledge of simples from Serapion, had misunderstood the *Historia naturalis*. Both stationed its author among the grammarians and orators, not the philosophers and physicians, and in consequence, modern medics did not consider him worth reading. The right conclusion, thought Leoniceno, for the wrong reasons. Pliny should be removed from his pedestal and seen for what he was: a confused compiler of natural science, a muddler of information derived from the Greeks. Thus placing the *Historia naturalis* on the same level occupied by a *codex descriptus* in Poliziano's textual criticism, Leoniceno then drew the radical conclusion that Pliny should be eliminated: confounding one type of germander (*polion*) with another kind of maritime plant (*tripolion*), he repre-

[103] P. 2ª. All references are to the successive versions of Leoniceno's work in the edition published at Ferrara in 1509. The first tract was published in 1958, with a useful introduction (and an unreliable text), by L. Premuda.

[104] On Pliny's medical information, see V. Nutton, "The Perils of Patriotism: Pliny and Roman Medicine," in *Science in the Early Roman Empire,* ed. R. French (London, 1986), pp. 30–58 (= Nutton, *From Democedes to Harvey,* pp. 30–58), and R. French, *Ancient Natural History: Histories of Nature* (London, 1995), pp. 223–25. Cf. P. Mudry, "La Médécine romaine: Mythe et réalité," *Gesnerus* 47 (1990): 133–48.

sented a danger to public health.[105] Far more useful and impressive was Galen, who, in order to ascertain the difference between two Lemnian herbs, had traveled to the island of Lemnos, gaining experience that the Latin bookworm failed to acquire.[106] Pliny could not grasp distinctions that, in the garden, were plain to see then as now.[107] Ancient Greek botany and medicine provided a reliable guide, but the present degenerate age was too absorbed in "garrulous and sophistical disputations" to open its eyes.[108] Dedicating his work to Poliziano, Leoniceno defined the point at issue as "not fleeting words but things on which the health and survival of mankind depends."[109]

From the contrast between *verba* and *res,* form and content, previously drawn by Pico,[110] a new theory of knowledge began to emerge. Its basis was not verbal, for the arts of language were subordinated, in *De Plinii . . . erroribus* 1, to observation of an unchanging nature. Even Dioscorides and the other Greek fonts of pure truth whom Leoniceno preferred to tainted Latin sources had to be verified by empirical practice. The Hellenism that he so vehemently asserted therefore remained, in his thought, a means to an end, reached by clearing from the path of progress obstacles erected by later tradition. If philology, for Leoniceno, was a vehicle, medicine was his goal: not an academic pastime of the ivory tower, but the applied—the supreme—science of life.

Philological humanism at Florence was confronted with an assault that threatened to topple the structure of *enkyklios paideia* that Poliziano was beginning to build. Not by chance, in the academic year 1489–90, he offered a private course on Pliny. A different, more public defense of this author was now needed, and the *grammaticus* sought assistance from Pandolfo Collenuccio—diplomat, politician, orator, and jurist.[111] The legal profession enabled Collenuccio to assume the mask of the feigned innocent. He was *supra partes,* he asserted (while actually remaining beneath them): "Not a professor of eloquence or of medicine, but the most illiterate man of letters, as jurists usually are."[112] The disingenuousness with which he sought to set himself apart from Poliziano, whose side he actually took, and from Leoniceno, whom he effectively opposed, is apparent from the place in which Collenuccio chose to publish his work. At Ferrara, the city where Pliny's critic held a chair and

[105] *De Plinii in medicina erroribus* 1 (ed. Premuda), p. 5[b].

[106] Ibid., p. 7[a].

[107] Ibid., p. 8[b].

[108] Ibid., p. 9[a].

[109] "Hic non de verborum momentis, sed de rebus agatur, ex quibus hominum salus ac vita dependet." Ibid., p. 21[b].

[110] See pp. 35–36 above.

[111] On Collenuccio, who deserves fuller study, see Varese, "Pandolfo Collenuccio umanista," pp. 149–246; and E. Melfi in *DBI* 27 (Rome, 1982), pp. 1–5, with bibliography.

[112] *Pliniana defensio,* aii.

where his defender was ducal counsellor, the *Pliniana defensio* was printed in 1493, equipped with a dedication to Ercole d'Este. This attempt to undermine, at his home base, the Ferrarese professor's authority ("1,400 years have passed, and no one has attacked Pliny. Now there appears . . ."[113]) was issued with the collusion of Poliziano and his circle. To him and to Pico, Collenuccio had shown the work, as he admitted in a separate letter;[114] and they had read it more than once. Their approval was seconded by that of two Florentine doctors. Of this joint effort directed against Leoniceno, Collenuccio breathes no word in his tract. Yet behind the *Pliniana defensio* stood, in tacit opposition, the Florentine champions of Pliny.

The ideal of *enkyklios paideia,* so dear to Poliziano, makes an appearance early in Collenuccio's work: "I have always thought that each and every discipline is contained in the compass of philosophy alone; that they are all bound together by a single bond and common ties of kindred."[115] The unity of knowledge, in Collenuccio's eyes threatened by Leoniceno's plea for medical specialization, is reasserted by appeal to "the great authors and *ipsa rerum experientia.*" This aspect of the *Pliniana defensio* is more cogent than its quibbles about the dating of Dioscorides.[116] Whether he lived during the reign of Cleopatra and had no time to publish a work on which Pliny could not have drawn is secondary to Collenuccio's prime insistence on "the force of experience and the majesty of reason." Writing about the *tripolion,* he refers to his observation of the plant at Venice, supported by the evidence of illuminated herbals.[117] Discussing the *pentaphyllon,* Collenuccio distinguishes its five curved leaves and illustrates them with one of the first woodcuts to appear in a tract of this kind (Plate 1).[118] Again at Venice, in the famous pharmacy "Del Moro," he had seen a splendid herbal with drawings of such plants. The manuscript still exists, as does the shop at the foot of the Rialto Bridge.[119]

Declaring, with partial justice, that his case depends not on the status of Pliny or the opinion of Leoniceno, but upon empirical research, Collenuccio then turns against his opponent his own aspersions: "Although a Latin, he insists more on Greek words than on Latin things"; "Dioscorides," in the opinion of this rabid Hellenophile, "is the greatest, and he is a Greek. Does he not mean that Dioscorides is the greatest *because* he is a Greek?"[120] On

[113] Ibid., a*iii*.

[114] See Santoro, "La polemica," p. 201.

[115] "Nam disciplinas omnes intra unius philosophiae ambitum contineri semper duxi, unoque omnes vinculo et communi cognatione coniungi." *Pliniana defensio,* a*ii*.

[116] Ibid., a*iii*.

[117] Ibid., b*ii*.

[118] Ibid., c*i*.

[119] For context and illustrations, see S. Toresella and M. Barini, "Gli erbari a impressione e l'origine del disegno scientifico," *Le scienze* [= Italian edition of *Scientific American*] 239 (July 1988): 70–71.

[120] *Pliniana defensio,* a*ii*.

τ angulosa fit: Nomen a numero folioꝝ habet τ ipsa haerba incipit τ desinit cuꝫ vite. De penthaphyllo igitˀ hoc est quinqꝫfolio haec habentur. Nullus eni quod sciam his auctoribus vetustior illam pingit. Nã Galenus eius tantuꝫ vires non figurã aperit.

Primũ illud ex his satis constat vulgarem illam Leoniceni quinqꝫfoliuꝫ non esse hanc de qua agimus: Naꝫ τ illi nec flos albidus nec in surculis fructus: nec radix rubra nec crassa: nec inarescens aut quadratur aut nigrescit: nec vitis egressum digressuꝫqꝫ sequitˀ. Sed perpetuo viret. Haec si quis neget haerbae ipsius inspectione cõuincitur. Sed τ illud quoqꝫ liquido constare arbitror cum Plinij auctoritate: tuꝫ Dioscoridis pictura Penthaphyllon hanc nostraꝫ fructũ quoqꝫ ferre: cum etiã Fraga gignẽdo cõmendari illam scribat Plinius. Cũ ramos vnius palmi tenues in quibus fructus sint habere illam Dioscorides referat. Foliũ vero non esse quale Leonicenus arbitratus est ex omniũ descriptõibus intueri licet: Nam Theophrastus foliũ habere illam viti simile prodidit. τ folia omnia quinqꝫ: Dioscorides vero folia habere illam sinuatim falcatimve diuisa quolibet in surculo quinqꝫ. Tum in nõibus Penthadactylon illaꝫ vocat quo nomine τ Cici quoqꝫ siue sylvestre sesamũ cognoiatur cuiˀ foliuꝫ palam est viti simili mũ esse: Tum pseudoselinon quod falsuꝫ apiũ dici põt. Plinius vero Chamaeselinon quasi humile apiuꝫ: eadem vterqꝫ ratõe cognominãt quod τ apium viti simile quiddaꝫ habere videatˀ τ folia ad hũc quoqꝫ moduꝫ sinuata: a quoꝝ deinceps numero quinqꝫfoliuꝫ τ quinqꝫpẽna dicta est. Quae cum ita sint: ideo qnqꝫ foliuꝫ dicta est quod huiusmõi integra folia quinqꝫ ab radice emittit: Nec foliusculis quinqꝫ (vt quam pedem coruinũ vocari supra diximus) aut vulgaris Leoniceni penthaphyllũ distincta: sed porrectioribˀ qnqꝫ (vt ita dixeriꝫ) angulis ad vitis apij qꝫ similitudinẽ in hunc ferme moduꝫ effigiata est. Haec τ Penthaphyllon illa est quae Dioscoride auctore fructus edit: quae Fraga a Plinio appellantˀ: Cuius eximiae a Dioscoride vires Plinioqꝫ tra

c i

pẽtadachilo
cici
siluestre sesamũ
pseudoselinõ

1. Pandolfo Collenuccio, *Pliniana defensio:* the *pentaphyllon.*

Leoniceno, advocate of the Hellenic and denigrator of the Latin tradition, Collenuccio projects the same attitudes that Poliziano, at *Miscellanea* 1.1, had attributed to Argyropoulos. With his neglect of *realia,* his ornamental elegance, and his pedantic obsession with details, the Ferrarese suffers from all the faults for which he vituperates the *grammatici.* He has no right to denigrate the Roman expert on natural history. Mixing up issues in a mass of confusion,[121] Leoniceno's portrait of Pliny offers a mirror-image of himself. Against such distortions, Collenuccio applies a method of examining the evidence by categories (*membratim*), analyzing individual details (*singula*) systematically (*ex ordine*).[122] This is pure Poliziano. Such terms of taxonomy, like the rhetoric of integrated learning and of cultural clash, derive from his writings[123] and provide the theoretical basis for Collenuccio's investigations into plants. For if Poliziano shrank from attacking, in his own name, a living adversary of Leoniceno's stature, the *Pliniana defensio* is nonetheless a work that bears his stamp.

. . . . .

The controversy about Pliny had thus become, by 1493, a focal point of tensions in Italian culture between different concepts of method and of its purpose. Both sides acknowledged a role for philology and assigned a place to natural science or medicine, but both evaluated them differently, in the light of incompatible objectives and their views of the relative importance of the Greek and Latin traditions. Collenuccio, in his *Pliniana defensio,* and Leoniceno, in the second version of his *De Plinii . . . erroribus,* similarly attempted to exploit to their own ends Ermolao Barbaro's *Castigationes Plinianae,* which had appeared in the same year. Collenuccio's eighth chapter compares Leoniceno's arguments with those of Barbaro, triumphantly concluding that the authority on Pliny came down on his side.[124] Dedicating *De Plinii . . . erroribus* 2 to Barbaro, Leoniceno also pretended that they spoke with one voice: "Barbaro leonizes or Leoniceno barbarizes, not because you have borrowed anything from me, or I from you, but because there is a harmonious meeting of minds."[125] His alleged double was then compared with Varro,[126] elevating Barbaro to the rank of encyclopedist previously denied to Poliziano. Why was it, Leoniceno pointedly asked, that its dedicatee had not

[121] Ibid., a*iiii.*

[122] Ibid.

[123] See pp. 65ff. above. Cf. *Panepistemon:* "Nam et dividam singula prope minuatim, et in summam summarum redigam, quo possit unumquodque vel facilius percipi vel fidelius retineri." *Politiani Opera,* 3:29.

[124] Discussed by Santoro, "La polemica," pp. 170ff.

[125] *De Plinii in medicina erroribus* 1 (ed. Premuda), p. 23[a].

[126] Ibid., p. 23[b].

replied to the first version of his work? Could it be that Poliziano was too occupied with the poets, orators, and philosophers? Are these studies to be deemed more serious than the defense of Pliny? And how could one delegate such a task to ignoramuses who knew nothing about medicine and still less about Greek?[127] So much for Collenuccio. Evoking criteria of comprehensive learning satisfied by Barbaro at Rome but unfulfilled at Florence, Leoniceno continued by affirming that "the professions are divided."[128] Not for him the hair-splitting of a mere *grammatista*. He was a physician.[129] Unlike Pliny and his Florentine defenders, Leoniceno presented himself as competent both in philology and in matters medical. No ground is given in *De Plinii . . . erroribus* 2. The challenge to Poliziano and the intellectual position that he occupied was reissued from Ferrara in 1493 with undiminished ferocity.

. . . . .

There are signs that he recognized the problem. In the spring of 1494, months before his death, Poliziano wrote to Collenuccio, then on a diplomatic mission to the emperor-elect Maximilian, to thank him for dispatching specimens of plants.[130] "The *gnaphalium* and the Gallic nard that you have recently discovered and sent gave me great pleasure. There can be no doubt that they are, as Plautus says, The Real Thing (*ipsissimae*)." Describing the colors and characteristics of both plants, he praises Collenuccio for his diligence in empirical research: "Particularly in this field, which is dimly perceived by the medicine of our age." The sentiment and the style of this remarkable letter, without precedent in Poliziano's writings, are worthy of Leoniceno, from whose *De Plinii . . . erroribus* they draw inspiration.

Collenuccio, Poliziano's collaborator, was, as his *Pliniana defensio* had shown, a man of many parts. With lively interests in medicine and botany, he also brought his legal training to bear on philological problems. From this living personification of his own encyclopedic ideal, a worthy second to Pico, Poliziano learned much: "You touch on out-of-the-way disciplines, in which you make daily discoveries of things unknown even to professors." Collenuccio had divined that the Greek term for edible grapes was missing in exemplars of the *Digest* known to him. Consultation of the archetype enabled Poliziano to confirm the suspicion, as he wrote in the same letter, which aligns his botanical and medical studies with the investigations into legal texts of his last years.[131]

[127] Ibid., pp. 22^{a-b}.

[128] Ibid., p. 44^{a}.

[129] Ibid., p. 45^{a}.

[130] *Politiani Opera,* 1:218. The letter is after 16 March 1494, when Collenuccio delivered an oration before the emperor Maximilian, to which Poliziano refers.

[131] On Poliziano's legal studies, see Branca, *Poliziano,* pp. 182–92; and Wilson, *From Byzantium to Italy,* pp. 109–11.

That alignment, developed in private correspondence, hardened into a methodological parallel when confronted with opposition. "The learned," as Poliziano sarcastically put it, to whom Collenuccio had reported his reading of the archetype, declined to accept the truth.[132] Between their refusal to acknowledge this primary evidence and their condemnation of his use of actual specimens of nard and *gnaphalium,* Poliziano drew an analogy: "You sent me not the form but the very plants or (to put it in your legal terms) specific instances (*species*)." In botanical as in codicological research, Poliziano advocated a return to first principles. To neglect them was to be left with nothing more than pseudo-erudition reliant on custom. "Usum populo concedimus," ends this letter citing Cicero, "scientiam nobis reservamus." Knowledge, possessed by the chosen few, is distinguished from popular habit in the manner of *Miscellanea* 1, but with a new and distinctive emphasis. Palaeographical study of manuscripts and empirical investigation of plants are now viewed as related aspects of the same activity. His eyes opened by Leoniceno and Collenuccio, Poliziano had begun to gaze on aspects of nature with the same intensity that he hitherto reserved for codices, inscriptions, and monuments.

. . . . .

A beginning, not the completion, of a fresh approach is detectable in these late letters. They suggest that, immediately before his premature death, under the pressure of Leoniceno's assault and with the help of Collenuccio, Poliziano was feeling the need to reorient his methods. Yet it would be premature to conclude that, in 1494, he was about to become a naturalist, because the first and second *Centuriae* reveal a conflict between Poliziano's potential openness to empirical method and his stricter sense of what was admissible in philological form. The indications are various. If plants and herbs seldom figure in the first *Centuria,* animals enter its domain; and none of them looms larger than the giraffe, which is discussed at *Miscellanea* 1.3.[133] This beast was not unknown at Florence. It had attracted interest there long before one had been presented to Lorenzo de' Medici in 1487.[134] More than fifty years earlier, in the third book of Mariano Paccola's influential *Liber de ingeneis ac edifitiis,* the giraffe had been (mis-)represented as a kind of elongated dog, scarcely recognizable as the elegant animal subsequently painted by that "stupendous realist," Piero di Cosimo.[135] Poliziano knew better. He

[132] *Politiani Opera,* 1:226–27.

[133] Ibid., 515–17.

[134] See above, p. 29.

[135] For Paccola's work, see BNCF, Palat. 766, fol. 34^{v}, illustrated in B. Schmitt and A. Degenhardt, *Corpus der italienischen Zeichnungen,* vol. 2, 4 (Berlin, 1982), plate 48^{a}. On the influence of this work (including its drawings), see J. H. Beck, "The Historical 'Paccola' and Em-

had not only seen the beast possessed by his patron but had viewed a drawing of one in the villa of Filippo Strozzi, as well as receiving information from Lorenzo who, on his visit to Naples in 1479, had sight of another. We know this from Poliziano's observations on Beroaldo's *Annotationes centum,*[136] where he also records that, in a course on Horace, he had stated that the ancient term *camelopardalis* was identical with the modern word *girafa.* That bonehead Beroaldo was not even aware that the Greek Πάρδαλις is, in Latin, *panthera.* He had never set eyes on the animal, and was therefore unable to interpret the evidence provided by Pliny.

Observation was thus considered by Poliziano, in at least one case, not only a stick with which to beat his competitor but also a means of understanding *realia,* antique and modern, one year before the publication of the first *Centuria.* When that book appeared, however, the same problem was treated differently. Maintaining his identifications of *camelopardis* with *girafa* and of the Latin *panthera* with the Greek πάρδαλις and continuing to insist on his own priority, Poliziano now chose to emphasize his philological learning, citing a range of ancient testimonies that his unnamed rival had failed to adduce. Heliodorus, Cassius Dio, Pliny, Solinus, and others display an erudite virtuosity that Beroaldo, like that ridiculous, if anonymous, *grammaticus* who listed the half-word *pardalis* in his "popular" lexicon, did not possess. How Poliziano had laughed at this error of Giuniano Maio![137]

The verbal humor and polemic accompany a discernible but limited shift of focus. Near the opening of the same chapter, Poliziano records his wonder at the "little horns" (*cornicula*) on the giraffe presented to Lorenzo, "because previously I had read nothing about them in ancient sources." The next step—to inquire why—he does not take. Classical literature, in the first *Centuria,* is never confronted with direct observation of the natural phenomena that it reports. Ancient writers could be compared with one another and criticized; yet their authority, on such grounds, was unchallengable, because it formed the basis of his own. Leoniceno thought differently. Collenuccio, reversing his conclusions, acknowledged and developed his views on the importance of empirical method. Poliziano, in his personal correspondence about botany and in his private animadversions on Beroaldo, did not deny

---

peror Sigismund in Siena," *Art Bulletin* 50 (1968): 318 n. 45; and F. D. Prager and G. Scaglia, *Mariano Paccola and His Book "De Ingeneis"* (Cambridge, Mass., 1972). On Piero di Cosimo, see E. Panofsky, *Studies in Iconology: Humanistic Themes in the Art of the Renaissance* (New York, 1962), pp. 46ff. with plate 18. Panofsky, from whom the cited phrase is taken, dates the painting to "sometime after November 11, 1487" (ibid., p. 47 and n. 44) on the assumption that the giraffe was drawn from life. Note the entry in Luca Landucci's diary (*Diario fiorentino dal 1450 al 1516,* ed. I. del Badia, p. 52) for 11 November 1487: "Gli mandava el Soldano . . . una giraffa molto grande e molto bella e piacevole; *com'ella fussi fatta se ne può vedere i'molti luogi in Firenze dipinte.*"

[136] *Commento inedito ai Fasti di Ovidio* (ed. Lo Monaco), p. 139.

[137] See Ricciardi, "Angelo Poliziano, Giuniano Maio, Antonio Calcillo," pp. 227–84.

the point, but refrained from developing its implications in *Miscellanea* 1. On publication, he withdrew his attack on Beroaldo's capacity as an observer of nature, in a gesture that points both to the purpose and to the limitations of the genre he practiced. The combative but calculating author of the first *Centuria* deemed it more prudent to skirt the issue of natural phenomena, where he might be outflanked, and engage instead in a battle of the books.

As with the giraffes, so with crocodiles. They are presented at *Miscellanea* 1.55,[138] as a dialectical puzzle derived from Quintilian (*Institutio oratoria* 1.10.5). The "horn fallacy" ("What you have not lost, you possess; you have not lost horns, therefore you have horns") as expounded by Aulus Gellius and Lucian, not the rivers and deltas of Egypt, is their habitat. Having begun at chapter 54[139] with the criterion, conventional in ancient and medieval dialectic, of reserve or suspension of judgment (*non temere*) in the interests of truthful investigation,[140] Poliziano swiftly abandons it for an account of the richness of the sophistical tradition. This leads him, via the crocodile, to the number of horns (one or two?) on the rhinoceros and the Egyptian bull at chapter 56.[141] An epigram by Martial provides the pretext for the transition, but its real motive is disagreement with Calderini. The sequence of thought, free and associative, recalls the disdain for linear progression expressed in the foreword to the first *Centuria,*[142] yet a certain order underlies all three chapters. Like crocodiles, the horns of the rhinoceros and the Egyptian bull are, or appear to be, what Quintilian calls "choice ambiguities" (chapter 55). They provide a dilemma of conflicting information solved by reference to Pausanias, whom Calderini had misconstrued. No matter that Poliziano had never seen either of the beasts, for actual observation of them, had it been possible, was irrelevant to his procedure, which reduces the natural world to a playground of language, where the philologist flexes his dialectical muscles.

That sport Poliziano continued to pursue up to the end of his life. The second *Centuria* of the *Miscellanea,* left incomplete in 1494, displays his adherence to the same rules of the game. This persistence is striking, in view of the changed circumstances. Barbaro's *Castigationes Plinianae* had appeared, as had the first version of Leoniceno's *De Plinii . . . erroribus,* and the second version, available to Poliziano, was even more pointed. But he remained faithful to the approach of *Miscellanea* 1, devoting only one chapter to a plant—saffron (*crocus*)—which, on his understanding, was hardly a plant at all.

138 *Politiani Opera,* 1:609–10.

139 Ibid., pp. 608–9.

140 Cf. Cicero *De finibus* 4.1; *De officiis* 2.7–8; and see W. Burkert, "Cicero als Platoniker und Skeptiker," *Gymnasium* 72 (1965): esp. 176ff.; and G. C. Garfagnini, "'Ratio disserendi' e 'rationandi via': Il 'Metalogicon' di Giovanni di Salisbury," *Studi medievali* 12 (1971): 915–54.

141 *Politiani Opera,* 1:610–12.

142 "At inordination istam, et confuseam quasi sylvam, aut farraginem perhiberi, quia non tractim et continenter, sed saltuatim scribimus et vellicatim." *Politiani Opera,* 1:482.

The starting point of *Miscellanea* 2.57 is the *fabula* narrated in the fourth book of Ovid's *Metamorphoses*.[143] Fable is the preserve of the *grammatici;* without them, poetry cannot be understood. Yet the ancient writers adduced are not only literary: Pliny, Galen, and Philo of Tarsus supplement Ovid and Nonnus, who serve to reconstruct the myth. Employing the type of text adduced by Leoniceno, Poliziano suggests the potential harmony between poetical and medical sources, before expressing a mild philological disagreement with Barbaro. It is not that he is insensitive to the kind of question raised by Pliny's critic: rather that, in writing about the colors and properties of the plant, Poliziano declines to yield ground to the claims of *ipsa rerum experientia,* preferring, for motives soon to be discussed, information culled from texts. The result is both a confident reassertion of his method and an uneasy compromise, implicit here and plain in the next chapter, where the philologist represents himself as a consultant, on linguistic matters, to other disciplines such as law.[144] The omnicompetent *grammaticus* of *Miscellanea* 1 had begun to evolve into a source of specialist reference in the second *Centuria.* Gradually, reluctantly, not without a struggle, Poliziano was coming to acknowledge Leoniceno's case that "the professions are divided."

That struggle is revealed by his taste for provocation, even more marked in *Miscellanea* 2 than in the previous volume. Rivalry with his competitors for intellectual leadership, the revered Barbaro and the resented Leoniceno, lies behind Poliziano's penchant for exotic subjects about which they had said little. Yet the choices that he made were never arbitrary. Each of them, motivated by the dialectical purpose of pitting ancient authorities against one another so evident in the first *Centuria,* reveals a distinct anti-empiricism. Each draws conclusions that, in the late Quattrocento, were hardly refutable by any of his contemporaries on the basis of firsthand observation. That is why, in *Miscellanea* 2, crocodiles recur.

Illustrated in manuscripts produced at Laurentian Florence—notably in a codex (BMLF, Plut. 40.52) containing *L'acerba* by Cecco d'Ascoli, and produced for Bonifacio Lupi (Plate 2)—the crocodile, conveniently, had not inspired a large literature. Barbaro was reticent on the subject;[145] Leoniceno silent; but Poliziano had already been voluble. The dialectical crocodiles of the first *Centuria* give way to the aquatic and terrestrian species at chapter 37 of the second,[146] for who could trust Ovid's word (*Ars amatoria* 3.270) that it was the Pharian variety that provided the excrement from which feminine cosmetics are made? The answer, given the premises, was apparent from the outset: only a philologist, capable of correcting Ovid on the basis of Pliny, supported by Horace and Galen, who is obligingly translated for numbskulls ignorant of Greek. Crocodiles are treated like *crocus,* in the same dialectic

143 *Miscellaneorum centuria secunda* (ed. Branca and Pastore Stocci), pp. 107–9.

144 *Miscellanea* 2.58 (ed. Branca and Pastore Stocci, p. 109, ll. 5–7).

145 *Castigationes Plinianae* 5.65.1 (ed. Pozzi, 2:357).

146 Ed. Branca and Pastore Stocchi, pp. 58–59.

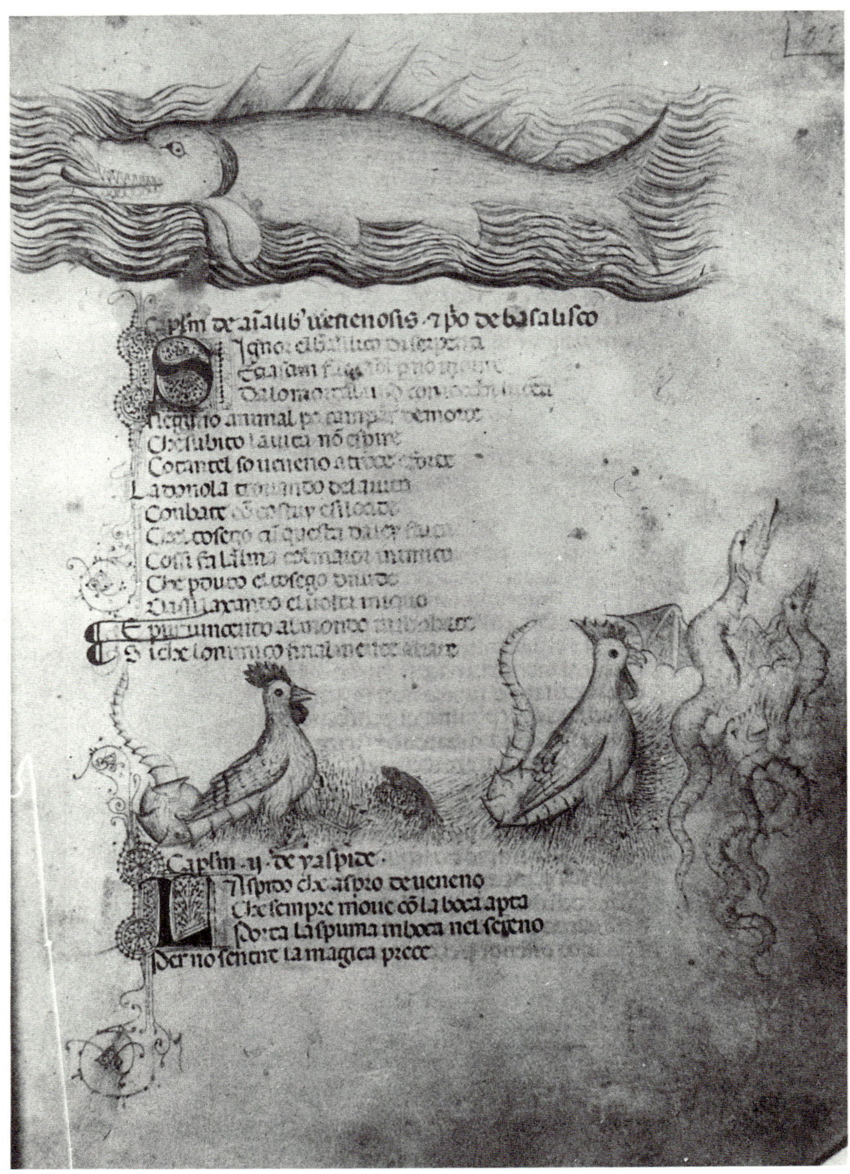

2. Biblioteca Medicea Laurenziana, Plut. 40.52: the crocodile.

between classical writers on medicine or natural history and the literary sources of Poliziano's preference. Both are instances chosen to demonstrate that, in areas where the approach of his rivals faltered, his valiantly advanced; and these pyrotechnics of one-upmanship led, by their perverse but coherent logic, to the weightier theme of elephants.

"Elephants!" exclaimed Pico, not once but three times, in the (otherwise scarce) marginalia that he made while reading Alamanno Rinuccini's Latin translation of Philostratus's *Vita Apollonii Tyanei*.[147] The subject was of lively interest to Poliziano's innermost circle. Still more absorbing were the divergent testimonies of antique authors on the vexed question of elephants' knees (*Miscellanea* 2.46).[148] St. Basil, in his *Hexaemeron,* provided the "astonishing and hitherto unheard of" information that, at this crucial point of their anatomy, the beasts lacked "knotty joints," which prevented them from lying down. St. Ambrose supported his view. In Aelian, Pliny, and Aristotle, however, Poliziano claimed to find indications to the contrary. He cited them all, adding for good measure the testimony of Nonnus, who, "although a Christian," thought that elephants slept on their feet while leaning on trees.[149]

A conflict was thus distinguished between two traditions, the sacred and the profane. Poliziano attached importance to a passage from Aelian's *De natura animalium* (7.37) that seems to support the view that elephants could kneel. What this shrewd selector of evidence did not quote is Aelian's chapter on the anatomy of the beast (4.31), which maintains that "the elephant sleeps standing upright, for it finds the act of lying down and of rising troublesome." Such information from an author whose integral text is frequently cited in the second *Centuria* was omitted by Poliziano, because it would have disturbed the clear lines of division that he needed to construct a problem to which no empirical solution was readily available. Hence the disingenuous avowal: "I have never seen real living elephants and dare not express a judgment." That did not prevent him from venturing an opinion: if Aelian (as reported by Poliziano), Aristotle (as translated by Theodore Gaza, a scholar criticized at *Miscellanea* 1.90 for his version of the same author, but here cited approvingly, on the grounds that he might have set eyes on the animal), and Pliny are to be preferred to the testimony of Ambrose, the Christian father could be excused. Why? Because reading the sixth book, chapter 27, of Caesar's *Bellum Gallicum,* he might have confounded the nocturnal habits of the elephant (African or Indian) with those of the (Gallic) elk!

Is this an argument—or a joke? Presenting the erring saint as a caricature

[147] BNCF, Fondo Nazionale, II.II.48, fols. 38^{v}, 39^{r}, 41^{v}. On the translation, see Giustiniani, *Alamanno Rinuccini, 1427–1499,* pp. 198ff.

[148] Ed. Branca and Pastore Stocchi, p. 82, ll. 60–61.

[149] On the issue, see generally H. H. Scullard, *The Elephant in the Greek and Roman World* (London, 1974); and, on the still-disputed questions of elephants' knees and sleeping habits, *Grzimeks Enzyklopädie,* vol. 4, *Säugetiere* (Munich, 1987), p. 509.

of book learning, it demotes Ambrose to the status of a mental midget. But if the humor is dubious, the intention is clear: the more esoteric the examples selected by Poliziano, and thus the less verifiable his interpretations, the better. His admirers might have marveled at his erudition (and, perhaps, at his wit) in chapter 46 of the second *Centuria*. His critics might have deplored both. Yet none of the scholars and thinkers—from Leoniceno to Pico, Barbaro, and Giorgio Valla[150]—who, in the last quarter of the fifteenth century, were less concerned with dialectical dexterity than with the substance of science, would have turned to Poliziano's book, had it been published, for information on the natural world. Is this because revision and accommodation of new approaches were forestalled by its author's death? Perhaps, although there is no reason to be more generous than Poliziano in attributing the benefit of doubt. He was well aware, in his last months, of Collenuccio's empiricism, which he enthusiastically praised; and he knew that the time had passed, in Italian culture, when Petrarch could make fun of useless knowledge about elephants and crocodiles.[151] Trapped in its own logic, Poliziano's method had begun to turn on itself. The result is atrophy. If *Miscellanea* 2 was never completed, one of the reasons was that, on the path that its author obdurately continued to pursue, there was no way forward. Introverted, self-referential, and increasingly self-parodic, the second *Centuria* displays the defiance of a philologist who had chosen to sever contact with reality.

. . . . .

Between reality and aspiration yawned a chasm of Poliziano's own making, which was not always perceptible to his students. The hagiography of The Master began during his lifetime. One of the first to style him a saint of learning was Girolamo Amaseo, who in 1493 migrated from Padua to Florence, pestering almost every eminent professor on the way.[152] Among the splendid architecture, pretty girls, and Spartan spirit that he esteemed in the Florentine Republic, nothing seemed more impressive to this bumptious prig than Poliziano. To his nocturnal habits Amaseo devoted the same attention that the great man paid to those of elephants. On retiring to bed, Poliziano (he relates) was wont to leave an oil lamp burning in a little vault with a door stationed above his bed. When he woke from his brief slumbers, he would raise his arm from the pillow, open the door, and caress the books in the vault,

[150] On Barbaro, see Pozzi in Barbaro, *Castigationes Plinianae,* p. cxlviii and n. 1. On Valla, see G. Gardenal, "Giorgio Valla e le scienze esatte," in *Giorgio Valla tra scienza e sapienza,* ed. V. Branca (Florence, 1981), pp. 9–54.

[151] *De sui ipsius et multorum ignorantia* (ed. A. Bufano et al.), p. 1038, with Bergdolt, *Arzt, Krankheit und Therapie bei Petrarca,* pp. 67ff.

[152] The source of these paragraphs is the letter discovered, edited, and illuminated by G. Pozzi (Amadeo, [*Epistula*], ed. Pozzi).

"which to him were like a wife and a girlfriend." With quasi-erotic joy Amaseo exclaimed: "I have seen him, I have seen him, our Mercury!"[153] If the means by which he had obtained access to his hero's bedroom are not revealed, the enthusiasm of this impecunious upstart may not be doubted. Poliziano had promised to lend Amaseo money.

The pupil's letter is charged with excitement at the rival of the Hellenism ("Day by day Italy is ever more set on fire by the study of Greek literature"[154]) that animated his teacher's new enterprises. They, as recounted by Amaseo, were now concentrated on philosophy, mathematics, and dialectic.[155] In 1493, Poliziano was lecturing on Aristotle's *Priora analytica,* while planning public courses for the next year on the *Analytica posteriora* and the *Isagoge* of Porphyry, together with a private one on Euclid.[156] The focus of his teaching interests had thus shifted to the quadrivial subjects of the traditional seven liberal arts, as he attempted, in his *Panepistemon* and other writings,[157] to complete earlier plans for an encyclopedic system of learning.[158] Yet Poliziano's concern with the exact sciences is sparsely documented. If, among his searches for Greek mathematical manuscripts,[159] he attempted to come to terms with geometry, a rare indication of what Amaseo meant is provided by *Miscellanea* 2.42,[160] which, taking its point of departure from Barbaro's discussion of the terms *decussare* and *decussatim* in Pliny, Columella, and Vitruvius,[161] applies an axiom, possibly derived from Euclid's *Elements,*[162] to the latitude and length of a line. In Euclid, that axiom is not an object of demonstration, and Poliziano appeals to the authority of Aristotle to justify his methodological rigor,[163] which does not amount to much. The problem treated was, and remains, one of the natural science to which geometrical categories are barely applicable, and, toward the end of his analysis,

[153] Amadeo, [*Epistula*] (ed. Pozzi), p. 195, ll. 92ff. On the name Mercury, see ibid., p. 216 n. 1.

[154] Ibid., p. 195, l. 112.

[155] Ibid., ll. 92 and 128.

[156] Ibid., ll. 106–11.

[157] Cf. S. Meltzoff, *Botticelli, Signorelli, and Savonarola: "Theologia Poetica" and Painting from Boccaccio to Poliziano* (Florence, 1989), pp. 32ff.

[158] Cf. I. Maïer, "Un édit de Politien: La classification des arts," *Bibliothèque d'humanisme et Renaissance* 22 (1966): 338–55; Cesarini Martinelli, "Sesto Empirico," pp. 327–58; and idem, "Un ritrovamento polizianesco: Il fascicolo perduto del Commento alle 'Selve' di Stazio,'" *Rinascimento* 20 (1980): 183–212.

[159] See P. L. Rose, *The Italian Renaissance of Mathematics: Studies on Humanists and Mathematics from Petrarch to Galileo* (Genova, 1975), pp. 10, 20–21, 32–35, 46–48, 63, et passim.

[160] Ed. Branca and Pastore Stocchi, pp. 65–73.

[161] *Castigationes Plinianae* 18.3 (ed. Pozzi, 2:802–3).

[162] *Euclidis Elementa* Iα', ed. E. S. Stamatis (Leipzig, 1969), p. 1 (not cited by Branca and Pastore Stocchi). The same axiom, however, occurs in other sources known to Poliziano, including Philoponus and Martianus Capella.

[163] Ed. Branca and Pastore Stocchi, p. 70, l. 43, with note ad. loc.

Poliziano loses faith in it, acknowledging that Barbaro may have been right.[164] Moving uncertainly in what was, for him, a new direction, the philologist of *Miscellanea* 2.42 was reluctant to abandon the old: investigation of words clutters, with erudite but irrelevant detail, a line of geometrical reasoning that he proved incapable of developing. Poliziano the mathematician is a theme that belongs to the legends of the lecture theater. More substantial, but no less problematic, was his wish (granted by Amaseo) to be regarded as an expert on philosophy and dialectic.

Both subjects had been in the forefront of Poliziano's mind since 1489. The *coronis* of the first *Centuria,* which announces his "conversion" to philosophy under Pico's guidance,[165] was followed by the *Praefatio in Suetonium,*[166] written under the impact of Leoniceno's indirect criticism of him and frontal assault on Pliny. It is notable that Poliziano, in his prolusion, responds to views that were being trenchantly expressed on this subject at Ferrara. Natural history is the second example that he chooses (after Aristotle's *Nicomachean Ethics*) to illustrate the necessity of historical understanding of philosophical problems, echoing Leoniceno's view that Pliny had been misclassified:[167] "Certain niggling philosophers of our age may happen to deny this, disapproving of Pliny's unique work on the grounds that its style is most elegant."[168] Just as the Ferrarese professor had condemned the "barbarian" tradition of medieval medicine and insisted on the primacy of Greek, so his junior colleague at Florence expressed admiration for the "most eloquent Aristotle" and disdain for his "most infantile, tongue-tied Teutonic" commentators or perverters.[169] While mobilizing Pandolfo Collenuccio to take the counteroffensive against the medical and botanical arguments of Leoniceno, Poliziano was advancing into his other field of study, brandishing the same standard of a Hellenic crusade.

Strictly parallel was his concern with dialectic, a member of the family of disciplines that constitute *enkyklios paideia* at *Miscellanea* 1.4. Was Poliziano competent to teach this subject? Some had their doubts, which he was at pains to dispel. He had studied dialectic in his youth—in part with frauds

[164] Ibid., p. 73, l. 69.

[165] See E. Garin, "L'ambiente del Poliziano," in *Il Poliziano e il suo tempo,* pp. 17–39; and above, p. 81.

[166] See above, pp. 52ff.

[167] See above, pp. 99ff.

[168] "Negent fortasse id argutuli quidam nostrae aetatis philosophi, ut qui nec Plinii singulare opus de eo negotio comprobent, iccirco videlicet, quia est elegantissime scriptum." *Politiani Opera,* 3:124. Cf. above, p. 104.

[169] "Commentaria in Aristotelem . . . ipsis etiam Getis barbariora. Deus bone, quae monstra in illis, quae portenta deprehendi! . . . Contuli et Graecum Aristotelem cum Teutonico, hoc est eloquentissimum cum infantissimo et elingui. Hei mihi, qualis erat! Quantum mutatus ab illo! Vidi eum, vidi, et vidisse poenituit, non conversum a Graeco, sed plane perversum." *Politiani Opera,* 3:124–25.

and charlatans who, knowing no Greek, had "besmirched the purity of all Aristotle's books with the hideous filth of their pedantry," moving him "sometimes to laugh and occasionally to throw up"; in part with others who, although they understood the original language, derived everything from the commentary tradition.[170] Poliziano represents himself as an autodidact, reliant, for knowledge of dialectic, on his familiarity with the seven liberal arts.[171] In that discipline, too, he plays the same role as Leoniceno, returning to the Greek springs of wisdom and affirming that instruction by a *grammaticus* offered an adequate preparation for any field of study. The natural consequence of this position was to base his own writings about dialectic on the arts of language.[172] Less consequent was Poliziano's reticence about the scholastic teacher of this subject, in whose dialogue, dedicated to him, a certain Angelus appears as a pupil.[173]

The *De negotio logico* of the Dominican monk Francesco di Tommaso, composed in 1480, represents Poliziano as an adept of rhetoric, neglectful of philosophy, with gentle irony. Yet in the course of the work, keen interest in dialectic and no mean command of its techniques is evinced by the persona of Angelus, to whom is attributed a passion for Thomas Aquinas that *Miscellanea* 1.1 supports.[174] In a version of the scholasticism for which his *Praefatio de dialectica* and his *Praefatio in Suetonium* express such disdain, lie the beginnings of Poliziano's acquaintance with that subject, while the image of an autodidact that he cultivates there is previewed in the flattery of the *De negotio logico*. "Will you manage to enable me to acquire dialectic without you?" asks Angelus. "I will do my utmost," replies Franciscus, "so that I shall seem to live with you, even when I am absent."[175] Little did Francesco di Tommaso know, in 1480, how literally Poliziano would take his words eleven years later.

The progression from the autodidact to the polymath announced in the *Praefatio de dialectica* is also anticipated in *De negocio logico*. Poliziano's thought about *enkyklios paideia* did not develop, as he suggests, through unmediated reflection on antiquity. Similar ideas had been voiced, many years before *Miscellanea* 1, by his scholastic teacher. In the opening sentence of his dedication, Francesco di Tommaso emphasizes the connection of dialectic with

[170] Ibid., p. 187.

[171] "Cum ad ipsam dominam affectarem viam, nequaquam postrema fuit cura etiam eius mihi ancillas & et pedissequas conciliandi, quae liberales a nostris artes appellantur. Earum me igitur scitis ad hanc usque diem familiaritate intima esse usum, quoniam non inutiles esse audieram, praesertim si praeparent ingenium . . . nam si philosophiam non docent, ipsae mox tamen percipiendae locum parant." Ibid., pp. 187–88.

[172] See Vasoli, *La dialettica,* pp. 116–31.

[173] F. di Tommaso, *De negocio logico* (ed. J. Hunt).

[174] Ibid., p. 50.

[175] "*Angelus:* Tu ergo facies ut dyalecticam nanciscar te sine? *Franciscus:* Huic rei do operam, ut me absente tecum videar vivere." Ibid., p. 58.

other branches of knowledge;[176] at its conclusion, he underlines the intimate links of that subject with eloquence. "Artibus enim illustrantur artes," announces Francesco: they develop by a principle of mutual aid and interdependence.[177] This is the thought that underlies Poliziano's definition of *enkyklios paideia* at chapter 4 of the first *Centuria,* where, beside the obvious influence of Quintilian, the unacknowledged traces of Francesco di Tommaso's ideas are detectable. When, in 1493, Girolamo Amaseo represented his hero as an implacable foe of the "barbarians" who had commented on Aristotle during the Latin Middle Ages,[178] he was faithfully reproducing the rhetoric of Poliziano, unaware that he, via Francesco di Tommaso, was a beneficiary of the heritage of the leading twelfth-century Aristotelian. "The *auctores,*" John of Salisbury had written, "interpret one another."[179] Phronesis has several sisters, first and foremost among whom is Philologia, critical seeker after truth.[180] The *grammaticus* is not only responsible for the *enarratio poetarum* but also for the exposition of philosophy.[181] It is not difficult, in this interdisciplinary context, so similar to his own, to understand why Poliziano laid stress on his knowledge of Greek. It appeared to place him in a different tradition from that of his medieval precursors, proximity to whom he sought to conceal by denigration. Too long taken at face value, Poliziano's invective reflects the discomfort of an advocate of *enkyklios paideia* who, at *Miscellanea* 1.4 and its continuations, expressed little that John of Salisbury, at *Metalogicon* 1.24 and elsewhere, had not said three hundred years before him.[182]

. . . . .

The prolusions on dialectic and on Suetonius report the criticisms of unnamed detractors who questioned Poliziano's competence as a philosopher. The issue had exercised him since 1479, when, in his translation of Epictetus's *Encheiridion,* he had distinguished between the thinker and his interpreters;[183] and when the question was posed afresh, by the reception of *Miscellanea* 1, he evoked the precedent set by Epicurus, whose "vain boast" that

[176] Ibid., p. 49.

[177] Ibid., p. 207.

[178] "Quamvis apud Latinos omnia sunt angusta et labyrinthea, saltem a barbaricis scriptoribus perplexa: proh divumque nominumque fidem, quantum omnia inverterunt!" Amadeo, [*Epistula*] (ed. Pozzi), p. 194, ll. 73–75. Cf. note 171.

[179] *Metalogicon* 3.1, ed. B. Hall (Turnhout, 1991), p. 105. Cf. John of Salisbury, *Historia pontificalis* 12, ed. M. Chibnall (London, 1956), p. 27, with von Moos, *Geschichte als Topik,* pp. 376ff.

[180] *Metalogicon* 4.30 (ed. Hall, pp. 166ff.).

[181] Ibid., 1.13 (ed. Hall, p. 32).

[182] Ed. Hall, pp. 51–52; with P. Godman, "*Opus consummatum . . . omnium artium imago:* From Bernard of Chartres to John of Hauvilla," *Zeitschrift für deutsches Altertum und deutsche Literatur* 125 (1995): 26ff.

[183] See A. Wesseling, ed., in Angelo Poliziano, *Lamia: Praelectio in Priora Aristotelis Analytica* (Leiden, 1986), p. 98 on 16 and 17.1–9.

he was a self-educated master of all subjects became, in the *Praefatio de dialectica,* Poliziano's own.[184] Hailed not only by Amaseo but also by Michele Acciari, in the spring of 1491, as "less an interpreter of the orators and the poets than a most eminent philosopher,"[185] Poliziano was awkwardly placed between the adulation of his students and the skepticism of his critics. Neither of them construed his position as he intended it, for when he had begun to lecture on Aristotle's *Ethics* in 1490, it was not in the institutional role of a professor of philosophy but as a *grammaticus* who wished to establish himself as an exegete of philosophical texts.[186] Without the abstruseness of a Ficino or the aridity of a schoolman, both of which he had mocked in the prolusion on dialectic,[187] Poliziano sought an approach to this subject that would mark his distinctive contribution. He found it in the veiled manner and integumental style exemplified by Pico's Platonizing "barbarian," and lent it expression in the *Lamia* of November 1492.

"Let's make up a fable," writes Poliziano in its first sentence, "but one that fits the facts."[188] To Aristotle, philosopher of factual realities and rigorous argumentation, is applied, at the beginning of a course on his *Priora analytica,* the mythopoeia of fiction. Justified, at the end of the *Lamia,* by Aristotle's own authority,[189] the style of this subtle work is Platonic. Like the Socrates of the *Dialogues* whom he invokes, Poliziano operates with irony[190]—deepened, for the Florentine audience to which the *Lamia* was addressed, by the historical resonance of his frequent declarations that he was no philosopher. They recalled a celebrated controversy at the Studio, in 1455, when Landino had competed for a chair obtained by Argyropoulos.[191] In his inaugural lecture on Aristotle of 1457, the Greek had rejected traditional praise of the disciplines as superfluous and boring, embarking instead on an analysis of the divisions of philosophy.[192] His thwarted rival, Landino, on appointment to a chair of rhetoric, had taken, as an alternative to Argyropoulos's course on the *Nicomachean Ethics,* Latin moral thought. Beginning his lectures on Cicero's *Tusculan Disputations* with the affirmation that he was a rhetor, Landino said: "I neither demand nor accept the name of philosopher."[193] This is what lies behind such protestations in the *Lamia* as: "You will easily understand

[184] *Politiani Opera,* 3:186, with Wesseling in Poliziano, *Lamia* (ed. Wesseling), p. 106 on 17.25–26.

[185] See p. 28 above.

[186] See pp. 81ff. above.

[187] *Politiani Opera,* 3:186–87.

[188] "Fabulari paulisper lubet, sed ex re." Poliziano, *Lamia* (ed. Wesseling), p. 3, l. 1 (with Wesseling ad loc., p. 21).

[189] Ibid., pp. 18, ll. 24–25, and 113.

[190] Ibid., p. 7, ll. 30ff. Cf. G. Vlastos, *Socrates, Ironist and Moral Philosopher* (Cambridge, 1991), pp. 21–44.

[191] See Field, *Origins,* pp. 77–106 (cited in note 35).

[192] *Reden und Briefe* (ed. Müller), pp. 4, l. 9, with Field, *Origins,* pp. 107–126, 241.

[193] Landino, *Scritti critici* 1, with Field, *Origins,* pp. 242ff.

that I am not a philosopher."[194] Recalling Argyropoulos's freedom to break with convention, Poliziano applies Landino's distinction between philosophy and rhetoric to his own sphere of *grammatica*.

What, then, was the role of this author of a *fabula ex re*? One capable of philosophizing without assuming the persona of the philosopher who, in the *Lamia,* becomes a figure of fun. Pythagoras and his followers, portrayed as the dictators of absurd fads, open their mouths only to bark out archaic imperatives ("Stateram ne transilito! Cerebrum ne comedito! Cor etiam ne comedito!").[195] Plato, that towering giant of truthfulness, is subverted by Socrates' arguments in favor of lies. The *Lamia,* like the *Misopenes* by Poliziano's friend Collenuccio, satirically portrays the philosopher in terms of his inactivity and his evasions. "What art do you profess?" Chrysius asks the thinker Misopenes in Collenuccio's work. "None, for I am a philosopher," comes the reply. Pressed to explain himself, Misopenes provokes the retort: "What you've described is smoke!" "Smoke is what we are, but we love wisdom," answers Misopenes.[196] Such is the gap between aspiration and achievement, which the *Lamia* attributes to the comic character of the philosopher. Professing that he is not one, while claiming the right to comment on philosophical texts, its author ironically evokes the Socratic paradox of knowledge identified with ignorance.

Irony is a form of dissociation, a means of multiplying the polyvalencies of Poliziano's theme, exemplified by the *fabula* of the cave at *Republic* 7.514*a*–517*c*.[197] The *Lamia* presents, in Latin translation, Iamblichus's allegory of Plato, and concludes by refusing to interpret it,[198] on the grounds that Florentines are too clever to require an explanation. Yet a moral is offered in a contrast between darkness and light, stupidity and learning. What kind of learning is required to penetrate this veil of obscurity? That of an interpreter: Donatus and Servius, for instance, among the Latins, or Aristarchus and Zenodotus among the Greeks.[199] All of whom, it is not idle to recall, were philologists.

By these indirect but convergent strategies, the nonphilosopher demonstrates the necessity of philological interpretation. His integumental *fabula* arrives at the point of indeterminacy, only to be rescued by the methods of the *grammaticus*. He is capable of understanding anything—even the works of Hippocrates. This dig at Leoniceno leads into a reaffirmation of the encyclopedic ideal outlined at *Miscellanea* 1.4. The philologist investigates

[194] Poliziano, *Lamia,* p. 4, ll. 8ff. Cf. "Nam et disciplinas illas vix attigi, quae philosopho competunt, et ab his, quos dixi, moribus et virtutibus absum longissime." Ibid., 8, ll. 18–19.

[195] Ibid., p. 7, ll. 30ff.

[196] *Operette morali: Poesie latine e volgari* (ed. A. Saviotti), pp. 32–33.

[197] Poliziano, *Lamia,* p. 13, ll. 38ff. (with Wesseling ad loc., pp. 89ff.)

[198] Ibid., p. 15, ll. 34ff.

[199] Ibid., p. 16, ll. 20ff.

"every kind of writing: poets, historians, orators, philosophers, doctors, jurists."[200] Beginning with a mock modesty, akin to Landino's, before the claims of the superior disciplines, Poliziano ends by proclaiming his competence over not only philosophy but all other branches of knowledge as well.

The modern age, he declares, has limited too narrowly the scope of this office. Resuming the ideas that had occupied him since 1489, Poliziano lends them final and forceful expression: over the undivided realms of *enkyklios paideia,* the *grammaticus* wields the censor's power. He is no schoolmaster, imparting *prima elementa.* Such lowly drudges of learning should not be called *litterati* or *grammatici* but *litteratores* and *grammatistae*[201]—the term, and the approach, that had revolted Pico. As to himself, Poliziano is not fussy: "Me enim vel grammaticum vocatote vel, si hoc magis placet, philosophastrum vel ne hoc ipsum quidem" ("Call me a *grammaticus* or, if you prefer, a philosophizing dilettante or not even that").[202] Employing one of the archaic imperatives with which he had mocked the Pythagoreans, the *grammaticus* suggests the arbitrariness of the terminology to which, sentences earlier, he had appeared to cling. Pico's "barbarian" could not have put it more ambiguously. Confronted with the complexity of manifold *res,* the philosopher who, like Aristotle, knows everything and, like Socrates, knows nothing must acknowledge that disputes about the equivocal *verba* that misrepresent them are subject to the philologist's arbitration. Such, in 1492, was Poliziano's reply to Pico's letter of 1485.

. . . . .

In the borderland between literature and philosophy, where meaning is plural, Poliziano, reflecting on Aristotle, wrote in the mythopoeic manner of Plato. The *Lamia,* culmination of years of thought on the place of the *grammaticus* in Quattrocento hierarchies of learning, is an introduction to a course on Aristotelian logic that, together the other lectures on philosophical subjects delivered by Poliziano in the 1490s, has not survived. It is therefore not easy to assess the nature of his interests in that subject, but the image of his devotion to the *vita contemplativa* in his letter on his patron's death[203] can be complemented, and modified, by Pico's dedication to Poliziano of *De ente et uno* in 1491.

Pico treats his governing theme—the concord of Plato and Aristotle—with marked originality, departing from traditional Neoplatonic interpretations of the *Parmenides* and the *Sophist,* and presenting the problem in terms, developed from the fourth book of Aristotle's *Metaphysics* by scholastic

200 Ibid., ll. 30–32.

201 Ibid., p. 17, ll. 8–9.

202 Ibid., p. 18, ll. 20–21.

203 See p. 23 above.

thought, of the doctrine of transcendental *universalia*. Whether Poliziano ever attempted such philosophical analysis may be doubted, and it is significant that the personal warmth of Pico's dedication to "my almost indivisible companion" is qualified by "above all in literary matters." Depicting his friend rather as "the champion of polished speech" than as a philosopher like himself, Pico concludes by repeating the message of his letter of 1485 with an elegant quotation from Manilius, privileging content over form.[204] To a convert to that doctrine who had renounced the allurements of literary style in favor of hard reasoning, Pico's point would not have needed to have been made.

That point is borne out both by the general character of Poliziano's interests up to 1494 and by the detailed evidence of his work on Aristotle in the second *Centuria*. At chapter 53, for example, he treats the term *universale,* which might have been linked with Pico's discussion of universals in *De ente et uno* and which was relevant to issues considered in the *Praefatio in Suetonium*.[205] Neither connection is made. Instead, Poliziano, following his usual dialectical practice of evoking a conflict between authorities, discusses a problem in two texts by Aristotle that, at least since Philoponus, had been recognized to contradict one another: *Analytica posteriora* (71*b*33–72*a*5) and *Physica* (184*a*16–24).

In the *Analytica posteriora,* according to Poliziano's paraphrase, Aristotle discusses the issue of *universalia*. This is not strictly true, but it accurately reflects medieval exegesis of the passage, and explains why the author of the second *Centuria* is so keen to denigrate Averroes and Thomas Aquinas—whom he had praised in the first—for their "pedantic quibbles," which "have no place in the *Miscellanea*."[206] Scholastic opponents had again to be mustered in order to assert this humanist's novelty; and when, at the end of the chapter, Florence's leading Hellenist quotes a passage in the original language (*Analytica priora* 64*a*28–30),[207] crowing in triumph over "a not unlearned but Greekless philosopher," with whom he had debated the meaning of *universale,* the Greek cited—τὸ καθόλου—is, in context, an adverbial expression signifying "generally," not a philosophical concept.

The triumph is hollow. Anxious to correct alleged mistakes of the schoolmen who had provided the terms in which he read Aristotle, Poliziano himself makes errors of Greek.[208] The structure of his argument reveals its bias.

[204] *De hominis dignitate, Heptaplus, De ente et uno, e varii scritti* (ed. Garin), pp. 386–88. For the quotation from Manilius, cf. Poliziano's *Panepistemon* in *Politiani Opera,* 3:29–30.

[205] Ed. Branca and Pastore Stocchi, pp. 99–102. For the *Praefatio in Suetonium* and Aristotle, see above, pp. 54ff.

[206] Ed. Branca and Pastore Stocchi, pp. 99, ll. 1–2; 100, ll. 41–45; and see above, p. 87. For Poliziano's use of medieval Latin Aristotelian commentaries, see Branca, *Poliziano,* p. 212.

[207] Ed. Branca and Pastore Stocchi, p. 102, ll. 86–96.

[208] Cf. Kraye, "Cicero, Stoicism, and Textual Criticism," pp. 79–110.

Reticent about the contribution of Simplicius to the solution of this problem,[209] he passes swiftly over the commentator, whose alleged obscurity of expression is condemned. Ample room, however, is made for Theodore Metiochita, a Byzantine philosopher who serves simply to demonstrate the breadth of Poliziano's learning, and to fill the lacuna left by his failure to engage with issues that Aristotle's theory of cognition, in the late Quattrocento, still raised. For his views about the route that leads from individual sense-experiences to apprehension of the universals that form their origin were not, as Poliziano asserts, themes done to death by scholastic captiousness. They were subjects that, in the near future, were to stimulate a lively discussion about the methodology of natural philosophy.[210] No anticipation of these debates penetrates the hermetic world of *Miscellanea* 2.53. Instead, one reference to a parochial dispute with an unnamed opponent over a point of translation, and another to a course on Aristotle's *Libri naturales* offered, four years earlier, to "certain men of learning."[211] To the chronology of his own exegesis Poliziano lavishes an attention that he denies to the implications of Aristotle's thought.

At the level of the individual word and the specific textual problem, his method, elaborated but essentially unchanged from *Miscellanea* 1, produces results.[212] It is when Poliziano attempts to extend it, and to effect a union between philological and philosophical approaches, that his work shows signs of strain and its conceptual weakness is laid bare. An instance is chapter 50 of the second *Centuria,* where Aristotle is accused of error,[213] on the basis of his discussion, at *Politics* 1.1252*a*ff., of the conditions needed to found a household. These are two: the relationships of a man with his wife, for purposes of procreation, and with a slave, who is to do the manual work. Aristotle cites Hesiod *Works and Days* 405. The verse, which states that a woman and an ox are required, proves, in Poliziano's view, the philosopher's dependence on the poet, because the ox is the slave of the poor man. The problem lies in the following line—not quoted by Aristotle—where Hesiod refers to a slave-woman (not a wife) who follows the plough.

The possibility that Aristotle might have been satisfied, for the purposes of his own argument, with citing a single verse out of context, Poliziano never entertains. Instead he affects perplexity. Because the *Politics* present the man's wife as responsible for the offspring, their author—a writer of "such carefulness in all matters"—should not be accused of philological inexactitude in omitting *Works and Days* 406. Rather, the text of Hesiod is peccant.

[209] Ed. Branca and Pastore Stocchi, p. 102, ll. 84–85.

[210] See N. Jardine, "Epistemology of the Sciences," in *Cambridge History of Renaissance Philosophy,* pp. 703–4 with bibliography.

[211] Ed. Branca and Pastore Stocchi, p. 101, ll. 62–63.

[212] E.g., *Miscellanea* 2.54 (ed. Branca and Pastore Stocchi, pp. 102–4).

[213] Ed. Branca and Pastore Stocchi, pp. 92–94.

Its grammar is odd; the sense curious; and, in a commentary by Demetrius Triclinius, the suspect verse is not mentioned.[214] But there is an explanation for this crux: a learned man, with a sense of humor but without taste for marriage—in short, a figure like Poliziano—had interpolated the offending line as a joke. In the margin of his manuscript of Hesiod he had written: "A bought, not a married, woman, to follow the oxen," and posterity, delighted or deluded by his impishness, had transmitted the result. The millennial mistake identified, it remained to effect the excision.

What began as a criticism of Aristotle ends as a defense—a defense against charges trumped up by a textual critic wishing to play Aristarchus. With mock solemnity, he advances his proposal "against the universal agreement of the manuscript tradition and the unanimous opinion of the interpreters. . . . More good will be done by defending Aristotle than bad by slaughtering a single verse." That ritual murder was only necessary because Poliziano posited a philosopher who thought like himself. The fidelity to a factitious logic, which he ascribes to Aristotle, like the interpolation of an erudite misogynist, which he hypothesizes in the text of Hesiod, mirrors his own mentality. As a contribution to the genre of oblique autobiography, *Miscellanea* 2.50 is ingenious. Yet its ingenuity contorts Poliziano's method into a mannerism and reduces philology to a prank. Recreating the past in his own image, the angel from heaven gazes upon it complicitly, and smiles at what he sees.

. . . . .

Not everyone shared his satisfaction. Satirical and scabrous epigrams on Poliziano's large nose, squint, and other supposed deformities evince the antipathy that his character provoked, especially among the Byzantine émigrés.[215] Yet only one of them commented on the nature and scope of his procedure, in a work that, for the penetration of its hostile insight, stands out from all the others: the poem addressed to Poliziano under the pseudonym "Ecnomus," or Monster, by that brilliant man of arms and letters, Michele Marullo.[216]

[214] On the problem, see M. L. West, *Hesiod: Works and Days* (Oxford, 1978), p. 260 ad loc.

[215] See Lascaris *Epigrams* 22–24, in Lascaris, *Epigrammi greci,* pp. 5–10, 129–35; and cf. Branca, *Poliziano,* pp. 194ff. and p. 261 n. 8.

[216] "'Dic aliquem sodes, dic, Ecnome, quaeso, colorem.' / 'Haeremus almis occupati legibus.' / 'Quid de legatis Falcitia, dic age, sancit?' / 'Sophiam magistri, iura non exponimus.' / (5) 'Ecquid stare potest sola virtute beatus?' / 'Virtutem inertem omitte, naturam inspice.' / 'Cor raro Arctois bacchantur fulmina lucis?' / 'Atqui libellos novimus, non fulmina.' / 'Quos, agedum, si fas, quos, Ecnome, quaeso, libellos?' / (10) 'Medicos, peritos, syderum et id alios genus.' / 'Fas ne paroxysmi febrem curare diebus?' / 'Ego ne valens de febribus verbum loquar?' / 'Num licet infaustos signorum avertere cursus?' / 'Quin, his relictis, ad studia vertere redi!' / (15) 'Incipe, sic capiti semper pater adsit Iachus!' / 'Non, Daphni, matutinus redis huc neve

An imaginary interlocutor requests from "Ecnomus" a *color.* The word is ambiguous, connotating both a pretext, a palliative, or an excuse, and a rhetorical figure of speech. "Ecnomus" replies that he is busy with the study of law. A question is posed about the *Lex Falcidia* of 40 B.C., which regulated the portion of dead man's estate that was to pass to his heirs. The problem is evaded on the grounds that teachers expound wisdom, not jurisprudence, and there follows the demand as to whether man can be happy by virtue alone. Another evasion: "Forget lifeless virtue and turn to nature." This is promptly done: "Lightning is rare in the far North, why?" "I know about books, not lightning." "What sort of books?" "Medicine, expertise in the stars etc. . . ." "How then do you cure a fever?" "How should I, a sick man, know?" "Is it possible to avoid the consequences of an ominous constellation?" "Let's give it all up and return to our old studies!" The nondialogue ends in acrimonious separation, with the Greek poet disparaging his opponent's knowledge of Latin, just as Poliziano had slighted Argyropoulos's command of Greek. Monster's barb concludes a series of venomous retorts: "We men of learning spurn such minutiae!"

The terms in which "Ecnomus" dismisses his interlocutor recall the criticisms leveled against Poliziano himself by Landino and his school.[217] This exponent of microscopic research turns against his tormentor the accusation of overexactness that Marullo's poem portrays him as claiming falsely. Each of its questions refers to one of Poliziano's areas of alleged expertise; each traces, in a painstaking detail that parodies his autobiographical style, the chronology of his studies. From rhetoric to jurisprudence, from moral philosophy to natural science, medicine, and astrology: every instance meets with an evasion. Against the elusiveness of "Ecnomus" is pitted his interlocutor's precision: one of the first examples (v. 3) not only alludes to Poliziano's research into Roman law but also echoes the legal language in which he had denied assuming the title of philosopher in the *Lamia,* as if it were a legacy that had become vacant because of the incapacity of the heir.[218] Same style, same problem, same sham is the implication: Poliziano is a fraud. The philosophical question of verse 5 evokes both his course of 1490–91 on the *Nicomachean Ethics* and his letter on Lorenzo's death, which represents the *virtus* of his patron in just such Aristotelian terms.[219] Books were what Poliziano knew about, not natural phenomena; even less was the capacity of this exegete of medical texts to cure disease (vv. 7–12). And the sympathy for astrology that is attributed to him at verse 13 acquires a

alius.' / 'Atqui non pes hic, non, Ecnome, sermo Latinus.' / 'Abi, homo, minuta haec spernimus docti viri.'" *Michaelis Marulli carmina,* ed. A. Perosa (Zürich, 1951), pp. 88–89. On Marullo, see the general account of C. Kidwell, *Marullus: Soldier-Poet of the Renaissance* (London, 1989).

[217] See above, p. 76.

[218] Poliziano, *Lamia,* p. 17, ll. 11–12 (with Wesseling, ad loc., p. 104).

[219] See above, p. 16.

double irony when it is remembered that Pico, at the beginning of his *Disputaiones adversus astrologiam,* portrays Poliziano as a "wondrous scoffer" at all such "superstitions."[220]

In an age characterized by satire and invective, Marullo's poem is unmatched for its exactitude. Systematically, point by point, it takes the subjects with which Poliziano concerned himself in his later years, and presents him as an incompetent with an alibi. To every question drawn from the field of *enkyklios paideia* that he had cultivated, "Ecnomus" avoids replying until, at the end, the implausible polymath is forced to repudiate his minute methods and admit the emptiness of his pretensions. The result is astonishing. For the first—and only—time in Renaissance literature, Poliziano is made to eat his words. And since words, in the poem, are all that he has, the dialogue form chosen for this masterpiece of malice acquires a subtle aptness. With such a double-tongued exponent of the verbal arts, suggests Marullo, dialogue was impossible.

. . . . .

The caricature contained an element of truth. Communication, for this professor of eloquence, was possible only on his own terms. The vituperation of the polemicist; the honeyed flattery of the courtier; the client's subservience; the expert's superiority: Poliziano's various poses find their unity, their coherence in forms of exclusion. On terms of intellectual equality he spoke solely to Barbaro and Pico—both, unlike him, of patrician or noble birth; both eminent figures in the *res publica litterarum;* both engaged in studies that touched on his own but remained reassuringly distinct from them. That was essential for all who had to deal with Poliziano, including his patrons. Piero de' Medici, accused by his former tutor of being too much under the influence of Piero da Bibbiena, wearily referred to Poliziano's "volatile nature and touchiness," his tendency—even in Lorenzo's lifetime—to "jump and scream."[221]

The intensity, bordering on hysteria, with which this *novus homo* conducted his professional and personal relations is not reducible to a combative period style. Frustration, felt acutely by an insecure man of humble birth and high ambitions, lies behind Poliziano's striving to establish his singularity, while denigrating the achievements of others. The only position of relative independence that he had achieved—that of professor—no longer satisfied him. Piero had promised him *otium,* leisured freedom for his research,

[220] "Semper omnium superstitionum mirus exsibilator." *Disputationes* (ed. Garin), p. 60.

[221] Piero de' Medici to Piero da Bibbiena: "Messer Agnolo, che parla come li decta la sua volatile natura et leggerezza et salterebbe et griderebbe chi gridassi a luj, anchora che havessi il torto, che sapete eius est contra stimulum calcitrare insino in vita di mio padre." Picotti, ed., *Ricerche umanistiche* (Florence, 1955), p. 124.

which efforts to secure the librarianship of the Vatican and the cardinal's hat had failed to deliver. In 1494 Poliziano still desired a change of occupation and, at the end as at the beginning of his career, he had no other means of effecting this than the backing of the Medici.

That is one reason why, in 1494, the bonds between the tutor and his ex-pupil were drawn ever tighter, and the polarization between their circle and its opponents became deeper and more dangerous. Continuing the campaign begun in the *Nutricia* and in his letter on Lorenzo's death to represent Lorenzo's son as his worthy successor,[222] Poliziano planned, in May of that year, to publish his *Liber epistolarum* with a dedication to Piero in the dual crisis caused by the external threat from Milan and France and the internal menace from the rival branch of the family headed by Lorenzo and Giovanni di Pierfrancesco de' Medici.[223] Allied with them was Bartolomeo Scala, to whom, weeks and days after his teacher's death, Piero was to write in Poliziano's acerbic manner, accusing his detractor of "lewd life, barbarous style, and dim intellect."[224] From beyond the grave, the arch-controversialist still possessed the capacity to deepen the divisions within the city's ruling elite. To defend Poliziano's memory, Florence's nominal first citizen, immediately before his fall from power, entered the lists against its honored First Chancellor.

Scala's troubled relations with Poliziano had erupted in controversy at the end of 1493.[225] At issue were not only private animosities—heightened, if a dubious tradition may be believed, by Marullo's marriage with the First Chancellor's daughter, whom Poliziano had courted—but also different conceptions of culture. The humanism of Bartolomeo Scala had little in common with the advanced Hellenism, the specialized erudition, for which his enemy stood. A high official, Scala viewed learning rather in terms of its practical utility than from the academic perspective of a professor. Cicero provided his single and authoritative model of stylistic purity: not for him the hybrid pluralism cultivated by Poliziano and his friends. In the eyes of this bluff bureaucrat, the new philology offered no more than frippery and frills. Barbaro, to Scala, appeared a *ferruminator*—a "scissors and paste" writer—and Poliziano seemed a gnat of scholarship, to be handled with caution because, if he counted for little in the real world of politics, he might sting.

[222] See above, pp. 19ff.

[223] See Martelli, *Angelo Poliziano,* pp. 210ff.

[224] "Tuae vitae obprobria et linguae barbariem et hebetem Minervam tuam subticuit: sed ita vulgu innotescere coegit, ut id nunc odii tu eius ossibus exerces et Politani manibus venenato isto thure arrideas." I. del Lungo, ed., "Tra lo Scala e il Poliziano," *Miscellanea storica della Valdensa* 4 (1896): 180.

[225] See Brown, *Bartolomeo Scala,* pp. 211ff.; and M. Martelli, "Narrazione e ideologia nella *Historia Florentinorum* di Bartolomeo Scala," *Interpres* 4 (1981–82): 21–22.

The Chancery contests the Studio in their correspondence of 1493–94. Or rather, the Florentine tradition of official humanism practiced by such celebrated chancellors as Salutati and Poggio is opposed, in Scala's letters and in the proemium to Book 4 of his *Historia Florentinorum,*[226] to the newfangled approach represented by Poliziano alone. Valla and Calderini, Beroaldo and Barbaro: the main precedents for, the chief analogues to, his methods derived from outside Florence. Within the city's living memory, not even Niccolò Niccoli had set a model for Poliziano's work. Eccentric and unproductive, Niccoli had left no publications to his name. Scala was different, more familiar, less esoteric. Like Landino, he advocated, with the prestige of his long-held office, a Latinate learning rooted in indigenous customs. Poliziano, reliant on the hegemony of the Medici, offered an import foreign to Florentine practices. Proudly conscious of his novelty, but lacking Scala's base in the city's institutions, he appealed to the illusion of an aristocracy of the intellect.

That illusion was precarious. Members of the elite, as selected by himself, were neither active nor numerous nor even alive. The deceased Lorenzo de' Medici had been portrayed by his client as sharing his philological interests in the dedication to the first *Centuria.* That the orthography of "Virgil" took second place to the statesman's more pressing concerns is not a matter of conjecture, nor does the anecdote, recounted at *Miscellanea* 2.7, about Pico's remarkable philological memory[227] alter the fact that the thinker whom he depicted as his partner was primarily engaged in studies, such as cabala, unconnected with those of Poliziano's preference. It was with the dead—with the ancient specter of Calderini (so often revived, so relentlessly persecuted) and with the more recent shade of Barbaro—that the lonely *grammaticus* continued to commune on his own terms; and nothing in the second *Centuria* discloses more poignantly the solitude that surrounded Poliziano at the close of his short life than these melancholy whispers with ghosts.

Without Florentine antecedents, without a stable social context for the philology that he declined to adapt to the temper of the times, he stood alone, preaching to the converted. Unlike Amaseo and Acciari, Scala was neither a pupil nor a fan. Lacking the reverence of the acolyte and the patrician's refinement, he had addressed Poliziano in gruff tones. And this irascible would-be aristocrat, remembering his superior pose but forgetting the isolation that underlay it, made the predictable but serious mistake of underestimating the First Chancellor.

. . . . .

[226] Martelli, "Narrazione e ideologia," pp. 18ff. For the term "official" (not "civic") humanism, see below, Chapter VII.

[227] Ed. Branca and Pastore Stocchi, p. 14, ll. 12ff.; and see below, p. 132.

"You have written much, I believe, but you have not published a great deal that has become a by-word" was one of Poliziano's first jibes at Scala.[228] A double-edged weapon in the hands of an author whose publications, in December 1493, were notable rather for their quality than their quantity. Yet no tactic was too underhand to disparage his antagonist's position: Scala's preference for Cicero, Poliziano insinuated, entailed contempt for later Latin authors; judging Barbaro by the same leveling standards, he usurped the power of censor.[229] Purists, from whom Scala is unconvincingly distinguished, have no sense of occasion, of context, of register. They are obtuse to the immense variety of Cicero's writings, so different from one another. Insisting that everything be trimmed to the same measure, these *maledocti* cannot tell what is authentically Ciceronian, because they read The Master's works in error-filled incunabula printed (to add insult to injury!) by Germans.

Caesar's precept that the unusual word should be avoided was valid at a time when Latin was a spoken language; in the present age, choice and recherché diction should be sought from a variety of models. Resuming the arguments for pluralism, stylistic and conceptual, in his letter about imitation to Cortesi,[230] Poliziano lent them a different emphasis. It was not creative liberty that he advocated when corresponding with Scala but critical restriction: the sense of one's own limits that comes from the awareness that Latin is no longer imbibed with the nurse's milk but learned, painstakingly, from modern *magistri*. Only with the modest diffidence that proceeds from the realization that even Ciceronians may extol a corrupt reading through ignorance of the textual tradition can one avoid the barbarisms perpetrated by Teutonic printers. Insidiously, this letter advances an argument for the cultural primacy of the higher scholarship that Scala held in scorn, an apologia for qualities of learned discrimination that Poliziano's "beloved, well-disposed friend" did not command.

To the old-fashioned *homme de lettres,* the traditional humanist of applied learning, Poliziano denied the status that he claimed for the new type of specialist, of whom Barbaro provided a paradigm. Defending his late ally, he was asserting his present authority. This Scala skillfully contested. Realizing that to accept Poliziano's terms of reference was tantamount to conceding him victory, he disputed that he was in any sense a scholar. "I am a man of the people (if you wish to know me)," wrote the First Chancellor, "a student of Latin eloquence, a champion and admirer of the *bonae artes*."[231] The first phrase contains a studied ambiguity: plebeian like Poliziano, Scala differed

[228] "Multa tu quidem, credo, scripsisti; non multa adeo tamen edidisti, quae vulgo ferantur." *Politiani Opera,* 1:131.

[229] See p. 90 above.

[230] See pp. 46ff. above.

[231] "Sum quispiam de populo (si nosse me vis) eloquentiae Latinae studiosus, assectatorque atque admirator bonarum artium." *Politiani Opera,* 1:133.

from him in his public role. Deflating the aristocratic pretensions of his correspondent by proclaiming his own humble origins, Scala shrewdly referred to functions of his office—the writing of state letters and the delivery of speeches—which, at Florence, lent the pursuit of Latin eloquence a meaning and a purpose that philology did not possess.

Feigning ignorance of that subject, Scala actually revealed a close acquaintance with Poliziano's philological writings, taking the orthography of "Virgil" as his example of an issue "too minute (believe you me) to go on tormenting good minds."[232] The terms of this taunt recall those of Landino, newly revived by Marullo;[233] and the "former teacher, now (so to speak) my colleague" was then adduced in the setting of his second career at Palazzo Vecchio, where Scala represented him as his collaborator in the composition of state letters. Gossiping together, these two humanists in a different mold found their favorite theme in Poliziano's *humanitas.*

The allusion, again, was intended to smart. *Humanitas* in the sense of "competence in the *literae humaniores*" could be attributed to this critic of his ex-master, but "humanity" or "kindness," as moral qualities, Poliziano notoriously did not possess. Beginning with *Miscellanea* 1.77, Scala went on to imply that, if Landino's approach seemed outmoded at the Studio, it found support at the Chancery. To the jibes that Poliziano's teacher was on the shelf in the first *Centuria,*[234] his colleague responded by intimating that his disloyal pupil's prowess, viewed from a larger vantage-point, might also seem to be less than overwhelming: "We are little men compared with the ancients," declared Scala; "when I compare our achievements in warfare, literature, philosophy, painting, and sculpture . . . with theirs, my spirits fall and I begin to be ashamed of our endeavors."[235] The attack on Poliziano's desire to equal antiquity, stridently proclaimed in *Miscellanea* 1, was thus mounted with arguments that inverted and distorted his own. The inferiority of the modern age, according to Scala, was redeemable only "if astrology brings aid and comfort to the prostrate," provocatively citing Poliziano's bugbear as a last resort in a situation depicted as hopeless. Inviting him to continue the debate in leisure at home, "should we fear the plebeian crowds of spectators," Scala—the pretended man of the people, the cultural pessimist masquerading as an ignoramus—proved himself a discerning reader of the first *Centuria.*

Poliziano dissimulated understanding.[236] Under the veil of courtesy, however, his tone became tarter. Of course Scala was no Ciceronian. If he favored that great author and wrote off later ones, it was because he had not

[232] "Minutior (mihi crede) res et, quam quae bona diutius ingenia torqueat." Ibid.

[233] See p. 123 above.

[234] See p. 82 above.

[235] *Politiani Opera,* 1:136.

[236] Ibid., pp. 137–43.

had the time to study them. The occupations of the humanist-bureaucrat became, in the eyes of his enemy, a reason for his want of learning. Comprehensible, added Poliziano more acidly, was Scala's aversion to his style: a *publicus scriba,* a Chancery drudge, could not approve what diverged from common usage. He wrote for the ignorant public: Poliziano, in a select diction, lectured to the cream of studious youth. The chancellor's antithesis between official humanism, with its public function, and professorial philology was twisted into a contrast between the superiority of the elite and the vulgarity of the masses.

The overbearing Poliziano was then likened by Scala to Hercules in triumph. This heroic image for the scholar, current at Florence since Salutati[237] and recently employed by Ficino, had a darker side, for Hercules' triumphal procession was also reserved for madmen who were paraded through the streets.[238] So, too, with Scala's epigram on the gnat, which was to be repeated and varied by the throng of Poliziano's detractors.[239] Pressure was mounting. Correcting Scala's mistakes of grammatical gender,[240] inveighing against his morals,[241] and engaging in a mock suit for the favors of his daughter Alessandra,[242] his antagonist sought, by delaying tactics, to skirt the real issue that their polemic had raised. For the First Chancellor had put his finger on a weakness in the assumptions of classical scholarship when he wrote: "You have triumphed in literature, you have had it in your power," and yet the past "was undoubtedly more fortunate than our age, at least as far as literary studies are concerned. When I say our age, I mean that about which you wail, in which there has been such an immense lack of the books and teachers needed to provide dependable sustenance for letters that everyone has tried his arm as best he could, producing many enduring faults."[243] In open debate with Scala, Poliziano might deny this charge, but privately, in the second *Centuria,* on which he was working at the same time, he came close to acknowledging the validity of his opponent's insight. At *Miscellanea* 2.5, discussing Calderini's tendency to invent missing evidence, the doubting philologist admitted: "There is no book in the Latin tradition that we professors understand with complete clarity, for we have lost too many of the ancient commentators to be able to explain everything, and our exemplars are so full

[237] Ibid., p. 144. Cf. Salutati, *De laboribus Herculis* 3.5 (ed. Ullman), p. 193, ll. 3ff.

[238] Martelli, "Nota a *Morgante* XX, 85, 4," pp. 263ff.

[239] See C. Vecce, "*Multiplex hic anguis,*" pp. 235–55.

[240] *Politiani Opera,* 1:380ff.

[241] Poliziano, *Prose volgari inedite e poesie,* pp. 273–74.

[242] See Kidwell, *Marullus,* p. 179 (cited in note 216).

[243] "Tulisti de litteris triumphum, idest eas habuisti in potestate. . . . Fortunatiora certe sunt ista tempora—quis negaverit?—nostris temporibus, quantum ad literas saltem pertinet, voco autem nostra vagitus illius tui tempora, in quibus et librorum et praeceptorum, ex quasi quodam certo literae hauriuntur, penuria permagna fuit, suo quisque Marte quid poscunt vires experiebatur, unde multa vitia inhaeserunt mentibus." *Politiani Opera,* 1:147.

of faults, in many places, that not even a trace of the original reading has survived."[244]

Scala knew the overweening author of the first *Centuria*. He was not, and could not be, acquainted with the less confident Poliziano of its unfinished sequel. The chancellor's case for the inferiority of the moderns touched the new Aristarchus to the quick, at a time when he was beginning to question the grounds for his mastery of the ancients. None of this, however, could be conceded during their acrimonious exchange. In vain did Scala refer to their common background, to careers made through Medicean support; in vain did he insist on his own achievements.[245] Worldly success meant literary failure, Poliziano taunted; he could outdo this incompetent even in his professional activity—the composition of state letters, which Lorenzo had charged him with rewriting.[246] In the poisoned atmosphere of 1494, the great mediator was cast as a partisan. Appealing like Scala to the memory of their mutual patron, Poliziano evoked past enmities between two types of Florentine humanism that had now become incompatible.

Scala, with his jibes about his enemy's shortcomings as a philosopher, was the kind of critic mocked with deft assurance in the *Lamia*.[247] Coarsely ridiculing him for his unclassical vocabulary and pomposity three years later, Poliziano was on the defensive. Assailed at Florence and thwarted at Rome, this gnat of literature had lost his sting. Not even Piero's abuse shook Scala's position, nor did the revolt of November 1494 remove him from the scene for long.[248] The First Chancellor was indispensable; and he remained, ever-vocal until his death in 1497, at the center of events. Marginal to the city from which he had failed to effect his departure, Poliziano, in the first *Centuria,* had expressed the cultural ideology of a part of the regime that was about to collapse. The aristocratic exclusiveness of the Medicean elite that he continued to voice in his correspondence with Scala was equivalent, on the intellectual plane, to behavior that was alienating Piero and his dependents from influential sections of the political oligarchy.[249] Turned in upon himself and an ever-dwindling circle, Poliziano sought the only consolation that remained. The first *Centuria,* dedicated to Lorenzo, stands in contrast to the second, which is inscribed "In nomine domini nostri Iesu Christi."[250]

[244] ". . . nullus apud Latinos sit liber (ut arbitror), quem professores ad liquidum intellegamus. Nam et commentariorum veterum iacturam maiorem facimus quam ut explicari iam cuncta possint, et exemplaria locis multis adeo mendosa sunt, ut ne vestigia quidem supersint integrae lectionis." Ed. Branca and Pastore Stocchi, p. 10, ll. 9–13.

[245] *Politiani Opera,* 1:393ff.

[246] Ibid., p. 398.

[247] Cf. Hunt, in *Politian and Scholastic Logic: An Unknown Dialogue by a Dominican Friar* (Florence, 1995), p. 27 n. 63.

[248] See Brown, *Bartolomeo Scala,* pp. 122–23.

[249] See Rubinstein, *Government of Florence,* pp. 230–31; and cf. below, p. 148.

[250] Ed. Branca and Pastore Stocchi, p. 3.

Whether persuaded by Pico or converted by Savonarola, its embattled author, in the last weeks of his life, had more than one motive for seeking refuge at San Marco.

. . . . .

In 1499, five years after Poliziano's death, Gregorio, the brother of his pupil and partisan, Girolamo Amaseo, in that vein of epistolary boastfulness which ran in the family, wrote: "Et quanto tu me dissese che studii de humanità non è philosophia, io ti respondo che li sonno da più cha philosophia . . . perché in humanità se contiene tutte le scienze del mondo."[251] From the lecture rooms of the Florentine Studio to the backwaters of the Friulian province, Poliziano's grandiloquent attempt to derive *enkyklios paideia* from the *studia humanitatis* echoed emptily in the bombast of this schoolmaster with upward ambitions. Amaseo was not content with the classroom. Coveting the social promotion that he believed would follow from the literary distinction of a polymath, he was attracted by Poliziano's distinction between the noble *grammaticus* and the lowly *grammatista*. Others had made the same point,[252] but none of them so determinedly as Florence's leading philologist, whose efforts to establish himself as the arbiter of letters placed censorship at the forefront of debate for the next generation.[253] At stake was intellectual primacy. Competitors, from Calderini to Scala, the imperative *grammaticus* would not brook. As peers in his project of universal learning, he acknowledged only Pico and Barbaro.

Barbaro was accordingly taken by Gregorio Amaseo as an example of the *homo universale*. He reputed this *humanista et artista* a god on earth. The *Castigationes Plinianae,* together with Barbaro's *Corollarium,* did indeed set out to reconstruct the ancient encyclopedia,[254] yet they differed from Poliziano's writings in their concentration on problems of textual criticism and in their restraint from the polemic that, in the second *Centuria,* became an end in itself. To his ally, to himself, to the cause of Hellenic scholarship Poliziano opposed two enemies, whom he often identified. One was the Greekless *opicus,* the other the erring theologian. What they shared was ignorance of the precise meaning of words, such as *synderesis*. Illustrating, with praise of Pico's linguistic competence and disregard of his philosophical message, the orthography and usage of the term at *Miscellanea* 2.7, this exponent of *verba* against *res* declared his indifference to its implications:

> About the doctrine itself I could not care less. Let men of ingenuity form their judgment of it as they see fit: may others grant me the right of having rescued

[251] Pozzi, "Da Padova a Firenze," p. 221.

[252] Ibid., with further references and bibliography.

[253] See pp. 160ff., 179 below.

[254] See below, pp. 219–22.

the Greek word from barbarism, since they have never achieved a command of polite literature, particularly in Greek.[255]

In these sentences, both the strengths and the weaknesses of Poliziano's method in 1494 find blatant expression. Announced under the cosmopolitan title of *enkyklios paideia,* his campaign, in practice, was confined to the province of language. There Poliziano was unquestionably a virtuoso. To textual research he brought not only the systematic spirit of an "Alexandrian" antiquarian but also the gifts of a sophisticated rhetor, arguing like an advocate and reasoning like a dialectican. That is what justifies the description of his work as an *umanesimo della parola*[256]—and what indicates its limitations, judged in its own terms and in the light of changes in Quattrocento culture.

To the questions being posed for the *studia humanitatis* by developments in the methodology of the natural sciences, medicine, and philosophy in the late fifteenth century, Poliziano offered no reply. His emphasis on the primacy of the word neither satisfied his own criteria of omnicompetent erudition nor dispelled the doubts of his critics. With the penetration of animus, Marullo had perceived his inconsistency on this score. Scala, from a different but related perspective, had thrown into relief Poliziano's limited social function and political insignificance. When Gregorio Amaseo, lauding the *studia humanitatis,* declared that "non è scientia né professione alcuna più politica de quella né più cossa da signor, principe, et re,"[257] he might have referred to the teeming Laurentian world of *Miscellanea* 1, not to the depopulated landscape of their continuation. Asserting his singularity, Poliziano had demonstrated his solitude.

The genre that he had elaborated was already exhausting its potential. *Miscellanea,* as Poliziano defined them in a passing aside, contained scholarly jokes.[258] Learned and jocose, the second *Centuria* resisted the admonitions voiced by the most intelligent of its author's few friends. To the insistence on content over form, repeated from Pico's famous letter to Barbaro in his dedication to Poliziano of *De ente et uno,* the *Lamia,* the *De dialectica,* and *Miscellanea* 2 responded by founding all knowledge on the arts of language. In a milieu that had begun to recognize the claims of empiricism and was reflecting on issues that they raised, that answer was no longer adequate. Exploiting the selectivity of the *miscellanea* form in order to concentrate on the verbal and textual aspects of problems that were understood to possess a philosophical or a scientific dimension, the specialist practice of Poliziano

[255] "Nam de doctrina ipsa minime equidem laboro. Liceat ingeniosis hominibus de ea ipsa pro arbitrio decernere: ius ipsum Graecae vocis a barbaris vindicandae nobis concedant alii, quoniam ipsi numquam politiores litteras maximeque Graecas attigerunt." Ed. Branca and Pastore Stocchi, p. 16, ll. 86–89

[256] Branca, *Poliziano,* pp. 193–296.

[257] Pozzi, "Da Padova a Firenze," p. 221 n. 1.

[258] *Miscellanea* 2.28 (ed. Branca and Pastore Stocchi, p. 43, l. 30).

was at variance with his encyclopedic theory. What began, in the first *Centuria,* as a strategy for conquering the empire of *enkyklios paideia* ended, in its sequel, as a tactic of evasion.

Sidestepping Pico's challenge, Poliziano was constrained to avoid another, more direct and determined, mounted from Ferrara. Among the many uneasy silences in *Miscellanea* 2, none is more revealing than the embarrassed hush that veils the name of Nicolò Leoniceno. And his onslaught, unrepelled, was followed by that of another Ferrarese whose message no one at Florence in the terrible winter of 1494 could afford to ignore.

IV

THE ELOQUENCE OF SOCRATES

SOCRATES from Ferrara, implacable censor of vice and imperturbable apologist of virtue, has recalled moral philosophy from long exile to the city and restored it to the state," wrote Giovanni Nesi in the second version of his *Oraculum de novo seculo,* published little more than a month before the papal bull excommunicating the hero of his work was promulgated at Florence on 18 June 1497.[1] Condemned at Rome for his teaching, Savonarola was applauded by the intellectuals of his adoptive *patria* in terms that recalled and reinterpreted their past.

Moral philosophy had not been exiled from Florence when Nesi's book issued from the press. His metaphor echoed both the preface to Poliziano's incomplete translation of Plato's *Charmides*[2] and the laments by members of the previous generation, such as Alamanno Rinuccini, who had campaigned to establish philosophical instruction at the Studio in 1455.[3] For Rinuccini, as for Donato Acciaiuoli, the appointment of Argyropoulos had filled a yawning gap;[4] and they and their contemporaries had flocked to his lectures on the *Nicomachean Ethics*—a text on which Francesco Filelfo, during his Florentine period, had already written a commentary and Poliziano, among many others, was to offer a course.[5] Brushing aside the academic tradition of the Studio in which he had been educated and to whose direction he was appointed, in the year of the *Oraculum*'s publication,[6] Nesi portrayed Savonarola as the renewer of a discipline that contained the secrets of statecraft. His Socrates was no abstract theorist, but a philosopher of life.

[1] "Ferrarensis igitur Socrates philosophiam, quae de moribus agit, diutius exulantem revocavit in urbem civitatique restituit vitiorum castigator acerrimus, virtutum laudator gravissimus." Ed. C. Vasoli, p. 161. On Nesi, see Weinstein, *Savonarola,* pp. 194–99, 202–4, 214; D. P. Walker, *The Ancient Theology: Studies in Christian Platonism from the Fifteenth to the Eighteenth Century* (London, 1972), pp. 51ff.; and Polizzotto, *Elect Nation,* pp. 102ff.

[2] ". . . philosophiam ipsam . . . longo iam tempore exulantem quasi postliminio in patriam revoces." Ed. Hankins, *Plato in the Italian Renaissance,* 2:65.

[3] See A. Field, *The Origins of the Platonic Academy of Florence* (Princeton, 1988), pp. 77–78. For a wider context, see Vasoli, "Uno studio tra scienza e 'humanae litterae,'" in idem, *Tra "maestri" umanisti e teologi* (Florence, 1991), pp. 1–58.

[4] Cf. his letter to Roberto Salviati of 24 November 1489: ". . . qui ante aetatem nostram humanitatis studia profitebantur, inter quos praeter unum Iannoctium Mannettum paucissimos in his philosophia peritos invenies." *Lettere ed orazione di Alamanno Rinuccini* (ed. Giustiniani), pp. 188–89. On Acciaiuoli, see Bianchi, "Un commento," pp. 29–55.

[5] See Kraye, "Renaissance Commentaries," pp. 99ff.; and Staico, "Esegesi aristotelica," pp. 1275–1371.

[6] See Verde, *Studio,* 1:250. Nesi was reappointed in 1499.

That claim illustrates one of the changes that occurred in Florentine culture after the expulsion of the Medici and under the impact of Savonarola's preaching: an exit from the ivory tower and a return to the values of the republican past already idealized, in his polemic with Poliziano, by Bartolomeo Scala. Among survivors from the ancien régime, there were casualities. To his present idol Nesi attributed the name and prestige of Socrates, which others had ascribed to Ficino, his former mentor. He, who called Plato "the doctor of souls" (*medicus animorum*), had pretended to the same title in his *Libri de vita,*[7] that appeared among the millenarian anxieties that were rife at the end of the Quattrocento.[8] But Ficino was now superseded, his aspirations to moral leadership realized by a different and sterner Socrates.[9]

One difference between Savonarola and that retiring scholar lay in his capacity for mediation. "A friend to all men," as he is represented in the *Oraculum de novo seculo,* "from the highways and byways . . . to the palaces of kings, the residences of the great, the philosophers' schools,"[10] this propitiator of all classes and interests shunned the exclusiveness that had contributed to the unpopularity of the Medicean circle.[11] That Nesi had its members in mind is evident from his language. "Who can stand those stage-show censors," he asked, "whose life is at such remarkable variance with their style of speech?"[12] Not just the issue of censorship posed by Poliziano is evoked in this sentence; it also borrows a neologism from the preface of the first *Centuria.*[13] And Nesi, whose own Latinity is as recondite as his hermetic symbolism,[14] paradoxically praises Savonarola for his simplicity of expression:

> His language is, and has always been, without pretense and artificiality: pure and uncomplicated, not reeking of the lamplight and affectation, but not careless; restrained not verbose and padded yet moderate and (when need be) truly laconic; not elaborate but chaste, modest, clothed in the garb of youth. . . . That

[7] See Vasoli, "Un 'medico' per i 'sapienti': Ficino e il *Libri di vita,*" in idem, *Tra "Maestri" umanisti e teologi,* pp. 120–41. For the image since Petrarch, see Garin, "Religione e filosofia," pp. 131ff., and, on the earlier tradition, J. Agrimi and C. Crisciani, *Medicina del corpo e medicina dell'anima: Note sul sapere del medico fino all'inizio del secolo xiii* (Milan, 1978).

[8] Vasoli, "L'attesa della nuova èra," pp. 370–432.

[9] See P. O. Kristeller, "Lay Religious Traditions and Florentine Platonism," *Studies in Renaissance Thought and Letters* (Rome, 1956), pp. 89–122. See further below, pp. 194ff.

[10] "Omnium hominum nihilo secius eorum, qui de pomeriis et triviis oblati . . . quam eorum, qui de regno vocati, de aula principali asciti, de philosophorum scholis delecti sunt amicissimus." Ed. Vasoli, p. 161.

[11] See above, pp. 130ff.

[12] "Quis ferat *censores* illos *pulpitarios,* quorum cum vita mirabiliter pugnat oratio?" Ed. Vasoli, p. 164.

[13] For "pulpitorii . . . censores," an expression that appears never to occur in classical or Biblical Latin (information courtesy of the *TLL*), see pp. 13 and 90 above; on censorship, pp. 299, 303ff.

[14] See Vasoli, "L'hermétisme dans l'*Oraculum* de Giovanni Nesi," in *Présence d'Hermès Trismégiste* (Paris, 1988), pp. 153–65.

is why Alcibiades was more moved and affected by the unadorned speech of Socrates than by the brilliant orations of Pericles.[15]

Seldom has simplicity been depicted in brighter shades of purple prose. Nesi's style reeks of the lamplight described at *Miscellanea* 1.4. Yet having sat at the feet of its author and absorbed his lesson about the desirability of choice diction,[16] he then proceeded to repudiate it, contrasting the "Asian" preciosity affected by Poliziano with the "Attic" purity that characterized Savonarola's every utterance. His words were "spirited, fiery, pungent"; "on his lips sat the Pythian goddess of persuasion; in the schools of Athens, as a professor, he might have interpreted the philosophy of Plato and Plotinus."[17]

So much for Ficino, some of whose best-known works expounded these two thinkers. So much, too, for the encyclopedic aspirations of a scholar-poet such as Poliziano. Savonarola wrote verse "with equal elegance and learning"; "he was a master, through daily practice, of all the disciplines that form *enkyklios paideia,* and a patron of those who taught them." Projects once formulated at the Studio, supported by Medicean munificence and staffed by Medicean protégés, were now transferred to the cloisters of the *Accademia Marciana.*[18] Casting the new Socrates in the humanists' mold, Nesi reveled in Savonarola's ability to break it: "Such is his teaching that the learned admit that, previously, they knew nothing."[19] So it was that, in the *Oraculum de novo seculo,* Poliziano's ideal, unfulfilled by himself, was appropriated to his spiritual mentor.

With its subject, this glowing encomium found favor. "A most elegantly written little book," observed the gratified Savonarola, "by a leading scholar, although a layman."[20] In that qualification are encapsulated key features of his intellectual attitude. The prior of San Marco was not, as is sometimes assumed,[21] at odds with the establishment of the Studio, among whose direc-

[15] "Est igitur illi (fuitque semper) non fucatus sermo et medicatus sed purus simplexque, non lucubratus et affectatus sed tamen non neglectus et sobrius, non verbosus et laciniosus sed modicus atque (si opus fuerit) etiam laconicus, non elaboratus sed castus, sed pudicus, sed praetextus. . . . Hinc Alcibiadem nuda illa Socratis quam Periclis luculenta oratio magis movit atque affecit." Ed. Vasoli, p. 164.

[16] See above, pp. 81 (lamplight) and 50 (choice vocabulary).

[17] "Sunt illi verba . . . animata, flammea, aculeata . . . insidet eius labiis persuasionis Dea Pitho illa . . . multiplicem philosophiam . . . ita possidet, ut et in Lycio antistes et in Academia non candidatus modo et imitatus sed etiam professus esse videatur, altissimos saepe Platonis Plotiniique sensus exquirens." Ed. Vasoli, pp. 164–65.

[18] For the expression, see Crinito, *Commentarii de honesta disciplina,* pp. 104–5, with Weinstein, *Savonarola,* pp. 110–11.

[19] "Scribit metro divinas odas . . . tam eleganter quam erudite . . . quotidie exercet . . . studiis disciplinisque omnibus, ut nulla sit ex earum orbe, quae ciclicae vocantur, in qua praestantes non adhibuerit praeceptores . . . ita docet, ut docti antea nihil se scisse fateantur." Ed. Vasoli, pp. 165–66.

[20] "Libretto di elegante litteratura," "uno laico, ma principe di scienza." *Dyalogo della Verità prophetica* (Florence, 1500), fols. 5^{v}–6^{r}, quoted by Polizzotto, *Elect Nation,* p. 106 n. 16.

[21] E.g., Verde, *Studio,* 4, 3:1171 et passim.

tors, both before and after his execution in 1498, numbered notable *piagnoni* such as Nesi.[22] Aware that, to his critics, he seemed to have forgotten Cosimo de' Medici's epigram that states are not governed by paternosters,[23] Savonarola insisted on the distinctness of sacred and profane culture; and in the vernacular preaching for which he became famous, he developed views that he had expressed in his now-neglected *Apologeticus*.[24]

That seminal work was written by the prophet of repentance in 1491—three years before Savonarola, with the optimism of success, had linked his teaching with traditional Florentine striving for primacy.[25] The *Apologeticus* offered a critique of formalism that was compatible with Pico's views, but diametrically opposed to the practice of Poliziano.[26] That critique, in and after 1494, was extended to other spheres. When Nesi praised Savonarola's capacities of mediation between the aristocracy and the people of a city in crisis, he was contrasting them with the lack of substance and relevance in the divisive approach of the humanists who had severed contact with reality. This contrast had point. Poliziano and Ficino, remote from the public life of Florence, served an elite. Savonarola, as Nesi perceived him, reached out to the elect.

Their basis was formed by the *fanciulli*. Children, more than 35 percent of a population of some 50,000,[27] were urged, in his sermons, to reject a degenerate secularism. When Savonarola spoke about literature and culture, his examples were chosen for them. The ribald poetry of Luigi Pulci was his prime instance of a work that deserved condemnation. On 1 November 1494, he exhorted those whose "homes were full of vanities and sinful books such as the *Morgante* and other verses contrary to the faith" to bring them to him and make a bonfire.[28] The licentious triviality of Pulci deserved to be consigned to the flames, in his opinion, because he wished to safeguard purity of morals among the chosen innocent. The same objective governed Savonarola's attitude to the classical *poeti cattivi*—that is, those who spoke of sex—"come è Ovidio De arte amandi, Tibullo, né Catullo e simili, né Terenzio dove parla di quelle metricule," as he defined them on 19 February 1496;[29] but his protectiveness did not exclude such moralists as Cicero and Virgil, recommended in the same breath as Holy Scripture.[30]

[22] Ibid., pp. 1160ff. For *piagnoni* teachers and administrators at the Studio, see Polizzotto, *Elect Nation,* p. 19 and n. 34.

[23] See Brown, *Bartolomeo Scala,* pp. 126ff., and below, p. 188.

[24] See above, pp. 31–33.

[25] See Weinstein, "Myth of Florence," pp. 15–44; and idem, *Savonarola,* chap. 1.

[26] See pp. 37ff.

[27] See Puelli-Maestrelli, "Savonarole," pp. 2–3, with the revised estimates of age from 6 to 17 (rather than 25) years by Verde, *Studio,* 4, 3:1218.

[28] *Prediche sopra Aggeo* (ed. Firpo), 1:20, ll. 19–23. For background, see Trexler, *Public Life,* pp. 474ff.

[29] *Prediche sopra Amos e Zaccaria* (ed. Ghiglieri), 1:92, ll. 2–5.

[30] Ibid., ll. 6–7.

The word of God occupied the supreme place in Savonarola's hierarchy of values, which he conveyed, to mercantile Florence, in metaphors of price and value. In search of gold, it was legitimate to pillage "the wise of this world," for gold signified wisdom, ethically interpreted; while oratory was silver, poetry resounding metal, grammar mute iron, and wood the rubbish produced by those without reason or sense.[31] Degrading the secular literature extolled by the humanists to a quarry for raw materials worked by a master craftsman of the intellect, Savonarola argued in favor of a hermeneutic principle contrary to theirs. For the priority of the text, classical and literary, which was the first postulate of their enterprise, he substituted, with the full rigor of medieval exegesis, the sovereignty of its interpreter.[32] His public was formed not by the academic coteries of the past but by the schoolmasters of the present holding in their charge the *fanciulli* in whom Savonarola invested his hopes for the future. They must be warned that the poets studied in the classroom contained dangerous fables: "E dove voi, maestri, trovate in quelli vostri libri di poesie Iove, Plutone ecc., dite loro:—Figliuoli miei, queste sono favole—, e mostrateli, che solo Dio è quello che regge el mondo."[33] The compassion of his pastoral care contrasted with the hauteur of the specialists, Savonarola exalted an audience on which they looked down. The *elementarii* at whom, from the comfort of the *cathedra,* Poliziano had sneered[34] were, to this preacher in the pulpit, the children of heaven.

How were their teachers to assume the grave responsibilities thrust upon them? With the guidance of a higher hermeneutic, capable of distinguishing between the husk and the core—between allegory, which applies only to Scripture, and the inferior forms of interpretation practiced by the humanists. In the Latin draft of his sermon on the psalm *Quam bonus,* Savonarola wrote: "This is against certain poets and grammarians who say that their branch of knowledge is theology."[35] Preaching about Amos 1:3, on 19 February 1496, he expanded on this view: secular literature not only lacked the qualities of allegory; it also failed to convey historical truth. History, for Savonarola, was polyvalent and tropological, its multiple meanings discernible only to the enlightened seer. Pagan *istorie,* cribbed and confined to the literal sense, had none of the Bible's predictive power, which Christian exegesis could unleash. Consider the example of Livy, who wrote not to foretell the future but to describe the past: "If you make war, you cannot determine what that war will signify in the future, in the first place because you

[31] *Prediche sopra Aggeo* (ed. Firpo), 11:182, ll. 23–30.

[32] See von Moos, "Was galt im lateinische Mittelalter als das Literarische an der Literatur?" pp. 431–51, and see further below, pp. 270ff.

[33] *Prediche sopra Amos e Zaccaria* (ed. Ghiglieri), 1:92, ll. 8–11.

[34] See above, p. 81.

[35] Verde, *Studio,* 4, 3:1142.

do not know how things will turn out in the future; in the second, you cannot do it because you do not know if you will succeed; and indeed you cannot know whether the future will turn out as you wish: that is in the gift of God alone."[36]

God's gift was not to be found at the low level of historical understanding offered, to his humanist enthusiasts, by an antiquarian like Livy.[37] Hence Savonarola's recurrent emphasis on the irrelevance, for his purposes, of the subjects from which the *studia humanitatis* claimed to derive universal knowledge.[38] "Every branch of learning has its limits," he wrote in the draft for his sermon on the psalm *Quam bonus,*[39] but those of poetry, oratory, and secular history were infinitely narrower than the majestic sweep of Scripture. Mediating, in the accessible vernacular, the sacred *auctoritas,* Savonarola stressed its actuality,[40] its bearing on the lives of all classes of Florentine society from which his following was drawn.[41] Comprehensive yet lucid, passionate but applicable, his teaching raised the issue of *utilità,* moral and political, which the Medicean intellectuals had evaded.

Imagine the impact of Savonarola's preaching on a pupil of Poliziano, such as Nesi, while he listened to the third sermon on Amos. Having heard the author of the *Lamia* disclaim, with Socratic irony, the status of a philosopher but arrogate that of the polymath,[42] Nesi was in a position to savor the contrast when, five years later, the new Socrates took up the same theme. No less provocatively than his namesake he beckoned: "Vien qua, filosofo—parlo de quello che gli pare sapere tutto,"[43] jesting with his public like Poliziano, and widening its scope. For this orator's audience was composed of both the

[36] "Dunque nota che così come Dio buono ha fatto le creature di questo mondo non solo per utilità del corpo nostro, ma *etiam* per utilità della anima per manifestare a lei la sua bontà, così la Scrittura lui l'ha ordinata e composta non solo perché narrassi quelle guerre e quelle istorie, ma per quelle significare altre cose, e ha fatto scriverle quelle Scritture e quelle istorie con quelli nomi e con quelli loci (come abbiamo dichiarato di sopra) non solo per dimostrare che così elle fussino, ma per significare altro. Non è così delle altre scritture: *vedi Livio che non scrisse perché quella scrittura significassi cose future, ma solo le passate; non lo può fare ancora uomo nessuno questo. Tu, se tu fai una guerra, non puoi designare che quella guerra significhi el futuro, primo perché non conosci le cose future, secondo non lo puoi fare perché non sai se la ti riuscirà; e non sai etiam se il futuro ti riuscirà a tuo modo: questo appartiene solo a Dio.* Però nessuna altra scrittura, se non la Sacra, ha allegoria." Ed. Ghiglieri, 3:74, ll. 28–75, 1–17.

[37] On the diffusion and use of Livy, see Billanovich and Ferraris, "Per la fortuna di Tito Livio," pp. 245–81. See further below, pp. 263ff.

[38] Cf. *Prediche sopra Giobbe* (ed. Ridolfi), pp. 131ff.

[39] Verde, *Studio,* 4, 3:1142.

[40] "Orsù, io te la esporro questa Scrittura di Amos e va'dove tu vuoi e ficcati in che cantone tu vuoi, ché questa Scrittura ti troverrà." *Prediche sopra Amos e Zaccaria* (ed. Ghiglieri), 2:54, ll. 22–25.

[41] See Guidi, "La corrente savonaroliana," pp. 31–46, esp. pp. 44–45; and idem, *Lotte, pensiero e istituzioni politiche,* pp. 321ff., with Polizzotto, *Elect Nation,* pp. 12ff.

[42] See above, pp. 117ff.

[43] Ed. Ghiglieri, 1:80, ll. 16ff.

students in the lecture room, who had hung on the professor's every word, and unlettered women, who were invited to poke fun at "the greatest ravings of scholars that you've ever heard." "Udite, donne," urged the satirical Savonarola, "listen and laugh at the absurdities of atom—and creation—theory, at the preposterous doctrine of *quodlibet est in quolibet*." Stripping from the high priests of humanism their mantle of universal knowledge, this skeptic of wordly wisdom then turned to celebrate the power of divine providence. Artfully simple, Savonarola opened to his hearers questions that these hermetic know-alls had kept closed; and he did so with a wit that neither his admirers nor his detractors have observed.[44] Publicly playing the role of intellectual scourge, while remaining privately receptive to the arguments of the one scholar whom he respected, Socrates from Ferrara developed a double persona that, both in his own age and later, has appeared inconsistent when considered out of context. If, as doyen of the *Accademia Marciana,* he could accept the potential compatibility with Christian doctrine of the Platonic and Aristotelian philosophies that, as prophet and exegete, he sometimes condemned,[45] only Pico, expert in both, was capable of convincing him of their harmony.[46] Mistrust of the *savi del mondo* Savonarola was inclined to project on the past because, with a single exception (deceased in 1494), it was justified by their inadequacy in the present.

There, with a zeal that has been exaggerated and a subtlety that has been ignored, he challenged the humanists on their own terms and demonstrated why they were to be deemed wanting. If Savonarola's exhortations to give to the poor money being spent on the Studio[47] might be shunned as the same impractical fervor that led him to call for the churches to be despoiled of their riches, at a time when the young, the wellborn, and the cultivated were abandoning the institutions of the university for the cloisters of San Marco,[48] his lesson could not be overlooked by Florence's professors. Nesi, at a sophisticated level of proselytism, magnified Savonarola's message: at the opposite extreme of semi-literacy and full fanaticism, Pietro Bernardino ("degli Unti"), sculptor by profession and demagogue by vocation,[49] amplified and distorted it, deriving from the ardor of his followers among the sect of the Anointed an obligation to burn all *libri disonesti*[50] and recommending, as a means of access to paradise, self-immolation.[51] When that fate befell him,

[44] Cf. D. Weinstein, "Hagiography," pp. 483–503.

[45] See Walker, *Ancient Theology,* pp. 42–51 (cited in note 1).

[46] Crinito, *Commentarii de honesta disciplina,* pp. 104–5.

[47] *Prediche sopra Aggeo* (ed. Firpo), 1:122, ll. 5–8.

[48] See Verde, "La congregazione domenica," pp. 151–237.

[49] On Bernardino, see Polizzotto, *Elect Nation,* pp. 119ff.

[50] "Fanciulli, havete ogni sapientia & lasciate . . . libri disonesti, come Terentio, Martiale, Iuvenale, Tibullo, Catullo, Propertio, Ovidio, & altri simili libri inonesti, perché se siate Christiani, siate obligati ad ardegli." *Prediche di Pietro Bernardino,* fol. 9ᵛ. Cf. p. 137 above.

[51] "Lasciatevi inanzi amazare, fanciulli mia, perché nandrete subito in paradiso." Ibid., fol. 6ᵛ.

in 1502, his entry into heaven passed unrecorded, nor had Savonarola, during his lifetime, deigned to acknowledge this crude caricature of his thought.[52] The "truly divine" philosopher, with whom Poliziano's friend, the refined Pandolfo Collenuccio, could enjoy long hours of conversation,[53] was as alien to the vulgar populism of a Bernardino as he was distant from other forms of extremism. In the cultural as in the political sphere, the secret of the new Socrates consisted in his ability to draw on, and transform, traditional values.[54]

. . . . .

No tradition of philological humanism had been established at Florence when Savonarola's ascendancy began. The position of the *grammatici* was weak. Neither capable of surmounting the limitations of their method nor able to silence the call for a restoration of past standards issued by Scala, they were placed on the defensive. Amid scandal and obloquy, Poliziano had passed away in September of that year, "vituperated less for his own vices than for the loathing in which Piero de' Medici was held."[55] His hegemony ended in the November revolt, the approach of his client fell on the wrong side of the caesura drawn in the intellectual history of the city by its First Chancellor's contrast between the detached erudition of the professoriate and the applied humanism of his predecessors in office.[56] Savonarola deepened that caesura, aligning himself, on grounds prepared by Scala, with the position of Leonardo Bruni.

The rapprochement was not total. When Savonarola dismissed Livy as the chronicler of an irrelevant past, he was not only contradicting Bruni, who, according to Vespasiano da Bisticci, had defended his loyalty to the Republic on the grounds that he had immortalized it in the Livian manner,[57] but also Donato Acciaiuoli, the preface to whose Italian translation of Bruni's

[52] Weinstein, *Savonarola,* p. 326.

[53] "Io me ho goduto a questi di e ancor godo Fra Hieronymo de Ferrara, homo veramente divino, maiore ancora in presentia che per scriptura. Li parlari insieme sono stati molti et longhi." Collenuccio to the duke of Ferrara, 4 October 1495, in "Pisa e Firenze" (ed. Negri), p. 56, and cf. p. 57.

[54] See Weinstein, *Savonarola,* pp. 181ff., and Polizzotto, *Elect Nation,* pp. 22ff.

[55] "Messer Agnolo Poliziano . . . passò di questa vita, con tanta infamia e publica vituperazione quanta homo sostenere potessi. . . . La vituperazione sua non tanto da'suoi vizii procedeva, quanto dalla invidia in cui venuto era Piero de' Medici nella nostra città." Parenti, *Storia fiorentina,* 1:100, 180–192. See Branca, *Poliziano,* pp. 193ff. and 322ff.; and Dionisotti, "Considerazioni sulla morte del Poliziano," pp. 145–56.

[56] See pp. 126ff. above.

[57] "Et non solo l'ho consigliata et fatto quello che s'apartiene a ogni buono cittadino, ma l'ho onorata et exaltata, quanto le mia debole forze hanno potuto, di scrivere le storie sua, et mandarle a memoria delle lettere, per farla eterna, quanto io ho potuto. Ché si vede Roma per i degni scrittori ha avuti, et maximo Livio, è stata celebrata et sarà per tutti i secoli." Bisticci, *Vite,* 1:476.

Florentine history asserted the civic utility and predictive qualities of a work that drew on this classical source.[58] Scala had taken the same model for his own *Historia Florentinorum,*[59] and in his polemic with Poliziano he had borrowed from Bruni ideas on the superiority of the ancients over the moderns.[60] Rejecting that value judgment, Savonarola accepted one of its premises, manipulating the idealization of pre-Medicean Florence that Scala promoted. Addressing the Signoria, on 13 December 1496, and speaking about the method of election to offices in the *Consiglio Maggiore,*[61] he cited Bruni's *Historiae Florentinorum* against the proposal to introduce sortition.[62] What the prophet set out to exploit was the historian's oligarchical ideology,[63] a useful weapon in his attempt to create consensus within the ruling elite or *reggimento.*[64] Radical in his religious teaching, the new Socrates was traditional in his sociopolitical thought; and that traditionalism determined the tone of public discourse in the years 1494–98. Even Savonarola's opponent at S. Maria Novella, Giovanni Caroli, presented his arguments against him in terms of a "contrast between past perfection and present decadence."[65]

Among the grounds for Caroli's criticism of Savonarola was his interference, although a priest, in political matters: witness the treatise that took as its title 2 Tim. 2:4: "Nemo militans deum [*sic*] implicat se negotiis saecularibus."[66] Nesi, praised by his hero on account of his learning "although a layman," was censured by Caroli for the same reason: he had no right to meddle in religious affairs.[67] And that was the problem that Scala, as spokesman for the Signoria, addressed with visible difficulty in his *Defense of the City of Florence Against Its Detractors* of 1496. Against a background of plots and conspiracies, at one of the many moments of crisis in the alliance with France of which Savonarola was a convinced advocate, the First Chancellor answered the charge that the city was being governed by friars, to the ridicule

[58] "Riguardando le cose passate possono meglio giudicare le presenti & le future: & ne bisogni della città piu savamente consigliare la loro republica." (Venice, 1476), a*z*.

[59] Scala, *Proemium* (ed. Jacobaeus), p. 1: ". . . minus, mihi crede, Livinianam tu in iis diligentiam facundiamque desiderabis"; with Fubini, "Osservazioni," p. 444; and idem, "Cultura umanistica," 1:440ff.

[60] See above, p. 129; and cf. Bruni, *Vita Quinti Sertorii,* proemium: ". . . nec in re militari, nec in gubernatione rerum publicarum, nec in eloquentia, nec in studiis bonarum artium tempora nostra antiquis respondere." *Humanistisch-philosophische Schriften* (ed. Baron), pp. 124–25.

[61] See Rubinstein, "I primi anni," pp. 151–94, 321–47; and Guidi, *Lotte, pensiero e istituzioni politiche,* 2:461ff.

[62] *Prediche sopra Ezechiele* (ed. Ridolfi), 1:97, ll. 6ff.

[63] See Fubini, "Cultura umanistica," p. 414, and idem, "Osservazioni," pp. 420ff, with Guidi, *Lotte, pensiero e istituzioni politiche,* 1:212 and n. 72.

[64] See Pesman Cooper, "Florentine Ruling Group," pp. 69–181.

[65] Polizzotto, *Elect Nation,* p. 63.

[66] Polizzotto, *Elect Nation,* pp. 61ff.

[67] Ibid., p. 87.

of the rest of Italy. Acknowledging that the *governo popolare* posed the danger of admitting the incompetent to the deliberations of their betters,[68] this apologist of established values appealed to the political slogan of *libertas,*[69] insisting on the separation of church and state, but then undermining his own insistence by an image of cooperation and mutual aid between the clergy and laity. This feeble attempt at conciliation, from the pen of the city's official defender, exposed the most vulnerable point of his case. Contrary to the conventions of government by the Signoria, against the trends to lay dominance in education, religion, literature and music that were notable features of Quattrocento Florence,[70] Savonarola, skillfully drawing on the ideology of republicanism and its oligarchical realities, had unleashed new forces, the political and spiritual elements of which seemed to many, for compelling reasons, indistinguishable. "Who would deny that the sacred and the profane are separate?" asked Scala with more rhetoric than conviction. The answer was evident. Those who witnessed the *fanciulli* policing the streets or processing, in numbers variously estimated but uniformly alarming, to the squares where products of Florentine secular culture—paintings, statuary, books—were tossed onto bonfires of the vanities and consumed in what appeared, to the disquieted gaze of the prophet's opponents, flames of fanaticism.[71] Nice distinctions of constitutional competence obscured in that heat and fury, it was not difficult to understand what Caroli meant when he moaned that the doctrines of Savonarola were "riddled with ambiguity."[72]

. . . . .

"Par morta tutta la città," wrote that lugubrious *laudator temporis acti* in 1497.[73] Caroli, in his nostalgia for bygone gaities of the Laurentian age, overlooked signs of life emanating from one of his younger colleagues at the Studio. In October 1494 a delicate appointment had been made. The vacant chair of Poliziano, reviled by his own and his master's enemies but mourned

[68] Scala, *Apologia,* fol. 9^b.

[69] Ibid., fol. 7^a. See Rubinstein, "Florentina libertas," pp. 3–26; and Witt, "Rebirth," esp. pp. 194–99.

[70] See Weinstein, "Critical Issues," pp. 265–70.

[71] See Parenti, *Storia fiorentina,* 1:311–12, 319–20; and cf. Landucci, *Diario fiorentino,* pp. 126–27. On processions and policing, see Trexler, *Public Life,* pp. 175ff.; on the bonfires of the vanities, H. Bredekamp, "Renaissance als 'Hölle': Savonarolas Verbrennungen der Eitelkeiten," in *Bildersturm: Die Zerstörung des Kunstwerkes,* ed. M. Warnke (Munich, 1973), pp. 41–64.

[72] "La varietà addunque di questa doctrina è cagione di varie opinioni, perché e tutta come la bugia aviluppata e rinvolta e inferma e instabile e in sull'acqua fondata . . . alchuna volta tutta sicura, alchuna volta piena d'ambiguità." Quoted from BNCF, Conv. Soppr. D.9.278, fol. 154^r by Polizzotto, *Elect Nation,* p. 54 and n. 1.

[73] Caroli, *Liber de discretione vanitatum,* in BNCF, Conv. Soppr. D.9.278, fol. 80^v.

by the friends of learning who viewed his death—a year after that of Barbaro, weeks before Pico's—as a calamity for the republic of letters,[74] had been filled by an unknown quantity: a scholar of thirty years with much promise and no publications to his name. His inaugural lecture, delivered on 1 November at a time of mounting tension,[75] eulogized Medicean patronage, to which he owed his promotion. Eight days later, Piero de' Medici was expelled from Florence.

No comfortable position, this, in which the new professor was placed; nor was Marcello di Messer Virgilio di Andrea di Berto Adriani a name with which to conjure at Florence in 1494;[76] although its bearer, from modest beginnings, went on to play a cardinal role in the development of Florentine humanism both before and after he became Machiavelli's colleague at the Chancery in 1498. Five years older than his famous contemporary, Marcello Virgilio was born, the second of four children, at 4 A.M. on Saturday, 2 July 1464. Baptized the following day at San Giovanni Battista, in the presence of his father's friends from the Guild of Lawyers and Notaries, he soon suffered his first trauma. His wet nurse, Monna Piera, who produced too little milk, had to be paid off and replaced.

This exhilarating information is provided by the *ricordanze* of Marcello Virgilio's father,[77] a cross between a diary and a ledger, which reveals much about the mentality and atmosphere in which his son was raised. Messer Virgilio combined a strong if conventional piety with attention to the worldly success that was never to be his lot. "May he find favor in the eyes of men," he prayed on the birth of his son, adding parenthetically, "and save his soul." Money, however, is the main theme that figures in the *ricordanze,* which chronicle its feckless pursuit through many and various transactions ending, invariably, with the same dismal result. Borrowing succeeded litigation, debt piled up upon debt, until nature intervened, leaving the impecunious sons of this speculator to settle the burden of taxation on his estate after his

[74] See Parenti, *Storia fiorentina* 1:100, 184–86, 196–203; and *Castigationes Plinianae* (ed. Pozzi), pp. clxivff.

[75] See Guidi, *Ciò che accade,* pp. 17ff.

[76] On the name, see Dionisotti, *Machiavellerie,* p. 242 n. 3 (not wholly accurate), and Verde, *Studio,* 3, 2:260. Unreliable are the monograph by Rüdiger, *Marcellus Virgilius Adrianus aus Florenz,* and G. Miccoli in *DBI* 1 (Rome, 1960), pp. 310–11. On confusions of Marcello Virgilio with his homonymous grandson (on whom see Miccoli, ibid., p. 310) and consequent misattributions of his work, cf. Godman, "Florentine Humanism," pp. 116ff., and L. Cesarini Martinelli in *Rinascimento,* ser. 2, 22 (1982): 183–85. Not modesty but plagiarism explains his grandson's omission of Marcello Virgilio from the history of academies in his unpublished oration to the Accademia degli Alterati in BMLF, Ashburnham, 559, fols. 60^v–61^r. Debts to his grandfather's writings are evident in his unpublished orations preserved in BNCF, Palat. 1166, I.

[77] ASF, Carte Strozziane, II, 21, fol. 8^r. On the problem of wet nurses, see P. Gavitt, *Charity and Children in Renaissance Florence: The "Ospedale degli Innocenti," 1410–1536* (Ann Arbor, 1990), pp. 227ff.

death.[78] To literature and learning Messer Virgilio paid no attention. Of books, in his *ricordanze,* there is never a word.

There lay one significant difference between the fathers of the First and Second Chancellors of the Florentine Republic. If Bernardo Machiavelli handled money matters with the same incompetence as Marcello Virgilio's prodigal parent, his *Libro di ricordi* reflects intellectual interests. On 22 September 1475, he obtained the Latin classic that was to serve his son in the *Discorsi*—*Le deche tutte di Livio,* from which he had compiled an index of "all the cities and mountains and rivers"—and had it bound.[79] He borrowed, or bought, Macrobius, Priscian, Ptolemy, Donato Acciaiuoli on Aristotle's *Ethics,* works by Cicero and by Flavio Biondo, and legal texts. While it is an exaggeration to describe Bernardo as a humanist,[80] it is not too much to attribute to Machiavelli's father a cultural curiosity that Messer Virgilio did not possess.

Socially the two families were more distinct from one another in appearance than in reality. The Machiavelli were a clan of repute. Twelve *Gonfalonieri* and sixty-three magistrates numbered among Niccolò's ancestors, at more than one remove. Yet the branch from which he descended was considered illegitimate by some,[81] and he did not qualify for membership of the *Consiglio Maggiore.*[82] Similarly lacking in luster was Marcello Virgilio's family, which in the fourteenth and fifteenth centuries had risen only twice to the priorate and had been excluded from the Medicean *reggimento* or ruling group.[83] Obscurity may have been an advantage for both these candidates at the elections to the First and Second Chancellorships in February and June 1498: lack of political affiliation, construed as neutrality, making their appointments acceptable both to the forces in favor of a broadly based regime (*governo largo*) and to those who advocated its restriction to influential families (*governo stretto*); while private opposition to Savonarola, discreetly communicated in the right quarters, skirted the issue that openly divided his enemies (the *arrabbiati*) and his partisans (the *frateschi*).[84] But that does not answer the questions of how the ascents of Marcello Virgilio and Machiavelli were engineered, and by whom.

[78] The "onera omnia tam imposita quam imponenda" on their estate were settled by Marcello and his brother Andrea on 22 April 1496. See ASF, Consigli della Repubblica, *Libri Fabarum* 71, fols. 27^{r}, 28^{v}, with Marzi, *La Cancelleria,* 1:281 n. 2.

[79] Ed. C. Olschki, pp. 14 and 35.

[80] Ibid., p. xv.

[81] See Ridolfi, *Vita di Niccolò Machiavelli,* pp. 4 and 180

[82] See Pesman Cooper, "The Florentine Ruling Group."

[83] Black, "Florentine Political Traditions," p. 12.

[84] Ibid., pp. 1–16; Black, "Machiavelli, Servant of the Florentine Republic," p. 81; and Rubinstein, "Beginning of Niccolò Machiavelli's Career," pp. 72–91. For Marcello Virgilio's early hostility to Savonarola, see above, p. 27.

Each of these men had fathers who were lawyers in contact with Bartolomeo Scala and his politico-legal circle. Bernardo Machiavelli appears as Scala's partner in his dialogue *On Laws and Legal Judgments*.[85] Messer Virgilio collaborated with the First Chancellor in a commission of 1489 appointed to scrutinize names eligible for the Guild of Notaries and Lawyers.[86] When his son took office as Scala's successor, one of his most important tasks was to record the deliberations preserved in the *Consulte e Pratiche*.[87] On 17 March 1498—little more than a month after his election on 16 February—Marcello Virgilio wrote, in his cursive script, the protocol of a debate about Florentine policy toward the papacy and Savonarola, conducted between those described as "the heart of the city."[88] Among prominent speakers were Antonio Malegonelle, Guidantonio Vespucci, and Angelo Niccolini, all of whom had served with Scala and Marcello Virgilio's father in the commission of 1489. If his son's first moves as chancellor were made in the company of a politically influential group of lawyers, linked with his parent and his predecessor, it is difficult to ascribe this to chance. The entry of Marcello Virgilio into Palazzo Vecchio, like that of Niccolò Machiavelli, was smoothed by the Scala connection.

Scala, from his brief dismissal and swift reappointment as First Chancellor in December 1494 to his death in July 1497, represented a counterbalance to Savonarola's pull. The First Chancellor was one of the few public figures with the authority to speak out in defense of secular culture. His weight can be gauged from the letters prefaced to his *Defense of the City of Florence Against Its Detractors* by Pietro Crinito, Poliziano's self-styled pupil, then engaged in preparing his works for publication, who fawned before the enemy of his alleged master: "You are the only one at Florence to possess authority and learning in equal measure."[89] Scala mattered, both intellectually and politically, not only to a marginal character such as Crinito but also to a pro-

[85] Ed. L. Borghi, pp. 256–82. See Gilbert, *Machiavelli and Guicciardini,* pp. 318–19; and Brown, *Bartolomeo Scala,* pp. 288–96.

[86] Brown, *Bartolomeo Scala,* p. 202.

[87] On the significance of which, see Gilbert, "Florentine Political Assumptions," pp. 187–214; on their function and membership, Guidi, *Lotte, pensiero e istituzioni politiche,* 1:76ff.

[88] ASF, Consigli della Repubblica, *Consulte e Pratiche* 64, fol. 41^r, 17 March 1497 (= 1498). The text is edited by D. Fachard, *Consulte e pratiche della Repubblica Fiorentina, 1494–1497* (Geneva, 1993), pp. 60–61. Fachard dates the protocol to "Die XVI*a* mensis Martii." With C. Lupi, "Nuovi documenti intorno a fra Girolamo Savonarola," *ASI,* 3d ser., 3 (1866): 53, I read "Die XVII*a* mensis martii": see Plate 3. Fachard does not identify Marcello Virgilio's hand in this document, and his attribution (in *Consulte e pratiche della Repubblica Fiorentina,* pp. 74 n. 1 and 75 n. 1) of *Consulte e Pratiche* 69, fols. 62^r–62^v, 63^r–64^v, to Marcello Virgilio is mistaken. The script appears elsewhere: e.g., ibid., fol. 61^r (first part). For the distinction between his two hands, see below, pp. 171ff.; for the debate, see further p. 169.

[89] "Tu unus Florentiae, cuius eruditioni non auctoritas auctoritati non eruditio desit." *Apologia,* p. 2^b.

fessor of the *studia humanitatis* who wished to play a central role on the civic stage.

Marcello Virgilio had matriculated at the Florentine Studio in 1480.[90] About his adolescence and student years, little is known. The family memoirs and funeral orations of his son and his grandson recall only the busy bureaucrat and distant father of later life.[91] Nonetheless, something can be established about his youthful sympathies and the friendships that he made. Marcello Virgilio's loyalties lay with Chalcondyles, not with Poliziano. Letters to and from the Greek émigré, after his move from Florence to Milan,[92] suggest a private reserve, a concealed dislike for the overbearing scholar whose position he inherited by making useful contacts. One of them was Roberto Acciaiuoli, son of the celebrated humanist Donato;[93] another was the well-placed member of a pro-Medicean family, Jacopo Segni. Their correspondence, which often mentions Marcello Virgilio in the warmest of terms, records with concern a domestic crisis (*rei familiaris angustia*) caused by the death of his father in October 1493;[94] and it was doubtless to the same hardships that Segni referred when commending him to Piero de' Medici, on 23 October 1494, as Poliziano's heir.[95]

Poor boy makes good. One day after Segni's request to Piero, it was granted. What his supporter discerned in Marcello Virgilio was *gravitas,* a political as well as a personal virtue in the turmoil at the end of the Medicean regime. Seriousness and dignity, learning and restraint are the qualities ascribed to him by Segni's recommendation: "He does not yield to the anxiety and worries that increasingly trouble us every day."[96] Two years earlier that had not needed to be said, nor would it have been considered a point in Marcello Virgilio's favor. But by October 1494 conditions had changed, and Segni wrote when factionalism was mounting. His eye was on the past, and he did not omit an analogy between the solicited patronage of Piero and Lorenzo's generosity to needy scholars. The desire to recreate a golden age of learning animates Segni's request to fill Poliziano's chair with so suitable a candidate: "No one among the entire throng of men of letters seems to me

[90] Verde, *Studio,* 3, 2:620.

[91] Primary sources are the *Funebris oratio in obitu Marcelli Virgilii [iunioris]* in BMF, Ms. B.III.65, fols. 190^{r}ff.; the autobiographical memoir of Marcello Virgilio's son, Giambattista (on whom see Miccoli, *DBI,* 1:310, and Albertini, *Firenze,* pp. 346ff.), ibid., fol. 248^{r} (partly edited by Bandini, *Collectio,* pp. xxiiff.); BNCF, Passerini 158 *bis,* n. 13; and ASF, Ms. 252, fol. 1244^{r}. See, too, Martines, *Lawyers and Statecraft,* p. 494.

[92] See above, pp. 27–29.

[93] See *DBI,* 1:90–93.

[94] BNCF, Magl. VIII.1452, fol. 31^{r}. Cf. ibid., fols. 18^{v}–19^{r}, 38^{v}, 49^{r}, 51^{v}. For Acciaiuoli's later correspondence with Marcello Virgilio, see below, p. 166.

[95] Verde, *Studio,* 3, 1:421–22.

[96] ". . . anxiasque sollicitudines non admictit, quibus quotidie magis magisque praemimur." Ibid., p. 422.

better suited to reproducing Angelo or resurrecting him in short order than Marcello Virgilio."[97]

Unaware that the candidate whom he proposed as Poliziano's successor was no admirer of his teacher, Segni had not been privy to the attitudes revealed in Marcello Virgilio's correspondence with Chalcondyles. After 1494 the latent reserve began to emerge in an oblique polemic and a stony silence occasioned by the revolt against the Medici and the birth pangs of the *governo populare.* Perceived (not without reason) as the creature of Piero, his house philologist had opposed the traditionalism and scorned the official humanism represented by Scala, with whose position the unarmed but mighty prophet of the city's future was aligned. To accept, without demur, Poliziano's legacy was dangerous in post-Medicean Florence. Disowning his master's methods and varying the terms of his legacy, Marcello Virgilio was to respond, with due caution, to the temper of the times.

The standing of this *novus homo* was precarious, his salary small, his contract annually subject to review. But he had learned the lesson that his father, on the day of his birth, had desired to impart; and he never forgot it. Marcello Virgilio needed and desired to "find favor in the eyes of men." Vaulting ambition, disguised by an imperturbable manner; sincere passion for learning; paternal debts and straitened circumstances; the insecurities of a struggle to make his way in the world; the consequent urge to make friends and win allies: all these factors focused the eyes of Poliziano's successor on the main chance. Machiavelli, from an equally simple milieu, believed that he could afford to scoff and scorn.[98] Never, in the course of more than a quarter of a century's public activity, did Marcello Virgilio lower his mask. The consequences of that difference between the First and the Second Chancellors were felt in 1512, when Machiavelli was expelled from Palazzo Vecchio, where his colleague remained ensconced.

Opportunism is too clumsy a term for this nimble survivor. Few (if any) among his generation at Florence pursued a different objective. And if lifemanship is an art and dissembling a virtue, according to the inverted criteria of *Il principe,* then Marcello Virgilio was a more accomplished Machiavellian than Niccolò Machiavelli. Their mutual friend, the historian Jacopo Nardi—executor, together with his wife and brother, of Marcello Virgilio's estate[99]—wrote of the regard in which, by common consensus, he was held by his fellow citizens, that, in 1502, "he held in his heart the perpetual and unbroken thread of the daily conduct of the Republic's affairs."[100] Day by day, year by

[97] "Nemo mihi ex omni litteratorum coetu visus est Angelum vel melius effingere vel nobis reddere maturius quam Marcellus Virgilius." Ibid.

[98] See below, pp. 239–41.

[99] ASF, Notarile antecosmiano, 21073 (notary Antonio Vespucci, 1481–1526), fol. 100^{v}.

[100] "Nel petto di questo uomo restava continuato, in quel modo che meglio si poteva, il

year, during one of the most turbulent periods in its early modern history, Marcello Virgilio stood at "the heart of the city" and attended to its beat. Neither Poliziano nor Machiavelli came close to attaining the position occupied by this pillar of the establishment. And because that establishment changed frequently during his career—from the dominance of the Medici to the apostolate of Savonarola, from the *governo populare* to the restoration of Lorenzo's dynasty—such tenacious tenure of office required more than a little dexterity. Marcello Virgilio displayed an almost unerring sense of the direction in which the wind was blowing; and if Machiavelli, theorist of *Realpolitik,* sought a practical lesson in that subject from one of his peers, he had only to look at the colleague with whom he worked for almost fifteen years.

Did their acquaintance predate their appointments to the Chancery in 1498? Many have thought so, making Machiavelli a pupil of Marcello Virgilio,[101] but not always distinguishing between him and his homonymous grandson, who put pen to paper long after Niccolò had died.[102] All rely on the testimony of Paolo Giovio. He says nothing of the kind, merely reporting that Machiavelli "inserted into his writings *flores* of Greek and Latin" taken from Marcello Virgilio.[103] This does not require us to imagine Niccolò, abstracted from the bank at Rome,[104] literally sitting at the professor's feet in the Studio of Florence or copying for him the text of Lucretius.[105] The debts were different; the process of influence, acceptance, and rejection subtler and more complex; and if it is hardly profitable to speculate on whether, in the years before his succession to Poliziano's chair, Marcello Virgilio, as a teacher of Greek,[106] might have kindled Machiavelli's interest in

---

filo perpetuo e continuo delle cose della repubblica che alla giornata seguiva." *Le storie di Firenze di Jacopo Nardi* (ed. Gelli), 1:232. On Nardi, see Albertini, *Firenze,* pp. 314ff.

[101] For the controversy, see Ridolfi, *Vita di Niccolò Machiavelli,* pp. 30–31 and p. 437 n. 17; Dionisotti, *Machiavellerie,* pp. 414ff.; Black, "Machiavelli, Servant of the Florentine Republic," p. 74; J. Stephens, review article in *Italian Studies* 47 (1992): 100.

[102] See Godman, "Florentine Humanism," p. 118.

[103] *Elogia clarorum virorum* 77 (ed. R. Meregazzo), p. 112. See further below, pp. 275ff.

[104] See M. Martelli, "L'altro Niccolò di Bernardo Machiavelli," pp. 39–100.

[105] The conjecture, for which there is no external evidence, that Machiavelli made his copy of Lucretius (Vatican, Ross. 884) for Marcello Virgilio (see S. Bertelli, "*Noterelle machiavelliane*—Un codice di Lucrezio e di Terenzio," *Rivista storica italiana* 73 [1961]: 544–53, and "*Noterelle machiavelliane*—Ancora su Lucrezio e Machiavelli," ibid. 76 [1964]: 774–90) derives from a misinterpretation of Paolo Giovio. See further below, pp. 277ff. Neither the marginalia nor the lacuna at Lucretius 1.1013 indicated in BMLF, Pluteo 35.32, fol. 21^r are in the hand of Marcello Virgilio (*pace* M. D. Reeve, "The Italian Tradition of Lucretius," *IMU* 23 [1980]: 47), and, for reasons set out below, nothing is less likely than the speculation (ibid.) that he occupied himself with the textual criticism of Lucretius in the 1490s.

[106] On Marcello Virgilio as a "maestro di greco" in 1490 (when Machiavelli was 21), see Segni's letter, ed. Verde, *Studio,* 3, 1:419.

that language, it is legitimate to ask, more precisely than hitherto, what Giovio meant. Which were the modes of reading and methods of interpretation that lie behind *Il principe* and the *Discorsi*?

. . . . .

The modes of reading that Marcello Virgilio promoted, the methods of interpretation that he developed in and after the year 1494 have never been analyzed, because his lectures and orations are largely unpublished and little known.[107] Only once did he venture into print—in 1518, with a translation of, and commentary on, Dioscorides' *Materia medica.*[108] More than 700 closely printed folios, in Latin, have not proved the most glamorous medium with which to attract the eye of fame, nor has attention been paid to the purpose of that weighty work in the culture for which it was produced.[109] Why Marcello Virgilio waited for twenty-four years after his professorial appointment to bring out a book is another problem that calls for explanation. Although reluctance to publish had precedents at Florence,[110] and a motive (or pretext) was furnished by the extinction of most of the city's printers in the last years of the Quattrocento,[111] even then pressure was being exerted on him by his admirers to prove his worth to a wider public. A Portuguese student, Enrico Caiado, writing from Bologna, where he had migrated to hear Filippo Beroaldo, assured Marcello Virgilio on 23 January 1495 of how much he missed his "majesty of speech," of how he longed for "the intensity" with which his former master "explained individual passages."[112] From the same city in which the productive Beroaldo was establishing a European fame, Caiado wrote again, on 20 November 1496, that no one believed him when he

[107] Extracts from the *praelusiones* of 1494 to 1498 are printed from *R* by Verde, *Studio,* 4, 3:1160ff. Perhaps unaware of the relationship between *R* and the uncensored versions of the speeches in *N,* Verde takes leave of Marcello Virgilio in 1498 (ibid., p. 1345), with a call for other scholars to occupy themselves with him, partly answered by McManamon's "Marketing a Medici Regime," pp. 1–41. Valuable work on *L* had previously been done by Richardson, "A Manuscript of Biagio Buonaccorsi," pp. 589–601; and see Godman, "Florentine Humanism," pp. 75ff. The affiliations of the manuscripts cited in sigla above and the parallel transmission will be examined in my edition of Marcello Virgilio's unpublished writings for the Studio and the Chancery.

[108] See below, pp. 212–34. I exclude the publication of his *Oratio . . . pro dandis Florentinae Reipublicae militaribus imperatoris signis magnifico Laurentio de Medicis* at Basle in 1518, because it was unauthorized.

[109] Dionisotti (*Machiavellerie,* p. 243) alone has pointed to its exceptional character.

[110] See Perosa, "Studi sulla tradizione delle poesie latine," *Studi in onore di M. E. Paoli* (Florence, 1956), pp. 539–62.

[111] Ridolfi, *La stampa,* p. 27.

[112] "Marcelli mei in dicendo maiestatem, in singulis quibusdam explanandis vehementiam." Ed. W. P. Mustard, *The Eclogues of Henrique Cayado* (Baltimore, 1931); and Verde, *Studio,* 4, 3:1160.

spoke of Marcello Virgilio's "remarkable learning," because nothing had been released from his well-stocked bottom drawer: "Come now, leave the shadows, go out into the world, and show your worth to the light of day! (That would give your fans the opportunity to speak about you more boldly!)"[113]

Which plea fell on deaf ears. A prudent administrator of his own reputation, Marcello Virgilio did not rush into print. Nor did he remain silent, choosing instead to confine to the audience for which they were originally intended the answers to the problems of a culture in crisis that he formulated in his lectures. Some of them, intended for oral delivery before the restoration of the Medici, were revised and censored by their author after 1512. Because a number of the original versions survive, analysis of his alterations and omissions offer us valuable insights into how he became, during the "popular" Republic, arbiter of letters. Valuable and piquant, for on 31 August 1507, by virtue of his office as First Chancellor, Marcello Virgilio was appointed—for the first time in Florentine history—state censor.[114] Equipped with draconian powers to imprison and to fine, he operated behind the scenes, independently of any magistrature. There we shall follow him, observing how he censored himself and reconstructing youthful opinions over which this éminence grise, with the wisdom of hindsight, thought it expedient to draw a veil.

. . . . .

A veil of ambiguity needed to be drawn over Marcello Virgilio's opinions at the beginning of November 1494. If, in his inaugural lecture, delivered days before the collapse of Piero's tottering regime, he could not afford to alienate the patron to whom he owed his chair, it was equally unwise to take the partisan line of Poliziano. But how to deal with a predecessor so notoriously bound to the house of Medici? Praise could not be avoided. It was required by the occasion. Better, therefore, to make a virtue of necessity, and render the encomium double-edged.

Equivocal and reluctant, for the first—and only—time in all his writings, Marcello Virgilio mentioned his master by name. Not, however, in the solitary splendor that Poliziano had desired but in the incongruous company of

[113] "Doleo quantum in me est, quod de singulari eruditione tua . . . nulla prorsus fides dicenti adhibeatur, praesertim cum nihil videant ex liberalissimis tuis scriniis depromptum. . . . Igitur prodi, exi foras, ut e tenebris virtus in claram lucem trahatur! (Quae res tuis dabit occasionem de te audacius loquendi.)" Ed. Verde, *Studio,* 2:476–77.

[114] ASF, Signori e Collegi, *Deliberazioni fatte in forza di ordinaria autorità,* 109, fol. 80^{v}, with Marzi, *Cancellaria,* p. 281 n. 2. The document is printed by Pettas, *The Giunti of Florence,* p. 292. The appointment is to be distinguished from unofficial "censorship," of which there are earlier instances; cf. H. Harth, "Niccolò Niccoli als literarischer Zensor: Untersuchungen zur Textgeschichte von Poggios *De Avaritia,*" *Rinascimento* 7 (1967): 29–53. See further below, pp. 294ff.

three scholars with whom he had been loath to exchange a word: Landino, whom he had snidely criticized; Chalcondyles, whom he had maneuvered aside; and Lascaris, with whom he had crossed swords.[115] And as if that were not enough for an audience at the Studio aware of the deceased professor's animosities, Poliziano was then represented as a follower of the teacher whom he had denied. "The father of literature," by virtue of his "singular learning and seniority," the living Landino was given precedence over the dead Poliziano. And what was he? A beneficiary of Medicean munificence—an interpreter and writer of poetry in a measure "which I should not venture to judge."[116]

Tepid eulogy of Poliziano's achievements contrasted with warm paeans to the ally of his enemy, Bartolomeo Scala, as Marcello Virgilio seemed both to laud the support given to culture by Lorenzo's dynasty and to intimate a reserve toward the unpopular client who had profited from it. The strategy was subtle. Proprieties outwardly deserved, who among the friends and the foes of the Medici could have quarreled with such a diplomatic exercise in due form? Its contradictions were implicit. Their sting lay in what remained unsaid.

Declarations of allegiance, in this shifting situation, were not to be taken at face value. Marcello Virgilio expressed his respect for tradition, from which he pledged he would not diverge.[117] Reversing the scorn poured on established practices a generation before him by Argyropoulos in his inaugural lecture,[118] the dutiful humanist proclaimed himself a student of Poliziano and Landino, before proceeding to demonstrate that he was a pupil of neither. To poetics, his chosen subject (and to much else besides), they had taken contrary approaches; and in the space left vacant by their differences, his own choices could be made. His own, announced with conscious anachronism, was the decision to speak "not about, but in favor of poetics," for that "most eminent of all the arts" lay "wholly destitute of support, torn apart by the abuse of its critics."[119]

[115] *R* fol. 1^{v}.

[116] *R* fol. 3^{v}: "Nam . . . Landinus, qui et ob singularem doctrinam, que in eo est, et ob etatem, qua ceteros nos anteit, pater litterarum a me appellandus habendusque est . . . quem secutus hac nostra etate Politianus, vir magni ingenii cultique iudiciique, qui et studio diligentiaque, quibus plurimum utebatur, fultus etiam ope liberalitateque domus Medice, cuius est unicum in hac urbe patrocinium litterarum, ea et ipse poetice prestitit docendo interpretando scribendoque, qualia non est animus mihi indicare."

[117] *R* fol. 1^{r}: "Ne quid in his mutetur, que utiliter semel excogitata a maioribus fuerint . . . nos itaque auctoritate magnorum virorum freti exemplo etiam maiorum hoc primo nostre interpretationis rudimento nihil de tota hac re mutare decrevimus."

[118] See above, p. 117.

[119] *R* fol. 1^{r}: ". . . [decrevimus] . . . non tam de poetice quam pro poetice dicere, siquidem una omnium prestantissima artium patrociniis omnibus destituta iacet obtrectatorum quorundam conviciis proscissa."

This sentence might have been written at the beginning, not the end, of the fifteenth century. Inconceivable from the pen of a specialist such as Poliziano, it was couched in the style of an old-fashioned defender of poetry against its detractors, like Coluccio Salutati. Drawing on the traditionalism that Scala had put in vogue, Marcello Virgilio ignored the fact that the discipline whose sole protector he styled himself had been rigorously treated, a handful of years previously, by no less than three writers: Fonzio, Poliziano, and Savonarola.[120] And if the purpose of this sleight of hand was to cast the unnamed author of the *Apologeticus* as an enemy of poetry, more militant than Giovanni Dominici,[121] it amounted to a travesty of the truth. Savonarola's criticisms, as Marcello Virgilio was well aware, had been leveled at what the prophet regarded as abuse of this medium. His criteria were moral. Judged by them, the subject that the new professor was paid to teach seemed irrelevant and trivial. Marcello Virgilio, in 1494, was not compelled by Savonarola to mount a general defense of poetry. He was faced with the more specific, and daunting, task of proving that secular verse, in a culture turning away from its recent history and back to its past, could meet the prophet's standards.

In this dilemma, neither of the humanists who had recently written on the subject were of much use to Marcello Virgilio. The theories of poetic frenzy, like the classifications of poetic genre and biography developed by Fonzio and Poliziano, were now beside the point. The *Nutricia,* inopportune in late Laurentian Florence, had been packed off to Rome. That is why, with the exaggerations of inaugural oratory, Marcello Virgilio depicted the state of his subject as desolate; shunned the work of his immediate predecessors; and focused his attention on the Horatian axioms of utility and pleasure that had served Salutati and others so well.[122]

Utilitas and *delectatio* were axioms, employed in epideictic rhetoric, of praise and blame. They had been used by Salutati and (in a different but related sense) by Landino to assess poetry in ethical terms.[123] The civic virtues figured in both their treatments, expository or apologetic, of the medium; but public affairs, in the poetics of Salutati and Landino, played a minor role.[124] Accepting their criteria, Marcello Virgilio altered their emphasis.

[120] See above, pp. 77–79.

[121] See Da Prati, *Giovanni Dominici;* and P. Denley, "Giovanni Dominici's Opposition to Humanism," in *Religion and Humanism,* Studies in Church History 17 (Oxford, 1982), pp. 103–14. For the parallel between Dominici and Savonarola, see Schnitzer, *Savonarolas Erzieher,* p. 108ff.

[122] For Salutati's views on poetry, see *Epistolario di Coluccio Salutati* (ed. Novati), 1:298–307, 321–29; 2:285–95 and 539–43; 4:170–240; and *De laboribus Herculis,* passim. Useful treatments include Witt, *Hercules,* pp. 209ff.; and Ullman, *Humanism of Coluccio Salutati,* pp. 53–70.

[123] See C. Kallendorf, *In Praise of Aeneas: Virgil and Epideictic Rhetoric in the Early Italian Renaissance* (Hannover, 1989), pp. 7–12 and 77ff.

[124] Ibid., pp. 142ff. and 167ff. (Landino); and Robey, "Humanist Views," pp. 11ff.

Poetry, to him, represented more than an instrument of art and education. It was a means of exerting intellectual control.

With "precepts and punishments," this moral medium is of use to man, because "with its charm it holds him, departing from the truth and on the verge of rebellion, in check."[125] Not the familiar position, derived from Cicero's *De inventione,* about poetry's civilizing force,[126] but a notion of corrective authority is advanced by Marcello Virgilio. That authority is comprehensive because the subject itself deals with all aspects of human inquiry. To attack poetry is thus to condemn philosophy and theology, with which it is inextricably linked.[127] The exponents of this omnicompetent art are capable of unlocking the secrets of nature: witness Aristotle's examples of Empedocles and Parmenides or the more dubious case of Lucretius, who, even if he did voice heretical opinions about atoms, lucidly explained the mysterious workings of the world.[128]

Its cognitive and social function affirmed, poetry still had to be defended from the originally Platonic charge, revived by Savonarola, that fiction deceives. That deceptiveness is inherent in the medium, Marcello Virgilio acknowledged, appealing instead to the idea of a *fraus utilis.*[129] When we read the poems about fornication and drunkenness by Martial or about whores by Juvenal, what we praise and admire are not the subjects that they treat, but the art with which they depict them.[130] Palpably ill at ease with this attempt, indirectly derived from Aristotle's *Poetics* (1448*b*ff.), to distinguish between mimetic pleasure and the images of its contemplation,[131] Marcello Virgilio hesitated to venture any formal definition of the medium that he defended. "It is hackneyed, and it is vulgar, to assert that, if the verse is subtracted, nothing remains of poetry: the criticism lays too much weight on one of its constituent elements, and that the worse."[132] "Nonetheless, from

[125] *R* fol. 1^{v}: ". . . utilitatem pariter et delectationem perfectissimumque rerum nature opus effecerit, quod et preceptis castigationibusque suis homini prodesset et a veritate ipsa discedentem et pene rebellem dulcedine sua retineret."

[126] See above, p. 63.

[127] *R* fol. 1^{v}: "Pleraque vero cum aliis scientiis et artibus ita communia, ut non possit poetice sine philosophia theologia etiam ipsa vituperari." Cf. ibid., 2^{r}: "Ea omnia que vix singula singule artes sibi proposuerunt in se una optime complexa est."

[128] *R* fols. 2f. For this echo of earlier controversies about Lucretius, see E. Garin, "Commenti lucreziani," *Rivista critica di storia della filosofia* 28 (1973): 83–84; and cf. V. del Nero, "Filosofia e teologia nel commento di Giovan Battista Pio a Lucrezio," *Interpres* 5 (1986): 156–99.

[129] *R* fol. 4^{r}.

[130] *R* fol. 4^{v}: ". . . nos lenocinia ebrietatesque Martialis impudicam Iuvenalis de mulieribus historiam legentes non res ipsas sed artem, que eas pulcre imitata est [*erased*] sit, laudamus et admiramur."

[131] See below, p. 201.

[132] *R* fol. 4^{v}: ". . . qui ad damnandam poetices accedant communiore et vulgari nimis accusatione utentes quod, soluta compositione illa numerosa carminum disturbatoque omnium

dialectic and rhetoric verse differs only in respect of its unique and intrinsic form."[133]

So the *Apologeticus* had argued on different grounds. Devaluation of form, like mistrust of formalism, were central topics over which divergence from Savonarola was, in late 1494, impossible. On the issue that had divided him and Pico from Poliziano and Barbaro, the advocates of content's primacy had won the day. It was no longer sufficient or expedient, at Florence, to defend poetry on aesthetic or historical grounds. Academic examples, presented with elegant learning, failed to meet the criteria set by the prophet, who had altered the tone of intellectual debate. Not all of them were satisfied by Marcello Virgilio, whose inaugural lecture scarcely addressed the hermeneutic difficulties raised by Savonarola's denial of allegorical status to secular literature and skirted the problem of poetic theology. There was much that the new professor did not say, still more that he left unsaid. Yet in this first public oration, improvised within a week by a humanist in a hurry, what were to become his principal themes during the following years had already emerged: utility and pleasure, conceived in an ethical and social context; a system of mutually dependent *artes,* linked not by a scholastic hierarchy but by a community of secular values; an atmosphere of crisis, attack, and defense that recalled the debates at the beginning of the Quattrocento. Back to the values of the republican past, away from the philology of the Medicean clients: such was Marcello Virgilio's response to the crisis of 1494, in which the traditionalism of Savonarola and Scala had become the order of the day. Within weeks of the new professor's debut, the French invaders had entered Florence; the scourge of Cyrus proclaimed from the pulpit had been felt; and the studious youth of the Florentine Studio, electrified by an oratory that dealt with these momentous happenings, was no longer disposed to attend lectures on subjects remote from the concerns of the moment.

. . . . .

The Studio, since its foundation in the fourteenth century, had not led one life with the city. Their uneasy coexistence had been marked, from the outset, by political interference in the affairs of the university.[134] One of the reasons (actual or fabricated) given for the transfer of the faculties of theology, medicine, and jurisprudence to Pisa in 1473 was a desire to safeguard

---

dictionum ordine et positura, nihil in poetice amplius remanebit, quod movere lectorem possit . . . animadvertentes se non integram iam poeticem sed partem eius—eamque deteriorem—vituperare."

[133] *R* fol. 5^r: ". . . neque enim est aliud quicquam quo poetice a dialectice et rhetorica differat, nisi forma ipsa, que sibi una et propria est."

[134] See Garfagnini, "Città e Studio," pp. 101–20.

students from the fleshpots of Florence.[135] There, among an abundance of temptations and a shortage of housing, had remained the literary subjects professed by Poliziano. And there, under Lorenzo's aegis, a teacher of the *studia humanitatis* had no need, no right to justify his pursuits in terms of their applicability to public issues. Quiescent men of letters, dedicated to research and sustained by patronage, went about the customary academic business of gossip, intrigue, and denigration of rivals. No voice was raised in protest against the Medicean regime. Cocooned in a comfort adequate to his needs but insufficient for his ambitions, Poliziano confined himself to admiring the style of the orations delivered by Pandolfo Collenuccio when his friend was *podestà*.[136] About their political content Poliziano said nothing, because there was nothing to say. The *protestationes de iustitia* of Lorenzo's lifetime[137] were as anodyne as the lectures of the professoriate.

In 1494 that idyll (or that illusion) was shattered. Pisa rose in revolt, and the teachers of the higher disciplines were transferred first to Prato, then to Florence, where they remained until 1503.[138] In the unfamiliar proximity of his colleagues from other branches of learning, it became increasingly difficult for a mere master of the *studia humanitatis* to sustain Poliziano's assertion that the literary subjects of his preference represented the sum of knowledge. The case had to be argued on different grounds, taking account of the new situation. The visceral link that bound the Florentine Studio to the city's politics[139] had tightened. If Poliziano's successor found it prudent to steer clear of controversy in November 1494, a year later it was imperative to take a stand and prove that the *studia humanitatis* were capable of reentering the mainstream of civic life.

At the Studio, where eloquence was so often extolled during the dominance of the Medici, empty rhetoric had reigned. As the generation previous to Marcello Virgilio's had left no viable models for political oratory, he had to look elsewhere—to traditions that were neither purely erudite nor exclusively academic,[140] whose distinguished exponents, combining refine-

[135] Documentation in Verde, *Studio,* 4, 1; still useful, for the perspective from Pisa, is G. B. Picotti, "Lo Studio di Pisa dalle origini a Cosimo Duca," *Bollettino storico pisano* 12 (1943): 37ff. See, too, Denley, "*Signore* and *Studio,*" pp. 203–16.

[136] See *Politiani Opera,* 1:220.

[137] See Santini, "La 'Protestatio de iustitia,'" pp. 33–106.

[138] Cf. R. Black, "Higher Education in Florentine Tuscany," in Denley and Elam, eds., *Florence and Italy,* p. 214.

[139] The expression is G. C. Garfagnini's ("Città e Studio," p. 117): "Lo Studio fu sempre visceralmente legato al potere politico di Firenze, a quella lotta di parte e di fazioni che coinvolgeva tutta la cittadinanza . . . che lo voleva e ne approvava il funzionamento, anche se con qualche mugugno, e poi lo dimenticava, letteralmente, assorbita in altre preoccupazioni più urgenti, dettate dalle convenienze e dalle circostanze interne o esterne."

[140] No recent study of this subject exists. The older work by Santini, *Firenze e i suoi oratori,*

ment of expression with a lofty conception of culture, had not been professors. Chief among them were Coluccio Salutati and Leonardo Bruni, the chancellors of Florence who were being cited by Scala and Savonarola. Marcello Virgilio, in his inaugural lecture, had already seen the point. Republican discourse was in the air. Now, at the opening of the academic year 1495–96, he had to pluck it from the winds of change and demonstrate the relevance and actuality of the discipline of rhetoric that he was paid to teach.

Demonstrate to whom? Not just to the students in his charge but also to the city fathers—in particular, the *Ufficiali dello Studio,* whom Marcello Virgilio addressed as *patres optimi.*[141] The allocution was a pun. It played on the double authority, paternal and political, of the members of his audience for whom, in the first place, his *praelusiones* were intended. They determined whether the fledgling professor's contract should be renewed, and on what terms. They held the key to eventual promotion. And they were not—in respect of their social, religious, or intellectual positions—homogenous, counting among their number both Savonarola's supporters and his opponents, advocates of a "closed" and proponents of a more "open" system of government. On them, without taking sides, Marcello Virgilio had to make an impression. On them his future depended.

There was one element in his predecessor's ideology that he hesitated to jettison, because it was shared by others. *Enkyklios paideia,* a complete and integrated culture, Marcello Virgilio located in the subject that he now turned to celebrate.[142] "Rhetoric," he declared, abandoning the mock modesty that had characterized his inaugural lecture, "would be treated by him with greater verve (*acrius*) than by all his predecessors, without exception, for they had dealt not with the substance of the discipline, but a shadow." And why had these miscreants, so recently praised, pursued a will-o'-the-wisp? Because for sixty years rhetoric had been taught and studied in a city that was unfree.[143] The allusion was polemical, the dating exact. In 1434 Cosimo de' Medici had returned from exile and established the primacy of his house. Under Medicean dominance, implied Marcello Virgilio (while managing not to mention the name), rhetoric had languished until now, with a change of fortune, the subject's importance to the resurgent Republic was again apparent. "With the arms of oratory" its champions would do battle in its de-

---

stands in need of revision and expansion. Valuable remarks by N. Rubinstein and C. Branca in *Leonardo Bruni, cancelliere della Repubblica Fiorentina,* ed. P. Viti (Florence, 1990), pp. 15–28, 227–45; and Baron, *Humanistic and Political Literature.*

141 *R* fol. 6^{r}.

142 Ibid.: "Est enim [Rhetorica] nobis velut encyclios quedam disciplina et in orbem reditus super his studiis a nobis traditus."

143 Ibid.: ". . . illi hactenus non rem, sed umbram persecuti sunt. Nec minus qui eam sexaginta annis in civitate parum libera studiosius didicerunt."

fense,[144] for rhetoric was both the guardian of laws and, "in democracies," the (with Pindar's translated words) "resplendent banner of liberty."[145]

The former Medicean protégé had become a spokesman of republican *libertas*. So Marcello Virgilio conceived the link between freedom and culture, in terms reminiscent of Leonardo Bruni.[146] His task, as he saw it, was "to educate your young men in those fields of study that improve and embellish the Republic."[147] *Arma et leges,* warfare and law, were the fundamental institutions of civil order that rhetoric upheld. Naturally, this did not mean that the master of the subject was an innovator: he was merely pursuing the goal set by the ancestors of his audience, while following a similar route.[148] Those *maiores*—before the invention of the *studia humanitatis,* after the "barbarian" invasions—had taught their young men, "with a new and ingenious commentary," to love liberty and fight for it. Not with arms, but with the weapons provided by such classic works as the *Aeneid,* Marcello Virgilio proposed to adopt the same method.[149] He would instruct his pupils on how to raise the sword and smite the tyrant. His gaze turned less to some unspecified era between the fall of Rome and the rise of the Medici than to a period of crisis that offered, for the politically astute among his hearers, analogies to the present age, Marcello Virgilio began to recreate the political eloquence of Salutati's *De tyranno,* to revive the chancellor's rhetoric during the War of the Eight Saints.[150]

A public role, never sought by his predecessor and antithetical to Poliziano's type of humanism, was evoked by Marcello Virgilio's choice of parallels. That aim was made explicit in the remainder of his speech. Rhetoric, as he described it, was not only a weapon in the struggle against

144 Ibid.: "Ut . . . mutata fortuna respub[lica] resurgeret, habere civitas posset quos oratoriis armis instructos ex umbra in veram aciem produceret."

145 *R* fol. 6v: ". . . ut quam nuper erexistis (ut Pindarus dicebat) 'fulgentem libertatis crepidinem,' eam adhuc altius tollentes servetis aeternam." The allusion (perhaps the first use, by a Florentine humanist, of Pindar in a political sense) is to fr. 77, 2 as transmitted by Plutarch, *De glor. Athen.* 350*a*. For context, see J. Irigoin, *Histoire du texte de Pindare* (Paris, 1952), pp. 364ff., 423.

146 Cf. E. Garin in *Leonardo Bruni, cancelliere,* p. 14, and idem, "La 'retorica' di Leonardo Bruni," pp. 40–41.

147 *R* fol. 6v: ". . . iuventutis vestre animos hiis studiis excolere possim, quibus Respub[lica] honestior et auctior reddatur."

148 Ibid.: "Non posse me sine piaculo ab institutis maiorum vestrorum discedere nec nisi iniuste ad eam, licet diverso itinere, non ingredi, quam illi sibi eruditionem iuventutis . . . [fol. 7r] optimam rationem proposuerunt."

149 *R* fol. 7r; and see further below, pp. 189ff.

150 See R. G. Witt, "The *De tyranno* and Coluccio Salutati's View of Politics and Roman History," *Nuova rivista storica* 53 (1969): 450ff.; and idem, *Coluccio Salutati,* pp. 53–56, 77–82, 84–85; Petrucci, *Coluccio Salutati,* pp. 17ff.; H. Langkabel, *Die Staatsbriefe Coluccio Salutatis* (Cologne, 1981), pp. 57ff.; and P. Herde, "Politik und Rhetorik am Vorabend der Frührenaissance," *Archiv für Kulturgeschichte* 47 (1965): 167ff.

tyranny and a guarantor of the laws; it was also a means of creating a consensus that, among the vicissitudes of the times, there existed "omnicompetent *signori* (*dominos*)" capable of determining, by perpetual and rational rules, the distribution of justice and the organization of the state: "Certain of the more distinguished among *us*," as Marcello Virgilio modestly defined them, whom, in the public interest, the others should elect and revere.[151]

Observe the magisterial pronoun: *nos* ('us'), rather than *nobis* ('for us'). Identifying himself with the Signoria—although, by birth and position, he was ineligible even for election to the Great Council[152]—Marcello Virgilio underlined the point in an example at the end of his lecture, imagining his audience transformed from "senators into professors" and elevating "professors into senators."[153] Rhetoric, once identified with intellectual wisdom,[154] was now employed as a means of social ascent. Adapting the elitarian and oligarchical ideology of Bruni,[155] Marcello Virgilio voiced an aspiration to join the ruling class. The gesture was noted. His salary, which had doubled from fifty to one hundred florins in 1495, was increased by a further twenty in the following year.[156] He was on the right track.

. . . . .

The Republic had been shipwrecked, and in two years of hardship the *studia humanitatis* had been jettisoned, announced the woe-washed orator in his *praelusio* on grammar on the beginning of the academic year 1496–97.[157] Should he lament the disaster or follow ancient conventions of the genre and write a dutiful but implausible panegyric? The tension, evident since Marcello Virgilio's inaugural lecture, between his obligation to preserve tradition[158] and his urge to depart from it, found expression in the metaphor of captivity used, by both the humanists and their critics, to describe their contested enterprise.[159] As defender of the *studia humanitatis,* the professor announced a cycle of annual lectures in praise of their constituent disciplines,[160] before abandoning precedent and claiming for himself, as

[151] *R* fol. 9^v: ". . . aliquos rerum omnium dominos, qui temporum vicissitudinibus has eternis legibus rectaque ratione distinguerent, quibus omnia accepta referenda essent . . . et *nos* prestantiores aliquos eligere, quos ceteri venerarentur et colerent." See further below, pp. 191ff.

[152] See above, p. 145.

[153] *R* fol. 11^r: ". . . ex senatoribus vos professores et ex professoribus senatores facere."

[154] See Vasoli, *I miti e gli astri,* pp. 254ff.

[155] Cf. R. Fubini, in *Leonardo Bruni, cancelliere,* p. 49.

[156] See Verde, *Studio,* 2:476–77.

[157] *R* fol. 12^r.

[158] Ibid.: ". . . ad servanda veterum instituta."

[159] Ibid.: ". . . ut mos est, ad res letas aliis atque aliis exultamus profecto ceu parentes receptis *ex longa captivitate* filiis suis." For the metaphor, see p. 31 above.

[160] *R* fol. 13^r: "Me vero nullus accuset, quod inauditum forte hactenus et insolitum de gram-

grammaticus, rights and responsibilities of which not even his most ambitious predecessors had dreamed.

Drawing an analogy between his function as an interpreter of language and the surgeon's interventions in the human body, Marcello Virgilio conceived the natural workings of language as imperfect and incomplete. They needed to be supplemented, regulated, and corrected with sharp incisions; and the instrument with which this professor proposed to effect the operation was the *virgula censoria.* But the mark and sign of critical activity that Poliziano had borrowed, in his *Lamia,* from Quintilian as a symbol of the censorial authority of the *grammaticus*[161] was neither precise nor pointed enough for Marcello Virgilio. He likened the power that he coveted to the cutting edge of the sword.[162]

Censorship, its rights and its privileges, was an office that he desired to revive on the model and with the justification of antiquity. This was Marcello Virgilio's claim, and it was patently untrue. No ancient grammarian had pretended to the critical absolutism asserted by this advocate of republican liberty.[163] He was aware of the discrepancy between his actual ideal and his feigned precedent, denying, with the ambivalence of Poliziano, that he was exchanging the role of defender for that of prosecutor,[164] while formulating his objective in terms of absolute control. Like ephors in the Spartan state, whose jurisdiction was superior to that of the royal writ, the *grammaticus*—as Marcello Virgilio imagined him—held sway over all authors, including Homer, "prince of literature and father of philology," commanding the right "to add to, subtract from, and athetize them" at will.[165]

---

matice sermonem ad vos afferam: hoc enim consilio huc accessimus, non ut veterem consuetudinem improbemus dicendi de bonis artibus, sed ut conculcatam grammaticam erigamus restituamusque in integrum unicam nostri animi interpretem. Et quia propositum mihi est, si et vos sic iudicabitis, singularum disciplinarum quotannis singulas laudationes dicere, ut (si fieri posset) ociosa hec iuventus vestra hiis laudibus ad hec studia erigatur."

[161] *Lamia* (ed. Wesseling), p. 16, ll. 28ff.: ". . . apud antiquos olim tantum auctoritas hic ordo habuit, ut censores essent et iudices scriptorum omnium soli grammatici, quos ob id etiam criticos vocabant, sic ut non versus modo (ita etiam Quintilianus ait) *censoria* quadam *virgula* notare sed libros etiam."

[162] *R* fol. 13^v: ". . . solamque cui ab antiquis *virgula illa censoria quasi gladii potestas* concessa sit in omnes pariter auctores."

[163] On the ancient tradition, see R. Kaster, *Guardians of Language: The Grammarian and Society in Late Antiquity* (Berkeley, 1988), pp. 15ff.

[164] *R* fol. 13^v: ". . . patrocinium enim hoc loco non censuram scriptorum agimus." Cf. p. 90 above.

[165] *R* fol. 13^v: "Nec aliud in litteris esse quamque in Spartana Republica ephori fuerunt: illis enim in reges etiam ius datum. Et huic in Homerum principem litterarum et totius philologiae parentem *libera potestas concessa addendi, detrahendi, signandique. . . .*" For a later analogy to the "censorship" of Homer in Codro Urceo, see Grafton and Jardine, *From Humanism to the Humanities,* p. 93; for the likeness to Sparta, cf. E. Rawson, *The Spartan Tradition in European Thought* (Oxford, 1969), pp. 139ff.

The language of power, the likeness to the higher—the supreme—magistracies, the similes of censors and ephors were adapted from a work upon which neither Poliziano nor any other *grammaticus* of the Laurentian era would have considered drawing in such a context. That model was the *Laudatio Florentinae urbis* of Leonardo Bruni.[166] The alignment with his humanism marked a further stage in the development of Marcello Virgilio's traditionalist thought: a return to a position analogous to that of the grammarian Guido da Raggiolo praised in Giovanni Caroli's *Vitae fratrum S.M. Novellae* (a work intended for laymen and clergy alike), who had served, or was presented, as a link between contemporary Florentine culture and the *studia humanitatis.*[167] And Marcello Virgilio effected more. His critical authority cast in political terms, he presented himself as the guardian of culture, holding it under strict control.

That control was secular. The distinction between the lay and the religious orders that Scala struggled to reassert in his *Defense of the City of Florence Against Its Detractors,* weeks before Marcello Virgilio delivered his oration, was fundamental to the professor's argument. Hence the significance that he attached to the issue of censorship, in order to offer an alternative to the theories of the Savonarolians. One of them, composed in 1496 and published a few months later, addressed the same problem: Gianfrancesco Pico della Mirandola's *De studio divinae et humanae philosophiae.* Following the rejection of lay learning, especially poetry, by his uncle on the eve of his life, Gianfrancesco called for what he regarded as "the vileness and obscenities" of the poets to be "utterly eliminated."[168] To the intransigence, on religious grounds, of the Savonarolian enemies of letters, Marcello Virgilio opposed his equally severe concept of secular authority. On that contested point, Florentine culture was now dividing into two opposing camps.

As the conflict intensified, a number of tacit borrowings were made from the heritage that Marcello Virgilio had claimed to repudiate. In refutation of his unnamed opponents, he again drew amply (and without acknowledgment) on Poliziano's writings, stating that grammar should not be confined in excessively narrow limits and attributing to it the right to dominate other disciplines.[169] This, with the addition of the likenesses to divine and royal

[166] Ed. Baron, pp. 260, ll. 12ff., 30ff.; 262, ll. 1ff.

[167] See Camporeale, "Giovanni Caroli," pp. 224ff.

[168] *De studio divinae et humanae philosophiae* 1.6, in *Giovanni Pico della Mirandola opera omnia,* 2:18. See Schmitt, *Gianfrancesco Pico della Mirandola,* pp. 34ff.; and B. Weinberg, *A History of Literary Criticism in the Italian Renaissance* (Chicago, 1961), pp. 255–57.

[169] *R* fol. 16^{v}: ". . . ideoque querentes maiores nostri sedem illi aliquam ceu materiam assignare, in qua versata ius suum exerceret, enarrationem illi poetarum dederunt, *non quia angustiore spacio cohercenda esset,* que parum iudicii vim in omnes alias disciplinas haberet, sed quia non secus quam nos celestes deos dicimus et arces in civitate regibus habitandas damus, altissimum omnium capax subiectum illi dandum fuit, non sane ut illhic tantam potestatem haberet, sed ut ex altiore illo munimento facilius dominaretur omnibus."

power, was essentially the argument of the *Lamia;*[170] and Poliziano's view of the contested relationship between grammar and philosophy lies behind Marcello Virgilio's verdict that "there is nothing (it seems to me) decided on by philosophy that is either so recondite or so difficult that it ought not, and cannot, be grasped by grammar."[171] Grammar was the discipline that, in times of sedition and strife, enforced the principle of solidarity between the competing branches of knowledge, as if by Solon's law.[172] Unity and harmony thus compared with the integrated cycle of the *studia humanitatis,* the grammarian represented his own primacy in terms of public order. A novel combination of the thought of Bruni and of Poliziano's intellectual ideal, Marcello Virgilio's ideas were expressed from the Studio, which he had transformed into a election forum. The moment had arrived to make a bid for office, and this academic politican seized the opportunity.

. . . . .

On 24 July 1497, Bartolomeo Scala died. When, in November, Marcello Virgilio delivered his *praefatio* at the opening of the new academic year, the post of First Chancellor was vacant. Proficiency in the humanities was a qualification for the appointment, and a distinguished tradition of scholars, from Salutati to Scala, had combined duties at Palazzo Vecchio with the pursuit of learning.[173] This precedent undoubtedly mattered in the election, on 16 February 1498, of Marcello Virgilio as Scala's successor. Piero di Marco Parenti, recording the event, noted the "young man's" competence in Greek and Latin literature and his "public lectures" at the Studio.[174] These criteria, however, do not wholly account for his success. Maintaining an appearance of engagement, while retaining the substance of nonpartisanship between 1494 and 1497, Marcello Virgilio had emerged, among many ambiguities, as the champion of secular culture. His plan to reintegrate the *studia humanitatis* with civic life was emerging with clarity and, to set the final stamp on his program, he chose to speak, while announcing courses on Virgil and Aristophanes, about the utility of subjects he professed.

[170] Ed. Wesseling, p. 16, ll. 32ff.: ". . . nostra aetas . . . *nimis brevi gyro* grammaticam *sepsit.*"

[171] *R* fol. 17ᵛ: "Mihi sane videtur nullum esse in philosophia placitum aut tam reconditum aut tam arduum, quod non debeat et possit novisse grammatica." For Poliziano's view of the philosophical competence of the *grammaticus,* see pp. 118–19 above.

[172] *R* fol. 17ᵛ: "[Mihi quadam videtur] . . . unam vero grammaticam fuisse, que secedentibus aliis omnibus in has aut in illas partes ceu ex lege Solonis, que cogeret in seditione omnes alteris adherere pariter se omnibus miscuerit."

[173] See Garin, "I cancellieri umanisti," pp. 1–32.

[174] "In cambio di messer Bartolomeo Scala primario nostro cancelliere . . . le cui lettere erano approvatissime, rimase eletto di più favore, nel Consiglio Grande, Marcello di messer Virgilio, giovanne d'anni 36, bene letterato in greco e latino, il quale in i studii di humanità qui publicamente leggeva." Ed. Tommasini, *La vita e gli scritti,* p. 95 n. 1. At the time of his election, Marcello Virgilio was aged 34, not 36.

Utilitas was now the standard that was perceived as dividing the "pure" learning of the Medicean intellectuals from the applied humanism of their forebears. Emphasized by Savonarola, it had been one of the points of contention between Poliziano and Scala. Choosing the same theme, Marcello Virgilio continued to associate himself with the applicable studies of earlier Florentine humanists: with the attitudes, for instance, expressed in Bruni's *De studiis et litteris,* which stressed the *utilitas* of literary learning,[175] representing Homer as a formative source for generals and political leaders,[176] and with Bruni's sympathizer and continuator, Nicolò Tignosi, who defended his own work on Aristotle against its critics on the same grounds.[177] A theory of education, cast in such terms, was conceived as an initiation into public life for future members of the governing class.[178]

They were set by Marcello Virgilio in a line of development—or rather, stationed in a process of decline. At the dawn of the Renaissance and the birth of the *studia humanitatis,* these subjects had attracted a large and enthusiastic public.[179] But, in the course of time, scholarship became more specialized, the audience restricted to those who were "of no use to the Republic." So much for the likes of Poliziano, who prided themselves on the anti-utilitarian character of their learning. They, of course, had not been excluded from educational opportunities, for (as Bruni had emphasized in his *Funeral Oration for Nanni Strozzi*[180]) meritocracy was a consideration, and talent should be encouraged. Declaring, again with Bruni, that noble birth should provide no measure of intellectual ability or progress in the literary arts,[181] Marcello Virgilio was hardly conceding much. Given his own background, what other position could he adopt?

One of sensitivity to where power and influence lay is the answer, expressed in the following figurative terms: "Our studies, however, instinctively rejoice at being in the hands of those who, in the state, are both of a rank

[175] *Humanistisch-philosophische Schriften* (ed. Baron), pp. 13, ll. 1ff.; 17, ll. 3ff.

[176] Ibid., p. 14, ll. 20ff.

[177] *Niclaii Tignosii Fulginatis ad Cosimum Medicem in illos, qui in mea in Aristotelem commentaria criminantur:* "Persium non legendum, sed cremandum predicant. Oratium, Iuvenalem *tamquam nullius utilitatis* homines abiiciendos, Livium non modo amplectandum sed penitus deperdendum et multos alios de medio removendos." BMLF, Pluteo 48, 37, fols. 12^{r}–12^{v}, and cf. fols. 22^{v}–23^{r}. On Tignosi, see Rotondò, "Niccolò Tignosi da Foligno," pp. 217–55; and Sensi, "Niccolò Tignosi da Foligno," pp. 359–495.

[178] Cf. Grafton and Jardine, *From Humanism to the Humanities,* pp. 27ff.; and see further below, pp. 118ff.

[179] *R* fol. 18^{r}: "Nam prodeuntibus quondam hiis studiis ex antiquo illo et informi situ, sub quo pene putruerunt, novitas ipsa rei facile efficiebat, ut vos frequentiores et sepius ad audiendum in hec loca veniretis et illi quasi ex intactis tesauris maiorem dictionis copiam sibi invenirent."

[180] Ed. G. D. Mansi, pp. 2–7 (translated in Bruni, *Humanism,* trans. Griffiths, Hankins, and Thompson, pp. 125–26).

[181] *R* fol. 18^{r}: ". . . in ingeniis et profecto ad bonas artes nullum sit ex nobilitate discrimen ponendum." Cf. Landino, *De vera nobilitate* (ed. Liaci), pp. 97, ll. 11ff. and 105, ll. 1ff.

and of means to command armies and enact laws for the Republic."[182] A bow to the governing elite or *reggimento,* to whose sons Marcello Virgilio had been presenting himself, for three years, as the ideal mentor. Now, however, his argument had undergone a change: it was not just, he contended, that political wisdom could be derived from the *studia humanitatis* but also that between them and the ruling class, restricted by birth and wealth to the *Consiglio Maggiore,* there existed a natural affinity.

How, then, to avoid taking sides in the struggle for power at Florence? By adopting a metaphor of craftsmanship that admitted several interpretations. As a sculptor in gold—not in stone, like that philistine enemy of literature, Pietro Bernardino[183]—Marcello Virgilio imagined himself. This contemporary of Leonardo da Vinci preferred to work in gold or ivory rather than in bronze or wood.[184] The imagery was polyvalent, but not dangerous. For who, among the members of the Great Council that, little more than three months later, would elect him to the chancellorship, would have quarreled with the idea that he was fit to rule the state or had sons worthy to be sculpted in figurative gold?

The same striving for consensus colored Marcello Virgilio's portrayal of the history of the *studia humanitatis* at Florence. "Under the protection of the entire state," "with the favor of all orders," the disciplines had once flourished among general applause.[185] In those halcyon days, before the upheavals of the "barbarian" invasions, a professor had been respected. Now world-weariness characterized the modern age; the treasures of the ancients were bankrupt; and, in the ensuing boredom, nothing new remained to be said.[186] The intellectual's position in the Florence of 1497, as perceived by Marcello Virgilio, stood in melancholy contrast with that of his forebears. They had prospered amid gregarious approval: he grubbed a living in poor solitude.[187] It had became fashionable to despise the humanist as a corrupter of the young;[188] and the condemnations of the bigots were reinforced by the hostility of the philistines.

[182] *R* fol. 18^{r}: ". . . sentiunt tamen nescio quo pacto et hoc studia hec nostra gaudentque in manibus eorum esse, qui in civitatibus et eo ordine et ea fortuna sint, ut regere imperiis exercitus et rempub[licam] legibus firmare possint." Cf. below, pp. 191ff.

[183] See above, p. 140.

[184] *R* fol. 18^{r}: "Non secus quam statuarius aliquis optimus in auro magis operari gaudet et ebore quam ere aut ligno."

[185] Ibid.: ". . . patrocinio totius civitatis viventes securius—"; and fol. 18^{v}: ". . . sentiebant nimium et illud favorabiles se esse apud omnes ordines in civitate laudarique passim ab omnibus et magno omnium plausu excipi."

[186] *R* fol. 18^{v}: "Nobis vero exhaustis iam pridem antiquis illis thesauris et fastidientibus omnibus nostratibus, ut vetera et obsoleta nihil superest, quod dicere gratum simul et novum apud vos valeamus."

[187] Ibid.: "Et nos pudet non nunquam in tanta solitudine concipere dicentis habitum."

[188] Ibid.: ". . . infestum nunc et odiosum omnibus hoc studium sequimur—damnatum etiam publice vanis quibusdam rationibus, quibus persuasi imperitiores inutile nos et impium et iuvenum animis noxium tractare opus credunt ob falsas rerum opiniones."

"What was the point, the applicability, the *utilitas* of his type of humanism," asked Marcello Virgilio, recurring to a theme of Salutati's, "when compared with the pursuit of medicine and law?"[189] Money was now what mattered.

> Since I have often been aware that my efforts have been condemned as useless . . . I have decided to speak to you today about their *utilitas:* the one and only word that (I hope) may make you prick up your ears because, by native tradition and natural inclination, in everything that you have to do, your immediate reaction is to calculate the dividend that it will yield you.

Industrious merchants and busy hustlers were what Marcello Virgilio's audience meant when it praised a man as good.[190]

Here, for the first time in three years, he voiced criticism of his audience. In the style of a lay preacher that was to shape his later oratory,[191] Marcello Virgilio recurred to the critique of the mercantile mentality voiced twenty years earlier by Giovanni Caroli. The decline of cultural standards, the enervating atmosphere in which intellectual life had to be pursued at Florence, was a consequence of commercial acquisitiveness—of the materialism that regarded venality as normal and considered everything up for grabs.[192] For such "ulcers of the mind" Marcello Virgilio offered, in a mixed array of medical images, his own prescriptions. His position now closer to that of Argyropoulos (which, in his inaugural lecture, he had shunned),[193] the systematic praise of the *studia humanitatis* announced the previous year had to be abandoned. An emergency loomed, demanding a swift response.[194]

In this dilemma Marcello Virgilio claimed flexibility, adaptability, and—above all—freedom. Freedom, in the first place, of speech. For him, as for Coluccio Salutati,[195] that right corresponded both to the natural order of the Republic and to the position of his pupils, who enjoyed unrestricted lib-

[189] Ibid.: ". . . sepius sensimus damnari tamquam inutiles labores hos nostros, quia nec corporis curam, ut medicina, nec patrocinium reorum habeant, ut iura." See Witt, *Hercules,* pp. 331ff.; and E. Garin, *L'umanesimo italiano,* 7th ed. (Rome, 1978), pp. 42ff.

[190] *R* fols. 18^v–19^r: ". . . constituimus de utilitate eorum hodie apud vos dicere, in quo speramus uno hoc 'utilitatis' verbo non fore vos in audiendo negligentes, ex eo maxime, quod omnes institutione hac patria et ingenio estis, ut in omnibus agendis rebus numeretis statim quanta sit vobis ex ea reditura annona. Ex quo et illud apud vos vulgare est, ut quem 'virum bonum' laudetis industrium [*sic*] mercatorem et assiduum institorem dicatis."

[191] See below, pp. 193ff.

[192] See Camporeale, "Giovanni Caroli," p. 219.

[193] See above, p. 152.

[194] *R* fol. 19^r: ". . . huius novationis veniam mihi facilem a vobis spero: repetentibus animo indesinentem rerum omnium mutationem et necessariam in nostris animis mobilitatem, in quibus hii precipue laudati sunt, qui urgente necessitate aliqua maiore aut occasione suadente voluntatem suam rebus, non eas sue voluntati submittere conati sunt."

[195] See A. P. McCormick, "Freedom of Speech in Early Renaissance Florence," *Rinascimento* 19 (1974): 235–40.

erty of choice.[196] Imagine a world, Marcello Virgilio invited his listeners, obsessed with the craving for power and forgetful of the *studia humanitatis*.[197] Like gaping invaders from beyond the Alps, they would enter an elegantly ornamented and splendidly built city, unable to appreciate the beauty or grasp the principles of the architecture that aroused their ignorant admiration. Florence and the French occupation of 1494 provided Marcello Virgilio's topical image of intellectual alienation; and in his role as censor of moral vice and cultivator of civic virtue, this professor of humane letters acknowledged that he had entered into competition with moral philosophy. Into that field which Giovanni Nesi, in a work published only a handful of months before this oration, had depicted as the special preserve of Savonarola,[198] Marcello Virgilio now advanced, proclaiming as his purpose the care of minds (*cura animorum*)[199]—not souls (*animarum*)—and asserting the diagnostic properties of examples drawn from the study of history in isolating the present ills of society and foretelling its future woes.[200]

So it was, in implicit polemic with Savonarola and his followers, that Marcello Virgilio offered an alternative to the preaching of the prophet. History—even ancient history—did have a predictive force, contrary to the third sermon on Amos;[201] the *studia humanitatis* were not turned to the past, but served to fathom the crisis of contemporary society. The Ciceronian theory of history as teaching by example (a humanist cliché) thus gained a fresh relevance: the writings of the ancients, for Marcello Virgilio, were not like the perfumes that lose their scent with the passing of time, nor were they incompatible with dogmas of the Christian faith.[202] Savonarola, his standing weakened by excommunication, was now faced with a competitor—hailed by Roberto Acciaiuoli, three days after the delivery of this oration, as the messiah of the imperiled humanities.[203] The prophetic tones

[196] *R* fol. 19^{v}: ". . . cum quia hec forma est reipublice vestre, tum quia iniquum est cogi aliquem consilii sui reddere rationem, presertim si apud eos dicat, quibus et elegendi et renuendi potestas libera concessa est."

[197] Ibid., fols. 20^{r}ff.

[198] See above, pp. 135ff., and cf. below, pp. 202ff.

[199] *R* fols. 21^{v}ff.

[200] Ibid., fol. 23^{v}: "Ad hec nos manuducimus timidiores hos multiplicique historiarum lectione exanclatis iam sepe hiisdam periculis quasi in tuto constitutos resumptis animis docemus non esse tantopere timenda, in quibus totiens conflictetur genus humanum . . . habere bella suos exitus, ex quibus semper plures incolumes evadant et in augenda civium virtute non mediocrem utilitatem . . . rerum omnium metum et inanis fortuitorum agonia, quorum tantam habet historia copiam, ut lectione diei unius et bellis cedibus ruinisque multis interesse possis et in malis tuis exitum ex similitudine et ex eventu remedium aliquod excogitare et utilitatem, si qua est, recognoscere."

[201] See above, pp. 138–39.

[202] *R* fol. 25^{v}.

[203] "Hac tempestate seu temporum angustiis, serieque fatorum seu hominum malignitate virtutes omnes labefactas esse videmus . . . tantum nobis relinquntur, ut te unum patronem, benefactorem et defensorem suum litterarum studia adclament." Ed. Bandini, *Collectio,* pp. 25–26.

were justified. An alternative Socrates, hardly less eloquent than his rival, had emerged. Within a handful of months, Marcello Virgilio was appointed Scala's successor.

. . . . .

A double authority was now possessed by this *homo novus*. Combining, for the first time since Carlo Marsuppini, the office of chancellor with a chair at the Studio, Marcello Virgilio personified a humanism engaged in public life. The identification had not been effected casually. A strategy, complementing the position of Scala while drawing on the work of his predecessors, had lent his oratory a political dimension neither achieved nor attempted by the Medicean professoriate. Voicing criticism in moderate and moralizing tones, expressing resistance in terms of constructive alternatives, Marcello Virgilio had assumed the role of advocate for the defense. What he defended, with republican rhetoric, were humane letters and the values of the ruling elite, which he portrayed as interdependent. And that was precisely what he was called upon to put into practice when, as secretary to the Signoria and composer of state letters written in its name, he attended the *pratiche* or consultative meetings that, in March 1498, were convened to decide the fate of Savonarola and guide the fortunes of Florence.

The character of those discussions—the arguments and images that were employed by the small group of potentates with whom Marcello Virgilio, through his father, was acquainted—reveal how closely his oratory at the Studio had captured the *koinê* of Florentine political discourse.[204] Divided among themselves as to how to react to the papal command that Savonarola should cease to preach and disquieted by the threat of interdiction that hung over the city,[205] they made common cause on one issue that Marcello Virgilio, throughout three troubled years, had often emphasized. That issue was *libertas:* the city's freedom when confronted with external menace but also its right, as an independent power, to decide on its internal affairs for itself. At the Studio, with ringing insistence, the professor had made use of this elusive slogan. Now, within the council chambers on the second floor of Palazzo Vecchio,[206] he was to learn, as First Chancellor, what it meant on the lips of those whose opinion counted.

Scarcely one of the speakers in the *pratica* of 14 March 1498 omitted a reference to liberty. Yet a tone of realism tempered their eloquence. The moment was sobering, the crisis pressing from many sides. Pisa had been

[204] See Gilbert, "Florentine Political Assumptions," pp. 7–48.

[205] For context, see Polizzotto, *Elect Nation,* pp. 11ff.; Weinstein, *Savonarola,* pp. 284ff.; and R. Ridolfi, *Vita di Savonarola,* pp. 342ff. (= *The Life of Girolamo Savonarola,* trans. C. Grayson [New York, 1959], pp. 234ff.).

[206] For the rooms used for the *Consulte e Pratiche* after 1494, see Rubinstein, *Palazzo Vecchio,* p. 40.

lost, and Florence had to pay for its reconquest with the overpriced aid of mercenaries. The conditions demanded by the *condottiere,* Paolo Vitelli, seemed outrageous to Francesco degli Albizzi. Nonetheless, during the deliberations of 28 February, he had acknowledged: "It is better to blush than blanch."[207] Confronted with the hostility of Venice, observed Bernardo Rucellai, one had to choose between dignity and security, and security was the wiser choice, "because whenever it has been preserved, dignity may return."[208] By mid-March, the problem of Savonarola and the papacy had become more urgent, menacing grave consequences for the city's merchants, and the discrepancies between high-flown theories and material necessity became pressing.

"The place for a *pratica* is where we are meeting: Palazzo Vecchio, not San Marco" was the argument of Giovanni Canacci, voicing a widespread suspicion of Savonarola's influence through the use of secret conventicles. Likening, with more learning than aptness, the *frate* to Helen of Troy and Anno of Carthage, Canacci argued that the papal command should be obeyed.[209] The same line, varied by the examples of Theodosius and Ambrose, was taken by Giuliano di Jacopo Mazzinghi, whose pyrotechnics of pedantry soon gave way to a calculation of possible losses to commerce.[210] Submission to the pope was unworthy of the city's liberty, argued Antonio di Simone Cavigiani, for Florence acknowledged no superior; and in any case, who needed instances taken from pagan literature, when one had the Old and New Testaments?[211] Giovanni Brunetti would not be silenced by this slight on learned references. He quoted the fate of Huss, burned for heresy at the stake in 1415, and cited the example of "most learned men" like Origen, who had committed grave errors.[212] In this exchange of allusions—this ping-pong of rival authorities—the exemplary style of historical argument defended by Marcello Virgilio months before at the Studio was applied to the prophet who had condemned it.

Subtler positions were adopted by two former colleagues of the First Chancellor's father. Paolantonio Soderini liked neither the tone nor the tenor of the papal bull (to the Perugians and others, Alexander VI would not have written in such tones!), but he was in favor of dissimulation. No good would come of isolating Florence. Better to conciliate the pope, while preserving Savonarola. And who should write the proposed letter of insincere obedience? "Your good and prudent chancellors"[213]—an idea that so impressed

207 *Consulte e pratiche, 1494–1505* (ed. Fachard), p. 37: ". . . è meglio arossire che impaladire."

208 Ibid., p. 39: "Havendo ad eleggiere la dignità o la sicuretà, che più presto sia di eleggiere la sicurità, perché ogni volta che altri si è conservato la dignità può tornare."

209 Ibid., p. 47.

210 Ibid., p. 55.

211 Ibid., pp. 55–56.

212 Ibid., pp. 56–57.

213 Ibid., p. 48.

Tommaso Fortini that he later proposed sending the same public servants as emissaries to the friar in order to convince him to stop preaching.[214] One of the strongest candidates for that invidious mission listened attentively, as themes that had already figured in his lectures were transposed into political debate. Listening, Marcello Virgilio learned. Some speakers indignantly contrasted the temporal and the spiritual powers;[215] others thought more soberly of the commercial goods that were being held up from dispatch to Naples;[216] but none captured the mood of the meeting, divided between a wish to assert Florentine *libertas* and a recognition of its possible consequences, more exactly than Guidantonio Vespucci, who argued that it was the lesser evil to satisfy the pontiff, because "we in Italy are what we are."[217]

Opinions remained divided. A solution had not yet been found. On 17 March, a further *pratica* was convened. Members gathered in numbers too large for reasoned discussion of so important a matter. The well-being of the Republic hung in the balance; less influential citizens withdrew; and the meeting was reduced to the smaller circle of those who effectively decided on affairs of state. That they were observed with attention by Marcello Virgilio can be demonstrated with certainty. Certainty, because it is in his cursive script that the decisions taken on 17 March 1498 are recorded (Plate 3).

The protocol was written in Latin, marking the formation of a restricted council to discuss an issue of historical significance, and the use of the learned language lent the decisions taken a solemn air of executive authority.[218] The *cor civitatis,* as those present were styled in the protocol, determined to give satisfaction to Alexander VI by persuading the friar not to preach, but to refuse the chief papal demands on the grounds that "they are beneath the dignity of our Republic." The First Secretary wrote to Rome. Two months later, after an exchange of diplomatic letters, he sought again to explain (or conceal) the Signoria's delaying tactics. Now the friar's fate was sealed. "Although we have continued to torture Girolamo Savonarola in the last few days," begins the disingenuous epistle of 6 May,[219] "we have not yet extracted the information that we need for our purposes, before we satisfy yours." The

[214] Ibid., p. 57.

[215] Ibid., pp. 50, 52, 55.

[216] Ibid., p. 53.

[217] Ibid., p. 49: "Et considerando l'uno et l'altro, cioè el fructo e l'danno, pare loro che sia più fructo satisfare al Pontefice. Noi siamo in Italia quegli che noi siamo."

[218] See I. Klein, "Leonardo Bruni e le Consulte e Pratiche," in *Leonardo Bruni, cancelliere,* pp. 164–65 (cited in note 140 above).

[219] "Cum torqueremus adhuc Hieronimum Savonarolam proximis diebus, nondum cognitis his, quibus ad Rempublicam nostram indigebamus . . . crescente in dies eo negotio et, ut fit in quaestionibus, volentibus nobis omnia, quae ab eo dicerentur, conferre rebus et testibus, alisque certioribus indiciis et signis confirmare, in hanc diem differre coacti sumus has litteras, quibus non auderemus . . . petere a S.V., ut de iure suo aliquis nobis cederet, nisi tot aliis rebus experti essemus." ASF, Signori, Missive, Prima Cancelleria, 51, fols. 66^{v}–67^{r}, ed. P.V. Marchese, "Documenti intorno alla vita e la morte di fra Girolamo Savonarola," *ASI,* App. 8 (1850), pp. 188–89.

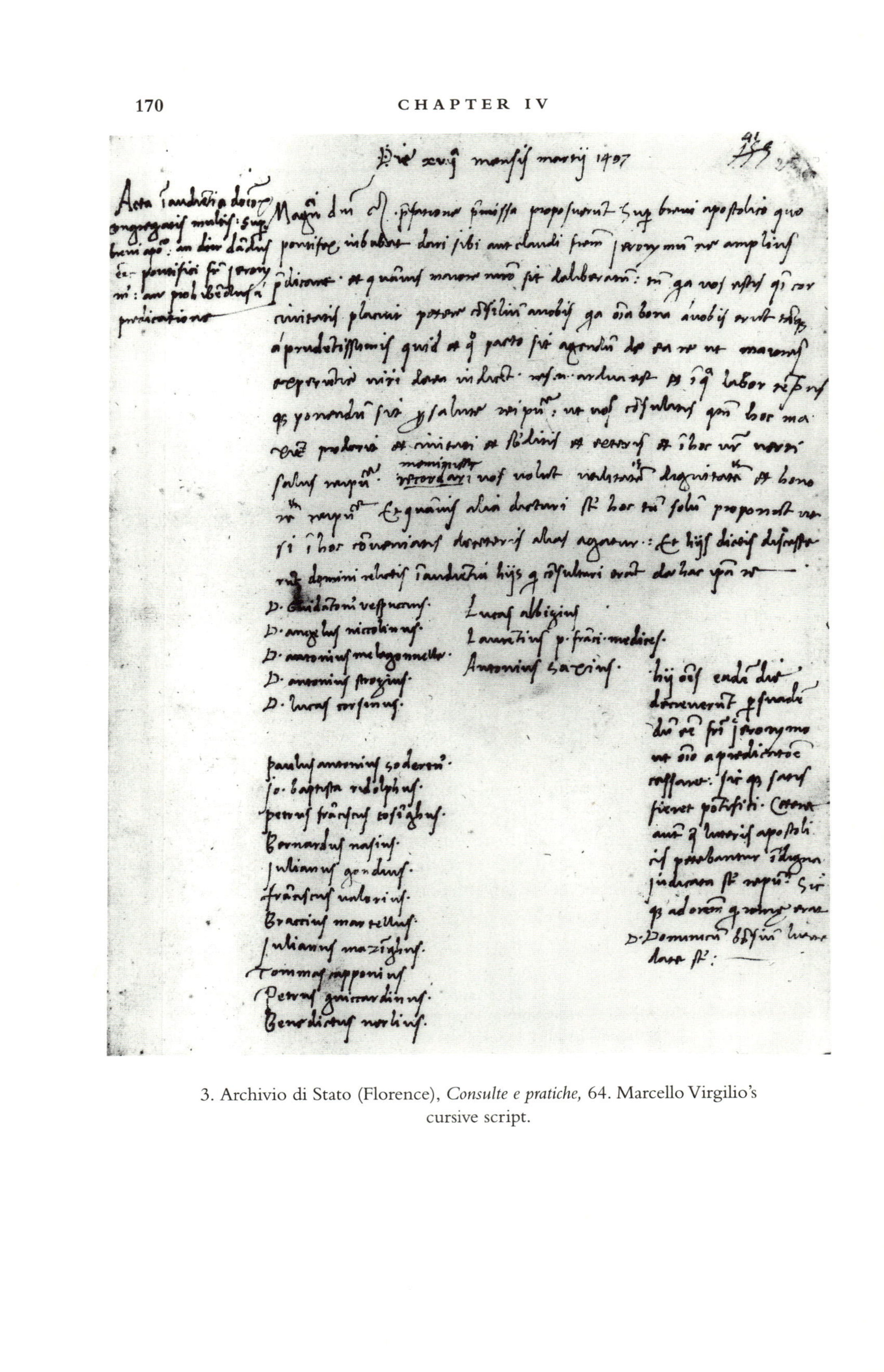

3. Archivio di Stato (Florence), *Consulte e pratiche,* 64. Marcello Virgilio's cursive script.

syntax is as tortuous as the process it describes; its hypothetical subjunctives attribute to the pope a concern for the security of Florence that was not his main objective; and the intricacies of this letter elaborate a sinister yet clear contrast between "the false sanctity that [Savonarola] simulated . . . among us (*apud nos*)" in the past and his "real punishment among us" in the present.

"Among us" is the key expression. No matter that the same Chancery had written to the selfsame pope less than two-and-a-half years earlier that "*frate* Girolamo from Ferrara . . . is a man to be admired for his saintly conduct and true faith,"[220] or that, on 30 June 1498, Marcello Virgilio would respond to King Louis XII of France with the transparent pretexts that his request for mercy on Savonarola's behalf had arrived too late and, in any case, the responsibility lay with Alexander VI: "That is why we are not responsible for his death, nor had we wished to do so . . . would we have been capable of saving his life."[221]

The diplomatic uses of humanism are graphically illustrated by such sentences. There can be no doubt about the attribution to Marcello Virgilio of public letters like this, copied by his adjutors, because no one in late Quattrocento Florence—not even Poliziano—employed the subjunctive of unreal condition with more deftness in the equivocalities of the Latin language than the First Chancellor. Dissimulating to the recipients of his evasive eloquence, he was well aware of the grim realities of political life in the city. What mattered, during the month that witnessed Machiavelli's election to the post where he served as Marcello Virgilio's colleague, was less the elimination of Savonarola than the decision that it should occur "among us." That is why, if it would be idle to seek personal conviction from such letters of state,[222] it is not irrelevant to reflect on the lessons of *Realpolitik* learned while writing them. Secretary and spokesman of the "heart of the city," Marcello Virgilio witnessed at first hand its divisions and tensions, participated in its ambiguous conduct of policy. His outlook, as expressed to his immediate colleagues, cannot but have been influenced by that role. It was, recording the issues on which Florence's ruling elite made common cause, to give voice to the ambiguous claims of *Florentina libertas*.

. . . . .

Libertas is a term that figures prominently in the *praefatio* to Statius that Marcello Virgilio delivered in November of the same year. At this moment, confirmed by recent success, he felt free to be expansive. How freely he voiced his newfound confidence is not wholly apparent from the official version of

[220] ASF, Signori, Missive, Prima Cancelleria, 50, fol. 5^v (28 December 1494).

[221] Ibid., 51, fol. 76^v (ed. Marchese, p. 193): ". . . quo fit, ut nec mortis eius nos auctores fuerimus nec, si voluissemus . . . vitae fautores possuissemus esse."

[222] See Black, "Political Thought," pp. 991–1003.

4. Marcello Virgilio's Chancery italic with the script (*ad fin.*) of his copyist (*R*).

the oration that, in his Chancery italic script, Marcello Virgilio made with the aid of a copyist after the restoration of the Medici in 1512 (Plate 4). To appreciate the manner in which the newly elected chancellor expressed himself fourteen years earlier, it is necessary to return to the original drafts, written in his cursive hand (Plate 5), and restore what this censor chose to cut.[223]

To his pupils was directed the official version, to their fathers the first of the drafts.[224] No longer was he a conservative follower of tradition: his lectures, Marcello Virgilio declared, had attracted criticism by their novelty (*novitas*). Brushing aside the accusation that literature corrupts, he asserted that, in teaching poetry, he was providing instruction in a subject necessary for life.[225] To the anticipated charges that he had "neglected the practice of the ancients"—meaning that of Poliziano and Landino[226]—and that he had digressed into themes above the heads of his audience and irrelevant to the subject he was treating, the guardian of letters responded with a spirited assertion of his singularity. Echoing Roberto Acciaiuoli's words of the previous year, he "alone at this time"[227] had dared, "in the gardens of the poets," to distinguish between flowers and weeds; he alone had been "bold enough to find fault with and emend with harsh censure the many things that they had said, as it were, with insufficient wisdom."[228]

This is hardly the language of textual criticism. Marcello Virgilio adapted and inverted the philological terminology (*censura, emendare, mutare*) of Poliziano, in order to plead for an approach contrary to that of his predecessor. Not historical fidelity to the letter of the text, alterable only when its tradition, reason, and context warranted an intervention, but the freedom to intervene and alter motivated his procedure: "[I alone have dared . . .] to teach, in my lessons on poetry, what should be added, subtracted, changed, or modified into other forms, in order that readers might gain useful plea-

[223] The two drafts of parts of this speech transmitted in *N* are distinguished by the sigla n^1 and n^2 and compared with the readings of *R*.

[224] "Ingenui Adolescentes" *R* fol. 26^r: "viri Florentini" n^1 fol. 50^r. (The opening of the address is missing from n^2 fol. 52^r.)

[225] "In poetis . . . erudire primam hanc etatem vestram, ut sine periculo bonorum morum que necessaria in illis vite humane precepta inveniuntur [*sic*]." *R* fol. 26^r: ". . . que necessaria vite humane in illis." n^1 fol. 50^r.

[226] "neglecta *veterum* consuetudine" n^1 fol. 50^r: "neglecta aliorum consuetudine" *R* fol. 26^r. Note the contrast between *veteres,* as applied to Poliziano and Landino, and Marcello Virgilio, drawn by his pupil and colleague Andrea Dazzi (on whom, see Verde, *Studio,* 3:1464–65) in his *De laudibus linguae graecae:* "Videbam enim quam plurimos *veterum* sed et memoria nostra Landinum et Politianum, novissime autem et Virgilium meum, quem praeceptorem in hac facultate confiteri non erubesco," in Dazzi, *Andreae Dactii,* pp. 301–2.

[227] "unus ego hac tempestate" *R* fol. 26^r and n^1 fol. 50^r.

[228] "aususque sim graviore censura multa tamquam parum sapienter ab illis dicta reprehendere et emendare" *R* fol. 26^r: "aususque sim multa ab illis tamquam parum sapienter dicta graviore censura mutare et emendare" n^1 fol. 50^r.

5. Marcello Virgilio's cursive script (*N*).

sure and, from their delight, draw profit."[229] The epideictic criteria of praise and blame, like the Horatian axioms of pleasure (*delectatio*) and utility (*utilitas*), voiced in Marcello Virgilio's earlier lectures, were now combined in a single image of censorship.

When did he adopt such methods? "In particular from the time when you became freer."[230] Note the comparative, tactful in a former Medicean protégé. But not tactful enough in the form secluded from his official version of the speech, where Marcello Virgilio wrote innocuously: "I considered that you should be trained and schooled, from your earliest years, in those opinions and judgments, according to which you shall be able to live gloriously and usefully for the Republic and yourselves."[231] In what kind of republic? Only the uncensored draft contains the assertion: "In a popular republic."[232] There the task of a teacher should be to teach his pupils to spurn "fear, folly, and craven spirits"; to desire liberty, defined by an antithesis that Marcello Virgilio found it opportune to suppress after the restoration of the Medici: "I did not think that your sons should be educated as we bring up slaves whom it is fitting to have at home in such a manner that they know nothing but abject servility and live with base humility, incapable of action unless they receive an order."[233]

Why this republican rhetoric was stripped from the official version of the speech after 1512 is not difficult to understand. But to whom was the original draft directed? Who, specifically, were the "most distinguished Florentines" courted by the professor in his oration at the Studio? Among the presiding officials nominated in the month when Marcello Virgilio delivered this stirring speech was that advocate of *libertas,* Alamanno Rinuccini, restored to influence upon the expulsion of the Medici.[234] When he died, on 12 May 1499, he was lamented by his colleagues at the Studio as its "patron and defender." During the funeral, "a most beautiful oration" (no longer extant) was

[229] "docereque in lectione eorum quibus additis, demptis, mutatisve aut in alia derivatis delectare se utiliter legentes possent et cum delectatione etiam prodesse" *R* fols. 26^{r-v} and n^2 fol. 50^r.

[230] "praecipue vero ex quo liberiores estis" *R* fol. 26^v and n^2 fol. 50^r.

[231] "ita erudiendos vos censui hisque opinionibus et placitis rerum omnium a prima etate imbuendos, quibus et reipublicae et vobis gloriose et utiliter viveretis" *R* fol. 26^v: "ita erudiendos censui filios vestros hiisque opinionibus rerum imbuendos quibus gloriose et utiliter sibi et reipublice viverent" n^2 fol. 50^r.

[232] "in republica populari" n^2 fol. 51^r.

[233] "Non enim sic arbitrabor erudiendos esse filios vestros ut servi a nobis educantur, quos ita domi habere oportet, ut nihil aliud quam servitutem servire sciant vivantque abiecti et humiles animo nihil nisi ex precepto agentes" n^1 fol. 51^r: "nec sic ratus sum erudiendos . . . filios nostros ut servi a nobis educantur, quos ita domi habemus sicque instituimus, ut abiecti animo vivant nihilque audere assuescant nec secreta domus intelligant" n^2 fol. 52^r. See further below, p. 188.

[234] Verde, *Studio,* 1:280; and Giustiniani, *Alamanno Rinuccini,* p. 38.

pronounced by Marcello Virgilio.[235] Still more beautiful must have appeared, to the late author of *De libertate,*[236] the *praefatio* that the same humanist had delivered the previous November. To Alamanno Rinuccini, defender of intellectual and political freedom against Medicean dominance, Marcello Virgilio's contrast between liberty and servitude had doubtless seemed music in the ears.

The process of self-censorship went further, extending from politics to scholarship. In 1498 Poliziano's successor had announced a break with the past—a "method of teaching that is not customary in the present age" as he boldly formulated it in the first of his drafts,[237] a "changed system of instruction" as he put it more discreetly in the official version[238]—abandoning with scorn the formalism that Poliziano, in his *Panepistemon,* had defined as the proper business of the grammarian: "I have jettisoned the entire discipline of glossaries and scansion and rhetorical analysis of the beauty of poems, in which it was once upon a time glorious to spend time and effort, striving to draw your attention to better, greater, and more elevated matters."[239] Marcello Virgilio poked fun at the dreariness and irrelevance of the "unhappy and ridiculous . . . problems set by the grammarians."[240] His examples were the triviality of scanning the first book of Homer; of seeking anticipations of the *Aeneid* in Virgil's earlier poetry; of asking what it meant, in the *Georgics,* when their author speaks of "the thriving of the fruits of the earth (*laetitia frugum*)," instead of considering the points of harmony and conflict in the natural world that that expert on agriculture knew so well; of puzzling over the problem of whether Livy begins his history with a hexameter.[241] All this pedantry of the past was beneath the attention of students being trained for political responsibilities. Plato was right: the state needed judges, custodians of morals, teachers who understood that, in reading Livy, what mattered was not "the prettiness of the style but the substance of Roman power and *virtus.*"[242]

Less than five months after Niccolò Machiavelli's appointment to the

[235] Verde, *Studio,* 4, 3:1338.

[236] See Giustiniani, *Alamanno Rinuccini,* pp. 243–48; Rubinstein, "Florentine Constitutionalism," pp. 461–62; and Martelli, "Profilo ideologico," pp. 131–43.

[237] *n*[1] fol. 51[r]: ". . . hanc inusitatam hiis temporibus docendi rationem."

[238] *R* fol. 26[v]: ". . . mutata hec docendi ratio."

[239] *R* fol. 27[v]: ". . . relictaque glossematum mensure carminum artificii pulchritudinisque disciplina omni, in quibus aliquando gloriosum fuit laborasse, ad meliorem quandam et maiorem erectionem animorum nostrorum conati sumus transferre vos ipsos." Cf. Poliziano, *Panepistemon:* "grammatice: . . . Hic littere, syllabeque cum suis vel fastigiis vel longitudinibus, hic orationis partes et proportio et inequalitas . . . et item pedes, metaplasmi, tropi, schemata, glossemata." *Politiani Opera,* 3:50.

[240] Ibid.: "infelices et ridiculas Grammaticorum questiones": "miserum et vile" *n*[2] fol. 52[r].

[241] *n*[2] fol. 52[r].

[242] *R* fol. 28[r]: "In Livio rem et virtutem Romanam potius admirari quam pulchritudinem sermonis."

Chancery, almost two decades before he composed that "commentary" on Livy entitled the *Discorsi*,[243] which compares Roman and Florentine history, his colleague at Palazzo Vecchio, in a programmatic speech, had denounced the philological approach to the same author and declared his intention to expound him in the light of republican politics—an aim that he never realized. In such a milieu, radical in tone but traditionalist in values, developed a mode of reading that differed profoundly from "grammatical" methods. Expressive of the ideology of the post-Medicean age, it was intended to be applied to texts that, since Machiavelli's boyhood, had been available in his paternal home.[244]

The conditions of culture had changed, affirmed Marcello Virgilio, not for the worse, as so many of his contemporaries lamented,[245] but for the better. Scholarship had moved forward, in a spurt of progress that motivated and legitimated his novel methods: "I was stimulated to adopt this method of teaching, which is not customary in the present age, because I perceived that Latin literature had reached such a point, in respect of a ready supply of books and a multitude of interpreters, that rudimentary education, on which past ages boasted that they spend time and effort, had become readily accessible to all."[246]

When were "past ages"? At a time unspecified but datable to 1493–94 by this patent allusion to fifth chapter of Poliziano's second *Centuria*,[247] which Marcello Virgilio excised from the official version of his speech. For the gloom of his predecessor—for Poliziano's laments on the lack of ancient texts and on the limitations of their modern interpreters—was substituted a sunlit conviction of advance and enlightenment. Not without a swipe of polemic. Anonymously reduced from the rank of a professor to that of the primary teachers whom he despised (*grammatista* in the lowly and conventional senses, not the new and elevated connotations of *grammaticus* in the *Lamia*), Poliziano, or his misrepresented approach, was implied to have been overtaken by the times. An ample supply of books, an abundance of exegetes, the march forward of Latin letters had left him behind. In his stead—in the vanguard of a revisionist humanism, adapted to the new age—Marcello Virgilio placed himself and his "new and unprecedented method of teaching."[248]

[243] On the *Discorsi* as commentary, see below, pp. 260–69.

[244] See further below, pp. 263ff.

[245] Cf. Crinito, *Commentarii de honesta disciplina,* pp. 316–17 and *Libri de poetis Latinis,* pref.

[246] n^2 fol. 51^r: "Impulit et illud etiam nos ad hanc inusitatam hiis temporibus docendi rationem, quod videbam eo pervenisse iam Latinas litteras copia librorum et multitudine interpretum, ut prima illa rudimenta, in quibus aliquando gloriosum fuit operam consumpsisse, omnibus in promptu erant."

[247] See above, p. 129. For Marcello Virgilio's knowledge of the unpublished *Miscellanea* 2, see below, pp. 204–5.

[248] n^1 fol. 51^r: ". . . nova et inusitata hactenus ratione dicendi."

What that involved was a critical, evaluative, and moralistic treatment of literature. Responding to the criticisms of the Savonarolians, he distinguished between the good that might be derived from poetry and its evils that were to be avoided.[249] "The poets are not always to be praised"[250] wrote Marcello Virgilio, repudiating their "superstitious" likeness to a temple with the mystique of divinity,[251] while portraying his own activity in metaphors of thickets and thorns, hornets and scythes.[252] Hence his newfound disdain for that "dirty story about women" in Roman satire cited tolerantly in his inaugural lecture;[253] his doubts about Cicero, whose works should not be read literally;[254] his hostility toward Epicurus, rebuked on the grounds that the misguided philosopher's views on "tranquility of spirit" could encourage passivity and thus enable "ambitious boasters to acquire power in the state."

"Critical philology" was repudiated. Literature, particularly poetry, was no longer to be studied on its own terms or in its historical context. It should be judged in terms of its utility, as raw material for moralizing discourse (*sermo*). The activity of the exegete, presented in medical imagery, was to be corrective. With reason, therefore, Marcello Virgilio now styled himself a censor and adopted the persona of Cato. Stern yet sensible, this critic was guided by reason—"the leader" and "charioteer" of Poliziano's *Nutricia*.[255] But where, in the work of his predecessor, the poetic medium was portrayed in ethereal images and Neoplatonic allusions, Marcello Virgilio described it with concrete exempla drawn from, and applicable to, urban politics, social ethics, and daily life.

What Nesi had attributed to Savonarola, he ascribed to himself: a moral leader's role and ability to mediate between the intellectuals and the governing class. The authority to which Marcello Virgilio aspired was that of Plato's guardian of the state. Like those supervisors of the young and their education in the *Republic* and the *Laws*,[256] he proposed to keep literature under his thumb. And he did so, quite literally, in the case of one of the most distinguished libraries at Florence. If the private collection of the Medici was not transferred from San Marco to the palace of the Signoria, as its members de-

[249] *R* fol. 28^{v}: "In poetis et lectione eorum carendum nobis est idque omni studio agere nos oportet, ut eorum bonis utamur et malis caveamus."

[250] n^2 fol. 52^{v}: ". . . non semper laudandi poete sunt."

[251] *R* fol. 32^{r}: "Neque oportet in poetis veluti in templo et in re divina superstitiose timere et colere deos."

[252] n^2 fol. 53^{r}.

[253] n^2 fol. 54^{v}, and see above, pp. 152ff.

[254] n^2 fol. 52^{r}.

[255] *R* fols. 27^{v} ("ratione duce") and 33^{r} ("auriga et gubernatore"). See above, p. 63.

[256] E.g., *Republic* 387*b*ff. and 595ff., with P. Murray, *Plato on Poetry: Ion, Republic 376e–398b, Republic 895–608b* (Cambridge, 1995), pp. 158 and 184ff. Cf. *Laws* 801*d*, with H. Fuchs, "Bildung," in *Reallexikon für Antike und Christentum* 2 (Stuttgart, 1954), pp. 346ff., and J. Dalfen, *Polis und Poesis: Die Auseinandersetzung mit der Dichtung bei Platon und seinen Zeitgenossen* (Munich, 1974).

manded on 7 May 1498, provisions were made on 12 December of the same year to place them under Marcello Virgilio's control at Badia Fiorentina, on condition that an inventory be kept by the First Chancery.[257] With his office at Palazzo Vecchio and his chair at the Studio, he was established as the arbiter of letters. That position was recognized and formalized, less than a decade later, by Marcello Virgilio's appointment as state censor. What had begun as a rhetoric of crisis ended as an institution. The oratory of the Florentine Cato had displaced the eloquence of Socrates from Ferrara.

[257] See E. Piccolomini, "Documenti intorno alle vicende della Libreria Medicea Privata," *ASI* 19 (1874): 268 and 270–72; Marzi, *Cancelleria,* p. 294; and Ullman and Stadter, *Public Library,* pp. 33–34.

V

THE PRINCE AND THE PLANT

PRINCES formed the audience to which Marcello Virgilio's lectures were addressed: "Princes and kings who, at home and abroad, were to administer the Florentine Republic."[1] An education less for scholars than for statesmen was offered, to the sons of the ruling elite, by the First Chancellor at the Studio, from which his successful and sustained career had been launched. This is perhaps worth bearing in mind, when considering the milieux in which moved the author of *Il principe*.

Niccolò Machiavelli's intellectual world was not restricted to the society of the Orti Oricellari or confined to communion with such figures from the past as Alamanno Rinuccini and Donato Acciaiuoli. For a decade and a half, as Second Chancellor, he worked with Marcello Virgilio. To understand the master's lesson, it was not necessary to sit at his feet. This public figure taught by his living example, which touched on the spheres of both action and reflection that interested Machiavelli keenly. Politics, which he observed with attention, and literature, which he pursued with taste, had provided the means by which his colleague at Palazzo Vecchio had engineered his rapid ascent. Throughout the "popular" Republic, to audiences that included some of Machiavelli's friends, the leading humanist of his generation at Florence combined the study of letters with commentary on current events. On the scene where, as professor of literature and as servant of the state, Marcello Virgilio played his double role, "una lunga esperienzia delle cose moderne e una continua lezione delle antique" was the order of the day.

Upon the restoration of the Medici, that order changed. A reversion to philology took place after 1512, a return to issues unsolved by Poliziano and his peers. In the many discussions of Machiavelli's relationship to humanism, this development has never been analyzed. To attempt to do so will require us to turn away from well-trodden paths of research, and follow less familiar routes taken by some of his contemporaries. Which modes of reading were in vogue among Florentine intellectuals of the late fifteenth and early sixteenth centuries? What forms of interpretation did they favor? How did the exegesis and practice of literature interact with one another? To this unexplored territory the work of Marcello Virgilio offers a privileged guide. It

[1] *N* fols. 65^{r} and 51^{r}: "reipublice nostre futuri . . . principes et reges," "qui rempublicam domi forisque administraturi sunt."

enables us to reconstruct what, at Florence during Machiavelli's generation, were the hermeneutics of humanism.

Florentine humanism did not represent a general or unified movement. Specific, competing, and incompatible tendencies that had erupted into conflict during the last years of Poliziano's life continued, in two distinct phases, to influence the work of his successor. Abandoning the political approach that he had adopted in 1495, Marcello Virgilio, after 1512, turned to technical scholarship, based on Greek texts, in which Machiavelli had limited interest. He continued to view the problems posed by the Medicean era in terms that recalled both the assumptions and the methods of intellectual life before his expulsion from the Chancery. There, in his opinion, he belonged; there his experience had been formative. Reflecting on politics, Niccolò Machiavelli remained, by inclination and nostalgia, a man of action.

That was exactly the combination of qualities fostered by Marcello Virgilio at the Studio. His teaching, however, was aimed at potential holders of political office: at a class from which he and Machiavelli did not spring. Florentines of modest birth and lofty aspirations, at Florence in the late Quattro- and early Cinquecento, did better to identify with the orthodoxies of the day, anticipating how they would alter the next, than to attempt to shape or challenge them. To others, of established background and higher rank, was entrusted the moment of decision. The chancellors played a part, secondary and subordinate, in the process of deliberation. Their task was less to formulate policy than to execute it. Thus it was—in the eyes of his multiple masters, the swiftly rotating Signoria—proper that Marcello Virgilio adopted the role of a pillar of the establishment. Seeking the advantages of belonging to it, while maintaining an independent spirit, Machiavelli, both before and after thrusting his unsolicited advice on the Medici, took a more expansive view of his mission. He was inclined to forget that, in his position at the Chancery, there was little inherent strength; and the wonder is not that he lost his job in 1512, but that he held it for so long. The qualities of insight and outspokenness for which he is celebrated today, dangerous during the Republic, were his undoing at the restoration. Apart from his work in the organization of the militia, there is little evidence that Machiavelli, the political theorist, was especially astute in the practice of Florentine politics.[2]

Politics affected his relationship with his colleague at the Chancery. It amounted to less the open and formal one of pupil to teacher than a covert dialectic that arose from fundamental differences of character, strategy, and tactics. Collaboration—or its absence—heightened the tension. The responsibilities of Marcello Virgilio were various, his burdens manifold. They were not always alleviated by Machiavelli. Enjoying the favor of Pier Soderini,

[2] See Rubinstein, "Machiavelli and the World of Florentine Politics," pp. 5–28.

which was denied to the First Chancellor, the Second was often absent on diplomatic missions; and Marcello Virgilio had to stand in for him—which he resented, because it got in the way of his own work. "The *Gonfaloniere* instructs me to tell you to stay at Imola," Machiavelli, while serving as ambassador to Cesare Borgia,[3] was informed on 7 November 1502, "and—God knows—you can imagine how willingly I do so, with my job and yours and the lesson on my back."[4]

Compassion may be felt not only for the writer but also for the recipient of this letter. Machiavelli, when absent, probably sighed with relief. Present in the cramped quarters of the Chancery, he cannot have avoided hearing all that he wished to know, and a good deal more besides, about his colleague's "lesson." Marcello Virgilio's was a didactic spirit, not given to brevity. Garrulous and verbose, prolix and repetitive, he reveled in the sound of his own voice. It boomed forth with the pomposity of a professor and the solemnity of a bureaucrat. Tempering (or heightening) these irritating qualities, he had a number of obsessions. Baldness and nakedness; parasites and prostitutes; wasting diseases, natural calamities, crabs, ringworm, serpents: all these constituted the imagery and the substance of lessons in Latin that, during the course of the long years that Machiavelli spent in his enforced company, Marcello Virgilio modeled on conversational style.[5] The conversation of the First Chancellor, to judge by his lectures, was interminable. Just as in his teaching he went on about his position at Palazzo Vecchio, so he may be visualized holding forth ex cathedra to his colleagues about subjects on which he spoke at the Studio. Niccolò Machiavelli, between 1498 and 1512, consorted with a windbag. More irritatingly still, with a windbag who had ability, shrewdness, and—among "the future princes and kings of the Republic" whom he instructed—conspicuous success.

Success with which budding statesmen? Consider an illustrious example: Francesco Guicciardini, whose first two extant letters voicing his enthusiasm for Marcello Virgilio's lectures are addressed to Alessio Lapaccini, who was to become his successor as chancellor.[6] Writing an academic Latin modeled on their master's style, Guicciardini ironically expressed his horror before the bugbear of a "two-bit *grammatista,*" whom he feared "like a censor."[7] This

[3] For context, see Ridolfi, *Vita di Machiavelli,* pp. 88ff.

[4] Machiavelli, *Opere,* p. 1044: "Il Gonfalioneri . . . mi ha decto ch'io . . . ti advertisca ad non partire; et se io lo fo volontieri, Dio lo sa, che mi truovo con le faccende mie, con le tue et con la lectione addosso." See further below, pp. 239ff.

[5] See below, p. 194.

[6] Guicciardini, *Le lettere,* pp. 3–4 and 6.

[7] "A Diobolari illo grammatista commonitus (iocari enim libet), ut censorem perhorrebam." *Sic* Guicciardini, *Le lettere,* p. 6, following P. Guicciardini, *Lettere inedite di Francesco Guicciardini* (Florence, 1935), p. 23, who comments (p. 30) on "Diobolari" that "della sua esistenza e tanto meno della sua celebrità nessun ricordo oggi. Non figura tra gli umanisti del tempo." Not surprisingly: *diobolari[u]s* is an adjective, not a noun.

antithesis between the tyranny of an elementary schoolmaster and the authority of an arbiter of letters recalled the debates of Poliziano's generation, amplified in the teaching of Marcello Virgilio. Guicciardini had learned his lesson well.

What did that lesson involve when the professor explicated a text? If he so roundly rejected the philological methods of his predecessor, what did he put in their place? Here again it is necessary to return to the manuscripts, in both their official and their private versions, recalling the strains in Florentine culture that influenced Marcello Virgilio's distinctive style of interpretation. He styled himself, and was regarded, as the champion of secular learning. Its defender against the criticisms of the Savonarolians and the slights of the philistines, he had to demonstrate that it had a high ethical worth and that it was applicable to contemporary problems. That is why Marcello Virgilio spoke so frequently of the *utilitas,* moral and political, of the subjects that he taught. He could not afford to dwell on the aesthetic qualities of literature or to linger over technical issues. It was the content that mattered—neither the style, nor the form—in a society that, by the end of the Quattrocento, had lost Ficino and destroyed Savonarola.

That entailed, first and foremost, an instruction that was actual and engaged: an approach that made limpidly clear (in Machiavelli's terms) the necessary and natural connection between "le cose moderne e . . . antique." In 1495 Marcello Virgilio had taken the *Aeneid* as an example of such a work, and likened it to a training ground for champions of the Republic to do battle with "the arms of oratory."[8] Here is how, at the beginning of the Cinquecento, he began to teach Virgil:

> For the exposition that we hope to finish in the course of this academic year—unless otherwise prevented—an immensely promising omen is provided by the first half-verse by Virgil ["Arms and the man I sing"] in which, *with two words,* he pledged to impart a method for improving the life of mankind.[9]

Observe the parenthesis ("unless otherwise prevented"): the bustle of business, here as elsewhere, entered Marcello Virgilio's lectures and lent them color. He never forgot, and never allowed his audience to forget, that he was rushed off his feet. Overseeing the work of the Chancery; writing instructions to ambassadors and officials; composing state letters; delivering public orations; preparing his courses: such activities, often undertaken during the absences of Machiavelli, lent plausibility to Marcello Virgilio's protestations of too much work and too little time. Yet there was another, more positive, side to his role that made an impact on his students. At the Studio, he ap-

[8] See above, p. 158.

[9] *N* fol. 60^{r}: "Ennarationis huius nostre, quam annuo labore—nisi quod obfuerit—absolvemus, ingens felixque auspicium nobis primus hic Maronis versiculus, in quo vite humane meliorem rationem duobus verbis complexus est [*erased*] docere policitus est."

peared not merely as professor but also as the functionary who, in the name of the eight Priors of Liberty and the *Gonfaloniere* of Justice, signed documents and dispatches issued with the authority of the state. When he invoked *libertas,* he was in a position to know what, in terms of current policy, that polyvalent term meant. This lent Marcello Virgilio's teaching presence and weight.

Weighty, if not ponderous, is the interpretation extracted from the words *Arma virumque*. Such were the *flores* that Paolo Giovio reported Machiavelli gathering;[10] and it seems not to have been noticed, by the many who have commented critically or credulously on his observation, that the term was technical. *Flores,* since the High Middle Ages, had been regularly contrasted with the systematic commentary or the selective gloss;[11] and the word characterized precisely Marcello Virgilio's method, in his lectures, of taking select passages from ancient authors and using them as a point of departure for political and ethical disquisitions.

That method presented the *Aeneid* as a basis, from which Marcello ranged freely over issues raised or implied by the text, for examining the Florentine present in the light of the classical past. As such, it amounted to the opposite of Poliziano's approach. His lectures had concentrated on the detail of each work, anatomizing individual passages, poring over single words. Analytic and exact, Poliziano had scrutinized ancient literature, in an attempt to reconstruct its historical sense. Even his infrequent generalizations were confined to particular genres or specific forms; while his "Alexandrian" ideology of scholarship led him away from the well-known classics to "minor," obscure, or difficult authors. Self-advertising though Poliziano was in practice, his theory entailed fidelity to the literature that he treated. Marcello Virgilio, by contrast, asserted, with a boldness equal to Savonarola's, the primacy of its exegete. Gone were the days when the act of learned interpretation sufficed to itself. Past was the time of esoteric relativism when any writer had an equal claim to attention. In the looming crisis, the value of literature was in doubt, and its worth could be affirmed only by the strongest of evidence. That meant, to one employed to teach Latin poetry, Virgil. And as the professor here, too, recurred to traditionalism, he was confronted with the example set by the leading Virgilian at Florence in the late Quattrocento.[12]

Cristoforo Landino, both in the third and fourth books of his *Disputationes*

[10] See above, p., 149.

[11] See Melville, "Zur *Flores,*" pp. 65–80, with further bibliography. This is distinct from (although related to) "un ideale florilegio o antologia," about which speaks Dionisotti, *Machiavellerie,* p. 414. See further below, pp. 273ff.

[12] On Landino's Virgilian exegesis, see A. Field, "An Inaugural Oration by Cristoforo Landino in Praise of Virgil (From Codex '2,' Casa Cavalli, Ravenna)," *Rinascimento* 21 (1981): 235–45; C. Kallendorf, *In Praise of Aeneas: Virgil and Epideictic Rhetoric in the Early Italian Renaissance* (Hanover, 1989), pp. 129–65; E. Müller-Bochat, *Leon Battista Alberti und die Virgil—Deutung der Disputationes camaldulenses: Zur allegorischen Dichter—Erklärung bei Cristoforo Landino* (Krefeld, 1968); and M. Murrin, *The Allegorical Epic: Essays in Its Rise and Decline* (Chicago and London, 1980), pp. 27–52.

camaldulenses (1473)[13] and in his commentary on Virgil of 1487–88,[14] had anticipated some of his pupil's central themes. "Maro's poem," he wrote in his proemium to the *Commentum,* "portrays every form of human life";[15] Aeneas offers a model of how it should be conducted.[16] This was the same conception of the exemplary character of the *Aeneid* voiced at the opening of Marcello Virgilio's lecture; and the terms in which he described its audience were virtually identical to those used by Landino: "Yours is the princely house in your republic," Piero de' Medici was assured in the dedication;[17] the competence of his father was universally recognized in "the administration of affairs at home and abroad."[18] Yet there was a significant difference. The titles of authority that Landino had applied to the Medici were attributed by Marcello Virgilio to the privileged youth of the post-Medicean Republic.[19] When his teacher had extolled Aeneas as a role model, he had imagined the objection: "But we cannot all be princes in the state or lead armies."[20] What Landino had denied, Marcello Virgilio affirmed, substituting for the Medicean model of a single *princeps,* uniquely distinguished by his culture and learning,[21] an entire class of capable princelings.

The subdued polemic introduced more radical divergences. Landino, advocate of "plain" exposition,[22] wished to exclude from his commentary on the *Aeneid* anything that smacked of what he regarded as triviality, such as the "superfluous quirks and empty ambiguities of dialectic" or "the fables without substance" of time-wasting fiction.[23] They were just what Marcello Virgilio desired to keep in. "Obscure and fabulous accounts of things sometimes reveal their deeper meanings,"[24] he stated, beginning with nature, to

[13] Dating according to R. Fubini, "Cristoforo Landino, le 'Disputationes camaldulenses,' e il volgarizzamento di Plinio: Questioni di cronologia e di interpretazione," in *Studi in onore di A. d'Addario,* vol. 2, ed. L. Borgia et al. (Lecce, 1995), pp. 535–57.

[14] Landino, *Scritti critici,* 1:205–35 (proemium and introduction).

[15] "Maronis poema omne humanae vitae genus exprimit," ibid., p. 215, ll. 23–24.

[16] "P. Vergilius, ut generi humano quam plurimum prodesset, eo potissimum consilio in uno Aenea absolutum omnino atque ex omni parte perfectum virum finxit atque expressit, ut omnes illum nobis tamquam unicum exemplar ad vitam degendam proponeremus." Ibid., p. 215, ll. 34–37–p. 216, l. 1.

[17] "Est iam diu, Petre Medices, *princeps in re publica* vestra domus tua." Ibid., p. 217, ll. 28–29.

[18] ". . . in rebus . . . domi forisque administrandis." Ibid., p. 223, ll. 21–22.

[19] See note 1 above.

[20] ". . . non omnes in re publica principes esse aut exercitibus praeponi possumus." Landino, *Scritti critici,* p. 216, ll. 14–15.

[21] Ibid., p. 225, ll. 1–4.

[22] "Itaque omittamus anxias interpretationes eaque solum assumamus, quae non modo in abdito non latent, sed ultro sese quaerentibus offerunt." *Disputationes camaldulenses* (ed. Lohe), 3:175, ll. 28–30.

[23] "Neque rursus levium futiliumque rerum est quaerenda doctrina, veluti qui in dialecticorum superfluis captiunculis ac vanis amphibologiis aut inanibus fabellis omne paene tempus terunt." Ibid., p. 208, ll. 23–26.

[24] *N* fol. 61^r: ". . . obscuris aliquando rerum . . . et fabulosis narrationibus graviores rerum sensus aperiuntur."

which he had already hailed the poet of the *Aeneid* and the *Georgics* an expert guide.[25] And natural science was linked, by Marcello Virgilio's view of *enkyklios paideia,* to the discipline of dialectic: "All that is taught or that we strive to learn refers either to nature or to civilized customs or to the method of education that the Greeks call dialectic."[26]

Of these three topics, it is the second—customs, manners, *mores*—that figures most prominently in his lectures. Landino had often adverted to the "civic" interest of the *Aeneid,*[27] but the social and political substance of such questions was beneath his notice. Heroizing his own role as critic,[28] he had interpreted the poem in the flickering light of his Platonic philosophy.[29] Metahistorical and allegorical, Landino stood for all that Marcello Virgilio rejected. Disinclined from abstractions, his concrete mind was hostile to the evasive rhetoric of the *vita contemplativa.* With abhorrence, in his *praelusio* of 1498, the newly elected chancellor had condemned those who, abandoning the trials and tedium of marriage, opted for celibacy "against nature and civilized custom." They were like usurers and crooks who, fearing the perils of honest trade and seafaring, made shady deals; like farmers who, shirking harsh labor in the fields, sold themselves into base servitude; like cowards who, fearing the rough-and-tumble of public life, sought refuge in solitude.[30] To flee the world into the mists of Neoplatonic contemplation seemed deplorable to this hard-nosed Aristotelian. The active life was his subject, the *vita civilis* his ideal. Marcello Virgilio's preferred brand of philosophy was consequently "moral"—ethics and (particularly) "economics" and politics, according to the tripartite division of university instruction.[31] In such terms he proposed to read the *Aeneid* as a work on the civic virtues—unlike Landino, unlike Poliziano, unlike any Virgilian interpreter at Florence before him. When, in 1498, elated by his dual appointment, this humanist had referred to his "new and unprecedented manner of teaching," he was telling the truth.

Or part of it. The model that Marcello Virgilio did not mention was indicated by his allusions to marriage and to honest commerce. These were fa-

[25] See p. 154 above.

[26] *N* fols. 65^{v}–66^{r}: "Omne quod docetur aut in quo discendo laboramus aut ad naturam pertinet aut ad mores aut ad rationem discendi, quam dialectices Graeci appellant."

[27] E.g., *Disputationes camaldulenses,* 3:153, ll. 22ff.; p. 174, ll. 27ff.; p. 176, ll. 14ff.; p. 177, ll. 7ff.

[28] See M. di Cesare, "Cristoforo Landino on the Name and Nature of Poetry: The Critic as Hero," *Chaucer Review* 21 (1986): 155–59.

[29] See Cardini, *La Critica del Landino,* pp. 1–84.

[30] *R* fol. 28^{r}: "Alter coniugii et rei uxorie labores fastidiaque fugiens, celibatum sibi contra naturam et bonos mores elegit. Cottidie offerunt se nobis, qui mercature et navigationis pericula veriti ad fenus turpesque alios questus se transtulerint. Sunt qui, ne in colendo agro se torqueant, ad ignavam servitutem se vertunt. Videre etiam licet qui, ne invidia laborant, ne pro repub[lica] laborem suscipiant, solitudinem sibi elegerint."

[31] See Kraye, "Moral Philosophy," pp. 303ff.

vored themes of Bruni—in his *Life of Dante,* for example, but particularly in his annotated Latin version of the pseudo-Aristotelian *Economics.*[32] That widely diffused work was not intended for a specialist audience. Bruni had dedicated it, as an example of practical philosophy, to Cosimo de' Medici. The applied interest of such subjects as the leadership of an army, the governance of the state, and the administration of a household, treated by pseudo-Aristotle and discussed by Bruni, was stressed in Marcello Virgilio's examination of the *Aeneid.* Qualified by Aristotelian standards (*Politics* 1283*a*) as future office-holders through property and rank, his students personified the contrast that he had drawn, while discussing the education of the ruling class in his *praelusio* of 1498, between liberty and servitude in language that recalled Bruni's comments on the *Economics.*[33] What pupils such as Guicciardini now sought, and obtained, from Marcello Virgilio was not philological exegesis or philosophical exposé of the *Aeneid* but a guide, through *flores* plucked from it, to the issues of the moment.

The moment was the academic year 1502–3. The financial situation of the Republic was grave.[34] Wealthy citizens had refused to grant further loans, and it was difficult to levy taxes. Arezzo had risen in revolt; the sinister figure of Cesare Borgia for several months maneuvered in the vicinity.[35] Failure to reform the institutions of government, often debated and always postponed, betrayed vacillation and weakness. In this *debolezza* of internal and foreign policy, declared Bernardo da Diacceto during the *pratica* of 5 July 1502, the choice lay between freedom and ruin.[36] Unity, affirmed Bernardo Rucellai, was worth more than the wages of fifty squadrons of cavalry.[37]

[32] See *Vita di Dante,* proemium, in *Humanistisch-philosophische Schriften* (ed. Baron), p. 51 and passim. On the ps.-Aristotelian *Economics,* see I. Soudek, "Leonardo Bruni and His Public: A Statistical and Interpretative Study of His Annotated Latin Version of the (Pseudo-) Aristotelian *Economics,*" *Studies in Medieval and Renaissance History* 5 (1986): 51–136, and "The Genesis and Tradition of Leonardo Bruni's Annotated Latin Version of the (Pseudo-) Aristotelian *Economics,*" *Scriptorium* 12 (1958): 260–68, with H. Goldbrunner, "Leonardo Brunis Kommentar zu seiner Übersetzung der pseudo-aristotelischen Ökonomik: Ein humanistischer Kommentar," in *Der Kommentar in der Renaissance,* ed. A. Buck and O. Herding (Bonn, 1975), pp. 99–118. All references are to *Aristotelis Stagiritae libri moralem philosophiam complectentes cum Averrois Cordubensis in Moralia Nicomachia expositiones* (Venice, 1560) (here shortened to *Aristotelis . . . libri*), pp. 162^{r}ff. A partial translation, with commentary, is given by Griffiths in Bruni, *Humanism,* pp. 300ff. On Bruni and *mercatura,* see P. Viti, *Leonardo Bruni e Firenze: Studi sulle lettere pubbliche e private* (Rome, 1992), pp. 197–222, and cf. pp. 339–63.

[33] See p. 142 above. Cf. Bruni on *Economica* 5: ". . . servos imbuere et docere et erudire illos, quos liberata negotia fuerint comittenda. Cum servis autem ita versetur scilicet dominus neque enim pati debet esse superbos." *Aristotelis . . . libri,* p. 163^{b}, ll. 48–52.

[34] See Gilbert, *Machiavelli and Guicciardini,* pp. 63ff.

[35] Cf. S. Bertelli, "La crisi del 1501: Firenze e Cesare Borgia," in *Essays Presented to M. P. Gilmore,* ed. S. Bertelli and G. Ramakus (Florence, 1972), pp. 1–19.

[36] *Consulte e pratiche . . . 1494–1505* (ed. Fachard), 2:816.

[37] Ibid., p. 821.

Liberty took precedence over change, argued Baldassare Carducci six days later:[38] better to bide time for reform. In this context of verbose indecision that eventually led to the compromise of electing Pier Soderini *Gonfaloniere a vita,*[39] Marcello Virgilio raised his voice. Speaking not on his own account but in the name of the Signoria, he reported on urban disorders, external threats, and the problems of raising money, before requesting the opinion of the Colleges, of the Dieci, and of "some seventy leading citizens present" on how "to organize the city and introduce good government."[40] These were the same issues about which, under the cover of lectures on the *Aeneid,* he reflected the same year before sons of the same politicians. Opinions that might not be expressed, *in propria persona,* by the chancellor during a public meeting of the ruling elite could be indicated at the Studio, where the interpretation of ancient literature was linked with discussion of current affairs for those who, in the future, would make the decisions. Small wonder that, to students like Francesco Guicciardini, Marcello Virgilio, among Florentine professors, seemed the man of the moment.

. . . . .

He was not without rivals—all the more formidable because they had connections with the Studio but came from the opposite camp. And they were active at the very time when Marcello Virgilio held his course on the *Aeneid.* One—perhaps the most daunting—was Giovanni Nesi, who, in the troubled year 1502–3, was preparing his *De moribus* for publication.[41] Like Marcello Virgilio, Nesi sought to adapt a work originally composed for Piero de' Medici to the needs of the youth of the post-Medicean Republic. His model was furnished not by Landino, but by an ethical tract of his own authorship. *De moribus* touched, too closely for comfort, on the themes that Marcello Virgilio was treating at the Studio: public order, commerce, the citizen as prince of the Republic. Yet the Savonarolian Nesi had little time for the active life. He dismissed it as a shadow. The substance of reality, according to him, was to be found in contemplation of the divine order.[42] What Marcello Virgilio presented as "a complete method for improving the life of mankind," Nesi regarded as propaedeutic to an *itinerarium mentis in Deum.* This was the other aspect of a scene that, at Florence, no lay sage could dominate un-

[38] Ibid., p. 829.

[39] Gilbert, *Machiavelli and Guicciardini,* p. 73; and R. Pesman Cooper, "L'elezione," pp. 145–85.

[40] *Consulte e pratiche . . . 1494–1505* (ed. Fachard), 2:818–19. It is misleading when Gilbert (*Machiavelli and Guicciardini,* p. 71 n. 1) represents Marcello Virgilio as making "an introductory speech to a *pratica* on 5 July 1502." Then, as always, he spoke in the name of the Signoria.

[41] See R. Bonfanti, "Su un dialogo filosofico del tardo '400: Il *De moribus* del fiorentino Giovanni Nesi (1456–1522?)," *Rinascimento* 2 (1971): 203–11.

[42] Ibid., pp. 215ff.

challenged. *Mores,* as Marcello Virgilio conceived them, were examined, in treatises addressed to the same audience to which he spoke, by *piagnoni* intellectuals such as Nesi, who asserted in forceful terms the values of a reforming spirituality. The shadow of Savonarola still hung over the city's culture.

That culture therefore had to be redefined in terms of its tradition. Florence, for many, was the heiress of Rome. The Roman past with which Marcello Virgilio sought to align contemporary society was consequently less that of the Christian capital than that of the *imperium* founded by Aeneas's descendants:

> Let us, first of all, follow the custom and sequence of the ancients and deal with ethics, passing then to marriage, the raising and education of children, management of the household and the state, for the practically limitless laws that govern them have been handed down by ancient tradition.[43]

From the *Aeneid* could be derived principles exempt from the religious overtones that might be read into the interpretations, by Salutati or Landino, of the poem as an allegory of the ages and progress of man. Resisting attempts such as Nesi's to lay down the law *de moribus,* Marcello Virgilio sought to demonstrate that secular literature was the distinct domain of the lay moralist, on which others encroached at their peril.

The territory staked out by his exposition of the *Aeneid* had limits, defined by his method of exposition. The professor paid little attention to the sequence of the base text—following its order when it suited him and, more often, springing from passage to passage or book to book. From aspects of *Aeneid* 1, for example, he turned to treat Book 4, and even then his commentary was eclectic and idiosyncratic. Over subjects like Aeneas's affair with Dido, Marcello Virgilio passed rapidly—not because he was a prude in matters sexual, but because he cast the poet in his own image as *morum censor.*[44] Probably the first (and possibly the only) exegete of the *Aeneid* to formulate the view that the Carthaginian queen was a chatterbox, Marcello Virgilio condemned her loquacity, while forgetting his own: "There is no more certain sign of a frivolous temperament in a woman than *loquacitas*. Its danger, united with other feminine vices, lies in the corruption of children."[45] Offspring was the issue: hence the attention paid to Ascanius, Aeneas's son, and the preference for Lavinia, his wife, over Dido, his mistress. A kingdom,

[43] *N* fol. 62^{r}: ". . . primumque, ut veterum morem et ordinem sequamur, de moribus agemus, in quibus precedunt coniugia, educationes eruditiones filiorum, cura rei domestice, cura et reipublice, quarum omnium infinite pene leges a veteribus tradite sunt."

[44] *N* fol. 67^{r}: "morum censor." See further below, pp. 272ff.

[45] *N* fol. 62^{v}: ". . . nullam certius argumentum . . . levis ingenii in muliere quam loquacitas, que una cum multis aliis vitiis quotidiano contubernio et exemplis domesticis subito facileque in filios transferta."

wealth, and honor had been acquired by the founder of the Roman empire in marriage.[46]

A future *princeps*—Virgil's Aeneas, or his own pupils, who were likened to the hero of the poem—should not forget that the "solid basis" of a family was "property and wealth."[47] An advantageous union in homely Latium, not passing flings in distant Carthage, constituted Marcello Virgilio's model. He interpreted the *Aeneid* in terms of marital and familial relationships described by the pseudo-Aristotelian *Economics,* with an emphasis on mutual responsibility that reflected the line taken by Bruni in his annotations on its fifth chapter.[48] Presenting the wife not as the slave or possession of her husband but as the subordinate partner in a common enterprise, the professor recalled Bruni's dissent from pseudo-Aristotle's use of Hesiod, with its implication that the wife should be reduced to the status of a domestic animal. This was the same issue treated by Poliziano in the second *Centuria.*[49] It is noteworthy that his successor, to whom the unpublished work was available,[50] passed over its interpretation in silence. For Marcello Virgilio, as for Bruni, the marital state was the norm, and the eccentricities of bachelor-philologists might be ignored.

Bachelors, on this view, led unbalanced lives—unlike Aeneas, his exegete's instance of a successful union between private and public affairs.[51] To achieve harmony, rather the practical than the theoretical branches of knowledge were required; and the advantage of studying Virgil (no less encyclopedic an author than Homer) was that he offered guidance, with the authority of a Hippocrates or a Galen, to such life sciences as agriculture and medicine.[52] The utilitarianism of lay culture, which privileged the applied subjects, was no longer disposed to assess the truth-claims of literature in terms of prophecy and redemption. If the *Aeneid* was worth pondering, it was because it contained empirical and verifiable observation of human affairs.[53]

The most pressing of them, in 1502–3, were the organization and gover-

[46] *N* fol. 66^{v}: "Exemplum nobis in Lavinia proponitur, que regnum in Italia tot aliosque honores Enee detulit et unde iam pridem Eneas sibi speravit 'Romanos rerum dominos gentemque togatam.'" Cf. Virgil *Aeneid* 1.282

[47] *N* fol. 63^{r}: ". . . rei domestice dispensatio, cuius quidem solida basis est patrimonium et opes." Cf. Bruni in *Aristotelis . . . libri,* p. 163^{r}, ll. 43–47.

[48] *Aristotelis . . . libri,* p. 163^{v}, ll. 10ff.

[49] See above, pp. 121–22.

[50] See below, pp. 204–5.

[51] *N* fol. 68^{v}: ". . . Eneas, qui nullam vite sue partem incultam reliquisset. Comitantur private et publice rei curam artes, quibus tamquam instrumentis vita nec nostra quottidie excolitur adeoque necessarias non aliam ob causam nec in alium usum omnes quottidie experimur."

[52] *N* fol. 69^{r}: "Nam agriculturam omnium medicinamque precipue signa primum et causas ostendens omnes, quas Hippocrates primum et Galenus . . . docuerunt."

[53] Ibid.: "Hoc ipsum dicendum nobis et diffinitione eius, quam hic intelligens esse collectionem multorum experimentorum ad aliquem finem utilem et necessarium vite humane."

nance of the state.[54] How to accommodate the recently established *Gonfalonierato a vita* with the nominally republican traditions of Florence's mixed constitution? Bruni, its leading theorist,[55] led Marcello Virgilio to Plato's and Aristotle's classification of regimes: monarchy, aristocracy, oligarchy, democracy, and, "in the rigor of the term, *politeía*."[56] This last distinction, derived from Aristotle (*Politics* 1297*b*), between legitimate government by the many and its populist corruption, was useful to an educator of "princes" aiming to reconcile access to high office by the political elite that formed the *Consiglio Maggiore* with the primacy of one head of state. Combining the ideal of an Aristotelian *politeía* with the figure of an enlightened *rex* that he derived from the *Aeneid,* Marcello Virgilio recommended that, below the level of quasi-sovereignty, other positions of power should be alternated by lot.[57] "Kingship" in this sense was a monarchical metaphor, legitimated by a hermeneutic license that asserted the versatility of literature. Not only Virgil's poetry was employed to justify the *Gonfalonierato a vita,* but also that of Pindar, whom, in 1495, Marcello Virgilio had cited as an authority on republican liberty. How times had changed in 1502! Was it now not obvious that Pindar had been of the same opinion as Virgil when he wrote (*Olympians* 1.113ff.), "The supreme and greatest of all goods culminates in kings"?[58]

"Kingship" had multiple meanings in the political vocabulary of republican Florence. *Rex* was the term that, in his letter of 1413 to Emperor Sigismund, Bruni had employed to designate rule by one man.[59] Lorenzo de' Medici's hegemony had been likened, by Aurelio Lippo Brandolini in his *De comparatione reipublicae et regni* (c. 1490), to "an image of royal authority";[60] and Ficino, in his epitome of the fourth book of Plato's *Laws,* had cited the instance of Dion, recommending a *regnum moderatum* on the basis of the *Let-*

[54] *N* fols. 69^{r-v}: "Adest iam nobis res publica, que vult et ipsa a nobis ostendi quod de se tantum senserit vates."

[55] See Moulakis, "Leonardo Bruni's Constitution," pp. 141–90; and Dees, "Bruni, Aristotle, and the Mixed Régime," pp. 1–23, esp. 5–9.

[56] *N* fol. 69^{v}: "Sunt autem eius alie atque alie species formeque a veteribus descripte, et ab hiis praesertim, qui huiuscemodi instituende vite humane monumenta reliquerunt, quales pre ceteris Plato et Aristoteles in hoc ordine conseritur: regna, aristocratie, oligarchie, democratie et—proprio dicte nomine—politie."

[57] Ibid.: "Rex erat Eneas nobis, et rex arva Latinus habebat et eam perfectam formam censuit, in qua princeps iuberet, populus pareret, et in ferendis rei publice muneribus sors regula esset."

[58] Ibid.: "Intelligerent omnes quod Pindarus ait: 'extremum et maximum bonorum omnium in rege terminari.'"

[59] Baron, ed., *Humanistic and Political Literature,* p. 182.

[60] BMLF, Pluteo 77, 11, fol. 164^{v}: ". . . aliquam etiam illius regii principatus imaginem." See I. G. Rao in *All'ombra del lauro: Documenti librari della cultura in età laurenziana,* ed. A. Lenzuni (Florence, 1992), pp. 101–3; and Hankins, "Humanism and Origins," pp. 132–33.

ters and the *Politicus*.[61] The ancient subtitle of that work, recorded by Diogenes Laertius (3.58), in Ficinian translation appeared as *De regno*.[62] In his interpretations of Plato's later political philosophy, as in his epitome of the *Republic,*[63] he struggled to come to terms with the tension between the myth of a governor, alone yet not absolute, and the "civic" order of a republican state.[64] That struggle, continued in Marcello Virgilio's reading of the *Aeneid* as a mirror for princes, was resolved by deference to the office rather than to its holder. Extolling the position to which one of "the kings and princes of the Republic" among his audience might, in the future, accede, Marcello Virgilio studiously avoided any reference to its present incumbent. No analogy was drawn between the glowing qualities of *rex Eneas* and the pallid person of *Gonfaloniere* Soderini.

Correctness marked relations between the first citizen of the Florentine Republic and its First Chancellor. Cordiality was not notable. If Marcello Virgilio, ex officio, was included in Soderini's bequest to members of the Chancery,[65] there is no sign that he was distinguished from them by the personal trust that the *Gonfaloniere* placed in Niccolò Machiavelli. The careers of the two colleagues, during the period 1502–12, displayed an inverse symmetry. When diplomatic missions were entrusted to the one, the other remained at Florence. Increasingly withdrawn from foreign affairs, where Machiavelli, as secretary to the Dieci, played a prominent role, Marcello Virgilio was given enhanced responsibilities in the domestic sphere of cultural politics. Censor of the press and adviser on the artistic embellishment of Palazzo Vecchio,[66] he won a degree of internal influence that hardly compensated for his failure to achieve political advancement. From 1503, by virtue of election to membership of the *Consiglio Maggiore,* Marcello Virgilio was eligible for the public offices secured by his predecessor Scala. That he never obtained them in the years of Soderini's *Gonfalonierato*—when his script, which had figured regularly in the protocols of the *Consulte e pratiche* from 1498 to 1502, became conspicuous by its absence—reflects a lack of crucial support. Too closely linked with the optimate oligarchy, and on suspiciously good terms with the Mediceans, Marcello Virgilio was kept at a distance by the *Gonfaloniere,* who had difficulties with both. The patronage that enabled the Second Chancellor, within the limits of his office, to involve

[61] Ficino, *Opera omnia* 1, 2:1497.

[62] Ibid., p. 1292.

[63] Ibid., p. 1406.

[64] See Vasoli, "Reflessioni sugli umanisti," pp. 146–68.

[65] For Soderini's will, see D. Silvano Razzi, *Vita di Pier Soderini* (Padua, 1737), pp. 153–54.

[66] See A. Cecchi, "Machiavelli o Marcello Virgilio Adriani? Ipotesi sul programma iconografico e l'assetto originario delle battaglie di Leonardo e Michelangelo per la sala del Maggior Consiglio in Palazzo Vecchio," *Prospettiva* 83–84 (1996): 102–15.

himself in political issues such as the militia was withheld from the First. As Machiavelli's star waxed, Marcello Virgilio's waned.

. . . . .

Reticence in public, during the decade (1502–12) of Soderini's rule, characterized the thwarted mandarin's response to the author of his marginalization. Unlike his pupil and colleague, Andrea Dazzi, Marcello Virgilio never dedicated a work, however occasional or ephemeral, to the *Gonfaloniere a vita*.[67] Never, in his lectures or speeches, did this professional eulogist praise, by name or allusion, Pier Soderini. But if, in his teaching, he followed a course parallel to, yet distinct from, that pursued by Bernardo Rucellai and the circle of the Orti Oricellari,[68] as civil servant he maintained a cautious distance from the gardens of the opposition to the republican regime. An outsider to the establishment like Pietro Crinito might trumpet his alleged connections with past and present generations of Florentine intellectuals who, in his unreliable opinion, mattered:[69] Marcello Virgilio, disfavored by the head of state, trained his gaze on those who might succeed him. From the chair that he regarded as a private pulpit, he transformed his lectures into sermons for future rulers of the Republic.

They were attuned to such an edifying approach. Vernacular preaching, by the laity, formed an established genre at Florence, the confraternities providing their occasion and context.[70] In the learned language, with attention to his youthful audience's needs and interests, Ficino "had turned the sermon into a classical oration . . . reclaiming for piety and true religion young men exposed to the intellectual corruption of the Aristotelian 'sophists' at the Florentine Studium."[71] In Marcello Virgilio's lectures, the Studio struck back. Continuing his attempt to replace the self-styled Socrates of the older generation in his role of moral and cultural leadership, the professor adopted the same persona in a style that was his own.

[67] For the dedication of Dazzi's poetry to Soderini, with its reference to a planned (but never completed) translation of Diodorus Siculus "tuis auspiciis," see Dazzi, *Andreae Dactii,* p. 5. Cf. the language of "Herrscherkult" in N. de' Nerli's panegyrics on Soderini, BRF 951, fol. 1^v: "Petro principi designato"; fol. 2^v : "Tu solus electus tanta ad gubernacula . . . tu solus rerum, tu ductor."

[68] On the chronology and rhetorical character of the discussions in the Orti Oricellari, see Gilbert, "Bernardo Rucellai";Cantimori, "Rhetoric and Politics," pp. 83–102; and Albertini, *Firenze,* pp. 67–85.

[69] E.g., Crinito, *Commentarii de honesta disciplina,* pp. 98–99.

[70] See J. Henderson, "Penitence and the Laity in Fifteenth-Century Florence," and R. F. Weissman, "Sacred Eloquence: Humanist Preaching and Lay Piety in Renaissance Florence," in Verdon and Henderson, *Christianity and the Renaissance,* pp. 229–71.

[71] Hankins, *Plato in the Italian Renaissance,* 1:298–99; and see above, pp. 135ff.

Marcello Virgilio combined the formality of the *politikos logos* with the more conversational and allusive manner of the *aphelês logos*.[72] The Greek terminology is pertinent,[73] because classical Latin models for the kinds of politico-philosophical sermon that he favored were neither numerous nor unfamiliar. With his taste for the new and the recherché, the alternative Socrates turned to a writer unused by Ficino: Maximus of Tyre, Neoplatonist of the second century, whose *Dialexeis* were beginning to be absorbed into Florentine culture of the late Quattro- and early Cinquecento.[74] A Latin translation, prepared before his death in 1513 by Cosimo de' Pazzi, archbishop of Florence, appeared at Rome in 1517 and at Basle in 1519—some forty years before the *editio princeps* of the Greek text. Marcello Virgilio was on good terms with the archbishop, who may have consulted him about his work, which he intended to dedicate to Pope Julius II.[75] Not good enough, however, to prevent this unscrupulous operator from drawing on the translation in its prepublication form and pressing it into the service not of the church but of the state—a state endowed with the strong leadership that, in the eyes of his enemies, Soderini had failed to provide.

Late in his *Gonfalonierato a vita,* during the winter of 1511, the designs of Pope Julius II to move against the Republic and restore the Medici became the subject of rumor. Against the intended dedicatee of Cosimo de' Pazzi's translation—unpublished and unpublishable in the hivernal climate of Florentine and papal relations—was directed a *praelusio,* delivered in November of the same year, in which Marcello Virgilio both voiced an ideal of rule at variance with Soderini's criticized policies and defined his own anti-Ficinian persona. Here is his self-portrait, composed months before the return of Lorenzo's dynasty:

> Do not be embarrassed that I call myself your wet nurse and midwife, pretending that I seek for myself unparalleled glory from my most menial and lowly services: these are the name and the function assumed by the wisest authorities whom I follow—Maximus of Tyre, professor of Platonic philosophy at Rome, who, in the oration in which he inquired whether what the Greeks term *enkyklios paideia* contributes anything to virtue, called poetry the gentle nurse of the youthful intellect, together with the famous Socrates, never sufficiently praised, himself son of a midwife who boasted that he had turned his mother's profession to a more honorable and better purpose by delivering daily newborn offspring from the minds of young men.[76]

[72] For the distinction, discussed below, between *politikos logos* and *aphelês logos,* see the *Ars rhetorica* attributed to Aristides, ed. W. Schmid (Leipzig, 1926).

[73] Cf. D. Russell, *Greek Declamation* (Cambridge, 1983), pp. 77–78.

[74] See Maximus of Tyre, *Dissertationes* (ed. Trapp), pp. xvii–xix. On Maximus of Tyre and Plato, see M. B. Trapp, in *Antonine Literature,* ed. D. A. Russell (Oxford, 1990), pp. 161–64.

[75] *Maximi Tyri philosophi platonici sermones,* p. 2.

[76] *R* fol. 33^{v}: "Neque pudeat vos quod nutricem et obstetricem vestram me profiteor ex

In a Latin that, here as elsewhere in this *praelusio,* echoed Cosimo de' Pazzi's translation,[77] Marcello Virgilio referred to the *Dialexeis* (37.3) by Maximus of Tyre. Mediating Plato's *Theaetetus* (148*e*–151*d*), with its image of Socrates' midwifery,[78] the *Dialexeis* served to justify and disguise Marcello Virgilio's appropriation to himself of the title of *nutrix* that Poliziano had bestowed on poetry, while claiming for his own teaching the encyclopedic ideal advanced in his predecessor's *Miscellanea* 1 and *Lamia.*

The recent past suppressed in silence, the modern Socrates loudly extolled the golden age of classical Athens, which he viewed through the optic of later Greek thought. Maximus of Tyre, in the sixth of the *Dialexeis* (to follow the sequence of Cosimo de' Pazzi's version), provided illumination in this dark hour of the Florentine Republic. Discussing the active and contemplative lives, he had interpreted Plato's later political philosophy in an interventionist spirit that contrasted sharply with Ficino's detachment. A convinced advocate of the monarchical principle, a sympathizer with aristocracy, but no friend to democracy,[79] Maximus had linked his "royalist" reading of the *Politicus* to a celebration of the political role of youth that he derived from the *Letters.* Young men should seize the initiative! Vacillation served no purpose. Dion had freed Syracuse from misrule by a coup d'état![80]

Piquant parallels occurred to Marcello Virgilio in the crisis of 1511. The *Gonfaloniere a vita* on whom he lost no love had been attacked by the *ottimati* for refusing to create the type of regime that, with only minor manipulation of the evidence, Plato via Maximus could be represented as advocating.[81]

---

vilissimis et sordidis ministeriis insolitam gloriam sapientie huius mihi affectantes: sunt enim appellationis et ministerii huius sapientissimi mihi auctores Maximus Tyrius Rome Platonem professus, qui in oratione qua quesivit 'an virtuti conferat aliquid que Greci cyclicas disciplinas dicunt,' poeticem iocundam iuvenilis animi nutricem appellavit et nunquam satis laudatus Socrates ille, qui obstetricis filius maternum studium ad honestiorem et meliorem rationem transtulit obstetricium exercere se iactans, quo novos ex animis iuvenum partus ad lucem quotidie proferret."

[77] Cf. the title of *sermo* 21: "Utrum circulares disciplinae conferant ad virtutem" and "poetica optima nimirum adolescentis animi nutrix et alumna," *Maximi Tyri philosophi platonici sermones,* pp. 85 and 86.

[78] Cf. R. M. Polawsky, *Philosophy and Knowledge: A Commentary on Plato's "Theaetetus"* (London, 1948), pp. 58ff.; and M. Burnyeat, "Socratic Midwifery, Platonic Inspiration," *Bulletin of the Institute of Classical Studies* (University of London) 24 (1977): 7–15.

[79] "Quarum [civitatum] quae beatissima est, gubernationem regiam aget, cedentibus nimirum reliquis partibus ei, quae ad Principatum moderandum genita sit. Quae verso huic felicitati inferior, secundaque est, ea aliquorum potentiam, qui coniunctim pro principe se gerunt, Aristocratia, id ut optimatum potentiam appellans. Regia quidem deterior est, sed Democratia, id est, populari potentia maior." *Maximi Tyri philosophi platonici sermones,* pp. 30–31.

[80] "Invenem omnia decent! Philosophus in iuventute negotiam gerat, oret, Rempublican capessat, militat, imperet! Nam Platonis in Siciliani cursus, labores, studiaque propter Dionem suscepta, opera fuerunt vigentis iuventutis." Ibid., p. 31.

[81] See R. Pesman Cooper, "Pier Soderini: Aspiring Prince or Civic Leader?" *Studies in Medieval and Renaissance History,* n.s. 1 (1978): 72ff.

Julius II, incensed by the flouting of the interdict that he had imposed on Florence, was harboring dark designs on the city. How to comment on this situation without overstepping the mark? By the time-honored technique of paraphrase: of Plato, who might express what Marcello Virgilio could not voice, interpreted in the spirit of Maximus of Tyre. Near the end of the *praelusio,* a summary of the Platonic *Dialogues* was offered. All but one of them were identified by title; all but one were described in the third-person singular. Abandoning this neutrality for a complicit second-person plural, the professor inserted, between his mini-epitomes of the *Theaetetus* and the *Charmides,* a sentence that ingenuous listeners might have taken to be an adaptation of *Politicus* 284*a*ff.: "*We have learned* that, in all human affairs, the utmost summit is kingship, and that there should be one king and one prince."[82]

The naive hearer would have been mistaken. The allusion was not to Plato but to Pindar. In 1511, as in 1502,[83] Marcello Virgilio employed the same monarchical metaphors—no longer distinguishing between the office and its holder but underlining the gap that divided the actual character of Soderini's "popular" regime from the desires of its patrician critics. In the hypothetical subjunctives so typical of his attempts to combine outspokenness with caution, this apologist for metaphorical monarchy described a golden age wholly different from the present troubled times: "There would be no bellicose prelates, advancing their worldly ambitions by aggression and slaughter. In the political idyll created by firm leadership, corruption would be eliminated and order restored. The state, regulated anew by a modern Solon, would be liberated by youth as enterprising as the Dion of the seventh *Epistle,* founder of a city no less perfect than that of the *Laws*."[84]

Pure Plato, of course. Any resemblance to persons living and identifiable was merely coincidental. Marcello Virgilio did not mean to refer to the reigning pope or to the *Gonfaloniere a vita.* If others read an allusion to Julius II or Pier Soderini into his innocent musings, that was the product of their heated imaginations. Imaginations were indeed heated in 1511, as the professor was well aware. Among the malcontents with Soderini's rule, in the ranks of the young with Medicean sympathies trained by him to regard themselves as *principes,* his "Platonic" language struck a chord. Three of the youthful aris-

[82] *R* fol. 37^{v}: ". . . *didicimus* omnibus in rebus mortalibus extremum fastigium in regibus culminari et unum oportere regem, principem esse."

[83] See above, pp. 185ff.

[84] *R* fols. 68^{r-v}: "Cui si similem habuisset, hec etas didicisset relligionis principes sanctius colere Deum et sanctioribus exemplis meliores mores nos docerent neque imperium, quod inane est, armis et humana cede affectarent nec simulata virtute, falsis exemplis et metu inferorum, quos ipsi non timent, docerent . . . ubique essent, qui Egyptum ad cognoscendas leges eius gentis penetrarent; qui ad Dionisii disciplinam bis terque in Siciliam navigarent; inveniretur passim Dion aliquis, qui Syracusas a tyrannide liberaret et qui Cretensem civitatem melioribus fundaret legibus et institutis."

tocrats who led the coup against the *Gonfaloniere* on 31 August 1512—Bartolomeo Vettori, Antonfrancesco degli Albizzi, and Paolo Vettori—had been his pupils, *studentes humanis litteris,*[85] to whom was attributed the desire to establish a principate.[86] Marcello Virgilio did not survive the restoration in office simply because, at Palazzo Vecchio, he maintained a bureaucratic neutrality. At the Studio, in a decisive moment, his lessons had sounded sweetly in the ears of Medicean *ottimati.* Machiavelli, perceived by his enemies as Soderini's creature, stood—and fell—on the opposite political side.

. . . . .

As the Second Chancellor was being deprived of office in November 1512, his former colleague delivered a *praelusio* from his professorial chair. Marcello Virgilio, after ten years of taking the back seat to Machiavelli, had now returned to public view, enjoying the favor of the Medici and their supporters,[87] restored to the prominence that—by inveighing against them and their cultural politics—he had temporarily attained in 1498. How prudent he had been not to publish the orations on the theme of republican *libertas* that he had delivered in and before that year! How judiciously, after 1512, he began to purge his drafts of indiscreet asides![88] Censoring the compromising evidence in his study, the First Chancellor turned his thoughts to finding employment for those who had lost it. With Niccolò Machiavelli, Biagio Buonaccorsi had been expelled from Palazzo Vecchio. That erring amanuensis, of dubious friendships but dependable calligraphy, could correct his solecisms and earn his keep by making copies of Marcello Virgilio's revised speeches.[89]

He could afford to be magnanimous. Having maintained, during a frustrating decade in which others had achieved their ambitions, an imperturbable appearance, he had voiced his disgruntlement only when the time was ripe. Now, in 1512, when for some, fortune's wheel had turned, he again raised his voice. About what did the solemn Socrates speak? About laughter—the unmalicious mirth of the philosopher, the superior merriment of the sage who, perceiving (in Machiavelli's terms) *res perditas,* did not exalt over the calamities of the less fortunate but surveyed them with a tranquil amusement derived from the knowledge that "established on a higher point of

[85] See Verde, *Studio,* 3, 2:781; 3, 1:112; 3, 1:164. For background, see Pesman Cooper, "La caduta di Pier Soderini," pp. 225–60; Gilbert, *Machiavelli and Guicciardini,* pp. 74–78; Devonshire Jones, *Francesco Vettori,* pp. 55–60; Stephens, *Fall of the Florentine Republic,* pp. 56ff.

[86] See Cerretani, *Storia fiorentina,* p. 442; and cf. Butters, *Governors and Government,* pp. 166ff.

[87] See below, pp. 242ff.

[88] See above, pp. 173ff.

[89] On *L,* see Richardson, "A Manuscript"; and cf. D. Fachard, *Biagio Buonaccorsi: Sa vie, son temps, son oeuvre* (Bologna, 1976), pp. 162–65.

observation within the colonnade, you shall look down from safety at the disasters of others."[90]

Naturally, no reference was intended to the circumstances of Machiavelli and Marcello Virgilio in November 1512. The complacent tone was not personal but generic—as generic as the colonnade, symbol of Stoic philosophy. Stoicism, he pontificated from the easy chair of authority, taught one to be content with one's lot. Just punishment awaited those with upward aspirations. Everyone, from the slave to the king, should accept his fate and refrain from striving for higher things. Ensconced at Palazzo Vecchio, with the comfort of a double salary, it was not difficult to voice satisfaction that all was right with the world. Summarily dismissed, heavily fined, and then prohibited from setting foot, for twelve months, in his erstwhile place of work,[91] Niccolò Machiavelli was inclined to take a different view. Relations between him and Marcello Virgilio, never warm, now chilled into antipathy.

Unmoved by the breach, the lay preacher continued to harangue his youthful audience. What he offered, in 1512, was a lecture-sermon on sorrow, and how it should be resisted. Christian consolation, which equated grief with lack of faith,[92] like monastic suspicion of laughter,[93] formed Marcello Virgilio's targets. From Seneca (*De ira* 2.10.5) he developed the theme of Heraclitus's tears and Democritus's mirth. True philosophical humor implied detachment from the arbitrary reversals of life. Democritus, content with *bonum suum,* set an example for others. The common qualities of mankind—its general susceptibility to pain and unhappiness—considered with ironical impartiality, could be a source of pleasure. Why whimper like Heraclitus? Undue compassion saps disciplined composure.

"Without discipline nature is blind, without nature discipline limps" is the proposition with which, in a later lecture, he pursued the same theme.[94] The professor of poetry and eloquence, who had already justified his claim to teach politics and "economics," was advancing into moral philosophy, aiming to link, in his integrative vision, a theory of the emotions with observation of nature. Too banal was the materialistic interpretation of the proverb "All my goods I carry about with me" attributed to Bians, one of the seven sages.[95] Properly understood, it referred not to such subjects as the distribution of property (debated in talking shops like the Orti Oricellari) but to the practical exercise of virtue. How Marcello Virgilio distinguished between a

[90] *R* fol. 41^{v}: ". . . quod in altiore specula et porticu constitutus ex tuto naufragia aliorum despicies."

[91] Ridolfi, *Vita di Machiavelli,* pp. 211–14.

[92] See Moos, *Consolatio,* 1:62ff.

[93] See Schmitz, "Ein Narr, der lacht," pp. 589–601.

[94] *R* fol. 56^{r}: "Natura sine disciplina ceca est et sine natura claudicat disciplina."

[95] Ibid.: ". . . quid sit quod a Pyreneo sapiente dictum aliquando fertur: 'Omnia mea mecum ecfero.'" Marcello Virgilio's sources for the attribution of the proverb are Cicero *Laelius* 59 and *Paradoxa Stoicorum* 1.8 (cf. Valerius Maximus 7.3.3).

correct and a mistaken interpretation of this principle was illustrated by his example of a soldier who, when Pope Julius II was beseiging Bologna in 1506, broke the coins that he had taken as booty into tiny fragments and swallowed them up. "Carrying all that he had about with him," this unenlightened follower of Bians suffered toxic consequences from his literal exegesis. The professor allowed himself an un-Stoical snicker.[96] More serious were the counterexamples of Aeneas, pious transporter of his family and household gods, or of those artists in South Germany who so conveniently hawked about anatomical drawings, for the human body, labeled with precision and portable for display, spared surgeons the bother of an autopsy. "All the goods" might be surveyed in the comfort of the home.[97]

Home truths facilitated perception of the moral life. It was perverted at Florence, argued Marcello Virgilio in his *praelusio* of 1515, by sycophants, flatterers, and parasites. Ingenious painters and ancient poets employed a natural symbol for these scourges of society when they depicted the river-crab.[98] Drawing on the descriptions of the beast by Pliny (*Historia naturalis* 9.97–99) and Dioscorides (*Materia medica* 2.10), the professor linked an account of its physical attributes to the ethical failings of *adulatores*. Claws armed with teeth reminded him of the biting tongues of gossips and slanderers; pop-eyes recalled the roving gaze of those who cast about for scandal; bloated bellies, the gluttony of the unscrupulous who fed on others. From the predatory images of Poliziano's *Lamia,* his successor's lecture took its inspiration: beasts inimical to learning, intellectual maladies, the remedy of ethical interpretation. Nature, like literature, could not be corrected by passive observation.[99] A purge was to be induced by the improvised lessons that their author, with more trenchancy than taste, called "spewings-forth."[100] And as his *cura animorum* or secular alternative to the religious care of souls began to assume more literal proportions, Marcello Virgilio, physician of the intellect, was turning to medicine. If politics did not recede from his thoughts and poetry, always present, took second place, his mind was primarily engaged with other things. Things such as river-crabs led him to reflect on the relationship between perceived and ideal reality so imperfectly conveyed by the language of the past, on the possibility of advance in the present, and on the obstacles to it posed by the cult of antiquity.

Antiquarianism and classicism, in the Florence of Marcello Virgilio's youth, had never enjoyed the dominance attributed to them by some modern scholarship. Even Poliziano, their arch-exponent, had resisted the contraints of purism with an open and subtle pluralism. His intellectual ally, Pico,

[96] *R* fols. 52^{v}ff.

[97] *R* fol. 53^{v}: ". . . haberet in medicine usum paratam domi tabellam."

[98] *R* fol. 66^{v}.

[99] *R* fol. 67^{r}: "Nobis vero non liceat ad sapientiam ex visis auditisque omnibus proficere."

[100] Ibid.: ". . . vomitiones (sic enim appello quottidianas et ex tempore dictiones)."

and his spiritual mentor, Savonarola, were devastating critics of the preference for form over content.[101] His successor, Marcello Virgilio, had taken a similar line, going on to link the study of the classics with the needs of contemporary society. From outside the city—in particular, at Ferrara—humanists of impeccable philological credentials had begun to assert that the ancients could err. The errors of Pliny, as Leoniceno had identified them on the basis of sound medical knowledge and an excellent command of Greek, were signs of a more critical approach to the Latin cultural tradition that Poliziano had championed. A change was occurring in Italian humanism, both of substance and style, as its practitioners, in the last quarter of the fifteenth century and the first decades of the sixteenth, turned away from the Roman world, once admired for its art of eloquence, to what seemed the more authentic, more scientific sources of Hellenic wisdom.

Wisdom and the search for the truth were the themes that Marcello Virgilio chose for his *praelusio* of 1514. Ever a convinced modernist, he found a new version of the familiar Quarrel of the Ancients and the Moderns.[102] Classical authority, for him, was no longer a help but a hindrance: little attention should be paid to the fame of the fathers.[103] Brushing aside previous generations' desires to emulate the ancients and be regarded as their peers, he emphasized that content, not labels, mattered; that nothing should be allowed to stand in the way of novelty and change.[104] Athens, until recently his political model, now became Marcello Virgilio's paradigm of cultural innovation.[105] Roman Italy was decadent, corrupt, and stagnant. Progress in learning and the arts implied a principle of perpetual motion. Once painting had relied on the simple depiction of lines and shades, medicine had depended on mere experiment and conjecture, while natural philosophy had amounted to little more than sense-perceptions. None of these subjects would have developed further had the postclassical world not dared to make its contribution.[106]

[101] See above, pp. 31ff.

[102] Cf. p. 51, with Black, *Benedetto Accolti,* pp. 195ff.

[103] *L* fol. 74v: ". . . aliquando fuerit id solum animo agere meminisseque semper utrobi veritas eamque *veterum auctoritate oppressam,* que in iudiciis aut nihil aut ad gratiam valere debet veluti ex tenebris in lucem proferre et in aperto constitutam unicam consiliorum et actionum vestrarum optimam ducem omnibus patefacere *nullibi enim minus quam in sapientia vetustatis maiorumque fame ratio habenda est.*"

[104] Ibid.: "Neque in tota humana re, si diligentius cuncta a vobis explicentur, quicquam invenietis, in quo minus conducat quam in bonis artibus, quecunque ille sint, earumque honore et utilitate *nomina pro rebus admirari* et in disciplina profectuque ad eas sic sibi constituere, ut inter has et mores legesque et relligionem nihil intersit, quibus *nullo scelere magis quam novitate et mutatione nocetur.*"

[105] *L* fols. 75rff.

[106] *L* fol. 75v: "Fuit cum pictura lineis tantum et vestigiis rerum imagines referret. Fuit cum medicine nulla ratione, sed ex sola experientia coniecturaque morbos curaret. Fuit etiam cum philosophia solo sensu in igne aere athomis omiomeriave naturam intelligeret. Quibus nisi

Hippocrates provided an example of this dynamism. He had transformed the primitive medicine of his predecessors. The Platonists and the Aristotelians had improved on the teachings of their masters by adding to them, subtracting from them, correcting their errors. Religious and ethical thought were areas in which advance was possible: not by returning to past standards, but by marching forward. Less restoration than reform was the goal, in attaining which the ancients should be viewed rather as leaders than as lords. Reverence toward them was as misplaced as an inferiority complex. In the discernment of truth, there was a difference between a man and a book.[107]

Books and the new techniques of printing indicated the right direction. To the immense benefit of mankind, more had been made available in a space of days than in the last millennium.[108] Imitation, if admitted, was free, imaginative, and natural. The Spartans had imitated the bees with their instinctive acceptance of regal power; the Romans mimicked them, adapting the institution of kingship to the dignity of the consuls.[109] Proceeding, like Aristotle, from the familiar into the unknown, true proponents of mimesis were to be viewed as adventurers and explorers. In this attempt to unite the axioms of *imitatio* and *libertas* that had governed his previous thought, Marcello Virgilio now sought a theory that would demonstrate the interdependence of the various subjects to which it referred. Nothing was excluded, all was relevant: an integrated culture demanded not only encyclopedic learning but ethical vision and critical spirit.

Originality, as Marcello Virgilio pursued it, therefore involved combining

---

adiectum in dies aliquid fuisset, quod certius et sapientius a posterioribus inventum esset, obscure sine gratia, sine honore, sine dignitate veritatisque luce discipline artesque omnes adhuc iacerent."

107 *L* fol. 76^{r}: ". . . quid enim homini turpius, quem ad sapientiam et veritatem factum natura protulit, quam ociosum maiores tantum audire *nec quasi duces sed dominos antiquiores quosque sequi cunctaque auctoritati tribuentem ex commentariis eorum tantum sapere et eoque vetustatem admirari,* ut non solum in cunctis deteriores estimemus, qui sero ad sapientiam accesserunt, sed nec posse illos quicquam melius hiis, que dicta decretave aliquando fuerint docere, tanquam opinari veritatem non invenisse oporteat nihilque *inter hominem et librum intersit*?"

108 *L* fol. 76^{v}: ". . . nos tamen intra centesimum annum nova signandi easdem litteras ratione nullo fere labore maximaque omnium gentium utilitate plus una aut altera die inprimi videmus quam vetusta illa ratione mille annis."

109 *L* fols. 81^{r-v}: "Quid aliud docuit nos quam principibus nostris regiam in summa arce collocare nos etiam, unde incolumes ipsi tueri alios possint senatum quasi sensus illis adiicere, quibus referentibus consulentibusque gloriosius et securius agant: plebem deinde iubere instar ignaviorum illarum partium in labore et opere occupatam melioribus inservire? An vos creditis Lacedemonios et, qui eos imitati sunt, Romanos—quorum alteri optimam, alteri felicissimam rempublicam habuerunt—aliunde quam ab imitatione hac nostra reges duos Sparte ex eodem semper Herculis genere et Rome consules ex eadem nobilitate ad imperium vocasse senatumque ambos illis addidisse mox ephoros et censores, aliosque magistratus ad gloriam et incolumitatem reipublice instituisse, nisi quia ratiocinati a principio fuerint felicissime publica privataque omnia sibi evenctura, si, sapientem magistrum secuti, in constituenda reipublica nihil ex pictura formulisque eius mutassent?"

the disparate strands of his interests in literature and medicine, Greek science and Latin moralism. Alert to unfamiliar Hellenic texts that had recently become available in Quattrocento Florence—witness his interpretation of Plato in the light of Maximus of Tyre—he had erected his instinct for novelty into a principle. Principled but provocative was the concern of the *censor morum* with ethics, both social and sexual. While this upholder of marriage as a base of stability for family and state[110] often moaned about its burdens and boredom, the erotic transgressions of others tickled his fantasy. Not for nothing, in his professorial robes, did Marcello Virgilio allude to nakedness. His audience was in its puberty; extramarital intercourse was frowned on; and the long series of attempts by the Florentine Republic to regulate prostitution had culminated, as recently as April 1511, in a draconian attempt to identify, by dress, members of the oldest profession.[111] Were whores, in early sixteenth-century Florence, so difficult to distinguish from ladies of good society?[112] Had Savonarola's preaching against lust and *lussuria,*[113] his efforts to reform women,[114] so dismally failed? The theme of prostitution to which Marcello Virgilio now turned in order to convey a moral message did not lack topical relevance.

The title given to this lecture, in one of the two autograph manuscripts that transmit it, regrettably incomplete, is "The Nature and Extent of the Harm Done to a Man by Seeming Good and Not Being It."[115] The allusion was to Sallust,[116] the reference to hypocrisy, a favorite theme of Marcello Virgilio's ethical observations. To develop them, he chose the erudite but arresting example of a woman so ravishing that her bosom, exposed in the midst of an trial for profanity, had produced a spontaneous verdict of innocence—Phryne, one of antiquity's most celebrated courtesans.[117]

This technique of linking erotic, tender, and learned elements with moral-didactic purposes was not new in the public oratory of Florence. Even speakers with a dour reputation were capable of such sauciness. Argyropoulos, in the lecture that he delivered on 1 February 1458 about the sixth book of

[110] See above, p. 190.

[111] See Trexler, "La prostitution florentine," pp. 983–1015. Cf. M. S. Mazzi, *Prostitute e lenoni nella Firenze del Quattrocento* (Milan, 1991), pp. 141ff., esp. pp. 180–81.

[112] The apposite question is Trexler's "La prostitution florentine," p. 1006.

[113] *Prediche sopra Amos e Zaccaria* (ed. Ghiglieri), 1:321.

[114] See F. W. Kent, "A Proposal by Savonarola for the Self-Reform of Florentine Women," *Memorie Domenicane,* n.s. 14 (1983): pp. 335–41.

[115] BNCF, Magl. VIII, 1493, no. 21c, fol. 321^{r}: "Quale et quantum homini malum sit videri bonum et non esse." A fragmentary version of the opening of the same speech is transmitted in *R* fol. 109^{v}, with the title "Quantum sibi et aliis noceat videri aliquem quod non sit."

[116] Cf. Sallust on Cato *De coniuratione Catilinae* 54 ("esse quam videri bonus malebat"), with R. Syme, *Sallust* (Berkeley, 1964), p. 114.

[117] See A. Raubitshcek s.v., in A. Pauly and G. Wissowa, *Realenzyclopädie der classischen Altertumswissenschaft* 20, 1 (Stuttgart, 1941), pp. 893–907.

Aristotle's *Nicomachean Ethics,* had compared his subject to a sexy virgin, as attractive as the goddesses of myth, likening the desire for scholarship to sensual impulses felt while falling in love.[118] With greater refinement and imagination, Savonarola, in his twenty-fourth sermon on Michea of 8 September 1498, had interpreted the milk given by Jahel to Sisera in the Book of Judges (4:19) as Christian doctrine, in contrast to the thin water of secular learning.[119] Like a protective mother, the wife of Heber, in his account, invited the bloodthirsty warrior to suck, implicitly transforming into a breast the bottle from which the Biblical Sisera drank. "Tu se' piccolino, tu hai bisogno di latte," she gently admonished. The Canaanite captain accepted, meek as a lamb. And to complete Savonarola's metamorphosis of this sanguinary pair, when Sisera was slain by Jehel with a hammer, that signified an allegory of the tongue. The tongue, to be sure, of reason by which "a big hypocrite" (*pinzerochone*) might be converted to love of Christ. Such was the winning way of the master understandably admired by a public that ranged from the intellectual Nesi to women in the street. Their feminine qualities underscored with delicacy, the prophet unarmed eschewed violence.

A difficult act to follow, that of a moral leader who, so skillfully appealing to maternal instincts, manipulated the Biblical authority that he claimed as the foundation of his own. Savonarola, as exegete and as preacher, was beguiling, ingenious, and shrewd. To match his living memory required all the qualities of audacity and inventiveness that Marcello Virgilio had recently praised. Abandoning the Bible for profane literature, he treated, by contrast, the example of a woman neither redeemed nor spiritual but sensual and fallen.

Poetry furnished his point of departure—specifically, the sixth elegy of the second book of Propertius. Phryne, a Theban hetaera who had grown rich through the exercise of her profession, promised to rebuild the city walls that Alexander the Great had torn down. This much, and no more, Marcello Virgilio had from Athenaeus (6.185ff.) and Propertius (2.6.5–6), whose work he freely quoted.[120] The remaining details—of Phryne's nudity, of her daily

[118] "Fingite igitur atque ante oculos vestrae ponite mentis ipsam scientiam virginis os habitumque gerentem omniumque rerum formas, quas ipsa complectitur, eidem adiungite: non haec profecto vobis tum Zeuxidis Helena, non ipsamet etiam Helena, non Pallas, non Iuno, non Diana, non Venus esse videbitur? Harum omnium formas vehementer sine dubio superabit atque huius etiam formae videbitur, quae mente quidem percipiatur, verbis explicari atque describi minime possit. O quantos ipsa tum amores, quantos ardores, quantas cupiditates, quantas denique, ut ita dicam, libidines ad sese adipiscendam, amplectandam atque fovendam, si qualis est ipsa perciperetur animo, quo quidem solo percipi poterit, excitaret!" *Reden und Briefe* (ed. Müllner), p. 43.

[119] *Prediche sopra Ruth e Michea* (ed. Romano), 2:263–64.

[120] BNCF, Magl. VIII, 1493, no. 21^{c}, fol. 321^{r}: "Thebana meretrix . . ., que *deletas* ab Alexandro quondam potuit *reponere Thebas,* Phryne *tam multis facta beata* procis ad licitandum venerem suam quotannis frequenter omni populo consueverat nuda in theatrum discendens,

provocations in the theater, of her shamelessness—not only were not sanctioned by classical tradition but were the opposite of what it recounted. Antiquity portrayed a Phryne famed for tasteful modesty and averse to vulgar display. Marcello Virgilio reversed this image, intending to shock by the unconventional moral drawn from his invention. Such behavior, he declared, invited one to reflect less on the naked and open conduct of men—on how bad it is to seem good, and not to be it—than on the subtler problem of how an appearance of evil may conceal goodness. At this point Phryne, the base and wanton prostitute of Marcello Virgilio's fantasy, began her ascent to the heights of virtue.

The *jeunesse dorée* of Thebes (bearing an uncanny resemblance to the gilded youth of Florence), he continued, was randy to a man. It lusted after ladies and could not wait even a couple of days to satisfy its desires.[121] To decide on which of the many local beauties deserved the prize, a sumptuous dinner was held over which—in a parody of Marcello Virgilio's mannerism—"one king, one lord, one prince" presided.[122] After the meal Phryne, regal as a queen, led the women to a well. Ordering them to imitate her, she washed her face—and appeared glowing with the divine radiance that had inspired the poetry of Virgil.[123] Not so her dining companions. Their make-up was ruined by the cold water. So much for the artificial sheen of Siconian oil! So much for the crocodile excrement applied to disguise sunburn and freckles! Phryne, by antithesis, became an paradigm of loveliness without lies, a model of substance against style. The youth of Florence, unlike that of Thebes, should not be deceived by fine appearances: hypocrisy was a social danger, sincerity an ethical quality. Propertius might be regarded as no less valid a teacher of *mores* than Plato or Lycurgus. A secular alternative thus offered to Savonarolian spirituality, Poliziano's heir neatly effected a deconstruction of his predecessor.

The mention of crocodile excrement raised the scent of the second *Centuria,* inaccessible to Pietro Crinito and Alessandro Sarti in 1498. That Marcello Virgilio knew this work is indicated by his allusion to its thirty-seventh chapter[124] and proved by his use of chapter 52.[125] There his teacher discussed

quo corpore amatoribus suis placitura esset ostendere." Cf. Propertius 2.6.5–6: "nec quae deletas potuit *componere Thebas* / Phryne *tam multis facta beata* viris," with P. J. Enk, *Sex: Propertii Elegiarum liber secundus* (Leiden, 1962), pp. 98–99 ad loc.

[121] BNCF, Magl. VIII, 1493, no. 21[c], fol. 321[v]: "Amabant omnes nullusque non ex famosis, qui tunc Thebis erant, aliquam in deliciis habebat, qua nec biduum carere posset et cum qua inhumanum egisse se crederat, si in voluptatum omnium suarum partem eam non vocasset."

[122] Ibid.: ". . . unum cene regem, unum dominum, unum principem esse." For the allusion to Pindar, see p. 158.

[123] BNCF, Magl. VIII, 1493, no. 21[c], fol. 322[v]: "claraque in luce refulxit: 'os umerosque dee similis.'" Cf. *Aeneid* 1.589.

[124] See above, p. 109.

[125] *Miscellaneorum centuria secunda* (ed. Branca and Pastore Stocchi), pp. 96–98.

Phryne, commencing with the same citation of Propertius employed by his pupil.[126] After recounting several details that either of them could have taken, independently, from common sources, Poliziano came to the one that was essential to Marcello Virgilio's oration. The account of the dinner at which Phryne triumphantly established her genuine beauty is transmitted, in ancient literature, only by Galen, and then in a text very rare in the Quattrocento, no manuscript of which now survives—the *Protrepticus,* chapter 10, from which Poliziano had made excerpts at Bologna in June 1491.[127] At Florence they fell into the hands of Crinito, but he was unable to secure the second *Centuria* because it was being read by Marcello Virgilio.[128] Not for motives of plagiarism, but with measured independence, he constructed from Poliziano's philological study of Phryne, abundant in learned detail but barren of moral insight, a sermon on ethics that was more faithful to the spirit of the *Protrepticus* than his master's method. Recapturing the intentions of Galen, who had exercised a therapy of souls,[129] Marcello Virgilio used his work to practice *cura animorum.*

The courtesan Phryne, in his thought, played the same role that the philosopher Epicurus had taken in that of his teacher Landino.[130] Beneath an appearance of shamelessness, both had exercised virtue. Virtue, for the unstoical manipulator of Stoic ethics Marcello Virgilio, was not its own reward, but an expression of character, socially formed. At the political level, this sometime republican rhetor accepted monarchical analogies for the head of state similar to those advanced in the first book of the *Camaldulensian Disputations.*[131] Yet he never abandoned his skepticism toward the *vita contemplativa* praised by Landino, and all that he wrote about the morality of public life was informed by his earlier lectures on politics and "economics."

After teaching them, Marcello Virgilio, in a reversal of the usual procedure,[132] began to give instruction in ethics, conventionally the beginning of moral philosophy. His thought circled around the problem of appearance and reality. The contingent and the particular, for him as for Aristotle in the *Physics* on which he drew, were preliminary levels of perception, from which one might achieve understanding of universal principles. All Marcello Virgilio's examples—from Bians and Phryne to river-crabs—posed the recurrent problem of illusion and truth. The seemingly base could be transformed, in the hands of an enlightened exegete, to reveal high probity. Morality was

[126] Ibid., p. 96, l. 1.

[127] For the excerpts, preserved in Munich, Bayerische Staatsbibliothek, clm. 807, see "Frammenti monacensi di Galeno" (ed. Pesenti), pp. 586–90; Perosa, *Mostra,* pp. 63–65 (no. 59); and Perosa, "Codici di Galeno," pp. 82–83. A wider context is provided by Nutton, *John Caius,* pp. 24ff.

[128] See further below, pp. 221ff.

[129] See M. Vegetti, "La terapia dell'anima," pp. 131–55.

[130] *Disputationes camaldulenses* (ed. Lohe), 1:58.

[131] See Skinner, "Political Philosophy," p. 429.

[132] See Kraye, "Moral Philosophy," p. 305.

to be determined by doubting the surface meaning of an action or an event, and seeking its underlying motives. Imitation was discounted, rivalry praised. Marcello Virgilio's concept of mimesis, literary and social, entailed criticism. Yet in linking critical evaluation to freedom and progress, he invariably referred to the culture of the classical past, not to the government of the present. The professor's courses after 1512 instilled a sense of duty, obedience, and hierarchy.[133] It was not for him to proffer advice to a prince but to train servants of state—energetic, pious, and aware of their place. The virtuous *civis,* beneath the level of the metaphorical monarch, should be untainted by ambition. "Carrying all his goods about with him," he was not to covet those of his betters. Candid, religious, yet conscious of fortune's fickleness and the malice of men, he was faithfully to perform his public duties while cultivating, in private, a detachment that masked mistrust.

The ethics taught, after the return of the Medici, by the First Chancellor represented a prudent withdrawal from the oratorical engagement of his youth. Discretion had served him well; passion was perilous. Only in the intellectual sphere did he show determination. There, with a tenaciousness unmatched in other areas of his experience, Marcello Virgilio continued his attempt to integrate the diverse parts of a culture that he desired to view in the round. The means at his disposal were various and impressive—literature, medicine, moral philosophy, a wide and deep knowledge of Greek and Latin—but they were not comprehensive. His cool and concrete mind never ventured into the heady sphere of metaphysics, left to his better-paid rival at the Studio, the Platonist Francesco da Diacceto.[134] Nor did Marcello Virgilio reflect on history. Unhistorical, unspeculative, fighting shy of abstractions, he sought a well-defined work to complete his enterprise, and made a timely choice when, at long last, he resolved to publish. How timely can be seen by considering the place of his single yet significant book among the other products of Florence's print culture during and after the "popular" Republic.

. . . . .

From the pages of Poliziano to which he was devoting his "most menial efforts" Pietro Crinito, on 15 February 1498, raised his dissatisfied gaze. Observing Marcello Virgilio's nomination (subject to approval by the *Consiglio Maggiore*) as First Chancellor,[135] he began to think of an academic career.[136]

[133] Cf. Grafton and Jardine, *From Humanism to the Humanities,* p. xiv.

[134] See Kristeller, "Francesco da Diacceto," pp. 187–336; and Verde, *Studio,* 2:218–19. Marcello Virgilio's salary never exceeded 300 florins; Diacceto's, by contrast, was 525 florins (ASF, Studio Fiorentino e Pisano [Ufficiali dello Studio], 8, fols. 64^r, 131^v, 134^r, 137^v–138^r, 139^r, 143^r, 146^r). On history, see below, pp. 263ff.

[135] ASF, Tratte, 286, fol. 61^r (in Rubinstein, "Beginning of Niccolò Machiavelli's Career," pp. 86–87).

[136] "Ego vero meis subindigissimis laboribus cogitare coepi de professione publicae lectionis." Ed. Verde, *Studio,* 4, 3:1331.

Whether Crinito hoped that Poliziano's chair might again become vacant or fancied that, via a professorship, he, too, might rise to higher things, his aspirations were to be disappointed. Publishing—at Venice—the works of the Medicean house-philologist was not the route to advancement in late Quattrocento Florence, as the career of Marcello Virgilio demonstrates.

He and Crinito are sometimes enrolled among Poliziano's pupils and counted as continuators of a "tradition" initiated by their master.[137] This claim is variously misleading. There is no clear evidence that Crinito ever studied with Poliziano. What he sought to do, by the exercise of posthumous piety, was to cast himself in the role of the great man's heir. Like his contrary tactic of toadying to Scala, Poliziano's archenemy[138]—like so many of Crinito's other ventures in self-promotion—that attempt fell flat. Success crowned the strategy of Marcello Virgilio, who, until the restoration, established his distance from the methods of the discredited client of the Medici.

Until their return from exile in 1512, silence fell, at Florence, on the activities that its greatest philologist had made his own. That silence, conterminous with the "popular" Republic, was nowhere more deafening than in Poliziano's own chair. Rarely broken, and then only by the few—Crinito, Alessandro Sarti, and Benedetto Riccardini—who desired to consolidate (or exploit) Poliziano's heritage, it persisted until Marcello Virgilio, addressing questions that his teacher had left unanswered, revived an approach peremptorily interrupted by himself. He did so without the aid of Poliziano's self-styled pupils, without mentioning so much as his name, in league with a guarantor of intellectual continuity between the *governo popolare* and the restoration: the publishing house of the Florentine Giunti.[139]

The beginnings of the Giunti were modest, and modest their production remained for several years. With the publication in 1497 of the Greek sophist Zenobius, prepared for the press by Benedetto Riccardini, the firm and one of its most active editors made their debut. Riccardini's pretensions were expressed in the misnomer *il filologo*. Of recension he had little knowledge; his conjectures, in the texts with which he tinkered, were not numerous; and when he rose to mediocrity, that was due to a technical competence in metrics. Riccardini was no more than a curator of the school classics central to the print culture of Florence in the first decade of the sixteenth century; and in that sphere the Giunti implemented a pragmatic accord with Aldo Manuzio.[140]

When, in the preface to his edition of Catullus, Propertius, and Tibullus

[137] E.g., Dionisotti, *Machiavellierie,* p. 236.

[138] See above, p. 146.

[139] The best succinct account is by Dionisotti, *Machiavellerie,* pp. 176–92. Fundamental remains Bandini, *Annales*. See, too, with Dionisotti's critique, D. Decia, R. Delfiol, and L. S. Camerini, *I Giunti tipografi editori di Firenze, 1497–1570* (Florence, 1978); and Pettas, *Giunti.* On the Giunti and vernacular literature, see Richardson, *Print Culture,* pp. 79ff.

[140] See P. Scapecchi, "Tra il giglio e l'ancora: Nomini, idee e libri nella bottega di Manuzio," in *Aldus Manutius and Renaissance Culture,* I Tatti Studies 15, ed. D. Seiberg (1997).

of 1503, Riccardini praised Aldo, upon whose earlier publication of the same authors his own was modeled, the eulogy was probably sincere. The Giunti had two branches: one at Florence, under the direction of Filippo, the other at Venice, headed by his brother, Marcantonio. Competition between them and the Aldine press was tempered by vested interests on both sides. During the lifetime of Aldo, Filippo di Giunta seldom ventured into the field of Greek scholarship, which that eminent publisher had made his own; and even in the principal area of their common concern—Latin literature—Giuntine copies of Aldine editions were few. Crinito, who at various stages of his career worked with them both, corrected the proofs of the Aldine Virgil, sent to "Florentine friends" in March 1501; while Scipione Forteguerri (*il Carteromacho*), to whom Riccardini inscribed, in 1506, his publication of the now deceased Crinito's *De poetis latinis,* acted as an intermediary at Venice between the scholars and libraries at Florence to which Aldo needed access. In collaboration with Manuzio, who had no right to print in their city, the small *équipe* of Giuntine editors went about their limited business. If they saw themselves as the continuators of Poliziano after his death in 1494, they were slow to do so.

Ten years passed before the admittedly young Crinito brought out a book in the mold of his alleged master. *De honesta disciplina* (1504) recalls, superficially, the eclectic form and heterogenous contents of the *Miscellanea.* Yet the likenesses (magnified by Riccardini) are less salient than the differences between them. Crinito adopted rather the antiquarian than the philological emphasis of Poliziano, substituting for the virtuoso selectivity of the *Centuriae* a pedestrian randomness. *De poetis latinis,* Crinito's posthumous best-seller, had been advertised previous to its publication in 1506 through excerpts that had appeared in Riccardini's earlier editions of Catullus and Valerius Flaccus. But when the much-heralded work issued from the press, it was apparent that it reduced Poliziano's interests in poetic biography and history to the Latin tradition and ignored the Greek, to which his most original research had been devoted. There his epigone did not attempt to follow him.

No matter that Riccardini, in his preface to *De poetis latinis,* compared Crinito with Suetonius. The encyclopedic *grammaticus* of Poliziano's ideal had shrunk to the dimensions of a compiler. No matter that, in his own collection of classical and neo-Latin eclogues (1504), Riccardini employed the rhetoric of textual criticism, priding himself on allusions to the obelus and the critics' rod (*criticorum ferula*), or that, in his edition of Terence (1505), he claimed to have completed the task of recension that Poliziano had planned to undertake. Knowledge of the textual tradition available to his teacher[141] was ignored by Riccardini, because what he wished to produce, in his usual

[141] See Ribuoli, *La collazione polizianea.*

hurry, was a handbook for *adulescentes* that offered guidance to the genres of comedy and to the types of Terentian verse-form, but made no lasting contribution to the improvement of the text. *Il filologo,* like most of the other industrious hacks employed by the Florentine Giunti during the "popular" Republic, was a negligible philologist. The only exception to this rule was Pier Candido,[142] whose edition of Lucretius in 1512, while lacking the exegetical scope and philosophical interests of work on the same author being produced, at the same time, by the Bolognese humanist Giovann Battista Pio,[143] made its mark at the level of emendation. Yet even there Candido acknowledged a primary debt not to Poliziano but to Pontano and Marullo.

From a production, neither large nor brilliant, of thirty-nine editions between 1497 and 1512, the overwhelming majority of Giuntine books was classical. Only six were religious in character.[144] Secular and "popular," the version of philology promoted by the firm under the *governo popolare* abandoned the aristocratic model that, in the previous generation, had lent that activity its invidious distinction. A tiny team of middling editors bidding for the favors of worthy half-notables—the Savonarolian Antonio Canigiani,[145] for example, to whom Riccardini dedicated his Sallust in 1506, or one Niccolò Machiavelli, to whose grandsons, under the pseudonym "Furius," was posthumously inscribed Riccardini's Latin grammar—supplanted the Medicean *princeps* and his client. Specialist pursuits of the study yielded to the quotidian needs of the classroom. Mundane purveyors of the textbook replaced the angel from heaven.

. . . . .

The pace quickened after 1512, and a new cast of characters entered the publishing stage. They were united, to a man, in the search for patronage that was to bind the Giunti to the house of Medici and make them the quasi-official printers of Florence. The ruling family and its supporters were bombarded with a hail of dedications, not all of them well directed. It was understandable that Mariano Tucci should inscribe his Apuleius to Cardinal Giovanni de' Medici, but the gesture was more dubious when, after his dedicatee's elevation to the papacy, Tucci offered, in October 1513, an edition

[142] On Candido, see P. Orvieto, in *DBI* 17 (1974), pp. 785–86.

[143] See E. Raimondi, "Il primo commento umanistico a Lucrezio," in idem, *Politica e commedia,* pp. 101–40; and V. del Nero, "Filosofia e teologia nel commento di Giovan Battista Pio a Lucrezio," *Interpres* 6 (1986): 156–99.

[144] For a statistical survey of the annual production of the Florentine Giunti, see L. Perini, "Firenze e la Toscana," in Santoro, *La stampa,* p. 437. A brief analysis is offered by C. di Filippo Bareggi, "Giunta, Doni, Torrentino: Tre tipografie fiorentine fra repubblica e principato," *Nuova rivista storica* 58 (1974): 321–23.

[145] See F. Troncarelli, in *DBI* 18 (1975), pp. 83–84

of Lactantius to Leo X's cousin, Innocenzo Cibo.[146] Grandson of both Lorenzo de' Medici and Innocent VIII, the aptly named Cibo owed his red hat to his ancestry. That bloated *bon viveur,* that syphilitic schemer, preferred the pleasures of the table and the flesh to those of the intellect. But Innocenzo Cibo, least suitable and most extravagant of Leo X's disputed creations to the cardinalate, was, by birth, a Medici. According to one of the simpler criteria that shaped the policy of the Giunti, he therefore deserved to be courted.

The impetus of that policy may be judged from Filippo di Giunta's success in mobilizing members of the Studio who had hitherto slumbered in the shades. A prime example is Niccolò Angèli, Marcello Virgilio's colleague since 1495 as professor of rhetoric. The culture and interests of such *minores,* before and after the restoration, reveal much about the tone and temper of intellectual life. Angèli, previous to being signed up by Giunta, spent his time translating, into Latin and Italian, the Greek letters ascribed to Brutus, role model of tyrannicides. *Amor della libertà* motivated his vernacular version, presented to its dedicatee, Giacomo Gianfigliazzi, in an elegant vanity copy.[147] A collector of proverbs[148] and a collator of manuscripts of the Neronian poet Calpurnius Siculus,[149] Angèli had a taste for miscellaneous information about birds, beasts, and fishes. In the circles that frequented the Orti Oricellari,[150] he played the role of an witty *causeur.* Viewing himself primarily as a rhetor,[151] he favored the pointed epigrams and telling anecdotes that his son published, after his death, under the title of *Facezie.*[152] The virtual opposite of Marcello Virgilio, that thoroughly political animal, his colleague resembled him solely in his aversion to venturing into print until 1512. During the period that witnessed a revised edition (March 1506) of Machiavelli's *Decennale primo* and, between 1505 and 1508, no less than 1,100 copies of Savonarola's *Prediche sopra l'Esodo,*[153] two of the principal holders of Florentine chairs of literature held back from publication. Both the mod-

[146] See F. Petrucci, in *DBI* 25 (1981), pp. 249–55.

[147] BRF 2692 (Latin version, BRF 1221 E). On Angèli, see P. Tentori, in *DBI* 3 (1961), pp. 199–200. On his translations, see G. Tanturli, "La cultura fiorentina volgare del Quattrocento davanti ai nuovi testi greci," *Medioevo e Rinascimento* 2 (1988): 234; and C. Bianca, "Tradurre nel Quattrocento: Le 'Epistolae' dello Pseudo Bruto," *Il cannocchiale* 1–2 (1994): 51–56.

[148] BRF 594, fols. 195^{r}–209^{v}.

[149] BRF 636, fols. 25^{r}–45^{r}.

[150] BRF 904, fol. 92^{r}: "Sedebamus nuper super vesperam in hortis Bernardi Oricellari."

[151] Cf. the autograph title of his *De genere deliberativo* in BNCF, Magl. VIII, 1442, fol. 293^{r}: "Nicolaus Angelius Rhetor Florentinus . . . *De genere deliberativo.*"

[152] Extracts in C. Speroni, *Wit and Wisdom of the Italian Renaissance* (Berkeley, 1964). See G. Folena, "Sulla tradizione dei 'Detti piacevoli' attributi al Poliziano," *Studi di filologia italiana* 9 (1953): 431–48.

[153] Perini, "Firenze et la Toscana," p. 435.

ern Socrates and the gentleman-scholar hesitated not only for motives of caution but also in response to a palpable lack of interest in what they had to contribute to learning. After 1512 that state of affairs changed, and even the languid Angèli stirred himself to join an enterprise accelerated by Giunta.

In a letter to Marcello Virgilio's friend Roberto Acciaiuoli, prefatory to the Quintilian edited by Angèli and published in October 1515, Filippo di Giunta spoke of his firm's wish to serve the common interest of men of letters by providing dependable editions of Latin authors.[154] That policy was not as new as his implied dating of its inception to 1512–13 suggested, but the restoration did entail a change of pace and a shift of emphasis. Angèli, for instance, now engaged in a frenetic sequence of classical editions—Plautus and Cicero in 1514; Macrobius, the *Scriptores rei rusticae,* Quintilian, and Cicero (again) the following year; the same author (his favorite) in 1516—equipped with reassuring subtitles (*maxima cura, summa diligentia, accuratissima castigatio*) at total variance with their slapdash execution. Complementing Angèli's precipitate labors, and extending them into Greek scholarship, was Poliziano's pupil and plagiarist, Eufrosino Bonini,[155] who, in his edition of Apollonius of Alexandria (1515), excused himself for his want of literary preparation on grounds of medical interests.[156] Compensating for his defects and seconding Bonini's efforts in later years were Antonio Francini and Andrea Dazzi. The team was expanding, effort was multiplying, as Hellenism, for reasons to be sought in Rome, became a chief concern of the Florentine Giunti.

When, on 11 March 1513, Giovanni de' Medici, munificent patron of Greek studies, was elected pope, one of the first to perceive the opportunity was Aldo Manuzio. In his preface to the edition of Plato that he published the same year,[157] Aldo extolled the renaissance of culture in the image of the pontiff's father. Filippo di Giunta swiftly rose to the challenge. The dedication of Angèli's edition of Plautus in 1514 compared the younger Lorenzo de' Medici with his grandfather, stressing the bonds between the ruling house and the tradition of scholarship that reached from Chrysoloras, Ficino, Chalcondyles, and Lascaris to the now-rehabilitated Poliziano. So began the operation of salvage that would continue with the printing, in 1517, of the poet-philologist's Latin version of Herodian, and, in the following year, of his *Stanze per la Giostra*—culminating, in 1520, with a letter by Francini to

[154] "Ad communem litteratorum utilitatem *circa biennium* usi in recensendis optimis quibusdam Latinis auctoribus, qui postea typis nostris in hominum manus emendatissimi evivere." Bandini, *Annales,* 1:51.

[155] See Hill Cotton, "Frosino Bonini," pp. 157–75.

[156] "Errata . . . nobis indulgeas, neque non Poetarum non Rhetorum non Grammaticorum praeceptis imbutum esse memineris, sed . . . febribus . . ., pellendis." Bandini, *Annales,* 1:98.

[157] *Aldo Manuzio editore* (ed. Dionisotti and Orlandi), 1:120–23 and 2:367–68.

Thomas Linacre, prefatory to his edition of Julius Pollux,[158] in which the identity of interest between Florentine philology and the Medici was declared to have found its most recent and convincing expression in the work of Marcello Virgilio.

Before that achievement could be celebrated, a number of obstacles had had to be surmounted. In July 1514 Leo X issued a comprehensive privilege in favor of Aldo Manuzio's Greek and Italic types.[159] The *Otto di Pratica* bristled at this untoward act. In the city from which the pope had sprung—not Venice—Greek printing had its origins, they declared; and the ambassador at Rome, Francesco Vettori, was ordered to intervene with Leo X and obtain for Giunta comparable rights. A letter by the Florentine publisher to Vettori, prefixed to Angèli's edition of the *Scriptores rei rusticae,*[160] recorded gratitude for efforts that bore fruit in February 1515—the very month in which Aldo, by a timely coincidence, died. The path was clear for Giunta to modify the terms of his *entente cordiale* and turn to the Greek studies lucratively sponsored by the pope at Rome. The following winter, Marcello Virgilio decided to translate and comment on Dioscorides.

. . . . .

Why Dioscorides? Why a new Latin translation with an elaborate commentary? A philological undertaking of such a scope and scale accorded neither with Marcello Virgilio's "new and unaccustomed method of teaching" nor with his previous refusal to publish. Yet his choice was a sign of the acuteness of his eye to the main chance—an attribute that others lacked. On 17 February 1513—while Machiavelli languished in prison, accused of being involved in an anti-Medicean conspiracy—Marcello Virgilio was received by the Medici at a soirée that graced the first performance of Jacopo Nardi's *I due felici rivali.*[161] The irony of that title, in the circumstances, could have engaged only the two ex-colleagues, for the cream of Florentine society, as skimmed by Cardinal Giovanni, had other preoccupations. Over the evening presided that urbane prelate, more than Marcello Virgilio's match in affairs of this world, absorbed in gossip about the promisingly poor health of Julius II.

Events moved swiftly. Three days later the pope was dead. Within as many weeks, Giovanni de' Medici was crowned at St. Peter's. "Wafted by sweet breezes," he returned in triumph to Florence in November 1515.[162] There

[158] Discussed by Dionisotti, *Machiavellerie,* pp. 214–15.

[159] For context, see Lowry, *World of Aldus Manutius,* pp. 156ff.

[160] Bandini, *Annales,* 2:88.

[161] Ed. A. Ferrajoli (Rome, 1901), pp. v–viii.

[162] See I. Ciseri, *L'ingresso trionfale di Leone X in Firenze nel 1515* (Florence, 1990). Cf. Marcello Virgilio's *praefatio* of that month in *R* fol. 52^{r}: "Ex adventu pontificis ad vos suaviori aura perflari animos omnium."

to greet him, at his entry into San Lorenzo, was (alone among Florentine intellectuals) the ubiquitous First Chancellor, author of a Latin inscription lauding the piety of the dynasty. For his pains Marcello Virgilio was presented with a brace of capons. Soon after this ambiguous gift of castrated cocks, there occurred a meeting of minds. Marcello Virgilio thought of Filippo di Giunta, with whom, in his capacity as censor of the press, he had had dealings for several years. For Giunta, who needed both a distinguished Hellenist a cut above the likes of Bonini, Dazzi, and Francini and a man of the world with the skill required to compose a manifesto of revived Florentine philology for the Hellenophile pope, no one could have better fitted the bill. Low calculation united with higher scholarship, in a joint effort to recreate the atmosphere in which, under Leo X's father, largesse had been showered on meritorious men of learning (and their publishers). So it was that Marcello Virgilio returned to a field of study cultivated by Poliziano.[163] Founder, in November 1513, of the first chair of simples in Europe and chronic sufferer from a femoral fistula, the pope had more than academic motives for being interested in Dioscorides' botanical and pharmacological writings.

So did Marcello Virgilio. Nonpartisan in his choice of subject, this chameleon of cultural politics remained ever-adaptable to his environment. Others were less versatile. Where Machiavelli sought the role of adviser to the Medicean *principi* bent on establishing their hold on the city, his former colleague perceived that the Florentine roost was ruled from Rome, by a donor of capons famed for his generosity to Hellenists[164] and friend of notable scholars like Nicolò Leoniceno.[165] When, in a famous letter to Francesco Vettori of 9 April 1513,[166] Machiavelli wrote with mock modesty that, lacking other skills, "mi conviene ragionare dello stato," the admission was intended to be winning, but it also pointed to a limitation that, in their common quest for advancement, did not inhibit the First Chancellor. Humanism had its uses. Translating and commenting on Dioscorides, rather than writing *Il principe,* Marcello Virgilio assumed more Machiavellian colors than did Niccolò Machiavelli.

[163] For the dating, cf. ". . . [quam] nos inter tot alias publicae privataeque rei sollicitudines et occupationes *non plene integris tribus annis* absolvimus." Statement to the reader, of October 1518, extracts from which are printed by Bandini, *Annales,* 2:126–127, and by Riddle, "Dioscorides," pp. 36–37. Where possible, for the reader's convenience, the extracts printed by Riddle are cited; otherwise the 1518 edition is used.

[164] See d'Amico, *Renaissance Humanism,* pp. 41ff., with D. Gnolli, "Il secolo di Leone X," in idem, *La Roma di Leone X* (Milan, 1938), pp. 341–84; J. Isewijn, "Poetry in a Roman Garden: The Coryciana," in *Latin Poetry and the Classical Tradition,* ed. P. Godman and O. Murray (Oxford, 1990), pp. 211ff.; R. Alhaique Pettinelli, *Tra antico e moderno: Roma nel primo Rinascimento* (Rome, 1991); and V. de Caprio, "Roma," in *Letteratura italiana,* ed. A. Asor Rosa, *Storia e geografia* 2, 1, *L'età moderna* (Turin, 1988), pp. 327ff.

[165] See Mugnai Carrara, "Profilo," p. 188 and n. 48.

[166] Macchiavelli, *Lettere a Francesco Vettori* (ed. Inglese), p. 110.

The *Materia medica* stood at the center of intellectual debate. Synonymous with the study of botany,[167] that work had been employed by Leoniceno, in his polemics on Pliny, to argue that it was no longer adequate for a humanist who advocated an ideal of *enkyklios paideia* to plead a specialist case. Dioscorides not only dealt with what Leoniceno presented as matters of life and death; he also posed afresh the long-standing problem of the relationship of medicine and philology within an integrated structure of knowledge. Despite the evasions of his second *Centuria,* Poliziano had grasped the point. He had translated medical texts and studied plants with Collenuccio,[168] providing Barbaro with codices of the *Materia medica* for the preparation of his *Corollarium,* and priding himself on that scholar's deference to his acquaintance with herbs and his knowledge of Dioscorides.[169]

That combination is characteristic of the "medical humanism" of the late Quattro- and early Cinquecento.[170] Empirical observation and philological reconstruction complemented one another, with the result that "in botany and, to some extent, in medicine, practical problems could easily be categorized as textual problems."[171] The reserve expressed by humanists such as Coluccio Salutati, in his *De nobilitate legum et medicinae,* toward the contingency of empirical method was not incompatible with the disdain voiced, in scholastic theory, for the base and "unscientific" *empyrici.*[172] These inherited attitudes reinforced the new approach of Leoniceno, whose philosophical premises implied congruence between nature, fundamentally unchanged since antiquity, and language, in the pristine purity of Dioscorides' Greek. Correctly to construe the *Materia medica* was tantamount to identifying a herb or a plant. Neither insensitive to nor uninterested in firsthand investigation of the *res* described by his source, Leoniceno was adept in the study of the original *verba.* For him, a separation between "two cultures," scientific and humanist, did not exist. Here he was in agreement with Marcello Virgilio. Where they differed was in their emphases and their objectives. The Ferrarese professor regarded philology as an instrument, a means to the end of medicine, the primacy of which was sanctioned by the prevailing hierarchy of learning. Wishing to preserve the unity of knowledge, his junior colleague at Florence aimed to prove that, on the basis of a text of medical in-

[167] The older bibliography is summarized, and new interpretations are advanced, by Dilg, "Die botanische Kommentar-Literatur," pp. 22–52; Reeds, "Renaissance Humanism and Botany," pp. 519–42; Nauert, "Humanists, Scientists, and Pliny," pp. 72–85; French, "Pliny and Renaissance Medicine," pp. 252–81; and Mugnai Carrara, *La biblioteca di Nicolò Leoniceno,* pp. 25ff.

[168] See pp. 105–6 above.

[169] *Politiani Opera,* 1:368.

[170] For a concise survey, see A. Wear, in *The Western Medical Tradition, 800* B.C.–1800 A.D., ed. L. I. Conrad (Cambridge, 1995), pp. 192–205.

[171] Nutton, "Greek Science," pp. 26–27.

[172] See Agrimi and Crisciani, *Edocere medicos,* pp. 34ff., 154ff.

terest much favored by the avant-garde, the old-fashioned values of literary studies could be maintained.

This was original. No one before Marcello Virgilio had thought of using the *Materia medica* for a defense of literature. (No one has thought of doing so since.) Moreover, the choice of this author reveals his paradoxical consistency. Throughout a long and intricate career, Marcello Virgilio remained faithful to one principle that he had taken over from Poliziano: *enkyklios paideia,* the ideal that had led him, in his teaching before the restoration, to align the classical poets with the ancient *auctores medici*. Galen's moralism informed his own ethical instruction,[173] and by the premium placed on literary culture in the same thinker's concept of *technê*.[174] Marcello Virgilio was attracted. He expressed himself in medical imagery with a frequency and a vividness unparalleled in the work of any Florentine humanist of his generation. Probably under Chalcondyles, he had studied and made notes on anatomy.[175] And he moved in a milieu where doctors and literary scholars traditionally shared interests in one another's fields of competence.[176]

That tradition, at Florence, was long-standing. Giovanni Baldo di Faenza, professor of medicine at the Studio during the first decade of the fifteenth century, composed a defense of poetry.[177] The polymath Paolo Toscanelli (†1464), personification of *enkyklios paideia,* was highly regarded in medical and humanist circles.[178] Such qualities of interdisciplinary learning were what that tragic figure, Lorenzo Lorenzi (1459/60–1502), admired in Hippocrates.[179] They furnished one of his motives for translating the Hippocratean *Aphorisms*—a model, as he claimed and as Marcello Virgilio acknowledged, for a culture integrated by ethics.

That culture, reflected in the libraries of doctors such as Bernardo Torni (1452–97) and—particularly—Antonio Benivieni (1443–1502),[180] combined scholastic learning with the more recent products of Florentine hu-

[173] See above, p. 205.

[174] See Vegetti, "Modelli di medicine in Galeno," pp. 47–64, esp. p. 52.

[175] *L* fols. 46^r–48^r; and BNCF, Magl. VIII, 1195, fols. 147^r–149^r. Cf. Verde, *Studio,* 4, 3:1200ff. with bibliography.

[176] See Park, *Doctors and Medicine,* pp. 225ff.; and cf. Schmitt, "La cultura scientifica," pp. 67ff.

[177] BMLF, Pluteo 19, 30, with Garin, *Il pensiero pedagogico,* pp. 119–20, and Robey, "Humanist Views," p. 17.

[178] See Park, *Doctors and Medicine,* pp. 228ff. Cf. Garin, "Religione e filosofia," pp. 313–34; and the older study by G. Uzielli, *La vita e i tempi di Paolo dal Pozzo Toscanelli: Ricerche e studi* (Rome, 1894).

[179] See F. Piovan, "Un umanista trascurato: Ricerche su Lorenzo Lorenzi e sulla sua biblioteca," *Atti dell'istituto veneto di scienze, lettere ed arti,* Classe di scienze morali, lettere ed arti 142 (1983–84): 191–216.

[180] See M. Messina, "Bernardo Torni," and S. Sclavi, "La biblioteca di Antonio Beniveni," *Physis* 17 (1975): 249–54 and 155–68. On Torni, see further M. Messina Montelli, ed., *Bernardo Torni: Opusculi filosofici e medici* (Florence, 1982).

manism. Benivieni, however, was no captive in what Savonarola called "the prison of antiquity." His *De abditis nonnullis ac mirandis morborum et sanationum curis,*[181] published by Giunta in 1507, drew not on ancient authority but on empirical practice[182]—the very method that Marcello Virgilio, in 1514, had condemned as inadequate by itself, while advocating a more critical approach to the classics.[183] More congenial to his outlook was Benivieni's distinction between "physicians of the body and the soul." A leader in the secular sphere where the Florentine doctors of his own and earlier generations practiced, he needed to demonstrate, in competition with sophisticated and popular scholastic encyclopedias of medical learning such as the *Medical Sermons* of Niccolò Falcucci da Borgo San Lorenzo,[184] that humanism could make a comparable contribution. Hence a further attraction of the encyclopedic Dioscorides—but not, significantly, the *Materia medica* in Greek. Like Manente Leontini, translator of Hippocrates for Leo X;[185] like the Ficino who had rendered Plato for the pope's father and grandfather, and whose combination of medical, literary, and philosophical interests Marcello Virgilio emulated, he chose to turn Dioscorides' work into Latin.

Latin versions of the *Materia medica* were available in 1515. The first was published in 1478, at Colle Val d'Elsa, and in 1514 another appeared at Venice with marginal notes drawn from the commentary of Peter of Padua (1307–11). This brutish book—"scholastic" in its two-column format, "Gothic" in its typographical style—is a world apart from the second edition of Dioscorides in Greek, brought out, again at Venice, only four years later by Aldo Manuzio's heirs. In the preface, his brother-in-law, Andrea Torresani, acknowledged the help that Leoniceno had provided by lending a codex in his possession that had enabled improvements to be made in the text of the *editio princeps*. It had issued from the Aldine press in 1499, its foreword resounding with echoes of Leoniceno's arguments for Pliny's dependence on Dioscorides, and had been presented by Aldo himself to Marcello Virgilio in October of that year with a honeyed plea for collaboration.[186] Providing, in his commentary, what the Aldine editions did not offer and following a familiar pattern, according to which "new material [was] published in Greek, and then given greater accessibility by . . . a Latin translation,"[187] he was both implementing a variant on Giuntine policy and steering clear of a looming obstacle. For behind the Greek text of Dioscorides first printed by Aldo and

[181] Translation by C. Singer (Springfield, Ill., 1954).

[182] See below, p. 265. Cf. L. Thorndike, *A History of Magic and Experimental Science,* vol. 4, *Fourteenth and Fifteenth Centuries* (New York, 1934), pp. 586ff.

[183] See above, pp. 200ff.

[184] See Park, *Doctors and Medicine,* pp. 50–51.

[185] See A. Campana, "Manente Leontini fiorentino, medico e traduttore di medici greci," *La Rinascità* 20 (1941): 513–15.

[186] Bandini, *Collectio,* p. 28.

[187] Nutton, "Greek Science," pp. 23–24.

later revised by his heirs stood the intimidating Leoniceno, who had worsted Poliziano. Recurring to the debates of the previous generation, his successor was aware that old scores had not been settled.

What he did not yet know was to be disturbing, both to him and to his publisher. In the excitement of the pope's visit to Florence in November 1515, Marcello Virgilio had set to work on Dioscorides, and Filippo di Giunta had puffed his labors. Puffing became pressure on 27 August 1517, when Giunta brought out Plutarch, with a dedication of the *Parallel Lives* to his favorite scholar. Marcello Virgilio had supplied him with the manuscript upon which the edition was based, and, paying tribute to this benefactor of learning, his publisher urged him to get on with his magnum opus: "As soon as you can, send to press your Dioscorides—*yours* I call it with reason, because you have translated it into Latin!"[188] Anxiety lay behind the emphatically personal pronouns. The expectant gaze of Florence and of all Italy, claimed Giunta, was trained on the prodigy that Marcello Virgilio was about to produce.

The reasons for Giunta's anxiety were pressing. In 1516, the French humanist Jean Ruel had prepared a Latin version of Dioscorides.[189] Worse still, in May 1517, Barbaro's ghost had risen from the grave, in the all-too-tangible form of yet another translation of the *Materia medica* and a *Corollarium*.[190] Exhumed by Barbaro's brothers, Luigi and Francesco, and edited by Giovanni Battista Egnazio, the posthumous work was intended as Italian philology's response to Ruel. Who, other than Giunta, could now respond to the preempted Marcello Virgilio? What he had been preparing so carefully since 1515 had been anticipated partly by an unknown Frenchmen and fully by the celebrated ally of Poliziano.

If Barbaro's specter haunted Marcello Virgilio, he was no less troubled by the shadow of Leoniceno. His interests were represented at Florence by the Pescian humanist Stefano Sterponi,[191] master of malice, who, during his brief sojourn in the city, managed both to stand in for Marcello Virgilio at the Studio in 1519 and to rouse the thunders of the scholar before whom he trembled. Behind the scenes, eight months before publication, Sterponi had been writing to Leoniceno, whom he hoped would be the fiercest critic of his rival's work.[192] This "public scribe and teacher of the *studia humanitatis*—in his own way, quite cultivated,"[193] reported Sterponi with complicit irony

[188] "Quampridem potes, Dioscoridem tuum—*tuum* iure appello, a te scilicet Latinitate donatum emittere velis!" Bandini, *Annales* 1:124.

[189] On Ruel, see Riddle, "Dioscorides," pp. 29–32; and Pozzi, "Appunti," p. 620.

[190] See Pozzi, "Appunti," pp. 619–40.

[191] See F. Inghirami, *Storia della Toscana* 14 (Fiesole, 1884), pp. 321–22; and cf. G. Ansaldi, *Cenni biografici dei personnaggi illustri della città di Pescia e suoi dintorni* (Pescia, 1872), p. 238. See further below, pp. 246–48.

[192] BRF 911, fols. 59^{v}–60^{v}, extracts from which are published by Bandini, *Collectio,* p. xx.

[193] "Publicus scriba et doctor humanitatis studiorum, homo in suo genere satis litteratus." BRF 911, fols. 59^{v}–60^{v}.

in February 1518, had composed a Latin version of Dioscorides, like Barbaro before him. As it was being edited for the press the anxious author would question Sterponi, on each of their frequent encounters, whether his opus might find favor with Leoniceno. "Of course," he replied ambiguously, "providing that is *emendatissimum,* in contrast to Barbaro's book." Sterponi knew that Leoniceno had dedicated *De Plinii . . . erroribus* 2 to Barbaro. He was aware, and recorded, that Marcello Virgilio "bites Barbaro in several places." How sharp were his teeth? Before inquiring into what Sterponi wished to insinuate, let us savor this scene of prepublication nerves.

Marcello Virgilio blushed (*subrubuit*). As well as he might. "This man who regards himself as an expert," observed the venomous Sterponi, "and who is, in my opinion, no fool in matters of grammar, seemed to dread your terrible judgment."[194] "Grammar," in this sentence, like "public scribe" in the previous paragraph, recalls the terms of Poliziano's polemic with Scala and the literary studies unconnected with higher disciplines such as medicine, which Leoniceno scorned. To him, stirring the waters further, Sterponi promised to send a copy of Marcello Virgilio's book as soon as it appeared. The promise was coupled with an invitation to comment,[195] and Sterponi kept his word. The Dioscorides of October 1518 did reach Leoniceno's library.[196] In this poisonous atmosphere, it is not difficult to understand why Giunta gasped with anxiety that the partner of his ambitions should complete his work ("Your Dioscorides—*yours* I call it with reason!")

How to resolve such a delicate dilemma? By the exercise of diplomacy, in which Marcello Virgilio excelled. With scrupulous care he redacted his preface to his readers—the most menacing of whom could be imagined in his study at Ferrara, red pencil poised. Four chronological stages of preparation were defensively distinguished: the initial study of a "most ancient codex written in 'Lombard' letters" (now Munich, clm. 337);[197] a subsequent reading of Ruel's version; a perusal of Barbaro's translation and *Corollarium;*[198] and, the inadequacy of previous efforts determined, a collation of five Greek codices.[199] If Marcello Virgilio did not abandon the enterprise—a thought that often entered his mind—it was because his two predecessors had not used the "more ancient rendering" (which in any case merited stylistic revision); because Ruel, reliant on a defective manuscript, had nothing to offer

[194] "Homo sua opinione non imperitus, nec mea quidem sententia in grammaticis ignarus, visusque est mihi reformidare gravissimum iudicium tuum." Ibid.

[195] BRF 911, fols. 60^r–60^v (not in Bandini, *Collectio*).

[196] See Mugnai Carrara, *La biblioteca di Nicolò Leoniceno,* p. 14.

[197] In Marcello Virgilio's possession since circa 1490, speculates H. Stadler, "Der lateinische Dioscurides der Münchner Hof- und Staatsbibliothek und die Bedeutung dieser Übersetzung für einen Teil der mittelalterlichen Medicin," *Allgemeine Medicinische Central-Zeitung* 15 (1900). See further A. Beccaria, *I Codici di medicina del periodo presalernitano* (Rome, 1956), pp. 272–73.

[198] Riddle, "Dioscorides," p. 37.

[199] 1518 edition, cit., AA ii^b.

his reader but *bona fides;* because Barbaro's premature death had prevented him from adding the medical information that the work required and deserved.[200] In short, the onerous task of textual criticism and exegesis had still to be completed, and Marcello Virgilio had set about it dispassionately: "With no desire to speak ill of others, without envying the praise earned by anyone, without the intention of making a reputation by identifying others' mistakes, which is the first aim of the ambitious in this kind of praiseworthy undertaking." His motive was pure altruism, a noble concern "for the health of mankind and the dignity of this writer."[201]

Humbug! To Marcello Virgilio's *antiquissimus codex,* little is owed by his Latin translation; from Ruel, while criticizing his version, he filches references to Paul of Aegina (especially in the translation of the pseudo-Dioscoridean *De venenis* as Book 6 of *Materia medica*); and against Barbaro—the resurrected Barbaro, so revered by Poliziano and his circle,[202] so inconvenient for their competitor—is directed the main thrust of his animus.

Naturally Marcello Virgilio could not admit this in his statement to the reader. Proprieties had to be observed, an alternative strategy had to be found. It is revealed in his prefatory playing-up to Leoniceno. Not only were medical matters missing, as a consequence of Barbaro's death, from the *Corollarium.* Incompetence abounded generally in the treatment of this subject. Confusion of terminology bedeviled Latin writings on botany and medicine. The problem was exacerbated by the presumptuousness of professors, tampering with the text and shedding more darkness than light with their accumulated erudition. Later tradition offered no help; it was necessary to return *ad fontes:* to Dioscorides, whose supremacy in these matters, acknowledged by all Greek writers, was proved by Pliny's dependence on him.[203] A tissue of topoi woven together from *De Plinii . . . erroribus,* in an attempt to enlist Leoniceno's sympathies for this rival of Barbaro.

Between Ermolao Barbaro and Marcello Virgilio there were more points in common than their evident differences of birth, station, and ability might seem to suggest. Both combined literary and political interests. Both were confronted with the challenge of Poliziano's example. Both worked on Aristotle and Dioscorides, whom they were united in regarding as a focus for their encyclopedic ideal. In the preface to his *Corollarium,* Barbaro wrote:

> When, at the urging of my friends, I decided to send this book to press, I was induced by the same youthful conviction that led me to undertake the great-

[200] Riddle, "Dioscorides," p. 37.

[201] ". . . nullo sane maledicendi studio, nullius laudi invidentes, nec ex erratis aliorum, quod primum sibi in hoc laudis genere arripit ambitio, gloriam nostram augere cogitantes . . . pro salute hominis et scriptoris huius dignitate." Ibid., pp. 36–37.

[202] Cf. Crinito, *Commentarii de honesta disciplina,* p. 69.

[203] Riddle, "Dioscorides," p. 36.

> est and most burdensome of all tasks—of making available Dioscorides and Pliny and, to speak freely, of illuminating the whole of literature with a new commentary, so that there would be nothing written by either the Greeks or the Latins up to this day that I had not gathered together in this treatise. I wished to call these books a *Corollarium* because they are an appendix and supplement to my justifiable and correct translation of Dioscorides—and not only to Dioscorides, but to absolutely all my studies and writings.[204]

The *Materia medica* presented Barbaro with the opportunity to compose his *summa,* and the *Corollarium* was designed as the new Varro's bequest to posterity.[205] Contesting his heritage, Marcello Virgilio sought to usurp the same title.

Which did not imply, despite his deference to Leoniceno, primary attention to medicine. Unlike the members of the school of Ferrara, who were concerned less with an impeccable text than with a working basis for empirical investigation,[206] this pupil of Poliziano viewed Dioscorides first and foremost with the eyes of a philologist—a philologist who was, by preference, a Hellenist, determined to affirm the authority of the Greeks: "My particular purpose is to render and confirm Greek antiquity with the arguments provided by the ancient Greeks."[207]

How far motives of rivalry with Barbaro incited Marcello Virgilio to depart, in public, from his unpublished utterances may be judged from the *praefatio* that he had delivered at the Studio in 1514: "Do not . . . defer so much to antiquity that you leave nothing to your freedom of choice and judgment!"[208] The *auctoritas* of the ancients, often questioned in Marcello Virgilio's lectures,[209] was maintained to be unshakable in the case of

[204] "Quem cum emittere vel hortantibus amicis vellem, eadem animi inductione quam a teneris hauseram promovendi opus omnium maximum ac laboriosissimum aggressus, Dioscoridis ac Plinii et, ut ingenue fatear, *omnis rei literariae illustrandae nova commentatione suscepi, ut nihil vel apud Graecos vel apud Latinos ad hanc diem extet in hoc scribendi genere, quod non in hosce commentarios regesserim*. . . . Hosce libros *Corollarii* nomine nuncupare volui, quod hi velut appendix additamentumque essent legitimo iustoque opere tralatiti Dioscoridis—*neque vero Discoridis solum, sed meorum plane studiorum scriptorumque omnium*." The text is conveniently printed by Pozzi, "Appunti," pp. 622–23.

[205] For the characterization, see Leoniceno in his dedication of *De Plinii in medicina erroribus* 2, p. 22[b]: "Hermolae, qui tantus in omnium doctrinarum genere litteris, ut *Marcum* illum *Varronem* Latinorum atque Graecorum habitum aliquando doctissimum solus aetate nostra repraesentes."

[206] See D. Mugnai Carrara, "Nicolò Leoniceno e Giovanni Mainardi: Aspetti epistemologici dell'umanesimo medico," *Alla corte degli Estensi: Filosofia, arte e cultura a Ferrara nei secoli xv e xvi,* ed. M. Bertozzi (Ferrara, 1994), p. 21.

[207] "Antiqua enim et Graeca antiquorum et Graecorum rationibus tradere et confirmare praecipuum nobis consilium est." 1518 edition, cit., AA *iii*[a]. Cf. Codro Urceo (1446–1500), professor of Greek at Bologna, *Sermones,* IX and X, with Nutton, *John Caius,* p. 21 and n. 21.

[208] *L* fol. 88[r]: ". . . nolite antiquitati tantum deferre, ut nihil electioni et iudicio vestro relinquatis!"

[209] See above, pp. 154ff., 160ff.

Dioscorides. A different type of work, to be sure, from the Latin poets and orators whom the professor had previously expounded, a source of untainted Hellenic truth that the *posteriores* had polluted. Criteria of textual purity, so familiar from Poliziano's writings and so foreign to Marcello Virgilio's earlier declarations, serve both to vaunt the claims of the *Materia medica* and to assert those of its interpreter.

That is why Marcello Virgilio departed from the *miscellanea* form developed by Poliziano; why, in the exhaustive length of more than 700 closely printed folios, he abandoned the laconicism of Barbaro's *Castigationes Plinianae* and the terseness of his *Corollarium,*[210] while recalling, in act of typographical imitation without parallel in the earlier output of the Giuntine press, the spacious layout and generous dimensions of both his rival's books (Plates 6, 7, and 8). The thoroughness of the systematic commentary replaced the principle of choice selection; and, despite his attack on the otiose accumulations of his predecessors, Marcello Virgilio inevitably yielded to the same tendency. Ruel skulks at the margins of his work, shunned or dismissed; at its center stands Barbaro—not only the commentator of the *Corollarium* but also the critic of Pliny. What he had done for the text of the *Historia naturalis* Marcello Virgilio aimed to achieve for the *Materia medica:* a precise yet imaginative determination of its meaning, eliminating the corruptions and ambiguities of tradition, by philological methods.

The philologist's task, as Marcello Virgilio presented it in his statement to the reader, was conceived in terms reminiscent of Poliziano. Like the *grammaticus* of the *Lamia,* Dioscorides' translator and commentator was described as an *interpres* with encyclopedic interests. The aesthetic of deliberate disorder formulated in the preface to the first *Centuria* reappeared in Marcello Virgilio's foreword, where, with the ambiguity of his predecessor, he proclaimed his Socratic ignorance. That pose was belied, however, by reflections on culture more searching than anything attempted by Poliziano or Barbaro: on the protean nature of knowledge, especially in the fields of botany and pharmacology, due to the variety, the multiplicity, and the contingency of human and natural history.[211]

This perception shaped the character of Marcello Virgilio's medical humanism, in line with his previous insistence on the truth-claims of literature, entailing accurate representation or "fabulous" rendering of nature, and with

[210] See Pozzi in Barbaro, *Castigationes Plinianae,* pp. clxff.

[211] "Difficilem in quotidiana multiplicique natura varietate fuisse semper et adhuc esse plantarum et medicae materiae disciplinam: temporibus siquidem locis, annorum temperamentis, humana cultura et ad utramque partem continuo naturae motu varietate raro easdem se undique ostendunt. Accessisse naturae difficultatibus his diversis gentium indicationes, quibus quod alioquin idem naturae semper fuit diversum et aliud saepenumero a scriptoribus creditum est. Auxisse postremo et paulo minus quam inextricabiles tam multas difficultates fecisse novam posteriorum scriptorum medicinam, quae mixtis cum antiquis Graecorum vocibus barbaris appellationibus suis quid qualeve hoc aut illud in antiquis scriptoribus fuerit aegre cognoscendum relinquit." 1518 edition, p. AA *ii.*

LIBER PRIMVS. II

ci alterum genus. Gangetidis nomine, ab fluuio Indię: qui montem, in quo nascitur: præfluit: uiribus languidũ, ut quod proueniat aquoso solo, proindeq; in maiorem altitudinem, q̃ Syriacum adolescat, pluribus ab eadem radice Aristis fruticantibus: implicatis, & redolentibus uirus. Odoratius uero, quod locis celsioribus gignitur spica breui, Cyperũ olente, In totũq; eisdem dotibus qbus Syriacũ. Habetur & Sampharíticũ frutice admodũ pumilo: a loco: ubi carpitur, dictum, spicis ingentibus: candidum: caule, qui e medio prosilit, aliquando hircum spirante, damnatur in totum. Ac uenũdari quidem hæc solet elota. Sed candore spicę, squaloreq; coarguitur, & ꝙ lanugine careat. Adulterant flatum stibio, cum aqua palmeoue uino. spissitatis & ponderis causa. In usu lutum: qui hęserit radici: decutimus, & puluerem ipsum cribro succretum reponimus, utilem futurum manibus lauandis. Nardo uis excalfacere: siccare: urinas mouere: quo fit, ut aluum sistat repercusso liquore: Abundantias certe fœminarum appositu, saniemq; cohibet. In nausea bibitur cum frigida: Tremoribus cordis: inflationibus stomachi: laborantibus Iocinore: morbo regio, renibus subuenit. Decoctũ in aqua inflamationes uuluę insidentium fouet. Pilorum defluuia in genis coercet, astringendo eos obiter, farciendoq;. Corporibus quoq; humetis comminutæ puluis inspergitur. additurq; in antidota. Ad oculorum desideria conditur nouo fictili: cui tectorium nõ sit inductũ. In uino trita & in pastillos coacta.

NARDVM GALLICVM VII

n Ardus Gallica in Ligurię alpibus nascitur, Aliuca uernaculo indigenis nomine. Nascitur & in Istria. Frutex pusillus cũ radice uellitur, & in fasciculos manuales digeritur. Folia ei longiuscula, leuiter flauescentia: Flos luteus. Vsus eius in caule tantum atq; radicibus, quoniam odorata solum hæc habentur. Cæterum pridie q̃ repurges, aspergere aqua manipulos conueniet, & pauimento humenti: sed charta prius istrato, componere. postridie eius diei terrenum & sordes eximere. Ita. n. paleatum, alienũq; omne ab eo, quod frugi, sincerumq; erit. lẽtitia, beneficio madoris quęsita, sine iniuria secernitur. Cũ Gallico Nardo reponi solet herba, quæ a grauitate odoris Hirculus uocat̃, qua maxime adulteratur. Alioquin distinctio facilis, Distat ꝙ sine cauliculo est: & ꝙ cãdidior & ꝙ minoribus foliis. ꝙq; radicis neq; amarę, neq; odorate, qualis uera Nardus. Radicẽ et caulẽ seponi oportet. foliũ abiici. Mox: si suare collibeat: e uino teri: & pastillos defingi, atq; in figlinũ nouũ cõponi debet: operculo probe, ac diligenter iniecto. Optimum, quod recentissimum odoratissimumq; est: Radice multiplici, plena nec fragili. Eosdem effectus habet: quos Syriacum: Nisi ꝙ urinam acrius ciet: stomachoq; utilior probatur. Inflammationibus quoq; Iocinoris confert. Item arquatis, & inflationibus stomachi, si cum decocto absinthii bibatur. Eodem modo lienibus, uesicæ morbis: ac Renum: Contra uenenatos uero ictus ex uino. Malagmatis: potionibus, unguentis ex calfactoriis miscetur.

A ii

6. Barbaro, translation of Dioscorides, *Materia medica* (Venice, 1517).

LIBER PRIMVS ;

lat,etiam ſi quibuſdam exemplaribus cypera legitur.Non poſſum nõ mirari quãobrem Laurẽ/
tius ualla cyperum in herodoto ſiler conuerterit.

CARDAMOMVM V

Ardamomũ Theophraſtus refert alios e Media putare, alios ex india cũ amomo atq;
c nardo & plurimis id genus aduehi. Simile amomo frutice toto prædicant,ſemine ob
longo.Quatuor eius genera uiridiſſimũ & pingue acutis angulis, Fricanti pertinax,
quod & maxime laudatur.Proximũ e Ruffo candicans.Tertiũ minutius atq; nigrius. Peius ua/
rium & friari facile,odoris ꝙ parui id quod uerius eſt.uicinius eſſe coſto debet.Precium optimi
ait Plinius in libras denarii.ii.Recentiores mauritani hoc nõ cardamomũ ſed cordumeni & ſyl/
ueſtre caros uocant.Cardamomi uero noïe genus aliud intelligunt in geminas diuiſum ſpeci/
es.Alterũ lentis amplitudine.Alterũ ciceris obnigri.In quo granũ albũ ſit guſtu mordaci.Vtrũq;
odoratũ.Quid ꝙ officinæ cardomomo utuntur alio,q̃ quod & a mauris & a Dioſcoride perſcri
bitur:duplicis faſtigii,minus & maius appellantes,cui ſimile id ſemẽ ſit: quod uulgo melligeta
dicitur prælatum uiribus:

NARDI SPICA VI

Ardum ſiue Nardus in Thracia exili odore naſcitur,ſiue ut Theophraſtus ſcripſit Radi
n culæ potius quædã imitãtes odore nardũ,ſed leuiter, q̃q̃ Plinius inuẽtam in Thracia
nuper herbã dicat,cuius folia nihil ab indica nardo ſpecie diſſentiant. Principatus in
unguentis nardo apud ueteres ſtetit.Frutex eſt graui & craſſa Radice,ſed minuta nigraq; ac fragi
li:q̃uis pingui,ſitũ Redolente,qualem cupreſſi,aſpero ſapore,folio paruo denſoq;.Cacumina
in ariſtas ſe ſpargunt,Ideo gemina dote nardi ſpicas & folia concelebrãt.Alterũ genus apud Gã
gem in totũ Reiicitur.Adulterãt Pſeudonardo herba,que ubiq; naſcit̃ Craſſiore atq; latiore fo/
lio,colore languido,in candidũ uergente.Sit hæc fortaſſe quã Dioſcorides ſamphariticã appel
lat.Item ſua Radice permixta,ut ſtibio ponderis gratia,et gũmi & argenti ſpuma & cyperi cor/
tice.Preciũ ſpicæ in libras denarii.lxxxx.foliorum uero eius quod maiora hæc habet Hadroſphe
ron uocatur, Denarii. xxx. eius autem quod minora & mẽſoſpheron dicitur denarii. lx. At eius
quod minima & ob id microſpheron appellatur laudatiſſimumq; eſt denarii.lxxv.odoris gra//
tia omnibus.Maior Recentibus.Nardo color:qui inueterauerit, nigriori melior. Indica ſyria/
cæ præfert̃ a Galeno.Nigrior & ualidior etiam nõnunq̃ ſyriaca.Reliqua genera in mẽtione gal/
lici nardi montaniq; dicemus.Sed poſcimur identidem,quæ ſint illæ nouem ſpecies,quas Nar/
dum indicum repreſentare Plinius exiſtimet. an gangetis prima. ozenitis ab odore uirulento
dicta. Secunda Pſeudonardus. Tertia ſyriaca. Quarta gallica. Quinta cretica: id eſt phu. Sexta
baccaris. Septima hirculus.Octaua aſſaron.Nona thracia.Quidã uſum nardi,oẽm abdicant ob
ancipitẽ ex ea medicinã,propterea ꝙ in nardo quiddã ueneni delibutorii uice naſci ferãt, e quo
Piſon illud uocatum indi conficiant.Exitiale nõ potu modo,ſed in ſudore corporibus appoſi/
tum etiã ſi ab legulis purgari & elui curioſiſſime moris ſit.fortaſſeq; hoc ſit aut nõ diſſimile quod
pharicon a Dioſcoride ac Plinio Phariacon ab athenæo dicitur guſtu nardi omnino. ſed Reſo/
lutionẽ faciẽs neruorũ cũ alienatione mentis atq; ſpaſmo.Aduerſari autẽ huic ueneno maxime
cydoniam philarchus prodidit.Notatu dignũ a Dioſcoride cæteriſq; ueteribus nardũ cyperi o/
dore commẽdari,a Plinio cupreſſi.Malim quidẽ librarii fuiſſe culpam ſed ſi Plinio tribuendus
error foret,affinitate uerbi lapſum eſſe dicerem.Cypariſſizin pro cyperizin legentem.Neq; dici
poteſt contra deceptũ eſſe Dioſcoridẽ nõ Pliniũ.Quando quidẽ cyperũ idem ipſe Plinius odo/
rem nardi referre alio loco ſcribat.Aduertendũ eſt & illud oĩa nardi genera herbas eſſe præter in
dicum.In iis probatio una,ne ſint fragilia & arida potius q̃ ſicca folia.Hirculus porro qua uitiari
nardũ ſincerã dicunt,nõ grauitate odoris modo,ſed ſimilitudine etiã,nonnullã animalis eius
nomen accepit.Græci tragon uocant.Illud,ne quem fallamus noſcendũ:Syriacã nardũ dupli/
cis eſſe generis unũ in india,ſed parte montis in ſyriã ſpectante,quã Plinius ſub indicæ uocabu
lo cõpleſtitur.Alterũ in orbe nr̃o id eſt ſyria,ciliciaq; hoc aliqui gallico præponũt.Aliqui Con/
tra,gallicũ ſyriaco tali præferũt.De gallico mox dicemus. Galenus indicã nardũ accipit quoti/
es abſolute ſtachyn id eſt ſpicã nardi nominat,quaſi ſpicam cæteræ non habeãt,ſed herbam dũ/
taxat,quẽadmodũ & Plinio uidet̃.In Gedroſia quoq; nardũ ẽ.Sed ſub indico ꝯtineri credimus

NARDVM GALLICVM VII

Ardum gallicũ ſiue ut græci appellant,celticũ,laudatur in orbe nr̃o poſt ſyriacũ, quip
n pe quod ſyriaco ſit leuius,neq; multũ ab indico differens ut Plinius exiſtimat. Preciũ
ſiclis.xiii.hoc & aliucã uocari Dioſcorides alpinis populis tradit.Credo ſaliuncã legẽ/
dum a uicinitate puto ſaliuncæ.Quã nr̃i folioſam quidẽ, Sed breuem & quæ necti non poſſit,
deſcribunt.Radici numeroſæ cohæret herba uerius q̃ flos.Denſa ueluti manu preſſa.Breuiterq;

A iii

7. Barbaro, *Corollarium* (1517).

LIBER. I. 10

lant ideoq; huic oculorum malo ex re assignatū. Quod in Isagoge sua inter alias oculorum labes Galenus his uerbis magis descripsit q̄ diffiniuit: Cōmunis uox μύδησις est omnibus quæ putrescentia pereunt: fit aūt hoc & in palpebris quæ tumidiores, hoc malo fiunt continueq; destillant: copioso circa eas concrescente adipe. Quam descriptionem nos etiam secuti palpebrarum cum destillatione defluuia & tumores diximus. μύδησις.

DIOS. DE NARDO GALLICA. Cap. vii.

Elticam. Romani Gallicam nardū dicūt. Nascitur Gallica nardus in liguriæ alpibus ab incolis gētis suæ uocabulo Gallica appellata. Nascit & in Istria breuis & exiguus frutex: qui una cū radicibus carpitur & in manuales fasciculos ligat. Folia habet oblonga: colore subflauo lutheū uero florē. Caulium tātū radicuq; usus ē solę enī hæ partes odoris bonitate cōmendātur. Ideoq; oportet per diē ante inspersos aqua fasciculos & amoto si quid terreni inhæserit: in humido pauimēto subiecta charta sternere: tum sequēti die purgare. hac. n. ratiōe aucta ex humore firmitate tenaciq; materiæ lentore: nō peribit dū tractabit in purgādo una cū inutilibus cremiis paleisq; & alieno omni quod utile ē. Adulterat euulsa primū mox reposita simul cōsimili herba quam ob odoris uirus Hirulū uocāt: facile tn̄ deprehēdit. Sine caule siquidē cādidiorq; ē: min⁹ oblōgis foliis frōdet: nec amara: nec aromatū mō odorata radice est quæ oīa habet uera gallica nardus. Sepositis igitur ad usum caulibus: radicibusq; folia abiicito. Et si seruare eam uolueris uino tritam excipito: conformatamq; in pastillos in nouo picato fictili diligenter operculatā reponito. Probatissima est nardus gallica quæ recens: odorata: multiradix: non facile fragilis: & plena erit. Potest Gallica quæcunq; Syriaca nardus: Maiore tn̄ ui ad ciendam urinā & stomacho magis accomodata hæc est: Prodest iocinoris inflammationibus: suffusis felle: & stomachi inflationibus cum decocto Absinthii pota. Prodest eodem mō & lieni: Renū uessicæq; uitiis: & cū uino cōtra ea quæ ictu morsu ue uenenū relinquunt. Miscet præterea malagmatis: potionibus: & unguentis quæ calefaciendo sunt.

INTERPRES.

Væ Indicā & Syriacam nardū sequuntur Celtica: & montana Nardus: Asaron: Phu: & Malobathrū sui generis herbæ: sola odoris similitudine in cognationem censum & nomen Nardi uenerunt: quod ex ꝓpria singulorum historia & ex his quæ in Malobathro mox dicentur: colligere omnibus facile est: Nec refert quod hic ait posse celticam nardum quæcunq; syriaca potest. Ex notis. n. quæ singulis paucioribus ue in eodē: aut non dissimili genere ꝓpriæ: magis q̄ ex uiribus quæ pluribus & in diuersis generibus cōmunes sunt: similitudinis cognationisq; plantarū ratio accipienda est: Qua obseruatione nos usi nō uidemus cur Gallica nardus impetrato ex similitudine alieno nomine Saliunca dici & illi eadē haberi possit: Cum ex Dioscoridis historia nardus hæc foliis oblongis sit: Lutheo colore floreat: & in caules erigatur: Saliunca si Plinio credim⁹ foliosa quidem sit: sed tā breuis ut necti in coronas nō possit: herba uerius q̄ flos & sui generis cespes: illa in liguriæ alpib⁹: hæc in noricis & pānonia nascat. Quod cōtemplatus Maro et in buccolicis suis in cōparatione carminis duorum pastorum tn̄ alteri cedere alterum dicebat: quantū Puniceis humilis cedit Saliunca rosetis: nihil aliud ut uidetur describens q̄ Saliuncæ breuitatē: & foliosum cespitē: quæ rosetis comparata longo interuallo eis cederet. Ex eo factū est ut sæpe alias demiratus ego sim eos qui Pliniū in hoc tā grauiter accusent obiiciantq; homini: ut nos etiā concedimus nō semper diligenti & oculato in his quæ scribebat Saliuncæ ignorātiā: quam Maro nouerit: & quā ipse dicebat tantæ suauitatis esse ut metallum & uectigal eē incœpisset: ex quibus non facile erat decipi: tā multæ erant utriusq; diuersæ & contrariæ notæ: tamq; ut erant eorum temporum fortuna & mores: quottidianus usus. Omnē ut uidetur doctissimorum nostra ætate uirorum ꝓ Saliūca & Gallica nardo disceptationē excitauit una Dios. in hoc capite uox: q nec una nec eadē in antiqs græcis ē Sed in aliqbus Saliūca: in aliqbus aliūca: in plerisq; et geminato. l. alliūca legitur: Ex q̄ tā multiplici lectione oborta nobis suspitio ē uitiū in ea uoce eē ut plerūq; fit: in his q [illegible] & a latinis græca [illegible] alterius liguæ librariis scribūt: nec Saliūcā illic legēdū eē: [illegible] quo sunt in qbus duplex. l. est & in oībus totā dictionē finit. ca. syllaba: Gallica p

b ii

8. Marcello Virgilio, Dioscorides, *Materia medica* (Florence, 1518).

his skeptical approach to Latin sources. Botanical research, conducted in a spirit of critical inquiry, was consequently one of the standards to which Marcello Virgilio appealed. In his commentary on the lucerne at *Materia medica* 2.133, he wrote: "For a long time past I have searched the length and breadth of Italy—my long-standing aim was a renaissance of the truth—and have attempted, by diligently interviewing the inhabitants of many regions and in various places, to restore to light knowledge of simples, wherever they were unidentified, and to reestablish the study of the countryside."[212] Commenting on the squill (2.159), he opposed "necessity" and "daily experience" to the "authority of the ancients" and "the testimony of the manuscripts," and came down on the side of the first.[213] Yet this contrast, which echoed Collenuccio's *Pliniana defensio,* is hardly sustained in Marcello Virgilio's work on Dioscorides. Empirical investigation, for him, was dominated by textual analysis;[214] and the primacy attributed to the text was intended partly to compensate for its lack of illustrations.

In the case of so concrete a subject as that of *Materia medica,* this represented a disadvantage.[215] Marcello Virgilio was conscious of the drawbacks of his pictureless commentary. But if his book lacked "graphic aids," that was not only because the drawings in Munich clm. 337 were of little use to him and the remainder of the tradition of the illustrated Dioscorides inaccessible.[216] Economic motives played a role. Marcello Virgilio's bulky volume was by far the largest, most imposing, and most expensive that the Giuntine press had ever produced.[217] The additional costs of woodcuts on the scale required would have been prohibitive, and the *Materia medica* had to await the commercial flair of that entrepreneur of botanical studies, Pietro Andrea Mattioli, whose picture book did not appear until 1554.[218] Marcello Virgilio, near the beginning of the craze for Dioscorides that was to outlast the sixteenth century, made his mark by other techniques.

One of them was to outclass Barbaro's *Corollarium,* butt of his frequent slights. The emulation, reaching beyond botany and philology, amounted to a different intellectual enterprise. Discussing, in the dry, concise, and factual

[212] "Quaesivimus nos iampridem tota Italia—antiquum enim renovandae veritatis studium in nobis est—diligentique multarum diversis locis gentium et incolarum percontatione sicubi incognita medica in lucem proferre et ruris disciplinae restituere conati sumus." Ibid., p. 135ᵃ.

[213] Ibid., pp. 148ᵃ⁻ᵇ, 149ᵇ.

[214] A different emphasis is given by Dilg, "Der botanische Kommentarliteratur," pp. 244–45.

[215] On Dioscorides editions without illustrations, see A. Touwaïde, "Un receuil grec du Xᵉ siècle illustré au XVᵉ siècle," *Scriptorium* 39 (1985): 51.

[216] For the tradition, see S. Torresella, "Dioscoride," in *Enciclopedia dell'arte medievale,* vol. 5 (Rome, 1994), pp. 655–63.

[217] See below, p. 235.

[218] On Mattioli and his context, see Palmer, "Medical Botany," pp. 151ff., esp. p. 153; on illustrations, see W. T. Stearn in *Herbarium Apulei 1481: Erbolario volgare 1522* (Milan, 1979), pp. lxvff.

manner of a lexicon article that is characteristic of his book, the cup-shaped plant known as *acetabulum* in Latin and as *cotyledon* in Greek, Barbaro had been content to distinguish it from the *cimbalaris,* even though Dioscorides had also used the term *cimbalion*. No less than nine alternative names are listed in Marcello Virgilio's version of *Materia medica* (4.83), but it is on the seventh of them—*umbilicus Veneris* ("the navel of Venus"), specifically identified as Roman—that he seized in order to write a mini-essay that begins with terminological difficulties and ends with "problems in carrying out intercourse."[219]

If the colorful medieval tradition that located the feminine libido in the navel[220] led him to single out this name for the plant, what attracted Marcello Virgilio even more were the manuscripts (not in Florence) that transmitted a choice of synonyms wider than that offered by the part of the textual tradition available to Barbaro.[221] Here as elsewhere in his commentary, they provided the Dioscoridean expert of the new generation with the opportunity to correct both his rival and the Latin author whom he defended. Pliny, like Barbaro, had called the plant not *umbilicus Veneris* but *cotyledon*—which, in Marcello Virgilio's eyes, proved nothing. The "facts of the matter" (*res ipsa*) and Apuleius supported his preference, for the origin of the name was capable of reconstruction by an approach of which the literal-minded had never dreamed. Gazing at the shape of the plant, he speculated, the ancients had been reminded of a navel; and they had linked the term with Venus in order to invest it with an aura of dignity. The symbolic power of the goddess accounted for the existence of similar expressions in Latin ("Venus's hair," "Venus's eyebrow"): Roman religion legitimated a natural process of association. Botany and pharmacology subordinated to a search for the mythical genesis of words, the philologist displayed his deftness with metaphor and etymology.

Etymology opened all doors. They led in the same direction—away from the natural world and into the domain of literature. Why was the plant called κῆπος Ἀπροδίτης? Because *kēpos* can mean not only "garden," but also a "hairstyle"—the wavy fashion in which Venus's flowing locks were depicted by the ancients (and Botticelli).[222] By the same analogy, the derivation of *cimbalion* from *cymbala* was explained: where Barbaro, discussing that word, was bent on eliminating its confusion with *cimbalaris,* Marcello Virgilio reveled in the polysemy that arose from an abundance of plants and a scarcity of names.

[219] 1518 edition, pp. 251^{b}–252^{b}.

[220] Isidore of Seville *Etymologiae* 2.1.98, with D. Jacquart and C. Thomasset, *Sexuality and Medicine in the Middle Ages,* trans. M. Adamson (Oxford, 1988), pp. 13 and 138.

[221] See *Pedacii Dioscuridis Anazarbei De materia medica libri quinque* (ed. Wellmann), 2:250, app. ad loc.

[222] See A. Warburg, "Sandro Botticellis 'Geburt der Venus' und 'Frühling,'" in Aby Warburg, *Ausgewählte Schriften und Würdigungen,* 2d ed., ed. D. Wuttke (Baden-Baden, 1980), pp. 11–64.

In the controversial area of Latin synonyms for Greek botanical terminology, Poliziano's successor identified new opportunities for the application and extension of the grammatical methods traditionally applied to *enarratio poetarum*. Drawing on the unpublished second *Centuria,* but offering answers to problems that his teacher had left unresolved,[223] Marcello Virgilio treated it as a source book (among many others) that helped him to depart from Roman writers. Ovid, discussing the excrement of the crocodile, had muddled the aquatic and terrestrial types of the beast.[224] Dioscorides, by contrast, was right to draw attention to the effect of the *umbilicus Veneris* on deformations of the sexual organs.[225] Against the entire medical and exegetical tradition, reaching from Pliny, Galen, Paul of Aegina, and pseudo-Apuleius to Barbaro, which he cited, Marcello Virgilio, former student of anatomy, attached importance to the anatomical anomalies mentioned in the *Materia medica.* This concern, bordering on obsession, with deformed genitalia was consistent with issues raised at the beginning of his commentary on the same plant: if *umbilicus Veneris* or κῆπος Ἀπροδίτης was the appropriate term, what had it to do with the goddess of love? The further, and relevant, question of whether Dioscorides was reliable in describing the plant's curative properties Marcello Virgilio left unanswered. "This is a task for doctors," he declared, recalling the deference to other fields of specialist competence in *Miscellanea* 2.[226] For him, as for Poliziano, plants were hermeneutic ciphers transmitted in literary code. Heterogenous and mutable, they reflected the human cultures that assigned them names.

Anthropomorphism, in one of its vulgar forms, was an obvious danger of such an approach. The mandrake root of *Materia medica* 4.70 provided Marcello Virgilio with an occasion to establish his distance from those who propagated the "lie" that "the plant in human form" possessed magical powers. Pseudo-Pythagoras lay behind the legend, followed by Columella, Theophrastus, and Pliny; but the real targets of Marcello Virgilio's attack were those peddlers of superstition whom he described as *Agyrtae.*[227] Such quacks, who claimed to provide charms for those crossed in love,[228] were

[223] See above, pp. 107ff.; and Lo Monaco, "Aspetti e problemi," pp. 318–25.

[224] 1518 edition, p. 320[a].

[225] Ibid., p. 252[a].

[226] See above, p. 109.

[227] 1518 edition, p. 247[a]: "*Qui mandragoram quotidie circumferunt Agyrtae* iactantquae tanto periculo effodi humana forma ignavae plebi eam ostendentes, ex uno (ut nos credimus) Pythagorae nomine eius Anthropomorpho mendacii sui occasionem arriperunt. Neque enim vox illa aliud quam humanae formae plantam significat." For *Agyrtae* in the derogatory sense, cf. Plato *Republic* 346*b.*

[228] *Materia medica* 4.125 (on the vetch): 1518 edition, p. 263[b]: ". . . a salutari exortu religionis nostre Christiani principes et ecclesiae auctores magicas vanitates quotidie et ubique exagitantes, in quibus perierunt quidem antiqua, sed aliunde nova irrepserunt: tam vana mortalitas est et in amoribus affectibusque aliis suis plus posse herbam quam formam, virtutem, laborem, industriam et operam hominis credit. Certiorem spem ab anu *Agyrteve aliquo* in votis suis concipit quam a natura moribusque et industria sua."

alive and kicking "*today*." A menace to public order and religion, they "*celebrated* the mandrake *even now*."[229]

The allusions were topical, the animus evident. It is worth recalling that, in February 1518, as the final touches were being put to this commentary before it was sent to press,[230] the Carnival was held, during which, it has been argued, was recited a drama in which the principal character pretends to be a doctor. With a display of pseudo-learning, satirically couched in the Latinate idiom of pedantry, "Callimaco" proposes a mandrake potion as a cure for impotence. "Today," "even now," while Marcello Virgilio wrote, the kind of charlatanism that he so solemnly condemned was being gaily celebrated in a comedy, entitled *Mandragola,* composed by his ex-colleague Niccolò Machiavelli.[231]

Slights against the "lies" of this mandrake merchant were counterbalanced by a robust defense of literature against the same charge. Employing the text of Dioscorides to reassert the value of *bonae litterae,* Marcello Virgilio answered the criticisms directed at their practitioners by Leoniceno. Tribute to his factual expertise and acknowledgment of his precedent[232] led into a nuanced distinction between the types, useful and pernicious, of mendacity. It was tolerated by the ancients in the interests of the common good, Marcello Virgilio wrote in the unpromising context of a commentary on *castor* (the strong-smelling substance derived from the inguinal glands of the beaver).[233] Plato, in the *Republic,* explained that the everyday and the well-worn have less power over the ignorant than what seems to have fallen from heaven with the charisma of novelty. That accounts for why there are so many magicians and frauds in the history of medicine. Take Pliny, by whom "are taught fabulous superstitions rather than natural medicine."[234] So is resumed a theme that Marcello Virgilio had announced in his preface: the progress of research and the decline of magic.[235] The advance toward truth, the reversal of entrenched prejudice, entailed eliminating such charlatans as Pliny and enlisting the aid of the poets conventionally but mistakenly branded as liars.

"Fabulous superstitions," as recounted by Leoniceno's bête noire, are compared unfavorably in Marcello Virgilio's commentary with "fabulous histories." These, as Poliziano had emphasized in his exegesis of the mythological

[229] Ibid., p. 247[a]: "His auctoribus et quasi per manus translata huiuscemodi superstitione verisimile est vanis periculorum relligionis et humanae formae mendaciis *celebrari nunc etiam mandragoram*."

[230] See above, p. 217.

[231] Cf. Raimondi, *Politica e commedia,* pp. 257ff. For the dating, cf. Ridolfi, *Vita di Machiavelli,* p. 271 (1518); and C. Dionisotti, "Appunti sulla 'Mandragola,'" *Belfagor* 39 (1984): 637 (composition 1519, performance 1520). See further below, p. 259.

[232] E.g., 4.110, 1518 edition, cit., p. 259[a]; and see the following note.

[233] 2.23, 1518 edition, p. 90[b].

[234] Ibid.: ". . . fabulosa magis superstitio quam naturalis medicina docetur."

[235] Ibid., AA *ii*[b]–AA *iii*[a].

names for the plants *milax* and *crocus*,[236] were integral to poetry; and in developing them further, in his account of the iris, Marcello Virgilio was expanding on a speculative dimension that he recognized to be present in Dioscorides' text.[237] Unlike Barbaro's *Corollarium,* the terse remarks of which were confined to *realia,* the Florentine reading of the *Materia medica* paid tribute to its author's exercise of imagination. Dealing with the black hellebore (4.142), Marcello Virgilio observed on the previous chapter's treatment of the white version of the same plant: "What Dioscorides relates [in 4.141] is fabulous and less essential for understanding the medicinal properties or history of the hellebore than for admiring it more fervently."[238] The *Historia naturalis* was different. There Pliny, inept and literal-minded, related the "history of herbs."[239]

"Herbal history" and "fabulous history": in the realm of botany, there were two different levels of reality. Only one was accessible to the pedestrian Pliny. Accuracy in reporting the appearance and properties of plants was demanded from him; and where he diverged from it, he could be branded as a fraud. Not so Dioscorides. His *Materia medica* was measurable not only by the standards of empirical method, but also by those of poetic myth—and that was highly relevant to the truth-claims of literature. As with the hellebore, so with the peony at 3.149: "If I have expounded all this length, it is in order that those who study humane letters may understand that what often seems absurd when one reads poetry sometimes has natural causes."[240] Literature, with its "fabulous" aspects, and nature, source of terminological polysemy, could illuminate one another. The prosaic Dioscorides shed light on poetry.

This was no light claim to make after Nicolò Leoniceno, whose discussions of a plant such as the bugloss displayed mastery of the ancient sources, exact textual criticism, and original research.[241] His example was cited by Marcello Virgilio when commenting on the thistle *cirsion,* also known as the "big bugloss" (*Materia medica* 4.110),[242] where the dispute over the name (*buglossa* or *borrago*?) was outlined, before being elaborated in a later chapter

[236] See above, pp. 108ff.

[237] For the iris, see 1518 edition, pp. 3ª–5ª; and below, p. 231; on Dioscorides, A. Touwaïde, "Strategie terapeutiche: I farmaci," in Grmek, *Storia del pensiero medico occidentale,* 1:357; and M. Mantegazza, "Per una nuova lettura della farmacologia antica a partire dall'opera di Dioscoride," in *Le piante medicinali e il loro impiego in farmacia nel corso dei secoli,* Atti del congresso internazionale di storia della farmacia (Piacenza, 1988), p. 33.

[238] 1518 edition, p. 269ᵇ: "Quae in extremo capite fabulosa et augendam rei admirationem potius quam medicinae aut historiae veratri necessaria a Dios[coride] referuntur."

[239] Ibid.: "Alter enim hic herbariam quam illi [= Dioscorides and Theophrastus] fabulosam historiam docet."

[240] 1518 edition, p. 215ᵇ: "Quae omnia longius dicta a nobis sunt, ut intelligerent humaniores litteras profitentes quae in poetis ridicula multis locis leguntur naturales aliquando causas habere."

[241] *De Plinii . . . erroribus,* 1:93ᵇff.

[242] 1518 edition, pp. 258ᵇ–259ª.

(4.119). Cato, in *De re rustica,* described how the unidentified *lingua bubula* was employed to shelter trees, after pruning, from the rain. This could only make sense, argued Marcello Virgilio, if its leaves were round—which is the case with the *borrago,* not the *buglossa.* Thus it follows that Cato referred to *borrago,* confirming Leoniceno's theory.[243]

Although the actual appearance of plants played a role in this train of speculative thought, it was not the same one discerned by Leoniceno. He sought, when confronted with divergent botanical evidence, to reduce it to a single medical fact. Less "scientific," Marcello Virgilio was interested in the tradition: "I shall leave it to others to discover the truth [about *borrago*] by thinking through the material that I have gathered. What concerns me is less the object (which everyone knows) than the terminology and history of *materia medica.*"[244] The practice of that subject, as he defined it in his voluminous commentary on the iris (1.1), dealt with "the science of things, not words and names." Those who professed medicine, like those who were herbalists, should draw rather on verifiable experience than on arbitrary *appellationes.*[245] Their task was botany; his, botany's lexicon and its development.

That development imported a natural philosophy colored by Marcello Virgilio's moralism. The river-crabs of his lectures[246] are treated again in his commentary on the *Materia medica* (2.10).[247] The ambiguity of the beast, like the polysemy of plants, now aroused his ire, for poets and painters abused emblems and metaphors. Enough of parasites and sycophants! As will be plain to even the meanest intelligence with the slightest grasp of science, the swollen belly of the beast is not a sign of gluttony but a gift of provident nature, which facilitates swimming. The pop-eyes of the crab are indicative less of unbridled curiosity than of judicious caution. Would that man had such attributes! exclaimed the indignant Marcello Virgilio. The figure of Janus demonstrated that antiquity was aware of these anthropological deficiencies. Nature never sets a wicked example and should not be maligned, admonished the agile dialectician, undaunted by the fact that, a handful of years previously, the interpretations that he was now rejecting had been advanced by himself.[248]

[243] Ibid., pp. 261[b]–262[a].

[244] Ibid., p. 262[a]: "Nos enim pro deprehendenda veritate cogitanda aliis haec tamen proponimus. Nec laboramus pro re (cunctis enim nota est) sed pro medicae materiae nominibus et historia."

[245] Ibid., p. 3[a]: ". . . ex aliarum plantarum similitudine aliqua multis nomina accrevisse, miscerique simul difficile intellectu in una eademque appellatione diversa penitus aliquando genera. Quod nunc etiam fieri deprehendimus ignota sibi plantarum nomina ex similitudine ad notum aliquid genus referentibus saepenumero herbariis nostris. Instabat postremo illud quod *rerum non vocum nominumve scientia haec est, decetque medicinae professores et herbarios omnis ex historia notisque et in utramque partem eventibus cunctis magis quam ex appelationibus medicam cognovisse historiam.*"

[246] See above, p. 199.

[247] 1518 edition, p. 86[b].

[248] Ibid.: ". . . monuisse haec placuit, ne quis ad turpitudinis exemplum aliquid naturam fe-

In 1518 the commentator on Dioscorides returned to a contention of his lectures on the *Aeneid* of 1502–3.[249] Natural facts provided the basis from which literature might provide verifiable exempla, while the "poetical" qualities of Dioscorides offered a means of mediating between scientific investigation and the *studia humanitatis*. In this attempt to combine the claims of empiricism with the aspirations of *enkyklios paideia,* the grammarian developed an argument *pro poetice* that was more compelling than all that he had written in twenty-four years of attention to his preferred subject. Literature integrated into the realm of *technē,* philology served the moralist, the censor, and the doctor. The methods developed by Poliziano reconciled with the standards set by Leoniceno, Marcello Virgilio's *summa* encompassed issues central to two generations of heated debate.

. . . . .

That debate was continued—not, at first, publicly, nor by Leoniceno himself, but by his pupil and colleague Giovanni Mainardi, who, in 1519, wrote to Marcello Virgilio.[250] Laid up in bed by gout, Mainardi had found solace in reading the recently published Dioscorides—a reaction not shared by its author on perusing this long and devastating critique. Replying to Mainardi on 8 March 1520, he excused his delay by injuries caused three years earlier in falling from his horse.[251] He had not noticed any response to his book—Mainardi's was the first—and had imagined the experts taking it to pieces (as, at Ferrara, they indeed were).

The correspondence of these medical invalids, framed by a comic symmetry, has nothing of the bedside manner. Mainardi was not only voicing inherited animosities; he was also defending Barbaro, to whom he acknowledged a personal debt.[252] Long-standing links with Florence—in particular with Pietro Crinito,[253] Marcello Virgilio's disgruntled rival—bound him rather to the First Chancellor's detractors than to his friends. A similarly critical view of tradition served only to widen the rift. Weeks before the publication of the Florentine Dioscorides, on 31 July 1518, Mainardi had com-

cisse credat; meminerimus omnes nihil magis hominem decere quam maledicto contumeliaque abstinuisse." See above, p. 200. For the argument, cf. Pliny *Naturalis historia* 7.1–5, and Lactantius *De opificio Dei* 1–2. On the tradition, see Kraye, "Moral Philosophy," p. 308.

[249] See above, p. 188.

[250] The letter in BRF 767, fols. 127^{r}–151^{r} (new foliation), together with two later epistles, was subsequently published in various editions of his *Epistolae medicinales* 8.1–3. Extracts are printed by Riddle, "Dioscorides," pp. 51–53.

[251] BRF 767, fol. 152^{r} (Marcello Virgilio's draft). The prolonged closure of the Biblioteca Ambrosiana (Milan) has prevented consultation of the fair copy sent to Mainardi in the Ms. S. 81, sup. fols. 192^{r}–197^{v}.

[252] See Zambelli, "La critica dell'astrologia," pp. 80ff.

[253] Cf. his letter (*Ep.* 1.4) to Crinito about *De honesta disciplina* in Mainardi, *Epistolae medicinales,* pp. 6^{a-b}.

posed a polemic against unthinking worship of ancient authority in terms that were strikingly similar to Marcello Virgilio's own.[254] At the end of a denunciation of the errors made by those inexpert in his own field of study, however, Mainardi wrote vehemently about "commentaries (as I hear) recently published," and about "new editions of Dioscorides . . . containing as many mistakes as words," with which he planned, in short order, to deal. The book in question was not yet in his hands, but Sterponi (we know) was preparing the post.

No less than three times, in long letters amounting to treatises published after Marcello Virgilio's death, Mainardi listed the solecisms—real or attributed—in his translation and commentary. Leoniceno's colleague took up cudgels for Barbaro, accusing his critic of misunderstanding and misrepresenting him, of lacking practical experience, of ignoring Galen's significance.[255] Marcello Virgilio parried the detail of the criticism, while evading its thrust: now advancing the bold assertion that his aim had not merely been to observe nature but to supplement it, *ingenio et experientia,* and "emend" Dioscorides;[256] now retreating into the feeble excuse that he had done just the opposite.[257] The culmination of his inconsistent self-apology came in its final sentence: "I have interpreted Dioscorides, not Galen; and it was my intention to harmonize others with him."[258]

Ringing and epigrammatic, this missed the point. Mainardi, exponent of empirical methods that found their theoretical justification in Galen's works, had argued in principle against such a separation.[259] Dioscorides, for him as for Leoniceno, was not a goal but a means of establishing factual truth. Suspicious of dialectic, dubious about the weighty commentary form, to which he preferred the nimbler vehicle of adversaria, unconvinced of the independent value of the *bonae litterae* that Marcello Virgilio often extolled by what seemed to him questionable appeal to natural philosophy, Mainardi, de-

[254] *Ep.* 1.1 (ibid., p. 1^{a-b}: "Ego . . . rem si ullo umquam tempore nostro saeculo summe necessariam puto hac in arte scribere eaque ingenuitate et audacia, ut veritate pro oculis habita neque autoritatis neque antiquitatis propter mille etiam annos ulla ratio habeatur. Ex ignavia etiam, et nimia in seniores observantia, factum est cognosco, ut non solum nihil arti a nostratibus sit adiectum sed et *priscorum commentaria sine delectu veluti oracula suscepta sint.*" Cf. above, p. 200.

[255] On which see Mugnai Carrara, "Nicolò Leoniceno e Giovanni Mainardi," p. 28 (cited in note 206). On the letters, cf. J. M. Riddle, "Three Previously Unknown Contributors to Pharmacy, Medicine, and Botany—Ioannes Manardus, Franciscus Frigimelica, and Melchior Guilandinus," *Pharmacy in History* 21 (1979): 144–46.

[256] BRF 767, fol. 152^r: "Fuerat ante omnia mihi consilium naturam, quatenus poteram, augere illique in eo scriptore favere; ingenio et experientia mutare emendareque multa in eo opere."

[257] Ibid., fol. 153^r: "Secutus . . . ego sum naturam et veterum codicum fidem."

[258] Ibid., fol. 157^r: "Ego enim Dioscuridem interpretatus sum, non Galenum; et alios illi concordes efficere mihi studium erat."

[259] See Premuda, "Un discepolo," pp. 43–56.

spite his wide humanistic culture, viewed the problem from a standpoint of incompatibility. An admirer of practicing doctors such as the late Antonio Benivieni, from whom his fellow Florentine differed,[260] Mainardi adopted the unflattering view of Marcello Virgilio fostered by Sterponi—regarding him as a mere *grammaticus,* a fumbling amateur, a trespasser on the autonomous territory of medicine.[261] A chasm had opened between two approaches that Marcello Virgilio's *summa* had sought to bridge, as the battle, begun by Leoniceno and Poliziano, between the professional and medical humanism of Ferrara and its literary-encyclopedic version at Florence continued into the declining years of their successors.

More receptive to Marcello Virgilio's book was its dedicatee, who summoned him to Rome soon after its publication. No effort had been spared to impress Pope Leo X with the gravity of the undertaking. For the Florentine Dioscorides a new typeface had been produced, Sterponi had reported to Leoniceno.[262] The printers had labored mightily, observed Antonio Francini two months after its publication.[263] Compared to Marcello Virgilio's "weighty work" (*grave opus*), the translation of Euripides' *Hecuba* and *Iphigenia in Aulis* by Erasmus that he had just seen through the press seemed light relief.

Lightness of touch does not distinguish the dedicatory epistle in which Marcello Virgilio bid for papal patronage. Following Aldo Manuzio's example,[264] he hailed the rebirth of learning after the devastation of war—the malady that (he claimed) accounted for his prolonged philological convalescence. Cured by the arts of peace, he offered the product of his restored intellectual health to their supreme practitioner: a Medicean pope, a *medicus* or doctor concerned with the health of the body, mind, and soul. For who would deny that "Leo X practices medicine"?

This ponderous pun, introducing a work that fills the lacuna in the history of classical scholarship between Poliziano and Vettori,[265] encapsulated a movement and a change in Italian humanism: from the skepticism of Petrarch[266] to a respectful admission of medicine's cultural importance. And it would have done the trick, winning Marcello Virgilio the favor he courted, had he not been stricken by an eye illness and by another malady, for which his Dioscorides provided no remedy.[267] Prevented from traveling to Rome

260 See Zambelli, "La critica dell'astrologia," p. 90. For Marcello Virgilio's contrary view, see above, p. 231.

261 Cf. Mugnai Carrara, "Nicolò Leoniceno e Giovanni Mainardi," p. 33.

262 Bandini, *Collectio,* cit., p. xx.

263 Bandini, *Annales,* 1:127–28: ". . . grave opus, et in quo multum excussores laboraverunt."

264 See above, p. 211.

265 See below, p. 298.

266 See above, p. 112.

267 See below, pp. 248–49.

and reaping the rewards he had sought, the thwarted invalid remained at Florence to fend off the barbs from Ferrara. His hour had come and gone; other actors were returning to a stage that he had dominated alone; but Marcello Virgilio had achieved something that none of his scholarly predecessors had attained. In a book issued with pomp and ceremony by the leading press at Florence and dedicated, in the city's interests, to its most illustrious son, had appeared the unprecedented subtitle: [*Pedacii Dioscoridis Anazarbei medica materia*] *interprete Marcello Virgilio Secretario Florentino*. Uniting the official and philological traditions of Florentine humanism, Marcello Virgilio had interpreted Dioscorides as chancellor of the Republic.

VI

THE SHADOW OF THE CHANCERY

ON 16 August 1521, at Florence, a disgraced civil servant published a blatant lie. From the Giuntine press issued the *Arte della guerra,* ascribed to one "Niccolò Machiavegli, cittadino e *Segretario Fiorentino*."

To the dignity that he claimed, Machiavelli had no right. It was not a publisher's interpolation. In the autograph manuscript, the words are written in his own hand[1]—despite the decision, taken by Florence's supreme executive board on 7 November 1512 and never revoked, to "dismiss, deprive, and totally remove [him] . . . from, and out of, the office of Second Chancellor."[2] Parallels with a modern politician who, after losing office, retains its honorific title may not be drawn. There was nothing honorific about Machiavelli's expulsion from Palazzo Vecchio or his imprisonment and torture on charges of involvement in an anti-Medicean conspiracy. Nor did the traditions of the Florentine Chancery warrant the retention, in such circumstances, of a status that Machiavelli knew that he had forfeited. Writing to Francesco Vettori, on 9 April 1513, he signed himself *quondam segretario.*[3] Weeks before the publication of the *Arte della guerra,* in letters addressed to Francesco Guicciardini during Machiavelli's mission to the Franciscan friars at Carpi, he referred to how he had come down in the world with the ironical formula "orator pro Republica Florentina ad Fratres Minores."[4] The ex-Second Chancellor was well aware of his loss of position. *Post res perditas* it rankled with him, and lent edge to his major writings.

The *Arte della guerra,* by its subject, recalled the peak of Machiavelli's public career. Between 1506 and 1512, he had been the *segretario fiorentino* who had played the leading role in the organization of the militia. Contemporaries who understood that allusion would have been struck by a precedent. Three years earlier, on the frontispiece of the grandest book yet produced by the Giunti, Marcello Virgilio, for the first time in Florence's brief history of

[1] BNCF, B.R. 29, fol. 108^r (new numeration)/fol. 177^r (old numeration).

[2] ASF, Signori e Collegi, *Deliberazioni fatte in forza di ordinaria autorità* 114, fol. 117^v: "Praefati magnifici et excelsi Domini et Vexillifer cassaverunt, privaverunt et totaliter amoverunt Niccholaum domini Bernardi de Machiavellis ab et de offitio Cancellarii secunde Cancellerie."

[3] *Ep.* 202, Machiavelli, *Opere,* p. 1132.

[4] *Ep.* 264, ibid., p. 1206 (18 May 1521). Cf. *Ep.* 264, ibid., p. 1204 (17 May 1521), with W. B. Rebhorn, "Machiavelli at Carpi: Confidence Games in the Republic of Wooden Clogs," *Italian Quarterly* 24 (1983): 27–40.

printing, had styled himself *secretarius Florentinus*.[5] How and why his former colleague pretended to the same title that, in 1521, he did not possess, are questions related to one another by two careers.

More important to Machiavelli than the belated (and minor) recognition conferred by his appointment, in April 1526, as chancellor to the Proctors of the Walls[6] was the rehabilitation implied, in the *Arte della guerra,* by the publishing house bound to the regime. By 1521 the Giunti had courted Medicean favor and followed Medicean policy for almost a decade.[7] Neither self-interest nor legislation allowed them to do otherwise. As recently as May 1518 they had printed the acts of the Florentine provincial synod of the previous year that, in the terms and spirit of the Fifth Lateran Council, imposed ecclesiastical censorship.[8] Three years and as many months later, with Leo X on the papal throne, it was not possible to present Machiavelli as *segretario fiorentino* without the sanction, or complicity, of the city's ruler. He was its archbishop—the pope's cousin, a discerning intellectual and, until he vacillated in the Vatican, a consummate statesman. His name was Cardinal Giulio de' Medici.[9]

With him Machiavelli's enemies had long been in contact. One of them was the secretary of Leo X, Piero Ardinghelli.[10] In the name of the cardinal he had written, on 14 February 1515, to quash the rumor that "Nicolò" had been taken into the service of Giuliano de' Medici.[11] The story had been spread at Florence by Paolo Vettori, Marcello Virgilio's pupil,[12] whose wagging tongue had also revealed the contents of private discussions at Rome with Lorenzo, who wished to become *del tucto signore di quella città*. That Machiavelli, both with his projected dedication of *Il principe* to Giuliano de' Medici[13] and with flattering verses offered to him,[14] was attempting to regain lost ground will surprise no one; nor should ill will be suspected on the part of Vettori, that indiscreet partisan of a principate disposed, through the

[5] See above, p. 234. Among the examples of printed works by Florentine chancellors, two of the most striking are the 1496 (Miscomini) edition of Scala's *Apologia contra vituperatores civitatis Florentiae* (see above, p. 142), written in the official persona of the city's defender, and the 1492 (Bartolomeo de' Libri) edition of Donato Acciaiuoli's translation of Bruni's history of Florence (see above, p. 142), undertaken at the command of the Signoria. Neither work attributes this title to Scala or Bruni.

[6] See Marchant, "Machiavelli cancelliere," pp. 235–48.

[7] See above, pp. 209ff.

[8] Extracts are printed in Pettas, *Giunti,* pp. 295–96. See R. Trexler, *Synodal Law in Florence and Fiesole, 1306–1518* (Vatican City, 1971), p. 112.

[9] See Guicciardini, *Storia d'Italia* 16, 12 (ed. Mazzali), pp. 1843ff.; and Vettori, *Sommario della storia d'Italia* (1523), in *Scritti storici e politici* (ed. Niccolini), p. 207.

[10] See L. Bertoni Argentini, in *DBI* 1 (Rome, 1962), p. 34; Villari, *Niccolò Machiavelli,* 2:382; and Sasso, *Machiavelli e gli antichi,* p. 265.

[11] Sasso, *Machiavelli e gli antichi,* p. 267.

[12] See above, p. 197, and Ridolfi, *Vita di Machiavelli,* p. 252ff.

[13] For the chronology, see *Il principe* (ed. Inglese), pp. viiff.

[14] After the restoration (not before the expulsion) of the Medici is more plausibly to be dated the poetry edited and discussed by Martelli, "Preistoria (medicea) di Machiavelli," pp. 377–405.

friendship of his brother Francesco with the unemployed servant of state, to find him a job.[15] More to the point of Ardinghelli's letter was the origin of the information that prompted it. Someone at Florence connected with Vettori had identified him to Giulio de' Medici as the source of a compromising leak. Someone was alarmed, in 1515, at the prospect that Giuliano might take up the author of *Il principe.*

If that work, by 1517, had a limited circulation in manuscript among Machiavelli's friends,[16] it, unlike the *Arte della guerra,* was never published during his lifetime under his own name. After the imposition of ecclesiastical censorship, *Il principe,* by a masterstroke of Medicean policy, was pressed into the service of the Church.[17] With the same period, not by chance, coincided the partial rehabilitation of the pseudo-*segretario fiorentino.* Before then, one man at Florence had been officially empowered to forbid or restrain subversive literature; and he was well placed to do so. Marcello Virgilio knew exactly what Machiavelli was about. Biagio Buonaccorsi, who was occupied in making copies of *Il principe,*[18] served as his amanuensis. Surveillance of the codices from the near distance was not difficult, and the First Chancellor had direct intelligence of the press. He was the leading collaborator of the Florentine Giunti, influencing and controlling what they might print, should a questionable writer be so rash as to submit a dubious manuscript. An expert in secret cipher,[19] Vettori's teacher was in touch with Cardinal Giulio. That may be why, apart from the trivial anecdote that Lorenzo was more interested in the gift of a pair of dogs than in the presentation of Machiavelli's book, there is no evidence that it ever reached the duke of Urbino or any other Medicean magnate at Florence. The gloved hand of the lay censor had reached out to Rome.

From the Holy City Giulio de' Medici returned to Florence after the death of Lorenzo in 1519. Only then did Machiavelli's fortunes change. Never had there been a "greater appearance of civility and liberty, a greater dissimulation of princely authority,"[20] than under the rule of that subtle cardinal. On 10 March 1520 Machiavelli was received in audience. On 8 November, the

[15] *Ep.* 243, in Machiavelli, *Opere,* p. 1193 (10 October 1516).

[16] See Stephens and Butters, "New Light on Machiavelli," pp. 54–69.

[17] See further below, pp. 253ff., 300.

[18] See Machiavelli, *De principatibus* (ed. Inglese), pp. 16ff.; and Martelli, "Da Poliziano a Machiavelli," pp. 248ff.

[19] E.g., ASF, Signori, Dieci di Balia, Otto di Pratica, *Legazioni e commissarie, Missive e responsive,* 10, fol. 397^{r}, ibid. 12, fols. 41^{r-v}. The numerous examples of Marcello Virgilio's use of cipher will be considered further in my edition.

[20] Nardi, *Istorie di Firenze,* 2:76: ". . . nè con maggiore apparenza di civiltà e di libertà, nè con maggiore dissimulazione di principato." Cf. Paolo Giovio, *Vita Leonis Decimi,* book 4 (ed. Cataudella), p. 92: "Laurentio vita functo, pontifex Iulium cardinalem Florentiam misit, ut ad clavum reipublicae sederet. Is incredibili humanitate atque munificentia singulos omnium ordinum cives complexus, ita rempublicam constituit, ut aequissimae libertatis status, renovata felici illa veterum temporum conditione, reductus esse diceretur." See Albertini, *Firenze,* pp. 31–33; and A. Prosperi in *DBI* 27 (1982), pp. 242–43.

Florentine Studio, headed by Giulio de' Medici, entrusted him with a task customarily assigned to Chancery officials: the writing ("in Latin or in Tuscan, as he pleased") of what were envisaged as the "annals or chronicles," which became the *Istorie fiorentine.*[21] And in December of the same year he composed, at the instigation of his newly acquired patron, the *Discursus florentinarum rerum post mortem iunioris Laurentii Medices* for Pope Leo X. The publication of the *Arte della guerra* solemnized Machiavelli's comeback. Yet his metamorphosis from the suspect of 1515 to the *segretario* of 1521 had not been achieved without overcoming enmities, and it was bought at a price. One reason why Machiavelli considered that price worth paying is indicated by the title that he was permitted, on paper, to reclaim. *Segretario fiorentino* not only implied a restoration of status, informal but significant; it also evoked a parallel, motivated by long-standing rivalry. How long-standing is a problem that now needs to be addressed.

. . . . .

The author of *Il principe,* intending to present it, after Giuliano's death, to Lorenzo de' Medici, planned to offer him something that he already had. A "mirror for princes," providing guidance to the problems of Florentine government and politics, had been composed, for the would-be *signore* of the city, by his uncle in 1513. What need of Machiavelli's work had the impulsive and unreflective Lorenzo when he possessed the *Instructiones* by Leo X?[22]

That useful document was concise and concrete. It advocated a policy not of institutions but of persons,[23] bound to the house of Medici. Among the individuals whom it named was Niccolò Michelozzi, former secretary of Lorenzo the Magnificent,[24] whom Leo X described as a "bono et fidatto instrumento," especially adept in dealings with the Signoria and the Dieci.[25] These were functions of the Second Chancellor, and it was Michelozzi who replaced Machiavelli in his post. Praising his trusted servant's qualities of reliability, discretion, and confidentiality, the pope defined, by tacit antithesis, those lacking in Michelozzi's predecessor.

Viewed from this perspective, it was irrelevant that Machiavelli, immedi-

[21] See below, pp. 286ff.

[22] *ASI* Appendice 1 (1843), pp. 299–306.

[23] Albertini, *Firenze,* p. 25.

[24] See Brown, *Bartolomeo Scala,* pp. 204–5: and V. Arrighi and F. Klein, "Segretari e archivi segreti in età laurenziana: Formazione e vicende delle carte Gaddi-Michelozzi," in *La Toscana al tempo di Lorenzo il Magnifico,* 3:1381–96.

[25] Cf. Vettori, *Ricordi . . . al cardinale de' Medici:* "E necessario che V.S. Rev.ma pensi come al presente queste Cancellerie si hanno a ridurre; e volendo che le faccende di stato si maneggino a'Dieci, bisognerebbe che Iuliano . . . avessi uno cancelliere che stessi a'i Dieci bene pratico delle cose di dentro e di fuora. . . . E quando voi vi abbattessi a questo istrumento che fussi pratico o fidato, e sarebbe in questo principio per lo Stato uostro un'ottima cosa." Ed. Albertini, *Firenze,* p. 359.

ately after his release from prison, hastened to write, on 13 March 1513, to Francesco Vettori, then ambassador at Rome, offering his services to Leo X.[26] The Medici perceived a difference between the tested loyalty of a Michelozzi and the temporary allegiances of a Machiavelli. Neither his bond with Soderini nor the animosities that he had aroused in the controversial performance of his duties[27] wholly account for his disgrace in 1512. Florence's new masters wanted their own man in his delicate office; and even a gray bureaucrat, more neutral and conventional than Niccolò Machiavelli,[28] would not have fitted the bill.

Why, then, was Marcello Virgilio not replaced by a Medicean partisan? The illusion of continuity is not a sufficient explanation, nor are political doubts valid. In November 1511 the First Chancellor had declared his hand—with suitable caution, of course, but in terms that had satisfied the agents of Soderini's overthrow.[29] Marcello Virgilio, however, had spoken not ex officio but ex cathedra. He had a forum—the Studio—to which Machiavelli was denied access. When the *Gonfaloniere* fell, his protégé, alienated from many of those cultivated by that deft operator of *clientela* and connections who had been his colleague, appealed to the Medici and to his friends, in order to counterbalance the influence of his enemies. In and after 1512 the precariousness of Machiavelli's position was exposed; and the mediations of Francesco Vettori at Rome were not equal to the machinations of Marcello Virgilio at Florence.

There, in the Chancery, Machiavelli and those linked to him had been difficult colleagues. The expulsion of the otherwise insignificant and unexceptionable Biagio Buonaccorsi[30] is the clearest sign of office tensions that reached back over fourteen years, some of which had political implications. In Palazzo Vecchio, where the official correspondence of the First and Second Chancellors and their assistants was often shared or conducted in common, there had existed, between 1498 and 1512, a clique of three facetious wags, headed by Niccolò Machiavelli. Applauding his sallies, urging him on, and (occasionally) counseling prudence were Buonaccorsi and Agostino Vespucci. The private letters of these bumptious bureaucrats, standing not high in the hierarchy but holding no low opinion of themselves, disclose much about the milieu of the Florentine Chancery before 1512.[31] They suggest why, by then, this trio of self-appointed wits had come to seem a thorn in the flesh of Marcello Virgilio.

Their correspondence with one another was bilingual—Latin, Italian, and

[26] *Ep.* 196, in Machiavelli, *Opere,* p. 1128.

[27] Lucidly analyzed by J. Najemy, "The Controversy Surrounding Machiavelli's Service to the Republic," in Bock, Skinner, and Viroli, *Machiavelli and Republicanism,* pp. 101–12.

[28] Cf. Black, "Machiavelli," pp. 71–100.

[29] See above, pp. 195–97.

[30] See Sasso, *Machiavelli e gli antichi,* 2:173–210.

[31] For an overview, see Marzi, *La cancelleria,* pp. 281ff.

a mixture of both. Much of its humor was verbal, deriving from puns, ribald asides, and surprising shifts of register.[32] The formal pomposity of the official medium was parodied in the written exchanges of Machiavelli, Buonaccorsi, and Vespucci, the complicity of the two coadjutors with the Second Chancellor usually counting to the cost of the First. Marcello Virgilio, for him, was a tiresome chief, Buonaccorsi suggested as early as 1499.[33] The mentality that his letter conjured up was that of the reluctant functionary, glorifying his attachments of choice and resenting those of obligation. Outwardly deferential, the circle at times pretended to open and include Marcello Virgilio. After recounting the menace of a *nobilissimus civis* that Machiavelli, if he continued to be absent, might lose his job, Vespucci, in 1500, painted a picture of the rapturous reception given to the letters of their absent colleague by a group at Palazzo Vecchio that included the First Chancellor.[34] But the harmonious idyll withered before Vespucci's customary malice. After hinting at Marcello Virgilio's impotence or inability to father a child, "he loves you like a brother," Machiavelli's correspondent assured him, "tametsi non baptizes."[35]

The joke was double-edged. What seemed a sign of unconventionality and flair to his underlings was deplored by their pious superior. Marcello Virgilio was the stuffed shirt at whom Vespucci and Buonaccorsi, with the collusion of Machiavelli, liked to poke fun. There was no moment during their long and lively correspondence from Florence, Rome, and elsewhere when the First Chancellor was ever drawn into the mirth—except as its butt.[36] And while he openly grumbled about the additional tasks that fell to his lot during Machiavelli's diplomatic missions,[37] Vespucci, behind his back, ran him down. On 14 October 1502, he described to Machiavelli the sorry scene at Palazzo Vecchio, where Marcello Virgilio neglected the letters that he ought

[32] See further below, pp. 259ff.

[33] *Ep.* 10, in Machiavelli, *Opere,* p. 1017: "Et io sono et da Marcello et da omni uno sbattuto, et stomi continue ad pregare et sollicitare che ne vegniate, ché ce n'è di bisognio. . . . Con messer Marcello, circa il respondervi presto etc, non vi sono più buono né voglio essere."

[34] *Ep.* 18, in Machiavelli, *Opere,* p. 1023: "Mihi enim quidam nobilissimus civis . . . insinuavit quod locum in Palatio tuum, ni adsis, perdis omnino. . . . Perlegi literas tuas D. Marcello, duobus aliis cancellariis et Blasio, qui omnes tenentur miro videndi tui desiderio. Jucundus enim sermo tuus urbanus et suavis."

[35] Ibid.: "Marcellus noster primarius se infra dicemnium non suscepturum prolem ex coniuge penitus assererat: quam ob rem nescio. Certo scio hoc, quod te in germani fratris loco diligit, tametsi non baptizes." Note the accuracy of Marcello Virgilio's prediction ("[non] infra dicemnium"): his eldest son, the historian Giambattista, was born in 1511.

[36] Cf. *Ep.* 22, in Machiavelli, *Opere,* pp. 1026–27; and *Ep.* 25, in ibid., pp. 1028–30.

[37] See above, p. 182, and cf. Vespucci's imputation of sloth, *Ep.* 33 (Machiavelli, *Opere,* p. 1034): "Marcellum tuis litteris excites, cohorteris, urgeas, iustes et ita flagites, ut velit aliquot dies, officio tuo fungens, onus dictandi litteras subire, non detrectare, connivere sed, ut facit, despicere. Murceam deam, postquam tu discessisti, is incolit arbitror, adeo murcidus, idest nimis desidiosus et inactuosus factus est."

to have written for irate members of the Signoria in lieu of the Second Chancellor,[38] while dreaming of moves to oust the First. "I wish that no one but you was my superior," the self-conscious slanderer declared to Machiavelli.[39] Empty words, coming from a political nonentity like Agostino Vespucci, but they indicate the atmosphere of back-biting in the Florentine Chancery.

It was worsened, in 1504, by a comedy that, Giuliano de' Ricci reported,[40] his grandfather had written at Marcello Virgilio's prompting. Aristophanic in inspiration, ominously entitled *Le maschere,* it gave voice to Machiavelli's satirical spirit. Marcello Virgilio's spirit was different, and less irreverent his suggestion had doubtless been. At the Studio he lectured on Aristophanes, frequently citing his works as moral exempla. But this academic politician never emphasized the political satire of the Greek playwright, and he would have shrunk in horror at the thought that any of his pupils—much less his colleagues—might have taken *The Clouds* as a model to criticize leading citizens of Florence. That was just what Machiavelli did, according to Ricci ("Sotto nomi finti va lacerando et mal trattando molti di quelli cittadini"); and the acerbity of its attack explained why his grandson suppressed *Le maschere* after his death.

Not for the first time in 1504 (nor for the last[41]) did the Second Chancellor cause embarrassment to the First. Like Marcello Virgilio, Machiavelli was an elected official who depended on the approval of the Signoria for renewal of his post. That, in the eyes of the cautious colleague, ought to have entailed a discretion that the author of *Le maschere,* with his two confederates in satirical provocation, flouted. Ill-advised sallies on prominent burghers; overwork, resented (and, whenever possible, avoided) during the travels of Machiavelli; office plots of little moment but lasting irritation, punctuated by snide comments and barbed asides; the successes of Soderini's favorite in contrast to the marginalization of Marcello Virgilio: such tensions, heightened by the dissatisfaction of many at the Second Chancellor's dilatoriness in public correspondence, indicate why he seemed, to this beleaguered bureaucrat, an awkward cuss. Among the factors that contributed to Machiavelli's "dismissal, deprivation, and total removal from and out of the Chancery," one may have been neglected: the push, concealed but comprehensible, that came from within.

. . . . .

[38] *Ep.* 33, in Machiavelli, *Opere,* p. 1033: ". . . vereor, ne maledicus habear et praesertim in Marcellum. . . . Marcellus tanquam rei, hoc est officii tui, neglector, onus scribendi reicit."

[39] Ibid.: "Velim equidem quod nullus praeter te astaret mihi essetque in Cancelleria superior."

[40] For the text of his *Priorista,* see F. Neri, "Sulle prime commedie fiorentine," *Rivista teatrale italiana* 14 (1915): 6; and Ventrone, *Gli araldi della commedia,* p. 194 and n. 82. For background, see Raimondi, *Politica e commedia,* pp. 235–52.

[41] Cf. *Ep.* 101, in Machiavelli, *Opere,* p. 1071 (6 February 1506).

Within and without the Chancery, the interests of members of the ruling house and of Marcello Virgilio converged and, during the long winter (1513–19) of Machiavelli's disgrace, his former colleague, unchallenged at Palazzo Vecchio, basked in the sun of celebrity. On two ceremonious occasions—the conferment on Lorenzo de' Medici of the *bastone* or truncheon symbolic of military command over Florentine forces, on 12 August 1515, and the funeral of his uncle Giuliano on 17 March 1516—the First Chancellor delivered orations. And if, at Leo X's triumphal entry into the city in November 1515, Marcello Virgilio had to content himself with offering verses to the pope, no other intellectual was permitted to make a speech.[42] Until 1519, at Florence, the monopoly of the official word belonged to this spokesman of the state.

The Florentine state was not yet the uncontested dominion of the Medici. Nor were Giuliano and Lorenzo, in practice, the happy rivals imagined by Jacopo Nardi in his comedy of that title.[43] Between the disputing Medicean dauphins, their respective roles yet to be defined, mediated with difficulty Leo X, seconded by Cardinal Giulio. Against the policy of moderation advocated by Rome, aimed at establishing a "civic principate" to reconcile the republican and oligarchical traditions of the city with the primacy of their house,[44] strove the ambitious Alfonsina Orsini, Lorenzo's mother, and her allies. Despite the misgivings of the head of the family in the Holy City and the opposition of such patricians at Florence as Giambattista Ridolfi and Jacopo Salviati, she and her supporters contrived to make her son captain-general of the Republic.[45] Had not Giuliano been recently created captain-general of the Church? Indeed he had, acknowledged the pope, but neither of his demanding relatives had any experience in military posts usually occupied by professionals. How they would perform in time of need, the perplexed pontiff had no idea.

Nor had Marcello Virgilio when he composed his oration for the ceremony. Only once before had he written a speech of this kind—in 1498, when the ill-fated *condottiere* Paolo Vitelli had been put in charge of troops sent to recapture Pisa.[46] Then the First Chancellor, new to his office, had been content to play variations on a theme of Bruni's.[47] Then Florence had

[42] See above, p 213.

[43] See above, p. 212.

[44] Cf. *Ep.* 226, in Machiavelli, *Opere,* p. 1172 (February–March 1514).

[45] For the context, see Giorgetti, "Lorenzo de' Medici," pp. 194–215; and Trexler, "Two Captains," p. 175. On the opposition, see H. Reinhard, "Lorenzo von Medici, Herzog von Urbino 1492–1515: Ein biographischer Versuch unter besonderer Berücksichtigung der Vermittlerrolle Lorenzos zwischen Leo X und Franz II von Frankreich im Jahre 1550," diss. phil., Freiburg, 1935, p. 33; Albertini, *Firenze,* pp. 31ff.; and Devonshire Jones, *Francesco Vettori,* pp. 111ff.

[46] *L* fols. 17^r–24^r. For context, see M. Mallett, *Mercenaries and Their Masters: Warfare in Renaissance Italy* (London, 1974), pp. 248–49.

[47] See C. C. Bayley, *War and Society in Renaissance Florence: The "De Militia" of Leonardo Bruni*

been a "popular" republic, ruled by a *governo popolare*. Now the expelled Medici had returned to power and Lorenzo was to command not only foreign mercenaries but also the Florentine militia.[48] Was the pope's nephew to receive his symbol of leadership as a citizen invested with the exceptional powers by the civic authorities? Or was he to accept the truncheon as homage paid by the city to its *signore*?

The orator was placed in a difficult position. Ex officio the mouthpiece of the Signoria, Marcello Virgilio was decidedly a Medicean. The Medici, however, were divided among themselves. If lordship, or an approximation to it, was to be had by maintaining a veneer of republicanism, as Leo X and Cardinal Giulio thought, Lorenzo, his mother, and their followers desired both the appearance and the substance of princely rule. To this quandary, Marcello Virgilio found an elegant solution. He feigned ignorance. About the art of war, he declared, he knew nothing; he was "a townsman ever occupied, up to now, with pursuits of peace."[49] One fact, however, was clear and must be spelled out: neither the influence of the pope nor the designs of his Florentine family had secured for Lorenzo this appointment as captain-general. It had emerged through felicitous collaboration between church and state, uniting public and private interests. Order was needed—a combination of wisdom and force, law and arms.[50] What that meant was, responsibility lay elsewhere. How judicious the fathers of the Republic had been to establish the militia! From that decision it followed logically that one citizen should be made commander—a *civis,* emphasized Marcello Virgilio, of unchallenged authority in this sphere. "One prince, one arbiter, one lord"—the refrain, Pindaric in origin, was repeated from his lectures—but only "in war."[51]

In peace a different and more mighty prince reigned: Leo X.[52] With him, of course, the budding warlord's relations were harmonious. How could they be otherwise? Consider Lorenzo's forebears: Cosimo, Piero, the great Medici who was his namesake—and there Marcello Virgilio stopped. No, it was not his task to write contemporary history. If his audience expected it, it was to be disappointed. Memories were fresh, the past demanded reflection. It was one thing to deliver an encomium on the militia and its command, which only required demonstration of their necessity and their utility: quite another

---

(Toronto, 1961), pp. 369–97, with P. O. Kristeller, review article in *Canadian Historical Review* 44 (1963): 65–69, and L. Gualdo Rosa, "L'elogio delle lettere e delle armi nell'opera di Leonardo Bruni," in *Sapere e/è potere: Discipline, dispute, e professioni nell'università medievale e moderna: Il caso bolognesi a confronto,* vol. 1, *Forme e oggetti della disputà delle arti,* ed. L. Avellini (Bologna, 1990), pp. 109ff.

[48] Trexler, "Two Captains," p. 175.

[49] *R* fol. 60^{v}: ". . . urbanus homo et in studiis pacis semper hactenus occupatus."

[50] *R* fol. 62^{r}.

[51] *R* fol. 64^{r}: "Vocatoque ad militare imperium uno et cive hoc vestro rempublicam tueri simul et ornare cogitastis. . . . Unum oportet esse principem in bello, unum arbitrum, unum dominum." Cf. pp. 158 and 191 above.

[52] *R* fol. 64^{v}.

to describe recent events, which demanded careful analysis of the *causae rerum* and a complete narrative of all that had happened.[53]

Completeness would have involved continuing the lineage of Lorenzo de' Medici to include his father. Piero, still hated at Florence, might have weakened the case for Medicean capacity in leadership. Better, therefore, not to mention him. No word either of Giuliano. Instead Marcello Virgilio extolled the Sforza at Milan, the Este at Ferrara, and the Orsini at Rome.[54] Alfonsina, the captain-general's mother, was an Orsini; and she, too, found a place in the international sweep of his eulogy. Lorenzo, it implied, was no provincial potentate. His connections outside Florence bolstered his local power, to which his military command permitted regal and imperial analogies.

On 12 August 1515, Marcello Virgilio nailed his changing colors to the mast. Beginning with praise of the captain-general's office, he ended by declaring allegiance to its holder: a "civic" prince, legitimated by just decisions of the Florentine authorities, supported by the pope, and comparable with the aristocratic rulers of other Italian cities. The contrast with the professor's lectures on Virgil of 1502–3, which had distinguished between the metaphorical monarchy of the *Gonfaloniere a vita* and the unadmired person of Piero Soderini, could not have been greater.[55] Like other Florentine humanists of the same period,[56] Marcello Virgilio now sought to attach himself to Lorenzo de' Medici. And as the thwarted dedicator of *Il principe* to the same patron observed his former colleague, on the public stage, making of his inability to compose an *arte della guerra* the pretext with which to support Lorenzo in his ambitions, the seeds of one of his future projects may have been sown in his mind. Four years and three months before receiving the commission to write the *Istorie fiorentine,* on hearing or being informed of the speech in which the First Chancellor balked at the task of narrating and analyzing contemporary events, Machiavelli glimpsed another of his undertakings. The history of Florence before and during the time of the Medici, together with the art of war—subjects that a *secretarius Florentinus* was entitled to treat—were to become his chief concerns. In 1515, however, his time had not yet arrived. From the podium, Marcello Virgilio aligned himself with what then seemed the winning side in the struggle for power, while Machiavelli, demoted and disgruntled, mingled with the crowd.

[53] *R* fol. 65^{r}: "Sentio expectari a vobis integram Medice gentis et eorum precipue, quos paulo ante memoravimus rerum gestarum historiam, sed nihil est quod iustius et libentius in labore hoc nostro omittamus, non quia pauciora sunt relatuve indigna . . . sed quod apud eos agimus, qui plura per se meminisse possint quam longiore meditatione ex omnibus commentariis dici hoc loco potuissent et quod aliud est de militia militarique imperio agere apud vos, aliud historiam scribere. Hec causas rerum et eventus omnes narrare exigit: illa satis habet, si demonstrata utilitate et necessitate honeste constituantur."

[54] *R* fols. 65^{r-v}.

[55] See pp. 192–93 above.

[56] Bausi, "'Extincta viret laurus,'" pp. 185–217.

An audience that included Bartolomeo Cerretani was favorable to Marcello Virgilio's oration. "Moltto bella" was Cerretani's comment on his speech.[57] Soon he had another to deliver. On 17 March 1516 Giuliano de' Medici died, and the unity of the regime was to be celebrated at his funeral.[58] Nothing of the kind had been provided for Cosimo or Lorenzo de' Medici, who had prudently declined such public honors.[59] But the aspiring *signore* of Florence wished to reconcile his standing with the aspirations of the city's elite, and Giuliano's death provided the occasion. The *bono et fidatto instrumento* who gave voice to Lorenzo's policy was the obliging First Chancellor.

This was an undertaking for which Marcello Virgilio was better prepared. His thought, even under the *governo popolare,* had never been egalitarian.[60] The apologist of the *reggimento* had always abhorred the faintest whiff of populism. Proper hierarchies were to be respected and true nobility defended: not the *nobilitas* of birth but an aristocracy of the intellect, soaring above the plebs by its lofty virtue and enlightened patronage. The one quality revealed and reinforced the other. Support for scholarship and, in particular, the encouragement of deserving professors proved the claim of the Medici to *virtus.*[61] (Poliziano had made the same claim.[62]) Viewed as a dynasty, their eminence was less inherited than merited by experience. Although some of that had been bitter, did not the study of nature teach that plants trampled underfoot blossomed with renewed strength? Were not the laurel and the plane trees, situated at the edge of the field, maltreated by passersby and buffeted by storms, similar, in their resilience, to Lorenzo's family?[63]

The commentator on Dioscorides was already at work; the professor was dreaming of patronage; and the First Chancellor, economical with effort, recycled his *praelusio* of 1514. Its analogies to Sparta and Rome[64] furnished his model of the Florentine polity: aristocratic but governed by a "civic" prince in alliance with an elite that held in check the demagogic urges of the people. This did not represent acceptance of the alleged "program" of the Orti Oricellari and the circle of Rucellai:[65] such ideas were shared by the pope himself and by Giulio de' Medici. Nor was the position that Marcello Virgilio assumed new. All his instincts had been moving in that direction, even before 1512. What had changed was the fact that he had a name and an individual to which they might be attached; and his panegyric on Giuliano was

[57] Cerretani, *Ricordi* (ed. Berti), p. 330.

[58] The speech is edited and discussed by McManamon, "Marketing a Medici Regime."

[59] See above, p. 14.

[60] See above, pp. 158–59.

[61] McManamon, "Marketing a Medici Regime," p. 30.

[62] See above, p. 3.

[63] McManamon, "Marketing a Medici Regime," pp. 33 and 34.

[64] See above, p. 201.

[65] *Pace* McManamon, "Marketing a Medici Regime," p. 13.

less concerned with the dead Medici whose few achievements formed its ostensible subject than with his living nephew. Namesake of the great Lorenzo, he would found a new Athens.[66] Learning, culture, and piety would flourish in the newfound harmony between religious and lay authorities. In March 1516, Marcello Virgilio visualized the fulfillment of the ideal for which he had yearned in November 1511.[67] Lorenzo de' Medici, the actual recipient of this encomium on his uncle, and Leo X, future dedicatee of Marcello Virgilio's Dioscorides, were to usher in a golden age. That illusion, shaken by the secular messiah's political misfortunes and disagreements with the pope after 1516,[68] was shattered by Lorenzo's death in 1519; and his encomiast, already weakened in health,[69] this time was seen to have espoused a lost cause. Fortune, of which the long-term survivor had made light in his oration, began to turn her wheel, and, by the law of inverse symmetry that governed their careers, the star of Niccolò Machiavelli commenced its reascent as Marcello Virgilio's declined.

. . . . .

The first indication of his fall from grace came swiftly. In May 1519 the First Chancellor did not deliver the funeral oration on Lorenzo de' Medici, although this was one of his official duties. The speech was made by Francesco da Diacceto, who, the following year, became *Gonfaloniere,*[70] a dignity for which his colleague was technically eligible, but which he never achieved. In 1520 Marcello Virgilio's contract at the Studio was renewed only for the months March to June.[71] During the remainder of the academic year he was replaced by Stefano Sterponi, the arch-intriguer from Pescia who, in 1518, had sought to incite Leoniceno against him.[72]

Sterponi had the characteristics of a river-crab described in the less flattering of Marcello Virgilio's two interpretations.[73] If not endowed with a bloated belly, his stand-in at the Studio possessed a forked tongue. While maligning Marcello Virgilio to those whom he hoped would harm his rival, he was toadying to others from whom he aspired to receive the professor's chair. When he obtained a teaching post in 1519, Sterponi turned to celebrating himself the skills that he had previously displayed in praising Florentine football.[74] On the point of departing for Ferrara with the offer of a good post,

[66] Ibid., p. 34.

[67] See above, p. 196.

[68] See Devonshire Jones, "Lorenzo de' Medici, Duca d'Urbino," pp. 299–315; and cf. A. Verdi, *Gli ultimi anni di Lorenzo de' Medici, Duca d'Urbino* (Este, 1905).

[69] See above, p. 231.

[70] Kristeller, "Francesco da Diacceto," p. 303.

[71] ASF, Studio Fiorentino e Pisano (Ufficiali dello Studio) 8, fols. 95^r, 136^v, 178^v, 182^v.

[72] See above, p. 217.

[73] See above, p. 199.

[74] See C. Nardini, ed., *Il giuoco del calcio: Lettera di Filopono a Francesco Onesti* (Florence, 1898),

he had been astonished (so he claimed on 22 February 1519) by appointment to a better one at Florence. Sterponi dismounted from his horse and, "with the instant agreement of the Signoria and to the great satisfaction of the entire city," accepted Marcello Virgilio's salary to teach what he described as "moral philosophy and rhetoric."[75]

Twice, in the course of a few lines, Sterponi expressed his glee at an income equivalent to that of the scholar whom he pretended to have supplanted, and to whom he momentarily warmed. The plodding *grammaticus* ridiculed in 1518[76] now became "the learned and good Marcello." This revisionism toward his predecessor was intended to justify the attribution to Sterponi of the same qualities. That it was as false as his other assertions is demonstrated by what he was actually paid: 90 florins—to teach not "moral philosophy and rhetoric" but poetry and oratory at a level below that of full professor—as opposed to the 300 that had been earned by Marcello Virgilio.[77] The *Ufficiali dello Studio,* unlike Sterponi himself, had no inflated notion of his merits; nor was the land of milk and honey that beckoned him in February 1519 slow to turn to dust. On 27 May he wrote to Cardinal Giulio, lamenting that Diacceto (with a salary more than five times the size of his own) had been chosen to speak at the funeral of the duke of Urbino. Importunate as ever, Sterponi solicited an audience, commended himself, and enclosed his unwanted oration.[78] He was ignored. In February of the following year, matters had become worse; and the unappreciated intellectual wrote, at greater length and with greater vehemence, tendering his resignation. Florence was thankless. It had failed to marvel at the pearls of wisdom that, in his allegorical reading of the *Aeneid,* Sterponi had cast before its youthful swine.[79] He was not a Marcello Virgilio (now re-demoted to a mere *homo grammaticus*[80]), but an eminent philosopher and a mistreated foreigner, like Chrysoloras. In a city where, after the restoration, it had become fashionable to pour forth floods of ink in praise of Florentine learning, Sterponi swam against the current. All the distinguished scholars who had taught there had been foreigners, he jibed; all had been mishandled, maligned, and subjected to envy. *Invidia* and denigration, pusillanimity and malice—attributes that Sterponi possessed in abundance—had been leveled, he protested,

---

with H. Bredekamp, *Florentiner Fussball: Die Renaissance der Spiele* (Frankfurt, 1993), pp. 17, 69, 75, 82, 92.

[75] "Inventutem Florentinam publice doceo tum moralem philosophiam tum oratoriam facultatem . . . cum iam equum ascenderem Ferrariam profecturus, ut illic publice bonas artes profiterer, continuo Marcello Dominorum scribae publico stipendio suffecti sumus, idque alacri consensu Dominorum nec sine magna voluptate totius civitatis." BRF 911, fol. 65^{v}.

[76] See above, p. 218.

[77] ASF, Studio Fiorentino e Pisano (Ufficiali dello Studio) 8, fols. 88^{v}, 95^{r}, 135^{r}, 136^{v}, 175^{v}, 178^{r}, 179^{v}.

[78] BRF, 911, fol. 11^{v}.

[79] Ibid., fols. 73^{r}ff.

[80] Ibid., fol. 76^{v}.

against his undervalued talent.[81] Not but what the misunderstood genius remained convinced of his superiority. He had proof. Had not Bologna offered him a higher salary? There he was recognized. There he would be paid according to his deserts. It was not that he was unworthy of Florence, but that Florence was unworthy of him.[82] And, thumbing his nose at its obtuse provincials, Sterponi remounted his horse and rode out of the city gates.

. . . . .

Behind him he left the *Ufficiali dello Studio* with little option but to reinstate Marcello Virgilio,[83] now recovering from his diplomatic illness. That his malady was not so superficial, nor its cure so simple, is suggested by a letter written from Rome by his financial agent, Michele Venturi, on 5 May 1520.[84] Venturi was no insignificant name in Italian commerce and politics. The Venturi had been partners in the Medicean bank,[85] and its representatives at Bruges and Rome. In the Holy City Michele had the ear of pope and cardinals, and what he had heard, seen, and reported to Marcello Virgilio chilled his blood.

It was not so much the *calumnia* and *malevolentia* recounted by Venturi that shook the First Chancellor. He, to judge from his agent's reply, was already aware of moves against him and had appealed to Venturi for help. What was disturbing, to Marcello Virgilio, was the news that his letters had "fallen by chance" (*temere inciderunt*) into the hands of Cardinals Salviati and Ridolfi, for Venturi implied that his client's correspondence had been intercepted by his foes. Both were relatives of the Medici. Giovanni Cardinal Salviati was among the first to receive a copy of the *Arte della guerra*.[86] His influential father, Jacopo, an opponent of Lorenzo de' Medici's desire to establish a principate, attempted to revive Machiavelli's career.[87] Niccolò Cardinal Ridolfi owned an autograph of the *Discorsi*.[88] Both, in person, wielded influence at the papal court; both, through their powerful families, had been linked with

[81] "Turpe duci vobis non inveniri alter, quem Marcello homini grammatico surrogetis! Quid aliud est quam malignus invidiae livore, quem duobus illis pretiosissimis feris iunctum avaritiae, sed atque superbiae vobis inesse manifesto clamavit Dantes Aligherius in ea poesi, quam vernacula lingua doctissime fecit? Hac ipsa de causa expulsus est Chrysoloras ille Bizantinus." Ibid., fols. 77^{v}.

[82] "Nos hinc discedimus hoc temporis puncto Bononiam profecturi, ut illic publice doceamus magno salario acciti. Tu tuis Florentinis prospice, ut facis!" Ibid., fol. 77^{v}.

[83] ASF, Studio Fiorentino e Pisano (Ufficiali dello Studio) 8, fols. 137^{v}–138^{r}, 184^{r}.

[84] Bandini, *Collectio,* p. 33.

[85] R. de Roover, *The Rise and Decline of the Medici Bank, 1397–1494* (Cambridge, Mass., 1963), pp. 36, 91, 249, 231.

[86] Ridolfi, *Vita di Machiavelli,* pp. 330, 555.

[87] Ibid., pp. 330ff.; and Devonshire Jones, "Lorenzo de' Medici, Duca d'Urbino," p. 305.

[88] Ridolfi, *Vita di Machiavelli,* p. 531.

aristocratic resistance to the designs of the duke of Urbino, which Marcello Virgilio had been seen to support. Deprived, by Lorenzo's death, of the patron who had guaranteed his position, he was being undermined at Rome by two Florentine cardinals acting in concert. His potent enemies were Machiavelli's highly placed friends. The consequences were plain and permanent. Again relegated to the wings of the stage on which he had strutted, in 1521 Marcello Virgilio passed into the oblivion that would last for half a millennium. Commemorated after his death by a monument that does not even mention his name,[89] the erstwhile éminence grise had been offered cold comfort by Venturi's assurance that both *amici* and *inimici* would not only praise his "supreme prowess in literature but also his unbelievable humanity."[90] The last word on Marcello Virgilio was, suitably, ambiguous.

. . . . .

While Lorenzo de' Medici lived and was served by the First Chancellor, the way to Machiavelli's rehabilitation was blocked. Only after the duke's demise and the marginalization of Marcello Virgilio could the second *segretario fiorentino* assert his dubious claim to that title. Sponsored by patricians whose cooperation the new ruler of Florence needed, Machiavelli's comeback was cast in terms that recalled Palazzo Vecchio. Giulio de' Medici understood his wish to wipe out his disgrace. Hence the tolerance showed toward the publication of the *Arte della guerra* with the fiction of its author's office; hence the commission to write the *Istorie fiorentine*. Issued from the Studio, Marcello Virgilio's haunt during more than a quarter of a century, it situated Machiavelli in the tradition of famous Florentine chancellors, such as Scala; and it pointed to a large lacuna. That history, like an art of war, represented an enterprise before which his rival had faltered. The desire to excel where Marcello Virgilio had failed; revenge for the humiliations that had followed 1512; the challenge of two undertakings with political overtones: the shadows that darkened Machiavelli's career on his expulsion from the Chancery were to be lightened and lifted by services rendered to a Medicean prince of the church.

In Giulio (not Giuliano nor Lorenzo) de' Medici—the central, most significant, and least studied *principe* in his checkered experience—were united the qualities that Machiavelli sought in a "civic" prince. At Florence, between 1519 and 1522, the cardinal practiced his own version of the policy advocated by *Il principe* with dexterity and guile. Why he was vital to Machiavelli

[89] For the inscription and bust in S. Salvatore al Monte, see A. Cecchi in *L'officina della maniera,* pp. 102–3 (no. 15).

[90] Bandini, *Collectio,* p. 33: "Hoc sane ad cumulum laudum tuarum adcedet, quod omnes amici tui pariter, et inimici non solum Te summa literaruum virtute, verum etiam incredibili praeditum humanitate praedicabunt."

requires no emphasis. How the author of the *Arte della guerra* and the *Istorie fiorentine* served Giulio's purposes is not wholly explained by the Florentine character of these works and their local setting. To appreciate the cardinal's intentions, it is necessary to look beyond the confines of the city to the wider European scene. There, in the years 1519–23, one ruler (seldom remarked on by Machiavelli) was of decisive importance to his Medicean master: the emperor Charles V.

His election, on 28 June 1519, had been backed by Giulio. In the struggle between Charles V and Francis I, king of France, the cardinal had consistently taken the imperial side.[91] The treaty that Leo X signed with the emperor on 8 May 1521 promised him the investiture of Naples in return for maintaining the Medici at Florence.[92] Against the "Lutheran poison" Charles offered antidotes, while a papal-imperial alliance raised hopes of regaining Italy's *libertas*. When the pope died in December 1521, and the cardinal de' Medici, after failing to obtain a majority in the conclave, proposed Adrian of Utrecht, the situation changed. Adrian VI displayed no gratitude, and intended to begin a reform of the Church with the Sacred College. No longer the principal adviser of the reigning pontiff, Giulio de' Medici returned to Florence in October 1522, where he pursued the same strategy that was to secure him the throne of St. Peter a year later with imperial support. By interest and by conviction, he had every motive for seeking to influence the emperor.

What, therefore, could have been more natural for this Florentine archbishop than to present Charles V with a Florentine "mirror for princes"? One was available, composed by a sometime *segretario fiorentino* dependent on his grace and favor. Its author was in no position to decline a request or refuse an order. Machiavelli was poised between past disrepute and partial restoration. And if *Il principe* did not correspond, in every respect, to Giulio's image of rulership, the mirror simply required adjustment by a Medicean courtier. Not only Niccolò Machiavelli was Machiavellian.

Medici was the adoptive name of a courtier much favored by the family. Its appearance on the title page of Agostino Nifo's *De regnandi peritia,* published at Naples in 1523,[93] intimated who stood behind the book, completed on 3 October 1522 at Sessa, the philosopher's hometown. The duke of Sessa was Charles V's ambassador at Rome. Nifo, too, was an academic diplomat, with a sense of time and place. Author of a *De re aulica,* modeled on Castiglione's *Il cortigiano* but distilling his own rich experience, he knew that success in his chosen art of lifemanship demanded more than the ability to flat-

[91] See Price Zimmermann, *Paolo Giovio,* pp. 30, 35.

[92] Nitti, *Leone X,* pp. 425ff. and 460; and K. Brandi, *Kaiser Karl V. Werden and Schicksal einer Persönlichkeit und eines Weltreiches* (Munich, 1959), pp. 122ff.

[93] On Nifo, see Mahoney, "Nifo, A.," pp. 122–24.

ter and entertain a prince.[94] It also involved writing—or, when need be, rewriting. Voluminous in his productivity, this opportunist weighed up the advantages of serving the most recent and powerful authority. Recognition, in the form of a series of handsomely paid professorships, led Nifo from Naples and Salerno to the Holy City where, in the chair of philosophy to which he had been called by Leo X, he attacked the views of his Paduan rival, Pietro Pomponazzi, on the immortality of the soul. Attracted to Pisa, where the pope to whom he dedicated that work had studied, by an enormous salary and deference to his fame,[95] he was created count palatine and granted the rights to use the name of his patron and to issue degrees. By 1520 Agostino Nifo was established as the house philosopher of the Medici.

In April of that year his links with their regime found concrete expression in a tract for the times. *De falsa diluvii prognosticatione,* published by the Florentine Giunti, which set out to refute prophecies of an apocalyptic flood in 1524,[96] was offered to the emperor. *Dialectica ludicra,* which lampoons in its preface the uselessness of philosophers in governing the state, followed in August with an inscription to Cardinal Salviati, supporter of Machiavelli. In April 1521, on the (for Florence) unusual subject *Quae ab optimis principibus agenda sunt,*[97] Nifo extended and established his claim to be viewed as the leading intellectual in Medicean cultural politics. That claim was encyclopedic—Nifo presented himself as omnicompetent—and it was recognized in the city both because he enjoyed the support of the ruling house and because he was regarded as the perfect candidate to complete a long-standing project initiated by the Giunti. In the preface to his edition of Alexander of Aphrodisias's commentary on Aristotle's *Analytica priora,* Antonio Francini, in December 1521, hailed Nifo as the natural heir to Marcello Virgilio's enterprise of *enkyklios paideia.* "We have done the poets, orators, and historians," declared this optimistic agent of the Giuntine press. "Now we shall do dialectic, presently ethics and politics." Nifo was just the man to take over where the firm's recently deceased collaborator had left off. The First Chancellor had prepared a complete edition of Aristotle, on almost all of whose works his designated successor would comment.

The legacy of Marcello Virgilio handed to him on a plate, Agostino Nifo turned it down in favor of more pressing tasks. On the first day of the month in which Francini made his offer, Leo X died; and Giulio de' Medici had

94 *De re aulica* 1.5 (*Augustini Niphi sua tempestate,* ed. Naudé, pp. 246ff.). On Nifo and Castiglione, see P. Burke, *The Fortunes of the Courtier* (Oxford, 1995), p. 48.

95 Turin, Biblioteca civica, Raccolte storiche, fondo Cosilla 62 (*Ufficiali dello Studio* to Francesco Vettori, 15 January 1519 [= 1520]).

96 On these prophecies, and the genre in which Nifo wrote, see Cantimori, *Umanesimo,* pp. 164ff.; and Zambelli, "Fine del mondo," pp. 291–368.

97 See Dionisotti, *Machiavellerie,* p. 132.

more need than ever of imperial support. Now began the period, which was to last for two years, when he most determinedly sought the ear of Charles V. And the restless Nifo, attentive to the desires of his patron yet pining for the south, discharged his debt to the cardinal before departing for Salerno and Naples. Florence was not stable, as a conspiracy against Giulio de' Medici in May 1522 was to show. That the emperor could intervene even at his power base was demonstrated by the imperial party's insistence, against the will of the cardinal, on harsh punishment of the conspirators.[98] But before seeking safety and advancement in the dominions of Charles V, Nifo completed *De regnandi peritia,* which combined his interests with those of Giulio de' Medici.

So it was, by a double irony, that having turned down the mantle of Marcello Virgilio, Agostino Nifo came to spin a new garment from Machiavelli's web. *De regnandi peritia* is not a mere plagiarism but a rewriting of *Il principe* in the light of Giulio's policy. It represents the second, more creative, phase of censorship to which that book was subjected after the *non imprimatur* of the first.[99] Discerning a potential *speculum principis* in the work, which Machiavelli intended for a secular ruler, this prince of the church initiated a course that the ecclesiastical authorities would follow, with variations, for many years. In 1594 the plan of Machiavelli's grandson, Niccolò, and of Giuliano de' Ricci to bring out an expurgated edition of his writings was not to be realized, because the cardinals responsible for the Index wished them to be printed under another name.[100] The price that the *segretario fiorentino* paid to Giulio de' Medici for his rehabilitation continued to be exacted, in a less subtle form of censorship, from his descendants.

The idea, so unthinkable to Machiavellian scholars,[101] that their hero was aware of what, in 1522 and 1523, was being done to his work is not only plausible but probably understated. Acquiescence in the will of his master was entailed by Machiavelli's desire for recognition. If he lost *Il principe* to Giulio, he gained from him the *Arte della guerra* and the *Istorie fiorentine*. What the cardinal needed was a civilizing model of a "civic" prince to lighten the heavy hand of his imperial ally that, as recently as the spring of 1522, he had felt at Florence. When, therefore, on 26 March 1523, *De regnandi peritia* appeared at Naples, the place was chosen not to spare Machiavelli's feelings in his native city, nor simply to further Nifo's aims in the south, but to continue the campaign to win Charles V's support from the heartland, strategic and financial, of his Italian realms.[102] Like the location, the timing was carefully

[98] Francesco Vettori, *Sommario della istoria d'Italia (1511–1527),* in idem, *Scritto storici e politici,* ed. E. Niccolini (Bari, 1972), pp. 133–246.

[99] See above, p. 237.

[100] See Appendix below.

[101] Dionisotti, *Machiavellerie,* p. 128 (citing Ridolfi).

[102] See G. Coniglio, *Il regno di Napoli al tempo di Carlo V* (Naples, 1951), pp. 250ff.; and

judged. On 23 April Giulio de' Medici, formerly out of favor with Adrian VI, entered the Holy City in triumph. A papal-imperial league for the defense of Milan was announced in consistory on 29 July, and signed on 3 August. The cardinal, regarded as its architect, declared Florence's adherence. The duke of Sessa had been informed by the emperor on 13 July that he regarded Giulio as his most faithful ally and that the backing of the imperialists should be given to him in the likely event of a forthcoming papal election. When that occurred, as predicted, after the death of Adrian VI on 14 September, Charles V's support was a necessary condition for the cardinal's elevation, prepared by a policy that included rewriting, for imperial consumption, a work composed by a critic of the church.

Machiavelli's chapter 11, *De principatibus ecclesiasticis,* was accordingly altered beyond recognition. Among Nifo's other revisions of the text,[103] some of the most far-reaching affected those chapters (24 and 26) that deal with war and the exhortation to free Italy from its invaders. Giulio de' Medici, even before the formation of the papal alliance with Charles V in 1521, had been opposed to the armed struggle involved in Leo X's attempt to regain Parma and Piacenza for the church. A bellicose emperor was the last thing he desired, and he had long believed that Italian freedom could best be obtained by conciliation between Rome and the Hapsburgs. Rather a pacific principate than an autocratic monarchy, wielding power through consensus, was the Florentine model of rulership that he charged Nifo to hold up to Charles V.[104] *De regnandi peritia,* not primarily designed for the local audience of feudal Naples,[105] was intended to play a part on the international stage of high politics that had recently witnessed the debut of Erasmus's *Institutio principis christiani.*[106] Nifo's patron had pondered his strategy.

Giulio de' Medici, like his cousin Giovanni, was a dialectical thinker. Caution, appearing to some of their contemporaries as indecisiveness,[107] characterized their conduct of papal affairs. Popes Leo X and Clement VII were inclined to see two sides of each question, and then to multiply them. Experience naturally counted in this respect, but so did training. If exile and the loss of power encouraged circumspection in its subsequent exercise, both had also been educated at the Studio of Pisa, where Nifo was to profess a

J. M. Headley, *The Emperor and His Chancellor: A Study of the Imperial Chancery Under Gattinara* (Cambridge, 1983), pp. 74ff.

[103] See P. Larivaille, in Nifo, *De regnandi peritia* (ed. Larivaille and Pernet-Beau), pp. viiiff.; Procacci, *Studi sulla fortuna,* pp. 3–26; and Richardson, "*The Prince* and Its Early Italian Readers," pp. 30–33.

[104] See Larivaille, "Nifo, Machiavelli," pp. 150–99, with the older bibliography.

[105] *Pace* Dionisotti, *Machiavellerie,* p. 134.

[106] *Operā omnia* 4, 1 (ed. Herding), pp. 133–219; and O. Herding, "Isokrates, Erasmus, und die *Institutio Principis Christiani,*" in *Dauer und Wandel der Geschichte: Aspekte europäischer Vergangenheit,* ed. R. Nierhaus and M. Botzenhart (Münster, 1966), pp. 101–43.

[107] See Price Zimmermann, *Paolo Giovio,* pp. 60ff.

subject dear to their hearts. When, in the preface to his *Dialectica ludicra,* he had inquired what philosophy could contribute to political practice, and poured scorn on the sophistries (as he viewed them) of the professionals, his polemic was motivated by animosity toward Lorenzo Valla's concept of dialectic.[108] Syllogistic rigor, not probability or polysemy, occupied the central position in Nifo's logic. Ambivalence, and the consequent emphasis on appearances, he sought to combat. This "antidialectical" method of dialectic was congenial to the nimble mind of Giulio de' Medici. His house philosopher provided an incisive scalpel with which to amputate *Il principe,* where needed, and to perform surgery on the equivocal elements in Machiavelli's thought.

The judgment of an action according to criteria of its outward effect, the stress on image and dissembling rather than sincerity and reality, key features of *Il principe,*[109] were accordingly regarded, by Nifo, as the tactics of the type of sophist presuming to advise the powerful against whom he had inveighed in *Dialectica ludicra.* He set out to eliminate them. On the delicate question of whether and how a prince, in a time of peace, should conduct military exercises discussed by Machiavelli in his fourteenth chapter, Nifo (*De regnandi peritia* 2.2) rejected the argument that the ruler's concern with warfare should be continuous, on the grounds that peace cannot be regarded as the end of belligerence, unless readiness for conflict is abandoned. Where Machiavelli advised princes to treat war and peace as the same, Nifo discerned a contradiction that he resolved into distinct ethical concepts.[110]

Such distinctions of the *quaestio* method, in *De regnandi peritia,* did not lead to formalism. The premise of Nifo's rewriting of *Il principe* was that only general propositions, not real actions, can be contradictory. When Machiavelli, in his sixteenth chapter on the generosity of the prince, began with the hypothetical and the ostensible, reasoning that what matter are the appearance of open-handedness and the political advantages that follow from a carefully crafted reputation, Nifo divided the arguments *pro et contra* into two classes, supported by opposing authorities. For Machiavelli, the ambiguous relationship between perception and reality implied that avarice could be admitted, if it served a purpose. By Nifo (4.1) this calculation of *Realpolitik* was lent a moral tone: stinginess, masked as generosity, required ethical legitimation.

Legitimation on the grounds of utility or of a disabused realism, in favor of which Machiavelli argued at *Il principe* 17 when treating the problem of whether it is better, for a prince, to be loved or feared, was presented by Nifo (4.4) as a logical contradiction. The example of God the Father demonstrated that the presence of fear and the absence of hatred were compatible, he argued, suppressing the view that love and dread may be evoked simultane-

[108] See Jardine, "Dialectic or Dialectical Rhetoric?" pp. 253–70.

[109] See further below, pp. 278–80.

[110] See further S. Anglo, "Machiavelli as a Military Authority: Some Early Sources," in Denley and Elam, *Florence and Italy,* pp. 326–27.

ously. Dissembling and lies, with which Machiavelli's prince was advised to deceive the gullible people in his eighteenth chapter, were, in *De regnandi peritia* (4.11), condemned as the tactics of a tyrant. Against Machiavelli, admirer of the Romans, Nifo set Roman rejections of insincerity, on the pragmatic grounds that unethical methods tended to produce incapable rulership. It was not desire for power that *De regnandi peritia* censured, but failure to grasp the opportunity to display virtue in the face of adversity.

For Machiavelli's dialectic of appearance, Nifo substituted one of directness. An unequivocal moral core remained, for him, in the shifting sphere of politics; religion might not be reduced to a means of social control; nor were princes of the Church comparable to lay magnates, kings, or emperors. Civility was rather the model than the means by which power might be acquired and held, as Machiavelli's revision of conventional ethics was supplanted by a scholastic argument for Christian values. What remained was Florentine. Retaining the ideal of a "civic" principate discussed in *Il principe,* Nifo's book set out to destroy the distinctive polyvalency of the original. But if, in his antidialectical dialectician, Giulio de' Medici found the right agent to correct what seemed to him the distorted features of Machiavelli's "mirror for princes," the Fortune whose fickleness it portrayed was subsequently to prove him wrong. Even the cardinal was not able to calculate that when, four years later, he reigned as Clement VII in the Holy City, Rome would be sacked by troops of the same emperor in whom *De regnandi peritia* was intended to inspire a policy of peace.

. . . . .

Toward humanism and its practitioners Niccolò Machiavelli, in and before 1523, had no reason to entertain tender feelings. One of his major works had been taken from him by the patron to whom he could not afford to say no and altered, by a humanist, in its substance and essence. Dressed in the cosmopolitan garb of Latinate learning, his book was sent an audience that the all-too-Florentine author could not yet hope to address. The posthumous publication, in 1532, of *Il principe,* sanctioned (perhaps as recompense for services rendered) by Clement VII, was no consolation to its author nine years earlier. By then Machiavelli's experience, during most of his adult life, with the intellectuals of the establishment had been tense and troubled. Nifo was only the latest of his tormentors. Another, recently deceased, had been no less of a bugbear. His relations with Marcello Virgilio, never warm, had cooled into antagonism after 1512 as the ex-Second Chancellor observed the First maneuvering himself, once again, into a position of prominence. For the ineffective theoretician of *Realpolitik,* Niccolò Machiavelli, it was galling that this humanist achieved, at Florence, a worldly success that he himself never attained.

The Studio and the Chancery, the lecture theater and the podium had been dominated, for more than two decades, by Marcello Virgilio. Behind him stood institutions to which Machiavelli had lost, or never gained, access. As a writer, as a thinker, even as a type of teacher,[111] the sometime *segretario fiorentino* was divided from his former colleague by tangible differences of opportunity, status, and talent. These factors are perhaps too often taken for granted. Not all of them worked to Machiavelli's advantage, and none of them should obscure the fact that he and Marcello Virgilio shared a basic similarity of purpose. Both wrote and thought and taught for the elite that did, or might, hold power.

That is why, when addressing the unsolved problem of Machiavelli's relationship to humanism, it may be worth pausing to reflect on what, at Florence during his lifetime, that ill-defined term actually meant.[112] Its meaning, ideology, and character altered, following his expulsion from the Chancery, from what they had been when he had worked alongside Marcello Virgilio,[113] and, after 1512, Machiavelli declined to follow suit. Much of his writing sprang from a dialectic with an older approach familiar to him during the period of the "popular" Republic. It does not diminish his achievement to appreciate that it had a more complex background than is supposed, nor is it irrelevant to understanding Machiavelli's intellectual stance to see that one factor in its development was the sustained aim of offering an alternative to the changing positions taken by the leading humanist of his own generation.

. . . . .

An early stage in this process can be observed in two letters written *post res perditas:* one, justly famous, was addressed to Francesco Vettori on 10 December 1513, and composed in the vernacular; the other, also to Vettori on 4 December 1514, has hardly been studied, although (or, perhaps, because) it is written in Latin.[114] While the first has inspired a large and valuable literature that renders insistence on its qualities superfluous,[115] there are some aspects of this splendid text that deserve further attention.

Describing his day on his farm at San Casciano, Machiavelli relates going into the wood, wandering from a spring to an aviary with Dante or Petrarch or "one of those minor poets such as Tibullus, Ovid, and their like" under

[111] See below, pp. 262ff.

[112] Cf. J. Najemy, review article in *Speculum* 52 (1977): 59.

[113] See above, pp. 181ff., 235ff.

[114] *Epp*. 216 and 232, in Machiavelli, *Opere,* pp. 1158–60 and 1180, with the commentary of G. Inglese, in Machiavelli, *Lettere a Francesco Vettori,* pp. 196–201, 255.

[115] See best J. Najemy, *Between Friends,* pp. 215–240, with his bibliographical note at p. 222 n. 11.

his arm. Reading the amatory authors whom Savonarola had condemned,[116] he recalls with melancholy pleasure his amours. A parallel between the past and the present ironically drawn, he then shifts direction to the road leading to the inn ("Transferiscomi poi in su la strada nell'osteria"). The gentleman of letters enters its rustic company. Meditation and silence give way to rough and tumble. A frugal meal, a game of tric-trac punctuated by vulgar quarrels and earthy abuse, and he returns home where, in the evening, he changes his mud-splattered garments to array himself in "royal and courtly robes" ("panni reali et curiali").

These are not the academic vestments of the professor, nor the chancellor's gown. From daily squalor—sartorial and social, literal and figurative—Machiavelli passes to nocturnal elegance and ceases to be a dismissed civil servant banished among country companions. Entering "the ancient courts of the men of antiquity," lovingly to be received and fed by them, he takes his fitting place among an aristocracy of the mind. Both images had precedents in the Florentine humanism of Machiavelli's lifetime. Aristocratic were Poliziano's pretensions;[117] emphatic was Marcello Virgilio's attempt to recreate and surpass classical culture.[118] Yet neither of them went so far, or so imaginatively, as Niccolò Machiavelli in his claim to fathom the motives of the ancients ("Domandarli della ragione dello loro actioni") by direct communion with them. Replying to their peer with a humanity denied to him by contemporary humanists ("Quelli per loro humanità mi rispondono"), these noblemen of learning enable him temporarily to forget boredom and troubles, poverty and death. "Tucto mi transferisco in loro": the humble road, recalled by the reflexive verb, to the gregarious solitude of the inn becomes the high route to intellectual empathy.

"I completely transfer myself to them" is not an adequate rendering of this metaphorical phrase. The metaphor is less one of movement than of metamorphosis. A total transformation of the self and the present that arises from immersion in the past is Machiavelli's meaning; and his witty but unrecognized allusion is to a cultural concept well known in the Middle Ages and Renaissance. That concept is *translatio artium/studii:*[119] the theory of the transmission and progress of scholarship from Greece to Rome, from France to Italy, culminating . . . on the farm of San Casciano. The idea, like the style, is Latinate, aptly capped by a quotation from Dante on the nature of knowledge. Aptly, because Dante's use of a cognate verb (*translatare*) provided one of the models for this elevated sense of *mi transferisco,* and Petrarch's practice

[116] See above, p. 137.

[117] See above, p. 83.

[118] See above, p. 201.

[119] See Worstbrock, "Translatio artium," pp. 1–22. Cf. G. G. Jongkees, "Translatio studii: Les avatars d'un thème médiéval," in *Miscellanea mediaevalia in memoriam J. F. Niermeyer* (Groningen, 1967), pp. 41–51.

another; while the authority of Bembo indicates, by analogy, its Latin flavor.[120] The active voice, rather than the passive employed by his predecessors, underscores Machiavelli's personal engagement and dynamism. In the uncouth exile of the Tuscan countryside, this subtle seigneur of the *volgare,* at one with the ancients, rivals the humanists at their own urbane game.

In Florence his letter was composed about Machiavelli's life far from the city. At his rural retreat in S. Andrea in Percussina he wrote, again to Vettori, a year later. The subject was a domestic dispute between an absent husband and an abandoned wife, recounted in Latin. Machiavelli said nothing, in the learned language, that could not have been expressed in the vernacular. Nor did he choose a *lingua curiale,* in the sense of his *Dialogue* on Italian,[121] but an administrative prose rigorous in its subordinate clauses, severe in its parallelisms. The erudition and eloquence, the sallies of wit and flowery flourishes that Vespucci, writing from Rome on 25 August 1501, expected that his friend would admire in the Latin oratory of the papal court[122] left no trace on the style of Machiavelli's letter. Only at its end, contemplating the splendors of a Florence under Medicean rule, did he permit himself the rueful allusion: "Soli mihi Pergama restant." The theme, derived from Ovid, was widely diffused in medieval and Renaissance Latin poetry of lament;[123] and the aside evoked a banished Machiavelli at home in the literary culture of the chanceries and embassies, to which Vettori and Vespucci continued to belong.

Acknowledging one of his friend's letters, in October 1500, Agostino Vespucci, in a reply that began with a parade of the Second Secretary's titles, had expressed his pleasure, "although it was written in 'Etruscan.'"[124] *Quamvis etrusce:* the irony derived from the occasion and the context. To private correspondence Vespucci transposed the linguistic standards that governed an official epistle. When he replied to Machiavelli in Latin, the solemn language of state became a means of heightening the humor of personal gossip. These were the bilingual resources on which Machiavelli drew, in 1514,

[120] Cf. Dante *Paradiso* 14.83, with A. Mariani in *Enciclopedia dantesca* 5 (Rome, 1976), s.v. p. 699; and Petrarch *Rime* 318.12, on which see P. Bembo, *Prose della volgar lingua* 3, in *Prose e rime* (ed. Dionisotti), pp. 302–3: ". . . *translato,* che disse il Petrarca, è latinamente, non toscanamente detto." Cf. Ovid *Met.* 15.120, and Cicero *Acad.* 2.69. For Machiavelli's use of Latinisms, see the concise remarks of F. Chiappelli, *Studi sul linguaggio del Machiavelli* (Florence, 1953), 11ff.

[121] Machiavelli, *Dialogo intorno alla nostra lingua* (ed. Castellani), pp. 237, ll. 38ff.; 245, ll. 58ff.; 251, ll. 78ff.

[122] *Ep.* 22, in Machiavelli, *Opere,* p. 1029.

[123] For the Ovidian allusion (*Met.* 13.507), see *Lettere a Francesco Vettori* (ed. Inglese), p. 255 and n. 2; for the tradition, A. Boutemy, "Le poème *Pergama flere nolo . . .* et ses imitateurs au XIIe siècle," *Latomus* 5 (1946): pp. 233–44; and F.J.E. Raby, *A History of Secular Latin Poetry in the Middle Ages,* 2d ed. (Oxford, 1957), 1:325ff.

[124] *Ep.* 18, in Machiavelli, *Opere,* p. 1023.

both humorously and seriously. From his exile in the province, he addressed the ambassador at Rome in the international medium of public communication. Applied to a parochial problem, his command of Chancery Latin served to point to the waste of his talents. What Machiavelli understated in the text was emphasized by its form and language.

Language and the kinds of knowledge that it conveyed are among the themes of *Mandragola*. Advised by the pander Ligurio to pretend to be a doctor and a man of letters in order to have his way with the wife of the ingenuous Nicia, Callimaco speaks in Latin or *grammatica* (1.3). "Nam causae sterilitatis sunt aut in semine aut in matrice aut in instrumentis seminariis aut in virga aut in causa extrinsica," declares that fraud in a parody of the language of scholastic medicine (2.4). The urine of the woman, he goes on to add (2.6), is of greater thickness (*maioris grossitiei*) and paleness, and is less beautiful, than that of the man. What this drivel means, is nothing. What its style connotes, is significant. Casting his pseudo-knowledge in a grotesque medieval Latin, Callimaco fills his false prescriptions with "barbarisms," such as *grossities,* which the humanists deplored. And the humanist who, at the time of *Mandragola*'s appearance, was completing a Latin version of Dioscorides' *Materia medica* that claimed to surpass in elegance all previous versions of that work[125] had linguistic and personal reasons for detecting a satirical intent behind Machiavelli's portrayal of mock medics and charlatans of scholarship. Inability to sire a child was not only a problem of Nicia's. It had made Marcello Virgilio a laughingstock among his former colleagues in the Chancery.[126]

When Machiavelli attributed to Ligurio a contempt for book-learning and ignorance of worldly affairs,[127] he was touching on a subject that he would develop in the *Vita di Castruccio Castracani*. Castruccio, the taciturn *condottiere,* speaks in blunt and brutal epigrams. He despises verbiage, echoing Dante's maxim (as it is interpreted in Machiavelli's letter to Vettori of 10 December 1513) that knowledge depends on understanding.[128] Comprehension, for this skeptic of the verbal arts, is hindered by prolix oratory.[129] The most prominent orator of Machiavelli's generation at Florence was Marcello Virgilio, a notable windbag both in his public speeches and in his lectures at the

[125] See above, p. 218.

[126] See above, p. 240; and cf. G. Sasso in Machiavelli, *La Mandragola* (ed. Inglese), p. 2.

[127] 3.1: "Pertanto io no vorrei che voi nel parlare guastassi ogni cosa, perché un vostro pari, che sta tutto dì nello studio, s'intende di quelli libri, e delle cose del mondo non sa ragionare."

[128] *Vita di Castruccio Castracani* (ed. Inglese), p. 132, l. 157: "Gloriandosi uno di avere letto molte cose, disse Castruccio: 'E'sarebbe meglio gloriarsi di averne tenute a mente assai.'" Cf. *Ep.* 216, in Machiavelli, *Opere,* p. 1160: "E perché Dante dice che non fa scienza sanza lo ritenere lo havere inteso."

[129] *Vita di Castruccio Castracani* (ed. Inglese), p. 134, l. 167: "Avendolo uno uomo simile con una lunga oratione infastidito et dicendogli nel fine: 'Io vi ho forse, troppo parlando, stracco.' 'Non hai,' disse, 'perché io non ho udito cosa che tu abbia decto.'" Cf. ibid., 166.

Studio.[130] There he had claimed to train future leaders for an active life in politics. Castruccio, whose *virtù* consists in political and military action, dismisses the superfluous eloquence of the intellectuals as the yelping of curs.[131]

Roman reticence and Roman valor, in Machiavelli's biography and in his dramas, are qualities to be admired. Athens, the utopia for which the Hellenophile humanists longed and which they planned to recreate, is treated by him as a joke. In the prologue to his *Clizia,* this advocate of imitation of antiquity in the present[132] denies that a situation that occurred in classical Athens could be repeated in Cinquecento Florence. "Athens is ruined. Its streets and *piazze* are unrecognizable. Moreover, its citizens spoke in Greek, a language that you do not understand." Part of the humor derives from a rejection, at the "popular" level of *Clizia*'s audience, of a correspondence between Athens and Florence crucial to the ideology of high culture.

In vain did Marcello Virgilio decry, in his commentary on Dioscorides of 1518, the vulgarity of popular superstitions connected with the mandrake root.[133] From *Mandragola* and *Castruccio* to *Clizia,* his former colleague pursued a polemic against humanism and its pretensions. Popular culture Marcello Virgilio might spurn, just as he looked down on the plebs, but none of these irreverent works was vulgar, and each of them undermined, indirectly and insidiously, what the First Chancellor stood for. With weapons sharpened in the Chancery, Machiavelli continued, in his drama and his biography, the satirical campaign against the intellectuals of the establishment that had been spearheaded by the onslaughts on *idées fixes* in *Il principe* and the *Discorsi.*

. . . . .

The *Discorsi* and *Il principe* are usually considered in terms of Machiavelli's written culture. To the spoken word, the oral discourse that contributed to these works, little attention has been paid except by linguists, understandably interested in their author's style and its place in the development of the Italian language, and by the many devotees of the Orti Oricellari. They, whenever the question of Machiavelli's milieu is raised, intone the names of the Rucellai and their garden guests with a confidence inversely proportional to the slender evidence. If what survives from the debates and discussions of Machiavelli's friends is precious little, it has been made to seem more than enough. Although the writings of Bernardo Rucellai inconveniently place

[130] See above, p. 182.

[131] *Vita di Castruccio Castracani* (ed. Inglese), p. 132, l. 154.

[132] See below, pp. 267ff.

[133] See above, p. 228. On popular and learned elements in *Mandragola,* see G. Aquilecchia, "Mandragola la favola si chiama," in *Collected Essays in Italian Language and Literature Presented to K. Speight* (Manchester, 1971), pp. 74–100.

him in the world of humanist learning,[134] other "pedants" and bores have been ignored,[135] for they might complicate the romantic image of an autodidactic genius.[136] Such are the orthodoxies of Machiavellian scholarship.

They rest on a shaky foundation. Shaky, because those who have dismissed a priori the notion that he might have been aware of his colleague's approach to issues that engaged them both have not troubled to read Marcello Virgilio's unpublished writings nor entertained the possibility that Machiavelli, in formulating his own positions, might have reacted against those held by a figure more successful than himself. Yet it is often profitable, in the case of a gifted thinker, not only to trace the paths that he followed but also to consider routes that he refused to take. They are indicated by Machiavelli in the repeated and negative allusions of *Il principe* and the *Discorsi* to "others," to "some," and to "many." When, in a well-known sentence of *Il principe* 15, he speaks of the "*many* [who] have imagined republics and principalities that have never been seen or known to exist," it is in order to "differ from the precepts offered by *others*." When, at *Discorsi* 1.2, Machiavelli refers to "*some* who have written of states," he compares them with "*some other* and, as many think, wiser men" in a manner that finds parallels elsewhere in the book. Who were these "others"?

Such references are generic, is the common response. At *Il principe* 15, for example, Machiavelli may have been thinking of "some ancient writers (e.g., Plato in his *Republic*) and to more recent ones who emphasized ideals and the duties of leaders."[137] This is possible, and can be contextualized;[138] but it does not do full justice to the problem. Machiavelli's skepticism toward misdirected book-learning, evident at chapter 15, is also attested in his later writings. The biographer of Castruccio Castracani, the energetic functionary who had undertaken diplomatic missions and organized the militia while others sat in the Chancery refusing to compose his official letters or pontificated ex cathedra, was voicing a pointed contrast when he wrote "Una lunga esperienza delle cose moderne e una continua lezione delle antiche" in the dedication to *Il principe*.[139] The point lay in the word *esperienza*. It was what the humanists of his generation lacked: not the desire to align antiquity with modernity, nor the wish to derive axioms for present conduct from the classical past—both of which animated Marcello Virgilio's teaching—but the

[134] Dionisotti, *Machiavellerie,* pp. 138ff.

[135] Ibid., p. 280.

[136] Cf., from a different point of view but with a similar conclusion, Martelli, "Schede," p. 303.

[137] Machiavelli, *The Prince* (trans. Skinner and Price), p. 54 and note ad loc. Longer, but essentially the same, are A. Bird's comments, *Il principe* (ed. Bird), pp. 382–83.

[138] See Inglese's helpful note ad loc. in Machiavelli, *Il principe* (ed. Inglese), p. 102.

[139] Cf., in general, G. Sasso, "La lettura degli autori antichi e la lezione delle cose moderne nella nascità del mondo moderno," *La cultura* 21 (1983): 192–210. See further below, pp. 227ff.

practical *esperienza* gained, during his long tenure of a sorely missed office, by Machiavelli.

Rather antagonism than dependence characterized his relationship to humanism, and it invites us to open our ears to some of the sounds that, during the enforced retirement when *Il principe* and the *Discorsi* were composed, continued to ring in their author's memory. Machiavelli knew how a humanist, by attuning his teaching of the classics to current affairs, had essayed what he would now accomplish; and he had witnessed the impression made by Marcello Virgilio on a youthful elite that included some of his friends. To appreciate the ways in which Machiavelli responded to that impetus, it is worthwhile examining the *Discorsi* in the light of hitherto unknown material with which, through the spoken word, their author was familiar.

"I have chosen not those who are princes," Machiavelli wrote in his dedication, "but those who because of their innumerable good qualities deserve to be." These phrases are generally taken to refer to Machiavelli's two friends from the Orti Oricellari and to his disappointment with the Medicean magnates whose favor he had sought to win by offering them *Il principe*. The explanation is plausible, but not necessarily complete, because it takes little account of those to whom the dedication was addressed. What was the resonance of this sentence to Zanobi Buondelmonti, sometime *studens humanis litteris*[140] and pupil of Marcello Virgilio during the "popular" Republic?

Buondelmonti had been trained to regard himself differently. He and fellow students like Francesco Guicciardini had been encouraged by the professor to think of themselves as princes. The course on the *Aeneid* of 1502–3 initiated a series of lectures in which Marcello Virgilio, by direct analogies between the rulers of antiquity and the members of his youthful audience, urged them to consider themselves future guardians of the state.[141] Princely parallels and monarchical metaphors had formed an essential part of his teaching to Florence's governing class. Now Machiavelli was informing Buondelmonti that he had been demoted—not through lack of merit, but because what he had been taught to consider his rightful place had been usurped. And not only his. The Medicean restoration, disenchanting many among the optimates, had discredited a former teacher of republican values. Another, implied the polemic of this dedication, was rising up to take his place.

Promptly, in the first sentence of the preface to Book 1 of the *Discorsi,* Machiavelli evoked the specter of envy. Envy felt by whom? Proclaiming his originality, he declared: "I have decided to enter a path not yet trodden by anyone." These, we are told, are humanist topoi. The term "topos," in itself, explains little. What was its reference, its function, and its purpose in the cul-

[140] Verde, *Studio* 3, 2:946.

[141] See above, p. 190.

ture for which it was produced? How did Buondelmonti understand Machiavelli's claim? "Discourses on the First Decade of Livy" was not a genre to which he or his contemporaries were accustomed. It did not help to think of Valla's *Emendationes Livianae.* That alternative teacher, Niccolò Machiavelli, was proposing something different, surprising, and new.

Surprise was justified. The innovation was real. Not in absolute terms, considered critically, for Livy's model had been imitated with skill in the Florentine history of Scala.[142] But if imitation amounted to an interpretative act, it was not the same as a commentary. A precedent for the historical subject of the *Discorsi,* in the humanism of Machiavelli's generation, did not exist. When he described himself as a pioneer, he raised the question of who might have trodden his chosen path before him. An exact response may be offered, with a precise dating. A handful of months after Machiavelli's election as Second Chancellor, in November 1498, his future colleague, in a key *praelusio* defending his teaching and announcing his intentions, had ridiculed the philological approach and pledged to relate the study of classical literature to political actuality. Among the examples that Marcello Virgilio selected was the history of Livy.[143] After that promising start, a deafening silence fell. Never, on the extant evidence, did he lecture on Livy at the Studio; nor did anyone else.[144] It is improbable that vicissitudes of transmission have distorted this picture. References to ancient historians, both Latin and Greek, are conspicuous by their absence in all the professor's writings; and their neglect cannot be explained by the later establishment of history as an academic subject[145] or by the terms and title of his chair.

Bartolomeo Fonzio, in an oration of 1482, had spoken about history and praised Livy while introducing his courses on Lucan and Caesar.[146] Marcello Virgilio omitted that subject while composing a cycle of *praelusiones* on the individual disciplines between 1494 and 1498. His alleged motive was the crisis of 1497, but a deeper disinclination continued to hold him back from treating even those ancient historians with whom his predecessor in the same chair of poetry and rhetoric had dealt. Poliziano's *Praelusio in Suetonium* encouraged specialization, focusing on later imperial writers; and by 1495 Bernardo Rucellai had to turn to the Neapolitan circle of Pontano for a broader discussion of Roman history and its leading representatives.[147] When Machiavelli composed the *Discorsi,* Livy had not been in vogue among Florentine humanists within recent memory. If his father Bernardo, outside

[142] See above, p. 142.

[143] See above, p. 176.

[144] Verifiable by ASF, Studio Fiorentino e Pisano (Ufficiali dello Studio) 4–8.

[145] See F. Gilbert, "Reflections on the History of the Professor of History," in idem, *History: Choice and Commitment,* pp. 441–56; and cf. A. C. Dionisotti, "Nepos and the Generals," *Journal of Roman Studies* 78 (1988): 35–49.

[146] See C. Trinkaus, *The Scope of Renaissance Humanism* (Ann Arbor, 1983), pp. 53, 57ff.

[147] See above, p. 59; and Gilbert, *Machiavelli and Guicciardini,* pp. 203–5.

the intellectual establishment, had compiled an index to an incunable of the *Decades,*[148] others had been content to treasure their manuscripts of the work—as elegant, as ornamental, and as unread as coffee-table books.[149] Behind Machiavelli's interest in Livy lay not only family and Chancery tradition but also a clear wish to establish his own approach. The unhistorical Marcello Virgilio, after promising in 1498 to deal with the *Decades,* had reneged on his word; and his rival now advanced where he had feared, or failed, to tread.

The republic of the Romans, the history of Livy: these were sobering choices in the heady Hellenism of Florence during the second decade of the sixteenth century. Medicine and moral philosophy were the topics to which Marcello Virgilio had turned, not neglecting poetry, but steering clear of other subjects that, after the restoration, might prove politically dangerous. Abdicating his position as a mentor to future princelings, he had become a trainer of obedient subjects.[150] The new pretender, Machiavelli, dedicating the *Discorsi* to Zanobi Buondelmonti and Cosimo Rucellai in terms that recalled their past aspirations and acknowledged their present disappointments, presented himself as less craven and more consistent. Years before, in his "*Ghiribizzi*" of 1506 to Giovan Battista Soderini,[151] after citing the examples of Hannibal's and Scipio's successes in maintaining military discipline, he had adduced instances of modern practice, on the grounds, sarcastically expressed, that it "is not customary to treat the Romans as authorities."[152]

This assertion, at the time when it was made and in the general terms in which it was couched, amounted to a blatant affront. The Romans, in 1506, were regularly being treated as authorities by Machiavelli's colleague. A decade later, however, the situation was different, and the claim received plainer but no less tendentious definition in the preface to Book 1 of the *Discorsi.* There Machiavelli again referred to prevailing neglect of examples taken from ancient history, this time specifying that it was their political and military value that was not appreciated. In 1506, that qualified claim had been true; and no Florentine intellectual during his lifetime was to present the case developed, on the basis of political and military exempla, by Machiavelli in the *Discorsi.* Yet the grounds on which he first argued it revealed the limits of his horizons:

> I am all the more struck with wonder and grief [at this neglect] when I perceive that, in the differences that arise between citizens in civil affairs or in the maladies from which men suffer, they have always had recourse to the maxims

[148] See above, p. 145.

[149] See de la Mare, "Florentine Manuscripts," pp. 177–200. Cf. L. Reynolds in *Texts and Transmission: A Survey of the Latin Classics,* ed. Reynolds (Oxford, 1983), pp. 206–8.

[150] See above, p. 206.

[151] See R. Ridolfi and P. Ghiglieri, "I Ghiribizzi al Soderini," *La bibliofilia* 72 (1970): 53–74; and M. Martelli, "I 'Ghiribizzi' a Giovan Battista Soderini," *Rinascimento* 9 (1969): 147–80.

[152] ". . . non si usa allegare e Romani," *Ep.* 116, in Machiavelli, *Opere,* p. 1182. For the argument, cf. *Del modo di trattare i popoli della Valdichiana ribellati* (ed. Marchand), pp. 98–119.

or the remedies that have been pronounced or prescribed by the ancients; for the civil laws are nothing else than the judgments delivered by ancient jurists that, restored to order, teach our jurists how to judge. And medicine, too, is nothing other than the experiments conducted by ancient physicians, on which present doctors base their diagnoses.[153]

Stuff and nonsense. Or a misleading simplification, to say the least. Empirical method, with scant reference to antiquity, already played a prominent role in Florentine medicine when Machiavelli wrote these sentences. In a book issued by his own publishers, the (posthumous) *De abditis nonnullis ac mirandis morborum et sanationum curis* of 1507, by Antonio Benivieni, a series of anatomical and technical cases had been made public, devoid of appeal to classical physicians.[154] In the long course of the Plinian controversy, at the heart of which stood matters medical and botanical, the issue—even for Pliny's defenders such as Pandolfo Collenuccio—was not merely ancient authority, but how far it could be verified or corrected by direct observation.[155] And if classical jurisprudence, especially Justinian, had attracted increasing interest during the Quattrocento, the legal reasoning of Paolo di Castro, expert on the *Digest,* about the qualifications of *cives ex privilegio* for office had demonstrated, much earlier in the same century, that rational modernization was being implemented, at Florence as elsewhere, in the civil law.[156] By the legal and medical instances that it selected, the earliest version of the proemium to Book 1 of the *Discorsi* revealed an author who was, in his own age and ambient, not in touch with the latest developments.

It was therefore prudent that Machiavelli suppressed the sentences beginning "For the civil laws are nothing else" when he revised his draft.[157] The

[153] ". . . non posso fare che insieme non me ne maravigli e dolga. E tanto più, quanto io veggo nelle diferenzie che intra cittadini civilmente nascano, o nelle malattie nelli quali li uomini incorrono, essersi sempre ricorso a quelle iudizii o a quelli remedii che dagli antichi sono stati iudicati o ordinati: perché le leggi civili non sono altro che sentenze date dagli antichi iureconsulti, li quali, ridutte in ordine, a'presenti nostri iureconsulti iudicare insegnano. Né ancora la medicina è altro che esperienze fatte dagli antiqui medici, sopra la quale fondano e'medici presenti e'loro iudizii." Book 1, proemium, in Machiavelli, *Opere,* p. 76.

[154] See above, pp. 216ff., with A. Costa and G. Weber, "L'inizio dell'anatomia patologica nel Quattrocento sui testi di Antonio Benivieni, Bernardo Torni, Leonardo da Vinci," *Archivio de' Vecchi per l'anatomia patologica* (Florence, 1963), pp. 429–878. Cf. G. M. Nardi, "Antonio Benivieni ed uno scritto inedito sulla peste," *Atti e memorie dell'Accademia di storia d'arte sanitaria* 4 (1938): 124–33, 190–97.

[155] See above, pp. 99–106.

[156] Kirshner, "Paolo di Castro," pp. 227–44; and idem, "*Ars imitatur naturam,*" pp. 289–331. On the problem in general, see Kelley, "Civil Science," pp. 777–94; M. Ascheri, "Giuristi, umanisti e istituzioni del Tre- Quattrocento: Qualche problema," *Annali dell'Istituto storico italo-germanico in Trento* 3 (1977): 42–43; C. Dionisotti, "Filologia umanistica e testi giuridici fra Quattro e Cinquecento," in *La critica del testo,* Atti del II° Congresso internazionale della società italiana di storia del diritto 1 (Florence, 1971), pp. 89–101. Cf. D. Osler, "Filippo Beroaldo e l'umanesimo giuridico," in *Sapere e/è potere,* 1:233–43 (cited in note 47).

[157] Pincin, "Le prefazioni," pp. 79ff.

cause to which he had ascribed neglect of ancient examples—"the enfeeblement into which the present *religion* has brought the world"—was also corrected, in the two *editiones principes* of 1532, from the original *religione* of the autograph to *educazione*.[158] That the emendation derived from the author is hardly open to doubt. It reflects the polemical tone of his dedication, and is mirrored in the course of his work. *Educazione,* for Machiavelli, did not imply instruction by *grammatici* groveling to the powerful, like Marcello Virgilio. A larger, more ambitious and political concept was entailed by this term; and it was to be implemented by the *uomini litterati* who, at 1.10, take their honorable place after heads and organizers of religion and founders of republics and kingdoms. Distinctions, however, had to be drawn. *Uomini litterati* were of so many kinds that they must be graded according to their respective ranks.

Uomini litterati is a Latinism. It renders *litteratores,* the rank to which, in 1494, Jacopo Segni had assigned Marcello Virgilio, while recommending him to Piero de' Medici.[159] The word was used to avoid the more technical and ambiguous *grammatici,* which, despite Poliziano's efforts, had acquired negative connotations during the Quattro- and Cinquecento.[160] At the grammarian's lower level Marcello Virgilio would have been graded by his rival, whose *Discorsi* 2.2 ascribed the current shortage of lovers of liberty to a difference between modern and ancient *educazione.* By whom was that training being provided at the Florentine Studio when Machiavelli wrote his chapter? By an erstwhile apologist of republican freedom transformed, during the second decade of the sixteenth century, into an educator of docile state servants. The oblique language of the *Discorsi* is neither generic nor vague. Casting scorn on the servile professoriate, Machiavelli recalled its abandoned rhetoric of liberty in a manner intended to sting.

What he had not forgotten, when he stressed *libertà* in the *Discorsi,* were the republican sentiments that had been revived by Marcello Virgilio, in stridently Brunian terms, during the *governo popolare.* If Niccolò Machiavelli, during the second decade of the sixteenth century, appeared to emerge as the "true heir of Bruni and his disciples,"[161] it was because he reacted against the betrayal of their legacy by the First Chancellor, who had not hesitated to manipulate and then to disown it when the time was ripe. That the time was not ripe between 1513 and 1519 so lightly to abandon the ideals current in the 1490s was Machiavelli's contention in the *Discorsi. Libertà* and *educazione:* the two concepts, for him, were intimately linked. He was thinking in terms of their association, which had been effected by Marcello Virgilio and which

[158] Ibid., p. 79.

[159] See above, p. 148. For context, cf. Feo, "'Litterae' e 'literatura,'" pp. 21–41.

[160] See above, pp. 81ff.

[161] Skinner, "Political Philosophy," p. 436, citing Baron, *Crisis,* pp. 428–29; and cf. Skinner, *Foundations,* vol. 1, *The Renaissance,* pp. 152ff.

he now turned against him. The expression *uomo litterato,* derived from the professional vocabulary of the humanists, at *Discorsi* 1.10 designated the nonprofessional intellectual—bolder, more consistent, more politically engaged—who was to supplant such invertebrate teachers as Buondelmonti's former mentor and Machiavelli's sometime colleague.[162]

Invertebrate (*debole*) the world had become because the Christian religion had exalted "the humble and the contemplative," rather than men of action. Examining what he saw as the causes of universal decline, Machiavelli appealed to the criterion of *esperienza. Educazione,* he continued, and the false interpretations that it had imposed produced fewer republics than in antiquity. Having located the blame in the types of training offered by pious professors, Machiavelli went on, at *Discorsi* 2.2, to draw a series of analogies between the state and the family, between wealth, liberty, and leadership, conceived in princely terms. Countries prospered when their populations were larger. Marriages were contracted, children begot and brought up, patrimony was secure. Born free and not slaves, men knew that, by their abilities, they could become *principi.* Behind this argument lay Bruni, mediated and elaborated. Mediated and elaborated by Marcello Virgilio's reading of Virgil in the light of Brunian annotations on the pseudo-Aristotelian *Economics.*[163] Adopting the material of his rival, Machiavelli altered its sense. This was what *esperienza,* not modern *educazione,* taught. Recalling the hermeneutics of 1502–3, he indicated how they had been betrayed by their time-serving exponent.

"La debolezza de' presenti uomini," *Discorsi* 3.27 continues, "is due to feeble *educazione* and slight knowledge of affairs." Again, the negative standard of didactic deficiency is contrasted with the positive one of practical experience. Modern notions were far from the truth: witness the failed policy toward Pistoia and Pisa. Effective understanding depended on just apprehension of the past and accurate prediction of the future. Human activity might vary from region to region, according to *la forma della educazione* from which people acquire their habits of life (3.43), but human nature remained constant. That was a fundamental premise of Machiavelli's enterprise as an alternative teacher, reiterated throughout his work and centered on its concept of imitation.

Imitation of antiquity was no less central to Florentine humanism.[164] For Poliziano and his successor, it amounted both to a principle of progress and to an agent of change. Emulative imitation, as conceived by the holders of the chair of poetry and eloquence at the Studio, was a means not of follow-

[162] Hence the malice (not, *pace* Martelli ["Schede," p. 287], the precision) of Benedetto Varchi's description of Machiavelli as "più tosto non senza lettere, che letterato," *Storia fiorentina* 4, 14 (ed. Milanesi), 1:199.

[163] See above, p. 190.

[164] See above, pp. 46ff. and 201ff.

ing the ancients but of equaling and surpassing their achievements. Rather divergence than correspondence stimulated their thought on this subject, and imitation was less their goal than their point of departure. Adherence to a model, single and strict, these Florentines rejected as conservative Roman purism. Modernity was their objective, pluralism their ideal, classicism their method. If they exalted the ancient past, it was because they desired to be regarded as the new Greeks. Hellenic thought and medicine, "Alexandrian" literature and learning should serve to erect a new and better Athens. From the colonnades of its academy, they looked down on reality with a philologist's gaze. And because the philologist's business is words, and language, as they were disposed to study it, remained ever subject to change, what they perceived when they observed a text, an event, or a plant was mutability, variety, contingency. This is the attitude that found expression in Marcello Virgilio's preface to Dioscorides.[165] It is the attitude that Florentine philology, by its emulative aims and pluralistic practice, was constrained to take. It is the attitude that, on different grounds and without approving its implication of relativism, even Savonarola might have sanctioned in part.[166] And it is the attitude that Niccolò Machiavelli decisively rejected.

As an intellectual, he, viewed in terms of Pico's letter to Barbaro,[167] was an advocate of the primacy of *res* over *verba*. For the humanists' stress on the mutability of language, the variety of cultures, and the contingency of circumstances, Machiavelli substituted the natural continuum, the stability and sameness of *esperienza* described at *Discorsi* 3.43. That chapter was not isolated. It developed a position asserted at key points of the work: in the proemium to Book 1, for example, with its denial that "the sky, the sun, the elements, men were changed in movement, order, and power from what they were in antiquity." There "the error of innumerable readers" was identified as taking pleasure in the *varietà degli accidenti* recounted by history, "without thinking of imitating them."

Imitation, for Machiavelli, therefore required a corrective hermeneutic. What he wished to correct was a mode of interpretation that divorced *storie* from real life. It failed "to draw that sense, to taste that flavor" that books on history "really have." Similar terms had been employed by Marcello Virgilio in 1497, when he had promised to bring the *studia humanitatis* back into the mainstream of civic activity. Denouncing the misplaced attention now being paid by his rival to the *varietà degli accidenti,* Machiavelli recurred to the humanist's former position with a postulate of uniformity that had been forgotten. Ignorance of the past and misplaced confidence in the future, censured in the proemium to Book 2, hindered comprehension of the depressing present. While Marcello Virgilio, in 1514, was urging the young with buoy-

[165] See above, p. 220.

[166] See above, p. 37.

[167] See above, pp. 34ff.

ant optimism not to enslave themselves to imitation of antiquity,[168] Machiavelli, at the somber conclusion of his second proemium, contradicted him flatly: "I shall make bold to say in plain terms what I understand about ancient and present times, in order that the young men who read my writings shall be minded and able to flee the present and prepared to imitate antiquity."

Not the glimmer of a renaissance hailed in humanist circles but the gloom of a decadence that should be recognized by all motivated this turning to the past. Nowhere in Machiavelli's critique of the humanism of his generation are his differences with it more forcibly stated than in the proemium to Book 2 of the *Discorsi*. Yet his pessimistic sense of general corruption, in contrast to Marcello Virgilio's belief in progress, also served to underline a fundamental similarity of intention. Both wrote, as teachers, for "the young." By the professor, his pedagogical status required no advertisement. For more than a quarter of a century Marcello Virgilio held a chair. By Machiavelli, who no longer had an institutional role, an alternative had to be created; and that is why this critic of conventional ethics was so determined to represent his didactic intent as a moral mission: "It is the duty of a good man . . . to teach others what he has been unable to effect." From a sense of failure in the world of action, the ex-Second Chancellor turned to the intellectual sphere, in order to save "others"—the "young," the likes of Buondelmonti—from the "errors" being disseminated by the First.

. . . . .

In the *Discorsi* Niccolò Machiavelli entered into a dialectic with the approach and the ideology that Florentine humanism had created during the "popular" Republic, in order to contest the forms that it assumed after the restoration of the Medici. The opportunist-intellectuals, as he perceived them, lacked his own seriousness of purpose. Yet in his attempt to voice a compelling alternative to what seemed to him the decayed *educazione* being offered during the second decade of the sixteenth century, Machiavelli was not only criticizing what Marcello Virgilio represented. The teacher was one of two personae adopted by the author of the *Discorsi*. The other, manifest to every reader of the apocalyptic rhetoric in the *exhortatio* that concludes *Il principe*,[169] was that of the prophet. And at Florence, during Machiavelli's lifetime, there had been one prophet, unarmed but powerful, whom he both suspected and admired: Girolamo Savonarola.[170]

[168] See above, p. 201.

[169] Cf. T. Hampton, *Writing from History: The Rhetoric of Exemplarity in Renaissance Literature* (Cornell, 1990), pp. 74ff.

[170] On Machiavelli and Savonarola, see Brown, "Savonarola, Machiavelli, and Moses," pp. 57–72 (= eadem, *The Medici in Florence,* pp. 263–81); and Weinstein, "Machiavelli and

Prophetic qualities were attributed to Machiavelli before he composed the *Discorsi*. Filippo Casavecchia, writing as one commissioner of the Florentine Republic to another on 17 June 1509, declared: "Day by day I discover in you a greater prophet than the Hebrews or other peoples have ever had."[171] The greatest of the Hebrew prophets, in the Old Testament that Machiavelli preferred, was Moses, a leader who, according to *Discorsi* 3.30, "in order to get his laws and orders adopted . . . was compelled to murder innumerable opponents." In the same chapter, Moses is compared and contrasted with "the tough Savonarola with his disturbingly anti-Christian paradoxes [who] impressed Machiavelli and made his work original and iconoclastic."[172] One feature that contributed to the originality of the *Discorsi* was their liberty of exegesis. Asserting that "anyone who reads the Bible judiciously" would share his view of that sanguinary prophet, their author matched the interpretative freedom claimed by Savonarola.[173]

Savonarola set a precedent for Machiavelli, not only in his hermeneutic license. Both of them deprecated the *savi del mondo*.[174] But if the friar's slights on worldly intellectuals were congenial to the author of the *Discorsi,* his book was intended to refute one of the contentions advanced in Savonarola's sermon on Amos 1:3 of 19 February 1496, which had attacked the study of Livy.[175] Denying the possibility of prediction on the basis of what seemed to him antiquarian texts like the *Decades,* Savonarola had asserted an ecclesiastical concept of history. Its course was theologically determined—its development decreed by God, revealed by prophecy, and guided by Providence. Only the Bible held the secrets of the future that Christian exegesis could unlock. Animated by the secularism that, during Savonarola's ascendancy and after his fall, had also provided one of the driving forces behind Marcello Virgilio's interpretations of the classics,[176] Machiavelli aimed to go further in the *Discorsi* and prove the modern prophet wrong.

A commentary of this kind on Livy thus represented a doubly polemical choice—intended to highlight shortcomings of the humanists and to achieve what Savonarola had deemed impossible. Hence the tendentiousness of the Biblical references in the *Discorsi* and other writings by Machiavelli—the "slightly dubious air" with which he cites Scripture, the holding of "his tongue in cheek when he inserted in his recommendations for a citizen army a Bible story interpreted along allegorical lines."[177] Trespassing on

Savonarola," pp. 251–64 (both superseding J. H. Whitfield, *Discourses on Machiavelli* [Cambridge, 1969], pp. 87–110).

171 *Ep*. 162, in Machiavelli, *Opere,* p. 1108.

172 Brown, "Savonarola, Machiavelli, and Moses," p. 65.

173 See above, p. 138.

174 See above, p. 140.

175 See above, pp. 138ff.

176 See above, pp. 153ff.

177 Gilbert, *Machiavelli and Guicciardini,* p. 168.

Savonarola's territory, he had to feel his way, and he was guided by the postulate of uniformity, his prop and stay. That is why Machiavelli laid such stress on imitation. The sameness of human nature, over cultures and time, which it presupposed and exemplified, served to ground his own predictive claims.

Imitation, for him, therefore entailed alignment of the past with the present, not the rivalry emphasized by the humanists. Only so could Livy be made to yield knowledge of the future, and even negative examples might, by analogy with what had happened, reveal what was to occur. Such is the argument of *Discorsi* 1.39, and 3.43, where the method and goal of imitation, within the limits of imperfect perception and changing circumstances, are linked to the theory of immutable constants and recurrent patterns.[178] Recurrence, in the cyclical form of *anakyklosis* borrowed from Polybius,[179] both lent a universal dimension to Machiavelli's theory and accounted for the element of dynamism that humanism was disposed, without explanation, to locate in emulative *imitatio*.

Here, at the point where Machiavelli's departures from the humanists of the establishment are evident, it is less pertinent to speculate on whether he acquired his knowledge of Polybius from the malcontent Bernardo Rucellai,[180] the outsider Pietro Crinito,[181] or a third party[182] than to recognize from whom it did not derive, and why. Neglected by Marcello Virgilio, the concept of universal history advanced by Polybius had been criticized in Poliziano's *Praefatio in Suetonium*.[183] In the individual and the particular—not the grand sweep, controlled by the recurrence and consequent predictability of men and events—the philologist had invested the full resources of his method. By Polybius's attacks on the monograph, on antiquarianism, on detailed but unphilosophical research, Poliziano had felt threatened; and in its place he had put an ideal of *enkyklios paideia* intended to justify the cultural ambitions of the *grammaticus*. That ideal, if not yet bankrupt, as Marcello Virgilio's Dioscorides attempted to demonstrate, was being savaged by the specialists. In agreement with their objections, Machiavelli declined to belong to their number. His classification of *uomini litterati* at *Discorsi* 1.10 reflected not only a desire to set himself apart from the ranks of the mundane professionals but also a wish to advance to the higher grade of an organizer of religion or founder of a republic. Hence the importance to him of Polybius's theory, in those universal aspects least congenial to Florentine humanism. It contributed to link Machiavelli's role as a political thinker and teacher

[178] See Larivaille, *La pensée politique,* pp. 25–31. Cf. Sasso, *Niccolò Machiavelli,* pp. 383ff.

[179] See Sasso, *Machiavelli e gli antichi,* 1:3–65; and G. W. Trompf, *The Idea of Historical Recurrence in Western Thought from Antiquity to the Reformation* (Berkeley, 1979), pp. 251ff.

[180] Dionisotti, *Machiavellerie,* pp. 138ff.; and Sasso, *Machiavelli e gli antichi,* 1:57ff.

[181] Richardson, "Notes," p. 34.

[182] For a recent survey of the problem, with bibliography, see L. Canfora, "Il pensiero storiografico," in *Lo spazio letterario di Roma antica,* ed. G. Cavallo, P. Fedeli, and A. Giardina, vol. 4, *L'attualizzazione del testo* (Rome, 1991), pp. 65ff.

[183] See above, pp. 54ff.

with that of the secular prophet. Aiming at an omnicompetence unmatched by even the advocates of *enkyklios paideia,* he pronounced, in the *Discorsi,* on the past, present, and future.

. . . . .

As a lay alternative to Savonarola's preaching, the political humanism of Marcello Virgilio during the "popular" Republic[184] provided a framework, traditional and Brunian, that Machiavelli filled with his own thought. Subtler, more penetrating, and more original, it sustained a tone to which the humanist had rarely risen. Only in times of crisis—during the perceived threat to the *studia humanitatis* in the 1490s, and the fear of the Holy League in 1511—had Marcello Virgilio assumed the prophetic persona; and if Machiavelli touched, at *Discorsi* 1.33, on the vision of a noble youth who would redeem the Republic with which the First Chancellor, shortly before the return of the Medici, had spurred on their aristocratic supporters,[185] it was to underline his differences.

In both his lectures and his public speeches, Marcello Virgilio had identified with the *reggimento,* expressing disdain for the people and horror at social disorder. The spokesman of the Signoria viewed *educazione* as a means of inculcating respect for the laws. They existed to guarantee the hierarchy that he unwaveringly supported, and to eliminate the dissensions that he regularly deplored. When, at *Discorsi* 1.4, Machiavelli derived Roman virtue from good *educazione,* good *educazione* from good laws, and good laws from the *conflicts* between senate and plebs,[186] he was reversing the line taken by the arch-conformist who had been his colleague. Skeptical of the role of the *grandi* to whom Marcello Virgilio deferred and wishing to involve in the political process the middle and lower orders that he spurned,[187] the alternative teacher detected in the harmony praised by his rival at the Studio a pretext for stifling freedom and furthering the ambitions of an optimate oligarchy. Small wonder, then, that Guicciardini criticized Machiavelli's theory of civil discord.[188] Among "the many who thoughtlessly condemn those dissensions" that threatened his class had been his mentor. If Marcello Virgilio called himself Socrates, Francesco Guicciardini was known as Alcibiades.[189]

[184] See above, pp. 158ff., 190ff.

[185] See above, pp. 195ff.

[186] See Bock, "Civil Discord," pp. 181–201.

[187] See Bonadeo, "Role of the 'Grandi,'" pp. 90–130. Cf. A. Parel, *The Machiavellian Cosmos* (New Haven, 1992), p. 124.

[188] *Considerazioni intorno ai Discorsi del Machiavelli* 1.4, with M. Gagneux, "Une tentative de démystification de l'idéologie républicaine: Les 'Considérations sur les Discours de Machiavel' de François Guichardin," in *Culture et société,* pp. 208–9.

[189] *Scritti autobiografici e rari* (ed. Palmarocchi), p. 212.

Attacked in the substance of the *Discorsi,* Marcello Virgilio influenced their form. Little attention has been paid to this problem, although it provides a measure of Machiavelli's antagonistic yet intimate relationship with humanism. "The *Discorsi* were conceived in the form of a traditional literary genre" is an influential view.[190] There reflection stops. Thick books have been written on the assumption that Machiavelli's work is a commentary without inquiring what, in his own time and place, that term meant.[191] "Traditional" the *Discorsi* were not; nor did there exist, in Quattro- and Cinquecento Florence, a single genre of textual interpretation that made their author's choice of form self-explanatory. Between the literary commentaries of Landino and the philological lectures of Poliziano, the divergences are great; and the hermeneutics of the next generation, as exemplified by Marcello Virgilio, are far freer than those of the *miscellanea* written by his teacher and by Crinito, with which they should not be confused.[192] Generally flouting the restrictions of consecutive order, while occasionally recurring to the original sequence of the base-text, the professor, during the "popular" Republic, proceeded discursively, submitting the classical writers whom he treated to his own digressive style of interpretation. This orator of "republican" freedom, in his reaction against a form of philological rigor associated with Poliziano, created a hermeneutic counterpart to the liberties taken with Scripture by Savonarola.[193] Such was the unmethodical method of commentary that Juan Luis Vives ironically defined as "writing one's own book rather than an exposition of another's."[194]

It was also the method to which Machiavelli referred in his title *Discorsi.* When Paolo Giovio, recalling his conversations with their author in the early 1520s, stated that Machiavelli had taken *flores* of Greek and Latin literature from Marcello Virgilio, he was referring not to ornamental learning, but to a principle of selective composition.[195] Plucking flowers from Livy in the second decade of the sixteenth century, Machiavelli wove them into a form current at Florence during the first. At the end of Book 1, for example, he

[190] F. Gilbert, "The Composition and Structure of Machiavelli's *Discorsi,*" in idem, *History: Choice and Commitment,* p. 132.

[191] E.g., H. C. Mansfield, Jr., *Machiavelli's New Modes and Orders: A Study of the "Discourses on Livy"* (Ithaca, N.Y., 1979).

[192] *Pace* Dionisotti, *Machiavellerie,* p. 258 (translated in *Machiavelli and the Discourse of Literature,* ed. A. R. Ascoli and V. Kahn [Ithaca, N.Y., 1979], p. 44).

[193] See above, pp. 191ff.

[194] ". . . non tam alieni operis expositores dici debeant, quam authores proprii." *De ratione dicendi* 3, in Vives, *Opera* (Basel, 1555), p. 151. For a general account, see J. Céard, "Les transformations du genre commentaire," in *L'automne de la Renaissance,* XXIIe Colloque international d'études humanistes, Tours, 2–13 July 1979, ed. J. Lafont and A. Stegman (Paris, 1981), pp. 101–15; cf. K. Stierle, "Les lieux du commentaire," in *Les commentaires et la naissance de la critique littéraire,* ed. G. Mathieu-Castellani and M. Plaisance (Paris, 1990), pp. 19–30.

[195] See above, pp. 149ff.

drew attention to his procedure: "I shall begin by discoursing on those things that happened inside [the city] and according to public deliberation that I judge worthy of fuller commentary, adding to them everything that depended on them."[196] On what authority was this declaration made? On that of the "potestas addendi, detrahendi, signandique" asserted in 1496 by Marcello Virgilio.[197] Comparing the rise of Rome with the examples of Sparta and of Athens at *Discorsi* 2.3, Machiavelli developed ideas that have little connection with the work on which he purported to be commenting, only to conclude his account of the policy that "made Rome great and very powerful" by referring it to Livy: "Il che dimostra Tito Livio in due parole, quando disse: 'Crescit interea Roma Albae ruinis.'"[198] "In two words": the very formula, and the same sleight of hand, employed by Marcello Virgilio when foisting the many words of his own interpretation on *Aeneid* 1.1.[199]

It follows that neither the incompleteness of Machiavelli's work[200] nor the revisions that it underwent allow us to draw chronological inferences from its structure. Intermittently pursuing continuous commentary, more often diverging from its base-text, what has been described as the "nonstructure" of the *Discorsi*[201] reflected an exegetical freedom established at Florence by their author's former colleague. To evoke an "*original* order of *successive* comments on Livy"[202] is to tie a dubious dating to the assumption that the *Discorsi* were conceived in "the form of a traditional literary genre"[203]—unproved, unprovable, and inconsistent with Machiavelli's ideological aims. Arbitrariness, viewed in terms of their sources, or liberty, as perceived by their exponents, distinguished the hermeneutics that provided the model for his work on Livy. Its exegetical form, redolent of the "popular" Republic, indicated Machiavelli's loyalty to the past. How it was being traduced in the present is vividly illustrated by comparison with the commentary on Dioscorides that, at exactly the same time as the *Discorsi* were being composed for those deserving "*principi*" Rucellai and Buondelmonti, Marcello Virgilio was preparing for a Medicean prince of the church. Reverting to

[196] "Io comincerò a discorrere sopra quelle cose occorse dentro e per consiglio publico, le quali degne di maggiore annotazione giudicherò, aggiungendovi tutto quello che da loro dependessi," in Machiavelli, *Opere,* p. 78.

[197] See above, p. 160.

[198] Machiavelli, *Opere,* p. 151.

[199] See above, p. 183.

[200] Cf. Bernardo Giunta's preface to the Florentine edition of 1532, edited and discussed by Pincin, "Sul testo di Machiavelli," pp. 163–64.

[201] Bausi, *I "Discorsi" di Niccolò Machiavelli,* p. 121, on which see G. Inglese, "Ancora sulla data di composizione dei *Discorsi,*" *La Cultura* 24 (1986): 98–117.

[202] Gilbert, "Composition and Structure," p. 124.

[203] See above, pp. 184ff.

the neutrality of systematic philological interpretation, the humanist disavowed the republican precedent set by himself.

. . . . .

Unprecedented, even in the writings of the scintillating Savonarola, were the "Attic" qualities of Machiavelli's prose. The epithet again stems from Paolo Giovio, who ascribed it to a talent nurtured by "no knowledge of Latin literature, or certainly a mediocre one." Such was the hauteur of the humanist, defender of a tradition that he knew was imperiled.[204] Its excesses had been mocked in the dedication to *Il principe,*[205] which distinguished Machiavelli from the mannerists of learning among whom his biographer belonged. Hence Giovio's aspersions on the vernacular "Atticist's" Latin, balanced by the compliment of a likeness to Boccaccio.[206] Safely relegated to the realm of the *volgare* (where, for most, he remains), Machiavelli posed no threat to defensive humanists. One might even approve the restraint of his style.

Stylistic restraint implied an intellectual position that Giovio understood, both in his polemic and in his praise. That position was not only defined in relation to Boccaccio. "Atticism" had been the criterion by which *piagnone* intellectuals like Nesi had judged the "new rhetoric" of Savonarola,[207] and contrasted it favorably with the "Asianism" of the humanists. Giovio, too, was thinking in such terms. Consider how he, elsewhere in the same work, described Poliziano: "In [the *Stanze per la Giostra*] he was thought to have gathered choice flowers from the Greeks and the Latins for the people to marvel at."[208] The reference was not to some hack of scholarship, stringing together faded *flores* of quotations, but to a selective transposition of humanist culture into the vernacular by the leading *érudit* of the age. In the same terms, of *flores,* Giovio described Machiavelli's debt to Marcello Virgilio. The First Chancellor had "a sophisticated and sweet manner of speech." From the

[204] Price Zimmerman, *Paolo Giovio,* pp. 92–96.

[205] Cf. Richardson, "*The Prince* and Its Early Italian Readers," pp. 20ff.

[206] "Quis non miretur in hoc Macchiavello tantum valuisse naturam, ut in nulla vel certe mediocri Latinarum litterarum cognitione ad iustam recte scribendi facultatem pervenire potuerit?" *Elogia clarorum virorum LXXVII* (ed. Maregazzo), p. 111; and ibid., p. 112: "Ipse quoque natura perargutus et docilis salsique iudicii plenus pedestrem patrii sermonis facultatem, a Boccacii conditoris vetustate diffluentem, novis et plane Atticis vinculis astrixerat; sic ut ille castigatior sed non purior aut gravior otiosis ingeniis existimetur." Cf. idem, *Dialogus de viris et feminis aetate nostra florentibus* 2 (ed. Travi and Penco), p. 245, ll. 33ff., on which see Raimondi, *Politica e commedia,* pp. 242ff.

[207] See above, pp. 135ff.

[208] Ed. Maregazzo, p. 69: "In id enim a Graecis atque Latinis delectos flores populo stupendos contulisse censebatur."

professorial chair and the public podium, he displayed "the marvelous variety of his many-sided learning."[209] Marcello Virgilio's teacher, in his Latin translation of Herodian, had combined "artificial ornaments" with "deceptive and pernicious *colores*" of rhetoric, in order to disguise his debts to a rival. *Ubertas* ('abundance') characterized Poliziano's style.[210]

Justly conveyed by Giovio, these were the "Asian" qualities of Florentine humanism during Machiavelli's lifetime—the preciosity of Poliziano, the cloying sweetness of his successor. To commend their works to their patrons, both deployed, in Latin, every trick of their meretricious trade. Poliziano, dedicating *Miscellanea* 1 to Lorenzo, and Marcello Virgilio, inscribing Dioscorides to Lorenzo's son, "embellished" their letters with "redundant *clausulae,* pompous, pretentious diction, specious allurements, and superficial ornamentation." These expressions derive from the terminology of Latin rhetoric. They are translated from the letter with which Machiavelli intended to present *Il principe* to the duke of Urbino.[211] And they introduce a contrast, drawn by the alleged ignoramus, between himself and "the many who are accustomed to write fancy descriptions of their works."

The merits of his own, in the same dedication, are described as intrinsic. They arose, simply and naturally, from "la varietà della materia e la gravità del subietto."[212] No mincing mannerist, of course the ingenuous Machiavelli was unaware of the Ciceronianism that practiced what he condemned.[213] Naturally he had no idea that his preference for content over form had been shared by some of the most influential critics of humanist eloquence in fifteenth-century Florence.[214] Nor is it legitimate to draw parallels between his preface and those of Christian Latin literature, in which such ideas had been current for centuries;[215] or to compare Machiavelli's taste for the "plain

[209] Ibid., p. 134: ". . . eximia huius fuit in blando vultu *cultoque sermone suavitas,* et quum e suggestu iuventutem doceret aut in corona loqueretur, doctrina multiplex ipsaque varietate mirabilis."

[210] Ibid., p. 69: "Exinde Herodianum Romane loquentem publicavit, cunctis haud dubie erepta laude, qui id generis munus ante susceperint, quanquam aemuli eam translationem, uti nos a Leone Pontifice accepimus, Gregorii Tifernatis fuisse dicerent; quod passim, *inducto fuco et falsis levorum coloribus interlita alieni styli habitum mentiretur.* Sed eadem praecellenti studiorum omnium *ubertate* florentem, post editam *Miscellaneorum centuriam* publicataque Latina poëmata, immatura mors oppressit."

[211] "La quale opera io non ho *ornata* né ripiena di clausule ample o di parole ampullose e magnifiche o di qualunque altro lenocinio e ornamento estrinseco." *Il principe* (ed. Inglese), pp. 4–5.

[212] See ibid., p. xxxvii.

[213] Cf. Cicero *De oratore* 2.72.94 and 3.177.5. For background, see Leeman, *Orationis ratio,* pp. 91ff.; and Fumaroli, *L'âge de' l'eloquence,* pp. 47ff.

[214] See above, pp. 31ff.

[215] See T. Jansen, *Latin Prose Prefaces: Studies in Literary Conventions* (Göteborg, 1964), pp. 128ff.

style" with the traditional criteria of *sermo humilis*.[216] No, this irreligious vernacular author may not be likened to St. Jerome.[217] Rhetorically denouncing rhetoric, he was as untutored as Castruccio Castracani. So it is that, despite the learning lightly and elegantly worn in the dedication to *Il principe*, Giovio's charge is deemed proven, and Machiavelli is found as innocent of Latin as many of his modern interpreters.

. . . . .

"Una lunga esperienza delle cose moderne e una continua lezione delle antiche": the second of these attributes might have been claimed by rival humanists, but not the first and, to Machiavelli, the most important. Both were produced from his *suppellettile*, an originally Latin term with oratorical flavor used by Poliziano[218] that characterized the resources of a different kind of intellectual who, claiming to have studied the subjects previously monopolized by the professors, set out to link antiquity with modernity in the light of his practical experience. This was the design that bound *Il principe* to the *Discorsi*: the completion of a project on which the Florentine humanism of his generation had faltered. Incapable of carrying it through, pipe-dreamers like Marcello Virgilio belonged to the unreal world of "theories and speculations," of "republics imagined and principalities never seen," of ornamental "Asianism" and empty bombast.

Thus the "Attic" austerity of *Il principe* 15, linking the critique of language and style in the dedication to one of content. No less of a teacher in that work than in the *Discorsi*, Machiavelli continued to employ a Latinate diction. His ideal reader, the *principe* or ruler of chapter 14, was urged to practice the *exercitatio animi* that formed a traditional part of medieval and Renaissance education by exemplum.[219] Reading Plutarch and Xenophon, he should study, in order to imitate, Alexander, Scipio, and Cyrus. Citation of exemplary leaders was not new at Florence, nor was this approach. Nothing

[216] See F. Quadlbauer, *Die antike Theorie der genera dicendi im lateinischen Mittelalter*, Österreichische Academie der Wissenschaften. Phil.-hist. Klasse, Sitzungsberichte 241, 2 (Vienna, 1962), s.v., p. 281; and cf. E. Auerbach, *Literary Language and Its Public in Late Antiquity and in the Middle Ages*, trans. R. Mannheim (reprint Princeton, 1993), pp. 25–82.

[217] ". . . in morem cotidiani eloquii . . . fideliter magis quam ornate interpretatus sum." *Origenis Homiliae in Canticum Canticorum*, prol., ed. O. Rousseau, *Origène: Homélies sur le Cantique des Cantiques* (Paris, 1966), p. 62.

[218] Cf. Cicero *Orator* 79; and see above, p. 42.

[219] *Il principe* 14.14: "Ma quanto allo *esercizio della mente*, debbe el principe leggere le storie." On the term and its use, see Moos, *Geschichte als Topik*, pp. 280ff. For exempla in Machiavelli, see J. D. Lyons, *Exemplum: The Rhetoric of Example in Early Modern France and Italy* (Princeton, 1989), pp. 35–71.

different had been recommended, by Marcello Virgilio, to the "princes" for whom he had interpreted the *Aeneid*.[220]

Rex Eneas, with whom he compared them, was construed as a proto-*Gonfaloniere a vita*. Attentive to power and wealth, this role model for future rulers had all the *pietas* of his namesake, and none of his flair. A solid patrimony and a sound marriage guaranteed, by pseudo-Aristotelian analogy, his responsible governance of the state. If passing indiscretions might be condoned, a mistress should be discarded swiftly. She was not to be possessed like Fortune, but to be avoided like the plague. Useful only as subordinate partners in a domestic undertaking, women, as exemplified by Marcello Virgilio's Dido and Lavinia, were less important than a son and heir. A son was the investment for the future recommended by the First Chancellor to the mercantile mentality of his audience. Properly equipped with the social advantages and the civic virtues enjoined by Bruni, a member of the elite might accede to high office. There, from an eminence observed with envy by his peers, he would exercise caution, sincerity, discretion. No names were mentioned. None of the potential *principes* was, or should be, singled out. Addressing them collectively, Marcello Virgilio used the second-person plural.

Machiavelli, after his dedicatory letter, preferred the third-person singular. His work was not directed to the ruling class, but to an individual ruler. Nor was its original title *Il principe*.[221] *De principatibus,* accommodating both the form of a republic and the reality of dominance by one man that, after the restoration of the Medici, characterized the Florentine state in flux, was Platonic in connotation and polyvalent in sense.[222] It did not signify the explicit *On Autocracy* or the euphemistic *On Principalities*. Its immediate antecedents lay in the Latin vocabulary of Florentine humanism during the Gonfalonierate of Pier Soderini. Applicable both to his primacy and to the dominance of the Medici, *On "Princely" Rule* is a nearer approximation to what Machiavelli meant by this ambiguous term.

Ambiguity and inversion are regarded as techniques that influenced the composition of *Il principe*. Machiavelli's image of the ideal ruler was informed, antithetically, by the qualities of leadership lacking in the deposed Soderini,[223] while chapters 15–19 were written as "a *polemical* reply to the traditional [humanist] catalogue of virtues."[224] Why polemic, if these were as stale, as generalized, and as un-Florentine as most of the "mirrors for princes" that have hitherto been cited? Because that tradition was not at its

[220] See above, pp. 184ff.

[221] See *Il principe* (ed. Inglese), p. v n. 2.

[222] See above, pp. 193–97; and cf. N. Matteucci, "Niccolò Machiavelli politologo," in Gilmore, *Studies on Machiavelli,* pp. 209ff., esp. pp. 243–46.

[223] See Pesman Cooper, "Machiavelli, Pier Soderini and *Il principe,*" pp. 119–44.

[224] Gilbert, "Humanist Conception," p. 114 (my italics), with idem, *Niccolò Machiavelli,* pp. 244–66.

last gasp, but alive in recent memory when *Il principe* was composed. In lectures held at the Studio and attended by Guicciardini, Buondelmonti, and others, the First Chancellor had held up to these "*principes*" a mirror that Machiavelli turned on its head. And in doing so, he demolished the model of moral conduct being constructed by his rival at the time when he wrote *Il principe*.

The bourgeois virtues that Marcello Virgilio had commended to the sons of the ruling elite during the first decade of the sixteenth century were being set, by him, on a new ethical basis during the second. That basis was furnished by a debate about the nature and kinds of knowledge, in which Machiavelli also participated. In his correspondence with Francesco Vettori, conducted while he was composing *Il principe,* its author pondered "the problematic nature of any *discorso* that pretended to analytical or empirical objectivity; the gap between the actions of princes and their *parole* and *dimostrazioni*."[225] The related issue of appearance and reality was addressed by Marcello Virgilio in his *praelusio* of 1514 on Machiavelli's favored theme of imitation.[226] The self-styled Socrates began by defending poetry from Plato's attack. Every discipline, he argued, derived from mimetic activity; and in the ontological gap between the original idea and the object that imitates it, a cognitive process was discernible. From the contingent and particular one proceeded, in the manner of Aristotle's *Physics,* to certain knowledge. Appearances, partial and imperfect, should be corrected in the light of ethical insight: such was the process that Marcello Virgilio exemplified in his orations on Bians and Phryne,[227] inducing rules for social and political conduct from ancient exempla. Some of them were ingenious, and all of them aimed to reduce the provisionality and ambiguity of experience to ideal order. Factual reality hardly concerned him. What exercised the state censor after 1512 was the development of a moralizing hermeneutic. With the *virgula censoria* that he had never relinquished since he had taken it up in 1496, he flailed semblances of being into what they ought to become.

"Because I want to write what will be useful to anyone capable of understanding, it seems to me better to concentrate on the actual truth, rather than the imagining, of reality." The problem raised at chapter 15 of *Il principe* was the same as that being discussed by Marcello Virgilio, but Machiavelli's solution was contrary to that of his former colleague. The distinction between how men should live and how they do; the flight into an imaginary realm of ethics; the dissolution of a concrete discourse about human conduct into speculative theories and general rules—all subjects on which the humanist, in his lectures, was attempting to lay down the law—were rejected on the grounds that the distinction being drawn between perception and

[225] Najemy, *Between Friends,* p. 149 (an excellent analysis).

[226] See above, pp. 200ff.

[227] See above, pp. 198ff., 203ff.

reality should be dismissed as meaningless. "One man *is considered* generous, another miserly . . . one *is considered* open-handed, another rapacious; one cruel, another merciful . . . and so on." So on throughout the sixteenth chapter into the next, where "every ruler should want *to be thought* merciful, not cruel." The insistent repetition hammered home the point: what, for the First Chancellor, was a hermeneutic *primum movens* that should be corrected by ethical intervention, Machiavelli regarded as the very nature of experience. Elusive, polyvalent, and manipulable, it was to be measured by its effect. In the sphere of political action, only a dreamer mused on the difference between what was and what might seem to be.

That dreamer was teaching moral and political philosophy while Machiavelli composed *Il principe*. Not by chance did dissembling, the Sallustian theme that Marcello Virgilio treated in his lecture on Phryne, appear in chapter 18 less as an affront to Christian ethics than as a virtue of *Realpolitik*. "Everyone has read the conspiracy of Catiline as narrated by Sallust," wrote Machiavelli at *Discorsi* 3.9,[228] but not everyone interpreted that author with the mentality, revealed (or satirized) in Vespucci's parenthesis "tametsi non baptizes,"[229] of a lay preacher to the young. Rather in the spirit of Bruni's *Oratio in hypocritas*[230] than in that of his reviver, Marcello Virgilio, Machiavelli dismissed motives and concentrated on *fama*. Fame and glory, to him legitimate aims of ambition in the public interest,[231] were being slighted at the Studio. The prime instance of success in acquiring both among the recent rulers mentioned at *Il principe* 21, Ferdinand of Aragon, manipulated religion to his political ends, hunted down Moors, and drove them out of his kingdom, noted Machiavelli with approval. The same monarch, related Marcello Virgilio in a *praelusio* on the satires of Horace,[232] received an ambassador from the Turkish sultan and was so impressed that a statue was erected to commemorate his *sapientia*. Which demonstrated that alien wisdom, interpreted in Horatian terms, could be derived as effectively from the pagan ancients as from an un-Christian envoy. The premise for such imitation was not the Machiavellian postulate of uniformity but difference—the difference that enabled Marcello Virgilio to regard Ferdinand of Aragon rather as an exemplar of religious tolerance than as a hero of the *Reconquista*. Inverting these pious illusions, Machiavelli's satire became tragedy. Dido was no longer Mar-

[228] On the Sallustian background, see Q. Skinner, "Machiavelli's *Discorsi* and the Pre-Humanist Origins of Republican Ideas," in Bock, Skinner, and Viroli, *Machiavelli and Republicanism*, pp. 123ff.

[229] See above, p. 240.

[230] See L. Gualdo Rosa, "Leonardo Bruni, l' 'Oratio in hypocritas' e i suoi difficili rapporti con Ambrogio Traversari," *Via monastica* 41 (1987): 1–23, esp. p. 22.

[231] See R. Price, "*Ambizione* in Machiavelli's Thought," pp. 383–445; and idem, "The Theme of *Gloria*," pp. 588–631.

[232] *R* fols. 67^{r-v}.

cello Virgilio's chatterbox and distraction from the mission of Aeneas,[233] but a queen poignantly voicing, at chapter 17 of *Il principe,* the "harsh necessity" that confronted *nuovi principi.*[234]

Underlining, by the Latin subtitles given to each chapter, his departures from the prescriptive style of the moralism that he was subverting, Machiavelli proposed a functional ethic of power for an individual prince to replace the standards that had been set, before 1512, for a class of "*principes*" by pseudo-Aristotle, "Brunian" humanism, and a miscellany of Christian clichés. But if he rejected the conventional values that Marcello Virgilio developed after that date, he shared his rival's disinclination to think in metaphysical terms. Both of them excluded all that was transcendental, mystical, ineffable. Products of the worldly culture of the Florentine Chancery, members of the generation that, against the religious hegemony that Savonarola and the *piagnoni* were thought to wish to erect, had asserted the claims of the laity, Machiavelli and Marcello Virgilio were united in their determination to assert the distinctness of the state. While the one tempered it with an observance of form that contributed to his long survival, the other took the same ambition to its extreme and made a moral mission of politics.[235] That is the sense of the redemptive rhetoric in chapter 26 of *Il principe,* where Machiavelli urged the cause of Italy's *libertas,* looked beyond Savonarola's vision of apocalypse, and assumed the mantle of the secular sage. And that is why, in the light of his prophetic persona and his views on the Christian religion,[236] it is instructive to compare the much-admired *Exhortatio ad capessendam Italiam in libertatemque a barbaris vindicandam* with an embarrassment to Machiavellian scholarship, the *Esortazione alla penitenza.*[237]

. . . . .

Can he have meant it sincerely? The usual answer is, "No." "A chatty joke" with a "certain veiled irony" for some,[238] the *Esortazione* appears to have been read in the light of Machiavelli's reply to the news from Francesco Guicciardini that he had been nominated to suggest a preacher for the Wool Guild.[239] Receiving (or pretending to have received) the letter while on the lavatory, the improbable intermediary of divine will recommended, on 17 May 1521, a preacher "slyer than Savonarola" to prepare the route to par-

[233] See above, p. 189.

[234] Cf. Najemy, *Between Friends,* pp. 210ff.

[235] Cf. Berlin, "Originality," pp. 168ff.; and Mansfield, *Machiavelli's Virtue,* pp. 6ff.

[236] See Tenenti, "La religione di Machiavelli," pp. 708–48. Cf. Preuss, "Machiavelli's Functional Analysis," pp. 171–90.

[237] Machiavelli, *Opere,* pp. 932–34.

[238] "Scherzosa cicalata," B. Croce, *Conversazioni critiche* 4 (Bari, 1951), p. 16; "Certa velata ironia," Villari, *Niccolò Machiavelli,* 3:200. See, too, Pacini, "Per una rilettura," pp. 125–36.

[239] *Epp.* 260 and 261, in Machiavelli, *Opere,* pp. 1202–4.

adise with a descent to hell. Was this the spirit of the *Esortazione*? Did Machiavelli play with Christian ideas of man's mutability into a devil, a slave, or a beast[240] with the same impishness that enabled him to poke fun at Pico's *De dignitate hominis* when, near the end of *L'Asino d'oro,* the pig declines to resume human shape?[241]

"No," is again the answer, but in a different and less embarrassed tone. Machiavelli's skepticism toward the Christian faith was coupled, and consistent, with the regard for ritual as a method of regulating civil society that is formulated in the eighteenth chapter of *Il principe*. Among the qualities of piety, faith, uprightness, and humanity, which the prince should have, or should appear to possess, "none" was "more necessary" than *religione*. That was the advice that Machiavelli followed, at his own level, in the *Esortazione alla penitenza*. The moral-didactic role that he played while delivering that work, after 1520, in the setting of one of the politically influential confraternities[242] had been previewed in the secular genre of his *Capitoli;*[243] and the *Esortazione* dealt with a subject of actual controversy. On 24 June 1520, the papal bull *Exsurge Domine,* formulated by a commission appointed by Cardinal Giulio de' Medici, who oversaw its deliberation in consistory, had condemned the views of Martin Luther.[244] Leo X's exhortation to penitence was flung into the flames on 10 December at Wittenberg by the unrepentant reformer.[245] Delivering his own version of a theme that had divided the cousin and predecessor of his patron from this rebel against Roman authority, Machiavelli had no option but strict orthodoxy. If respect for religious form need not entail belief, self-interest did not permit irony. The *Esortazione alla penitenza,* like the *Allocuzione ad un magistrato,* also composed in or after 1520,[246] was an exercise in an official genre, a sign of Machiavelli's gradual return and partial acceptance.

. . . . .

That acceptance lent fuel to the fire that Machiavelli brought to his dialectic with humanism. Here was the subject in which the *esperienza* he had

[240] "Diventa pertanto l'uomo, usando questa ingratitudine contro ad Dio, di angelo diavolo, di signore servo, di uomo bestia." *Esortazione,* in Machiavelli, *Opere,* p. 933.

[241] Ibid., p. 973.

[242] Cf. Weissman, "Sacred Eloquence," pp. 250ff., esp. p. 258. Cf. J. Henderson, *Piety and Charity in Late Medieval Florence* (Oxford, 1994).

[243] *Capitoli* (ed. Inglese). See Dionisotti, *Machiavellerie,* p. 99.

[244] *Dokumente zur Causa Lutheri (1517–1521),* vol. 2, *Vom Augsburger Reichstag 1518 zum Wormser Edikt 1521,* ed. P. Fabisch and E. Iserloh (Münster, 1991), pp. 317 and 322. For the controversy, cf. pp. 414ff.

[245] See H. A. Oberman, *Luther: Mensch zwischen Gott und Teufel* (Berlin, 1987), pp. 33ff.

[246] Edited and discussed by Marchand, in Machiavelli, *Allocuzione ad un magistrato* (ed. Marchand), pp. 209–21.

gained while organizing the militia amounted to expertise—the subject that Florentine chancellors, from Bruni to the Brunian reviver of his own generation, had recognized as a challenge, because it confronted them with the realities of military action, about which they knew little or nothing.[247] As in the *Discorsi,* so in the *Arte della guerra,* the failings of humanism were underlined by the choice of a form cultivated by its exponents. The dialogue, with its opening allusion to Cicero's *De oratore,*[248] is dominated by Fabrizio Colonna, celebrated among his contemporaries as a distinguished tactician.[249] In the persona of this master of warfare, Machiavelli (whose own militia had performed miserably in 1512) instructed his readers on the actuality of the example set by Roman writers on the same subject,[250] advancing a thesis of the unity of civil and military power opposed to the humanists' fragmented fantasies of peace.

Outside their circle, Machiavelli's Roman exempla had currency and resonance. Acknowledging his gift of the *Arte della guerra,* Cardinal Salviati hoped for a revival of ancient practices in the present age.[251] During the debate about the election of Lorenzo de' Medici to the office of captain-general of the Florentine forces, on 23 May 1515, the *Gonfaloniere* of Justice had supported the proposal with analogies to republican Rome.[252] Holding fast to its model and disparaging "the many who have held and hold the opinion" that civil and military life were distinct and unrelated, Machiavelli had at least one proponent of this view in mind: Marcello Virgilio, who, in 1515, from the public podium, had excused, on such grounds, his failure to produce an *arte della guerra.*[253] If words are so vehemently contrasted with actions throughout Machiavelli's work, it was because the time

[247] On Bruni and Machiavelli, see Bayley, *War and Society,* pp. 360ff., and the analysis of H. Baron's positions by Najemy, "Baron's Machiavelli," pp. 119–29.

[248] Dionisotti, *Machiavellerie,* p. 261; and V. Cox, *The Renaissance Dialogue: Literary Dialogue in Its Social and Political Contexts* (Cambridge, 1995), pp. 20–21. Cf. Senesi, "Niccolò Machiavelli," p. 309.

[249] It is misleading when Dionisotti (*Machiavellerie,* p. 261) describes Colonna (†20 March 1520) as living—a description applicable to part or whole of the period of composition (1519–20) of the *Arte della guerra,* but not to its time of publication (August 1521). On Colonna, see F. Petrucci in *DBI* 27 (1982), pp. 288–93.

[250] See Burd, "Le fonte letterarii," pp. 187–261. Cf. Sasso, *Machiavelli e gli antichi,* 1:401–536; and Gilbert, *Machiavelli and Guiccardini,* pp. 182ff.

[251] *Ep.* 266, in Machiavelli, *Opere,* p. 1202.

[252] "Nè trovando alcuno italiano esterno, per essere la milizia italiana molto mancata di capi, mossi dallo esemplo delle repubbliche passate et externe et italiane et *potissimum* della Repubblica Romana, la quale con li suoi Capitani proprii governò in modo li suoi eserciti et guerre che si fece gloriosissima et quasi madonna di tutto il mondo, pensorono che facilmente potesse essere che alla Repubblica fior.[na] succedessi, se non in tutto, almanco in qualche parte, simile cosa, quando si cominciasse ad usare qualche suo huomo in Capitano del suo esercito." Quoted by Giorgetti, "Lorenzo de' Medici," p. 209.

[253] See above, p. 243.

had come to replace the rhetoric of Hellenophile humanism with stout Roman virtues.

Hence continuity between the *Arte della guerra,* the *Discorsi,* and *Il principe*—a continuity of polemic developed by Fabrizio Colonna, at the beginning of the first book, not as a professor lecturing in the Studio but as a soldier-sage imparting his wisdom to the young.[254] Machiavelli's previous attempts to define the figure of an alternative teacher culminate in that martial mentor. Colonna exemplifies, more completely than the author, the principle of "una lunga esperienza delle cose moderne e una continua lezione delle antiche" that, throughout his previous writings, Machiavelli had advocated. The general is not at ease among the elegant amenities of the Orti Oricellari. To him, they reek of *ozio,* of indolence, of luxury. Colonna admonishes his audience to endure the harsh heat of the sun, to suffer the *cose forti e aspre* of "true and perfect antiquity,"[255] rejecting the notion that times have changed and ascribing the failure to achieve correspondence between the past and the present to the mutability of men.[256] Having touched on a theme of personal as well as intellectual relevance to Machiavelli, he recalls another discussed in the letters to Vettori, and cites Swiss performance in warfare as an example of successful implementation of Roman practice.[257] What, for Colonna, impeded understanding of "gli antichi modi e . . . l'anticha virtù" was degenerate modern *educazione.*[258] The young men of Florence, deluded by being taught to prefer *verba* to *res,*[259] should grasp that even modern artillery could be interpreted in ancient terms,[260] for in arms—as in poetry, painting, and sculpture—*le cose morte* might be revived.[261]

The authority that Machiavelli could not claim, Fabrizio Colonna possessed, substituting for the humanists' model of progress through emulative imitation one of reform conceived as restoration. Berating their shortcomings as teachers, he usurped their role as sages with an eloquence that, on the subject of warfare, a Florentine professor of rhetoric had recently lacked. It is through hard necessity that generals become orators, states the soldier at the end of Book 4—the necessity that "compels you either to vanquish or

[254] "Molte cose utili alla vita non solamente militare, ma ancora civile, saviamente da uno sapientissimo uomo disputate, imparino." Machiavelli, *Opere,* p. 303.

[255] "Quanto meglio arebbono fatto quelli, sia detto con pace di tutti, a cercare di somigliare gli antichi nelle cose forti e aspre, non nelle delicate e molli, e in quelle che facevano sotto il sole, non sotto l'ombra, e pigliare i modi della antichità vera e perfetta, non quelli della falsa e corotta." Ibid.

[256] Ibid., p. 306.

[257] See Najemy, *Between Friends,* pp. 156ff.

[258] Machiavelli, *Opere,* p. 313.

[259] Ibid., p. 326.

[260] Ibid., p. 342. Cf. F. Gilbert, "Machiavelli: The Renaissance of the Art of War," in P. Paret, ed., *Makers of Modern Strategy from Machiavelli to the Nuclear Age* (Princeton, 1986), pp. 11–31; and Mansfield, *Machiavelli's Virtue,* pp. 191ff.

[261] Machiavelli, *Opere,* p. 389.

to die."[262] The "Atticism" of the dedication to *Il principe* gives way to the laconicism of the *Arte della guerra,* pointing toward the contemptuous curtness with which, in Machiavelli's next work, Castruccio Castracani was to dismiss the mouthings of the rhetors as the "yelping of curs."[263]

. . . . .

The biography of Castruccio was completed, in haste, by 29 August 1520 at Lucca, where Machiavelli was representing the interests of Florentine merchants affected by the bankruptcy of a Lucchese citizen. On 6 September, Zanobi Buondelmonti commented on a draft that had been circulated among several of its author's friends. Although Buondelmonti's letter,[264] which foreshadows the commission to write the *Istorie fiorentine,* has often been discussed, one of the its most significant features has been overlooked. Alone in Machiavelli's extant correspondence after November 1512, it addresses him as *segretario fiorentino.*

No other writer committed that solecism. When the *Ufficiali dello Studio,* on 8 November 1520, drew up their contract, it was in the following simple and accurate terms: "Conduxerunt Nicholaum de Machiavellis *civem florentinum* . . . ad componendum annalia et cronacas florent."[265] That this formulation did not correspond to Machiavelli's desires in at least two respects can be demonstrated. He, in a letter to Francisco del Nero, had defined his wishes as "sia condocto . . . con obligo che debba et sia tenuto scrivere *gli annali o vero le storie* delle cose facte da lo stato et città di Firenze."[266] No mention was made, in his official contract, of the personal preference expressed in the distinction *o vero le storie;*[267] no word of the title "ciptadino et *segretario fiorentino,*" which is transmitted by all four manuscripts of the *Istorie fiorentine.*[268] Both reflected the private ambitions of their author, to which Buondelmonti was complicit.

His complicity was less ambiguous than that of the patron upon whom Machiavelli depended and by whom he was being used. From his return to Florence in 1519 until the conspiracy of May 1522, Giulio de' Medici pursued that apparently liberal policy which led many to believe that, following the signorial regime of the duke of Urbino, there had been a complete change.[269] It was in this context, at the cardinal's instigation, that the *Dis-*

[262] ". . . che ti costringe o vincere o morire." Ibid., p. 254. Cf. E. Raimondi, "Machiavelli and the Rhetoric of the Warrior," pp. 1–16.

[263] See above, p. 260.

[264] *Ep.* 254, in Machiavelli, *Opere,* pp. 1199–1200.

[265] Villari, *Niccolò Machiavelli,* 3:121.

[266] *Ep.* 255, in Machiavelli, *Opere,* p. 1200.

[267] Discussed by Rubinstein, "Machiavelli storico," pp. 699ff.

[268] See Martelli, "Machiavelli e la storiografia umanistica," pp. 128–29.

[269] ". . . pare che egli avesse interamente mutato cosi la persona propria, come l'ufficio, per-

cursus florentinarum rerum post mortem iunioris Laurentii Medicis, which advocated the restoration of a republic after his death and that of Leo X, were written. By tactics of division and rule that the writer of *Il principe* might have approved, had they not been turned against himself, Giulio, appearing to encourage the supporters of a *governo libero,* contrived to make them seem his supporters. Simultaneously reassuring the Medicean partisans that, in reality, he intended to alter nothing, he transformed the thinkers of the potential opposition into encomiasts of his cause.[270] Far from emerging as a champion of republicanism, Machiavelli, comparing the Florence of 1520 with a monarchy,[271] fell into a trap. Even in the eyes of his friend, Jacopo Nardi, he was perceived as the cardinal's man.[272] No Medici, not even the Magnificent Lorenzo, manipulated Florentine intellectuals with more shrewdness than the illegitimate Giulio.

He had reasons to be displeased with Machiavelli's rival. Compromised by his support for the ambitions of the duke of Urbino, Marcello Virgilio was frowned on by the cardinal seeking to emphasize his distance from Lorenzo's style of rule. If the merits of long-standing service and the tradition of lifelong tenure of office precluded the First Chancellor's removal, he could be taken down a peg at his other position of influence. There, in the Studio, Marcello Virgilio's appointment was allowed to lapse and that scourge of professors, his ex-colleague at Palazzo Vecchio, was hired by the *Ufficiali.*

In their name the cardinal commissioned Machiavelli to undertake a task that was different from what he had envisaged with the formula *gli annali o vero le storie.* What Machiavelli wished to write was an account of Florentine history before 1492:[273] hence his continuation and correction of the work of Bruni and Poggio. What he did not desire was specified, in his contract, by the phrase *annalia et cronacas:* the redaction, assigned to the Chancery since its reform in 1483, of *res gestae* or contemporary events. That is why it is hardly surprising that Machiavelli did not use the archival sources at Palazzo

ciò che egli si mostrò a tutta la nostra cittadanza umanissimo ne' fatti, e nelle udienze pazientissimo." Nardi, *Istorie,* 2:66, cited by Rubinstein, "Machiavelli storico," p. 713. Cf. Albertini, *Firenze,* pp. 37ff.

[270] ". . . cominciò, mediante d'alcuni molto buoni e forse troppo creduli cittadini, a seminare nell'universale qualche parola di voler rendere la libertà al popolo fiorentino; e cosi tenne viva quella oppinione, intanto che quasi non si dubitava punto che questa fusse simulazione." Nardi, *Istorie,* 2:69.

[271] "Parci, considerato tutto questo ordine come repubblica, e senza la vostra autorità, che non le manchi cosa alcuna, secondo che di sopra si è a lungo disputato e discorso: ma se si considera vivente la Santità Vostra e monsignore reverendissimo, ella è una monarchia." Machiavelli, *Opere,* p. 30, with Silvano, "Florentine Republicanism," pp. 57–60.

[272] ". . . alcune persone . . . composero alcune formule di governo libero, e alcune orazioni in lode singularissima della persona del cardinale, del numero de' quali principalmente fu Niccolò Machiavegli, il quale scrisse poi le Istorie Fiorentine ad istanza del medesimo cardinale." Nardi, *Istorie,* 2:70. Cf. the reaction of Antonio Brucioli, discussed by B. Richardson, "*The Prince* and Its Early Italian Readers," p. 34.

[273] Rubinstein, "Machiavelli storico," pp. 700–707.

Vecchio.[274] The material available to him when he wrote the *Decennale primo,*[275] the notes made by Marcello Virgilio on which Guicciardini drew for his *Storia d'Italia,*[276] the extracts from and comments on documents that Machiavelli and Buonaccorsi had compiled while working together in the Chancery[277] were all concerned with the history of Florence after 1492. Of that perilous territory he intended to steer clear.

On it he would have been a trespasser, with attendant political risks. They can be judged by the account of the French invasion composed, in embryo, by his former colleague. To this purpose, Marcello Virgilio made extracts from letters of state to and from the Dieci between April 1497 and June 1499.[278] He commented on them ("Si vuole dire ecc."), admonishing himself and his collaborators on how to develop, narrate, and analyze the raw material that he had gathered ("Vuolsi in questi tempi narrare," "Vuolsi descrivere"). An extension of this work was what Giulio de' Medici had in mind when he entrusted Machiavelli with the composition of *annalia et cronicas;* and if the reluctant historian admitted to Donato Giannotti his misgivings about writing, for a Medicean patron, an account of Florence from Cosimo to Lorenzo,[279] they applied a fortiori to the recent past. Flinching at the danger of discussing *le cause universali delle cose,* Machiavelli (as Giannotti reported him) privately echoed what Marcello Virgilio had publicly admitted in 1515.[280] They were at one in their hesitation before a subject still too hot to handle: the unwritten, but partly prepared, history of Florence after Lorenzo the Magnificent, a theme more suitable for that independent aristocrat, Bernardo Rucellai, than for a vulnerable ex-servant of state.

If Florence's recent history was to be avoided, its origins were a humanist theme par excellence. Combining scholarship with patriotism, they had provoked a controversy between generations. Poliziano had challenged Bruni's views on the subject,[281] and Machiavelli had attempted a synthesis of their opinions in the first chapter of Book 1 of the *Discorsi.*[282] He, who had been

[274] Ibid., pp. 721–22. On Machiavelli's sources, see G. M. Anselmi, *Ricerche sul Machiavelli storico* (Bologna, 1979), pp. 115–70; Cabrini, *Interpretazione;* and, in general, A. Matucci, *Machiavelli nella storiografia fiorentina* (Florence, 1991).

[275] Ridolfi, *Vita di Niccolò Machiavelli,* pp. 460–61.

[276] See Gerber, *Niccolò Machiavelli,* p. 21, with Pieraccioni, "Note su Machiavelli storico II," pp. 67ff.

[277] Gerber, *Niccolò Machiavelli,* pp. 14–16; Pieraccioni, "Note su Machiavelli storico I," pp. 637ff.

[278] In N. Machiavelli, *Opere,* vol. 2, ed. L. Passerini and G. Milanesi (Florence, 1873), pp. 129–56.

[279] Ridolfi, *Vita di Niccolò Machiavelli,* pp. 310ff.

[280] See above, p. 244.

[281] See N. Rubinstein, "Il Poliziano e la questione delle origini di Firenze," in *Poliziano e il suo tempo,* pp. 101–10.

[282] See the note, ad loc., of G. Inglese in Machiavelli, *Discorsi sopra la prima Deca di Tito Livio* (ed. Inglese), p. 193.

jocularly accused by Vespucci of writing in "Etruscan,"[283] had urged imitation of their forebears on the present Tuscans at *Discorsi* 2.4.[284] The exhortation reflected the lively interest in antiquities that had led Marcello Virgilio to write to Francesco Soderini in 1508 about an Etruscan inscription discovered in a tomb in the Val di Chiana,[285] and the cardinal in turn to send him, on 1 January 1509, an extract from Tacitus's *Annals* 1.79, which indicated the honor in which the Florentines had been held by the Romans fifteen hundred years earlier.[286] This is the information that Machiavelli incorporated into *Istorie fiorentine* 2.2, citing Tacitus in support of Poliziano's polemic against Bruni's belief that the original name of the city had been *Fluentia*.[287]

To read Tacitus, Machiavelli did not have to wait for the publication, at Leo X's wish, of the first six books of the *Annals* in 1515. This chapter was known to his circle since 1509 and copied, from Soderini's letter, into the collection of Marcello Virgilio's correspondence and *praelusiones* being made by Biagio Buonaccorsi.[288] If the extract was not used in the earlier *Discorsi,* it was not because it was inaccessible or unfamiliar to Machiavelli when he wrote that work, but because source-criticism had no place in the commentary that he used to conduct political polemic against contemporary humanists.[289] By 1520, the genre and the situation were different; and the Chancery tradition of historical writing, from Bruni to Poggio, was firmly rejected. Weighing up opinions on the names and origins of Florence at *Istorie fiorentine* 2.2,[290] Machiavelli cultivated the appearance of scholarly balance, in order to voice his deeper divergence from Bruni.

The alleged, and the real, reason for that difference was Bruni's (and Poggio's) neglect of internal conflicts.[291] Machiavelli would treat what they had omitted. "It is not my intention," he wrote in the proemium to Book 1, "to occupy the place of others." No more ironical sentence is to be found in his entire oeuvre. Since 1513 Machiavelli had been actively engaged in "occupying the place" of humanist chancellors of the Florentine Republic, while implementing a scorched-earth policy. It was pursued, in the *Istorie fiorentine,*

[283] See above, p. 258.

[284] Cf. Tommasini, *La vita e gli scritti,* 2:154–55.

[285] See K.J.P. Lowe, *Church and Politics in Renaissance Italy: The Life and Career of Cardinal Francesco Soderini, 1453–1524* (Cambridge, 1995), pp. 258–60; for Soderini's reply, see Bandini, *Collectio,* pp. 31–32.

[286] "Videtis enim nostros homines supra millesimum et quingentesimum annum Florentinos appellatos apud Populum Romanum." Ed. C. Fea, *Miscellanea filologica critica e antiquaria . . .,* vol. 1 (Rome, 1790), p. 328.

[287] Machiavelli, *Opere,* pp. 659–60, with Rubinstein, "Machiavelli e le origini di Firenze," pp. 952–59.

[288] *L* fols. 50^r–52^r, with Richardson, "A Manuscript," pp. 589–90.

[289] See above, p. 268.

[290] Cf. Rubinstein, "Machiavelli storico," p. 724.

[291] See Najemy, "*Arti* and *Ordini,*" pp. 161–91.

with a moralism that links him with the concerns of his rival. Writing about the corrupting peace of the Laurentian age in Book 7.28, for example, he condemned the decadence of "the young men of Florence, forgetful of the customs of the past," who spent extravagantly on clothes and banquets, games and women. Given over to the pursuit of idleness and frivolities, they typified decadence.[292]

This was the same theme treated by Marcello Virgilio in his oration on Phryne,[293] where the dissipation of Theban youth was compared to that of the Florentines. The official moralist, however, had treated the levities of high society with indulgence. Sumptuousness and whore-mongering were not, for him, symptomatic of a cultural malaise that led to "the politics of factionalism and hegemony."[294] What mattered was sincerity: the ability to distinguish between the concealed virtue of a prostitute and the specious allurements of a grande dame. If they were symptomatic of corruption, decadence derived from misapprehended rules of social conduct, which might be adjusted. The First Chancellor had no interest in penetrating the masks of public behavior and revealing the political disengagement that lay behind them. History—even Florentine history—was viewed by Marcello Virgilio as a manifestation of contingency, beyond which one should look. Patterns or parallels, if discernible, arose from similar ethical attitudes. The censor's rod was wielded only in the realm of letters. No history, little politics after 1512: rather, a sententiousness tempered by deference to social forms that might be corrected but not controlled. To this flaccid formalism Machiavelli opposed, with Colonna's toughness, the proemium to Book 5 of his *Istorie fiorentine*.

The concept of *anakyklosis* formulated there is not the same as that discussed in the *Discorsi*. No room is made for contingency, even as a consequence of imperfect perception; and cyclical movements of recurrence both order and transcend the uniformity of human nature in time and space.[295] Here the paradoxes of Machiavelli's thought are evident. Departing from Polybius's model and altering his own, he is restrained, by the logic of his theory, from taking the further step and denying that classical authorities, divorced from their context and differing among themselves, can shed light on the present. That view, however, is implicit in the manner in which Machiavelli presents decline. Rejecting the interpretations of Sallust and Tacitus, which linked the flourishing of the arts with periods of political freedom, he claims that philosophy and literature, hallmarks of decadent *ozio,* inevitably follow a golden age of military virtue.[296] This rejection of the ide-

[292] Machiavelli, *Opere,* p. 811.

[293] See pp. 202ff. above.

[294] Najemy, "Machiavelli and the Medici," p. 573.

[295] Ibid., pp. 575–76; and G. Sasso, *Studi su Machiavelli* (Naples, 1967), pp. 210–14.

[296] Machiavelli, *Opere,* p. 738, with F. Gilbert, "Machiavelli's 'Istorie fiorentine,'" pp. 86 and 98.

ology of *renovatio,* essential to the humanist image of Lorenzo de' Medici that had recently been given a new lease on life,[297] posed an embarrassing question. If such a dim view of learning and letters was to be taken, what were its implications for the author of the *Istorie fiorentine*—an *uomo litterato,* developing his own philosophy of history?

It would not do to decry the age—the *tempora,* the *mores.* Machiavelli was part of them, his writing vulnerable to the charge that he had leveled against others. His solution to this problem was suggested by Marcello Virgilio, who, in 1498, had selected as his model Cato the censor.[298] Evoking, in the proemium to Book 5, the same Cato who had expelled philosophers from Rome, Machiavelli not only turned away from the Athenians to the Rome of his hero Colonna, but also purged it of all *uomini litterati* engaged in activities less serious than his own. Hence the irony of the sentence: "It is not my intention to occupy the place of others." Others, such as Marcello Virgilio, were displaced in terms that they would have understood, as the authority of Bruni's reviver was undermined by appropriating his language of censorship.

Rejecting Bruni, historian and apologist of the Florentine optimates, and taking up such writers of the opposition to Medicean primacy as Giovanni Cavalcanti,[299] Machiavelli transformed the figure of the youthful hero, endowed with *virtù istrordinaria,* which had been central to the myth of the redeemer propagated by Marcello Virgilio since 1511.[300] In its place were put the less ostentatious Medici, the figures from the shades—Vieri and Giovanni, who had avoided the appearance or the substance of tyranny[301]—reinforced by examples that contained a veiled warning. At *Istorie fiorentine* 8.2, for instance, after relating Lorenzo's harsh measures against the rival Pazzi, Machiavelli attributes an admonition to Giuliano de' Medici: "If you wish [to take] too much, you stand in danger of losing everything." These ominous words were dated to the period immediately before the Pazzi conspiracy in which Giuliano, the cardinal's father, had been assassinated. Written after the plot to murder Giulio de' Medici in 1522, they acquired a more immediate menace.

In the *Istorie fiorentine,* the tensions latent and present in Machiavelli's previous writings are brought to a head. His polemic, sustained in each of his works, was more actual and more specific than has been allowed. Discussions

[297] See p. 244.

[298] See above, p. 178.

[299] See Anselmi, *Ricerche,* pp. 125ff. (cited in note 274); and M. Marietti, "Machiavel historiographe des Médicis," in *Les écrivains et le pouvoir en Italie à l'époque de la Renaissance,* ed. A. Rochon (Paris, 1974), pp. 127ff.

[300] See above, p. 196; and Najemy, "Machiavelli and the Medici," pp. 560ff.

[301] Marietti, "Machiavel historiographe," pp. 148ff.; cf. eadem, "L'uso dell' 'antologia' nelle 'Istorie fiorentine,'" in *Culture e société,* pp. 197ff.; and Rubinstein, "Machiavelli storico," pp. 716ff.

with like-minded garden guests in the Orti Oricellari fail to account for the edge and the satire with which Machiavelli denounced the shortcomings of "others," of "some," and of "many." These references, which to us seem generic or vague, held for his contemporaries point and sting. Humanism, in its political and ethical versions all too opportunely professed by a figure of the establishment, provided one of Machiavelli's targets. Religion offered another, for Savonarola had taught him a lesson in how it could be manipulated to political ends. Styling himself a prophet and a teacher, he employed terms and ideas that were current at Florence from the last decade of the fifteenth century to the second quarter of the sixteenth. And if it is undeniable that Machiavelli stamped them with his own imprint, it has not been recognized that they were intended, in their original context, to represent the obverse of a medal molded by Savonarola and Marcello Virgilio.

Late in 1525, Machiavelli found a measure of the detachment required for self-irony. Writing then to Francesco Guicciardini, he imprecated against "the *principi,* who have brought us to this pass," and signed himself "historico, comico, et tragico."[302] The tragi-comic fate of a historian, as he now regarded it, made it unnecessary to insist on the title *segretario fiorentino*. Guicciardini knew the truth. Such illusions were for the broader public, which could not sense their bitter private resonance. Almost to the end, the dark *flores* of Niccolò Machiavelli's originality blossomed in the shadows cast by the Chancery.

[302] *Ep*. 291, in Machiavelli, *Opere,* p. 1224.

VII

PHYSICIANS OF THE INTELLECT

MEDICAL metaphors are recurrent in the political and intellectual discourse of Florentine humanists during the High Renaissance.[1] Malady and corruption, disease and decline: such are the images with which these physicians of the intellect diagnosed the ills of their culture and prescribed a *cura animorum*.[2] Their rhetoric of crisis mounted to fortissimo at what is now considered one of the highest and healthiest points of European civilization. Not all of their laments should be taken seriously. There has been no period in its long history when humanism, according to its exponents, has not been in crisis.[3]

The history of Florence, in the period from Poliziano to Machiavelli, may seem to lend substance to these topoi. Invasion by the French, the expulsion of the Medici, divisions between Savonarola's supporters and opponents both during and after his ascendancy, the loss of Pisa, and the travails of the *governo popolare* were factors that led intellectuals, turning away from a depressing present and recalling the liberties (real or imagined) of the past, to amplify an alarm sounded, in previous emergencies, by Salutati and Bruni. Whether this republican nostalgia amounted to yet another crisis in the late Quattro- and early Cinquecento may be doubted. Behind the facade of humanist eloquence, there lurked a confidence that derived from a stable oligarchical tradition.

Bruni and Salutati had employed the deceptive language of freedom, and appealed to the elusive standards of republicanism.[4] As chancellors of the Florentine Republic, this was their task. Marcello Virgilio manipulated the same illusions, in order to defend the city's independence and serve the interests of its ruling elite. Despite the slogan of a *governo popolare*, the compo-

[1] Cf. L. Zanzi, *I "segni" della natura e i "paradigmi" della storia: Il metodo di Machiavelli: Ricerche sulla logica scentifica degli "umanisti" tra medicina e storia* (Mandura, 1981).

[2] On the theme of cultural pessimism, cf. K.A.A. Enenkel, *Kulturoptimismus und Kulturpessimismus in der Renaissance: Studie zu Jacobus Canters "Dyalogus de solitudine" mit kritischer Textausgabe und deutscher Übersetzung* (Frankfurt, 1995), pp. 17ff.

[3] E.g., John of Salisbury *Metalogicon* 1; Curtius, *ELLMA,* foreword; Baron, *Crisis,* passim; Kristeller, *Iter Italicum* 5 (Leiden, 1992), p. xxii; Hankins, *Plato in the Italian Renaissance,* 1:365–66.

[4] Cf. Caroli's distinction (*De suis temporibus,* Vatican lat. 5878, fol. 188^{v}) between "vera libertas" and "fucata et vulgaris." See Hankins, "Humanism," pp. 120ff.; and Q. Skinner, "The Republican Ideal of Political Liberty," in Bock, Skinner, and Viroli, *Machiavelli and Republicanism,* pp. 293ff.

sition of that restricted group changed little after 1494.[5] What altered were its ideology and cultural politics, which had to be distinguished from those of the Medici. Marcello Virgilio accordingly repudiated the philological approach tainted by its link with Lorenzo's house, becoming the successor of both Poliziano and Scala—only to revert, after 1512, to the technical scholarship that he had appeared so decisively to discard. Two tendencies in Florentine humanism—the official and the philological—that are sometimes regarded as mutually exclusive were combined in this protean persona. What united them was politics—the politics that required a layman excluded, by birth and background, from the *reggimento* to make his way in the world through institutions controlled by the government of the day: the Studio and the Chancery. Angelo Poliziano belonged to one; Marcello Virgilio to both; Niccolò Machiavelli, *post res perditas,* to neither.

The position and career of the secular intellectual, at Florence, was defined in terms of these institutions—not of "civic" humanism, the concept that has shaped and influenced the study of the Italian Renaissance.[6] "Civic" humanism, during the late Quattro- and early Cinquecento, did not exist. Its origins lie in the political and intellectual history of the Weimar Republic;[7] and its typological distinctions between "individualism" and "public" engagement obscure the fact that its self-styled champion, in the years 1495–1512, provided the republican rhetoric used to promote the cause of the oligarchy.

If Marcello Virgilio, like several of his predecessors as chancellor, changed position, that was not because he betrayed the cause of liberty to make capital, after the restoration, as a Medicean partisan. Adaptation was necessary in his institutional role. The office that he and his subordinates occupied was not, could not be, and never had been independent. No humanist at Palazzo Vecchio was permitted to speak, in his own voice, on political matters. The occupation and duty of Machiavelli's colleague were to act as spokesman for the *governo popolare* and then to do the same for the new masters of the city—"trimming his sails to the buffets of fortune," in Poliziano's metaphor.[8] Was this the Aristotelian virtue of a Lorenzo de' Medici? Or the unscrupulous opportunism of a Talleyrand?[9]

[5] See Pesman Cooper, "The Florentine Ruling Group," pp. 71–171, esp. pp. 113–15; Rubinstein, "Oligarchy and Democracy," pp. 107–10.

[6] See Hankins, "The 'Baron Thesis,'" pp. 309–38; and J. Najemy's review of H. Baron, *In Search of Florentine Civic Humanism,* pp. 340–50. Cf. A. Rabil, Jr., "The Significance of 'Civic Humanism' in the Interpretation of the Italian Renaissance," in *Renaissance Humanism: Foundations, Forms, and Legacy,* vol. 1, *Humanism in Italy,* ed. A. Rabil, Jr. (Philadelphia, 1988), pp. 142–74.

[7] See, best, Fubini, "Renaissance Historian," pp. 541–74.

[8] See above, p. 17.

[9] Cf. the metaphors of J. Orieux, *Talleyrand ou le sphinx incompris* (Paris, 1970), p. 824: "Pour lui, les tempêtes ne se paraient d'aucun prestige et le malheur d'aucune poésie. Ce n'étaient

Such questions may be answered by moralists, according to their point of view. Marcello Virgilio, on the second floor of Palazzo Vecchio, had a different perspective. The public orator of Machiavelli's generation was permitted to voice his opinions, within limits, not from the Chancery but ex cathedra. When he did so, his tones were authoritarian. The pretense of liberty, equality, and freedom of speech in the restored Republic was exposed by the disciplinarian drive of the censor; and the *reggimento* acknowledged his claims when, in 1507, it gave him custody of the province of letters.[10] There, with the rigor of a Platonic guardian of the state, he submitted Homer, Virgil, and a host of classical authors to the sway of his arbitrary interpretations. Yet if Marcello Virgilio was a literary despot and his "civic" humanism a sham—readily assumed on the rise, and jettisoned with equal facility after the fall, of the regime that it supported—that was what made him a true heir of Salutati and Bruni. The real continuity in the positions of the humanists who held the office of chancellor at Renaissance Florence lay less in their republican convictions than in their subordination to power.

No one understood this better, or felt it more keenly, than Niccolò Machiavelli. The difference between being and seeming, like the political uses of a carefully crafted reputation, figures prominently in his works, not only because it was a current theme of debate. Experience, prolonged and bitter, of a humanist in a similar station taught Machiavelli the meaning, at his own social level, of feigning, dissembling, and *Realpolitik*. Just as he penetrated the veneer of Marcello Virgilio's moralism and revealed the emptiness of his eloquence, so he saw through the rhetoric of republicanism with which self-interest might be masked and careers advanced or made. These were hardly the insights of heroism. More searching and innovative (if less successful) than his rival, Machiavelli played a variant on the same theme. When, in the course of his writings from the *Discorsi* to the *Istorie fiorentine,* he took an increasingly critical view of such intellectuals of the establishment as the Brunian reviver of his own generation and, ultimately, of Bruni himself,[11] that was because he failed to achieve even their honorary membership of it. Tolerable during the years 1502–12, when he enjoyed the favor of the *Gonfaloniere a vita,* Machiavelli's situation became harder to bear after his removal from office. Having breathed no word of dissent under Soderini, he then emerged as an acute but circumspect critic, striving to rehabilitate himself in institutional terms. Both as an alternative teacher and, especially, as a *segretario fiorentino*—the dignity that he no longer possessed and never regained—

---

que les formes de la brutalité et de l'imbécillité du monde. Néanmoins, puisque le monde était tel, il sut s'en accommoder, naviguer sans naufrage, trouver un port, quel qu'il fût, et y débarquer avec autant de désinvolture que s'il eût abordé Cythère. Il se fit un bonheur comme d'autres se font une situation."

[10] See below, pp. 151ff.

[11] Cf. above, pp. 226ff.; and see Najemy, "Baron's Machiavelli," pp. 123ff.

Machiavelli attempted to recover a lost identity in terms of the only professional categories that he knew.

. . . . .

During Machiavelli's youth, the changing role of the intellectual was a topic that had been brought to the forefront of discussion by philologists, who had more reason than the officials of Palazzo Vecchio to employ the language of crisis. Following Lorenzo's death, and in the absence of his restraining influence, a controversy erupted between Scala and Poliziano.[12] It was not a struggle between "civic" and philological humanism but, specifically, a feud between a bureaucrat and a professor. Heightened by personal animus, it illustrated the differences between two types of thinker at Florence. Poliziano caricatured Scala as an ignoramus: the chancellor dismissed him as a gnat. Command of Greek and Latin was rather the issue than the cause of the conflict. At stake was the meaning and purpose of the specialized erudition practiced by an elite as opposed to an applied learning with roots in the politics and administration of the city. Old-fashioned in the eyes of a newfangled Hellenist like Poliziano, Scala regarded him as marginal to the mainstream of public life. At Florence, after 1494, it was the chancellor's view that prevailed.

The precariousness of philological humanism was evident to its Renaissance practitioners. With a mixture of pride, concern, and defiance, they recognized the problem and were not slow to draw its consequences. When Lorenzo was still young and Poliziano, in 1480, had returned to Florence from Venice, where he had made the acquaintance of Ermolao Barbaro, the twenty-six-year-old philologist received from his new friend a premonition of death:

> I demand from you two things, as if by right. First, that you do your utmost to lead a long life, not for your own sake—although for your own sake as well, to be sure—but primarily in the cause of literature and scholarship, which (Heaven knows!) in their state of decay, decadence, and imminent danger of collapse need to be rescued by men of expertise who should take urgent measures to succor them. Second, that you either enroll me as an ally in this enterprise or that you calmly permit me to enroll you.[13]

It is a patrician who writes, treating a plebeian as his equal in a common undertaking of cultural revival. An emergency is announced by Barbaro, an ur-

[12] See above, pp. 126ff.

[13] "Postulo autem a te quasi meo iure duo. Primum, uti vivere diu studeas, non tibi—sed et tibi sane—dum litteris primum et bonis artibus, quibus (hercule!) succurrendum est ruinosis et nutantibus brevique casuris, nisi per solertissimos homines ope summa prospiciatur. Alterum uti aut tu me socium in haec adhibeas, aut a me adhibitus aequo animo patiare." *Politiani Opera,* 1:14.

gent threat to learning; on the verge of collapse, it needs to be shored up; yet the team of rescuers numbers precisely two.

One of them was alive to the scholarly strength and social weakness of his position. To Barbaro's hyperbole, Poliziano replied with studied irony, mingling praise with reserve:

> The words with which you, like a good commander, urge me, your soldier, to mount a rescue operation on behalf of rigorous scholarship that is under assault, as it were, on both fronts, affect me less [by their flattery] because, in point of fact, I see very few of your caliber whom I would be willing to follow as leaders.[14]

The primary sense of this figurative language is military. *Imperator,* however, can mean not only "commander" or "general," but also "emperor"—a double entendre that captures Barbaro's imperious tone. From the lower ranks of the intellectual infantry, the foot-soldier Poliziano perceives "very few *duces*." Few, not none. The compliment to his superior's singularity is relativized by the adjective and by the noun. *Duces* signifies both authoritative "leaders" and more companionable guides. Barbaro, stationed by Poliziano on a pedestal, is wryly reminded that there is room for two.

Their alliance of mutual admiration admitted, as equals, Pico and Lorenzo, both of them "not men but heroes."[15] Heroization of scholarship entailed denigration of the vulgar craving for fame. "These specious signs of good-willed popularity," wrote Poliziano to Barbaro, "which are like artificial tricks, you (it seems to me) do not desire and I abhor."[16] The illusion of a self-sufficient republic of letters could be sustained, in its fragility, only so long as the heroes remained in their places. Movement was fatal and, in 1491, it occurred with Barbaro's promotion to the patriarchate of Aquileia. Writing to congratulate him, Poliziano noted that the still waters had been stirred, and that his own reflection had changed shape:

> Of highest birth and amply endowed background, having achieved outstanding success in your career, you command the heights of virtually all the disciplines and so lovingly embrace professors and scholars (although we are generally of low station) that you lower the banner and standard of your quasi-regal authority as a token of submission to us all.[17]

[14] "Verba porro, quibus velut me militem bonus imperator hortaris, ut rectis studiis utroque quasi cornu laborantibus succurram, eo minus moverunt, quod sane quam paucos tui similes video, quos duces sequar." Ibid., p. 15.

[15] "Testis Medices Laurentius meus, testis hic item Mirandula Picus, heroes (ut arbitror) duo, non viri, quos aut auditores habeo laudum tuarum attentissimos, aut benevolentissimos praedicatores." Ibid., p. 16

[16] "Speciosa ista et popolaria benevolentiae ostentamenta quasi fucum et praestigias neque tu (arbitror) desideras et ego abominor." Ibid., p. 17.

[17] "Et enim summo loco natus, amplis opibus innutritus, egregiis honoribus perfunctus et fastigium disciplinarum prope omnium tenes et professores ac studiosos artium bonarum

What had begun as an ambiguous *courtoisie* between peers became deference to a hierarchical superior. Barbaro, in his institutional eminence, reinforced by birth and wealth, could no longer be regarded simply as an ally, a collaborator, or a colleague. He had also to be acknowledged as a potential patron. The mirage of an aristocracy of the intellect dissolved before the reality of a prince of the church; and the client-canon Poliziano, with unfulfilled designs on a cardinal's hat, perceived that all he had achieved was a professor's chair. These are not the exultant and introverted tones of the preface to *Miscellanea* 1.[18] A growing sobriety is detectable in the writings of Poliziano's last years, a heightened awareness that, as Scala taunted, he was no more or less than the house-philologist of the Medici.

Scala was right. Philology was not identical with Florentine humanism, but a divergence from the main route of its official tradition. That is why the crisis proclaimed by the *grammatici* deserves closer analysis. In its exclusiveness lay both the attraction and the weakness of their approach, revealed by its permanent vulnerability and temporary collapse on Poliziano's death. And if his legacy was capable of revival after 1512, it was not only because he had taught Marcello Virgilio how to collate a manuscript or establish a text. Such techniques, as their pioneer saw clearly, were instrumental, a means to an end. That end was the defense of *enkyklios paideia*. No Florentine humanist was more sensitive, more attentive, more alert than Poliziano to the criticism that the technical scholarship that he glorified belonged in the schoolroom.

The age-old charge[19] had recently been compounded by the skepticism of the Ferrarese medical humanists, who denied the universality of philological pursuits. To them and to others, Poliziano had offered an incomplete apology for the humanities when he died in 1494. The task that he left unfinished was taken up, after the restoration and in the interests of his patron's dynasty, by Marcello Virgilio, whose Dioscorides amounted to a continuation, on the same battlefields and with the same weapons, of the war fought by his teacher from Florence to defend, against the onslaught of the new specialists, the venerable ideal of an integrated culture. With the encyclopedic aims of a new Varro, Marcello Virgilio planned, in the manner of Ermolao Barbaro,[20] to extend this enterprise to the Aristotelian corpus. And here, at the point where Agostino Nifo declined to further a project launched by two generations of Florentine humanists, Pier Vettori entered the scene.

Vettori, the patrician excluded by the Medici from politics, expressed his patriotism by other means. His philology—in particular, his work on Aristotle—appears enigmatic, if it is separated from the wider context of his

(quamvis humili fortuna plerique sumus) ita complecteris et amas, ut aeque cunctis tuae quasi maiestatis fasces ac vexilla submittas." Ibid., p. 19.

[18] See above, pp. 89ff.

[19] Cf. Fubini, "L'umanista," pp. 435ff.

[20] See above, p. 219.

teaching.[21] The dedication of Vettori's commented edition of the Aristotelian *Poetics*[22] cites the names of Poliziano and Marullo as Florentine *poetae docti,* asserting the public utility of literature in providing moral correction and examples of how to govern the state, in the manner of Marcello Virgilio.[23] It was therefore natural that Vettori turned to Aristotle's political writings,[24] ethics, and rhetoric that, in his lectures, he presented as parts of an indivisible whole.[25] In the city that had witnessed the first publication of the *Organon* (1520),[26] where its author's complete writings had been commented on by Marcello Virgilio,[27] Vettori, holder of the same chair of poetry and oratory, transferred to the Aristotelian corpus his predecessors' enterprise of *enkyklios paideia.*

Defense of the unity of learning, with its center in the verbal arts and its focus on the ruling class, was the ideal that lay behind his scholarship. At Florence, Vettori was not an instigator but a continuator and modifier of the tradition developed by both Hellenists who had occupied his post. If the philological methods of Poliziano were received with more enthusiasm north of the Alps, in the city where they were criticized, rejected, and eventually restored, a sense of their cultural purpose was never lost. When, in June 1539, "Ambrosius Nicander" wrote to Vettori from Ancona, expressing the hope that he would perform for Florence the same services rendered by Poliziano and Marcello Virgilio,[28] he coupled their names because he understood that the recently appointed professor had not one teacher or model, but two.

. . . . .

The discontinuous history of philological humanism at Florence, throughout and beyond Machiavelli's lifetime, had little of the triumphalism and none of the teleology that still characterize some accounts of classical scholarship. If the purveyors of *enkyklios paideia* were defensive, they had reason

[21] Grafton, *Joseph Scaliger,* 1:52ff.

[22] See A. Porro, "Pier Vettori editore di testi greci: La 'Poetica' di Aristotele," *IMU* 26 (1983): 307–60; and Kraye, "Renaissance Commentaries," pp. 114ff.

[23] *Petri Victorii commentarii in primum librum Aristotelis de arte poetarum,,* pp. *aiii–iiii:* "Quis enim nescit Marullum Politianumque in bonis valde poetis enumerandos? . . . mores simul vitamque ab omne labe culpaque emendare . . . quantum vero studium veteres pöetas adhibere soliti sint, ut vitae hominum prodessent."

[24] *Petri Victorii commentarii in VIII libros Aristotelis de optimo statu civitatis.*

[25] *Petri Victorii epistolarum libri X, orationes XIIII et liber de laudibus Ioannae Austriacae,* pp. 1, 4, 9, 17.

[26] See Schmitt, *Aristotle in the Renaissance,* p. 31; and F. E. Cranz, *A Bibliography of Aristotle Editions, 1501–1600,* 2d ed., revised by C. Schmitt (Baden-Baden, 1984), pp. 117–18.

[27] See above, p. 251.

[28] *Clarorum Italorum et Germanorum epistolae ad Petrum Victorium* (ed. Bandini), p. 8; and cf. pp. 2 and 25.

to be so. Scorned as schoolmasters, parodied as pedants, the *grammatici* struck back with an image of their activities intended to demonstrate their contested superiority. The image was that of the censor. One of the intellectual origins of Italian censorship lies in the Florentine Quattrocento, long before its formal establishment at Rome in the Congregations of the Inquisition and the Index.[29] Niccolò Perotti's call, in 1470, for press correction to be overseen by a scholar appointed by the pope was not identical with the control exercised in the banning of a number of Pico's nine hundred theses[30] or with the edict of 1487 ordering publishers to submit to the ecclesiastical authorities the works that they intended to bring out.[31] Nor was the Church alone in its aspirations to surveillance. Laymen, at Florence, claimed less official rights of intervention. Poliziano, affecting to decline the title of censor, had aspired to that informal status.[32] Such was the point of his insistent polemic: to establish his dominion in the republic of letters by eliminating critics and rivals; and the imperative character of his scholarly persona was lent an absolutist stamp by Marcello Virgilio. Rather than banishing the poets like Plato, the First Chancellor "added to, subtracted from, and athetized them." In an age when the printed book was being hailed by humanists as a sign of progress,[33] and scholars and nonspecialists alike regarded publication as an advance,[34] that authority was not negligible. Conceived as a counterbalance to the influence that Savonarola had exerted, Marcello Virgilio's institutional appointment as censor was complemented and strengthened by the role of the lay sage taken over from Ficino and played out on the stage of the Studio.

. . . . .

These were some of the strains in Florentine high culture, to and against which Niccolò Machiavelli reacted after 1512. They are hardly intelligible in terms of the traditional antitheses between "civic" humanism and individualism, republican conviction and support for a principate. In the crucial

[29] See further the Appendix.

[30] See J. Monfasani, "The First Call for Press Censorship: Niccolò Perotti, Giovanni Andrea Bussi, Antonio Moreto, and the Editing of Pliny's *Natural History*," *Renaissance Quarterly* 41 (1988): 1–31, with M. Davies, "Making Sense of Pliny in the Quattrocento," *Renaissance Studies* 9 (1995): 248 and n. 33. On the censorship of the *Conclusiones*, see G. Blasio, *Cum gratia et privilegio: Programmi editoriali e politica pontificia, Roma, 1487–1527* (Rome, 1988), pp. 11–19. Cf. Pico della Mirandola, *Conclusiones nongentae* (ed. Biondi), pp. xxxiff.

[31] Still fundamental is Hilgers, *Der Index der verbotenen Bücher*, pp. 3ff. Cf. R. Hirsch, "Pre-Reformation Censorship of Printed Books," *Library Chronicle* 21 (1955): 103; Lopez, *Sul libro a stampa;* and Grendler, *Roman Inquisition*, pp. 63ff.

[32] See above, pp. 90ff.

[33] Cf. Davies, "Humanism in Script and Print," pp. 53ff.

[34] See above, p. 201.

period of his partial rehabilitation (1519–22), that ambiguous "republican" Machiavelli was confronted with a prince who shared, and implemented, some of his views. Giulio de' Medici exploited the appearance of conciliation with all the guile of the ruler described in *Il principe*. He was prepared to permit the harmless fiction of an illegitimate title published by Machiavelli on the title page of a work that was in the public interest. He was willing to tolerate, for a time, that modest proposal for a return (in the unspecified future) to republican forms contained in the *Discursus rerum florentinarum,* which was composed at his own instance. At his own instance, was the point. Machiavelli was made to seem the cardinal's man; and when there was need of his writing, it fell victim, at the hands of Nifo, to the *Realpolitik* that it advocated.

If Machiavelli's vulnerability is understandable and his critique of humanism justified, his unwillingness to deal directly, in the *Istorie fiorentine,* with events after 1492 is a matter for regret. A portrait by his hand of Cardinal Giulio de' Medici between 1519 and 1522 would undoubtedly have matched or surpassed the splendor of Guicciardini's picture of Pope Clement VII in the *Storia d'Italia*. Undoubtedly, because we already possess it in outline. The "civic" prince—subtle and unscrupulous, urbane and calculating—so brilliantly depicted in *Il principe* bears no resemblance to the blunt features of that autocratic bonehead, Lorenzo, duke of Urbino. It is a sketch, had Machiavelli known it, of Cardinal Giulio, the patron (and censor) who would take his work from him. Retaining a dubious dignity and an arduous task, the author of the *Istorie fiorentine,* from seven years after his expulsion from Palazzo Vecchio until his death, was not a *segretario fiorentino* but the *bono et fidatto instrumento* of a Machiavellian Medici.

Cardinal Giulio and Savonarola, leading figures in Florentine culture of the late Quattro- and early Cinquecento, understood its weaknesses and exploited them. Machiavelli stood closer to both of them than has been suspected. As an "Atticist" critic of humanist "Asianism" and a prophet surveying the past, present, and future, this antitype and antagonist of the friar shared the fascination of his contemporaries with Savonarola. Religious fervor was scarcely Machiavelli's motive. Many of the ideas of this martyr to the sinister cause of *Florentina libertas* had a wide and deep appeal because they seemed, in the claustrophobia of the city's humanism, fresh, cogent, and liberating. Most of the criticisms leveled by Savonarola against its exponents were true. Posterity, which has revered or reviled him as a fanatic, might pay him the compliment that Florentine thinkers did not deny him—and consider Socrates from Ferrara, in his own terms, as an intellectual.

The humanist who offered a secular alternative to Savonarola's spiritual message, Marcello Virgilio, began by rejecting the cultural politics of the Medici and ended by furthering them. Unwitting, reluctant, or complicit, his former colleague, after 1512, followed a parallel course. The actuality and originality of Machiavelli's writings, particularly *Il principe* and the *Discorsi,* cannot be assessed solely in terms of their influence. If before them stands their reception—heroizing or demonizing, but usually inclined to view their author alone—behind him stood a culture that he shared with others. At Florence, for a quarter of a century, Machiavelli did not stand in isolation at "the heart of the city." Its beat, irregular but audible, was also measured by less famous physicians of the intellect. Among these figures was an éminence grise who, through the turbulences that shook Palazzo Vecchio, remained in office while his rival languished at San Casciano; who lectured on nakedness at the Studio in his professorial robes; and who remembered the last years of Lorenzo the Magnificent, in which he and Machiavelli had passed their youth—a time past, unrecoverable yet unforgettable, when there was leisure to reflect not only on politics and princes, but also on the knee-joints of the elephant, the crocodile's excrement, the horns of the giraffe.

APPENDIX

MACHIAVELLI, THE INQUISITION, AND THE INDEX

ARDENT bibliophilia coexisted, in the Catholic Reformation, with fiery bibliophobia. Nothing was dearer to his heart, declared Pope Paul IV in January 1559, than the Vatican Library. Under the direction of his grandnephew, Cardinal Alfonso Carafa, he hoped that its holdings would be conserved and increased.[1] On 2 June of the same year, at the command of the selfsame pontiff, the learned *custos* of that library, Guglielmo Sirleto,[2] arranged for "five large sacks of books" to be deported to the Holy Office. "A very long list" of them, deemed heretical and deserving to be burned, had been prepared by the Inquisition, as Bernardo Navagero, the Venetian ambassador, reported to the Doge in a dispatch of 7 September 1557.[3] The pope approved of the plan, but thoughtfully recommended that it be implemented in stages (*poco a poco*), in order to limit the losses to booksellers. Among the authors whose works were to be consigned to the flames were Boccaccio, Erasmus, and Machiavelli. We do not know whether Sirleto's sacks contained the Roman edition of the *Istorie fiorentine,* dedicated to one of Paul IV's predecessors, Clement VII, and issued with papal privilege in 1532 by Antonio Blado, but we may be sure that, if they did not, Machiavelli's book was intended for the next delivery.

His name figured in the "first class" of the Index of 1559, to which lip service was paid at Florence (a city "poor in inquisitors"),[4] before reappearing in the Index of 1564 as one of the heretical authors whose writings were prohibited entirely.[5] In the meantime, at the third session of the Council of Trent, an attempt was made to moderate the rigor of Paul IV's condemna-

[1] "Cum Bibliotheca nostra Vaticana . . . in primis cordi sit . . . speramus hoc in negotio tractando tantum eum usui futurum, ut tam in veteribus libris sarciendis, restituendis, exscribendis, tam vero in novis conquirendis et diligenter dispondendis . . . maximum sit incrementum." Ed. G. Monti, *Ricerche su Papa Paolo IV Carafa* (Benevento, 1975), p. 306.

[2] On Sirleto and the Vatican library, see Bignami Odier, *La Bibliothèque Vaticane,* pp. 44–52. Cf. G. Denzler, *Kardinal Guglielmo Sirleto (1514–1585): Leben und Werke* (Munich, 1964); and P. E. Commodaro, *Il cardinale Guglielmo Sirleto* (La Fanzaro, 1985). See further below.

[3] "Una lista molto longa di libri, che dicono esser heretici, et hanno da essere bruciati." Ed. P. Paschini, "Letterati ed Indice nella Riforma Cattolica in Italia," in his *Cinquecento romano e Riforma Cattolica,* p. 239.

[4] Panella, "L'introduzione a Firenze," pp. 11–25. Cf. C. de Frede, "Roghi di libri ereticali nell'Italia del Cinquecento," in *Ricerche storiche ed economiche in memoria di C. Barbagallo* 2 (Naples, 1970), pp. 325ff.; and idem, *Ricerche per la storia.*

[5] See De Bujanda, *Index de Rome 1557, 1559, 1564,* pp. 125, 195, 626.

tion and save Machiavelli, by censoring him. To his defender, Guidobaldo II della Rovere, duke of Urbino, that enterprising expurgator, Girolamo Muzio, sent samples of his "corrections" of the author whose language he had denigrated and whose opinions he had reviled, in the hope that they would "open the path to emendations of others."[6]

Muzio's purged versions of the *Discorsi* and the *Arte della guerra* were available at Trent in September 1562. On the twenty-fourth of that month, Giovanni Strozzi, Cosimo I's representative at the council,[7] wrote to the duke of Tuscany, relating the opinion that the same services should be performed for Boccaccio, "per l'onore della lingua fiorentina e di lui fiorentino."[8] So it was, in the interests of Florentine patriotism and linguistic preeminence, that, with the approval of Cosimo de' Medici, plans to prepare expurgated editions of Boccaccio and Machiavelli were linked.[9] The long and tormented story of the censorship of the *Decameron* has often been told:[10] for more than a century, nothing new has been written about the still more protracted and tortuous attempt to "emend" the works of Machiavelli. Undertaken by his grandsons, the homonymous canon and Giuliano de' Ricci, with the approval of the Congregation of the Index, communicated by its secretary on 3 August 1573; completed before 17 May 1578, when Pier Vettori wrote to Sirleto, intervening on behalf of their work; but still unpublished in 1594, because the correctors refused to agree to the condition that it be published under another name: this is the tale recounted in book after book, all of them reliant on the evidence of Ricci.[11] He provides us with the family perspective on this problem up to 1594. It continued further and ascended higher,

[6] See Bertelli and Innocenti, *Bibliografia machiavelliana,* pp. xliiff.; and cf. L. Menapace, "L'ombra del Machiavelli sul Concilio di Trento," in *Studi machiavelliani* (Verona, 1972), pp. 275ff.

[7] On Strozzi, see H. Jedin, "La politica conciliare di Cosimo I," *Rivista storica italiana* 62 (1950): 354ff.

[8] See J. Šušta, *Die römische Kurie und das Konzil von Trient* 2 (Vienna, 1909), p. 348.

[9] "Joannis Boccacii opera, Pontificis sententia damnata, veluti ex exilio revocavit et, ut emendata publice legeretur, impetravit: quod et de Machiavelli scriptis facere constituerat." D. Mellini, *Ricordi intorno ai costumi, azioni, e governo del Sereniss. Gran Duca Cosimo I* (Florence, 1820), p. 5.

[10] See Tapella and Pozzi, "L'edizione del *Decamerone* del 1573," pp. 54–84, 196–227, 366–98, 511–44; Chiecchi, *Dolcemente dissimulando;* Chiecchi and Troisio, *Il Decamerone sequestrato.* Cf. Sorrentino, *La letteratura italiana,* pp. 145–87. See further below.

[11] "Perché *levatene alcune poche cose* elle restanno tali che si possono ammettere, fu dato cura l'anno 1573 a me Giuliano de' Ricci, et a Niccolò Machiavelli mio cugino . . . come appare per una lettera scritta alli detti dall'Ill. mi Signori Cardinali deputati sopra la rivista dello Indice, data in Roma alli 3 d'Agusto 1573, sottoscritta da frate Antonio Posi allhora segretario di detti cardinali, et sebbene si faticò attorno alla detta revisione, et si corressono tutte, e a *Roma si mandò le correctioni delle historie,* sino adesso che siamo nel 1594 non si e condotto questa opera a fine, perché nello stringere il negotio volevano quelli signori che si ristampassono sotto altro nome, al che si diede passata." Quoted by Bertelli and Innocenti, *Bibliografia machiavelliana,* pp. xlvii–xlviii (italics mine).

reaching the loftiest levels of the Congregations of the Inquisition and the Index.

. . . . .

When Muzio produced his censored versions of Machiavelli in 1562, the Roman Inquisition was barely twenty years old,[12] and the Congregation of the Index did not yet exist. The *deputati* of the Florentine Academy, headed by Vincenzio Borghini (and including Marcello Virgilio's son), responsible for expurgating the *Decameron* worked closely with the Master of the Sacred Palace, Tommaso Manrique,[13] whom Pius V, in 1570, had charged with "correcting prohibited books and making them available to readers,"[14] and with the pope's confessor, Eustachio Locatelli, bishop of Reggio. The pontiff himself oversaw and approved the emendations made at Rome.

Machiavelli was not accorded the same honor. Although censures of his writings were planned and conducted at the same time as those of the *Decameron,* Boccaccio remained the priority of the Florentine *deputati* and the Roman authorities. The earliest traces of the attention paid by both to Machiavelli emerge in correspondence between Locatelli and Ludovico Martelli, gentleman of letters in the service of Cardinal Niccolò Ridolfi.[15] The cordiality of their exchange is one of its most interesting features. Writing on 7 December 1571 to Borghini, *spedalingo* (director) of the Ospedale degli Innocenti,[16] Martelli described Locatelli as a charmer.[17] A charmer

[12] On the problem, see A. Prosperi, "Per la storia dell'Inquisizione romana," in *L'Inquisizione Romana in Italia nell'età moderna: Archivi, problemi di metodo, e nuove ricerche* (Trieste, 1991), pp. 27–64; Henningsen and Tedeschi, *The Inquisition in Early Modern Europe;* Tedeschi, *Prosecution of Heresy.*

[13] For the office, see Catalani, *De magistro Sacri Palatii Apostolici libri duo;* Hilgers, *Index,* pp. 510–13; and Reusch, *Der Index der verbotenen Bücher,* 1:433ff. and 440ff. On Manrique and the censorship of Boccaccio, see Tapella and Pozzi, "L'edizione del *Decamerone* del 1573," passim. On Borghini, see G. Folena in *DBI* 12 (1970), pp. 680–89; and cf. note 10 above.

[14] The quotation is from Pius V's *proprius motus* to the Master of the Sacred Palace, 19 November 1570.

[15] On Martelli, see Bertelli, "Egemonia linguistica," p. 250. On Ridolfi, see above, p. 248.

[16] On the office of "Spedalingo degli Innocenti," see P. Gavitt, *Charity and Children in Renaissance Florence: The "Ospedale degli Innocenti," 1410–1536* (Ann Arbor, 1990), pp. 151ff. On Borghini's activities as *spedalingo,* see Folena in *DBI* 12:682ff.

[17] An extract from the text printed below has been published by Tapella and Pozzi, "L'edizione del *Decamerone* del 1573," p. 210; for Borghini's response, see ibid. The source is BMLF, Pluteo 90, sup. 111, 1, fols. 197^{r}–198^{v}: "Al molto R.do Mons. mio oss.mo Mons. lo Spedalingho delli Innocenti—Firenze // Molto R. Mons. mio oss.mo // Domenica passata mi trovai a lungo con Mons. di Reggio, al quale parlai con mia grandissima satisfactione et comodità, et lo ritrovai tanto informato delle cose di tutto il Mondo che certo n'hebbi grandissima consolatione. . . . Sua Signoria R.ma aspetta con desiderio il restante de l'opera per poterla quanto prima dare alla stampa, et quanto a quello che si è racconcio ne resta molto satisfatto et gli pare che le SS. VV. habbino come si dice dipinto. Mi disse che sempre che li sara mostro che le pa-

with literary sense, who desired, orthodoxy permitting, to preserve the original wording of the authors he was "emending." Seldom has a purge been organized in a spirit of such joviality. Martelli poked fun at the corrected Castiglione ("non vole dir Cortigiano ma buffone"),[18] warming with complicity to Locatelli's wish that the censored *Decameron* should not appear under the name of the Florentine Academy or of its members. That had the advantage of concealing the part played by *questi Signori di Roma,* who desired not to be seen making a concession that they were willing to grant secretly. A similar treatment was to be meted out to Machiavelli, whose works Locatelli had by now "almost completely expurgated."

The sunlit optimism of that genial bishop was clouded by few doubts. Although it was awkward, he admitted to Martelli (who reported this to Borghini in another letter—undated but assignable to between 8 and 15 December 1571), that Machiavelli's name appeared among authors of the first class in the Index of 1564, if it could be ascertained that he had not come to the attention of the Inquisition, the project might go ahead.[19] On 22 February 1572, Locatelli wrote to Martelli (now at Florence), informing him that

---

role dell'authore non sieno scandalose sempre cerchera di conservarle come per esempio ha fatto di quelle del homo di corte, che non vole dir Cortigiano ma buffone, et di cio ne ha avuto piacere per mantenimento di quella novella. Quanto a quello che V.S. R. dice che non è bene che si stampi ne sotto nome dell'Accademia ne di chi l'ha avuto nelle mani, il che a me pare necessario omninamente non ho avuto difficulta con S.S. cognoscendo essa che questa domanda è honestissima, et pare che si contenti, che lo stampatore faccia lui la lettera avanti, et narri come da se che ha messo di nuovo in luce questo libro per publica utilità et cetera et dove fussi manchevole in qualche parte che fra poco tempo si darà fuora tutto senza mai accennare che questi Signori di Roma habbino havuto questo pensiero perche in vero non vorrebbono apparire di concedere cosi fatto authore, ma lo permetteranno bene volentieri come di gia se n'è visto l'effetto. Non sono venuto con seco a particulare nessuno perche eravamo in Palazzo dove desinammo insieme nelle stantie di Mons. Sangalletti insieme con molti altri Monsignori. Tutto questo negotio, et altri di simil portata è in petto di Sua Signoria, la quale ancora mi ha detto di volerci rendere il Macchiavello et che di gia l'ha quasi tutto expurgato, ma perché gli pare che vi possa essere di molti errori di lingua mostra desiderio, che potendosi commodamente fare si rassetti et di questo ne dara la cura come ha fatto del Boccaccio alla S.V. Rev.ma. Gli dava noia che il numero delle Cento Novelle non fussi intero. . . . In questo Monsignore ho trovato tanta amorevolezza et elegantia che io sono rimasto suo pregione et perche mi rinquoro ottenere da lui molte cose accennatemi quelle che vi paiono da esser conservate che le tentero seco volentieri. . . . // Di Roma alli vii di Dicembre 1571 // Lodovico Martelli."

[18] For the censorship of Castiglione, see Cian, "Un episodio," pp. 661–722; and J. Guidi, "Reformulations de l'idéologie aristocratique au xvie siècle: Les différentes rédactions et la fortune du 'Courtisan,'" in *Ré-écritures I: Commentaires, parodies, variations dans la littérature italienne de la Renaissance* (Paris, 1983), pp. 121–84.

[19] BMLF, Pluteo 90, sup. 111, 1, fols. 201^{r}–203^{v} (text incomplete in Tavella and Pozzi, "L'edizione del *Decamerone* del 1573," p. 211): "Appresso mostra desiderio grandissimo di contentarci anco del Machiavello et dell'Historia et de discorsi. Solo gli da noia che cotesto authore fussi messo nella prima classe, ma se ritrova che egli non sia mai stato inquisito, ve le rendera in ogni modo. . . . // Di Roma alli." For Borghini's reply, see Tavella and Pozzi, ibid., p. 210.

Machiavelli's memory was not in bad odor and, in a phrase that deserves to be famous, that the Inquisition "had nothing against him." Another touch of the censor's brush, and the works could be sent for stylistic embellishment to Florence, where, restored to respectability like Boccaccio, a new lease on life might be taken by "this fine fellow" (*questo valentuomo*).[20]

If, during the Catholic Reformation, there was a more engaging censor than Eustachio Locatelli, his name has not been recorded. Nonetheless, his high hopes fell flat. Borghini, still involved in the delicate and wearisome task of emending the *Decameron,* declined to perform the same service for Machiavelli,[21] and, at this point, his grandsons offered their own. Locatelli remained their intermediary with Rome, but not their chief point of reference. By 1573, he and the Master of the Sacred Palace had become *consultores* to a new and superior authority: the Congregation of the Index.[22]

. . . . .

When, on 5 March 1571, Pius V announced in consistory his intention to create the Congregation,[23] that experienced and powerful figure in curial politics, Giulio Antonio Santori[24]—cardinal of Santa Severina, future papal candidate and Grand Inquisitor—recorded perplexity ("non potui bene percipere").[25] It was justified. If the bull of Gregory XIII on 13 September 1572[26] charged the Congregation with removing "obscurities and difficulties" in the Index, not a few of them remained in its own ill-defined brief. One of the most salient was how the functions of that body were to be distinguished from those of the Inquisition. The question remained open for

[20] "Ho avuto molto caro intendere la diligenza usata nel ricercare il fatto del Machiavelli conforme a quanto pregai V. S. R. e mi piace che non sia in memoria d'uomini in cattivo concetto, e che nell'Ufizio non sia cosa alcuna contro di lui. Ora si dara un altra rivista alle sue opere, e poi si penserà a pregare le SS. VV. che le voglino corregere nella lingua, come avrano fatto il Boccaccio, acciò il mondo abbi le fatiche di questo valentuomo." Pacini, *Cinquecento romano,* p. 256.

[21] For Borghini's refusal to participate in the expurgated edition, see Tavella and Pozzi, "L'edizione del *Decamerone* del 1573," pp. 212 and 219.

[22] There are few modern studies of the early history of the Index, and none on its internal development. Valuable recent contributions include Rotondò, "Nuovi documenti," pp. 145–211; idem, "La censura ecclesiastica," pp. 1399–1492; idem, "Cultura umanistica"; Longo, "Fenomeni di censura," pp. 15–50, 275–84; Simoncelli, "Documenti interni," pp. 189–215; and Fahy, "The *Index librorum prohibitorum,*" pp. 52–61. See further below.

[23] Hilgers, *Index,* p. 513. See Del Re, *La Curia Romana,* pp. 325ff.

[24] In the absence of a biography, see Jedin, "Die Autobiographie," pp. 3–34. Among the most significant sources for the life of Santori are his *Diario consistoriale* (ed. Tacchi Venturi) and his autobiography (up to 1592) (ed. Cugnoni). Cf. R. de Maio, *Riforme e miti nella chiesa del Cinquecento,* 2d ed. (Naples, 1992), pp. 173ff. See further below.

[25] *Diario consistoriale* (ed. Tacchi Venturi), p. 28.

[26] Hilgers, *Index,* 2:514–15.

more than a quarter of a century, and it was rather addressed than closed by Pope Clement VIII's judgment, delivered *vivae vocis oraculo* on 20 January 1600, to Cardinal Cesare Baronio (Baronius), then prefect of the Congregation of the Index, that its authority extended over books, authors, printers, and readers but not matters of heresy, which lay in the competence of the Inquisition.[27] This was a distinction without a difference, in many cases. One of them bore the name of Niccolò Machiavelli.

The diffusion of his works was of concern to both Congregations. At Venice, that intrepid publisher of prostitutes' names, fees, and addresses (*Tariffa delle putane*), Girolamo Calepin, was found, in 1568, with prohibited writings by Machiavelli.[28] Others committed the same crime in Tuscany.[29] Expurgated editions were called for in the 1570s,[30] and refused by the Inquisition. The Congregation of the Index, headed by Guglielmo Sirleto—now a cardinal—was concerned to defend not only orthodoxy but also the reputation of the papacy. That was the principal objective of Sirleto and other censors as they worked on the historical writings of Carlo Sigonio,[31] to which one of them objected that "he says that the ruin of Italy was caused by the popes. Aside from the fact that this is the opinion of Machiavelli in the *Discorsi,* it is a danger in these times."[32]

The censor's view appears to have been shared by Vincenzio Borghini when, in 1542, he removed his copy of the *Discorsi* from his private library, also excluding the *Istorie fiorentine,*[33] on which Giuliano de' Ricci, in his account of his own and his cousin's efforts, laid particular stress. Entrusted by Antonio Posi, first secretary to the Congregation of the Index (1570–80),[34] with the revision, they corrected the complete works and sent to Rome, as a sample of their efforts, the expurgated *Istorie fiorentine.*[35] In reply to a letter, probably by Locatelli,[36] dated 3 September 1573 and received a week later, Machiavelli's grandsons had affirmed his piety and appealed to living

[27] Reusch, *Der Index der verbotenen Bücher,* pp. 432–33.

[28] Grendler, *Roman Inquisition,* pp. 160–61.

[29] See Prosperi, "L'Inquisizione fiorentina," pp. 113 and 115.

[30] Grendler, *Roman Inquisition,* p. 197 n. 53.

[31] See McCuaig, *Carlo Sigonio,* pp. 251–90.

[32] Ibid., p. 258.

[33] Folena, in *DBI* 12:681.

[34] On Posi, see Hilgers, *Index,* p. 514; J. H. Sparalea, *Supplementum et castigatio ad scriptores trium ordinum S. Francisci a Waddingo aliisque descriptos* (Rome, 1906), p. 88; and C. H. Lohr, "Renaissance Latin Aristotle Commentaries, Authors Pi-Sim," *Renaissance Quarterly* 33 (1980): 670–71. On the office, see Catalani, *De secretario.*

[35] See note 10 above.

[36] The sender of this letter has been taken by Pacini (*Cinquecento romano,* p. 256) to be Posi. The grandsons' reply (note 38 below) acknowledges intervention, on their behalf, with the Congregation of the Index. Its secretary, whose role was administrative, did not possess such authority. Locatelli, already involved in an attempt to "emend" Machiavelli, was among the most influential of the *consultores.*

(but unnamed) witnesses who would attest the frequency of his attendance at confession and communion.[37] More plausible was their argument that, if he had spoken with excessive license about the popes, Machiavelli had been employed, *in più di un negozio,* by Clement VII, who commissioned him to write the *Istorie fiorentine.*[38] It was prudent that Ricci and his cousin excised the original mention of the grand-duke of Tuscany from their draft. Cosimo I's policy toward the papacy in general and the Index in particular veered between obedience and independence,[39] and he appears to have wished to stay in the background. Nor was it necessary to insist, for, in the grandsons' correspondence with the Congregation, the name of the most relevant Medici had been dropped.

There lay the nub of the matter. In Machiavelli, the Roman authorities were confronted not merely with a writer "of the first class" but also with a Medicean protégé who had dedicated to the pope a now-prohibited work that had been published, some forty years earlier, with papal approval. This, even for a rigorist such as Cardinal Sirleto, was a trifle embarrassing. What were he and the Congregation to do? Machiavelli's grandsons had made a concrete proposal, submitting to them a copy of the *Istorie fiorentine* printed in 1551 at Florence, from which they had canceled the name of the author and "all expressions contrary to the Roman Church." That book (at present, untraced) came into the possession of Pasquale Villari,[40] who recorded that the same hand that had marked the passages expurgated and made a few alterations wrote at the end: "Questo libro è 194 carte, Historie di Niccolò Machiavelli, riviste prima da Niccolò Machiavelli e Giulia' de Ricci, e poi del teologo dell'Ill. Cardinal Alessandrino, per ordine de' superiori." This provides a clue to Roman policy.

The mention of "Cardinal Alessandrino"—Michele Bonelli, *cardinal nipote* of Pius V[41]—brings us directly into the ambit of the Congregation of the Index. Bonelli, one of its founding members, took his title from Santa Maria sopra Minerva, the Dominican monastery in which, until 1870, the secretaries resided. Locatelli could not be described as Bonelli's theologian, but Paolo Constabili could. Noted for his theological studies and for his activities as inquisitor, Constabili owed to "Cardinal Alessandrino" his promotion, in 1573, to be Manrique's successor.[42] Ex officio member of the Congregation of the Index and personally responsible for censorship in the Holy City, the new Master of the Sacred Palace took precedence over Locatelli, who

[37] On the theme, see Procacci, "Frate Andrea Alamanni," pp. 5–12.

[38] Ed. Bertelli, "Egemonia linguistica," p. 278.

[39] See note 4 above, and D'Addario, *Aspetti della Controriforma,* pp. 144ff., with Diaz, *Il Granducato di Toscana,* pp. 191ff.

[40] Villari, *Niccolò Machiavelli,* 2:424 n. 1.

[41] On Bonini, see A. Prosperi, *DBI* 2 (1969), pp. 766–74.

[42] See Catalani, *De magistro,* 2:133; and A. Foa in *DBI* 28 (1983), pp. 60–61.

Ex libro Censurar. m.s. Rome confecto signato C. pag. 15. ... 463

Censura, e correttione fatta a gli otto libri della Historia di Nicolò Machiavelli. Le carte che si citaranno, sono di un libro in 4°

stampato in Fiorenza per Bernardo di Giunta. l'anno 1522 in 4°.

Nel Proemio. Ne consideratono come l'attioni, che hanno in se grandezza, come hanno quelle dei governi, et degli Stati, comunche elle si trattino, qualunque fine habbino, pare sempre portino a gl'huomini piu honore che biasmo. (Si lieva.)

Nel libro p.o a car. 12. Pieri, Giovanni, e Mattei, Henrici, Federichi, e Corradi. si corregge. I miracoli. (Si corregge) la verità.

Pure. (Si lieva.)

A carte 13. Miseri. si corregge, Mortali.

Dio dovessino ricorrere. (Si corregge) fosse la vera religione, et oue dovessero ricorrere.

A carte 16. Di modo che tutte le guerre che dopo questi tempi furono da Barbari fatte in Italia, furono in maggior parte dai Pontefici causate, et tutti i Barbari, che quella inundarono, furono il piu delle volte da quelli chiamati; il qual modo di procedere dura ancora in questi nostri tempi, il che ha tenuto, et tiene la Italia disunita, et inferma. (Si lieva.) mescolate con l'Indulgentie (Si lieva.)

Et come per haver usato male l'uno, e l'altro, l'uno hanno al tutto perduto, dell'altro stanno a discrettione d'altri (Si lieva.)

A carte 17. Et si arrogarono tanta riputatione, massime poi che egli...

470

9. Censure of Machiavelli, *Istorie fiorentine*.

died in 1575. It was therefore understandable that, on or shortly after that date, the cardinals comissioned an expurgation of the *Istorie fiorentine.* A text corrected by outsiders such as Ricci and his cousin was not sufficient for their purposes. It was customary for the Congregation to form its own judgment on the basis of suggestions for elimination, adjustment, and rewriting made by one of their collaborators. That was where "Cardinal Alessandrino's theologian" came in. *Per ordine de' superiori* Constabili made a sample censure that, according to routine procedure, was to be decided on by Sirleto, Bonelli, and others. It follows that, if the labors of this cleric were later combined with those of Machiavelli's grandsons in the 1551 edition of the *Istorie fiorentine* that they had sent to Rome, the book owned by Villari can only represent an indirect witness to what was originally laid before the authorities. To recover the fourth attempt (after those of Muzio, Locatelli, and the grandsons) to make that "fine fellow," Niccolò Machiavelli, fit for presentation to the reading public, it is time to enter the archives.

There, among an abundance of documentation that attests the feverish activity of the reforming Church, is preserved a copy of the censor's work. Let us read Machiavelli with his eyes. We are in Rome between 1575 and 1577, at the heart of the Congregation of the Index. Under pressure, it has embarked on its attempt to stem and control the flood of heretical publications; the Inquisition, its superior, ally, and rival, is vigilant; and before us lies the problem of the *Istorie fiorentine* (Plate 9).

Transcription

ACDF, Indice, Protocolli, V [= IIa, 19]

FOL. 467r (OLD NUMERATION) = FOL. 470r (NEW)

Ex libro censurarum m.s. Romae confecto signato .E. pag[in]a 15

Censura,[43] e correttione *fatta*[44] *à gli otto libri della*[45] Historia di Nicolo Machiavelli. Le carte che si citaranno, sono di un libro in 4° stampata [*sic*] in fiorenza per Bernardo di Giunta, l'anno 1522 [*sic*] in 4°.

(1) *Nel prohemio* [*F,* A ivr-v: *M,* p. 633]. Ne considerarono come l'attioni, che hanno in sé grandezza, come hanno quelle dei governi, et degli stati, comunche elle si trattino, qualunque fine habbino, pare sempre portino àgl'huomini più honore che biasmo *si lieva*

[43] The siglum *M,* with subsequent pagination, refers to M. Martelli's edition of the *Istorie fiorentine;* the siglum *F,* with subsequent pagination, refers to the 1532 edition used by the censor. The passages censored are numbered for convenience of reference below. The censor's instructions are italicized. His punctuation and orthography are maintained.

[44] *negli* suprascript.

[45] *nella* inserted.

(2) *Nel libro p.º à car. 12* [*F,* 12ᵛ: *M,* p. 637]. Pieri, Giovanni, e Matthei / Henrici, Frederichi e Corradi *si corregge*. I miracoli *si corregge* la verità. Pure *si lieva.*

(3) *À carte 13* [*F,* 13ʳ: *M,* p.637]. Miseri *si corregge* mortali.

Dio dovessino ricorrere *si corregge* fosse la vera religione, et ove dovesseno ricorrere.

(4) *À carte 16* [*F,* 16ʳ: *M,* pp. 640–41]. Di modo che tutte le guerre che dopo questi tempi furono da'Barbari fatte in Italia, furono in maggior parte da i Pontefici causate, et tutti i Barbari, che quella inundarono, furono il più delle volte da quelli chiamati, il qual[46] modo di procedere dura ancora in questi nostri tempi, il che ha tenuto, et tiene la Italia disunita, et inferma *si lieva* mescolate con l'indulgentie *si lieva*

Et come per haver usato male l'uno, e l'altro, l'uno hanno al tutto perduto, dell'altro stanno à discrettione[47] d'altri *si lieva*

(5) *À carte 17* [*F,* 17ʳ: *M,* p. 642] et si arrogarono tanta riputazione, massime poi che eglino[48]

FOL. 467ᵛ = FOL. 470ᵛ

escluseno il Popolo Romano dall'[49] eleggere il Pontefice, che rade volte la elettione di quello usciva del numero loro, onde *si lieva*

(6) *À car. 18* [*F,* 14ʳ (= 18ʳ): *M,* p. 643] per vendicarsi con li Romani tolse à quelli *si corregge* tolse a Romani

qualunque di essi haveva altro intento che torre la riputazione, e l'authorità l'uno a l'altro *si lieva*

(7) *À car. 21* [*F,* 21ᵛ: *M,* p. 646] e sottomessesi à quello iuditio un'tanto Rè, che hoggi[50] un'huomo privato si vergognarebbe[51] sottomettervisi *si lieva*

Tanto le cose che paiano, sono più discosto, che d'appresso[52] temute *si lieva*

(8) *ÀA car. 22* [*F,* 22ʳ: *M,* p. 646] et cosi l'acque fecero più favore a'Mahumettisti,[53] che le scommuniche a' Christiani, perche queste frenorono l'orgoglio suo et quelle lo spensono.[54]

(9) *À car. 23* [*F,* 23ᵛ: *M,* p. 648] più certi *si corregge* altri

(10) *À car. 24* [F, 24ʳ: *M,* pp. 648–49] e cosi i Pontefici, hora per carità della religione, hora per lor propria ambitione non cessavano di chiamare in Italia humori[55] nuovi, et suscitare nuove guerre, et poi che eglino haveano

[46] *quale F.*

[47] *discretione F.*

[48] *egli F.*

[49] *dallo F.*

[50] *oggi F.*

[51] *vergognerebbe F.*

[52] *da presso F.*

[53] *Maumettisti F.*

[54] Instruction missing.

[55] *homori F.*

fatto potente un'Prencipe, se nè pentivano, et cercavano la sua rovina, nè permettevano, che quella Provincia, la quale per loro debolezza non potevano possedere, che altri la possedesse, et i Prencipi ne temevano perche sempre o' combattendo, o' fuggendo vincevano, se con qualche inganno non erano oppressi, come fù Bonifatio 8.° et alcuni altri, i quali sotto colore di amicitia, furono dall'Imperatore presi *si leva*
Huomo audace, et ambitioso *si leva*

FOL. 468r = FOL. 471r

[*F,* 24v: *M,* p. 649] Et fù il primo de Papi, che[56] mostrasse la propria ambitione, et che disegnasse[57] sotto colore di far' grande la Chiesa, honorare, et beneficare i suoi, e' come da questi tempi indietro non si è mai fatta mentione de nipoti, o' di parenti di alcun'Pontefice cosi per l'avenire[58] ne fia piena l'historia tanto, che noi ci condurremo a' figliuoli, ne manca altro à tentare à i Pontefici, se non che come eglino hanno disegnato[59] infino à tempi nostri, di lasciarli[60] Principi, cosi per l'avvenire[61] pensino di lasciar' loro il Papato hereditario, bene è vero, che per infino a' qui i Principati ordinati da loro hanno havuto[62] pocha vita, perche il più delle volte i Pontefici per vivere poco tempo, o' ei non forniscono di piantare le piante loro, o' si pure le piantano, le lasciano con si poche, e deboli barbe, che al primo vento, quando è mancata quella virtù che le sostiene, si fiaccano *si leva.*

(11) *À car. 25* [*F,* 25r: *M,* pp. 649–50] I cieli, i quali sapevano come el doveva venir tempo, che i Franciosi, e i Tedeschi si allargherebbono da Italia, e che quella Provincia restarebbe in mano al tutto delli Italiani, accio' che il Papa, quando mancasse[63] delli ostacoli oltramontani, non potesse ne fermare, nè godere la potenza sua, fecino[64] crescere in Roma due potentissime famiglie, Colonnesi, et Orsini, acciò che con la potenza, et propinquità loro tenessero il Pontificato infermo, onde che Papa Bonifatio, il quale conosceva questo, si volse à voler' spegnere i Colonnesi, et oltre all'havergli scommunicati, bandi loro la cruciata contro, il che se bene

FOL. 468v = FOL. 471v

offese alquanto loro, offese più la Chiesa, perche quell'arme, quale per carità della fede haveva virtuosamente adoperato, come si volse per propria ambi-

56 *apertamente F:* omitted.
57 *disegniasse F.*
58 *lo avenire F.*
59 *diseguato F.*
60 *lasciargli F.*
61 *lo avvenire F.*
62 *havuta F.*
63 *manchasse F.*
64 *feciono F.*

tione ai Christiani, cominciò à non tagliare, et cosi il troppo desiderio di sfogare il loro appetito, faceva che i Pontefici à poco à poco si dissarmavano *si leva, et si racconcia cosi* Nel cui tempo crebbero in Roma due potentissime famiglie Colonnesi, et Orsini, delle quali giustamente dubitando il Papa, si volse à volere spegnere i Colonnesi, et oltre all'haverli merevolmente scommunicati, bandi loro la Cruciata contro, e privo

Rabbioso [*F,* 25^{v}: *M,* p. 650] *si leva*

(12) *À car. 27* [*F,* 27^{r}: *M,* p. 651] anchora che fingesse il contrario *si leva*

(13) *À car. 28* [*F,* 28^{v}: *M,* p. 653] le terre dell'Imperio per non essere[65] ancora egli[66] meno liberale delle cose d'altri, che si fosse[67] stato il Papa *si leva, et si corregge* quelle

(14) *À car. 29* [*F,* 29^{r}: *M,* p.653] con la rovina *si corregge* contra[68]

Per questo benefitio [*F,* 29^{v}: *M,* p. 654] *si leva*

(15) *À car. 30* [*F,* 30^{v}: *M,* p. 655] perche non volse[69] fare un suo nipote Prencipe di Capua *si leva*

per farsi riputatione *si leva*

(16) *À car. 31* [*F,* 31^{v}: *M,* p. 655] per fare più ricca la Chiesa *si leva*

(17) *À car. 32* [*F,* 32^{r}: *M,* p. 656] come sono quasi sempre[70] tutti i Prencipi *si leva*

(18) *lib.° 2° À car. 35* [*F,* 35^{r}: *M,* p. 659] per non essere nei Prencipi alcuno appetito di vera gloria et nelle Republiche alcun'ordine de [*sic*] meriti di esser'lodato *si corregge* per non esser'molte volte in alcuni Prencipi, alcun'appetito di vera gloria, et nelle Republiche moderne quest'ordine che tanto merita di esser'lodato.

Fol. 469^{r} = Fol. 472^{r}

(19) *À car. 53* [*F,* 53^{r}: *M,* p. 677] dalla fortuna *si leva*

(20) *À car. 54* [*F,* 54^{r}: *M,* p. 678] la Fortuna *si leva*

(21) *lib.° 3° ÀA car. 72* [*F,* 72^{r-v}: *M,* p. 696] et erano chiamati santi, ancora che eglino havessino stimato poco le censure, e le Chiese de beni loro spogliate, e' sforzato il Clero co' celebrare gli offitii, tanto quelli Cittadini stimavano all'hora più la patria, che l'anima, e dimostrarono alla Chiesa come prima suoi amici l'havevano difesa, cosi suoi nemici la potevanno affliggere, perche *si leva*

(22) *À car.* 77 [*F,* 77^{r}: *M,* p. 700] di maggiore esperientia *si corregge* de più malvagi

[*F,* 77^{v}-78^{r}: *M,* p. 701] per conscientia *si leva*

né conscientia *si leva*

[65] *egli* cancelled.

[66] Suprascript.

[67] *fussi F.*

[68] Reading uncertain.

[69] *volle F.*

[70] Suprascript.

E della conscientia noi non debbiamo tener' conto, perche dove é come è in noi la paura della fame, et della carcere, non può, nè debbe quella dell'Inferno capire *si leva*

(23) *À car. 78* [*F,* 78ʳ: *M,* p. 701] tutti *si corregge* la maggior parte
E quelli i quali o' per poca prudentia, o' per troppa sciocchezza fuggono questi modi nella servitù sempre, é nella povertà affogano, perche i fedeli servi sempre sono servi, e gl'huomini buoni sempre sono poveri, nè mai escono di servitù, se non gl'infideli, et audaci, e di povertà se non i rapaci, et frodolenti, perche Iddio,[71] e la natura ha' posto tutte le fortune dell'huomini loro in mezzo, le quali più alle rapine che all'industria, et alle cattive, che alle buone arte sono esposte, di qui nasce che gl'uomini mangiano l'un l'altro, et vanne sempre còl peggio chi può meno *si leva*

(24) *lib.º 4º À car. 99* [*F,* 99ʳ: *M,* p. 722] Essempio veramente degno di quella lodata antichità, é tanto è piu mirabile di quelli, quanto è più rado *si leva*

(25) *À car. 113* [*F,* 113ᵛ: *M,* p.735] imputando ogni cosa più a' Cieli che volevano cosi *si corregge* imputando scioccamente ogni cosa più à i Cieli, che volessero cosi

Fol. 469ᵛ = Fol. 472ᵛ

(26) *lib.º 5º ÀA car. 116* [*F,* 116ᵛ: *M,* p. 738] e cosi sempre *si corregge* e cosi spesso

(27) [*F,* 118ʳ: *M,* p. 739] Ancorche il Conte all'ingiuria dello haverla occupata vi havesse aggionto il dispregio, perche nel segnare il luogo, dove scriveva à suoi genti, le lettere con parole latine, secondo il costume Italiano, diceva, ex Girfalco nostro Firmiano, invito Petro, et Paulo, *si leva*
Una vituperosa pace *si corregge* dannosa

(28) *ÀA car. 128* [*F,* 128ᵛ: *M,* p. 750] il cedere al Romano Pontefice, dispiacesse nondimeno *qui si aggionge* volendo cio' il dovere, per essere la fede una, et il capo della Chiesa il Pontefice Romano Vicario di Christo, e' successore di San Pietro

(29) *lib.º 6º À car. 144* [*F,* 144ᵛ: *M,* p. 765] il che tutto nasceva dal[72] disordine, con il quale quelle guerre si trattavano, perchè spogliandosi gli inimici[73] vinti, e non si ritenendo nè amazzando tanto quelli à rassalire il Vincitore, differivano, quanto ei penavano[74] da chi gli conduceva, di essere di armi, et di Cavalli riforniti *si leva*

(30) *À car. 149* [*F,* 149ʳ: *M,* p. 770] sempre dalla fortuna aiutate *si leva*

(31) *À car. 154* [*F,* 154ʳ: *M,* p. 775] ne lo riteneva il timore, o' la vergogna di rompere la fede, perche gl'huomini grandi chiamavono vergogna il perdere, non con inganno acquistare *si leva*

[71] *i Dio F.*

[72] *da il F.*

[73] *li nimici F.*

[74] *penavono F.*

(32) *À car. 157* [*F,* 157r: *M,* p. 778] de malvagi huomini amico *si corregge* sostegno

(33) *À car. 163* [*F,* 163v-164r: *M,* p. 785] i malvagi costumi de Prelati *si leva* ma' sopra tutto gli ne davano speranza quelli versi del Petrarca nella canzona che comincia, Spirto gentile, che quelle membra reggì, dove dice

Sopra il monte Tarpeio canzon vedrai
Un'Cavalier' ch'Italia tutta honora
Pensoso più d'altrui, che di se stesso

Sapeva M. Stefano molte volte i Poeti essere di spirito divino

Fol. 470r = Fol. 473 r

e profetico ripieni, tal che giudicava dovere ad ogni modo intervenire quella cosa che il Petrarca in quella canzona profetizava, et essere egli quello che dovesse essere di cosi[75] gloriosa impresa essecutore, parendoli, per eloquentia, per dottrina, per gratia, e per amici esser' superiore ad ogni altro Romano *si leva*

(34) *À car. 164* [*F,* 164v: *M,* p. 785] da qualcuno la Intentione di costui lodata *si leva*

(35) *À car. 169* [*F,* 169r: *M,* p. 790] l'ambitione del quale si conosceva *si leva*

(36) *À car. 172* [*F,* 172r: *M,* p. 792] immeritamente *si leva*

(37) *lib.o 7o ÀA car. 174* [*F,* 174r: *M,* p. 794] e perche Iddio paresse *si corregge* fosse

(38) *À car. 187* [*F,* 187r: *M,* p. 807] e come molte cose chiamate per lo adietro errori, si potevano sotto la pontificale autorita nascondere *si leva*
figliuoli *si corregge* nipoti
ambitioso *si leva*

(39) *À car. 193* [*F,* 193r: *M,* p. 813] vilmente *si corregge* humilmente

(40) *À car. 203* [*F,* 203r: *M,* p. 823] ricompensava *si corregge* pareva che ricompensasse

(41) *lib.o 8o A car. 205* [*F,* 205r-v: *M,* p. 825] e poi che il Papa si era[76] dimostro lupo, e non Pastore, per non essere come colpevoli devorati, con tutti quelli modi potevano, l'accusa loro giustificavano, e tutta l'Italia del tradimento fatto contro à lo stato loro, riempierono, mostrando la impietà del Pontefice e la ingiustitia sua, et come quel Ponteficato che egli havea male occupato, male esercitava, poiche gl'haveva mandato quelli che alle prime Prelature havea tratti in compagnia de traditori, et parricidi, e commettere tanto tradimento nel tempio, nel mezzo del divino offitio, nelle celebrationi[77] del sacramento, et dopoi, per che non gl'era successo amazzare i Cittadini, mutare lo stato della loro Città et quella a' suo modo

[75] *si F.*
[76] *s'era F.*
[77] *nella celebratione F.*

FOL. 470^{v} = FOL. 473^{v}

saccheggiare, la interdiceva, et con le pontificali maleditioni la minacciava, et offendeva, ma' se Dio era giusto, se a lui le violenze dispiacevano, gli dovevano quelle di questo suo Vicario dispiacere, et esser'contento, che gl'huomini offesi, non trovando presso à quello luogo, recorressero a lui, per tanto non che i fiorentini ricevessero l'Interdetto, e à quello ubidissero, ma' sforzarono i Sacerdoti à celebrare il divino uffitio *si leva*

(42) *À car. 213* [*F,* 213^{r}: *M,* p. 833] e' cosi la forza, e la necessità, non le scritture, et gl'obblighi fà osservare à i[78] Prencipi la fede *si leva*

(43) *À car. 217* [*F,* 217^{r-v}: *M,* p. 837] o' perche fosse[79] il termine di sua vita venuto, o perche il dolore della pace fatta, come nimico di[80] quella, l'amazzasse *si leva*

haveva sempre *si corregge* era sempre stata

Analysis

"Books" or collections of censures were kept by the secretaries of the Congregation of the Index. When they were bound into the present registers,[81] the chronological order of their composition was seldom preserved. From one of the earliest such *libri,* marked "E," the above censure was taken, as the superscription in the hand of Antonio Posi indicates. That the transcribed document is a copy, its attention to form and its carelessness toward content reveal.

Errors made by the copyist suggest that he was reading the original with difficulty or in haste. The mistake of grammar in the second line of the censure may be immaterial, but not the false dating of the Giuntine edition of the *Istorie fiorentine,* which arose from a misinterpretation of MDXXXII. The system, otherwise strictly observed by the censor, of placing his comments immediately after the passage to which they refer, is muddled at **(2)**; the instruction (probably *si lieva*) at **(8)** is omitted. Such confusions in transcribing the exemplar contrast with the rarity of cancellations or alterations made in the copyist's own text. He was a competent calligrapher. The first words cited on each new page are written at the bottom of the one that precedes it, in flowing script and spacious format. Such finer details of presentation are unusual among original documents from the 1570s in the registers of the Congregation of the Index. The autographs of its censors are seldom distin-

[78] Om. *F.*

[79] *fusse F.*

[80] *a F.*

[81] Cf. the decree of 17 June 1587: "Decretum proponere Secretario ob multas expurgationes Romae et alibi factas, ut in unum colligerentur et ex pluribus a diversis super eodem libro factis censuris unica perficeretur ex multis et tunc recognosceretur a consultoribus et per Con[gregatione]m approbetur." ACDF, Indice, Diarii 1 [= 1.1], fol. 22^{v}.

guished by their elegance—which may be why, in the interests of legibility, this copy was made.

If our transcription is a copy, where was the original? What did Posi mean when he wrote "ex libro censurarum . . . E"? Both questions can be answered because, in the same archive, there is a list, made by Paolo Constabili in 1577, of "expurgated books, censures of which have been handed into us and which are kept by us."[82] Among the works that, in the second column, he indicated, appear:

In Nico. Macchiavellu[m]
Dell'arte della Guerra
l'historie.

At fol. 203^{r} Constabili prepared an index of the contents of *censurar[um] . . . Tom. 2.* On the fifteenth folio were the passages expurgated or altered in the *Arte della guerra.* Beginning on the sixteenth and ending on the seventeenth folios were those censored in the *Istorie fiorentine* by a hand sufficiently minuscule to fit onto four cramped sides. We therefore know which of Machiavelli's works had been examined for the Congregation of the Index by 1577, and where and how they had been classified. What are the implications of this evidence?

The censure of the *Arte della guerra*—a book with which even Muzio found little to quarrel[83]—has not (yet) been found. Probably brief, it may have been lost or discarded. More significant is the absence from Constabili's list of Machiavelli's other writings. No *Discorsi,* in 1577, although they had already aroused disquiet;[84] nor *Il principe,* perhaps because the job, so thoroughly done by Nifo, could await a later turn;[85] nor any of the works, such as *Mandragola,* that might seem to have invited expurgation. Although it is possible that, amid the stress of the prolonged purge that led a brow-beaten official, in 1575, to throw up his hands and lament that the Church "needed a halt to printing for many years,"[86] the Congregation of the Index, two

[82] "Liber expurgati, quorum censure nobis tradite sunt et apud nos asservantur." ACDF, Indice, Protocolli A [= 2^{a}.1], fol. 204^{r} (cf. fol. 232^{r}), to be edited and discussed in my forthcoming "Machiavelli and the Censors."

[83] "La Arte militare di Machiavelli, il qual in questa parte non mi ha data molto fatica, chè non ho levate se non due parole di quella sua opinione, che la religion christiana faccia gli uomini poltroni." Muzio, *Lettere inedite di Girolamo Muzio* (ed. Zenatti), p. 28.

[84] Cf. Muzio: "Scrissi i passati giorni al R. i Patriarca di Ierusalem che V. Ecc. avrebbe indirizzato alle mani sue le cose del Macchiavelli, e ne ho per l'ultimo corriere avuto lettere sue, che egli le aspetta, masimamente essendo stato fatto in quelle congregazioni particolar menzione di voler che i *Discorsi* si riformino." Ibid., p. 26, and see above, p. 308.

[85] See above, pp. 253ff., and below, p. 323.

[86] "La santa chiesa havria più biosogno che per molti anni non vi fosse stampa." Cited by Rotondò, "Nuovi documenti," p. 157.

years later, had not yet proceeded to a complete censure,[87] we should hesitate before assuming that this was its aim. The grandsons, and perhaps Locatelli, wished to expurgate, for republication, all of Machiavelli's works, but Cardinal Sirleto, his colleagues, and their agents did not necessarily share the same purpose. What they required, and had obtained by 1577, was a sample, to verify the feasibility of the project; and the choice of an "easy" book to purge, such as the *Arte della guerra,* balanced by that of a more difficult one, such as the *Istorie fiorentine,* may reflect, in the hectic conditions in which the Congregation worked, a principle of economy with effort. No time was wasted with writings that ought never to have been printed, and might be irredeemable. Only authorized publications of a semiofficial character were taken into account. That is why the *Arte della guerra,* censored against the Venetian edition of 1534, and the *Istorie fiorentine,* corrected against what is described as the Florentine issue of 1522, appear in a list of "suspect books" made in 1577, which Roman booksellers were prohibited from selling until they had been set to rights.[88] How this was to be done, in the case of the *Istorie,* is illustrated by the work of our censor.

. . . . .

In the impersonal passive, five forms of censorship are proposed:

1. elimination (*si l[i]eva*),
2. correction (*si corregge*),
3. "repair," "adjustment," or "setting to rights" (*si racconcia*),[89]
4. addition (*si aggionge*),
5. a combination of the above.

Unlike the justifications offered by his predecessor, Manrique, for the emendations made in the *Decameron;* unlike the refutations, arguments, and polemic ("He is neither a philosopher nor a theologian," "Here he slaughters himself with his own sword") presented by the "committee" that expurgated the *De rerum natura* of Bernardino Telesio,[90] Constabili's style is laconic, peremptory, unreasoned. He was not diagnosing the ills of Machiavelli's work, but operating on the symptoms of its cancer. Surgery was his method; amputation his preferred technique. If the grandsons had found lit-

[87] On the slowness of the Congregation in the case of Sigonio and others, see Prodi, *Il cardinale Gabriele Paleotti,* 2:240ff.; and Dejob, *De l'influence,* pp. 59ff.

[88] ACDF, Indice, Protocolli A [II^{a}.1], fol. 250^{r}.

[89] For the sense of this euphemism, cf. Strozzi's letter to Cosimo I (ed. Šušta, *Die römische Kurie* [cited in note 8 above], 2:348): "Ora è accaduto che il duca d'Urbino ha mandati loro i *Discorsi* e il *Libro dell'arte della guerra* del Machiavello *racconci, cioe: levatone quel che era scandaloso e contra la nostra religione.*"

[90] Firpo, "Filosofia italiana e Controriforma," pp. 40ff.

tle to excise in the *Istorie fiorentine* ("Levatene alcune poche cose, levati quei pochi luogi dove alle volte con troppa licenza par che parli de pontefici"), he was less indulgent.

The first and most sustained purpose of "Cardinal Alessandrino's" theologian was to remove Machiavelli's slights on the papacy. This was less self-evident than it perhaps now seems because, in the rules of the Index of 1564, such a criterion is not explicitly formulated.[91] The Congregation decreed where the pope remained silent, implementing, in the case of the *Istorie fiorentine,* guidelines established by Manrique for censoring the *Decameron.*[92] They were open to interpretation, and it is instructive to consider not only what was altered or suppressed in Machiavelli's text, but also what was allowed to pass.

Istorie fiorentine 1.4 was an obvious target. Although the view that the wars and disunity of Italy were caused by the popes is eliminated at **(4)**, only the reference to indulgences is purged in the critical sentences that follow. Machiavelli's account of the expansion of papal power, of sanctions and arms, of the awe and terror that they inspired is permitted to stand. The temporal might of Rome, and the means by which it had been established, were beyond denial: what disturbed Constabili was implied abuse of spiritual authority. So, too, at **(5)**, the attack on the Sacred College is excised from *Istorie fiorentine* 1.11, but not the double reference to the Church and the papacy acquiring the privileges and status of empire. Revenge was inadmissible as a motive for abolishing the Roman people's right to elect the emperor in the following chapter **([6])**. Difficulties with the urban populace are acknowledged at **(7)**, but neither the humiliation of King Henry of England, which Machiavelli, in the nineteenth chapter of his first book, describes as an action intolerable in his own times, nor the deprecation of papal hegemony. This approach is taken to its logical conclusion at **(10)**, in the extensive eliminations from chapter 23, which serve to defend Nicholas III and to remove the allegation that he wished to make the throne of St. Peter hereditary.

Nepotism, a current theme of debate[93] signaled at **(15)**, is treated with striking discretion at **(38)**. Sixtus IV, who at *Istorie fiorentine* 7.20 is represented as favoring members of his family rumored to be his sons, is exculpated from that charge—only to be found guilty, by the "emendation" *nipoti,*

[91] *Index de 1564* (ed. Bujanda), p. 813.

[92] "Nota hauta da Roma dal R.mo Mons.r del Sacro Palazzo. Avvertimento per rassettar il Boccaccio . . . terzo: che per niun modo si parli in male o scandalo de' preti, frati, Abbati, Abbadesse, monaci, monache, piovani, provosti, vescovi, o altre cose sacre, ma si mutino lj nomi, o si faccia per altro modo che parrà meglio." Quoted by P. M. Brown, *Lionardo Salviati: A Critical Biography* (Oxford, 1974), p. 162.

[93] See W. Reinhard, "Nepotismus: Der Funktionswandel einer papstgeschichtlichen Konstante," *Zeitschrift für Kirchengeschichte* 86 (1925): 145–85. Cf. B. McClung Hallman, *Italian Cardinals, Reform, and the Church as Property* (Berkeley, 1985).

of another. It is worth recalling that this alteration was made by the protégé of Michele Bonelli, *cardinal nipote* of Pius V. If Machiavelli's criticism is modified, it is not struck out. Acknowledged abuses could be impugned, even at the heart of the Congregation of the Index, in an atmosphere of reform that foreshadows the measures taken against nepotism a decade later, in Sixtus V's bull *Romani Pontificis providentia* (April 1586).[94]

Although ambition is excised from the characteristics attributed to Sixtus IV in the same chapter, ambitious fear is not censored from the description of Nicholas III at *Istorie fiorentine* 2.11, despite the fact that the anxiety of that pope and his successors before rival rulers is presented as a cause of "the frequent tumults and changes" in Italy that is suppressed elsewhere. The "avarice and pride" of papal legates at 3.7 remains unchanged. Compared with these concessions to Machiavelli's critique, the removal, at **(27)**, of Niccolò Fortebraccio's jibe against Saints Peter and Paul in *Istorie fiorentine* 5.2 is a minimal intervention.

That the work was read closely by "Cardinal Alessandrino's" theologian is revealed by his corrections and reformulations. The common names listed at *Istorie fiorentine* 1.5 are substituted by ones of Germanic origin in **(2)**, avoiding blasphemy of the Apostles Peter, John, and Matthew. Machiavelli's ironical contrast between the "habits of the old religion" and "the miracles" of the new becomes the uncompromising "truth." "If indeed" (*pure*) introduces too critical a hypothesis about the unity of Christianity, and is meticulously emended into "if." "Mortals," not "the wretched," seek God's aid. About Him there is no room for doubt. Uncertainty clouds only human understanding of "the true religion" and the source of succor **([3])**. While, at **(8)**, Machiavelli's epigram about the waters and excommunications, on the death of Barbarossa, is predictably excised from *Istorie fiorentine* 1.19, the famous speech of 3.13 is attributed not to one of the "more experienced" Ciompi but to one of the "more wicked" at **(22)**, whose unorthodox views on conscience are removed.

Not all those who come to wealth and power achieve them by fraud or force; merely "the greater part" **([23])**. The idea that men are born equal, in the woolworker's speech, was acceptable to the censor, but neither the subversive notion that "faithful servants are always servants" nor Machiavelli's opinions on the law of the jungle. Without hesitating to "correct," at **(25)**, the author's statement into the opposite of what he says, this erstwhile inquisitor left unaltered the appeal to force in *Istorie fiorentine* 3.13. Although the self-sacrifice of Biagio del Melano—the example "worthy of praised antiquity," which he set by preferring death to rescue by the enemies of his fatherland at 4.12—proved intolerable **([24])**, the ruthless observation that

[94] *Bullarium Romanum* 8 (Turin, 1863), pp. 685–90, with Del Re, *La Curia Romana,* p. 66.

"great men must either not be touched or, if touched, be eliminated" at 4.30 remains unscathed. Fortune, regularly censored,[95] is treated at **(33)** with the same strictness as Petrarch's prophetic verse in *Istorie fiorentine* 6.28.[96] Yet despite his disavowal of any agency other than God's purpose as a motive or explanation for human behavior, what Paolo Constabili removes, at **(26)**, from the proemium to Book 5 is slight and insignificant. *Anakyklosis,* with its potentially disturbing implications for theories of divine providence and free will, is allowed to pass. If tolerance is not extended to the hint of reason of state in the preface to the *Istorie fiorentine* **([1])**, the inexorable laws of Machiavellian history—so long as they pose no direct threat to the Catholic religion, the Church, and the pope—are treated with leniency.

This is neither a harsh nor a superficial censure. More might have been excised from Machiavelli's work, more emended—as Nifo, in the case of *Il principe,* had already shown. Apart from the alterations to and subtractions from the speech at 3.13, the internal history of Florence, as Machiavelli presents it, is scarcely changed, and, even on controversial points, his account is modified with discretion.[97] A notable measure of tolerance characterizes the censure laid before the Congregation of the Index; and if Constabili was not authorized to make a personal recommendation, the sense of his labors was clearly that the "corrected" *Istorie fiorentine* could be republished. Moreover, it can be proven that his work was received in the spirit in which it was undertaken, for Machiavelli's work was included in the first catalogue, made during the late 1570s, of expurgated books that, in the Congregation's judgment, "might be singled out as particularly useful."[98]

. . . . .

[95] Cf. (**19**), (**20**), (**30**). On the subject, see J. Usher, "The Fortune of 'Fortuna' in Salviati's 'Rassettatura' of the *Decameron,*" in *Renaissance and Other Studies: Essays Presented to P. M. Brown,* ed. E. A. Millar (Glasgow, 1988), pp. 210–22.

[96] For the hostility of the Congregation to both, cf. Simoncelli, "Documenti interni," pp. 197ff.; and Vatican, lat. 6207, fol. 175^{v}.

[97] To the examples listed above, add the instances from Book 8 that strict censorship might have eliminated: chapters 17 (lack of confidence in the pope, perhaps redeemed by the reference to his "spiritual power and reputation"), 23 ("God's gratitude"), 28 (the pope's responsibility for war in Italy), 33 (Innocent VIII's son and nepotism), 36 (Lorenzo de' Medici raising his second son, Giovanni, to the cardinalate).

[98] "Ex primo catalogo, qui continet libros purgatos iussu Ill[ustrissi]me Congreg[ation]is, hi seligi posse videntur utpote utiliores." ACDF, Protocolli A [II^{a}.1], fol. 128^{r}. The prolonged closure of the Biblioteca Ambrosiana (Milan) has prevented consultation of its copy of the Giuntine edition of the *Istorie fiorentine* (1551), which Gerber (*Niccolò Machiavelli, Handschriften,* 2:82–83) describes as containing expurgations similar to those recommended in the text transcribed above. As, however, one of his three examples (3.13) differs significantly from the Roman censure and the other two (1.19 and 23) were obvious targets for elimination, dependence cannot be postulated without further evidence.

Hopes of republication blossomed in the spring of 1578. In May, after this censure had been laid before the authorities, Pier Vettori wrote to Sirleto.[99] Much time had passed, he reminded the cardinal, since his last letter. The reference was to that skilled piece of diplomacy which he had composed, on 6 February 1573, about the expurgated *Decameron;*[100] and Vettori's purpose was to revive the parallel enterprise of issuing the corrected works of Machiavelli. The grandson's efforts had not been seen by this literary politician, but he was confident of their thoroughness and orthodoxy. The emended author posed no threat. He would delight those who took pleasure in *memorie antiche,* being very clever and experienced in worldly affairs. By his own generation, Machiavelli had been thought to have penetrated to the core of history, especially in the *Discorsi.*[101]

Vettori's second letter to Sirleto was no less diplomatic than the first. Urging publication in the near future, he was at pains to represent the menace of Machiavelli as a legend of the past. He was an author for lovers of antiquity, not a subversive or enemy of the Church. Sirleto, responsible for the revision of the Index, took a different view of the problem. By 1578 the name of Machiavelli had become emblematic of heresy and sedition, and if it was desirable that the *Istorie fiorentine* be both censored and separated from their author, other writings were to remain beyond the pale.[102] That this treatment was not reserved for Niccolò alone is demonstrated by an address, delivered in Latin, on 18 March 1579, to the Congregation of the Index about a book composed *adversus Niclaum Machiavellum.*[103]

The name of its author and its title were omitted, as were its place of publication and printer. Since the theme of the speech was censorship of "commentarii de regno aut quovis principatu recte administrando," and a marginal note recorded "hic liber prorsus damnatus est," the reference may have been to the *Discours sur les moyens de bien gouverner et maintenir en bonne paix un royaume ou autre principauté contre Nicolas Machiavel, florentin,* issued anonymously

[99] *Clarorum Italorum et Germanorum epistolae* (ed. Bandini), pp. lxxiii–lxxiv; and Dejob, *De l'influence,* p. 396.

[100] Ed. Dejob, ibid., pp. 393–94. For context, see R. Mordenti, "Le due censure: La collazione dei testi del *Decameron* 'rassettati' da Vincenzio Borghini e Leonardo Salviati," in *Le pouvoir et la plume,* pp. 253ff.

[101] ". . . stimo bene, che trattone tutto quello, che potesse nuocere alla vita Christiana, il darle di nuovo fuora emendate, e viste prima, e approvate da V.S.R.^{ma} non potesse essere se non di giovamento a chi si diletta delle memorie antiche, perché egli fu uomo di grande ingegno, e molto pratico nelle cose del mondo, e io sentiva dire in que'tempi, che elle uscirono fuora, che egli aveva insegnato cavar vero frutto dalle istorie, e massimamente in que'suoi discorsi."

[102] Cf. Dejob, *De l'influence,* pp. 72ff.; and see further below.

[103] ACDF, Indice, Protocolli, C [II^{a}.3], fol. 192^{r} [= 182^{r}]. The speech records a decision taken on 14 March 1579. Ibid., fol. 86^{r} (minutes of the meeting), and cf. ACDF, Indice, Diarii 1.1, fol. 6^{v}.

in 1576 but written by Innocent Gentillet.[104] Seeking to pass for a moral writer, declared the orator, this monster of deception was "a Cyclops who belched forth thick smoke, thoroughly to obscure the splendor of respect for religion."[105] He was to be condemned not because he slighted the papacy but on the grounds that, as an obscurantist of Christian truths, he undermined the foundations of the faith. Little effort is required to imagine the reaction of the censor to the inversion of ethical language in *Il principe*.

Such was the view being formed of both Machiavelli and his enemies in the Congregation of the Index during the spring of 1579. General suspicion was qualified by partial tolerance; and the cardinals, prepared to countenance an expurgated edition of the *Istorie fiorentine,* demanded that they should appear under a different name. When the grandsons refused, an impasse was reached. The Roman authorities having arrived at the limits of their powers, appeal to higher authority remained the only solution. Sirleto went to the pope. His judgment was delivered in no uncertain terms. At a meeting of the Congregation of the Index, held on 21 October 1579, the following decision was recorded:

> The most illustrious Cardinal Sirleto, at the command of our Holy Lord on the same day, reported that the oracle of His spoken word had declared that the works of Machiavelli are to be totally condemned, with the effects, moreover, that no one should presume to expurgate them and that they are to be wholly removed from the hands of the faithful, as is decreed by the statute of the Congregation to be found in Book A, folio 86.[106]

Censorship, the "liberal" alternative to complete prohibition, was ruled out by Gregory XIII. There, it might be thought, the matter would be allowed to rest.

. . . . .

Not a bit of it. In 1585 both the pope and Sirleto died. In February 1587, Sixtus V, a former member of the Congregation, ordered a new Index to be prepared; and in a bull of 20 June 1582, he sought to enlist the aid of the Universities of Paris, Louvain, Salamanca, Alcalá, and Coïmbra. Their help

[104] ACDF, Indice, Protocolli, C [II^{a}.3]: "Ex consensu Theologorum . . . condemnaverunt, reprobaverunt et supprimendum decreverunt librum *Commentariorum de Regno aut quovis principatu recte administrando*."

[105] ". . . (ut ita dicam) Ciclops, qui densos evomuit fumos, ut omnino pietatis splendorem obscuraret." Ibid.

[106] "Ill.^{mus} Card. Sirletus eodem die ex mand[at]o S.D.N., vivae vocis oraculo habito, retulit opera Macchiavelli omnino reprobanda, ita ut de caetero nullus audeat illa expurgare, et a manibus fidelium prorsus amoveantur, prout Cong[regatio]nis statuto decretum est, ut habeas lib. A. fol. 86." ACDF, Indice, Diarii 1 [= 1.1], fol. 7^{r}. The reference is to ACDF, Indice, Protocolli, A [II^{a}.1], fol. 86a^{v}.

was needed. Neither consistency nor coherence distinguished the policy of the Congregation, the members of which, in their insecurity, were likened to "reeds buffeted by the wind."[107] Nominally one of their number, Cardinal Gabriele Paleotti, powerless at Bologna, had found to his bemusement, in 1577, that the *Manipulus curatorum* that, during his first diocesan synod, he had prescribed as required reading for all his curates was considered inadmissible by his colleagues at Rome.[108] In this fluid and unstable situation, not even the latest pronouncements by the papal oracle were regarded as sacrosanct. The attitude taken toward Machiavelli provides a sign of the times. On 3 December 1587, the *Istorie fiorentine* were again being discussed by the Congregation,[109] and, in the same year, Tommaso Zobbio, Master of the Sacred Palace, commissioned Roberto di Roberti, *conservatore del inclito popolo Romano,* to censor the *Discorsi.*[110]

Already singled out by Vettori and others,[111] the *Discorsi* contain some of Machiavelli's most stringent criticisms of the Christian religion and the Catholic Church. To the author's provocations, his censor responded in tentative tones. Roberto di Roberti began by composing a *parere,* or diagnostic censure, its views modestly formulated in the conditional (*io levarei*). When Machiavelli, in his proemium, described the *ozio* to which "many provinces and Christian cities" had fallen prey, the censor proposed the removal of the epithet, on the understated grounds that it appeared to confine an acknowledged evil to Christianity. It was undesirable, he thought, to retain passages in which the *Discorsi* spoke *troppo* [*sic*] *male* of the Roman Curia or subordinated religion to reason of state. Nor was it expedient to permit allusions to Savonarola, who had been condemned by a pope.[112] And if Machiavelli had to attack St. Gregory, he might have done so better and more fairly. . . .

The censor was leading in a clear direction. Both by his restraint in elimination and by the mildness of his emendations to the remarkably few pas-

[107] "Harundines . . . vento agitatas." Cited from F. A. Zaccaria, *Storia polemica della proibizione de' libri* (Rome, 1777), p. 165, by Rotondò, "La censura ecclesiastica," p. 1403; and see Frajese, "La revoca dell'*Index* sistino," pp. 20ff.

[108] Prodi, *Il cardinale Gabriele Paleotti,* 2:240–41. Note, however, that the *Manipulus curatorum* was crossed out from a list of prohibited and suspect books, which Roman booksellers were forbidden to sell, with the annotation "admittitur," in ACDF, Indice, Protocolli, A [II^{a}.1], fol. 242^{v}.

[109] ACDF, Indice, Protocolli, B (II^{a}.2), fol. 66^{r}. Cf. ibid., fol. 263 [= 269]: "Quid de Historiis Machiavelli, quae parvo admodum negocio expurgari possunt."

[110] For the full text and context of this censure, extracts from which are printed below, see my "Machiavelli and the Censors" (forthcoming). The source is ACDF, Indice, Protocolli, C [II^{a}.3], fols. 187^{r} [= 177^{r}]–189^{v} [= 179^{v}].

[111] See above, p. 323.

[112] On the censorhip of Savonarola, see M. Scaduto, "Laínez e l'Indice del 1559: Lullo, Sabunde, Savonarola, Erasmo," *Archivium Societatis Iesu* 24 (1955): 14ff.; and M. Firpo and P. Simonicelli, "I processi inquisitoriali contro Savonarola (1588) e Carnesecchi (1566–1567): Una proposta di interpretazione," *Rivista di storia e letteratura religiosa* 17 (1982): 200–52.

sages that he singled out, Roberto di Roberti revealed a wish to preserve the *Discorsi* for publication. He declared as much, with measure and clarity, at the end of his *parere,* which, shifting from the vernacular to Latin, concluded with a *iudicium:*

> I should say that it was quite right that the entire work was condemned, because from time to time [Machiavelli] impugns the authority of the Church, vituperates those in holy orders, teaches that religion is inferior and that, for reasons of state, anything is permitted, and because, in particular, he speaks like a pagan and one either ignorant of the Christian religion or contemptuous of it.
>
> On the other hand, I admire his style. Many of the things that are fundamental to the governance of the state, the drawing up of troops in battle order, and the practice of arms he treats so fully and eloquently that nothing could surpass him.
>
> In conclusion, this book could be republished if a few things were pruned, altered, and set to rights. I am inclined to regard this as a simple matter, and I am confident that it would be of great utility and instructiveness.[113]

Tactfully conceding the justice of previous condemnations, this positive judgment proceeds to reverse them. Anticipating a favorable reception, Roberto di Roberti submitted his censure to the Master of the Sacred Palace. Not only Machiavelli's enemies occupied high places.

. . . . .

Pressure to allow an expurgated edition continued. In a petition of 1593,[114] Count Aloisio Mariani and Giulio Areti requested the right to purge, among a large number of suspect works (including some as recent as the Genoese translation of Jean Bodin's *Les six livres de la République*[115]), the *Discorsi* and

[113] "Totum opus prudentissime damnatum dicerem, quod aliquando ecclesiam concutat, in sacris ordinibus constitutos vituperet, et posthabita religione omnia regnandi causa permitti edoceat et quod precipue loquatur tamquam etnicus et Christiane religionis vel ignarus vel conte[m]ptor.
"Contra admiror modum dicendi. Multa etiam que ad gubernandam rempublicam, ad exercitus instruendos, ad arma tractanda sunt necessaria ita plene ac diserte declarat, ut nihil magis.
"Denique si liber iste quibusdam resecatis, immutatis, et ad normam redactis—quod quidem haud difficile existimarem—in publicum denuo prodire posset, id non sine magna utilitate ac documento fore confiderem." ACDF, Indice, Protocolli, C [II^{a}.3], fol. 178^{r} [= 188^{r}]–179^{v} [= 189^{v}].

[114] ACDF, Indice, Protocolli I [II^{a}.8], fol. 512^{r} [= 534 ^{r}]. The petition was referred to the Inquisition on 27 March 1593. ACDF, Diarii, 1.1, fol. 67^{r}.

[115] *I sei libri della Republica del Sig. Giovanni Bodino tradotti di lingua francese nell'italiano da Lorenzo Conti, gentiluomo genovese* (Genua, 1588), in N. Giuliani, *Notizie sulla tipografia ligure sino a tutto il secolo XVI* (Genoa, 1869), p. 489.

the *Istorie fiorentine*. This document, together with Roberto di Roberti's *parere* and *iudicium* of 1587, points to the confusion in the early history of Roman censorship. Outside the Congregation of the Index, Gregory XIII's renewed prohibition of Machiavelli was unknown both to the Mariani-Areti partnership and to Giuliano de' Ricci, who, having no idea that his proposal had been refused fifteen years earlier by the pope, was still waiting for news of a decision in 1594. Inside that body which, in the late 1580s, was beginning to reorganize and expand, members were better informed. The ruling of 1579 was registered among acts that had been filed and classified;[116] and if the "reeds buffeted by the winds" of changing policy considered the possibility of a new expurgation, that can only have been because, in full possession of the facts, they were inclined to temper Gregory XIII's ban. Less clear is their ability to implement their plan, had they so wished. Among the increased powers that Sixtus V, in his general reform of the Curia, attributed to the Inquisition in 1588[117] were the censorship and prohibition of books. Not one but two bodies were now responsible for the same activity, and the stage was set for a clash. If no single Congregation at Rome was capable of defining how long a period was implied by the formula *donec expurgatur,* what hope was there for Giuliano de' Ricci at Florence?

Machiavelli's grandson was not alone in having difficulties with the Index. As he ruefully noted, in 1594, that nothing had become of his attempt to expurgate the works, Clement VIII was encountering opposition to the severity of recent efforts to modify the Sistine list of prohibited books. When, on 27 March 1596, that leading member of the Congregation of the Index, Cardinal Agostino Valier, ordered the Clementine version to be promulgated, it was to find his command suspended, a month later, at the instance of Cardinal Santori, the Grand Inquisitor.[118] Against this background of institutional conflict, the question of Machiavelli reemerged.

On 5 June 1596, Cesare Baronio, despite his protests, was created cardinal. The pope's confessor since 1594 and his librarian three years later, this leading historian of the Church stood at the pinnacle of his fame and influence. He was also, through his work for the Congregation of the Index,[119] involved in the attempt to settle the disputes that had arisen, particularly with

[116] With note 106 above, cf. the registration of Machiavelli's "opera omnia prorsus prohibentur" in the alphabetical list of heretical authors and books drawn up for the Congregation on 17 November 1580, in ACDF, Indice A [II^{a}.1], fol. 9^{v}.

[117] *Bullarium Romanum* 8 (Turin, 1883), pp. 985–99, with Del Re, *La Curia Romana,* p. 94.

[118] See Frajese, "La revoca dell'*Index* sistino"; and Grendler, *Roman Inquisition,* pp. 256ff.

[119] There exists no adequate treatment of this subject, ignored by H. Jedin, *Kardinal Caesar Baronius: Der Anfang der katholischen Kirchengeschichtsschreibung im 16. Jahrhundert* (Münster, 1978), and by A. Pincherle in *DBI* 6 (1964), pp. 470–78. Brief remarks in G. Calenzio, *La vita et gli scritti del cardinale Cesare Baronio della congregazione del Oratorio* (Rome, 1907), pp. 570–80, and C. K. Pullapilly, *Caesar Baronius: Counter-Reformation Historian* (Notre Dame, 1975), pp. 88–89.

Venice,[120] over the Clementine version. On September 14 a compromise was reached with the Venetian authorities and solemnized by a concordat, which substituted "local expurgation for outright prohibition."[121] In the same spirit, two weeks later, Baronio proposed a solution to an older and lingering problem.

On 28 September 1596, the cardinal suggested, at a meeting of the Congregation of the Index, that a "correction" of Machiavelli's works should be made by his canon-grandson.[122] The proposal approved, a decree of 9 November specified that the reappointed censor should work with "deputies" appointed by the archbishop of Florence's vicar-general, subject to the written approval of the *ordinarius* and the local inquisitor. The product was to be submitted to the Congregation.[123] So it was that a plan that had laid dormant for two decades was revived at the instance of one of the Church's most eminent scholars. Baronio's tolerance had been displayed in the winning grace with which, three years previously, he had urged Justus Lipsius to emend his *Politics* to avoid their being placed on the Index;[124] and if, in 1596, the cardinal was sensitive to Venetian objections to Roman censorship, he had equal reason to attend to those emanating from Florence, with which, as its ambassador's dispatches reveal, he was in contact during the last months of that year.[125].

Ferdinand I, grand duke of Tuscany, was determined to assert his own powers of control in that disputed domain between Church and State.[126] What the Congregation proposed was a variant on the model that had been used to expurgate Boccaccio. While that precedent hardly inspired confidence, as Lionardo Salviati's fresh efforts to undertake the same operation showed, history was being invited to repeat itself: the attempt to prepare yet another emended *Decameron* was again linked with an effort to win back, for Florence, as much as could be redeemed of Machiavelli. Cardinal Baronio

[120] See Grendler, *Roman Inquisition,* pp. 266ff.

[121] Ibid., p. 278.

[122] "Card. Baronius proposuit correctionem operum Machiavelli per quendam canonicum Florentinum eiusdem familie faciendam et decretumque eidem canonico per litteras committatur negotium." ACDF, Diarii 1 [= 1.1], fol. 92^r [= 97^a].

[123] "Decretum quod expurgatio Machiavelli committatur canonico Machiavello cum aliis a vic.° Archiepiscopo deputatis, ex quorum approbatione in scriptis et ordinarii et inquisitoris censura ad congregationem transmittatur." Ibid., fol. 94^r [= 97^b].

[124] "Te . . . meorum scriptorum habere cupio cognitorem, monitorem, atque censorem" (letter to Lipsius of 31 July 1593), in Burmann, *Sylloges epistolarum,* 2:678. See G. Oesterreich, *Antiker Geist und moderner Staat bei Justus Lipsius (1547–1606)* (Göttingen, 1989), pp. 201–2; and R. Bireley, *The Counter-Reformation Prince: Anti-Machiavellianism or Catholic Statecraft in Early Modern Europe* (Chapel Hill, N.C., 1990), pp. 90–91.

[125] ACDF, Diarii, 1, fol. 94^v [= 97^v] (9 November); and ASF, Mediceo del Principato, filza 3312 (September–December 1596).

[126] See A. Panella, "La censura sulla stampa," pp. 140–51; and cf. Frajese, "La revoca dell'*Index* sistino," pp. 45ff.

was amenable, but he was not the only factor in this complex calculation; and the grand duke made the mistake of intervening at a higher level, in order to gain the approval of the Inquisition. His choice of target and moment could scarcely have been more untimely. Against the background of the bitter struggle between the secular and ecclesiastical authorities in Italy over the Clementine Index, Ferdinand I sought the cooperation of a prelate who, with the intransigence of Paul IV, terrified other members of the Sacred College—that tireless, omnipresent, unrelenting inquisitor, Guilio Antonio Santori.

Not sweetened by his defeat in the papal election of 1592, adamantly opposed to censorship being undertaken by the friends or family of condemned authors,[127] the cardinal of Santa Severina was approached, in the name of the grand duke, by the Florentine ambassador, Giovanni Niccolini, in the first week of December 1596.[128] Less than a month after the Congregation of the Index, at Baronio's suggestion, had formally approved the expurgation of Machiavelli and prescribed how it should be carried out, Santori imposed his veto on the project.[129] No, it was not that he objected to a revision of the prohibited works. That might have been feasible, had only they been condemned. The Church's ban, however, covered the writings, the name, and the memory of Machiavelli; and, in an atmosphere where "a purge had become a privilege,"[130] it would never be conceded to this condemned author. Ferdinand I would do better to stay out of the matter, which had no chance of success. Interpreting the Index in a sense at direct variance with that of its own Congregation, Santori showed the grand duke's emissary to the door. Such was the style, such were the tones of the Grand Inquisitor: uncompromising harshness and unrelieved gloom. Even the pope called him Cassandra.[131]

Cassandra-Santori had reasons for the stand that he took. Behind him stood two other oracles: Paul IV and Gregory XIII. His position was further

[127] See Rotondò, "Nuovi documenti," p. 174.

[128] On Niccolini, see M. del Pazzo, *Gli ambasciatori toscani del principato (1537–1737)* (Florence, 1956), p. 154.

[129] ASF, Mediceo del Principato, filza 3312: "Conforme al commandam[en]to di V[ostra] A[ltezza] ho fatto offitio col S[ignor] Card[inale] Santa Sev[eri]na per ché quelli della famiglia de Machiavelli possin' far' ristampare l'opere del Machiavelli riviste et ricorrette, ma S[ua] S[antità] Ill[ustrissi]ma m'ha risposto, che se fussero dannate solam[en]te l'opere di quell'autore, questo potrebbe forse succedere, ma che essendo dannato insieme con l'opere il nome et la memoria di d[ett]o autore, quest'è una cosa che non si concederà mai, et che à S[ua] S[antità] Ill[ustrissi]ma pare, che non si deva interporre il nome et il favore dell'A[ltezza] V[ostra] in questo negotio, massime non c'essendo speranza che ne deva sortir' l'effetto che si desidera, però io non farò offitio con altri Card[ina]li sopra qu[es]to sin' che l'A[ltezza] V[ostra] non lo comanderà . . . // Di Roma il di 7 di dicembre 1596 // Humilissimo e devotissimo // Giovanni Niccolinj."

[130] Frajese, "La revoca dell'*Index* sistino," p. 45.

[131] Santori, autobiography (ed. Cugnoni), p. 169.

reinforced by the Clementine Index of 1596, which, among its new rules, condemned Machiavelli's doctrine of *raison d'état.*[132] In the context of the "anti-Machiavellianism" of the late sixteenth century—of the sequence of polemical attacks on his thought and character by Antonio Possevino, Tommaso Bozio, and a host of others[133]—the cardinal represented a dominant strand of orthodoxy. Yet it was not the only strand. Cesare Baronio, fledged in dealings with the Inquisition,[134] was inclined to grant the privilege of a purge, which, for twenty years, had been entertained by the Congregation of the Index.

The limitations of its powers and competence, relative to those of the Holy Office, are graphically illustrated by this episode. Not even the revered favorite of the reigning pope could withstand the Grand Inquisitor. Personal animus may be dismissed as a motive. Santori knew who his enemies were, and Baronio was not among them. He had been recommended, while still a poor scholar, for a bishopric by the cardinal,[135] who thought highly of his work. The point at dispute was institutional. The Holy Office would brook no challenge to its supremacy among the Congregations of the Curia, either at Rome or elsewhere. On 22 April 1596, Santori wrote to the Florentine inquisitor, observing that "the Secretary of the Congregation of the Index of Prohibited Books finds [*sic*] that he has sent the Index [of 1596] to Your Reverence without discussing it in advance in this Sacred Congregation of the Holy Roman and Universal Inquisition."[136] A number of corrections and clarifications followed. Their aim was to make it plain where authority lay—with Santori, in the Inquisition, not in the Congregation of the Index. The theme of the subordination of the body to which Baronio belonged is pursued, with typical thoroughness, in the cardinal of Santa Severina's later letters.[137] In one written on 27 April, Santori, referring to *La république* of Jean Bodin, declared: "Although in this new Index [it] is suspended until it can be expurgated, it actually does not qualify for expurgation, but should be treated as condemned in whatever language and edition, as was directed by Pope Gregory XIV."[138]

If the contradiction is glaring, the policy is plain. This was precisely the view that, in December of the same year, the cardinal took of Machiavelli.

[132] See J. Bujanda et al., in *Index de Rome 1590, 1593, 1596,* p. 350.

[133] See De Maffei, *Dal premachiavellianismo,* pp. 237ff.; Procacci, *Studi sulla fortuna di Machiavelli,* pp. 319ff.; and Rotondò, "Le censura ecclesiastica," pp. 1468ff.

[134] See J. Pérez Villanueva, "Baronio y la Inquisicion espagnola," and L. Osbat, "Baronio a Napoli per un procedimento d'inquisizione," in *Baronio storico e la Controriforma,* ed. R. de Maio et al. (Sora, 1982), pp. 3–182, 185–95.

[135] Calenzio, *La vita et gli scritti,* pp. 258–60.

[136] Edited and translated by J. Tedeschi, "Florentine Documents for a History of the *Index of Prohibited Books,*" in *Prosecution of Heresy,* pp. 282–83.

[137] Ibid., pp. 284ff.

[138] Ibid., p. 285.

Between the man, the reputation, and the works a distinction had been drawn since the grandsons, in their censure of the *Istorie fiorentine,* had canceled his name. If they were not willing to countenance a substitute, nor was Santori—for different reasons. He maintained that the author, his writings, and his memory had been, and should be, condemned in their entirety. So the Grand Inquisitor understood the "first class" of the Index, not only explicitly correcting its Congregation,[139] but also, by appeal to the ruling of Gregory XIV, implicitly ticking off his successor as pope. And there are signs that Clement VIII received the message, because in 1598, when a Venetian noble, Agostino Michele, claimed to have been encouraged by the local inquisitor to prepare an expurgated edition of Machiavelli's writings, he was refused permission to publish it, on the grounds that "His Holiness did not consider it expedient to grant such a license, the author being condemned in the first class, and most pernicious to read."[140] That judgment had been delivered by the pontiff on 19 February, at one of the twice-weekly meetings of the Roman Inquisition assiduously attended and regularly hosted by the cardinal of Santa Severina.[141] Santori had given his rival Aldobrandini a lesson in how to interpret his own Index.

While the papal monarchy of the Catholic Reformation established its absolutism by dividing the Sacred College into competing Congregations,[142] one of them—the Inquisition—remained capable of asserting itself.[143] To the acrimonious strife that surrounded Machiavelli's reputation and works in the sixteenth century must be added a none-too-latent tension between the defeated candidate in the conclave of 1592 and the victor. Not surprisingly, the other parties to this quarrel fell into line. When, on 27 December 1602, Fabio Albergati submitted his dismal polemic against Bodin, the Congrega-

[139] For the moderate spirit in which the Congregation of the Index viewed not only Machiavelli but prohibited books in general, cf. its response (*ante* 9 March 1589) to the fifth rule of the Sistine Index: "Hereticorum libri, qui de Religione ex professo tractant, prohibentur omnino. Permitti vero poterunt nonnulli eorum libri, sed admodum pauci—ex eo his, ii tantum, qui hactenus prodierunt, quique possint esse alicuius utilitatis, si modo de religione non tractent ex professo, sitque eorum expurgatio a Cardinalibus deputatis approbata." ACDF, Indice, Protocolli, V [2ª.19], fol. 13ʳ.

[140] "A sua Beatitudine non è parso espediente di concedere tal licenza, per esser l'autore dannato della prima classe, e di perniciossima lettione." (21 February 1598) recorded by the Venetian Inquisition in *Anima del Sant'Officio spirata dal Sopremo Tribunale della Sacra Congregatione raccolta dal Padre Predicatore F. Giacomo Angarano da Vicenza l'anno del Signore MDCXLIV* = Vatican, lat. 10945, fol. 149ᵛ and cf. fols. 113ᵛ and 114ᵛ.

[141] ACDF, Sant'Uffizio, Decreti, 1597–1598, 1, fol. 118ʳ; cf. L. Pastor, *Storia dei papi* (Rome, 1958), p. 464.

[142] See Prodi, *Papal Prince,* pp. 17ff. and 79ff.; and idem, *Lo sviluppo dell'assolutismo nello stato pontificio (secoli xv–xvi)* 1 (Bologna, 1968), pp. 87–114.

[143] Cf. L. Firpo, *Il processo di Giordano Bruno* (Naples, 1944), pp. 64, 86ff., 96ff., 100, 103. For the earlier history, see P. Simonicelli, "Inquisizione romana e riforma in Italia," *Rivista storica italiana* 100 (1988): 5–113, esp. 66ff.

tion of the Index applauded his efforts and urged him to continue them by writing against Machiavelli.[144] After being arrested in possession of his works and those of Bodin, a certain Cesare di Pisce was tortured eight years later.[145] When the cardinals of the Holy Office petitioned the pope to be allowed to read prohibited books, they received, on 14 September 1667, the reply from Clement IX that this was permitted—with two exceptions, one of which was Machiavelli.[146] For presuming to praise him, Angelo Maria Bandini was denounced to the Inquisition and instructed, by the Congregation of the Index, on 16 May 1753, to remove from the *Collectio* both his eulogy and his claim that the works had been proscribed, during the pontificate of Clement VIII, at the instigation of Bozio and Possevino.[147] The correction was just. These supine censors instigated nothing. The prime movers of anti-Machiavellianism in the Catholic Reformation sat on, or near, the throne of St. Peter.

. . . . .

The censorship of Machiavelli forms part of a colorful and dramatic tale, much of which remains to be told.[148] The cast of characters is long. Muzio, Locatelli, and Martelli; Machiavelli's grandsons and "Cardinal Alessandrino's" theologian; Roberto di Roberti and Tommaso Zobbio; Count Aloisio Mariani and Giulio Areti; Grand Duke Ferdinand, Cardinals Sirleto and Baronio: the point is less to make a list of Italian intellectuals who wished to save, by censoring, this "fine fellow," than to number the few who did not wish to do so. Their names, which have never figured in the history of Machiavelli's fortunes, were Pope Gregory XIII, Pope Clement VIII, and—above all—Grand Inquisitor Santori. At stake was not only the work of a prohibited author, but also the respective authority of two Roman Congregations jointly responsible for censorship. Parallel in theory, they were by no means united or equal in practice. Conflict was one product of this situation, irony an-

[144] Firpo, "Filosofia italiana e Controriforma," p. 157.

[145] Procacci, *Studi sulla fortuna di Machiavelli,* p. 327 n. 2.

[146] ACDF, Indice, Stanza storica, 0 2–C (6). The reference is to Urban VIII's decree of 1632. See Catalani, *De secretario,* p. 56.

[147] Procacci, *Studi sulla fortuna di Machiavelli,* p. 351. For the continuing suspicion of Machiavelli, cf. the letter to Bandini on 21 July 1753 by the Secretary of the Index, Ricchini, about "documenti qui esistenti circa l'empietà, e la morte del Machiavelli": BMF, Ms. B.1.27, 9, fol. 157^r, and the letter of Bandini's brother Giuseppe (2 July 1753), explaining that expurgation was necessary in order not to seem to "approvare la sua doctrina . . . avendomi il Padre Ricchini confidato che qua nel Sant'Uffizio ci sono dei documenti autentici dai quali manifestamente apparisce che Machiavelli fosse un empio e morissse bestemmiando." Ibid., fol. 13^r. Ed. E. Levi, "Nota su di un falso machiavelliano," *Il pensiero politico* (1969): 462–63.

[148] See my forthcoming *Inquisition and Index: The Theory and Practice of Censorship.*

other. For if the Holy Office remained (as its successor is still called) *la Suprema*[149] during the struggle over the Index, its own Congregation, defeated in the attempt to accord Machiavelli the privilege of a purge, did less violence to his works than some of their more recent inquisitors.

[149] Del Re, *La Curia Romana,* pp. 89ff.

SELECT BIBLIOGRAPHY

INDEX OF MANUSCRIPT SOURCES

Florence

ARCHIVIO DI STATO

Carte Strozziane. II, 21: 144n
Consigli della Repubblica. *Libri Fabarum* 71: 145n
———. *Consulte e Pratiche,* 64: 146n, 170
———. *Consulte e Pratiche,* 69: 146n
Manoscritti, 252: 147n
Mediceo del Principato, 3312: 328n, 329n
Notarile antecosmiano, 21073: 149n
Signori, Dieci di Balia, Otto di Pratica, Carteggio. Responsive originali, 10: 237n
———. *Legazioni e commissarie, Missive e responsive* 10: 237n
Signori e Collegi. *Deliberazioni fatte in forza di ordinaria autorità* 109: 151n
———. *Deliberazioni fatte in forza di ordinaria autorità* 114: 235
Signori. Missive, Prima Cancelleria 50: 171n
———. Missive, Prima Cancelleria 51: 169n, 171n, 248n
Tratte, 286: 206n
Studio Fiorentino e Pisano (Ufficiali dello Studio), 8: 206n, 246n, 248n, 263

BIBLIOTECA MARUCELLIANA

Ms. B. I, 27, 9: 332n
Ms. B. III, 65: 147n

BIBLIOTECA MEDICEA LAURENZIANA

Ashburnham, 559: 144n
Pluteo 19, 30: 215n
Pluteo 35, 32: 149n
Pluteo 40, 52: 110
Pluteo 45, 15: 84n
Pluteo 48, 37: 163n
Pluteo 60, 14: 60–61
Pluteo 77, 11: 191n
Pluteo 90, sup. 37 [*P*]: 3–26
Pluteo 90, sup. 39 [*L*]: 150, 197, 200–201, 215, 220n, 242, 288n
Pluteo 90, sup. 111, 1: 305n–306n
Strozzi, 106 [*S*]: 3–26

BIBLIOTECA NAZIONALE CENTRALE

Banco Rari 29: 235
Conventi Soppressi D. 9. 278: 143n
Fondo Nazionale II. II. 48: 111n

Fondo Nazionale II. V. 78 [*N, n, n*[1]]: 173–78, 180, 183, 185, 186, 189–91
Magl. VIII, 1195: 215n
Magl. VIII, 1439: 13n, 19n
Magl. VIII, 1442: 210n
Magl. VIII, 1452: 147n
Magl. VIII, 1493: 202–4
Palat. 1116, 1: 144n
Palat. 776: 106n
Passerini, 158 (*bis*): 147n

BIBLIOTECA RICCARDIANA

121: 74n
594: 210n
636: 210n
767: 231–32
811 [*R*]: 150–78, 186, 194–99, 212n, 243–44, 280n
904: 210n
911: 217–18, 247–48
951: 193n
1221 E: 210n
2692: 210n

Milan

BIBLIOTECA AMBROSIANA

S. 81 sup.: 231n

Munich

BAYERISCHE STAATSBIBLIOTHEK

Clm. 337: 218, 225
Clm. 745: 39n
Clm. 807: 205n

Paris

BIBLIOTHÈQUE NATIONALE

Grec 3069: 60n
Ital. 1543 [*P*[1]]: 3–26
Lat. 7723: 39n

Turin

BIBLIOTECA CIVICA

Raccolte storiche, fondo Cosilla 62: 251n

Vatican City

ARCHIVIO DELLA CONGREGAZIONE PER LA DOTTRINA DELLA FEDE

Indice, Diarii, I: 317, 323n, 324, 326n, 328
Indice, Protocolli A: 318, 319, 322, 324n, 327n
Indice, Protocolli B: 325n

Indice, Protocolli C: 323n, 324n, 325–26
Indice, Protocolli I: 326n
Indice, Protocolli V: 310–17, 331n
Sant'Uffizio, Decreti, 1579–98, I: 331n
Stanza Storica 0 2–C (6): 332

BIBLIOTECA APOSTOLICA VATICANA

Lat. 3867: 84n
Lat. 5878: 292n
Lat. 6207: 322n
Lat. 10945: 331n
Ross. 884: 149n

PRINTED PRIMARY SOURCES

Adriani, Marcello Virgilio. *Oratio. . . pro dandis Florentinae Reipublicae militaribus imperatoris signis Magnifico Laurentio de Medices.* Basle, 1518.

———. *Oratio . . . habita in funere Magni Iuliani Medicis illustrissimi ducis Nemursie.* In McManamon, "Marketing a Medici Regime."

———, ed. and trans. *Pedacii Dioscoridae Anazarbei medica materia libri sex interprete Marcello Virgilio Secretario Florentino cum eiusdem annotationibus nuperque diligentissime excussi addito indice eorum, quae digna notatu visa sunt.* Florence, 1518.

Amaseo, G. [*Epistula.*] Edited by G. Pozzi. In "Da Padova a Firenze nel 1493." *IMU* 9 (1966): 191–227.

Angèli, N., ed. Cicero, *De natura deorum, De divinatione, De fato, De legibus, Academicarum Quaestionum libri II, De finibus bonorum et malorum, De petitione consulatus, De universitate.* Florence, 1516.

———, ed. Cicero, *Orationes.* Florence, 1515.

———, ed. Cicero, *Philippicae.* Florence, 1515.

———, ed. Cicero, *Rhetorica.* Florence, 1516.

———, ed. Cicero, *Verrinae.* Florence, 1515.

———, ed. Macrobius and Cicero, *Somnium Scipionis, Interpretatio in Somnium . . ., Saturnalia.* Florence, 1515.

———, ed. Quintilian, *Institutio oratoria.* Florence, 1515.

———, ed. *Scriptores de re rustica.* Florence, 1515.

Barbaro, E. *Castigationes Plinianae et in Pomponium Melum.* 4 vols. Edited by G. Pozzi. Padua, 1979.

———. *Epistolae, orationes, et carmina.* 2 vols. Edited by V. Branca. Florence, 1943.

———. *Ioannis Baptistae Egnatii Veneti in Dioscoridem ab Ermolao Barbaro tralatum annotamenta. Hermolai Barbari patritii Veneti Corollarii libri quinque non ante impressi.* Venice, 1516 [= 1517].

Bembo, P. *Prose e rime.* Edited by C. Dionisotti. Turin, 1960.

Benivieni, A. *De abditis nonnullis ac mirandis morborum et sanationum causis.* Florence, 1507.

———. *Ἐγκώμιον Cosmi ad Laurentium Medicem.* Edited by R. Piattoli. Florence, 1949.

Bernardino, P. *Prediche di Pietro Bernardino de' fanciulli della città di Firenze mandata a 'ipsi fanciulli. . . .* Florence, 1497.

Bisticci, V. da. *Vite.* Edited by A. Greco. 2 vols. Florence, 1976.

Bruni, L. *Funeral Oration for Nanni Strozzi.* In *Stephani Baluzii Tutelensis Miscellanea novo ordine digesta . . . et aucta,* vol. 4, edited by G. D. Mansi, 2–7. Lucca, 1764.

———. *The Humanism of Leonardo Bruni: Selected Texts.* Translated by G. Griffiths, J. Hankins, and D. Thompson. Binghamton, N.Y., 1987.

———. *Humanistisch-philosophische Schriften.* Edited by H. Baron. Leipzig, 1928.

———. *Laudatio Florentinae Urbis.* Edited in H. Baron, *From Petrarch to Leonardo Bruni,* 232–63. Chicago, 1968.

———, trans. and commentary. Ps.-Aristotle, *Oeconomica.* In *Aristotelis Stagiritae libri moralem philosophiam complectentes cum Averrois Cordubensis in Moralia Nicomachia expositionibus.* Venice, 1560.

Burmann, P., ed. *Sylloges epistolarum a viris illustribus scriptarum.* 2 vols. Leiden, 1727.

Caiado, E. Letters to Marcello Virgilio, 23 January 1495, and 20 November 1496. Edited by A. F. Verde, *Studio* 4.3:1160; 2:476–77.

Candido, P., ed. Lucretius, *De rerum natura.* Florence, 1513.

Capranica, D. [Attributed.] *Arte del bene morire.* Florence, 1472 [BRF, Banco Rari 175].

Cerretani, B. *Ricordi.* Edited by G. Berti. Florence, 1993.

———. *Storia fiorentina.* Edited by G. Berti. Florence, 1994.

Collenuccio, P. Letter to the duke of Ferrara, 4 October 1495. Edited by P. Negri, "Pisa e Firenze nell'ottobre 1495 in due lettere inedite di Pandolfo Collenuccio." In *Scritti di storia in onore di C. Manfroni.* Padua, 1925.

———. *Operette morali: Poesie latine e volgari.* Edited by A. Saviotti. Bari, 1927.

———. *Pliniana defensio Pandulphi Collenucci Pisaurensis iurisconsulti adversus Nicolai Leoniceni accusationem.* Ferrara, 1493.

Consulte e pratiche della Repubblica Fiorentina, 1494–1505. Edited by D. Fachard. Geneva, 1993.

Consulte e pratiche della Repubblica Fiorentina, 1505–1512. Edited by D. Fachard. Geneva, 1988

Cortesi, P. *De cardinalatu.* Castrum Cortesianum, 1510.

———. *De hominibus doctis dialogus.* Edited by G. Ferraù. Palermo, 1979.

Crinito, P. *Commentarii de honesta disciplina.* Florence, 1504. Edited by P. Angeleri, Rome, 1955.

———. *Libri de poetis latinis.* Florence, 1506.

Dazzi, A. *Andreae Dactii Patricii et Academici Florentini poemata. . . .* Florence, 1549.

Dioscorides. *Pedacii Dioscuridis Anazarbei: De materia medica libri quinque.* Edited by M. Wellmann. 4 vols. Berlin, 1906.

Erasmus, D. *Institutio principis christiani.* In *Opera omnia* 4, 1, edited by O. Herding, 133–219. Amsterdam, 1976.

———, trans. Euripides, *Hecuba, Iphigenia in Aulide.* Florence, 1518.

Ficino, M. *Opera omnia.* 2 vols. Introduction by P. O. Kristeller. Turin, 1962.

———. Plato, *Phaedrus* (commentary). Edited by M.J.R. Allen, *Marsilio Ficino and the Phaedran Charioteer.* Berkeley, 1981.

———. Plato, *Philebus* (commentary). Edited by M.J.R. Allen, *Marsilio Ficino: The Philebus Commentary.* Berkeley, 1975.

———. Plato, *Sophist* (commentary). Edited by M.J.R. Allen, *Icastes:. Marsilio Ficino's Interpretation of Plato's Sophist: Five Studies and Critical Edition with Translation.* Berkeley, 1981.

———. *Supplementum Ficinianum.* Edited by P. O. Kristeller. Florence, 1937.

———. *Theologia platonica.* Edited by R. Marcel, *Marsile Ficin: Théologie platonicienne: De l'immortalité des ames,* vol. 2. Paris, 1964.

Filelfo, F. *Cent-dix lettres grecques à François Filèfe.* Edited by E. Legrand. Paris, 1892.

Fonzio, B. *Bartolomeus Fontius, epistolarum libri III.* Edited by L. Juhàsz. Budapest, 1931.

Francini, A., ed. Alexander of Aphrodisias, *In Sophisticos Aristotelis Elenchos commentaria.* Florence, 1521.

Giovio, P. *Dialogus de viris et feminis aetate nostra florentibus.* In *Pauli Iovii opera,* vol. 9, *Dialogi et descriptiones,* edited by E. Travi and M. Penco. Rome, 1984.

———. *Elogia clarorum virorum* 77. In *Pauli Iovii opera,* vol. 8, *Gli elogi degli uomini illustri (Letterati—artisti—uomini d'arte),* edited by R. Meregazzo. Rome, 1972.

———. *Vita Leonis Decimi.* In *Pauli Iovii opera* vol. 6, bk. 1, edited by M. Cataudella. Rome, 1987.

Guicciardini, F. *Lettere.* Vol. 1, *(1499–1513).* Edited by P. Jordogne. Rome, 1986.

———. *Scritti autobiografici e rari.* Edited by R. Palmarocchi. Bari, 1936.

———. *Storia d'Italia.* Edited by E. Mazzali. Milan, 1988.

Landino, C. *Disputationes camaldulenses.* Edited by P. Lohe. Florence, 1980.

———. *Scritti critici e teorici.* Edited by R. Cardini. 2 vols. Rome, 1974.

———. *De vera nobilitate.* Edited by M. T. Liaci. Florence, 1970.

Landucci, L. *Diario fiorentino dal 1450 al 1516.* Edited by I. del Badia. Florence, 1883.

Lascaris, G. *Epigrammi greci.* Edited by A. Meschini. Padua, 1976.

Leoniceno, N. *De Plinii et plurium aliorum medicorum in medicina erroribus opus.* 1–4. Ferrara, 1509.

———. *De Plinii in medicina erroribus* 1. Edited by L. Premuda. Milan, 1958.

Machiavelli, B. *Libro di ricordi.* Edited by C. Olschki. Florence, 1954.

Machiavelli, N. *Allocuzione ad un magistrato.* Edited by J.-J. Marchand, "Una *Protestatio de iustitia* del Machiavelli: L'*Allocuzione ad un magistrato,*" *La Bibliofilia* 76–77 (1974–75): 209–21.

———. *Capitoli.* Edited by G. Inglese. Rome, 1981.

———. *Del modo di trattare i popoli della Valdichiana ribellati.* In *Niccolò Machiavelli: I primi scritti politici (1499–1512): Nascità di un pensiero e di uno stile,* edited by J. J. Marchand, 98–119. Padua, 1975.

———. *De principatibus.* Edited by. G. Inglese. Rome, 1994.

———. *Dialogo intorno alla nostra lingua.* Edited by O. Castellani Polidori, *Niccolò Machiavelli e il "Dialogo intorno alla nostra lingua."* Florence, 1978.

———. *Discorsi sopra la prima Deca di Tito Livio.* Edited by G. Inglese. Milan, 1984.

———. *Esortazione alla penitenza.* In *Opere,* 932–34.

———. *Historie di Niccolò Machiavelli cittadino et Segretario Fiorentino.* Florence, 1532.

———. *Lettere a Francesco Vettori e a Francesco Guicciardini (1513–1527).* Edited by G. Inglese. Milan, 1989.

———. *Libro della Arte della Guerra di Niccolò Machiavelli cittadino et Segretario Fiorentino.* Florence, 1521.

———. *La Mandragola.* Edited by G. Inglese. Milan, 1996.

———. *The Prince.* Translated by Q. Skinner and R. Price. Cambridge, 1988.

———. *Il principe.* Edited by A. Burd, *Il Principe by Niccolò Machiavelli.* Oxford, 1891.

———. *Il principe.* Edited by G. Inglese. Turin, 1995.

———. *Tutte le opere.* Edited by M. Martelli. Florence, 1992.

———. *La vita di Castruccio Castracani e altri scritti.* Edited by G. Inglese. Milan, 1991.

Mainardi, J. *Epistolae medicinales.* Ferrara, 1521.

Manuzio, A. Dedicatory prefaces. Edited by C. Dionisotti and G. Orlandi, *Aldo Manuzio editore: Dediche, prefazioni, note ai testi.* 2 vols. Milan, 1975.

Marullo, M. *Carmina.* Edited by A. Perosa. Zürich, 1951.

Masi, B. *Ricordanze di Bartolomeo Masi calderaio fiorentino dal 1478 al 1526.* Edited by S. O. Corazzini. Florence, 1906.

Maximus of Tyre. *Dissertationes.* Edited by M. B. Trapp. Stuttgart, 1994.

———. *Maximi Tyri philosophi platonici sermones.* Trans. Cosimo de' Pazzi. Basel, 1519.

Medici, L. de'. *Lettere.* Edited by R. Fubini and N. Rubinstein. Florence, 1977–.

———. *Scritti scelti.* Edited by E. Bigi. Milan, 1977.

Muzio, G. *Lettere inedite di Girolamo Muzio.* Edited by A. Zenatti. Capodistria, 1896.

Nardi, J. *Istorie di Firenze di Jacopo Nardi.* Edited by I. Gelli. 2 vols. Florence, 1855.

Nesi, G. *Oraculum de novo seculo.* Edited by C. Vasoli, "Giovanni Nesi tra Donato Acciaiuoli e Girolamo Savonarola: Testi editi e inediti," *Memorie Domenicane,* n.s. 4 (1973): 103–79 (= Vasoli, *I miti e gli astri,* 51–128 [Naples, 1977]).

Nifo, A. *Augustini Niphi sua tempestate philosophi omnium celeberrimi opuscula moralia et politica.* Edited by G. Naudé. Paris, 1645.

———. *Dialectica ludicra.* Florence, 1520.

———. *De falsa diluvii prognosticatione.* Florence, 1520.

———. *De his, quae ab optimis principibus agenda sunt.* Florence, 1521.

———. *De regnandi peritia.* Edited by P. Larivaille and S. Pernet-Beau, *Une re-écriture du Prince de Machiavel: Le De regnandi peritia de Agostino Nifo,* Université Paris X—Nanterre, Documents du centre de recherche de langue et littérature italiennes 32. Paris, 1987.

Parenti, Piero di Marco. *Storia fiorentina I, 1476–78. 1492–98.* Edited by A. Matucci. Florence, 1994.

Petrarca, F. *De sui ipsius et multorum ignorantia.* In *Opere latine di Francesco Petrarca,* vol. 2, edited by A. Bufano. Turin, 1977.

———. *Invective contra medicum.* Edited by P. G. Ricci. Rome, 1978.

———. *Laurea occidens.* Edited by G. Martellotti. Rome, 1968.

———. *Triumphi.* Edited by M. Ariani. Milan, 1988.

Pico della Mirandola, Gianfrancesco. *De studio divinae et humanae philosophiae.* In *Gianfrancesco Pico della Mirandola opera omnia* 2:2–39. Basel, 1557; reprint Hildesheim, 1969.

Pico della Mirandola, Giovanni. *Conclusiones nongentae.* Edited by A. Biondi, *Giovanni Pico della Mirandola: Conclusiones nongentae: Le novecento tesi dell'anno 1486.* Florence, 1995.

———. *De hominis dignitate, Heptaplus, De ente et uno, e varii scritti.* Edited by E. Garin. Florence, 1942.

———. *Disputationes adversus astrologiam divinatricem.* Edited by E. Garin. 2 vols. Florence, 1946.

Polenton, S. *Scriptores illustres linguae latinae.* Edited by B. Ullmann, *S. Polentoni scriptorum illustrium linguae latinae libri XVIII.* Rome, 1928.

Poliziano, A. *Angeli Politiani Opera.* 3 vols. Lyons, 1533.

———. *La commedia antica et l' "Andria" di Terenzio: Appunti inediti.* Edited by R. Lattanzi Roselli. Florence, 1973.

———. *Commento inedito all'epistola ovidiana di Saffo a Faone.* Edited by E. Lazzeri. Florence, 1971.

———. *Commento inedito ai Fasti di Ovidio.* Edited by F. Lo Monaco. Florence, 1991.

———. *Commento inedito alle Selve di Stazio.* Edited by L. Cesarini Martinelli. Florence, 1978.

———. *"De laudibus artium liberalium."* Edited by I. Maïer, "Un édit de Politien: La classification des arts." *Bibliothèque d'humanisme et Renaissance* 22 (1960): 343–44.

———. *Lamia: Praelectio in Priora Aristotelis Analytica.* Edited by A. Wesseling. Leiden, 1986.

———. *Miscellaneorum centuria secunda* (ed. min.). Edited by V. Branca and M. Pastore Stocchi. Florence, 1978.

———. *Nutricia.* In *Prose volgari inedite e poesie,* 369–442.

———. *Panepistemon.* In *Politiani Opera,* 3:28–55.

———. *Praefatio in Persium.* In *Angelo Poliziano: Commento inedito alle Satire di Persio,* edited by L. Cesarini Martinelli and R. Ricciardi. Florence, 1985.

———. *Prose volgari inedite e poesie latine e grece edite e inedite.* Edited by I. Del Lungo. Florence, 1887; reprint Hildesheim, 1976.

———. *Stanze per la giostra del Magnifico Giuliano di Piero de' Medici.* Florence, 1518.

———. *Sylva in scabiem.* Edited by A. Perosa. Rome, 1954; and edited by P. Orvieto, Rome, 1989.

———. *Sylvae.* Translated and commentary by P. Galand, Ange Politien, *Les Sylves.* Paris, 1987.

———. Preface to Plato, *Charmides.* In Hankins, *Plato in the Italian Renaissance,* 2:623–26.

———, trans. Herodian, *Historiae.* Florence, 1517.

———, transcrib. Galen, *Protrepticus* [frag.]. Edited by G. Pesenti, "Frammenti monacensi di Galeno," *Rendiconti del real istituto lombardo di scienze e lettere* 53 (1920): 586–90.

Quintilian. *Institutio oratoria.* Milan, 1476 [BNCF, Banco Rari, 379].

Redditi, F. *Exhortatio ad Petrum Medicem.* Edited by P. Viti. Florence, 1989.

Reden und Briefe italienischer Humanisten. Edited by K. Müller. Vienna, 1899; reprint Munich, 1970.

Riccardini, B., ed. Sallust, *De coniuratione Catilinae, De bello Iugurthino, Invectiva in M. T. Ciceronem. . . .* Florence, 1504.

———, ed. Terence, *Comoediae in sua metra iterum restitutae.* Florence, 1505.

——— [*pseudo* Furius]. *Uni Trinoque Gloria: Erudimenta grammatices linguae Latinae.* Florence, 1510.

Rinuccini, A. *Lettere ed orazione di Alamanno Rinuccini.* Edited by V. R. Giustiniani. Florence, 1953.

———. *Ricordi storici di Filippo di Cino Rinuccini dal 1282 al 1460 colla continuazione di Alamanno e Neri suoi figli fino al 1506.* Edited by G. Aiazzi. Florence, 1840.

Salutati, C. *Epistolario.* 4 vols. Edited by F. Novati. Rome, 1891–1905.

———. *De laboribus Herculis.* Edited by B. L. Ullman. Zürich, 1961.

Santori, G. A. Autobiography. Edited by G. Cugnoni, *Archivio della società romana per storia patria* 12 (1889): 329–72; 13 (1890): 151–205.

———. *Diario consistoriale.* Edited by P. Tacchi Venturi, *Studi e documenti di storia e diritto* 23 (1902): 297–47; 24 (1903): 73–142.

Savonarola, G. *Dyalogo della verità prophetica.* Florence, 1500.

———. *Prediche sopra Aggeo.* Edited by L. Firpo. Rome, 1965.

———. *Prediche sopra Amos e Zaccaria.* Edited by P. Ghiglieri. 3 vols. Rome, 1971–72.

———. *Prediche sopra Ezechiele.* Edited by R. Ridolfi. 2 vols. Rome, 1955.

———. *Prediche sopra Giobbe.* Edited by R. Ridolfi. 2 vols. Rome, 1957.

———. *Prediche sopra Ruth e Michea.* 2 vols. Edited by V. Romano. Rome, 1962.

———. *Scritti filosofici.* Edited by G. C. Garfagnini and E. Garin. 2 vols. Rome, 1982 and 1988.

Scala, B. *Apologia contra vituperatores civitatis Florentiae.* Florence, 1496.

———. *De legibus et iudiciis.* Edited by L. Borghi, *Bibliofilía* 42 (1940): 256–82.

———. *Proemium.* In idem, *Historia Florentinorum,* edited by O. Jacobaeus. Rome, 1677.

Statuta concilii florentini. Florence, 1518.

Suetonius. *Vita Caesarum et scriptores historiae augustae.* Milan, 1485. [BNCF, Banco Rari 91].

Tommaso, F. di. *De negocio logico.* Edited by J. Hunt, *Politian and Scholastic Logic: An Unknown Dialogue by a Dominican Friar.* Florence, 1995.

Tucci, M., ed. Apuleius, *De Asino aureo libelli xi, Floridorum libri quatuor.* . . . Florence, 1513.

———, ed. Lactantius, *Divinarum institutionum libri septem.* . . . Florence, 1513.

Urceo, A. C. *Sermones.* Basel, 1540.

Valla, L. *Antidotum primum.* Edited by A. Wesseling. Amsterdam, 1978.

———. *Laurentii Valle epistolae.* Edited by O. Besomi and M. Regoliosi. Padua, 1984.

———. *Laurentii Valla opuscula tria.* Edited by M. J. Vahlen. In *Sitzungsberichte der kaiserlichen Akademie der Wissenschaften,* phil.-hist. Klasse 61. Vienna, 1869.

———. *Orazione per l'inaugurazione dell'anno academico, 1455–1456.* Edited by S. Rizzo. Rome, 1994.

Varchi, B. *Storia fiorentina.* Edited by G. Milanesi. Florence, 1857.

Vettori, F. *Scritti storici e politici.* Edited by E. Niccolini. Bari, 1972.

Vettori, Paolo. *Ricordi . . . al cardinale de' Medici sopra le cose di Firenze.* Edited by R. von Albertini, in Albertini, *Firenze,* 357–59.

Vettori, Pier. *Clarorum Italorum et Germanorum epistolae ad Petrum Victorium.* Edited by A. M. Bandini. Florence, 1758.

———. *Petri Victorii epistolarum libri X, orationes XIIII et liber de laudibus Ioannae Austriacae.* Florence, 1581.

———. *Petri Victorii commentarii in VIII libros Aristotelis de optimo statu civitatis.* Florence, 1576.

———. *Petri Victorii commentarii in primum librum Aristotelis de arte poetarum.* Florence, 1560.

Vives, J. L. *Opera.* Basel, 1555.

SELECT SECONDARY SOURCES

Agrimi, J., and C. Crisciani. *Edocere medicos: Medicina scolastica nei secoli XIII–XV.* Milan, 1988.

Albertini, R. von. *Firenze dalla repubblica al principato: Storia e coscienza politica.* Turin, 1970.

Ames-Lewis, F., ed. *Cosimo "il Vecchio" de Medici, 1389–1464: Essays in Commemoration of the 600th Anniversary of Cosimo de' Medici's Birth.* Oxford, 1992.

Bandini, A. M. *Collectio veterum aliquot monimentorum ad historiam praecipue litterariam pertinentium.* Arezzo, 1752.

———. *De florentina Iuntarum typographia eiusque censoribus annales.* 2 vols. Lucca, 1791.

Baron, H. *The Crisis of the Early Italian Renaissance: Civic Humanism and Republican Liberty in an Age of Classicism and Tyranny.* Princeton, 1966.

———. *Humanistic and Political Literature in Florence and Venice of the Quattrocento.* Cambridge, Mass., 1955.

———. *In Search of Florentine Civic Humanism: Essays on the Transition from Medieval to Modern Thought.* 2 vols. Princeton, 1988.

Bausi, F. *I "Discorsi" di Niccolò Machiavelli: Genesi e strutture.* Florence, 1985.

———. "'Extincta viret laurus': L'imagine umanistica di Lorenzo de' Medici il giovane." *Studi umanistici* 3 (1992): 185–217.

———. *Nec rhetor neque philosophus: Fonti, lingua e stile nelle prime opere latine di Giovanni Pico della Mirandola (1482–1487).* Florence, 1996.

Bergdolt, K. *Arzt, Krankheit, und Therapie bei Petrarca: Die Kritik an Medizin und Naturwissenschaft im italienischen Frühhumanismus.* Weinheim, 1992.

Berlin, I. "The Originality of Machiavelli." In Gilmore, ed., *Studies on Machiavelli,* 147–206.

Bertelli, S. "Egemonia linguistica come egemonia culturale e politica nella Firenze cosmiana." *Bibliothèque d'humanisme et Renaissance* 38 (1976): 249–83.

Bertelli, S., and P. Innocenti. *Bibliografia machiavelliana.* Verona, 1976.

———, eds. *Florence and Venice. Comparisons and Relations.* Florence, 1979.

Bettinzoli, A. *Daedaleum iter: Studi sulla poesia e la poetica di Angelo Poliziano.* Florence, 1995.

Bianchi, L. "Un commento 'umanistico' ad Aristotele: L' 'Expostio super libros Ethicorum' di Donato Acciaiuoli." *Rinascimento* 30 (1990): 29–55.

Bigi, E. *La cultura del Poliziano e altri studi umanistici.* Pisa, 1967.

Bignami Odier, J. *La Bibliothèque Vaticane de Sixte IV à Pie XI: Recherches sur l'histoire des collections du manuscrits.* Vatican City, 1973.

Billanovich, G. "Auctorista, humanista, orator." *Rivista di cultura classica e medioevale* 71 (1965): 143–63.

Billanovich, G., and M. Ferraris. "Per la fortuna di Tito Livio nel Rinascimento italiano." *IMU* 1 (1958): 245–81.

Black, R. *Benedetto Accolti and the Florentine Renaissance.* Cambridge, 1985.

———. "Florentine Political Traditions and Machiavelli's Election to the Chancery." *Italian Studies* 40 (1985): 1–16.

———. "Machiavelli, Servant of the Florentine Republic." In Bock, Skinner, and Viroli, eds., *Machiavelli and Republicanism,* 71–99.

———. "The Political Thought of the Florentine Chancellors." *Historical Journal* 29 (1986): 991–1003.

Bock, G. "Civil Discord in Machiavelli's *Istorie fiorentine.*" In Bock, Skinner, and Viroli, eds., *Machiavelli and Republicanism,* 181–201.

Bock, G., Q. Skinner, and M. Viroli, eds. *Machiavelli and Republicanism.* Cambridge, 1990.

Bonadeo, A. "The Role of the 'Grandi' in the Political World of Machiavelli." *Studies in the Renaissance* 16 (1969): 90–130.

Branca, V. *Poliziano e l'umanesimo della parola.* Turin, 1993.

Brown, A. *Bartolomeo Scala, 1430–1497, Chancellor of Florence: The Humanist as Bureaucrat.* Princeton, 1979.

———. "Lorenzo and Public Opinion in Florence." In Garfagnini, ed., *Lorenzo il Magnifico e il suo mondo,* 61–85.

———. *The Medici in Florence: The Exercise and Language of Power.* Florence, 1992.

———. "Savonarola, Machiavelli and Moses: A Changing Model." In Denley and Elam, eds., *Florence and Italy,* 57–72 [= Brown, *The Medici in Florence,* 263–81].

Bullard, M. M. *Lorenzo il Magnifico: Image and Anxiety, Politics and Finance.* Florence, 1994.

Burd, L. A. "Le fonte letterarii di Machiavelli nell' 'Arte della Guerra.'" *Atti dell'Accademia dei Lincei* 5 (1896): 187–261.

Butters, H. *Governors and Government in Early Sixteenth-Century Florence.* Oxford, 1955.

Cabrini, A. M. *Interpretazione e stile in Machiavelli: Il terzo libro delle "Istorie."* Rome, 1990.

The Cambridge Companion to Renaissance Humanism. Edited by J. Kraye. Cambridge, 1996.

The Cambridge History of Renaissance Philosophy. Edited by C. Schmitt and Q. Skinner. Cambridge, 1988.

Camporeale, S. C. "Giovanni Caroli e le 'Vitae Fratrum S. M. Novellae': Umanesimo e crisi religiosa (1460–1480)." *Memorie Domenicane,* n.s. 12 (1981): 147–267.

———. *Lorenzo Valla: Umanesimo e teologia.* Florence, 1972.

Cantimori, D. "Rhetoric and Politics in Italian Humanism." *Journal of the Warburg Institute* 1 (1937–38): 83–102.

———. *Umanesimo e religione nel Rinascimento.* Turin, 1975.

Cardini, R. *La Critica del Landino.* Florence, 1973.

Cardini, R., E. Garin, L. Cesarini Martinelli, and G. Pascucci, eds. *Tradizione classica e letteratura umanistica: Per A. Perosa.* 2 vols. Rome, 1985.

Catalani, G. *De magistro Sacri Palatii Apostolici libri duo.* Rome, 1751.

———. *De secretario Sacrae Congregationis Indicis libri II.* Rome, 1751.

Cesarini Martinelli, L. "In margine al commento di Angelo Poliziano alle *Selve* di Stazio." *Interpres* 1 (1978): 96–145.

———. "'De poesi et poetis': Uno schedario sconosciuto di Angelo Poliziano." In Cardini et al., eds., *Tradizione classica e letteratura umanistica* 2:455–87.

———. "Sesto Empirico e una dispersa enciclopedia delle arti e delle scienze di Angelo Poliziano." *Rinascimento* 20 (1980): 327–58.

Chiecchi, G. *Dolcemente dissimulando: Cartelle laurenziane e Decameron censurato.* Padua, 1982.

Chiecchi, G., and L. Troisio. *Il Decamerone sequestrato.* Milan, 1984.

Cian, V. "Un episodio della storia della censura in Italia nel secolo xvi: L'edizione spurgata del Cortegiano." *Archivio storico lombardo* 14 (1887): 661–722.

Culture et société en Italie du moyen âge à la Renaissance: Hommage à A. Rochon. Paris, 1985.

Curtius, E. R. *European Literature and the Latin Middle Ages.* Translated by W. R. Trask, with a new afterword by P. Godman. Princeton, 1990.

D'Addario, A. *Aspetti della Controriforma a Firenze.* Rome, 1972.

D'Amico, J. F. *Renaissance Humanism in Papal Rome: Humanists and Churchmen on the Eve of the Reformation.* Baltimore, 1983.

Da Prati, P. *Giovanni Dominici e l'umanesimo.* Naples, 1965.

Davies, M. "An Emperor without Clothes? Niccolò Niccoli under Attack." *IMU* 30 (1987): 95–148.

———. "Humanism in Script and Print." In *The Cambridge Companion to Renaissance Humanism,* 53–62.

De Bujanda, J. M., ed. *Index de Rome 1557, 1559, 1564: Les premiers Index romains et l'Index du Concile de Trente.* Index des livres interdits 8. Sherbrooke, 1990.

———. *Index de Rome 1590, 1593, 1596: Avec étude des Index de Parme 1580 et Munich 1582.* Index des livres interdits 9. Sherbrooke, 1990.

Dees, R. "Bruni, Aristotle, and the Mixed Régime in the 'On the Constitution of the Florentines.'" *Medievalia et humanistica* 15 (1987): 1–23.

Dejob, C. *De l'influence du Concile de Trente sur la littérature et les beaux-arts chez les peuples catholiques.* Paris, 1884.

Del Re, N. *La Curia Romana: Lineamenti storico-giuridici.* 3d ed. Rome, 1970.

De Maffei, R. *Dal premachiavellianismo all'antimachiavellianismo.* Florence, 1969.

Denley, P. "*Signore* and *Studio:* Lorenzo in a Comparative Context." In Mallett and Mann, eds., *Lorenzo the Magnificent,* 203–16.

Denley, P., and C. Elam, eds. *Florence and Italy: Renaissance Studies in Honour of N. Rubinstein.* London, 1988.

Devonshire Jones, R. *Francesco Vettori, Florentine Citizen and Medici Servant.* London, 1972.

———. "Lorenzo de' Medici, Duca d'Urbino: 'Signore' of Florence." In Gilmore, ed., *Studies on Machiavelli,* 299–315.

Diaz, F. *Il Granducato di Toscana: I Medici.* Turin, 1987.

Dilg, P. "Die botanische Kommentarliteratur in Italien um 1500 und ihr Einfluß auf Deutschland." In *Der Kommentar in der Renaissance,* edited by O. Buck and R. Herding, 22–52. Bonn, 1976.

Dionisotti, C. "Considerazioni sulla morte del Poliziano." In *Culture et société,* 145–56.

———. *Machiavellerie: Storia e fortuna di Machiavelli.* Turin, 1980.

Fahy, C. "The *Index librorum prohibitorum* and the Venetian Printing Industry in the Sixteenth Century." *Italian Studies* 35 (1980): 52–61.

Feo, M. "'Litterae' e 'literatura' nel medioevo e nell'umanesimo." In *Acta Conventus Neo-Latini Hafnensis,* 21–41. Binghamton, N.Y., 1994.

Firpo, L. "Filosofia italiana e Controriforma." *Rivista di filosofia* 41 (1950): 150–73, 390–401; 42 (1951): 30–47.

Frajese, V. "La revoca dell'*Index* sistino e la Curia Romana (1588–1596)." *Nouvelles de la République des Lettres* 1 (1986): 15–49.

Frede, C. de. *Ricerche per la storia della stampa e la diffusione delle idee riformate nell'Italia del Cinquecento.* Naples, 1985.

French, R. K. "Pliny and Renaissance Medicine." In *Science in the Early Roman Empire: Pliny the Elder, His Sources and Influence,* edited by R. K. French, 252–81. London, 1986.

Fubini, R. "Ancora su Ficino e i Medici." *Rinascimento* 27 (1987): 275–91.

———. "Cultura umanistica e tradizione cittadina nella storiografia fiorentina del 400." In *Storiografia umanistica,* 1, 2:399–443.

———. "Ficino e i Medici all'avvento di Lorenzo il Magnifico." *Rinascimento* 24 (1984): 3–52.

———. "Osservazioni sugli *Historiarum Florentini populi libri xii* di Leonardo Bruni." In *Studi di storia medievale e moderna per E. Sestan,* 403–48. Florence, 1980.

———. "Renaissance Historian: The Career of Hans Baron." *Journal of Modern History* 64 (1977): 541–74.

———. "L'umanista: Ritorno di un paradigma? Saggio per un profilo storico da Petrarca ad Erasmo." *ASI* 147 (1989): 439–508.

Fumaroli, M. *L'âge de l'éloquence: Rhétorique et "res literaria" de la Renaissance au seuil de l'époque classique.* Geneva, 1980.

Gaisser, H. *Catullus and His Renaissance Readers.* Oxford, 1993.

Garfagnini, C. E. "Città e Studio a Firenze nel XIV secolo: Una difficile convivenza." In *Luoghi e metodi di insegnamento nell'Italia medioevale (secoli XII–XIV),* 101–20. Galatina, 1989.

Garfagnini, G. C., ed. *Lorenzo il Magnifico e il suo mondo.* Florence, 1994.

Garin, E. "'Ενδελέχεια e ἐντελέχεια nelle discussione umanistiche." *Atene e Roma* 3 (1937): 177–87.

———. "I cancellieri umanisti della Repubblica Fiorentina da Coluccio Salutati a Bartolomeo Scala." In idem, *Scienza e vita civile nel Rinascimento italiano,* 1–32. Rome, 1983.
———. *Il pensiero pedagogico del umanesimo.* Florence, 1958.
———, ed. *Prosatori latini del Quattrocento.* Milan, 1952.
———. "Religione e filosofia nella cultura fiorentina." In idem, *La cultura filosofica del Rinascimento italiano: Ricerche e documenti.* Florence, 1961.
———. "La 'retorica' di Leonardo Bruni." In idem, *Dal Rinascimento al Illuminismo: Studi e ricerche.* Pisa, 1972.
———, ed. *La disputa delle arti nel Quattrocento.* Florence, 1947.
Gerber, A. *Niccolò Machiavelli: Die Handschriften, Ausgaben und Übersetzungen seiner Werke im 16. und 17. Jahrhundert.* 3 vols. Gotha, 1912; reprint Turin, 1962.
Gilbert, F. "Bernardo Rucellai and the Orti Oricellari: A Study in the Origins of Modern Political Thought." In idem, *History: Choice and Commitment,* 215–46.
———. "Florentine Political Assumptions in the Period of Savonarola and Soderini." *Journal of the Warburg and Courtauld Institutes* 20 (1957): 187–214.
———. *History: Choice and Commitment.* Cambridge, Mass., 1977.
———. "The Humanist Conception of the Prince and *The Prince* of Machiavelli." In idem, *History: Choice and Commitment,* 91–114.
———. *Machiavelli and Guicciardini: Politics and History in Sixteenth-Century Florence.* New York, 1968.
———. "Machiavelli's 'Istorie fiorentine': An Essay in Interpretation." In Gilmore, ed., *Studies on Machiavelli,* 73–99.
———. "Machiavelli: The Renaissance of the Art of War." In *Makers of Modern Strategy from Machiavelli to the Nuclear Age,* edited by P. Paret, 11–31. Princeton, 1986.
———. *Niccolò Machiavelli e la vita culturale del suo tempo.* Bologna, 1964.
Gilmore, M. P., ed. *Studies on Machiavelli.* Florence, 1972.
Giorgetti, A. "Lorenzo de' Medici, capitano della Repubblica Fiorentina." *ASI,* 4th ser., 11 (1883): 194–215.
Giustiniani, V. R. *Alamanno Rinuccini, 1427–1499: Materialien und Forschungen zur Geschichte des florentinischen Humanismus.* Cologne, 1965.
Godman, P. "Florentine Humanism between Poliziano and Machiavelli." *Rinascimento* 35 (1995): 67–122.
———. "Poliziano's Poetics and Literary History." *Interpres* 13 (1993): 110–209.
Gombrich, E. "From the Revival of Letters to the Reform of the Arts." In idem, *The Heritage of Apelles,* 93–110. London, 1976.
Grafton, A. *Defenders of the Text: The Traditions of Scholarship in an Age of Science.* Cambridge, Mass. 1991.
———. *Joseph Scaliger: A Study in the History of Classical Scholarship.* Vol. 1, *Textual Criticism and Exegesis.* Oxford, 1983.
Grafton, A., and L. Jardine. *From Humanism to the Humanities: Education and the Liberal Arts in Fifteenth- and Sixteenth-Century Europe.* London, 1986.
Grendler, P. *The Roman Inquisition and the Venetian Press, 1540–1665.* Princeton, 1977.
Grmek, M., ed. *Storia del pensiero medico occidentale.* Vol. 1, *Antichità e Medioevo.* Bari, 1993.
Guidi, G. *Ciò che accade al tempo della Signoria di novembre–dicembre in Firenze l'anno 1494.* Florence, 1988.
———. "La corrente savonaroliana e la petizione al papa del 1497." *ASI* 147 (1954): 31–46.

———. *Lotte, pensiero e istituzioni politiche nella Repubblica Fiorentina dal 1494 al 1512.* Vol. 1, *Tra politica e diritto pubblico.* Florence, 1992.

Hankins, J. "The 'Baron Thesis' after Forty Years and Some Recent Studies on Leonardo Bruni." *Journal of the History of Ideas* 56 (1995): 309–38.

———. "Humanism and the Origins of Modern Political Thought." In *The Cambridge Companion to Renaissance Humanism,* 118–41.

———. "Lorenzo de' Medici as Patron of Philosophy." *Rinascimento* 34 (1994): 15–53.

———. "The Myth of the Platonic Academy of Florence." *Renaissance Quarterly* 44 (1991): 429–75.

———. *Plato in the Italian Renaissance.* 2d ed. 2 vols. Leiden, 1991.

Henningsen, G., and J. Tedeschi, eds. *The Inquisition in Early Modern Europe: Studies on Sources and Methods.* Dekalb, Ill., 1986.

Hilgers, J. *Der Index der verbotenen Bücher in seiner neuen Fassung dargelegt und rechtlich- historisch gewürdigt.* Freiburg, 1904.

Hill Cotton, J. "Frosino Bonini: Politian's Protégé and Plagiarist." *La Bibliofilia* 71 (1969): 157–75.

L'Inquisizione Romana in Italia nell'età moderna: Archivi, problemi di metodo, e nuove ricerche. Trieste, 1991.

Jardine, L. "Dialectic or Dialectical Rhetoric? Agostino Nifo's Criticism of Lorenzo Valla." *Rivista critica di storia della filosofia* 36 (1981): 253–70.

Jedin, H. "Die Autobiographie des Kardinals Giulio Antonio Santorio (†1602)." In *Abhandlungen der Mainzer Akademie der Wissenschaften und der Literatur,* Geistes- und sozialwissenschaftliche Klasse 2 (1969): 3–34.

Kelley, D. R. "Civil Science in the Renaissance: Jurisprudence Italian Style." *Historical Journal* 22 (1979): 777–94.

———. *Foundations of Modern Historical Scholarship: Language, Law, and History in the French Renaissance.* New York, 1976.

Kenney, E. J. *The Classical Text: Aspects of Editing in the Age of the Printed Book.* Berkeley, 1974.

Kent, F. W. "*Lorenzo . . . Amico degli uomini da bene:* Lorenzo de' Medici and Oligarchy." In Garfagnini, ed., *Lorenzo il Magnifico e il suo mondo,* 43–60.

Kirshner, J. "*Ars imitatur naturam:* A *Consilium* of Baldus on Naturalisation in Florence." *Viator* 5 (1974): 289–331.

———. "Paolo di Castro on *Cives e privilegio:* A Controversy over the Legal Qualifications for Public Office in Early Fifteenth-Century Florence." In *Renaissance Studies in Honor of H. Baron,* edited by A. Molho and J. A. Tedeschi, 227–44. Dekalb, Ill., 1971.

Kraye, J. "Cicero, Stoicism, and Textual Criticism: Poliziano on Κατόρθωα." *Rinascimento* 23 (1983): 79–110.

———. "Moral Philosophy." In *The Cambridge History of Renaissance Philosophy,* 301–86.

———. "Renaissance Commentaries on the *Nicomachean Ethics.*" In *The Vocabulary of Teaching and Research between Middle Ages and Renaissance,* Etudes sur le vocabulaire intellectuel du Moyen Age 8, edited by O. Weijers, 96–117. Turnhout, 1995.

Kristeller, P. O. "Francesco da Diacceto and Florentine Platonism in the Sixteenth Century." In idem, *Studies in Renaissance Thought and Letters* [vol. 1], 187–336. Rome, 1984.

———. *Iter Italicum: A Finding List of Uncatalogued or Incompletely Catalogued Humanistic Manuscripts of the Renaissance in Italian and Other Libraries.* London, 1977–.

———. "Philosophy and Medicine in Renaissance Italy." In idem, *Studies in Renaissance Thought and Letters* 3:431–42. Rome, 1993.

Larivaille, P. "Nifo, Machiavelli, principato civile." *Interpres* 9 (1989): 150–99.

———. *La pensée politique de Machiavel: Les "Discours sur la première décade de Tite-Live."* Nancy, 1982.

Leeman, A. D. *Orationis Ratio: The Stylistic Theories and Practice of the Roman Orators, Historians, and Philosophers*. 2 vols. Amsterdam, 1963.

Longo, N. "Fenomeni di censura nella letteratura italiana del Cinquecento." In *Le pouvoir et la plume,* 275–84.

Lopez, P. *Sul libro a stampa e le origini della censura ecclesiastica*. Naples, 1972.

Lorenzo dopo Lorenzo: La fortuna storica di Lorenzo il Magnifico. Exhibition catalogue. Edited by P. Pirolo. Florence, 1992.

Lorenzo Valla e l'umanesimo italiano. Atti del convegno internazionale di studi umanistici (Parma, 18–19 October 1984). Edited by O. Besomi and M. Regoliosi. Padua, 1986.

Lowry, M. *The World of Aldus Manutius: Business and Scholarship in Renaissance Venice*. Oxford, 1979.

Mahoney, E. P. "Nifo, A." In *Dictionary of Scientific Biography,* vol. 10, edited by C. C. Gillespie, 122–24. New York, 1976.

Maier, I. *Ange Politien: La formation d'un poète humaniste (1469–1480)*. Geneva, 1966.

Mallett, M., and N. Mann, eds. *Lorenzo the Magnificent: Culture and Politics*. London, 1996.

Mansfield, H. C. *Machiavelli's Virtue*. Chicago, 1996.

Marchant, J. J. "Machiavelli cancelliere sotto i Medici." *Italianistica: Rivista di letteratura italiana* 7 (1978): 235–48.

Mare, A. de la. "Florentine Manuscripts of Livy in the Fifteenth Century." In *Livy,* edited by T. A. Dorey, 177–200. London, 1971.

Martelli, M. *Angelo Poliziano: Storia e metastoria*. Lecce, 1995.

———. "L'altro Niccolò di Bernardo Machiavelli." *Rinascimento* 14 (1974): 39–100.

———. "Machiavelli e la storiografia umanistica." In *Storiografia umanistica* 1, 2:128–29.

———. "Nota a *Morgante* XX, 85, 4 (con una postilla su Bartolomeo Scala e Angelo Poliziano)." *Interpres* 3 (1986): 263–69.

———, "La politica culturale del ultimo Lorenzo." *Il ponte* 36 (1980): 923–41, 1040–69.

———. "Da Poliziano a Machiavelli: Sull'epigramma *Dell'occasione* e sull'occasione." *Interpres* 2 (1979): 230–54.

———. "Preistoria (medicea) di Machiavelli." *Studi di filologia italiana* 29 (1971): 377–405.

———. "Profilo ideologico di Alamanno Rinuccini." In *Culture et société,* 131–43.

———. "Schede sulla cultura di Machiavelli." *Interpres* 6 (1986): 283–330.

Martines, L. *Lawyers and Statecraft in Renaissance Florence*. Princeton, 1968.

Marzi, B. *La cancelleria della Repubblica Fiorentina*. 2 vols. Reprint. Florence, 1987.

McCuaig, W. *Carlo Sigonio: The Changing World of the Late Renaissance*. Princeton, 1989.

McManamon, J. M. "Marketing a Medici Regime: The Funeral Oration of Marcello Virgilio Adriani for Giuliano de' Medici (1516)." *Renaissance Quarterly* 44 (1991): 1–41.

Melville, G. "Zur *Flores*—Metaphorik in der mittelalterlichen Geschichtsschreibung." *Historisches Jahrbuch* 90 (1970): 65–80.

Momigliano, A. *The Classical Foundations of Modern Historiography*. Berkeley, 1990.

Monaco, F. Lo. "Aspetti e problemi della conservazione dei secondi 'Miscellanea' di Angelo Poliziano." *Rinascimento* 29 (1989): 318–25.

———. "Poliziano e Beroaldo: Le *In Annotationes Beroaldi* del Poliziano." *Rinascimento* 2ª, ser. 32 (1992): 103–65.

Moos, P. von. *Consolatio: Studien zur mittellateinischen Trostliteratur über den Tod und zum Problem der christlichen Trauer.* 4 vols. Munich, 1971.

———. *Geschichte als Topik: Das rhetorische Exemplum von der Antike zur Neuzeit und die "historiae" im "Policraticus" des Johannes von Salisbury.* Hildesheim, 1988.

———. "Was galt im lateinischen Mittelalter als das Literarische an der Literatur? Eine theologisch-rhetorische Antwort des 12. Jahrhunderts." In *Literarische Interessenbildung im Mittelalter,* DFG-Symposium 1991, edited by J. Heinzle, 431–51. Stuttgart, 1993.

Moulakis, A. "Leonardo Bruni's Constitution of Florence." *Rinascimento* 26 (1986): 141–90.

Mugnai Carrara, D. *La biblioteca di Nicolò Leoniceno: Tra Aristotele e Galeno: Cultura e libri di un medico umanista.* Florence, 1991.

———. "Una polemica umanistico-scolastica circa l'interpretazione delle tre dottrine ordinate di Galeno." *Annali dell'istituto di storia della scienza in Firenze* 7 (1983): 31–57.

———. "Profilo di Nicolò Leoniceno." *Interpres* 2 (1979): 169–212.

Najemy, J. M. "*Arti* and *Ordini* in Machiavelli's *Istorie fiorentine.*" In *Essays Presented to M. P. Gilmore,* edited by S. Bertelli and G. Ramakus, 1:161–91. Florence, 1978.

———. "Baron's Machiavelli and Renaissance Republicanism." *American Historical Review* 101 (1996): 119–29.

———. *Between Friends: Discourses of Power and Desire in the Machiavelli-Vettori Letters of 1513–1515.* Princeton, 1993.

———. "Machiavelli and the Medici: The Lessons of Florentine History." *Renaissance Quarterly* 35 (1982): 551–76.

———. Review of *In Search of Florentine Civic Humanism,* by Hans Baron. *Renaissance Quarterly* 45 (1992): 340–50.

Nauert, C. G. "Humanists, Scientists, and Pliny: Changing Approaches to a Classical Author." *American Historical Review* 84 (1979): 72–85.

Nitti, F. *Leone X e la sua politica.* Florence, 1892.

Nutton, V. *From Democedes to Harvey: Studies in the History of Medicine.* London, 1988.

———. *John Caius and the Manuscripts of Galen.* Cambridge, 1987.

———. "Greek Science in the Sixteenth-Century Renaissance." In *Renaissance and Revolution: Humanists, Scholars, Craftsmen and Natural Philosophers in Early Modern Europe,* edited by J. V. Field and F.A.J.L. James, 15–28. Cambridge, 1993.

L'officina della maniera: Varietà e fierezza nell'arte fiorentina del Cinquecento fra le due repubbliche, 1494–1530. Exhibition catalogue. Venice, 1996.

Pacini, G. P. "Per una rilettura della *Esortazione alla penitenza* di Niccolò Machiavelli." *Rivista di storia e letteratura religiosa* 27 (1991): 125–36.

Palmer, R. "Medical Botany in Northern Italy in the Renaissance." *Journal of the Royal Society of Medicine* 78 (1985): 149–57.

Panella, A. "La censura sulla stampa e una questione giurisdizionale fra Stato e Chiesa in Firenze alla fine del secolo XVI." *ASI* 43 (1909): 140–51.

———. "L'introduzione a Firenze dell'Indice di Paolo IV." *Rivista storica degli archivi toscani* 1 (1929): 11–25

Park, K. *Doctors and Medicine in Early Renaissance Florence.* Princeton, 1985.

Paschini, P. *Cinquecento romano e riforma Cattolica: Scritti raccolti. . . . Lateranum* 14. Rome, 1958.

Perosa, A. "*Febris:* A Poetic Myth Created by Poliziano." *Journal of the Warburg and Courtauld Institutes* 9 (1946): 74–95.

———. *Mostra del Poliziano nella Biblioteca Medicea Laurenziana: Manuscritti, libri, rari, au-*

tografi e documenti. Florence, 23 September—30 November 1954. Catalogue. Florence, 1955.

Pesman Cooper, R. "La caduta di Pier Soderini e il 'Governo Popolare.'" *ASI* 143 (1985): 225–60

———. "L'elezione di Pier Soderini a Gonfaloniere a vita." *ASI* 143 (1985): 145–85.

———. "The Florentine Ruling Group under the Governo Popolare, 1494–1512." *Studies in Medieval and Renaissance History* 7 (1985): 69–181.

———. "Machiavelli, Pier Soderini and *Il Principe*." In *Altro Polo: A Volume of Italian Renaissance Studies,* edited by C. Condren and R. Pesman Cooper, 119–44. Sydney, 1982.

Petrucci, A. *Coluccio Salutati*. Rome, 1972.

Pettas, W. A. *The Giunti of Florence: Merchant Publishers of the Sixteenth Century*. San Francisco, 1980.

Piccolomini, E. "Documenti intorno alle vicende della Libreria Medicea Privata." *ASI* 19 (1874).

Picotti, G. B. "Tra il poeta e il lauro." In idem, *Recerche umanistiche,* 3–86. Florence, 1955.

Pieraccioni, G. "Note su Machiavelli storico I." *ASI* 146 (1988): 633–64.

———. "Note su Machiavelli storico II." *ASI* 147 (1989): 61–98.

Pincin, C. "Le prefazioni e la dedicatoria dei 'Discorsi' di Machiavelli." *Giornale storico della litteratura italiana* 143 (1966): 72–83.

———. "Sul testo di Machiavelli, I 'Discorsi.'" *Atti dell'Accademia delle Scienze di Torino* 94 (1959–60): 506–18.

Pocock, J.G.A. *The Machiavellian Moment: Florentine Political Thought and the Atlantic Republican Tradition*. Princeton, 1975.

Polizzotto, L. *The Elect Nation: The Savonarolan Movement in Florence 1494–1545*. Oxford, 1994.

Il Poliziano e il suo tempo. Atti del IV convegno internazionale di studi sul Rinascimento. Florence, 1957.

Le pouvoir et la plume: Imitation, Contrôle, et Répression dans l'Italie du XVIe siècle. Actes du colloque international organisé par le Centre interuniversitaire de recherche sur la Renaissance italienne et l'institut culturel italien de Marseille. Aix en Provence-Marseille, 14–16 Mai, 1981. Paris, 1982.

Pozzi, G. "Appunti sul 'Corollarium' del Barbaro." In *Tra latino e volgare: Per C. Dionisotti,* edited by G. Bernardoni Trezzini et al., 1:621–40. Padua, 1974.

Premuda, L. "Un discepolo di Leoniceno tra filologia ed empirismo: G. Manardo e il 'libero esame' dei classici della medicina in funzione di piu spregiudicati orientamenti." In *Atti del convegno internazionale per la celebrazione del V centenario della nascità di Giovanni Manardo, 1462–1536,* 43–56. Ferrara, 1963.

Preuss, J. S. "Machiavelli's Functional Analysis of Religion: Context and Object." *Journal of the History of Ideas* 40 (1969): 171–90.

Price, R. "*Ambizione* in Machiavelli's Thought." *History of Political Thought* 3 (1982): 383–445.

———. "The Theme of *Gloria* in Machiavelli." *Renaissance Quarterly* 30 (1977): 588–631.

Price Zimmermann, P. C. *Paolo Giovio: The Historian and the Crisis of Sixteenth-Century Italy*. Princeton, 1996.

Procacci, G. "Frate Andrea Alamanni confessore del Machiavelli." *Dimensioni e problemi della ricerca storica* 2 (1993): 5–12.

———. *Studi sulla fortuna del Machiavelli*. Rome, 1965.

Prodi, P. *Il cardinale Gabriele Paleotti (1522–1597)*. 2 vols. Rome, 1967.

———. *The Papal Prince: One Body and Two Souls: The Papal Monarchy in Early Modern Europe*. Translated by S. Haskins. Cambridge, 1987.

Prosperi, A. "L'Inquisizione fiorentina dopo il concilio di Trento." *Annuario dell'istituto storico italiano per l'età moderna e contemporanea* 37–38 (1985–86): 97–124.

Puelli-Maestrelli, C. "Savonarole, la politique et la jeunesse à Florence." In *Théorie et pratique politiques à la Renaissance,* XVIIe Colloque international de Tours, 1–13. Paris, 1977.

Raimondi, E. "Machiavelli and the Rhetoric of the Warrior." *Modern Language Notes* 92 (1977): 1–16.

———. *Politica e commedia: Dal Beroaldo al Machiavelli*. Bologna, 1971.

Reeds, K. M. "Renaissance Humanism and Botany." *Annals of Science* 33 (1976): 519–42 [= Reeds, *Botany in Medieval and Renaissance Universities,* 519–42. New York, 1991].

Regoliosi, M. "Lorenzo Valla e la concezione della storia." In *Storiografia umanistica* 1, 2:549–71.

Reusch, H. *Der Index der verbotenen Bücher*. 3 vols. Bonn, 1883.

Ribuoli, R. *La collazione polizianea del codice bembino di Terenzio*. Rome, 1981.

Ricciardi, R. "Angelo Poliziano, Giuniano Maio, Antonio Calcillo." *Rinascimento* 2 (1968): 227–84.

Richardson, B. "A Manuscript of Biagio Buonaccorsi." *Bibliothèque d'humanisme et Renaissance* 36 (1974): 589–601

———. "Notes on Machiavelli's Sources and His Treatment of the Rhetorical Tradition." *Italian Studies* 26 (1971): 24–48.

———. "*The Prince* and Its Early Italian Readers." In *Niccolò Machiavelli's 'The Prince': New Interdisciplinary Essays,* edited by M. Coyle, 19–39. Manchester, 1995.

———. *Print Culture in Renaissance Italy: The Editor and the Vernacular Text, 1470–1600*. Cambridge, 1994.

Riddle, J. M. "Dioscorides." In *Catalogus translationum et commentariorum: Medieval and Renaissance Latin Translations and Commentaries,* edited by F. E. Cranz and P. O. Kristeller, 36–37. Washington, D.C., 1980.

Ridolfi, R. *La stampa a Firenze nel secolo XV*. Florence, 1958.

———. *Studi savonaroliani*. Florence, 1935.

———. *Vita di Niccolò Machiavelli*. 7th ed. Rome, 1978.

———. *Vita di Savonarola*. 6th ed. Florence, 1981.

Rizzo, S. "Il latino nell'umanesimo." In *Letteratura italiana,* vol. 5, edited by A. Asor Rosa, 379–408. Turin, 1986.

———. *Il lessico filologico degli umanisti*. Rome, 1973.

———. "Una prolusione del Poliziano e i commentatori greci di Aristotele." In *Studi in onore di A. Ardizzoni,* vol. 2, edited by E. Livrea and G. Privitera, 759–68. Rome, 1978.

Robey, D. "Humanist Views on the Study of Poetry in the Early Italian Renaissance." *Journal of the History of Education* 13 (1984): 7–25.

Rotondò, A. "La censura ecclesiastica e la cultura." In *Storia d'Italia* 5, 2:1399–1492. Turin, 1973.

———. "Cultura umanistica e difficultà di censori: Censura ecclesiastica e discussioni cinquecentesche sul platonismo." In *Le pouvoir et la plume,* 15–50.

———. "Niccolò Tignosi da Foligno: Polemiche aristoteliche di un maestro del Ficino." *Rinascimento* 9 (1958): 217–55.

———. "Nuovi documenti per la storia dell' 'Indice del libri proibiti' (1572–1638)." *Rinascimento* 3 (1963): 145–211.

Rubinstein, N. "The Beginning of Niccolò Machiavelli's Career in the Florentine Chancery." *Italian Studies* 2 (1956): 72–91.

———. "Cosimo *optimus civis*." In *Cosimo "il Vecchio" de Medici,* edited by F. Ames-Lewis, 5–20. Oxford, 1992.

———. "Florentine Constitutionalism and Medici Ascendancy in the Fifteenth Century." In *Florentine Studies,* 442–62.

———. "Florentina libertas." *Rinascimento,* ser. 2, 26 (1986): 3–26.

———, ed. *Florentine Studies: Politics and Society in Renaissance Florence.* London, 1968.

———. "The Formation of the Posthumous Image of Lorenzo de' Medici." In *Oxford, China, and Italy: Writings in Honor of Sir H. Acton,* edited by E. Chaney and N. Ritchie, 94–106. London, 1984.

———. *The Government of Florence under the Medici, 1434–1494.* Oxford, 1966.

———. "Lorenzo's Image in Europe." In Mallett and Mann, eds., *Lorenzo the Magnificent,* 297–312.

———. "Machiavelli e le origini di Firenze." *Rivista storica italiana* 79 (1967): 952–59.

———. "Machiavelli storico." *Annali della Scuola Normale di Pisa. Classe di lettere e filosofia* 3, 18 (Pisa, 1987): 695–733.

———. "Machiavelli and the World of Florentine Politics." In Gilmore, ed., *Studies in Machiavelli,* 5–28.

———."Oligarchy and Democracy in Fifteenth-Century Florence." In Bertelli, Rubinstein, and Smyth, eds., *Florence and Venice,* 99–112.

———. *The Palazzo Vecchio, 1298–1532: Government, Architecture, and Imagery in the Civic Palace of the Florentine Republic.* Oxford, 1995.

———. "I primi anni del Consiglio Maggiore di Firenze (1494–99)." *ASI* 112 (1954): 151–94, 321–47.

Rüdiger, W. *Marcellus Virgilius Adrianus aus Florenz: Ein Beitrag zur Kenntnis seines Lebens und seines Werkes.* Halle, 1889.

Sabbadini, R. *Il metodo degli umanisti.* Florence, 1922.

———. *Storia del ciceronianismo e di altre questioni letterarii nell'età della rinascenza.* Florence, 1885.

Santini, E. *Firenze e i suoi oratori nel Quattrocento.* Milan, 1922.

———. "La 'Protestatio de iustitia' nella Firenze medicea del sec XV." *Rinascimento* 10 (1959): 33–106.

Santoro, M. "La polemica pliniana fra il Leoniceno e il Collenuccio." *Filologia Romanza* 3 (1956): 162–205.

———, ed. *La stampa in Italia nel Cinquecento.* Atti del convegno Rome (17–21 October 1989). Rome, 1992.

Sasso, G. *Machiavelli e gli antichi e altri saggi.* 3 vols. Milan, 1988.

———. *Niccolò Machiavelli: Storia del suo pensiero politico.* 2d ed. Naples, 1980.

Schmitt, C. *Aristotle in the Renaissance.* Cambridge, Mass., 1983.

———. "La cultura scientifica in Italia nel Quattrocento: Problemi d'interpretazione." In idem, *The Aristotelian Tradition and Renaissance Universities,* 55–70. London, 1984.

———. *Gianfrancesco Pico della Mirandola, 1469–1533, and His Critique of Aristotle.* The Hague, 1967.

Schmitz, G. "Ein Narr, der lacht . . . Überlegungen zu einer mittelalterlichen Verhaltensnorm." *Bibliothèque d'humanisme et Renaissance* 36 (1974): 589–601.

Schnitzer, J. *Savonarolas Erzieher und Savonarola als Erzieher.* Berlin, 1913.

Seigel, J. E. *Rhetoric and Philosophy in Renaissance Humanism: The Union of Eloquence and Wisdom, Petrarch to Valla.* Princeton, 1968.

Senesi, M. "Niccolò Machiavelli, *L'arte della guerra* e i Medici." *Interpres* 8 (1988): 297–309.

Sensi, M. "Niccolò Tignosi da Foligno: L'opera e il pensiero." *Annali degli studi di Perugia* 9 (1971–72): 359–495.

Silvano, G. "Florentine Republicanism in the Early Sixteenth Century." In Bock, Skinner, and Viroli, eds., *Machiavelli and Republicanism,* 41–70.

Simoncelli, P. "Documenti interni alla Congregazione dell'Indice 1571–1590: Logica e ideologia dell'intervento censorio." *Annuario dell'istituto storico italiano per l'età moderna e contemporanea* 35–36 (1983–84): 189–215.

———. "Inquisizione Romana e riforma in Italia." *Rivista storica italiana* 100 (1988): 5–113.

Siraisi, N. *Avicenna in Renaissance Italy: The "Canon" and Medical Teaching in Italian Universities after 1500.* Princeton, 1987.

Skinner, Q. *The Foundations of Modern Political Thought.* 2 vols. Cambridge, 1978.

———. "Political Philosophy." In *Cambridge History of Renaissance Philosophy,* 387–452.

Sorrentino, A. *La letteratura italiana e il Sant'Uffizio.* Naples, 1935.

Staico, U. "Esegesi aristotelica in età medicea." In *La Toscana al tempo di Lorenzo il Magnifico,* 3:1275–1371.

Stephens, J. N. *The Fall of the Florentine Republic, 1512–1530.* Oxford, 1983.

Stephens, J. N., and H. C. Butters. "New Light on Machiavelli." *English Historical Review* 97 (1982): 54–69.

La storiografia umanistica. Convegno internazionale di studi, Messina (22–25 October 1978). 2 vols. Messina, 1992.

Tapella, C., and M. Pozzi. "L'edizione del *Decamerone* del 1573: Lettere e documenti sulla rassettatura." *Giornale storico della letteratura italiana* 165 (1988): 54–84, 196–227, 366–98, 511–44.

Tedeschi, J. *The Prosecution of Heresy: Collected Studies on the Inquisition in Early Modern Italy.* Binghamton, N.Y., 1991.

Tenenti, A. "La religione di Machiavelli." *Studi storici* 10 (1989): 708–48.

Timpanaro, S. *Contributi di filologia e di storia della lingua latina.* Rome, 1978.

———. *La genesi del metodo del Lachmann.* 2 vols. Padua, 1981.

Tommasini, O. *La vita e gli scritti di Niccolò Machiavelli nella loro relazione con il machiavellismo.* 2 vols. Turin, 1914.

La Toscana al tempo di Lorenzo il Magnifico: Politica, Economia, Cultura, Arte. 3 vols. Pisa, 1996.

Trexler, R. "La Prostitution florentine au XVe siècle." *Annales* 36 (1981): 983–1015.

———. "Two Captains and Three Kings: New Light on the Medici Chapel." In idem, *Church and Community, 1200–1600: Studies in the History of Florence and New Spain,* 169–244. Rome, 1987.

———. *Public Life in Renaissance Florence.* New York, 1980.

Trinkaus, C. *The Scope of Renaissance Humanism.* Ann Arbor, 1983.

Ullman, B. L. *The Humanism of Coluccio Salutati.* Padua, 1963.

Ullman, B. L., and P. A. Stadter. *The Public Library of Renaissance Florence: Niccolò Niccoli, Cosimo de' Medici and the Library of San Marco.* Padua, 1972.

Varese, C. "Pandolfo Collenuccio umanista." In Varese, *Storia e politica nella prosa del Quattrocento.* Turin, 1961.

Vasoli, C. "L'attesa della nuova èra in ambienti e gruppi fiorentini alla fine del Quattrocento." In *L'attesa dell'Età Nuova nella spiritualità della fine del Medioevo,* Convegni di studi sulla spiritualità medievale 3, 370–432. Todi, 1962.

———. *La dialettica e la retorica dell'umanesimo: "Invenzione" e "Metodo" nella cultura del XV e XVI Secolo.* Milan, 1968.

———. "L'hermétisme dans l'*Oraculum* de Giovanni Nesi." In *Présence d'Hermès Trismégiste,* 153–65. Paris, 1988.

———. "Reflessioni sugli umanisti e il principe: Il modello platonico dell' 'ottimo governante.'" In *Per F. Chabod: Lo stato e il potere nel Rinascimento,* edited by S. Bertelli, *Annali della facoltà di scienze politiche* 17, 146–68. Perugia, 1980–81.

———. *Tra "maestri" umanisti e teologi.* Florence, 1991.

Vecce, C. "*Multiplex hic anguis:* Gli epigrammi di Sannazaro contro Poliziano." *Rinascimento* 25 (1990): 235–55.

Vegetti, M. "Modelli di medicine in Galeno." In *Galen: Problems and Prospects,* edited by V. Nutton, 47–64. London, 1981.

———. "La terapia dell'anima: Patologia e disciplina del soggetto in Galeno." In *Galeno: Le passioni e gli errori dell'anima: Opere morali,* edited by M. Vegetti and M. Menghi, 131–55. Venice, 1984.

Ventrone, P. *Gli araldi della commedia: Teatro a Firenze nel Rinascimento.* Pisa, 1995.

Verde, A. F. "La congregazione domenicana di San Marco: Il 'reale' della predicazione savonaroliana." *Memorie Domenicane,* n.s. 14 (1983): 151–237.

———. *Lo Studio fiorentino, 1473–1503: Ricerche e documenti.* Florence, 1973–.

Verdon, J., and J. Henderson, eds. *Christianity and the Renaissance: Image and the Religious Imagination in the Quattrocento.* Syracuse, 1990.

Villari, P. *Niccolò Machiavelli e i suoi tempi.* 3 vols. Milan, 1912.

Viti, P., ed. *Pico, Poliziano e l'umanesimo di fine Quattrocento.* Florence, 1994.

Weinstein, D. "Critical Issues in the Study of Civic Religion in Renaissance Florence." In *The Pursuit of Holiness in Late Medieval and Renaissance Religion,* edited by C. Trinkaus and H. A. Oberman, 265–70. Leiden, 1974.

———. "Hagiography, Demonology, Biography: Savonarola Studies Today." *Journal of Modern History* 63 (1991): 483–503.

———. "Machiavelli and Savonarola." In Gilmore, ed., *Studies on Machiavelli,* 251–64.

———. "The Myth of Florence." In Rubinstein, ed., *Florentine Studies,* 15–44.

———. *Savonarola and Florence: Prophecy and Patriotism in the Renaissance.* Princeton, 1970.

Weissman, R. "Sacred Eloquence: Humanist Preaching and Lay Piety in Renaissance Florence." In Verdon and Henderson, eds., *Christianity and the Renaissance,* 250–71.

Wesseling, A. "Poliziano and Ancient Rhetoric." *Rinascimento* 30 (1990): 191–204.

Witt, R. *Hercules at the Crossroads: The Life, Works, and Thought of Coluccio Salutati.* Durham, N.C., 1983.

———."The Rebirth of the Concept of Republican Liberty in Italy." In *Renaissance Studies in Honor of H. Baron,* edited by A. Molho and J. A. Tedeschi, 173–99. Dekalb, Ill., 1971.

———. *Coluccio Salutati and His Public Letters.* Geneva, 1976.

Worstbrock, F. J. "Translatio artium: Über die Herkunft und Entwicklung einer kulturhistorischen Theorie." *Archiv für Kulturgeschichte* 47 (1965): 1–22.

Zambelli, P. "La critica dell'astrologia e la medicina umanistica." In eadem, *L'ambigua natura della magia: Filosofi, streghe, riti nel Rinascimento,* 76–118. Milan, 1991.

———. "Fine del mondo o inizio della propaganda? Astrologia, filosofia della storia e propaganda politico-religiosa nel dibattito sulla congiunzione del 1524." In *Scienze, credenze occulte, livelli di cultura,* 291–368. Florence, 1982.

POSTSCRIPTUM

SINCE this book was sent to press, three excellent monographs on subjects relevant to its main themes have become available to me: R. Fubini, *Quattrocento fiorentino: Politica, diplomazia, cultura* (Pisa, 1997); G. Procacci, *Machiavelli nella cultura europea dell'età moderna* (Rome, 1995); and A. Prosperi, *Tribunali della coscienza: Inquisitori, confessori, missionari* (Turin, 1996).

INDEX